BUDGETING FOR LOCAL GOVERNMENTS AND COMMUNITIES

D1615565

BUDGETING FOR LOCAL GOVERNMENTS AND COMMUNITIES

DOUGLAS F. MORGAN
KENT S. ROBINSON
DENNIS STRACHOTA
JAMES A. HOUGH

Routledge
Taylor & Francis Group
LONDON AND NEW YORK

First published 2015 by M.E. Sharpe

Published 2015 by Routledge
2 Park Square, Milton Park, Abingdon, Oxon OX14 4RN
711 Third Avenue, New York, NY 10017, USA

Routledge is an imprint of the Taylor & Francis Group, an informa business

Library of Congress Cataloging-in-Publication Data

Morgan, Douglas F., 1943–
  Budgeting for local governments and communities / by Douglas F. Morgan, Kent S. Robinson, Dennis
Strachota, and James A. Hough.
     pages cm
  Includes bibliographical references and index.
  ISBN 978-0-7656-2780-3 (pbk. : alk. paper)
  1. Local budgets—United States. 2. Local finance—United States. 3. Budget—United States. I. Title.

HJ9147.M67 2014
352.4'82140973—dc23   2013047528

ISBN 13: 9780765627803 (pbk)

CONTENTS

PART II. REVENUES AND BUDGETING

PART IV. EXECUTIVE PRIORITIES, BUDGET ADOPTION, AND IMPLEMENTATION

PREFACE AND ACKNOWLEDGMENTS

This text on local public budgeting draws on our several decades of instructional experience, scholarship, and professional practice focused on the improvement of local public service. We are grateful that much of our experience has been acquired through our work in the Mark O. Hatfield School of Government's Center for Public Service (previously known as the Executive Leadership Institute) at Portland State University. The Center for Public Service (CPS) serves as a two-way transfer station that integrates the practical knowledge of public service professionals with the academic research and knowledge generated by the university. CPS has provided a fertile ground where practitioners and academics come together to coproduce better public service knowledge and practices through joint engagement in applied research, leadership development, and technical assistance. This book is both a product of this coproduction process and a testimonial to the important role that such a partnership plays in improving public service practices. We have sought to capture the lessons we have learned from this experience and pass them on to our students who wish to devote their lives to public service in local nonprofit and governmental organizations. In the sections that follow, we summarize the role of this text in preparing students for careers in local public service.

FOCUS OF TEXT

This text is aimed especially at graduate students in master's degree programs in public policy, public administration, urban planning, nonprofit management, political science, health, social work, and public affairs. Since these programs vary widely in the background of their students and in the priority they give to courses in local government and budgeting, we have tried to be mindful of this diversity in writing the text.

In some programs, public budgeting is the first introductory course in a public finance sequence; in other programs, budgeting is a second course following an introductory course in accounting and management control. In some programs, public budgeting is a mandatory core course; in others, it is an elective. Students tend to enter public budgeting classes with a broad array of technical skill levels and backgrounds. Within this diversity, however, there is a common denominator: Most students have limited backgrounds in statistics and analytic methods, economics, and an understanding of the public policy process, especially at the local level of government. To make this text accessible to students and practitioners at *all* levels, we have kept the mathematics, computations, and accounting to the basic level of first-year college algebra and analytic geometry. And we have increased our emphasis on local government structures and processes of governance. Other available public budgeting texts provide effective content and instruction at a higher analytic level. Furthermore, we have assumed a minimum level of understanding of the local public policy process and the varieties of models that seek to make sense out of local governing processes.

A large portion of students enrolled in public budgeting courses work at the local government level. This book makes a special effort to take into account the variety of experiences these students have in all forms of county, city, and special districts. Another large portion of students who are typically enrolled in public budgeting courses work for nonprofit organizations and foundations. Again, the text makes a special effort to take into account the wide variety, size, and complexity of nonprofit organization, ranging from the smallest micro nonprofits providing social services with one part-time administrator and volunteers, to major hospitals, universities, and intermediaries with budgets in the hundreds of millions of dollars. While there are important differences, nonprofit administrators are faced with many of the same budget process requirements and challenges as their peers in local government. Nonprofit budgeting includes planning and accounting for revenue generation, expenditure development, account balancing, and the political aspects of budget adoption through an executive director and board. For these reasons, we attempt throughout the text to discuss the applicability of the material and budgeting principles to nonprofit organizations. But this coverage falls short of what nonprofit managers need to know in order to be fully successful in performing their fiduciary roles. We encourage faculty and students with a primary interest in nonprofit finance to consult other, more advanced texts.

The variation in course requirements among graduate public administration programs also reflects inconsistent mandatory degree requirements. Many topics closely related to public budgeting are covered in elective courses. A public budgeting course may provide students with their only exposure to strategic planning, contracting and procurement, management control and accounting, nonprofit finance, performance measurement, or public finance. We have provided foundational summaries of these topics as they link to the public budgeting process.

CORE THEMES

Most public budgeting texts focus on the federal budgeting process despite the fact that local governments are by far the most important unit of government in the lives of most citizens. Local government units throughout the United States number about 87,500. This text is organized around the following four local government themes, which are more fully developed in chapter 1:

- Local governments play a central role in building and sustaining the trust of American citizens in democratic governance.
- Local government career administrators play a critical role in making the local budgeting process work successfully.
- The common good at the local level is the product of collaboration between government, nonprofit service providers, private market-sector organizations, and other community partners.
- The reality of severe resource constraints faced by most local governments for the foreseeable future increases the urgency of taking what we call a *polity-centered* approach to local public budgeting.

ORGANIZATION OF TEXT

We have divided the text into four parts or sections, each of which opens with a demonstrative teaching case. The purpose of each case is to illustrate the core themes of the section and to provide students with an opportunity to test the practicality of what they have learned in the section chapters. Part I establishes the context of local public budgeting within the larger historical framework of American government. It defines the purposes of public budgeting and establishes the importance of governance as the driving force behind government and community budgeting.

The section then reviews the major actors in the government budgeting process and introduces the budget process cycle.

A familiarity with revenue sources is critical to understanding the potential for spending and program services delivery. Part II of the text reviews the sources of public revenues, explains the role of property tax and retail sales tax in detail, reviews methods for forecasting revenues, and provides an overview of nonprofit revenues and community governance of tax expenditures and tax rebates. It then reviews budget funds and basic accounting concepts that play an important role in defining the parameters and standards for measuring the success of local public budgeting systems. Students need to understand these concepts to fully understand the public budget documents they read. This part of the book closes with an important chapter on budget process planning.

Part III of the text focuses on department- and program-level budget preparation. We devote a chapter to each of the following four traditional approaches to local government budgeting: line-item budgeting; the planning, programming, budgeting system (PPBS); performance-oriented budgeting; and zero-base budgeting (ZBB) and priority-based budgeting. The goal of these chapters is to illustrate the following four types of accountability that are important for measuring the success of local public budgeting:

- Line-Item Budgeting → Financial Accountability
- Planning, Programming, Budgeting System → Effectiveness Accountability
- Performance Budgeting → Efficiency Accountability
- Zero-Base and Priority Budgeting → Innovation Accountability

The order of discussion for the format-focused chapters in Part III is based on the historical evolution of various systems of accountability. However, the chapters are written as independent, stand-alone essays, thus allowing instructors to sequence the discussions to accommodate the goals and purposes of a given course.

Part IV of the text reviews the processes for the development of an integrated executive budget and its adoption by the legislative body. The section begins with a chapter on the process for budget approval, which is composed of budget assembly by the central budget office, review and approval by the executive, and finally, review and adoption by the elected or appointed council or board. Part IV also includes a chapter on capital budgeting. A primary outcome of the budgeting process is its actual application over the fiscal year or biennium. With this in mind, the section explains the procedures that are used as part of the budget execution process, including monthly reporting and cash flow management adjustments. Finally, Part IV provides an overview of the post-budget auditing process.

Our teaching experiences have confirmed the benefit of having a series of prepared technical exercises and datasets to support the topics presented in the course text. To this end, we have provided the following series of laboratory exercises that can help students gain a basic understanding of key concepts and budgeting techniques. The website at **www.pdx.edu/cps/budget-book** provides exercises and data for:

- Revenue forecasting
- Budget fund accounting
- Line-item budgeting
- PPBS budgeting and performance budgeting
- Zero-base budgeting
- Making the department budget request
- Budget integration and balancing
- Capital budgeting

We have included an extensive glossary at the end of the book for all terms that have technical or special meaning to those in the professional budgeting community. All boldface terms in the text can be found in the Glossary.

ACKNOWLEDGMENTS

We would very much like to thank those students who reviewed the text and laboratory exercises over the years. The Oregon State Fiscal Association provided the initial grant that supported the development of our precursor text, *Handbook on Public Budgeting*. We also wish to acknowledge the support, advice, and suggestions of Jon Yunker, Drew Barden, David Jarvis, Mary Gruss, Susan Walker, Cathy Huber Nickerson, Cece Clitheroe, Mary Ripp, Sandra Reese, and Mark Sayler. In particular, we would like to thank Rick Mogren, our production coordinator, who has performed stellar work in bringing this finished product to the final production stage; our executive editor, Harry Briggs; and the editorial staff at M.E. Sharpe, for their continued enthusiastic and high-quality editorial support. Finally, we would like to thank Ron Tainmen, Director of the Hatfreld School in Government, for financial support in the preparation of this manuscript.

PART I

GENERAL CONCEPTS OF LOCAL PUBLIC BUDGETING

A CASE OF DRASTICALLY FALLING NONPROFIT REVENUES

CASE NARRATIVE

Sonia Albertson, executive director of the nonprofit Upper Cascade Women's Support Project (hereafter referred to as the Support Project) sighed as she reviewed the numbers and then looked over at her finance officer, Brenda Johnson.[1] As usual, Brenda had reduced the ever-changing flow of contracts, grants, major donations, and fees for service into a reality of hard, clear numbers. Several of the revenue sources that the Support Project had come to rely on were being discontinued. Revenues for the coming year's budget would be much lower than they had been in recent years, and the organization would need to make major changes to adapt. Next year's budget would have to become the blueprint for defining and making these radical changes.

It was now mid-September, and Sonia needed to present a proposed budget to the Support Project's board of directors by November 15. This would allow sufficient time for debate by the board and for the adoption of a new budget by January 1, which was the beginning date of the new fiscal year. Fortunately, Brenda had organized a budget process for the organization. Budget preparation instructions had been sent out to each major program in late July, and the staff analysts, program directors, and division directors were currently completing the technical groundwork for their budget requests. Brenda had provided them with the best possible forecasts of the different revenue sources, but revenues were falling steadily from the forecast levels. The directors and staff were scrambling to make adjustments and still meet their October 1 due date for budget request submission. By this time, Brenda was working closely with the different programs to develop cutback packages. This was a whole new experience for Sonia, Brenda, the program directors, and the staff, but the Support Project simply could not go on in its current form.

Sonia and Brenda had hoped that the local community foundation would supply several emergency grants to help offset the loss in state government and country grant revenues, but a recent telephone call from the foundation's director had convinced Sonia there was no chance of receiving any new funds. In past years, government grants had funded about 65 percent of the project's programs and staff. Sonia and Brenda would need to use the proposed budget to sketch out major reductions in programs, staff, and the elimination of two grants to partner organizations. The Support Project would likely maintain its strategic direction and program goals but respond to community and client needs in a much smaller way.

Sonia turned to Brenda and said, "I will schedule a large block of time at our October board meeting to lay out the situation. This will allow us time to provide a briefing and information session before the budget presentation at the November board meeting. It will give the board members time to process the situation before decisions are required. In the meantime, I'll update the board chair, and we will need to brief each of the other board members ahead of time." "As soon as we have an organization level proposal," she went on, "we will need to hold a staff family meeting to discuss the situation and the likelihood of layoffs. At that point, you will need to contact the Shelter and Respite House and the Youth Response Project and explain the situation." Both Sonia and Brenda knew that this would be a challenging month with devastating news for everyone.

Sonia Albertson had been the chief executive officer (CEO) of the Upper Cascade Women's Support Project for the past nine years. Over those years, the organization had grown from a small women's crisis hotline and shelter service to a multiservice organization with more than 120 employees. The project had taken on new grants from the local community foundation and two regional community intermediary nonprofits.[2] These nonprofit-sector grants complemented several major contracts from county and state social service agencies. The Support Project continued to provide telephone crisis intervention and safe shelter services for battered and threatened women and their families, but it also now provided a range of other social and support services to women and their families. The Support Project shelter could provide emergency and short-term shelter for 20 single women and three women with children. Through a state human services grant, the Support Project had established a drug and alcohol group treatment program for both women and men, and using a county grant it had established a small mental health services program. The Support Project provided a counseling and referral service to help women identify and access services. To assist women in their efforts to gain and retain employment, the Support Project established a business clothes bank, employment preparation counseling, and child care services for toddlers through kindergarten. The Support Project's board had carefully reviewed each new program for strategic conformance with the organization's mission—to help women in need), and for its financial ramifications. Sonia was proud of the organization's growth and its steady and increasing service to the community.

As the Support Project organization grew, attention to administrative services had lagged. After utilizing the services of a succession of bookkeepers and outside financial service providers, Sonia and the board realized that the organization had grown to the point that it needed a chief financial officer (CFO). Brenda Johnson was hired to bring order to a chaos of budgets, grant requirements, audits, and limited professional staff capacity. In filling the CFO position, the board sought a candidate who could develop complex financial systems and internal controls, lead budget development, bring consistency and quality to procurement and contracting, and improve the organization's performance.[3] Brenda applied for the position as a CPA with extensive nonprofit experience. She had successfully grown into the other aspects of the position. Brenda reported directly to Sonia as the chief executive and was an important member of the executive team. Additionally, through her continued presence and quality work, Brenda had developed strong credibility with the board members. Brenda maintained a direct relationship with the board, especially on financial matters. She managed this relationship carefully, most often closely coordinating with Sonia but, on occasion, advocating independent opinions to the board chair and board members.

Brenda and Sonia had worked especially hard to diversify the organization's revenues between private grants, state agency and local government contracts, smaller charitable donations, and client user fees. This formula had worked well up until the recent major economic downturn. The Support Project had consistently covered expenses and put away a small reserve for tough times. But the severe economic recession of the last year had overwhelmed these carefully laid plans and strategies.

Brenda had pushed Sonia to follow the development of the economic recession over the last year and a half. A sputtering national economy and the downturn of the stock market had stalled business hiring. Faced with employment uncertainty, consumers had put off purchasing new cars and other large discretionary capital purchases. Another major outcome of the recession was severely limited tax revenues to the state government: Reduced purchasing by consumers and businesses resulted in reduced retail sales tax revenues. Automobile use taxes and transfer fees, and lodging and entertainment sales taxes were also down considerably. Caution by businesses had led to increased unemployment. Weak employment and reduced business activity led to a strong reduction in state income tax revenues.

The reduced revenues had left the state government with revenue shortfalls of over $800 million. With state revenues so severely depressed, the legislature would be forced to reduce revenue sharing and grants to counties and local governments. These intergovernmental revenues were the primary source of funds for many of the Support Project's programs.

Early in the previous December, following state constitution requirements, the governor had presented a balanced budget filled with extensive cuts and program reductions. The balanced budget responded to the $800 million revenue shortfall with major cuts to numerous programs. The governor could have shifted the timing of expenditures, used one-time monies, emptied the rainy day fund, and/or borrowed short-term funds to soften the blows, but she relied on her budget office analysts to present a truthful picture without gimmicks. This approach forced the legislature to make the policy and spending decisions that would respond to the reality of reduced revenues. The structure of the state budget, however, greatly limited what the governor could modify. Over 70 percent of the state budget was protected by constitutional requirements to fund K–12 schools, public safety, and the state police. Other required spending included matching funds to obtain federal grants and debt service payments on funds borrowed by the state. The difficulty of the state's revenue situation was demonstrated by calls to close both a youth corrections camp and the least efficient unit of the adult state prison system. But because social services were not constitutionally protected, the deepest cuts fell on health and social service programs. About 10,000 clients would be left ineligible for the state health plan, thus freeing up $150 million in savings. Secure crisis residential centers for youth were eliminated in favor of lower cost residential service for $9.4 million in savings. Nursing home reimbursement rates under the state's Medicaid program were reduced by 5 percent, yielding another $46.2 million savings in both state and federal dollars. Funding for mental health services was reduced by $30.5 million. And the general assistance to unemployable adults and alcohol and drug addiction treatment funds were cut by $160 million. Though it was balanced, even the governor publicly lamented that the budget was unjust.

Sonia and Brenda had followed the governor's budget—and the subsequent legislative action on it—quite closely. In January, the state legislature had convened for a general session, a primary task of which was to prepare a new biennial budget. Committee hearings in the state house and state senate laid out the issues. The quarterly state revenue forecast told of further revenue shortfalls. But analysts from the state's service caseload forecasting team predicted strongly increasing needs for social services, job training, and postsecondary education services because of the poor economy. Sonia had gone to the state capital and testified before the House Health and Social Services Appropriations Subcommittee on the growing need for services. Other nonprofit executives and county commissioners had testified before state senate committees. Social service advocates and lobbyists had worked the halls and delivered constituent communications as best they could. While the lawmakers had blunted the worst cuts in the governor's budget, the fiscal realities resulted in about a $325 million reduction spread across emergency housing, low-income health, mental health, drug and alcohol recovery, developmental disabilities, juvenile services, and job training programs.

Just after the legislature convened in January, the Upper Cascadia County Commission also began its work on a budget for the coming fiscal year. As executive director of the Support Project, Sonia kept in close contact with the county director of community and social services. At every chance, Sonia stressed the continuing need for crisis services, shelter services, and treatment services for mental health, drug abuse, and alcohol addiction. The county director was quick to recognize the growing service demand and caseload but was also quick to caution that if funding from the state fell drastically, so would the county programs and service contracts.

By late April, the county executive released his proposed budget: Community and social services would take a 10 percent reduction. County-delivered programs would be reduced by 7 percent. Major existing service contracts for housing, veterans, mental health, children's and family services, and developmental disabilities would continue, but without an inflation escalation in payments. This matched the minimal inflation rate across the regional economy. But most important, several drug and alcohol treatment, mental health, and homeless services contracts would be wound down and not renewed. The number of new service contracts in community and social services was reduced to near zero.

Sonia and Brenda worked through the county executive's proposed budget in detail and winced at many of the cuts. These cuts would be devastating to their organization and to their clients. Sonia contacted the county director of community and social services to explain the situation and its implications. The county citizen budget advisory committee met in early May to review the executive's proposed budget. Sonia requested, and was granted, a slot to testify before the committee to explain the implications of the combined cuts. The county commission then held three public hearings on the proposed budget. Again, Sonia requested a slot, and she was granted five minutes at the second public hearing. In her presentation, Sonia explained the implications of the reductions on women in the community and on the nonprofit partners that carried out county and state programs. The commissioners listened, but one politely reminded Sonia of the major cuts in state funding to the county, and of flat and declining property and sales tax revenues. Another commissioner was more blunt and asked Sonia how she would apportion a $2.5 million cut to social services to minimize the impact on clients.

By early June, the commissioners understood the full impact of state funding reductions and adjusted the worst of the reductions through amendments to the county executive's proposed budget, but in the end reduced services for alcohol and drug treatment, homelessness, mental health issues, the elderly, and children by 15 percent. The county commission adopted a balanced annual budget in mid-June—in time for the new fiscal year, which would begin on July 1.

The reductions in government funding were difficult enough, but Sonia and Brenda's communications with the local community foundation presented another challenge. The economic downturn had rocked the stock market and created uncertainty in the foundation's other endowment investments. Personal charitable giving had also dropped off because of the economic insecurity. The community foundation completed its budget cycle in late August, which allowed it to follow and react to decisions by the state and county governments in their budgets. In early August, the foundation's chair had convened a meeting with its nonprofit grantees, contractors, and partners. Sonia and Brenda attended that meeting and related the difficulties the Support Project was facing because of reductions in government funding. The community foundation chair and chief executive officer could only empathize and report that the foundation, too, would be cutting its grants and contracts to service providers. The foundation would examine all components of its programs and strategically adjust its grants to prioritize and support services, and where possible, compensate for the reductions in government funding. The Support Project would benefit from some of these adjustments, but the larger message was that the foundation was going to significantly reduce grants to its service delivery partners. These developments knocked another leg out from under the Support Project's revenue sources.

The impacts of the drastic government and foundation cuts would hit the Support Project in the next fiscal year. The new budget had to reflect major structural changes in the organization's programs. Preliminary scenarios indicated that about 40 percent of the programs would need to close, and staff layoffs would follow a proportional reduction. The two grants with partner organizations would need to be terminated if the Support Project's budget were to remain balanced.

The dire revenue situation caused Sonia and Brenda to go back and reconsider their organization's mission and purpose. The Support Project had been established to empower and support women in the community as they gained personal stability and self-sufficiency. This mission still seemed highly relevant and appropriate, but the current program goals of comprehensive services and annual objectives of well-developed service delivery—though once appropriate—were now lofty and overstated. Resizing and restating the goals and objectives would be a critical task in developing a new budget. Sonia and Brenda agreed that the board and the staff would need to be involved in such an effort, even though the budget schedule left very limited time for such an effort.

Brenda stated that she could quickly convene the department and program directors and the budget analysts to conduct a downsizing exercise. The group would take on the details of reducing all programs and then develop a series of alternative budget scenarios with 30, 20, and 15 percent reductions. Brenda quickly outlined a meeting agenda. Sonia would convene the group and explain the overall revenue and strategic situation. Brenda would then give a more detailed look at the reduced funding levels for each of the major programs. Next, she would break the leadership team into small groups and give each one a program area for analysis. A paper exercise would follow with the required reductions to reach a balanced budget. At the end of the day, the group would reflect on their exercise results and develop recommendations to Sonia and to the board of directors.

Sonia paused a moment over whether to follow Brenda's suggestion. Should the staff take the lead in defining major program reductions and reorganizations? The department directors and staff analysts were well into the alternative development process as part of the budget preparation task. The budget process would allow the board a full chance to review the situation and to evaluate any proposed reductions and reorganizations, but should she focus first on the board and let them give initial guidance on alternatives? She was sure that she could "sell" staff-developed alternatives and a recommended course of action, but would it be better to let the board provide strategic guidance and program priorities on how best to transform the organization and its programs? Allowing the board to take the lead would allow the board members to make contact with the Support Project's service delivery partners and subcontractors, key donors, advocacy groups, community leaders, clients, and even staff. Sonia turned to Brenda and asked, "Would you please hold off on convening a staff work group until I consult with our board chair and we can figure out our next steps forward?"

CASE ANALYSIS

The Upper Cascade Women's Support Project case opens up the subject of public budgeting on numerous levels. At least three major levels stand out in the scenario: (1) the networked delivery of services and issues of community governance and responsibility; (2) the structuring effects of the public budgeting process; and (3) the contrasting values and success criteria of political actors and professionals.

First, the Support Project has defined itself as a comprehensive, one-stop service delivery agency, but providing such a program depends on numerous sources of revenue and the support of several major benefactors. These supports include state social service and health agencies, county government departments and social service programs, community foundations, and community intermediary nonprofits. Each of these contributors is an independent organization, even if they have partial reliance on each other for funding or policy direction. For example, state social service agencies may contract with county governments for service provision. The county may deliver programs with in-house staff or may partner and contract with nonprofit organizations like the Support Project. The Support Project is, however, an independent provider—it receives funding from multiple sources and answers to its own board of directors. It follows county or state government direction only to the degree required in its contracts, and out of common policy intention and goodwill. The Support Project, in turn, contracts with two subgrantees or subcontractors to deliver part of its services. These subcontractors are again independent organizations. The service providers in this community are interlinked in a complex network of resource and service organizations. The network arrangement may be beneficial for performance effectiveness and resilience, for building a competitive vendor community, and for nurturing civic capacity and civil society. But the diffusion of authority and responsibility over the network can be problematic. Who governs the network and sets its strategic direction to benefit the community and its needs? And, as we have seen in this case, who takes final responsibility to ensure that sufficient resources are budgeted and channeled to meet client needs? Once services are provided, who reviews the efficiency and effectiveness of the service program? Governance of the network raises additional issues. Should governance of the network generate from community energy and local relationships, or should network leadership and decision making draw from a larger funding organization that can enforce performance and resource allocation? In this case, should the Support Project as the primary service delivery group closest to the ground have primary responsibility, or should the community foundation, or a major community intermediary, or the county have responsibility as a primary donor? More defined and effective network governance might provide a more focused answer to these issues.

Second, the case demonstrates that public budgeting follows a well-defined process. We explain the generic budget cycle and the major budget process steps in detail in chapter 5, and the budget actors who use the process in chapter 4. The case, however, offers glimpses of the state government, county government, and nonprofit organization budget procedures. The case demonstrates that while these governmental and nonprofit organizations may be in very different political and economic contexts, the budget development procedures have many features in common. A budget cycle will typically begin with a planning phase initiated by the executive, followed by a budget request preparation phase by agency, department, or program staff. The organization executive, a governor, county executive, mayor, special district executive, or nonprofit executive then presents a proposed consolidated organization budget to a legislative group for evaluation, public review, likely modification, and final adoption. Legislative groups include state legislatures, city councils, county commissions, special district boards, or nonprofit boards. Once the budget is adopted, the organization will implement it and spend its resources over a single fiscal year or fiscal biennium of two years. When the fiscal year or biennium ends, an audit phase reviews the agency's financial and organizational performance. But the case demonstrates a complexity specific to public budgeting: The timing of cycles used by different governments and nonprofits does not always mesh. For example, the county government was trying to build a budget at the same time that the state legislature was undecided on funding for state grants to counties for social services. This made it hard for county and other local governments to plan and budget effectively. The community foundation recognized this timing mismatch and scheduled its budget process to follow the adoption of the government budgets. The foundation's retrospective approach allowed it to prioritize its funding allocations to partially compensate for government funding shortfalls.

Third, the case gives some indication of the many actors involved in the public budgeting process. Each actor has a different perspective on the process, along with different criteria for demonstrating successful participation. Professionals in the process—as modeled by Brenda Johnson, the Support Project's department and program directors, and the staff analysts—judge their success by professional standards and by legal compliance with state regulations and rules. For finance professionals and analysts, the Government Finance Officers Association (GFOA 2000) distinguished budget presentation criteria; professional accounting and auditing standards (see chaps. 9 and 18) provide such criteria. For program professionals, designing, funding, and conducting responsive, effective programs to meet client needs and professional expectations stand as the success criteria. In contrast, executives and elected officials face a less sufficiently defined and more politically tangled set of success criteria. Budgeting must be of special help to these actors as they respond to political pressures, communicate with activists outside the organization, and connect with the community and its many groups. The budget process provides an important communication path for executives, legislatures, councils, commissions, and boards building confidence in government and its ability to deliver services. These two conflicting perspectives, the professional and the political, raise tensions throughout the budget process. As the closing moment in our case demonstrates, professional standards and efficiency may often need to give way to the political needs of building support for action and governance agreement.

NOTES

1. Though hypothetical, this instructional case is drawn and integrated from real-world events and conditions. As examples of major nonprofit service provider cutbacks, see VanderHart (2010); state government reductions (State of Washington 2008, 18–20, 2009); and county government reduction (Hannah-Jones 2011). For an example of a social service delivery nonprofit with state and government grants, see the Cascadia Behavioral Healthcare website at www.cascadiabhc.org/ (accessed January 19, 2014).

2. *Intermediary* nonprofit organizations (chap. 3, 8; glossary) raise money from a broad number of sources and then partner and contract with service provider organizations to deliver programs and services. An intermediary typically does not engage in service provision, but might provide community leadership planning and coordination services. Widely known community and regional intermediary organizations include regional and local United Way chapters, as well as religious affiliated service providers that draw donations from member churches, parishes, and synagogues (e.g., Catholic Charities Community Services; Lutheran Community Services). Rather than identify specific organizations, we use the generic term of *intermediary nonprofit* throughout the book. Community foundations play a similar role, but through a slightly different mechanism. A *foundation* is a type of intermediary nonprofit. Foundations may use collected revenues for making direct grants to service providers and groups, but foundations often collect money from donors to feed an investment endowment. Income generated from the investments provides revenue for grants to service providers and community groups.

3. The responsibilities of this position are similar to those handled by the finance director of a small- or medium-sized city or special district. A clerk of a small town would have similar duties, but on a smaller scale.

1 | LOCAL PUBLIC BUDGETING AND THE CHALLENGES OF DECENTRALIZED GOVERNANCE

THREE SCENARIOS

Scenario 1: The Complexity of Local Government and the Need for Interjurisdictional Cooperation

Following several unsuccessful attempts to pass local **property tax** levies to finance public services, four separate governing jurisdictions took action: They initiated a strategic planning process and enlisted help from their local university to assist in creating a tax levy plan and citizen outreach strategy for funding local services. The four governing units (a unified school district, a county, a city, and an independent parks and recreation district) realized that citizens were confused about how local services were funded and believed that too many governments were making too many requests for increased taxes. The goals of the strategic planning process were (1) to generate a better understanding of the priorities citizens placed on the separately funded public services; (2) to educate citizens on the mutual needs and funding sources of the various entities; and (3) to create a plan for property tax revenue requests by the four independent entities.

In the face of growing urbanization, government leaders in this large urban area were struggling to meet increased service demands without dramatically increasing property taxes or compromising the existing property tax base upon which the various jurisdictions relied for funding. The major governing entities in the region agreed to create a joint task force to develop governance options. Ultimately, the task force recommended the creation of a new regional government and the transfer of regionwide functions to the new entity (e.g., regional land-use and growth planning, management of the zoo and the Exposition Center, solid waste disposal, and parks and open space), with the taxing authority to fund these functions. Citizens and government leaders alike supported the recommendations of the task force.

Scenario 2: The Financial Fragility of Local Governments

On average, 40 percent of the funding for services provided at the local level comes as transfers from the state and federal government (Tax Policy Center 2008). Since the **economic downturn** of 2007–2009, 46 states plus the District of Columbia have initiated major budget cuts. These cuts resulted in the reduction of health care (31 states), services to the elderly and disabled (29 states and the District of Columbia), K–12 education (34 states and the District of Columbia), and higher education (43 states) (Johnson, Oliff, and Williams 2011). These cuts are occurring at a time when local debt has risen by more than 76 percent between 2000 and 2008 (U.S. Census Bureau 2003, 2012b).

Scenario 3: The Creative Governance Role of Career Administrators in Local Public Budgeting

Unable to fund the growing social service needs of its citizens, county administrative leaders facilitated a community envisioning process with citizens and stakeholders. The exercise served to identify shared aspirations and map existing resources in the nonprofit, business, religious, and governmental communities that might be better coordinated and leveraged to meet these unmet social service needs. The county created a new 501(c)(3), called the Vision Action Network, to serve as the holding company for addressing these needs, and it committed to using this new network as the governing entity for dispersing county-funded social service activities.

Struggling to find ways of replacing seriously undermaintained old buildings, a local school district entered into a **partnership agreement** with the Boys and Girls Club, the city, the development commission, and the private sector to develop a new mixed-income residential community large enough to require a new school. The new school includes a community and recreation center, which is partly owned and operated by the Boys and Girls Club and the city parks department. The school has full use of the athletic facilities for all of its school functions but only pays for a share of the total costs. Because the new development includes neighborhood businesses located within the new community and is built within a low-income area of the city, the development qualifies for low-interest federal loans. The old school building and land have been donated to the city in exchange for the land in the new community development.

We begin this book with these three scenarios to illustrate why local public budgeting deserves special attention. Budgeting is not simply a technical exercise about how best to expend the revenues collected from citizens through fees, charges, taxes, and other sources. It is ultimately about determining what the community values and generating the support necessary to fund these values. The support is reflected not only in dollars but in patterns of relationships that have been developed through time and have acquired institutional status. The local school, library, Boys and Girls Club, chamber of commerce, rotary club, friends group, community center, or a long-enduring citizen group may symbolize this institutional role. While the national and state budgeting processes are greatly influenced by well-financed lobbyists speaking on behalf of well-organized interest groups, this is not the case in most of the 88,657 local government jurisdictions in the United States (see Exhibit 1.1). Instead, the budgeting process is shaped by deeply embedded local institutional entities that have a vested interest in how government officials use the process to promote the common good of the community. This makes the budgeting process political, but it is a different kind of politics than the interest group model used to explain what happens at the state and federal levels of government.

Most books on public budgeting focus on the federal and, to a lesser extent, state budgeting processes. Moreover, most of these books view budgeting more narrowly as an interest-based lobbying activity that determines how various revenue sources will be allocated to support what government does. This model is less applicable to the state and especially local levels of government (Carroll and Johnson 2010). The reasons are an artifact of a legal and political structure that gives local citizens large amounts of control over the discretionary authority of elected officials to collect various kinds of revenue and to expend those revenues to support what government does.

We have organized this book around four core themes that, taken together, explain why government budgeting at the local level deserves to be given special attention. First, there are 88,657 local governments (see the aforementioned Exhibit 1.1) in the United States. These local governments are responsible for providing services that matter most to the average citizen, including those related to schools, land-use planning, public safety, water, sewer, transportation, and mental health. The complexity of this arrangement creates the need for cooperation across organizational and jurisdictional boundaries and provides a multitude of opportunities for the

Exhibit 1.1

Number of Governmental Units by Type, 1952–2007

Type of Government	1952[1]	1962	1967	1972	1977	1982	1987	1992	1997	2007	% Change[4] (1952–2007)
					Year						
Total, All Types	116,807	91,237	81,299	78,269	79,913	81,831	83,237	85,006	87,504	89,272	–23
U.S. Government	1	1	1	1	1	1	1	1	1	1	0
Native American Tribes[2]	n/a	n/a	n/a	n/a	n/a	n/a	n/a	n/a	n/a	564	0
State Governments	50	50	50	50	50	50	50	50	50	50	0
Local Governments	116,756	91,186	81,248	78,218	79,862	81,780	83,186	84,955	87,453	88,657	–24
Counties	3,052	3,043	3,049	3,044	3,042	3,041	3,042	3,043	3,043	3,033	–0.60
Municipal	16,807	18,000	18,048	18,517	18,862	19,076	19,200	19,279	19,372	19,492	16
Townships and Towns	17,202	17,142	17,105	16,991	16,822	16,734	16,691	16,656	16,629	16,519	–4
School Districts[3]	67,355	34,678	21,782	15,781	15,174	14,851	14,721	14,422	13,726	14,561	–78
Special Districts	12,340	18,323	21,264	23,885	25,962	28,078	29,532	31,555	34,683	35,052	84

Sources: U.S. Census Bureau, 2002, *Census of Governments*, Vol. 1, No. 1, *Government Organization*, Series GC02(1)-1, Washington, DC: U.S. Government Printing Office, 2002; and U.S. Census Bureau 2007a.

[1]1952 adjusted to include units in Alaska and Hawaii, which adopted statehood in 1959.

[2]The U.S. Census Bureau does not track the number of Indian tribes. As of May 2013, the Bureau of Indian Affairs (BIA) listed 566 tribal entities as eligible for funding and services from the BIA by virtue of their status as Indian tribes. The basic legal framework for tribal sovereignty was established by Chief Justice John Marshall in a trilogy of cases adjudicated in the 1830s and affirmed by more recent courts. See *Johnson v. McIntosh*, 21 U.S. (8 Wheat.) 543, 5 L. Ed. 681 (1823); *Cherokee Nation v. Georgia*, 30 U.S. (5 Pet.) 1, 8 L. Ed. 25 (1831); *Worcester v. Georgia*, 31 U.S. (6 Pet.) 515, 8 L. Ed. 483 (1832) and *United States v. Wheeler*, 435 U.S. 313, 98 S. Ct. 1079, 55 L. Ed. 2d 303 (1978). For a list of federally recognized tribes, see U.S. Department of the Interior, Bureau of Indian Affairs, http://bia.gov/cs/groups/public/documents/text/idc1-023762.pdf (accessed February 4, 2014).

[3]Includes dependent school districts, which are under the control of the state, county, or other governing body.

[4]Calculation of percent change does not include Native American tribes.

exercise of creative leadership on the part of career public administrators as they carry out their local budgeting responsibilities.

A second reason for giving special attention to local public budgeting is that for the foreseeable future, local jurisdictions will be facing a financial crisis that requires the invention of new approaches to local service delivery and civic engagement strategies to enlist the support and confidence of the local community. Because local governments are the legal creatures of the state within which they exist, they operate within a more constrained environment than do their federal and state counterparts. Despite this constrained environment, we argue that local administrators have opportunities to exercise creative leadership that are not as readily available to those with budget responsibility at the state and federal levels of government.

Policy decisions for most local governments are made by part-time and unpaid elected officials who depend on their career administrators for innovative problem solving. This is a third reason we believe local public budgeting deserves separate consideration.

Finally, local governments in the future will be increasingly responsible for what we call **polity** budgeting—that is, a concern for how the community's assets across the nonprofit, for-profit, and government sectors can be identified and mobilized to make the highest and best contribution to the community's common good. This goes beyond the traditional jurisdiction-centered concern for using the budget process to preserve the delivery of high-quality government services, even in the face of diminishing resources. In the future, we believe local governments will increasingly use their *soft power* of influence rather than relying on their smaller sphere of constrained *hard power* and formal legal authority in the local public budgeting process.

In the sections that follow, we will elaborate more fully on each of the four core themes of the book, summarized here:

- the unique role of local governments in building democratic legitimacy;
- the perfect financial storm, a transformational opportunity;
- the unique politics of local public budgeting; and
- polity budgeting and the rebuilding of local communities.

THE UNIQUE ROLE OF LOCAL GOVERNMENTS IN BUILDING DEMOCRATIC LEGITIMACY

In the United States, local governments play a decisive but legally subordinate role in building and maintaining the legitimacy of democratic government. The Tenth Amendment to the U.S. Constitution makes explicit that "the powers not delegated to the United States by the Constitution, nor prohibited by it to the States, are reserved to the States respectively, or to the people." The states, in turn, have delegated their powers down to a wide variety of local governing bodies that provide the services about which the majority of citizens care most. This legal arrangement reflects the historical reality that many local governments existed prior to statehood, but it also embodies a conundrum: On the one hand, local governments play a significant, practical role in making democratic governance work; on the other, they are legally subordinate to their parent state authority. This conundrum will be explored more fully in the sections that follow.

The Practical Importance of Local Governments in the United States

In his travels across the United States in the mid-1830s, the French historian Alexis de Tocqueville was struck by the high levels of decentralization of governmental authority and the advantages this provided in building the trust of America's citizens in their public officials:

What I admire most in America are not the *administrative* effects of decentralization, but the *political* effects. . . . Often the European sees in the public official only force; the American sees in him right. . . . As administrative authority is placed at the side of those whom it administers, and in some way represents them, it excites neither jealousy nor hatred. . . . Administrative power . . . does not find itself abandoned to itself as in Europe. One does not believe that the duties of particular persons have ceased because the representative of the public comes to act. (Tocqueville 1835–1840/2000, 90)

If Tocqueville were to travel across the United States today, he would likely be even more impressed by the extraordinary expansion of the process of decentralization that has occurred over the past two centuries. As of the 2007 Census there were, 88,657 separate local governmental entities in the United States, each levying taxes or charging fees to deliver services to the citizens it serves. Exhibit 1.1 provides a summary overview of the kinds and growth of these governing bodies over the past 50 years. During this time, **special districts** have increased by more than 143 percent, growing from 12,340 in 1952 to 35,052 in 2007 (U.S. Census Bureau 2002, 2007a). In contrast, school districts have undergone a dramatic consolidation and contraction.

While all local governments in the United States are the legal creatures of the state within which they exist, the long-standing American tradition of *bottom-up governance* has resulted in the creation of a rich array of models that set local governments off from their counterparts around the world. First, there is a very large degree of discretionary authority at the local levels of the system, resulting in a wide variety of governing structures and processes. Neither the central government nor a controlling political party dictates how the majority of money raised from local citizens shall be spent by local government officials. This is not the case in many *single party* systems or in countries like France, whose local governing bodies are the administrative agencies of the central government. While local officials are elected in countries like France, Japan, South Korea, and Italy, their discretionary authority is severely limited in comparison to local government officials in the United States. For example, in Japan and South Korea, local government officials have very limited taxing authority. This is also the case for European democratic states like France and Italy, where local governing bodies have limited powers to collect taxes for services like public safety, transportation, waste collection, and street lighting. In these centralized governments, most of the revenue flows downward through the central ministries to local offices. This contrasts with the United States, where local governments exercise significant discretionary authority over the collection and expenditure of taxes (Tax Policy Center 2008).

Most Americans are surprised to learn that so many local budgeting entities hold the authority to levy taxes, charge fees, and borrow money to pay for the services they provide. A typical citizen may be a taxpayer of up to a dozen local jurisdictions: city, county, borough, township, state, school district, fire district, water district, soil conservation district, library district, hospital district, parks and recreation district, just to mention a few of the more common possibilities. One of the authors of this book resides in a county with 33 separate governing jurisdictions and pays taxes to six separate entities. This complexity of the local government landscape creates unique budgeting and revenue issues both for citizens and for elected officials, which we will discuss in more detail in the section that follows.

The Legal Subordination of Local Governments to Their Parent State: Dillon's Rule[1]

Each state defines by statute the types and kinds of local jurisdictions that can exist within its borders. This enabling authority is codified in state statutes, for which a dizzying array of models exist.[2] For example, the state of Pennsylvania organizes its local government code authority by county, subdividing each county into cities, class 1 townships, class 2 townships, and boroughs. By contrast, the state of South Carolina organizes its code authority by counties (Title 4), municipal corporations (Title 5), and Local Government Provisions Applicable to Special Purpose Districts and Other Political Subdivisions (Title 6). The state of Washington represents the extreme in specification of local government authority. It provides separate code authority for cities and towns (Title 35, which provides for the creation of class 1 cities, class 2 cities, and towns), home rule jurisdictions (Title 35A), counties (Title 36), library districts (Title 27), fire protection districts (Title 52), port districts (Title 53), public utility districts (Title 54), sanitary districts (Title 55), and water-sewer districts (Title 57).

Along the eastern seaboard of the United States, many local governments predated those of the states. These small governmental bodies provided the milieu for cultivating significant degrees of local autonomy—as well as direct and indirect democratic governance—decades in advance of the ratification of the U.S. Constitution. A U.S. Advisory Commission on Intergovernmental Relations report (1993, hereafter referred to as ACIR report) observed that during the colonial and revolutionary periods, "the custom and practice of local self-government was strong and pervasive," and local institutions exhibited varied forms and functions (1993, 28–29). Most commonly known are the New England town governments, which operated under colonial town laws and practiced direct democratic governance. However, local governments in other colonies also exercised considerable "local privilege," manifested in many instances through independent democratic decision processes, and in some cases were even empowered to send delegates with instructions to their colonial legislatures (1993, 27–30).

With the ratification of the U.S. Constitution came some drastic changes to the power structure at the local level. This dominant, national legal doctrine set forth the supreme laws of the land and, in general, treated local governments as mere creatures of the states—as products of the reserve powers ceded to the states under the Tenth Amendment to the Constitution. Technically, local governments in the United States are not even "guaranteed a republican form," as the Constitution requires of the state governments in Article IV. The states, it is held, provide for the establishment of local governments, and they delegate authority to local governing bodies that otherwise hold no independent authority.

The tidy legal doctrine just described is now commonly referred to as **Dillon's Rule**, after John Forest Dillon, a jurist from Iowa who had served on both state and federal courts and who articulated the doctrine in an 1868 Iowa case (*Clinton v. Cedar Rapids and the Missouri River Railroad,* 24 Iowa 455 [1868]). Dillon derived his analysis in part from Chief Justice John Marshall's (served 1801–1835) jurisprudence as expressed in cases such as *Fletcher v. Peck* (10 U.S. 87 [1810]) and *Dartmouth College v. Woodward* (17 U.S. 518 [1819]), and from Federalist legal commentaries such as James Kent's 1827 treatise on American law. In the *Fletcher* and *Dartmouth College* cases, Marshall—holding to strong Federalist views—outlined a theory of contract and property rights that favored centralized governmental interventions and policy to spur economic development over local self-determination. He deemed local governments a strong source of parochial interests that would likely do more to retard economic development than encourage it. For this reason, it was important that state governments possess strict authority over local governing entities as creatures of their own making. However, Marshall's jurisprudence did not preclude limited protection by state and federal courts of local initiatives that did spur economic development or that established important mediating institutions for socializing and educating local citizenry. Marshall thus left at least an opening for local governments to play their own role in these affairs (see Barron 1999, 506).

Judge Dillon narrowed this thinking in the 1860s and 1870s. Basing his jurisprudence in part on the popular laissez-faire and classical liberal doctrines of the late nineteenth century, he asserted that governments were constitutionally obliged to play strictly neutral roles over private civic and economic development. He proffered a bright-line distinction between public and private spheres of life, and state governments were obliged to strictly control local governments toward that end (Barron 1999, 507–509). If state legislatures failed in this effort, then "enlightened state judges would enforce the private boundary that public politics would likely breach" (509).

Though Dillon's Rule is still considered authoritative, it is not the only legal doctrine recognized in statutes and case law. Thomas Cooley, a highly regarded state supreme court jurist from Michigan, immediately attacked the Dillon doctrine, arguing in his then-influential *Treatise on Constitutional Limitations* (1868, see also his concurring opinion in a Michigan case, *People v. Hurlbut*, 24 Mich 44 [1871]):

> It is axiomatic that the management of purely local affairs belongs to the people concerned, not only because of being their own affairs, but because they will best understand and be most competent to manage them. The continued and permanent existence of local government is therefore *assumed* in all the state constitutions, and is a matter of *constitutional right*, even when not in terms expressly provided for. It would not be competent to dispense with it by statute. (emphasis added, Cooley 1868, 378)

As indicated, Cooley did not rest his defense of local autonomy on specific constitutional or statutory language, but rather "on a more general assertion of basic, unwritten constitutional norms" that derived from a more "organic approach to constitutionalism"—an approach associated with the Jacksonian common law perspective popular in that era (Barron 1999, 512, 518–519; see also Carrington 1997; Kahn 1992; Jones 1987; Paludan 1975; Siegel 1984; and Williams 1986). This amounts to a kind of inherent constitutional power, though a very limited one. Cooley "sought at once to embrace and to tame popular rule" by envisioning a "local constitutionalism in which public municipal corporations—such as towns and cities—would be responsible for imparting important values to the public in much the same manner that Marshall had previously imagined private civic corporations such as Dartmouth College would" (Barron 1999, 511–512). Cooley viewed the Constitution "not [as] a privatizing charter that protected individuals from government," but as "a publicizing document that protected the community from self-interested public officials, corrupted by powerful private interests" (Barron 1999, 512). Living as he did in the Gilded Age (the late nineteenth century) of massive corporate monopolies and urban political machines, this twist on constitutional purpose was neither surprising nor uncommon, especially among reformers (ironically, a group with whom Cooley was not then associated; see Barron 1999, 509–520).

Cooley wanted to shelter local governments from powerful private interests that were often protected by state politicians as they perverted the public interests of communities for private gain. He witnessed this dynamic firsthand through cases involving railroad monopolies—a problem he took on more directly upon being appointed head of the Interstate Commerce Commission a few years later (see Rohr 1986, chap. 7). With Jacksonian fervor, Cooley championed the "autonomy and liberty of persons to order their own affairs, subject to general laws which do not create favored or disfavored classes of citizens" (quoted in Barron 1999, 514).

Cooley believed that local governments played a vital role in preserving Jacksonian conceptions of democratic equality; such theories allowed for the socialization of local people into public life via civic and entrepreneurial associations, and enabled them to participate in local self-governance. Cooley's organic view of constitutions as facilitating the evolution of governing principles in the same way the common law does—through accreted habits, customs, lived experiences, and "common thoughts of men"—acknowledged the "from-the-ground-up" aspects of local governance and community life that the dominant, more positivistic jurisprudence ignored. From this perspective, he conceived a "structural defense of the practice of local self-government" (Barron 1999, 516–518):

Local political institutions provided the fora through which people could engage in the practice of constitutionalism for themselves. The practice of local self-government would directly inculcate constitutional values in the public sphere by affording the local citizenry an opportunity to practice democracy with constitutional limitations. Through the practice of public politics at the local level, citizens would be forced in a direct and immediate way to determine for themselves which decisions would serve the "public" interests of their own communities and which would not. That experience would provide citizens with a greater understanding of what it meant to govern themselves in accord with constitutional limitations that would be possible under a regime of either centralized state legislative control or judicial supremacy. (518)

Cooley's structural defense of local constitutionalism failed to become a more prominent legal doctrine for local governments in the United States. Dillon's Rule imposes an arid legal standard on local entities—a standard that fails to account for their rich and varied nature and leaves them quite vulnerable to the vagaries of state legislative meddling. In effect, it forces them to govern their own affairs with one hand tied behind their backs. The ACIR report strongly recommended that a more balanced and consistent relationship between state and local governments was needed, and the report specifically cited Cooley's doctrine as an important legal element in "refocusing the debate over how to balance state control and local autonomy" (1993, 7). The dominance of the Dillon Rule, however, has not been absolute. The organic or "from-the-ground-up" aspects of local self-determination and governance could not help but manifest themselves in law as well as in political life, and thus have been recognized in a more tenuous form through the adoption of *home rule* charters and related legislation.

Some scholars locate American precedents for home rule in the colonial and revolutionary eras (ACIR report 1993, 32–34), but Cooley's doctrine clearly gave the home rule movement more impetus. "Although Cooley's views were unequivocally adopted only in Indiana, Nebraska, Iowa, Kentucky, and Texas, they articulated a resurgence of values that would soon be embodied in institutional reforms designed to widen the scope of local choice" (1993, 34). These included the insertion of **ripper clauses** and more general state constitutional provisions against "special legislation," which was commonly used to interfere with local powers and prerogatives relating to social and economic development in their jurisdictions. Ripper clauses specifically forbade state legislatures from delegating powers of interference in municipal functions to special commissions, private corporations or associations, or any other entities that would work on behalf of private interests over local public interests. "By 1880, 28 of 38 states had incorporated similar restrictions in their constitutions" (ACIR report 1993, 35).

Going beyond self-imposed legislative restraints, states also began thinking in terms of "empowering local citizens with the ability to articulate their preferences over institutional forms and functional powers within their communities" (ACIR report 1993, 41). Missouri first experimented with what later came to be called *home rule provisions*, a term originally associated with local or regional self-determination movements in Ireland and England, and then eventually around the world. The Missouri Constitutional Convention of 1875 conferred charter-making power on the city of St. Louis, though it was hedged about with many conditions and restrictions. Charter-making power was considered to be strictly a sovereign power of state legislatures, so this broke new legal ground. Discussion in the state convention centered on two concerns—curbing the extensive "corruption and favoritism by the state legislature in the management of the affairs of the city," and recognizing "the principle of local self-government" (ACIR report 1993, 41).

These arguments notwithstanding, the Missouri legislature retained essential prerogatives and asserted its authority over St. Louis in clear language that subsequent state court decisions would strictly enforce. This set a pattern among states—one that remains largely in place to this day—of legislatures conferring various types of autonomy on specific local governments (or in general to all cities/towns of certain classifications), but retaining powers of express and implied preemption that state courts would often interpret strictly. States such as Illinois, New Jersey, and California have mandated liberal construction by state judges of municipal powers under law in the attempt to reverse the impact of Dillon's Rule, but the judges have not always acted accordingly.

Beyond the conferral of chartering power, however limited it was in the Missouri Constitution, another key provision granted "the power to act without prior authorization by the state legislature"—as long as those actions were authorized in the local charter, "did not conflict with a statute, and did not run afoul of a constitutional prohibition" (quoted in ACIR report 1993, 42). This caught on in many states as cities grew in number and size to the point that state legislatures could no longer maintain the degree of control they once exerted. Cities needed to exercise their own initiative on many local matters without constantly seeking legislative authorization. This developmental imperative led to the formulation of a "devolved powers" model of home rule, which provides for "a general grant of powers subject to enumerated restrictions" (ACIR report 1993, 44).

Frank Johnson Goodnow (1895/2008) had articulated an early version of this model, and, significantly, used English and Prussian models of organization, departing "from 'the cross-checks and intersecting lines of divided responsibility' of the federal idea in favor of 'a simple pyramid' of efficient, rationalized functional administration" (quoted in ACIR report 1993, 44). This model's influence became widespread and contributed to the development of the council-manager model of local government during the Progressive reform era. It was used by University of Pennsylvania Law School dean Jefferson Fordham in 1953 as the basis for the American Municipal Association's model home rule provision, and has since been referred to as the **Fordham Rule**.

Finally, a Supreme Court case arose from a dispute over a diverse structure of courts provided for in the Missouri Constitution of 1875. In *Missouri v. Lewis* (101 U.S. 22 [1879]), the court unanimously asserted each state's "full power to make for municipal purposes political subdivisions of its territory and regulate their local government, including the constitution of courts, and the extent of their jurisdictions" (30). In sweeping language, the court affirmed states' rights to adopt diverse legal systems, processes, forms, and institutions for carrying out municipal functions within its jurisdiction, even to the point of grafting foreign legal systems and practices into a part of the state (the example of Mexico was used in this case; see *Missouri v. Lewis* 1879, 32).

Ironically, the Missouri Constitution's home rule provision for St. Louis required a form of government based on the federal constitutional model, with a "chief executive and two houses of legislation, one of which shall be elected by general ticket" (quoted in ACIR report 1993, 41). Few cities would follow this lead as Populist and Progressive reforms ensued. Indeed, as they developed over the twentieth and now twenty-first centuries, cities have cultivated even more diverse forms of operation, largely out of a need for more extensive interlocal cooperation in order to leverage resources as federal and state governments pare back their support. As the 1993 ACIR report indicated, local governments must now address "such matters as dissolution and annexation, consolidation and separation, joint participation in common enterprises, interlocal cooperation and [new forms of] intergovernmental relations," while "clarify[ing] rules concerning the formation, operation, and dissolution of special districts" (46). The report notes with emphasis the shift that has occurred over many decades "from a preoccupation with conflict to a recognition of the pervasive collaboration through contractual arrangements that [can be obtained] in modern state and local government" (46).

In general, states are embracing diversity in forms of local government institutions; however, as local governments try to adapt to changing conditions, states' treatment of local autonomy and self-determination remains mixed at best. Over the twentieth century, the spheres of local autonomy have alternately expanded and contracted, though it is safe to say that since the nineteenth century, they have expanded more than they have contracted. They possess a limited variety of taxing and other revenue powers, eminent domain powers, and contracting powers typically associated with sovereignty, while never enjoying sovereign status. State legislatures still meddle and courts still invoke Dillon's Rule from time to time, with the result that local governments continue to exist in an uneasy relation with their state masters. They continue to govern with one hand tied behind their backs.

In the sections that follow, we will summarize the major types and kinds of local government jurisdictions and forms of government, pointing out the wide variability from state to state with respect to the legal authority extended to the same types of governmental units. It is important for those who have budgeting responsibility to know what kind of authority and budget duties they have under their state statutes. The general summary of the types of local governments and their forms of governance in the following two subsections is not a substitute for knowing this more specific information.

Types of Local Government

There are six basic types of local government in the United States: counties and parishes; cities and towns; townships; boroughs; school districts; and special districts. Each will be discussed in greater detail in the sections that follow.

Counties and Parishes

All states except for Rhode Island and Connecticut have **county** units of government. Louisiana and Alaska subdivide the state into parishes and boroughs, respectively, instead of counties. While states rely heavily on counties to provide services, they vary widely in the power and functions delegated to them. In New England, counties serve as judicial court districts and provide sheriffs' services. In the mid-Atlantic and midwestern states, counties provide a broader range of services, including courts, public utilities, libraries, hospitals, public health services, parks, roads, law enforcement, and jails. Counties in western and southern states have even broader authority, including the provision of public housing, child/family/elder services, airports/recreation/convention centers, zoos, health clinics, museums, welfare/mental and public health services, animal control, veterans' assistance services, probation/parole supervision, historic preservation, food safety regulation, and environmental health services.

Counties vary widely in the number and kind of elected offices used for county leadership. Most counties provide for a county registrar, recorder, or clerk (the exact title varies). The clerk collects vital statistics, holds elections (sometimes in coordination with a separate elections office or commission), and prepares or processes certificates of births, deaths, marriages, and dissolutions (divorce decrees). The county recorder normally maintains the official record of all real estate transactions. Other key county officials may include the district attorney, coroner/medical examiner, treasurer, assessor, auditor, and controller.

In New England, regional councils have been formed to fill the void left by the abolition of county governments. The regional councils' authority is far more limited than that of a county government. For example, regional councils have no taxing authority or authority to issue permits; the aforementioned powers are delegated to the town governments. However, the regional councils do have authority over infrastructure and land-use planning, distribution of state and federal funds for infrastructure projects, emergency preparedness, and limited law enforcement duties.

Counties vary widely not only in their authority and the number and kinds of officials who are elected to office but also in their governance structures (Berman 1993; Coppa 2000; Jeffrey,

Salant, and Boroshok 1989; National Association of Counties [NACo 2011a] www.naco.org). Approximately 60 percent of all counties use the commission form of government. (See explanation later in this chapter under the heading *What Difference Do the Forms of Government Make to Local Public Budgeting?*) Under this system, three to five commissioners share administrative responsibility for the functions not performed by the other elected officials described above (i.e., sheriff, coroner, district attorney, clerk, registrar, recorder, and so on). There is no person specifically designated to carry out executive functions; rather, commission members share executive functions. Approximately 13 percent of the counties provide for an elected executive who serves as an equal member of the commission but has responsibility for operational oversight and budget management for the jurisdiction. The remaining 26 percent of the counties use a council-manager system, in which the commission hires a professional career administrator to provide administrative oversight for the county while working at the pleasure of the commission. Less than one percent of the counties have merged with cities. For example, Denver, Philadelphia, and San Francisco are simultaneously cities and counties. Just over half of the 3,033 counties in the United States have home rule with the delegated authority to operate with much greater independence regarding their taxing and budgeting control.

An important budget issue for many counties in the western part of the United States is the large amount of land owned by the federal government. More than 660 million acres of land—one-third of the entire United States—is exempt from state and county taxation due to federal ownership. Yet, many of the counties adjoining this land provide search and rescue services for recreationists who use the national parks and forested areas. In 1976, Congress recognized the need to compensate counties for the loss of tax revenue as well as the increased costs of providing services on the adjoining federal lands. They adopted a system of funding called payment in lieu of taxes (PILT), which in some counties in the West has accounted for more than 80 percent of the entire county budget.

Cities and Towns

Cities and towns are by far the most numerous units of general purpose government in the United States, comprising 40 percent of the total. There is no agreed-upon definition distinguishing a **city** from a **town**, but most citizens commonly think of cities as larger versions of towns. From a legal point of view, most states recognize a legal distinction within their enabling legislation that either authorizes the establishment of one form rather than another or, more commonly, allows for the creation of class 1 and class 2 cities/towns. By contrast, the state of California treats towns and cities as legally equivalent. In New England, *towns* are the norm, in contrast to most other parts of the United States, where *cities* is the term of choice.

Both towns and cities are created and operate under several legal frameworks, including home rule charter, special act charters, or general law jurisdictions. Most cities and towns are general law jurisdictions, which means that they operate under the general enabling legislation provided by state statute. Home rule (or charter) cities and towns operate under a special charter approved by the local voters pursuant to state law. The charter lays out in considerable detail the governance structure, processes, and authority of the local jurisdiction. If chartered cities have the legal authority to amend their charters without state approval, they are considered home rule jurisdictions.

Cities provide the core services most citizens have come to rely upon, including public safety (police, fire), utilities (water, sewer, and franchising electricity, telephone, Internet, etc.), land-use planning and permitting, and overall quality of life. In sparsely populated areas of the United States like Maine and parts of the western United States, small towns and unincorporated areas rely on the county for law enforcement.

Townships

Most Americans would be surprised to learn that they live in a **township**. In fact, most of the United States has been divided up into townships as part of the General Land Survey System that was created with the passage of the Land Ordinance of 1785. This act provided that the land west of the Appalachian Mountains, north of the Ohio River, and east of the Mississippi River was to be divided up into ten separate states. This act, along with the Northwest Ordinance of 1787 (commonly known as the Northwest Territory Act), resulted in organizing most of the states into townships. The townships were mapped by the Public Land Survey System (PLSS) into square blocks that were six miles on each side, with mile-square subdivisions called sections, as illustrated in Exhibit 1.2.

Exhibit 1.2

Public Land Survey Method for Numbering and Dividing Township into 36 Mile-Square Sections

6	5	4	3	2	1
7	8	9	10	11	12
18	17	16	15	14	13
19	20	21	22	23	24
30	29	28	27	26	25
31	32	33	34	35	36

Source: U.S. Bureau of Land Management 1974.

The creation of townships was not merely a land survey and mapping exercise. It was also an exercise in local public budgeting. For example, the original Northwest Ordinance of 1787 provided that section 16 of each township be reserved for a public school, thus guaranteeing that local schools would have an income and that the community schoolhouses would be centrally located for all children. In most of the western states, both sections 16 and 36 (or an equivalent) were designated to be held in trust by the state as a condition of statehood (Souder and Fairfax 1996; for an example, see Arizona State Land Department, "State Land Department Historical Overview," www.azland.gov/history.htm). The land survey system put in place by the Northwest Ordinance has served as the basis for creating townships with governing authority (called civil townships) in most of the midwestern states. According to the U.S. Census, 20 states currently use the township form of government (U.S. Census Bureau 2007b). In the early years, these townships cared for the poor, maintained the roads, preserved the peace, registered brands, and fulfilled the needs of local government generally. Today, townships in midwestern states provide services in the following broad areas:

1. public safety (including law enforcement, fire protection, and building code enforcement),
2. environmental protection (including sewage disposal, sanitation, and pollution abatement),
3. public transportation (including transit systems, paratransit systems, streets, and roads),
4. health,
5. recreation,
6. libraries, and
7. social services for the poor and aged.

Six East Coast states have created charter townships (Connecticut, Maine, Massachusetts, New Hampshire, New York, and New Jersey) that perform municipal-type functions that resemble the services traditionally provided by cities and towns.

Boroughs

The term **borough**—derived from the word *burgh,* meaning fortified town—originated in the Middle Ages and was used to describe settlements that were granted some self-governing rights from the central authority. Only six states use boroughs for governance and budgetary purposes. Most often, the present-day use of the word *borough* refers to a single town with its own self-government; in New York City, however, it refers to one of five subdivisions of the city (the Bronx, Manhattan, Queens, Brooklyn, and Staten Island). In the state of Alaska, the term is used instead of *county* and designates regions much larger than counties in other states. Alaska, unlike other states, does not recognize towns, cities, and townships as legal units of government in its codified law. Instead, it has only two tiers: the state and the boroughs (Title 7). Towns and cities acquire legal status by special charter on a case-by-case basis.

In Connecticut, boroughs are legal entities usually created within the populated center of a town, but they are still part of, and dependent on, the town within which they exist. This contrasts with both Pennsylvania and New Jersey, where boroughs are recognized as one of the authorized forms of municipal government under state law. In Pennsylvania, boroughs are self-governing units smaller than a city; in New Jersey, boroughs are one of the five recognized types of municipal government (the others are townships, towns, cities, and villages) (Cerra 2007). In Virginia, when multiple local governments consolidate to form a consolidated city, the consolidated city may be divided into geographical subdivisions called boroughs, which may be the same as the existing (1) cities, (2) counties, or (3) portions of such counties. Those boroughs are not separate local governments (VA Code, Title 15.2–3534).

School Districts[3]

As we indicated earlier in our discussion of townships, schools that are controlled by local citizens have been a cornerstone of American democratic governance (Spring 2008). This is in contrast to most parts of the world, where school funding and operation is controlled by the central state. While the number of school districts has declined through consolidations by nearly 80 percent over the past 50 years, more than 90 percent of the school districts in the United States are operated independently of other units of government (e.g., states, counties, cities, towns, and boroughs). Exhibit 1.1 shows a 6 percent growth in school districts between 1997 and 2007. This growth is largely due to the creation of independent education service districts, which provide supplementary services to other independent school districts and help fund services that would otherwise be jeopardized by funding shortages at the state and local levels. (We will elaborate more fully on these kinds of districts in our discussion of special districts in the section that follows.)

There are some important exceptions to the general rule that schools are independent units of government. In Maryland, all school systems are run by the county; in New York State, some school districts are independent and others are subordinate to cities (e.g., New York City). Hawaii is the only state that functions as a statewide school district. The *2002 Census of Governments* (U.S. Census Bureau 2002) lists the types and numbers of school systems in the United States as shown in Exhibit 1.3.

School districts have traditionally been funded by local property taxes. Exhibit 1.4 indicates that slightly more than 44 percent of the revenue for K–12 education is provided by local sources, with the states providing just over 44 percent and the remainder (12.5 percent) coming from federal

Exhibit 1.3

The Number and Kinds of School Districts in the United States

- 13,506 school district governments
- 178 state-dependent school systems
- 1,330 local-dependent school systems
- 1,196 education service agencies (agencies providing support services to public school systems)

Source: U.S. Census Bureau 2002, 17.

government grants. But there is considerable variation among the states with respect to reliance on local revenue sources versus reliance on state funding. For example, state funding in Hawaii and Vermont comprises nearly 90 percent of the total school revenue, in contrast to Nevada and Illinois, where the states provide about 30 percent of the total (Kenyon 2007, 47; National Center for Education Statistics, Table 2, http://nces.ed.gov/pubs2010/expenditures/tables.asp).

The variations in approaches to school funding are an integral part of the ongoing debate about the fairness of various strategies in supporting local public education. For example, school funding on a per student basis in 2011 averaged from a low of $6,212 in Utah to a high of $19,076 in New York (U.S. Census 2013, p. 8). Such disparities are caused not only by differences in state support but also by differences in the value of local property, which determines the amount of property taxes that can be assessed. These disparities have resulted in lawsuits throughout many states to equalize the provision of educational support as a requirement of the equal protection clauses found in most state constitutions. Such suits have prompted more than a dozen states to

Exhibit 1.4

Percentage Distribution of Revenues for Public Elementary and Secondary Education in the United States, by Source, Fiscal Year 2011

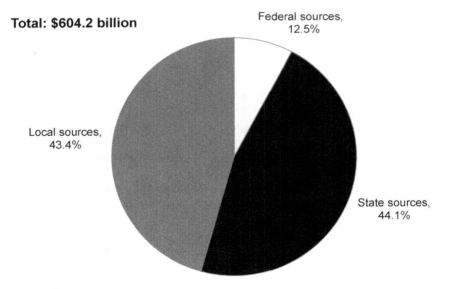

Total: $604.2 billion

Federal sources, 12.5%

State sources, 44.1%

Local sources, 43.4%

Source: U.S. Department of Education, National Center for Education Statistics, Common Core of Data (CCD), "National Public Education Financial Survey (NPEFS)," fiscal year 2011, preliminary version 1a.

consider school finance restructuring, with litigation actively ongoing in about 20 states (Kenyon 2007, 12).

We will not devote extensive attention to school district budgeting in this text because it is a specialized field that is already covered in several excellent publications (see endnote 2). Note, however, that most of the principles we cover in each of the chapters in this book can be applied to school budgeting. More important for the purposes of this text, those responsible for local public budgeting need to understand the interactive relationship between local school budgets and the budgets of other local jurisdictions. This is illustrated in our opening scenarios, where local school funding is viewed by voters as competing for the funding of other public services. While similar to special districts discussed in the next section, school districts frequently hold the highest priority among local citizens for the allocation of scarce resources (Maher and Skidmore 2009).

Special Districts[4]

Special districts (also special-purpose districts, special service districts) are the most rapidly growing unit of local government, increasing by 84 percent over the past 50 years. As with all local governments, the authority for creating special districts and the rules governing their operation are provided by state law. They have been created to furnish specific services that are typically not provided by general-purpose governments. These services include hospitals, ports, sewer and surface water treatment, water supply, fire and police protection, mosquito abatement, soil and water conservation, supplementary educational service, and upkeep of cemeteries. Most special districts provide only a single service, which makes them popular with citizens who want to live outside an incorporated city or town, pay lower taxes, but receive a higher level of service than is normally provided by the rural jurisdiction within which they reside. Special districts usually have their own governing boards and separate revenue authority from some combination of property taxes, fees, excise or sales taxes, and the issue of bonds.

Since the New Deal (1933–1938), five factors have greatly influenced the growth and autonomy of both cities and special districts. First, the process of expanding local jurisdictions began with President Franklin D. Roosevelt, who encouraged the creation of public corporations to float revenue bonds as a way of avoiding municipal defaults. He urged the creation of water, sewer, and electric power districts, arguing that "these governments should be used to circumvent debt limits and referendum requirements for issue of bonds" (Burns 1994, 53). Roosevelt provided model legislation for enabling citizens to form housing authorities and soil conservation districts, and tied federal funding exclusively to the creation of these jurisdictions.

Second, the impetus for expansion of special districts occurred under the pressure for economic development in the post–World War II period. The expansion of industry and housing, for example, caused the real estate industry to reorganize and apply political pressure to establish new cities and special districts.

Race played heavily as a third factor in the expansion of special districts. It was common practice prior to the 1950s for neighborhood improvement associations to create restrictive covenants that excluded individuals based on race. The U.S. Supreme Court declared in 1948 that race-based restrictive covenants were unconstitutional, and this encouraged cities to use their zoning authority in new and creative ways (Burns 1994, 60, 54–55).

Fourth, new pressure to expand cities and special districts occurred during the 1960s, with the New Frontier administration of President John F. Kennedy and the Great Society administration of President Lyndon B. Johnson. In this period, federal aid to cities almost doubled. It came in the form of programs for housing, urban renewal, mass transit, education, job training, poverty reduction, model cities, and grants-in-aid (Burns 1994, 62). These initiatives yielded two results. First, they changed the expectations of the role that cities could play in meeting the redistributive social needs of the community. In addition to planning for growth and providing infrastructure, New Frontier and Great Society programs laid the groundwork for a larger community-building role to be played by public administrators. A second consequence of the Kennedy/Johnson program initiatives is that they increased the complexity of local government and placed new challenges of interorganizational and interjurisdictional coordination on local government leaders. For example, transportation planning had to be coordinated with a growing number of local jurisdictions as well as with newly created administrative bodies. The elected and career officials responsible for these new arrangements were placed in the catbird seat.

The fifth factor that spurred the growth of cities and special districts was the significant increase in state and local taxation during the 1960s. Starting in 1961, taxpayers at the local level experienced the largest increase in taxes since the 1930s. This increased burden induced businesses and residents to create new cities and special service districts in the attempt to escape these tax burdens. New special districts also gave the public options in deciding whether they wished to purchase additional services (Burns 1994, 62). For example, if suburban dwellers wished to live in the pastoral setting of the countryside but still have access to city-level police and fire services, how could their desires be funded? One answer has been to provide everyone in the countryside with a base level of rural/county-level service and the option to purchase additional levels of police, fire, health, education, or other services through a special district. During the decades following the local taxation crisis of the 1960s, special districts grew in number from 21,264 in 1967 to 35,052 in 2002, an increase of more than 60 percent.

The expansion in the number, complexity, and role of local government jurisdictions since the New Deal has greatly increased the challenges for those who govern. At an administrative level, managers and elected officials have to coordinate more of their work with other jurisdictions. For example, how many special levies will voters support during any given election? How can jurisdictions coordinate their need for voter support while demonstrating that they are wise and prudent stewards of the community's resources? At a political level, the challenge becomes even greater, as communities balkanize into relatively isolated pockets that are organized by socioeconomic status, race, ethnicity, and business opportunities for employment. Under such circumstances, it becomes difficult for administrators to meet the needs of the community in ways that create a shared sense of common interest across many boundaries established by narrow self-interests.

What Difference Do the Forms of Government Make to Local Public Budgeting?

For the forms of government, let fools contest,
That which is best administered is best.
(Alexander Pope 1732–1733/1994)

Alexander Pope's epigraph, taken from his *Essay on Man*, has proved to be less true than he might have wished. This is because citizens trust themselves more than they trust others when it comes to spending their money. If they have to trust others, they would rather trust those over whom they have the most direct control than those over whom they exercise only indirect control, like professional career administrators. This principle has been institutionalized into the majority of local systems of government, which do not have the traditional tripartite system of checks and balances and separation of powers. Most local governments have more of a *fused power* model that structurally resembles the parliamentary system. While there are important exceptions, the prevailing practice in local governments is for part-time elected officials to make policy decisions that are implemented by a professional career administrator who works at the pleasure of the elected council.

This local government model reflects the spirit of the American Revolution, which memorialized the principle that elected representatives of the people shall have the authority to levy taxes and approve spending. For that reason, the U.S. Constitution requires that all appropriation bills originate in the U.S. House of Representatives (the People's House). However, at the local level, this legal authority is exercised by part-time and unpaid elected officials who depend heavily on the expertise of career administrators to assemble the details of taxing and spending plans. For that reason, the forms of government play an important role in shaping how the budgeting process gets carried out in each of the following four types of local government structures: the strong mayor form, the council-manager form, the weak mayor form, and the commission system.

Strong Mayor

The **strong mayor form of city government** consists of a mayor and a city council, each elected independently through predominantly nonpartisan elections. Both share in making policy, although the mayor has near-complete authority over the executive branch of government and commonly takes the initiative in making policy recommendations. The mayor appoints officers of the executive branch—the city attorney, assessor, treasurer-comptroller, and heads of departments—who serve at his or her pleasure, although these appointees generally must be confirmed by the council. The city council, in its role as the legislative branch, approves key mayoral appointments and ordinances prior to their becoming effective.

The objective of the strong mayor form of local government is to centralize control over the executive agencies of government. This control is defended on a variety of grounds. From a partisan political point of view, many proponents of democratic accountability argue that the mayor should be able to control the policy directions of a city by appointing department heads who share his or her policy agenda and political affiliation (especially in some larger cities that have partisan elections). From a "good government" perspective, proponents argue that democratic accountability necessitates unswerving attention be paid to issues of administrative efficiency and effectiveness. Without the supervening oversight of a strong mayor or professional chief executive officer (i.e., city manager, county administrator, etc.), many believe these values may be compromised by the self-serving and self-aggrandizing interests of individual departments, programs, and their constellation of stakeholders.

In keeping with the desire of the strong mayor system to centralize executive authority, the budget is prepared and presented to the legislative body in a fashion similar to the role of the U.S. president or a state governor in presenting a budget to the legislative body for deliberation. One of the major differences is that most local and many state legislative bodies do not possess the kind of analytic capacity exhibited by the Congressional Budget Office (CBO) or the congressional appropriations committees. This limits the ability of elected legislators to undertake their own independent analysis of financial impacts and outcomes of various funding options—particularly at local levels of government where part-time elected officials are heavily reliant on the work undertaken by the mayor or city manager's budget office.

Council-Manager

The **council-manager form of city government** is the most widely used system in the United States. According to the International City/County Management Association (ICMA 2006), the council-manager form is used in 63 percent of cities with populations of 25,000 or more; in 57 percent of cities with populations of 10,000 or more; and in 53 percent of cities with populations of 5,000 or more. According to a 1996 survey of municipal forms of government by the National Civic League, 61 percent of council-manager cities have popularly elected mayors (National Civic League 1996). More than 80 percent of all cities (mayor and manager) in the 1996 survey reported having appointed a chief official such as a city manager. This means that many mayor-council cities have a chief administrative officer who answers to the mayor or the council, much like a city manager does. In the other cities, the mayor administers the day-to-day operations of the government.

The council-manager form of government consists of a city council (the members of which are elected predominantly in nonpartisan elections), a mayor (in most cases selected from the membership of the council but elected at-large in others), and a city manager (appointed by the city council). In this system, the council determines city policy and the mayor merely presides over city council meetings. The executive branch of government is administered by the city manager, who is a professionally trained administrator. The city manager appoints executive officers, supervises their performance, develops the city budget, and administers programs.

Theoretically, the city manager cannot make policy, but as a practical matter, the recommendations of the manager are usually given great weight by the council. But it is also the case that when the city manager makes recommendations, he or she has done so based on prior conversations with each member of the council. This process plays a decisive role in shaping the city manager's recommendations to the council. For this reason, many scholars argue that the relationship between the city manager and the council should be understood as a process of coproduction (see endnote 5).

The council-manager form of government was created by the "good government" advocates of the Progressive Era at the beginning of the 1900s. The objective of the council-manager plan was to take the politics out of city government by turning over its administration to a professional manager. Beyond this, as a practical matter, it was difficult for citizens to evaluate the administrative performance of their elected officials. The council-manager plan was developed in the early days of the Progressive movement as a response both to this reality and to the influence of political parties and party politicians over city government under the mayor-council plan. Party and personal loyalty were attacked as an inappropriate basis upon which to run local government. Critics argued that there is nothing political about operating sewer, water, transportation, parks, garbage, and other local infrastructure systems. They pointed out that such systems could be run more effectively by a professionally trained administrator taking general directions from an elected city council. The council-manager system attempted to divide policy or politics from administration. While more recent studies have documented that this bright-line distinction does not exist very clearly at the local government level (Svara 1985, 1990, 1991, 1999, 2006; Montjoy and Watson 1995), there is a general consensus that the council-manager form of government is "less political." If the members of the council are elected in nonpartisan elections, the influence of party politics is even further reduced.

The council-manager system has important implications for the budgeting process. Both the development and implementation of the jurisdiction's budget is in the hands of the council-manager. In putting the annual budget together, the city manager has extensive discretionary authority in shaping the spending priorities of the various departments. The manager works with members of council to meet their personal and collective priorities. Once the budget is ready for presentation to council, this anticipatory work by the city manager makes the budget approval process more routine than contested.

Once the budget is approved by the council, the manager has the discretionary authority to implement the budget within the broad policy and fiscal guidelines established by council. Usually these guidelines give the city manager broad discretion, especially through control over filling vacancies and authorizing new positions.

Weak Mayor

Most smaller cities, and a few larger ones (i.e., Minneapolis, Minnesota), have a **weak mayor form of city government**, with a mayor who performs mainly ceremonial functions. Unlike the strong mayor system, a weak mayor does not have the power to veto council decisions, to oversee city government operations, or to draw up and implement the annual budget. Most "weak mayor" cities are very small; the mayor does not have separate executive authority, and the staff performs primarily clerical and direct service functions. The weak mayor system is the product of the Jacksonian democratic belief that too many government officials with too much power endanger the ability of the majority of middle-class Americans to control their government and keep it accountable.

Under the weak mayor system, the budgeting process is controlled by the council as a whole. The mayor facilitates the public participation activities that are part of the council's budgeting role and serves as the ceremonial leader of the council's deliberations over the budget adoption process. The mayor is "first among equals" when it comes to voting on the budget and exercising influence over the outcome.

Commission System

The **commission form of city government** fuses executive and legislative functions almost completely in the hands of elected commissioners. They hold the power to pass legislation and participate directly as administrators in overseeing the executive implementation of policy and adjudicated appeals, usually dealing with personnel and land-use issues. Members of the commission (which is like a city council) are elected in nonpartisan elections, and one member is designated (or in some cases is elected) chair of the board to preside over meetings. Again, as in the council-manager plan, the mayor has little power. The commission makes policy for the jurisdiction and appoints some of the executive officers, such as the city attorney, assessor, treasurer, and chief of police. However, in addition to making appointments of departmental/bureau executive officers, the commissioners themselves act as heads of the various city administrative units (the park commission and the public works commission, police, fire, and the like). Each commissioner is ordinarily assigned as head of one or more commissions and is charged with their administration. The elected board of commissioners as a whole coordinates policy and approves the city budget. Thus, the members of the commission act as legislators, administrators, and judges.

The commission system was created in 1901 in specific response to the terrible hurricane on the island city of Galveston, Texas, in the Gulf of Mexico. On September 8, 1900, hurricane winds of at least 120 miles per hour ripped across the Texas coastline, killing over 5,000 people and reducing the city of Galveston to ruins. During the 18-hour storm, tidal waves swept through sea-level streets, destroying homes and buildings and wiping out electricity, roads, and communication systems. As news of the disaster spread, supplies, including tents for the nearly 8,000 homeless, poured into Galveston from across the nation.

Influential business leaders in the community feared that the city might never recover its prosperity under the leadership of the incumbent city council, so they seized the initiative, prepared a plan, and requested that the governor appoint them as a commission to govern the city during the rebuilding period. To appease opponents who argued that appointed government was undemocratic, the plan was altered to provide for popular election of two of the five commissioners. Subsequent court challenges to the constitutionality of the partially appointive government led the Texas legislature to make the office of all five commissioners elective, and in this form, the commission plan became popular across the nation (Bradley 2010).

The commission system was viewed by many of the business-oriented reformers of the day as the right answer to getting things done quickly, effectively, and efficiently. Experienced and knowledgeable business leaders could take single-minded control over a given functional area and mobilize the resources needed to complete a plan of action. At its peak in 1918, 500 cities had adopted the commission system, but by 1984, the number had dwindled to just 177. Portland,

Oregon, is the largest city of its size still governed by the commission form, and it is widely regarded as a "strange anomaly" (Morgan, Nishishiba, and Vizzini 2010).

The commission system gradually fell out favor as it was replaced by the city-manager system, which was increasingly viewed as being much more effective in harnessing the growing and complex functions of local government under a single executive who had been specifically trained in the business of "making government work." Galveston abandoned its own child when the island city adopted the council-manager form of government in 1960 (Rice 1977).

Ironically, the commission form of government fell out of favor for some of the very reasons that it was created in the first place. First, the commission system was criticized for its lack of professionalism. For example, a commissioner, who typically has considerable private-sector expertise in financial management and budgeting, may end up having oversight responsibility for transportation, police, fire, or other departments for which he or she has no special competence, training, or experience. The city manager movement aggressively advanced the view that managing the public's business required special people who were committed to public service as a calling—people who were armed with the modern management tools necessary to transform this commitment into efficient and effective delivery of services carried out by technically trained career professional administrators. While the critics of the commission system agreed with their opponents on the need for management expertise, they doubted that private-sector business experience would provide that expertise. Public-sector work was regarded as uniquely different from the substantive competence necessary in managing for-profit enterprises in the private sector.

In addition to assuming responsibility for hiring and managing a professional cadre of public administrators, proponents of reform argued that a city manager could do a much better job than a group of independent commissioners in coordinating all of the complex activities associated with the delivery of local public services. While initially seen as a take-charge system that could get results in a hurry, the commission system came to be viewed as seriously defective in its ability to coordinate activities among diverse city functions. For example, the commissioner of environmental services might announce a new initiative to mitigate erosion through a partnership with local volunteer organizations to "plant a 100 trees per month," with little or no discussion with other commissioners who may have tree-planting responsibility in their roles as commissioners for the transportation or parks bureau. A city manager system was viewed as the solution to this problem because it created a single focus of responsibility for coordinating the disparate sets of expertise and organizational units that need to work together in order to achieve a common purpose.

Finally, in addition to the challenges of coordination posed by the commission system, there is also the problem of providing adequate representation to a diverse population. Take, for instance, the issues associated with at-large elections. At-large balloting is intrinsic to the commission concept, but elections of this type have been known to dilute minority voting strength. For this reason, most southern cities were forced to abandon the commission plan because of suits brought under the Voting Rights Act of 1965 and subsequent amendments (Rice 2010).

Despite the variety of governing models at the local level of government, they all share some common characteristics that enable us to talk about the distinctiveness of local public budgeting as opposed to state and federal budgeting processes and systems. First, a confluence of forces has created a moment of truth for many local governments. While both the state and federal systems of government are asking whether they can continue to do business as usual, no one is questioning their continued existence. This is not the case with some local governments, where increased attention is being given to their ability to declare bankruptcy, go out of existence, or transfer authority for some provision of services back to the state. On average, eight municipalities per year for the last 30 years have filed for chapter 9 bankruptcy protection. The city of Detroit has captured national attention by successfully filing for bankruptcy after Kevyn D. Orr, the state-appointed emergency financial manager, failed to find alternative solutions to paying off the city's 18 billion dollar debt. The city's bankruptcy, like most that have occurred, is a result of a combination of years of mismanagement and unanticipated financial calamity. Only a few bankruptcy cases have been the result of fraud (McGee 2011). With growing concern that local government revenues may not be adequate to meet ongoing financial obligations, chapter 9 bankruptcy has grown in importance as an option (Christie 2010; McGee 2011). When this occurs it puts the jurisdiction's public assets like art and historical museum treasures in competition with unfunded legal mandates and pension liabilities as well as the normal list of private-sector creditors.

From a legal point of view, local jurisdictions that pursue bankruptcy do not have access to the same options as the private sector in dealing with their financial challenges. The rule-of-law framework governing local governments creates the following limitations: (1) Local governments are subordinate legal entities of the state and subject to the state's supervening authority. (2) Local governments do not have the reorganization option that the private sector has in bankruptcy proceedings. (3) Local governments do not have the "liquidation of assets" option that the private sector has in bankruptcy proceedings. (4) The only option available to most cash-strapped local governments is to pay their debts, but such payments are subject to the state's supervening authority and the adjudication of the priority these debts have under the jurisdiction's legally binding contract obligations.

In addition to the financial legal framework shared by most local governments, a second commonality is the frequent blurring of the lines between the executive and legislative functions of government. This may be the artifact of the formal structure of authority, as with the commission or city manager forms of government, or it may be the artifact of part-time elected officials. In either case, there tends to be a much closer working partnership between the executive and legislative branches of local government than is the case at the federal and state levels of government. This has important implications for local budgeting, as we will explain in greater detail in the next two sections.

THE PERFECT FINANCIAL STORM: A TRANSFORMATIONAL OPPORTUNITY

The complexity in number and types of local government in the United States and the significant role they play in funding and providing local services are reason enough to devote a book to local public budgeting. But there is another reason that local public budgeting deserves special attention. Over the past decade, two forces have come together to create the perfect local government funding storm, and we believe this convergence will transform our traditional approach to local government budgeting. On the revenue side, local governments are facing growing constraints on their ability to generate revenue. On the expenditure side, there has been an expansion of federal unfunded mandates, an explosion in employee benefit costs (e.g., health care and pensions), a continuing and rapid deterioration of infrastructure, and growth in demand for services that often outstrips local revenue capacity. All of these developments have reduced the discretionary control by local administrators and elected officials over the budget process.

The Revenue Limitations

Exhibit 1.5 indicates that 38 percent of local revenue comes as transfers from the state and federal government, and another 28 percent comes from property taxes. Both of these sources of revenue have fallen dramatically since the collapse of the housing mortgage market in 2008. When combined with the political psychology surrounding increased taxation, local governments face a steep uphill climb in persuading voters to pay higher taxes for government services. This has forced local officials to think of alternative ways of funding local services—an issue we will deal with in much greater detail in chapter 8.

Exhibit 1.5

Local Government Revenue by Source, 2010

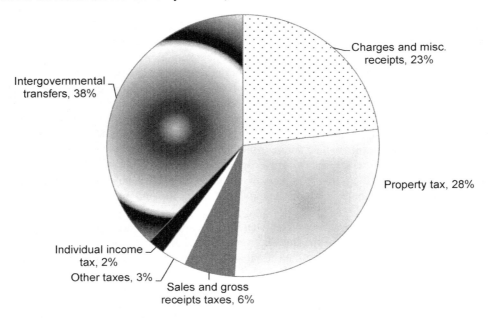

Source: Tax Policy Center, State and Local Government Finance Data Query System http://www.taxpoli-cycenter.org/taxfacts/displayafact.cfm?Docid=530.

Property Tax Limitations

The dependence of local governments on property tax revenue hit the wall in 2008, when the private market for home mortgage financing dropped from nearly 60 percent of the total to less than 5 percent (Phillips 2011). While government-guaranteed loans increased, it was not enough to close the private-market mortgage gap. In the wake of the Wall Street mortgage crash in 2008, home values dropped 23 percent in the Phoenix, Arizona, area in just one year. In California's Riverside County, budget officials witnessed an 11 percent drop in property tax receipts. Las Vegas, Nevada, experienced the first property tax decrease in at least 30 years. Since property tax revenue accounts for 50–60 percent of a typical county budget—funding everything from schools and police to trash pickup—many jurisdictions have had to cut personnel and benefits, freeze hiring, and require employees to take furloughs in order to balance the budget (Allen 2009). Schools are especially vulnerable to the downturn in property taxes. Nearly half of the property taxes collected by counties across the United States goes to fund elementary and secondary education (Kenyon 2007). This constitutes about 50 percent of the total revenue that schools receive, the other half coming from state and federal funding sources (Biddle and Berliner 2002).

As we suggested in our introductory scenarios, local governments may be the most vulnerable to economic downturns of all governments. In chapter 7, we will show that heavy dependence on property tax revenue by local governments has been severely constrained by various property tax limitations put in place either by a vote of the state legislature or by an initiative process of the citizens. This so-called taxpayer revolt began in 1978, with the passage of California's Proposition 13, (also known as the Jarvis initiative) which established a maximum property tax of 1 percent of the full cash value of such property. It decreased property taxes by assessing property values at their 1975 value and restricted annual increases of assessed value of real property to an inflation factor, not to exceed 2 percent per year. It also prohibited reassessment of a new base year value except for (a) change in ownership or (b) completion of new construction. In addition to decreasing property taxes, the initiative contained language requiring a two-thirds majority in both legislative houses for future increases of any state tax rates or amounts of revenue collected, including income tax rates. Proposition 13 also required a two-thirds majority vote in local elections for local governments wishing to increase special taxes. Variations on Proposition 13 have been adopted in 37 states (Mullins and Joyce 1996; Winters 2008). Proposition 13 added insult to an already injured system of local government financing. In 1971, seven years before its passage, school districts in California were hit with a court-ordered school-funding equalization mandate that forced the state to pick up a greater portion of the tab for school funding (*Seranno v. Priest,* 5 Cal.3d 584 [1971]).

State interference in local government decision making has not been limited to property tax. Over time, restrictions have been placed on many sources of local tax revenue, either through limits on the *amount* that can be raised (through tax rate or revenue caps) or on the uses of the revenue. Special interest groups have also persuaded federal and state legislators and voters to preempt local governments from levying certain taxes altogether. Depending on the state, these kinds of restrictions affect taxes on retail sales, Internet sales, real estate sales, income, payroll, hotel and motel revenue, fuel, cigarettes, liquor—in short, virtually anything that a local government might tax.

Decline in State and Federal Intergovernmental Revenue

In addition to limitations on property and other tax revenues, intergovernmental revenue from the state and federal government is on the decline. In the two years following the 2007–2009 economic downturn and Wall Street collapse, 46 states plus the District of Columbia initiated major budget cuts that resulted in the reduction of health care (31 states), services to the elderly and disabled (29 states and the District of Columbia), K–12 education (34 states and the District of Columbia), and higher education (43 states) (Johnson, Oliff, and Williams 2011). These cuts were both broad and deep.

On the revenue generation side of the budget-balancing equation, local jurisdictions have pushed for increased reliance on user fees and the creation of various kinds of special districts that can generate new revenue for identified categories of service. For example, some districts are intended to encourage urban renewal and economic development by reliance on tax-increment financing (TIF). TIF diverts property tax revenue (up to a certain threshold) in the targeted renewal district from local taxing jurisdictions, thus encouraging private investments in buildings and land to spark redevelopment efforts. Property values in redeveloped areas invariably rise, generating greater property tax revenues that, in turn, cover the cost of the improvements in the district. Other special service districts provide residents with the opportunity to purchase higher levels of police, fire, and additional services contingent on their willingness to approve higher levels of property taxes to pay for the services. These strategies to increase taxes and fees are an inherent part of Populist democracies where voters have the freedom to decide what services they want and what they are willing to pay (for further elaboration on this issue, see the section titled *The Proximity Imperative: The Political Psychology of Taxation v. Expenditures and Their Consequences for Local Government Budgeting* on page 39.

Expenditure Control Pressures

Local revenue has been increasingly constrained at times of upward pressure on expenditures from employee benefits, increased demand for services, and rapidly deteriorating infrastructure.

Employee Benefit and Retirement Programs

Publicly funded employee-benefit costs (retirement and health care) became a cause célèbre with the crash of the Wall Street mortgage market, and they will continue to garner front-page attention for the foreseeable future. Since then state and local jurisdictions have undertaken considerable strides to reduce employer contributions. Since 59 percent of the contributors to the state plans are local government employees whose jurisdictions provide the financial support for employee participation, there is considerable pressure on local governments to make continuing changes (GAO 2012, 4). Despite these on-going efforts, the GAO study concluded that "most plans have experienced a growing gap between actuarial assets and liabilities over the past decade, meaning that higher contributions from government sponsors are needed to maintain funds on an actuarially based path toward sustainability (GAO 2012, 8).

In 2010, the Pew Charitable Trusts reported that the total accrued retiree pension and nonpension benefits totaled $3.35 trillion nationwide, but only $2.35 trillion (85 percent) in assets had been set aside to cover these benefits, leaving a trillion dollars of unfunded liability (Pew Center on the States 2010a). In 2013 Pew reported that pension and retiree health care costs were responsible for the unfunded liabilities in 42 out of the 50 states. In the other 8 states, public debt was the primary cause for unfunded liabilities. As of fiscal 2010, the largest of these long-term obligations was for unfunded pension liabilities in 31 states, unfunded retiree health care costs in 11 states, and public debt in 8 states. Some studies have pointed out that these retirement benefits enjoy protected legal status, much like one's personal property, and therefore cannot be reduced quickly or easily. Taking this factor into account means that a lower discount rate should be used to calculate the unfunded retirement and benefit liabilities of public entities. Doing so increases the liability to more than $3 trillion (Collins and Rettenmaier 2010, 5). Whether one uses Pew's admittedly conservative number or the higher number that reflects a lower discount rate, it still leaves local governments with serious long-term expenditure control issues.

Local Government Infrastructure

At the eye of the local government funding storm (when decreasing revenue meets increasing expenses) is the financing of local government infrastructure, which is in a serious state of disrepair. The American Society of Civil Engineers (ASCE) has maintained an inventory of the growing infrastructure needs that exist at the federal and local levels of government throughout the United States. The ASCE estimates the total infrastructure costs to be more than $3.6 trillion (see the total needs column in Exhibit 1.6) to maintain and improve roads, bridges, transit systems, airports, schools, waterworks, sewers, dams, solid waste disposal, and more. The second column in Exhibit 1.6 provides a summary of the estimated existing level of funding for each of the infrastructure categories. The final column provides a summary of the additional amount of funding that is needed each year over an eight-year span (2013–2020) in order to bring American infrastructure up to a B-level standard.

In 2002, the U.S. Congressional Budget Office estimated that for the years 2000–2019, the annual costs for investment in the nation's water and waste water systems would average between $24.6 billion and $41 billion. The CBO projected that the annual costs (in 2001 dollars) over the period for operations and maintenance (O&M), which are not eligible for aid under current federal programs, will average between $25.7 billion and $31.8 billion for drinking water and between $21.4 billion and $25.2 billion for wastewater (CBO 2002). In 2013 the EPA calculated, based on 2011 data, that local water treatment infrastructure needs totaled $384 billion, consisting of $247.5 billion to replace or refurbish aging or deteriorating water lines, $72.5 billion to construct, expand, or rehabilitate water treatment infrastructure, and $39.5 billion to construct, rehabilitate, or cover

Exhibit 1.6

2013 Report Card for America's Infrastructure (in billions)

Infrastructure Systems	Total Needs	Estimated Funding	Funding Gap
Surface Transportation[1]	$1,723	$877	$846
Water/Wastewater Infrastructure[1]	$126	$42	$84
Electricity[1]	$736	$629	$107
Airports[1,2]	$134	$95	$39
Inland Waterways and Marine Ports[1]	$30	$14	$16
Dams[3]	$21	$6	$15
Hazardous and Solid Waste[4]	$56	$10	$46
Levees[5]	$80	$8	$72
Public Parks and Recreation[6]	$238	$134	$104
Rail[7]	$100	$89	$11
Schools[8]	$391	$120	$271
Totals	$3,635	$2,024	$1,611
Yearly Investment Needed	$454	$253	$201

Sources: American Society of Civil Engineers (ASCE) 2013. In previous versions of the Report Card, investment estimates were based on a five-year period. In 2013, ASCE completed its economic study series (*Failure to Act*) on America's current and future infrastructure investment needs. These studies provided investment need estimates until 2020, which is the time period used for all estimates in Exhibit 1.6.

[1]Data taken from ASCE *Failure to Act* report series published 2011–2013.

[2]Airport needs and gaps include anticipated cost of NextGen: $20 billion by 2020 and $40 billion by 2040.

[3]Total needs are federal and nonfederal high hazard dams.

[4]Funding includes only publicly funded remediation, not funds from the private sector.

[5]Total needs numbers are based on discussions with the National Committee on Levee Safety,

[6]Total needs and funding include all costs associated with Parks and Recreation. Funding gap is capital needs only.

[7]These numbers are based on market projection and current investment trends.

[8]These numbers are based on the last available national data collection and brought to current market dollars.

finished water storage reservoirs (U.S. EPA 2013). What is troubling about these numbers is that the local government gap between infrastructure funding and replacement needs is widening at the very time that the national government is shifting increased attention away from infrastructure support to local government and toward reducing the federal deficit. This is illustrated by the allocation of funds under the American Recovery Act of 2009.

Traditionally, spending money on infrastructure has been viewed by many economists as a sound strategy for priming the economy during periods of downturn. But, contrary to public perceptions, only a small portion of the American Recovery Act of 2009 was dedicated to infrastructure investment. According to calculations in a study conducted for the New America Foundation (a nonprofit policy institute in Washington, D.C.), of the $787 billion originally allocated for the Recovery Act, only about $92.5 billion was spent on infrastructure, or roughly 12 percent of the final package. The majority of the funding provided by the act took the form of tax cuts, transfer payments to individuals, and assistance to state and local governments, as illustrated in Exhibit 1.7 (Sherraden 2011). While President Obama's 2012 budget proposal to Congress included increased spending for selected infrastructure programs designed to bolster the nation's economic competitiveness, there is little reason to believe that local government infrastructure needs will receive significantly increased and sustained support in the coming years from the federal government as it struggles to reduce the federal deficit.

Exhibit 1.7

Allocation of Spending under the Recovery Act of 2009 (in billions)

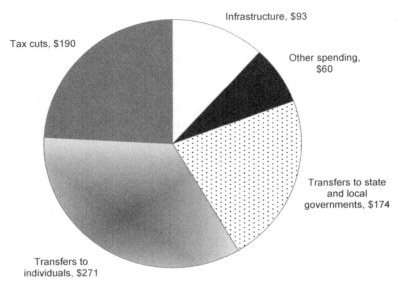

Source: Sherraden 2011.

What makes the local infrastructure issue so problematic is the decline of the municipal bond market triggered by the Wall Street crash of the home mortgage market in 2008. Traditionally, local governments have sold bonds to fund such things as roads, sewer systems, and government buildings. Because they are guaranteed by the general fund revenue from property taxes or the rates charged to sewer and water customers, municipal bonds were viewed as nearly risk free. That is no longer the case. Today, state and local government debt is at an all-time high of 22 percent of the U.S. gross domestic product (GDP) (usgovernmentspending.com, 2014). Unlike the federal government, if state and local governments want to spend more than they bring in, they must borrow it from investors. However, if investors believe that governments can no longer pay off the bonds, local jurisdictions will have to raise taxes and/or dramatically reduce services instead of borrowing. According to some observers, this is a strategy that local governments will readily pursue in order to maintain a high bond rating from private-sector investors (Hunsberger 2011). The average citizen is largely unaware of the indirect interactive consequences that bonding authority has on local public budgets. This is an issue discussed in greater depth in chapter 16.

At the same time that the national and state governments have restricted local revenues, they have also put pressure on the expenditure side through a growing series of mandates. These increase local government costs directly, as in the case of requirements to obtain permits for storm drains that discharge to streams, or requirements to provide medical services to jail inmates, or indirectly through such things as mandates to pay inflated wages for public works contracts or to restrict or eliminate the ability to terminate nonperforming employees.

Expenditure Reduction Strategies

As local revenue has declined and expenditures have increased, local jurisdictions have resorted to various cost-cutting strategies to complement new revenue-generation strategies discussed in the previous section. On the cost reduction side of the equation, local governments are making greater use of **intergovernmental agreements** with other jurisdictions and **contracts for services** (Cooper 2003; LeRoux 2007) and are applying new outcome-based performance and management strategies to reduce administrative transaction and overhead costs (Osborne and Hutchinson 2004). Many of these initiatives are treated as part of the new public management (NPM) movement to find ways of "making government run like a business" (Osborne and Gaebler 1992; Osborne and Hutchinson 2004; Osborne 2006). Intergovernmental agreements are increasingly common legal agreements among local jurisdictions to share police, fire, and fleet maintenance, or to take advantage of bulk purchases for materials and supplies. Some jurisdictions may be too small to provide specialized services, whether it be a library, convention center, or a public transportation system. Two local jurisdictions even used an intergovernmental agreement to share a director of budget and finance. Each jurisdiction by itself could not afford to pay a competitive salary to attract the kind of experienced administrator needed to deal with pressing and complex local finance issues, but together they could offer a competitive salary. It has become increasingly common for local governments to contract out solid waste, custodial services, building maintenance, food services, construction projects, computer services, transportation services, mental and public health services, and even public safety services.

There are growing examples of local governments contracting out the entire management of all city services. One of the first models of a contract city dates back to 1954, in the city of Lakewood, California. Dubbed the Lakewood Plan, the model was followed by several Southern California cities that contracted primarily with other governments. This model contrasts with the Sandy Springs Model, where, in 2005, Atlanta's Sandy Springs contracted out its city functions to the Colorado-based CH2M Hill consulting firm. The city entered into a five-year contract for $27 million per year for the first two years; leaders asserted that the results had "created a new model for twenty-first century municipal government." At least a dozen other communities in the Atlanta metropolitan area were inspired to follow the lead of Sandy Springs and hire private contractors to run their cities. "I think everybody across the country, from the federal level down to state and local, are seeing that resources are becoming harder and harder to come by, and you have to start doing things differently," noted Sandy Springs city manager John McDonough. "You can't just keep raising people's taxes. That was not a model Sandy Springs wanted. They wanted fiscal restraint and accountability, and that's what this model has provided them" (quoted in Peisner 2006).

The defenders of these private contracting arrangements argue that the costs to the city's taxpayers in the form of corporate profit is more than offset by cost savings resulting from the private firm's freedom from state mandates and interference in operations. Despite these arguments grounded in the values of efficiency and effectiveness, contracting out local services to private-sector firms remains a hotly debated topic. This is an issue we will explore in greater detail later in this chapter in the section titled *The Special Role of Nonprofits in Polity Budgeting*, on page 47.

While few local jurisdictions have been pushed to the extreme exemplified by Lakewood and Sandy Springs, the majority has joined the wave of reform over the past decades to implement what has come to be called "outcome-based" or "performance" management governance (Osborne and Hutchinson 2004). The notion is fairly simple in principle. Instead of focusing all of one's energies on managing the dollar costs of an activity and the rules to ensure process compliance, managers are encouraged to shift the focus to measurable performance outcomes. Commonly identified with the NPM movement, this strategy is said to (1) help eliminate unnecessary rules and process controls, and (2) result in reduced costs, increased efficiency and effectiveness, and improved customer satisfaction. A new cottage industry of consultants has been spawned by this results-oriented expenditure control strategy.

While local governments face a variety of financial challenges that will require forceful and creative leadership in the decades ahead, there are good reasons to be optimistic. As we argue later in this chapter, local governments are blessed by a long tradition of taking initiatory responsibility; they possess systems of government that promote the coproduction of solutions among elected officials and career administrators in collaboration with community partners. Building on this tradition, we believe that local governments will be able to operate successfully in even more complex **networks** of local government partners.

THE UNIQUE POLITICS OF LOCAL PUBLIC BUDGETING

We have already examined the complex organizational and jurisdictional considerations that affect the local public budgeting process, as well as the financial crisis that dominates budgetary concerns at the local level. A third reason to give special attention to local public budgeting is that, in most cases, the politics of the budgeting process is quite different at the local level from the politics at the federal level. From a public administration viewpoint, local governments are different because they establish their own budget processes. National and state governments can too, in theory, but their bureaucracies are typically too large to respond to principles of good management very quickly or extensively, and in any case, very few public administrators within those governments have much influence over the larger processes within which they carry out their budget activities.

The classic view of public budgeting at the federal level is that it is governed by the interplay of major large and well-organized interest groups. Over the course of his remarkably productive and highly influential academic career, Aaron Wildavsky explicated the "interest-based" political logic that drives the federal budgeting process (Wildavsky 1961, 1966, 1978, 1984, 1988, 1993). It is a logic that can best be understood in term of *interest group politics* that dominate the policy and budget allocation process at the subgovernment level of the U.S. Congress. Scholars have documented the key role played by a predictable coalition of vested interests that include key lobbying groups, elected officials, and agency career public servants who make the decisive policy and budget appropriation decisions at the subcommittee levels of Congress. Once an agreement to fund an activity is reached among the vested interest groups making up the *iron triangle* (i.e., elected officials, agency administrator, and lobbying group), it becomes very difficult to make significant changes from one year to the next. This dynamic is one of the major explanations of the incrementalism that characterizes the federal budgeting process and is put into operational practice through the principles of *base budget* and *fair share* increases and decreases from the base, depending on whether spending is on the rise or the decline.

While there are variations on this model,[5] scholars are in fundamental agreement that the federal budgeting process is largely controlled by *peak* interest groups. These groups use their relationships with administrative agencies and the subcommittees of Congress to form coalitions to ensure (1) successful passage of legislation (authorization), and (2) the funding to support it (appropriations). Such a process serves the reelection interests of political officials and the administrative interests of bureaucrats whose ability to provide services for clients usually falls short of demand.

Based on our own experience with many different types of local public budgeting processes, our work as consultants, and our role as educators of career public administrators, we have identified three major factors that create a different political logic at work in most of the nearly 89,500 local government jurisdictions. First, local governments are closest to the citizens and more accessible in bearing the burden of frustration that citizens experience in paying their taxes. Second, the large number of government jurisdictions at the local level encourages a spirit of cooperation. Third, most local governments have a different political structure than the tripartite systems of checks and balances and separation of powers that exist at the federal and state levels of government. The local system encourages greater cooperation between the legislative and executive functions of government. Taken together, these factors create a political logic at the local level that is far different from the logic dominating the budgetary process at the federal level. We will discuss these differences in more detail in the rest of this chapter.

The Proximity Imperative: The Political Psychology of Taxation v. Expenditures and Their Consequences for Local Government Budgeting

> In a democratic society, the division of resources between the public and private sectors is roughly determined by the desires of the electorate. But because it is such a complex and time-consuming task to acquire adequate political information, the electorate is chronically ignorant. . . . This ignorance causes governments to enact budgets smaller than the ones they would enact if the electorate possessed complete information. . . . The resulting misallocation of resources becomes more and more serious as the economy grows more complex. (Anthony Downs 1960, 541)

And, we would add the following to that last statement: The seriousness of this misallocation of resources also increases as government becomes more Populist. Anthony Downs reminds us that there is an important psychological dimension to the public budgeting process. Because citizens lack knowledge about (1) what is in the budget, and (2) what ends the budget items are intended to achieve, the majority will always opt for the trade-off of spending the money themselves rather than have it spent by elected officials on unknown activities with uncertain benefits. This is another way of saying that the economic rationality of the budgeting process is less important to the electorate than the political rationality of whether the citizens think they are "getting their money's worth." Since the benefits of the budget are indirect and longer term, it is hard for taxpayers to believe that government is doing all it can to eliminate waste and reduce spending on programs that are out of alignment with their personal priorities. This places a very heavy burden on public officials to educate the citizenry as to what is in the budget and what benefits are achieved with the dollars that are being spent. As we will see in our review of budget formats in Part III of this text, much of the history of public budgeting is driven by a push for efficiency and effectiveness: Experts working for the executive branch of government want to make use of their analytic expertise and training to ensure that the taxpayers are getting their money's worth. But, as Downs suggests, no matter how successful public officials may be in undertaking this challenge, they will never be fully successful in overcoming the relative ignorance of the electorate regarding the contents of the budget and the intended outcomes of public expenditures.

Citizen anxiety over taxation and spending is not only the result of the rational calculation of individuals; it is also an issue of political principle that goes to the heart of America's founding: respect for the private interests of individuals. This and other topics are addressed at length by Alexander Hamilton, John Jay, and James Madison in the 85 essays that make up *The Federalist Papers*. As Hamilton observed:

> Tax laws have in vain been multiplied; new methods to enforce the collection have in vain been tried; the public expectation has been uniformly disappointed, and the treasuries of the States have remained empty. The . . . popular government, coinciding with the real scarcity of money incident to a languid and mutilated state of trade, has hitherto defeated every experiment for extensive collections and has at length taught the different legislatures of the folly of attempting them. (Hamilton 1787, Federalist No. 12, quoted in Rossiter 1961, 92–93)

Hamilton's reminder that you can't substitute taxation for wealth generation without undermining the legitimacy of government itself continues to pose a political problem for all government leaders, but especially those at the local levels, where control over the conditions of economic prosperity are severely limited. Unable to do much about economic development and limited by what can be collected from property taxes even when development is robust, public officials are left with the difficult task of triaging and coordinating efforts among multiple jurisdictions to assuage the concerns of taxpayers (see opening scenarios). Even 150 years ago, Tocqueville was struck by the general "stinginess" of American citizens. "To judge what sacrifices democracies know how to impose on themselves, we must therefore await a time when the American nation is obliged to put half of the revenue from goods into the hands of its government, like England" (Tocqueville 1835–1840/2000, 213). That has not happened and probably never will.

The Local Government Cooperation Imperative

In addition to the challenge of having to produce and maintain a budget that balances expenditures with revenues, local officials face another ordeal—namely, managing the competition among multiple jurisdictions for the "taxpayer's willingness to pay." Imagine three separate governing bodies that independently decide to ask taxpayers for approval of new bond measures in the same election cycle or during the same budget process. All may risk failure if they do not coordinate their conversations with each other and explain to taxpayers (1) why the proposed measure should be passed, and (2) what people's support of the proposed measure will mean in terms of the collective benefit to the community. As an alternative, public officials may simply decide to have these conversations at different times with the citizens by sequencing their approval requests for additional revenue over a period of years. In either case, there is a need for local governing bodies to coordinate their interface with a common pool of taxpayers and to demonstrate their good faith efforts to maximize the use of scarce resources through visible signs of cooperation.

Local Government Partnership Between Elected Officials and Career Administrators

As the preceding discussion of the various forms of local government makes clear, one of the important characteristics that many local governments share is that they are run by part-time elected officials who may receive little or no pay for their work. As a result, career administrators bear an especially heavy burden of successfully managing the multiple and intersecting relationships of community stakeholder groups, elected officials, and career administrators. Managing these relationships is especially difficult in the United States because of the deep and long-abiding distrust of government in general and public officials in particular (Karl 1987; Morgan, Green, Shinn, and Robinson 2013, chap. 5). Citizens are not certain that they can trust their government officials to be good stewards of their tax dollars, especially when these officials are perceived as having a self-interest in growing pet programs and organizations. There is a large and well-developed body of research that seeks to describe and explain how this tripartite set of relationships among citizens, elected public officials, and career administrators is most successfully managed.[6] A relative lack of success is reflected in the rather short tenure of city and county administrators. The International Association of City and County Managers Association reports that the average tenure for city and county managers was 7.5 years in 2006 (ICMA 2009).

While public officials at the federal government level have to deal with the same challenge of managing the conflicts between the pains and fairness of revenue generation with the public demands for services that usually exceed revenue, there are two important differences that distinguish local from national government budgeting. First, the federal government has the legal authority to carry deficits, while all state and local governments have to create and maintain a balanced budget. While local governments can borrow money, the constraints on local governing units (as we will see in Part II) are far more stringent than is the case with the national government.

Taken together, we believe the psychology of getting and spending money, the number and kinds of local governments, and the *fused power* structure of authority that characterizes most of these forms creates a different political logic that distinguishes the politics of local budgeting from the politics of budgeting at the federal and state levels of government. A combination of reliance on professional career administrators, part-time elected officials, the requirement to create a balanced budget, nonpartisanship, and proximity to citizens results in the need for more transparency and greater cooperation among those who have the responsibility of developing a budget and getting it approved.

POLITY BUDGETING: BUILDING LOCAL COMMUNITIES[7]

A fourth and final reason that local public budgeting deserves to be treated separately is that local government leaders are not simply budgeting for the government; they are budgeting to achieve the larger good for the community. While this can also be argued for those involved in the federal and state budgeting processes, the common community good is more tangibly visible at the local level, where decision makers are in face-to-face relationships with nonprofit service providers, other jurisdictions, and the business community on a regular basis. The common good is less of an abstraction and is less capable of being reduced to ideological principles or formulaic solutions to budget constraints. Typically, the effects of *local* budget cuts are far more immediate and glaring to citizens than cuts that result from the consequences of decisions trickling down from state and federal budgeting levels. With most state and federal grant funds, the target populations who are helped or hurt by funding decisions are less visible, not always well organized, and benefit from a layer of professional career administrators who serve as a buffer that obscures and tempers the adverse consequences for the local community. Ultimately, when these efforts by the professional cadre of grant administrators cannot quietly solve the problem created by reduced funding, local officials have to engage the community in discussions about how best to deal with decreased federal and state funding.

We call this budgeting for the common good *polity budgeting*. By *polity,* we mean the organic wholeness of a political system that contributes to the distinctive way of a life of a political community. Such an approach emphasizes the synergistic influence of history, institutions, and culture in creating a shared system of values, as well as shared agreement on governance processes and structures, both formal and informal. Since the late 1990s, there has been a resurgence in the scholarship that uses *polity* or *regime* as the unit of analysis for understanding political change, governance, and leadership development (Rohr 1989; Morgan, Green, Shinn, and Robinson 2008; Ozawa 2005; Elkin and Soltan 1993; Johnson 2002; Stone 1989; Leo 1997, 1998; Lauria 1997). Our use of the term *polity* throughout the book is consistent with this scholarship. It is also consistent with what others have described as *networked governance* (O'Toole 1997, 2006; Provan and Milward 2001; Provan and Kenis 2007; Isett et al. 2011). In addition, we recognize extensive intergovernmental cooperation and partnerships, and **intergovernmental** and **interlocal agreements** as networked elements of a community polity (LeRoux, Brandenburger, and Pandey 2010; LeRoux and Carr 2007). These relationships are illustrated in Exhibit 1.8.

Exhibit 1.9 shows a local problem that needs attention. It might be affordable housing for a given target population; it might be social services for individuals with mental illness; it might be crime-fighting efforts. Pick your favorite. In the exhibit the problem is the need for a school district to build a new school. This book argues that local governments will be called upon with increasing frequency to use their budgeting process not necessarily to solve such problems by themselves, but to play a leadership role that leverages all of the assets in the community to maximize the community good. Notice in Exhibit 1.8 that the government sits as an equal partner with other institutions in the community. This contrasts with the depiction in Exhibit 1.9, where a governmental entity is taking the lead to enlist the support of other partner organizations and institutions

Exhibit 1.8

Civic Infrastructure Budgeting Model

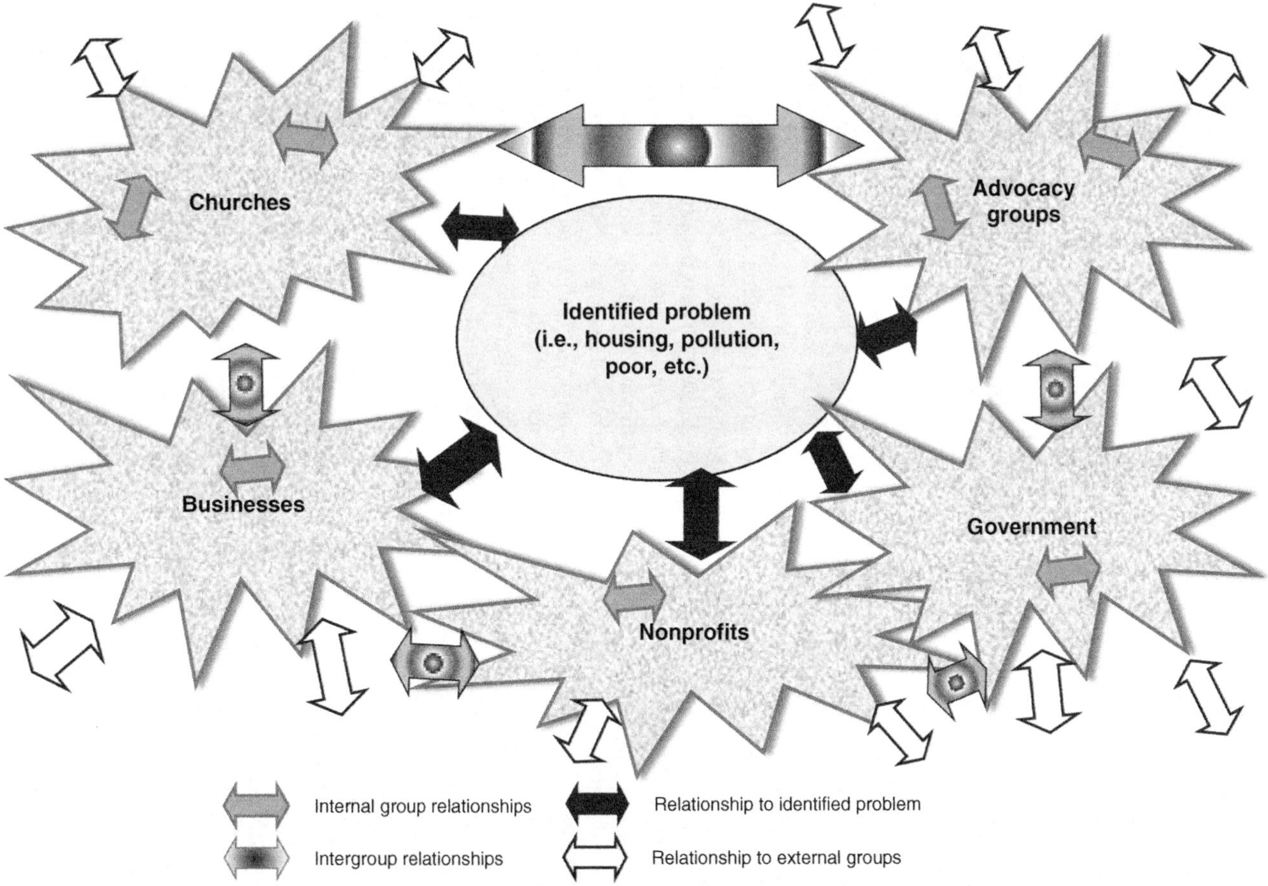

Exhibit 1.9

The Relationship Between the Public, Private, Nonprofit, and Special District Sectors

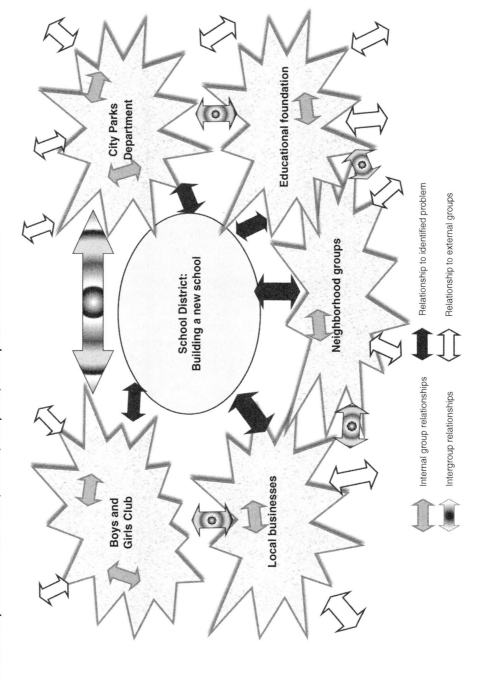

43

in the community to leverage scarce resources. Our opening scenario on building a new school illustrates this kind of leveraging role. The school district enlists the support of the city, the Boys and Girls Club, members of the business community, neighborhood associations, and a school foundation to (1) generate sufficient funding, (2) pool resources, and then (3) build a new shared multiuse facility that is jointly funded and owned by a variety of community partners. In both types of polity leadership illustrated in Exhibits 1.8 and 1.9, budget officials are required to coordinate resources across interjurisdictional units of government to include actors in the market economy as well as in the nonprofit civic sector. Polity budgeting requires local government officials to bring both an intersectoral and an institutional perspective to their budgeting roles. We will elaborate more fully on each of these polity budgeting components in the next two sections.

The United States possesses a mixed economy that relies upon the contributions of the public and governmental sectors, along with private, nonprofit, and for-profit sectors, to contribute to the common good of the community. No single sector can be counted on to do it all. This simple principle underpins American democratic governance and is legally recognized in our state and federal constitutions, statutes, administrative rules, and judicial opinions. The private sector has confidence that its private property will be protected and that businesses have constitutionally guarded rights to advance their interests in the political process. The nonprofit sector enjoys special legal recognition at both the national and state levels of our political system, including exemption from taxation on its income at the federal level and in most states. Citizens are free to join these nonprofit organizations, knowing their rights of association and advocacy will be protected. In addition, if these outlets for meeting the collective needs of groups of individuals are not adequate, and if general-purpose governments are not responsive, citizens in most parts of the United States can exercise their political rights to form special governmental units to assist them in their efforts. This legal system has produced a complex array of entities that contribute to the public good, but in doing so, it has made coordination and cooperation difficult.

The variety and complexity of the mixed economy can produce confusion about the role of the parts and how the parts contribute to the larger common good, not to mention the expenditure of energies that sometimes work at cross-purposes to the common good. To simplify this complexity, Exhibit 1.10 summarizes the essential differences among the sectors based on how they arbitrate value differences and the breadth of interests they serve. Private-sector agencies and firms negotiate value differences through the market, and their interests are parochial. The interests of nonprofit organizations, on the other hand, are usually regarded as part of the larger common good. Special districts and general-purpose public agencies arbitrate value differences through the political process but differ in the scope of interests they embrace. Special districts are established to pursue parochial interests in contrast to the broader common interests of general-purpose governmental units. The distinctive characteristics summarized in Exhibit 1.10 are not meant to be exhaustive; they simply illustrate that each of the sectors has its own logic and that there is complex interplay among these sectors, marked by mutual dependence in serving the larger common good.

The public sector plays a pivotal role for organizations operating in the private, nonprofit, and special district sectors of the economy. Markets cannot sustain themselves without a stable infrastructure of roads, communication systems, defense systems that protect and maintain international lanes of commerce, banking systems that provide security for loans, a legal system that enforces contracts, and a regulatory system that stabilizes the rate and complexity of change in markets as well as their relationships with consumers and communities. The nonprofit sector also relies on this infrastructure, depending heavily upon the grants, contracts, and other forms of sponsorship by governments at all levels, not to mention its privileged tax exempt status. The elaborate legal and procedural environment of many governments helps provide stability for the other sectors, but it also presents impediments to highly efficient operations. Private-sector firms and nonprofit organizations enjoy substantial advantages over the public sector in this regard.

Exhibit 1.10   **Institutional Forms**

| | | Scope of interests | |
		Parochial	Common
How values are arbitrated	Political	Special district governments	General governments
	Market	For-profit private agencies and firms	Nonprofit organizations

The private sector's concern for innovation, creativity, and customer satisfaction is assumed to be the best mechanism for efficiently maximizing the allocation of society's resources. This may be the case—as long as the goals of society are compatible with those of individuals and the demands of customers can be arranged to induce a market response. But there are numerous instances when these private marketplace conditions do not exist. The following are the most common examples of market failures or exceptions that have provided justification for public-sector intervention: (1) the provision of **public goods**, such as national defense; (2) the amelioration of some of the *diseconomies* or *externalities* of collective action, pollution of the environment and drug abuse among them; (3) the avoidance of *tragedy of the commons* problems, such as natural resource depletion; (4) reaping the collective benefits of *public economies,* such as education and early childhood development programs; and (5) taking advantage of *natural monopolies,* such as water, sewer, and other public utilities. In these and other instances, the public sector is encouraged to intervene in the private marketplace in the interest of promoting greater equity (Okun 1975; Wanat 1978, chap. 2).

Neither the public nor the private sectors are as capable as the nonprofit sector of meeting individual clientele needs with the fewest rules and lowest costs to the client. This is partly because nonprofits rely on the extensive passion of volunteers and because they are free from a variety of legal mandates imposed on local governing bodies. Soup kitchens and shelters for the homeless, runaway youth, and domestic violence victims rarely require clients to meet some extensive eligibility requirements. Those who provide these kinds of services to narrow target populations are passionate about what they do, and this passion—combined with flexible, adaptive approaches to care—is clearly reflected in the quality of treatment that is extended to each person in need. Because of these factors, more service can usually be provided for fewer dollars than is the case with either the public sector or the private marketplace. Nonprofits are also created in response to a variety of impulses, including government failure to provide sufficient public goods (for example, United Way); the American tradition of self-help (Alcoholics Anonymous); a commitment to helping others (Catholic Charities); or a desire to advance the interests of a target community (National Education Association, American Association of Retired Persons, the National Rifle Association, the Native Fish Society, the Boy Scouts of America, the Sierra Club, and the like).

Exhibit 1.11   **Comparative Characteristics of Sectors**

Private Sector	Nonprofit Sector	Public Sector	Special Districts
Mission driven	Clientele driven	Legal/rule driven	Purpose driven
Results oriented	Needs oriented	Process oriented	Service oriented
Entrepreneurial	Meeting needs with few rules and questions asked	Bureaucratic	Technical expertise
Motivating others for high performance	"Doing the right thing"	Constitutional agent of a sovereign power	Bounded legal authority
Customers	Target populations	Citizens	Target population
Flexibility	Service	Control	Service
Innovation	Flexibility for target population	Following rules	Service within narrow legal authority
Customer satisfaction	Clientele needs	Citizen rights and responsibilities	Client satisfaction
Incentives	"Doing good"	Regulations	Service
Employee empowerment	Voluntary commitment	Hierarchy	Functional competence
Delegation of authority	Informal coordination	Centralization of authority	Parochially governed
Self-interest	Responsibility	Accountability	Efficiency
Interests	Values	Rights	Service
Preferences	Needs	Equity	Effectiveness
Profit	Moral duty	Duty to the law	Duty to clients

The special district sector offers still another alternative to providing public services. Unlike general-purpose governments that administer a broad range of services, special districts are established to administer one specialized activity on a cost-of-service basis. Fire, hospital, police, water, sewer, library, and other services can be provided by creating a unit of government whose sole purpose is to administer that service at a specified cost to each member of the district. The advantage of this approach is twofold: It allows citizens to purchase additional levels of service that government may not be able to provide, and it controls the price they are willing to pay. One of the disadvantages of special districts is that they further balkanize public service delivery and allow those with more financial resources to obtain more and better service than the poor. As Nancy Burns points out in her study of local government, special districts are frequently a product of race and class motivations (Burns 1994). Under such circumstances, it becomes more difficult to build a shared sense of the common public or community interest.

In short, organizations operating in the public, private, nonprofit, and special district sectors are suited to perform quite distinctive tasks. It is important for local public budgeting officials to know what each sector can do particularly well and why, as they increasingly reach out across the sectors to obtain assistance in rethinking how to budget for the common good. The distinct characteristics of each sector are summarized below in Exhibit 1.11. The summary is not exhaustive but rather illustrates that each of the sectors has a logic of its own, and that there is a complex interplay among the sectors with mutual dependence of one upon the other. These characteristics also have important implications for shaping the ethical obligations of those responsible for budgeting for the common good. We will illustrate this more concretely in the next section, where we focus on the special role of nonprofits in the local public budgeting process.

The Special Role of Nonprofits in Polity Budgeting[8]

An important but largely ignored development over the last several decades has been the rapid rise of nonprofits in providing local services to the community. This is a result of an important shift that has occurred in the role of government in funding social services. Federal government spending on social services increased by 259 percent in inflation-adjusted dollars between 1965 and 1980 (Salamon 1999, 61). However, beginning in the late 1970s, government spending began a sharp reversal and experienced a 15 percent decline in inflation-adjusted dollars between 1977 and 1994 (116).

Despite the decline in government funding, support for the social service sector continued to grow as a result of the increased role played by the nonprofit and for-profit sectors. For example, between 1977 and 1992 (Salamon 1999, 116):

- Private social service agencies grew by 130 percent.
- The number of employees working for these agencies grew by 140 percent.
- The revenues of these agencies rose nearly 240 percent above what they had been in 1977, even after adjusting for inflation.

Exhibit 1.12 summarizes the key trends in social service delivery between 1977 and 1996. The paradox of declining government support and expansion of spending is explained by the shift of service provision to nonprofits and the private sector, which have relied increasingly on fee income and greater support from private giving. By 1996, "fees came to outdistance both government and private giving as a source of nonprofit human service agency income" (Salamon 1999, 117). As of 1980, "approximately 25 percent of all government spending in the fields where nonprofit organizers were active flowed to such organizations" (63). In Massachusetts, the dollar amount of purchase-of-service contracts with private nonprofit service agencies more than doubled between 1977 and 1981, increasing from $36 million with 380 contracts to $84 million and over 1,000 contracts (Smith and Lipsky 1993, 56). In addition to these **contracts for services**, federal block grants and federal programs providing funding for Head Start, runaway shelters, and an extensive array of other social services have been funneled to nonprofit organizations.

What are the consequences of this enlarged role for nonprofit organizations in becoming major providers of public goods and services? From one point of view, it represents the triumph of America's reliance on associations to achieve the common good of the community. Huge numbers of volunteers become enlisted in supporting these associations and in the process, to quote Tocqueville, "sentiments and ideas renew themselves, the heart is enlarged and the human mind is developed" (Tocqueville 1835–1840/2000, 491). But from another perspective, the mutual dependence of government and nonprofit organizations raises significant questions. Smith and Lipsky ask, "If the state no longer directly delivers services, but authorizes private parties to conduct its business, where shall we locate the boundaries of the state? Massive contracting for services should also have significant implications for the limits of government and the autonomy of nongovernmental community affairs. . . . More dependence on nonprofit organizations means not less but more government involvement in the affairs of voluntary and community agencies" (Smith and Lipsky 1993, 5).

Why is it the case that more contracting out is likely to undermine rather than strengthen the nonprofit sector? To answer this question, we need to return to the distinctions made in the previous section between the public, private, and nonprofit sectors. The public sector's emphasis on providing maximum service to as many citizens as possible conflicts with the nonprofit sector's emphasis on providing as much service as possible to its chosen clientele population (see Exhibit 1.12). In addition, the public sector is held to a different standard of accountability than the non-

Exhibit 1.12

Comparison in Social Services Delivery by Sector, 1977–1996

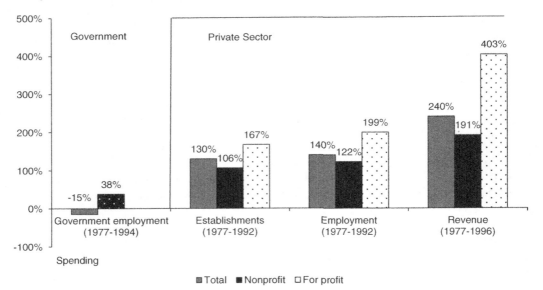

Source: Salamon 1999, 116. Copyright © 1999, 2012 The Foundation Center. Used by permission.

profit sector. The dual principles of equity and accountability for public-sector officials create an incentive to write contracts that require nonprofit organizations to deliver specified levels of service to given numbers of clientele with the dollars available. To accomplish this goal, nonprofits may have to alter their mission to accomplish the specifications of the contract. For example, instead of providing homeless shelter services to a given client for as long as it is needed, the nonprofit may be required to restrict the service to a client in order to meet its contract goals with respect to target numbers. It may even be subject to direct control by government "over admission, treatment and discharge decisions" (Smith and Lipsky 1993, 229, 122–132).

In addition to the need for a nonprofit to rearrange its service mission to accommodate the specifications of a contract, the accountability requirements of the contract may require the agency to hire professionals in accounting, financial management, personnel, and fundraising in order to meet its elevated eligibility standards and reporting procedures. This pressure to professionalize the management of nonprofit organizations can displace volunteers, thereby losing much of the passion, flexibility, empathy, and singleness of focus that they bring to such organizations (Smith and Lipsky 1993, 83–87, 100–108).

There is a final, unintended consequence of government's reliance on the contract for services process as a substitute for providing direct service. As public dollars have become increasingly scarce, the pressure to squeeze greater results from the contractors tends to rise. As a result, nonprofit service providers are being asked to deliver more for less, as are government agencies in general. When this occurs in the private business sector, the results are quite predictable, and so is the case with nonprofit organizations. To meet this demand for greater economies and efficiencies, nonprofit organizations have consolidated and merged their operations, leaving many fewer providers in the community than in the past (Smith and Lipsky 1993, 177–182). Smith and Lipsky conclude that the nonprofit sector now reflects "a shift . . . from the informal to the formal care systems, greater homogeneity of service within particular service categories, a diminished role of the board of directors in agency governance, and destabilization among nonprofit agencies" (215). In short, they have become more instrumental than constitutive in their mission and culture, and are thereby weakened in their ability to promote citizen engagement in governance. Those responsible for the public budgeting of services play a decisive role not only in providing efficient and effective services but also in ways of doing so that preserve the vitality of local communities, including the ability of nonprofit organizations to perform their distinctive role in contributing to the common good. For this reason, we believe it is important for those who are responsible for local budgeting to thinking institutionally in their approach to budgeting for the common good. What does it mean to think and to act institutionally? We will address this question next.

Importance of an Institutional Perspective

As we have argued in this section on polity budgeting, local officials will be increasingly required to enlist the support of others across jurisdictional and organizational boundaries in promoting the common good through the exercise of their discretion in the budgeting process. This boundary-spanning leadership requires identifying long-term partners who have acquired the trust and legitimacy of the community. Such partners are frequently an integral part of what citizens associate with the very identity of the community itself and, because of that, enjoy institutional status, not just an organizational identity. As Philip Selznick has argued, "Institutions are established, not by decree alone, but as a result of being bound into the fabric of social life" (Selznick 1992, 232).

This process of institutionalization establishes cultural identity that makes the whole greater than the sum of an organization's parts (Powell and DiMaggio, 1991). The Green Bay Packers, for example, mean far more to their fan base and their community than winning games and making money. The team engenders ways of dressing, of conversing, and of living during the season. It is literally and figuratively "owned" by the community. It is the pride of the community. Likewise, the transformation of a set of religious practices into something like the Catholic Church, the development of the market economy in the United States, or the role of the U.S. Forest Service in public land management exemplifies public institutions built through such processes and illustrates why institutions have to be understood historically in order to fully grasp their significance. Every local community has its own examples of such entities.

There are at least three major advantages to taking an institutional approach to local public budgeting: (1) It greatly influences our understanding of how change occurs; (2) it significantly improves our understanding of the interface between public- and private-sector activities; and (3) it enriches our understanding of the processes for generating legitimacy. All three will be increasingly important for those who have local public budgeting responsibility. The future will require local budget leaders to redefine the government's role in promoting the common good in partnership with institutional leaders across multiple sectors. In order for this change to add up to a difference that counts and to acquire legitimacy, it must be embedded in the institutional agents who can hold and sustain these agreements over time.

As the lead partner in this process of redefining what the community values, it is important for local public officials to be clear about the ethical role responsibilities they have as agents of a rule-of-law system bounded by state and federal constitutional and statutory authority. Since many of these officials operate within a fused power model similar to a parliamentary system (e.g., weak mayor, city manager, commission), the ethical role of administrators in the budgeting process is confusing and frequently conflicting. It certainly belies the traditional bright-line distinction between the legislative and executive functions. How do these local forms of government square with the conventionally held view of American democracy, where responsibility for policy development is lodged in the legislative branch and responsibility for policy implementation is the purview of the executive branch? What legislative role does the city manager play with part-time elected officials? How do council members and commissioners who hold both legislative and executive functions balance these roles in ways that ensure legislative responsiveness while also giving appropriate attention to the executive capacity to implement policy with energy, effectiveness, and efficiency? These are questions we will address in the next chapter, titled "Local Public Budgeting and Democratic Theory."

We conclude this chapter with some final reflections on the purposes of the text. Our goal is to show how the budgeting process and the role of its participants contribute to the overall functioning of our many systems of local democratic governance. We argue that our system of checks and balances and separation of powers necessitates a strong role for career administrators, citizen activists, elected officials, and technical experts. This view does not do much to help resolve conflicts in the budgeting process, but it does help reframe the conflicts so that they are seen as a natural and necessary by-product of our peculiar form of democracy. We believe this reframing has a sobering influence on expectations. By viewing conflicts as an important part of the process of our system of democratic governance, participants are less likely to see conflicts as artifacts that can be made to disappear through the magic of budget reform or restructuring. This book, therefore, is intended to serve as a corrective to what some might call the corrosive consequences of the somewhat obscured perspectives of participants in the public budgeting process. It is not designed to make one a technical expert on budgeting. Instead, it is written with the following three specific goals in mind:

- to help participants understand the overall logic of the public budgeting process and the respective role performed by each of the participants;
- to provide the reader with a historical understanding of the limits and possibilities for budget reform initiatives; and
- to demonstrate the need for participants in the budgeting process to view their activities as an essential element in our system of democratic governance.

In fact, this book assumes that you cannot be a responsible agent in the budgeting process without possessing a theory of democratic governance. In the absence of such a theory, participants simply become instrumental functionaries in a mechanical kind of process.

Given the broad focus taken by this text, readers cannot expect a quick read to provide them with what they need to be fully proficient with the microdetails of their jurisdiction's budget process. The information in this text clearly needs to be supplemented by the detailed technical information and organizational requirements that are unique to the public budgeting process for each jurisdiction and organizational unit.

STUDY QUESTIONS

1. How many and what kinds of local governments do you pay taxes to support? What kinds of services do you receive in return for these payments?
2. What authority does each of the jurisdictions to which you pay taxes have to raise various kinds of revenue (i.e., bonds, taxes, fees for service, etc.)?
3. What are the consequences of having so many local government jurisdictions to meet the needs of citizens?
4. What is the structure of the various local governments that you pay taxes to support? How are budget allocation decisions made? What kind of influence do you have over these decisions?

5. In many states, county governments provide a wide variety of local and regional services. The County Governance 1.1 exercise on the textbook website (www.pdx.edu/cps/budget-book) provides an opportunity to investigate county governance and service delivery. If you live in a state without strong county governments, adapt the exercise to a nearby medium or large city or township government.

6. In what ways does the local budgeting process differ from the processes at the federal and perhaps the state level?

NOTES

1. For this section, we have drawn heavily from Green and Morgan's "Making the Constitution Relevant to Local Governments, Special Districts, and Authorities," paper presented at the National ASPA Conference, March 13–17, 2014, Washington, D.C.

2. States vary widely in the number and kind of local jurisdictions that have been created under state authority (U.S. ACIR report 1993; "Local Governments in the United States," chapter 1 of *State Laws Governing Organizational Structure and Administration.* Report M-186, 1993. Washington, DC: U.S. Government Printing Office). For example, the State of Colorado in 2009 listed 3,183 local government units (cities and counties) and an additional 3,628 special districts (including school districts) (State of Colorado, Department of Local Affairs 2009). This contrasted with New Jersey's 2002 listing of 587 local units and 825 special districts (City-data.com 2010b). In 2002, Louisiana listed 362 local units of government and 110 school and special districts (City-data.com 2010a).

While there is wide variation in the number and kinds of local units of government that exist in the United States, it is generally true that the farther west one lives, the greater the number of local units of government you will find. This is largely a relic of the influence of the Populist era at the close of the nineteenth century. Frustrated first by the unwillingness of legislative bodies to control the growing abuses by private business and second by the unresponsiveness of elected officials to the electorate, Populist reformers introduced a variety of new accountability mechanisms that included recall, the initiative, and the referendum. While some scholars include these reforms as part of the Progressive movement in the early decades of the twentieth century, they were Populist in origin and were included in the national Populist Party platforms of 1892 and 1896 (Johnson and Porter 1973, 110). In fact, most of the electoral reforms advocated by the Populist movement became reality decades later under the banner of the Progressive movement. One of these structural changes included recall by voters of some elected public officials prior to completing their term of office. Another instrument of direct democracy included the initiative, which enables voters to place measures directly on the ballot without having to go through the legislative process. Such measures can include changes in statutes as well as alterations to a state constitution. A third reform, the referendum, allows the legislative body to refer a controversial piece of legislation directly to the voters for final approval. These instruments were first introduced in the West. Oregon became the first state to establish the statewide initiative and popular referendum. In the early days of the twentieth century, these institutions became widely known as the Oregon System. They fell into disuse in the middle decades of the twentieth century before being revived in 1970s and 1980s as a way of dealing with citizen dissatisfaction and loss of confidence in government policies—especially in connection with taxation and spending. A final pillar of Populist accountability was put in place with the successful campaign to broaden the use of direct popular election for officials such as secretaries of state, education commissioners, treasurers, district attorneys, clerks, auditors, and sheriffs (see Morgan, Green, Shinn, and Robinson 2013, chap. 5, 100–105).

3. School district budgeting will not be a primary focus of our attention in this book, largely because the topic is covered quite well by other texts (see Poston 2010; Hartman 2003; Sorenson and Goldsmith 2006; Kratz 1996) and because each local system varies widely as a result of the way in which state, local, and federal funding creates various mixes of discretionary authority by local school boards over the budget expenditure process. In general, local discretionary authority has been significantly reduced in recent years as a result of the federal No Child Left Behind Act and the increased role of state governments in supporting school funding.

4. We have relied heavily in this section on our previous treatment of this issue (see Morgan, Green, Shinn, and Robinson 2013, 44–47, 116–118). See Burns (1994) for a detailed analysis of the reasons for the rapid growth in local governments during the period between 1960 and 2000.

5. For variations on the interest-based model, see Lowi (1979), Wilson (1989), and Ripley and Franklin (1991). For actor-based models, see Anderson 2003; Lowi and Ginsberg 2000; Rourke 1984; Kingdon 1995; and Meier 2006. For advocacy-coalition models, see Sabatier and Jenkins-Smith (1993). For inter-

governmental relations models, see Scherberle 2004; Goggin, Lester, and O'Toole 1990; Elazar 1987; and Grodzins 1960.

6. See Lazenby 2009, chap. 3; Morgan and Kass 1993; Nalbandian 1994, 2000; and Svara 1990, 1991, 1998, 1999, 2006. For a history of the debate on the role of city managers in local government, see White 1927; Stone, Price, and Stone 1940; Childs 1963; Stillman 1974, 1977; Ammons and Charldean 1989; Green 1989; Hale 1989; Banovetz 1994; Teske and Schneider 1994; Hinton and Kerrigan 1995; Svara 1985, 1990, 1991, 1999, 2006; Montjoy and Watson 1995; Crewson and Fisher 1997; Rove 1999; Wheeland 2000; and International City/County Management Association 2008a.

7. We have relied heavily in this section on our previous treatment of this issue (see Morgan, Green, Shinn, and Robinson 2013, pp. 44–47, 470–471; Robinson and Morgan 2014, chap. 12.).

8. We have relied heavily in this section on our previous treatment of this issue (see Morgan, Green, Shinn, Robinson 2013, 44–47, 113–115, 470–471).

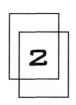

LOCAL PUBLIC BUDGETING AND DEMOCRATIC THEORY

In 1940, in what is still the best discussion of the subject, V.O. Key lamented "The Lack of a Budgetary Theory." He called for a theory which would help answer the basic question of budgeting on the expenditure side: "On what basis shall it be decided to allocate X dollars to Activity A instead of Activity B? . . . [T]he task, as posed, is impossible to fulfill. . . . A theory which contains criteria for determining what ought to be in the budget is nothing less than a theory stating what the government ought to do. . . . A normative theory of budgeting, therefore, is utopian in the fullest sense of that word; its accomplishment and acceptance would mean the end of conflict over the government's role in society.

(Aaron Wildavsky 1961, 183–184)

Political rationality is the fundamental kind of reason, because it deals with the preservation and improvement of decision structures, and decision structures are the source of all decisions. . . . There can be no conflict between political rationality and technical, legal, social or economic rationality, because the solution of political problems makes possible an attack on any other problem. . . . In a political decision . . . action never is based on the merits of a proposal, but always on who makes it and who opposes it. . . . Compromise is always a rational procedure, even when the compromise is between a good and a bad proposal.

(Paul Diesing 1982, 198, 203–204, 232)

UNDERSTANDING PUBLIC BUDGETING IN THE
CONTEXT OF DEMOCRAT THEORY

Wildavsky and Diesing remind us that public budgeting is not about numbers, but about the interests and values that produce the numbers. These interests and values are grounded in different perceptions of the role of government in society and who should have what kind of say in shaping this role. For these reasons, it is important for those responsible for the budgeting process to have an understanding of the various theories of democratic governance and the role that citizens, elected officials, professional administrators, nonprofit organizations, and the private market sector play in each model. Each local government's annual budget provides a snapshot understanding of how these contending parties and roles intend to work together for the common good of the community.

In this chapter, we will explore various theories of local democratic governance and the implications they have for understanding the relationships among the sectors, particularly the role of government and the role of career public administrators who are frequently in the catbird seat in developing and implementing local public budgets. The discussion in this chapter extends the argument made in chapter 1 about the importance of understanding the different kinds and forms of local government. Each of the forms we discussed in chapter 1 rests on a theory of democratic governance that has important implications for the local budgeting process and its outcomes. We will develop an understanding of some of these theories and explore the implications for the participants in three steps. First, we will summarize the conflicting theories that most citizens have about how the local budgeting process works. In doing so, we will explain how these theories align with the forms of government discussed in chapter 1. In the second part of this chapter, we will explore the debates between the Federalists and Anti-Federalists and abstract the governing traditions, values, and principles that continue to shape our thinking about the role of citizens, experts, voluntary associations, and the business community in the public budgeting process. We will also explore how these two governing traditions have combined to create four models of governance organized around the questions, Who should govern? and What is the proper role of government in society? In the final section of this chapter, we will draw on our discussion of the constitutional founding debates to present a theory of governance for local public budgeting and the various administrative leadership roles that are required by this theory.

We place considerable emphasis on the importance of understanding the underlying democratic theory that guides and supports local public budgeting for two reasons. First, it can help to reduce the frustrations of participants in the process; second, it ennobles the activity of public budgeting by making it an integral part of the community's ongoing debate about how best to achieve the collective well-being of its citizens.

Reducing Frustration

Frequently, actors in the budgeting process forget that their responsibilities are profoundly shaped by the jurisdiction's peculiar system of governance. Participants sometimes become so preoccupied with their "own knitting" that they seldom pause to reflect on how their work interfaces with the work of others to achieve a larger common good both within the organization and throughout the larger community. One of the consequences of this narrow perspective is that expectations are created at each stage of the budgeting process, many of which exceed the capacity of others to meet them. The result is that everyone is disappointed with the performance of everyone else. Before venting our frustrations on individuals and processes, it is useful to stop and ask how often these frustrations ultimately stem from the design of our democratic processes of governance—a design that tries to accommodate multiple and competing public purposes in the debate over the allocation of public resources.

Ennobling the Budgeting Process

Once we view public budgeting as part of our jurisdiction's larger structure of authority, the practical task of developing a budget becomes a window to the community's heart and soul. The budgeting process is the focal point for competing claims (1) about who should rule; (2) about social, economic, and political justice; (3) about the role of experts and citizens; (4) in short, about the well-being of the community. This text assumes that those with budget responsibility participate actively in shaping what the public good means. Whether they like it or not, those with fiscal and budgetary responsibility are not simply instrumental agents of their job descriptions but constitutive agents of the public interest (Morgan, Green, Shinn, and Robinson 2013, chaps. 1–2; Cook 1996, chap.1). By *constitutive,* we mean that these agents have the opportunity to exercise a proactive role in making policy recommendations and undertaking implementation strategies that shape the form, substance, and meaning of democratic government in the hearts and minds of ordinary citizens. To the extent that career public servants play this larger role, it is imperative that participants understand how their given role in a particular structure's budgeting process shapes the public interest. *More fundamentally, it is essential for participants in the budgeting process to have a theory of governance that both explains and justifies their respective roles.* In the absence of such a theory, participants cannot legitimatize their discretionary authority, which is the threshold requirement for governing by the rule of law. It is not enough for a participant in the budgeting process to say that we should do X rather than Y, "because I like it better," because it is more efficient, because it is more effective, or because it is more in alignment with what the "public sector does best." All of these are appropriate responses, depending on one's role responsibility, but they are not sufficient. It is important for each of these responses to be grounded in the principles of democratic governance. If, for example, we see issues of effectiveness and efficiency as business principles imported from the private sector rather than principles of democratic governance, we inadvertently put government budgeting at odds with private-sector budgeting. While there most certainly are differences, the importance of efficiency and effectiveness is not one of them. But without knowing how the principles of good budgeting are tied to the principles of good democratic governance, we will not be able to articulate a governance-centered rationale as to, say, why efficiency and effectiveness matter, or why some argue that it is a good idea for governments to steer and let nonprofit organizations be the direct service providers to clients. In the sections that follow, we will set forth a theory of democratic governance that we believe is consistent with legal, historical, and constitutional principles—principles that have guided and should continue to guide the agents of democratic governance in carrying out their budgetary responsibilities in the multitude of political systems that populate the American landscape. In the process of developing this theory, we will revisit three of the themes that we introduced in chapter 1: (1) the unique role of local governments in building democratic legitimacy, (2) the unique politics of local budgeting, and (3) the importance of the polity to local governance.

CONFLICTING THEORIES OF LOCAL DEMOCRATIC GOVERNANCE IN THE UNITED STATES[1]

In the previous chapter we summarized the four basic forms of local governance in the United States. We concluded by pointing out that most local governments depart from the *separation of powers* model that is characteristic of the national government, yet the average citizen continues to hold an espoused theory that assumes career administrators should carry out a subservient instrumental role in the governing process. According to this espoused theory, the bureaucracy is fully subordinate to the executive branch of government, as illustrated in Exhibit 2.1. Under this model, the citizens elect legislators who make policy and then hand off this policy to an elected or appointed head of the executive branch, who implements the policy based on the technical competence of trained professionals. This theory aligns best with the **strong mayor form of government**, where the executive function of government is controlled by an elected head that has the responsibility of implementing the policy priorities within the parameters established by the legislative body. Administrative officers and agencies interact with the legislative body through the office of the mayor similar to the way executive department heads at the national level interact with Congress. The exception is when the legislative body takes the initiative to request information directly from a department/agency head. Most large nonprofit organizations follow this model. The expectation is that the executive director is the main source of interaction with the governing board and has the responsibility of directing staff in the implementation of board policy.

However, at a level of practice, or "theory in action" (Schon 1983, especially chap. 2), the story is often quite different, especially in local systems of government where part-time elected officials rely heavily on career administrators for policy advice and counsel. Public administrators at all levels are expected to take a proactive role in setting policy and budget agendas that flow from complex

Exhibit 2.1

Theory of Local Government in Action

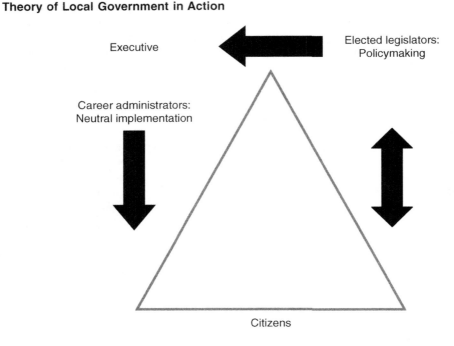

and diffuse structures of authority. In fact, in many local jurisdictions, it is frequently the case that career administrators play the dominant role in the budget and policymaking process. This theory in action is illustrated in Exhibit 2.2. The feedback arrow in Exhibit 2.2 at the chief executive and administrative levels illustrates the dominant role this part of government has in the budget and policymaking process. In this second model, policy development, implementation, and budgeting are fluid and collaborative processes of exchange: It is difficult to determine where to draw the line between the instrumental role of administrators and the constitutive policy role of board members or elected officials. At the level of practice, board members and career administrators are shaping both policy development and implementation in ways that confound any bright-line distinction between policy development and implementation. For example, in most local governments and small nonprofit organizations, the executive leadership team takes the initiative in preparing the budget. In doing so, they spend considerable time understanding the priorities of individual board members. This usually occurs informally through conversations but is also often done formally through priority-setting planning sessions (Ott 2001; see also endnote 6 in chap. 1 for documentation of this conclusion).

The challenge for governmental administrators in managing this tension between the instrumental and policy-shaping roles of their work has grown exponentially in the past 40 years. During the 1960s and 1970s, the federal government expanded regulatory and entitlement programs significantly as a result of initiatives undertaken by the New Frontier administration of John F. Kennedy and the Great Society administration of Lyndon B. Johnson. These initiatives focused on the elimination of poverty and racial discrimination and the promotion of education, medical care, and transportation infrastructure and increased funding to address urban problems. And although these programs expanded during the Republican administrations of presidents Richard Nixon and Gerald Ford in the 1970s, things changed radically with the administration of President Ronald Reagan in 1981. Since then, there has been a concerted effort to reverse the expansion of

Exhibit 2.2

Theory of Local Government in Action

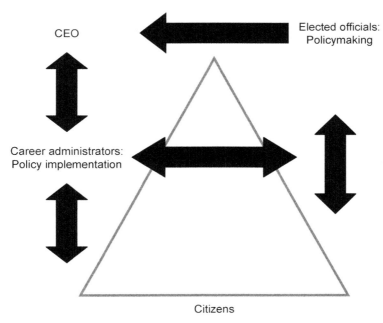

government and strengthen the private sector by reducing tax rates, deregulating the economy, and cutting back on government spending. Such policies reflected a growing doubt on the part of the American public about the capacity and legitimacy of various systems of U.S. government to solve some of the most intractable problems of the day—poverty, racial equality, improvement of educational outcomes, protection of the environment, economic growth, and creating livable communities. This doubt has resulted in a three-decade trend to deregulate, decentralize, and devolve greater responsibility for service provision away from the national governments to state and local governments and away from local government to the private and nonprofit sectors.

The most important implication of the developments over the past 30 years for local government administrators in both nonprofit and public organizations is the shift away from an emphasis on legal accountability and a shift toward more emphasis on marketplace principles for achieving efficient and effective outcomes. This new entrepreneurialism is reflected in the goals of the reinvention of government and **new public management (NPM)** movements initiated in the 1990s to liberate career administrators from a variety of bureaucratic constraints and to encourage them to take the initiative in introducing greater market incentives into public organizations (Osborne and Hutchinson 2004; Osborne and Gaebler 1992; Gore 1993). The NPM movement assumes that public managers will steer the needed changes, as is illustrated in Exhibit 2.2, and let actors in the private and nonprofit sectors do much of the rowing by contracting out for services. The growth of unfunded federal mandates and the rise of the federal debt in the first decade of the twenty-first century have further exacerbated the tension between the formally espoused instrumental role of administrators and the reality of their new entrepreneurial constitutive role. Local government administrators are facing increased performance criteria as a condition for receiving federal and state grants, and they in turn pass this *performance-driven* orientation on to contractors who are receiving tax dollars to provide public services for special target populations.

The increased emphasis on government accountability that can be measured has been aided and abetted by combinations of public power and private interests over the past decade (2000–2010)—a trend that has resulted in widespread corruption, performance failures, and excessive profits for a few. Critics cite the British Petroleum Louisiana oil spill in 2010, defense and public security contracts in the aftermath of the 2003 Iraq War, oversight of the banking industry preceding the collapse of the home mortgage market in 2008, and inside trading and the creative use of Wall Street financial instruments (e.g., derivatives, hedge funds, Ponzi schemes, stock options for executives, etc.) during the first decade of this century as vivid examples of the abuse of private power in the face of inadequate regulatory oversight. Such examples are used by critics of new public management to argue that reliance on business models of efficiency and effectiveness, combined with deregulation, has contributed to a decline in accountability, open-government practices, and appropriate legal norms, all of which help guarantee our liberties (Green 2012; Cooper 2003, 2009; Moe and Gilmour 1995).

The abuses or excesses arising from efforts to "make government run like a business" widen the gap between the claims of entrepreneurial management and the more complicated realities of American governance. Administrators in both the nonprofit and private sectors are caught in the crossfire between those who demand more accountability and those who demand more entrepreneurial initiative. But the conditions necessary for success in achieving these two goals are in conflict. Accountability requires rules, procedures, adherence to reporting, and evaluation processes, while entrepreneurialism emphasizes the removal of these barriers so that managers, programs, and organizational entities can be judged on results. Local government administrators are at the center of this crossfire between two competing theories of democratic governance.

As the first decade of the twenty-first century comes to a close, the American polity at all levels of government is confronted with an ever-widening divergence between our espoused theories of public administration and the theories we actually use. At the level of espoused theory, we continue to claim that "administrators are on tap, not on top." Under this model, administrators simply use their technical, neutral competence in the service of the policy directives set by the elected officials and appointed board members. This theory maintains a sharp distinction between politics and administration, as illustrated in Exhibit 2.1. It also captures the common view held by those on the outside viewing the work of both government and nonprofit organizations.

But to the average citizen, the policymaking and implementation process appears as a free-for-all, in which every special interest has its leg in the self-promotional game. The difference is that career administrators appear to have more than the nose of the camel inside the tent. Exhibit 2.3 illustrates this model. It is a perceived theory of democratic governance that puts administrators under a constant cloud of suspicion. Nothing they do or say is trusted because there is an assumption that they simply go through the motions of adhering to various administrative processes to arrive at a predetermined result. The dubious outsiders and critics assume that bureaucrats have a stake in protecting the status quo. This is a recipe for cynicism, burnout on the part of chief administrative officers, and avoidance of hard public policy choices by elected officials (Morgan and Kass 1993). Ambiguity and suspicion are less of an issue for most nonprofit organizations, where the clients are not expected to provide accountability oversight and where part-time board members rely on the executive administrative team to undertake the policy analysis work necessary for them to affirm and sometimes change the priorities of the organization.

In the section that follows, we will set forth a theory of democratic governance that we believe better describes the role responsibilities of administrators in the local public budgeting process than the three models discussed above. We believe that local officials can successfully use this theory to ameliorate the perception that local public administrators, who are frequently in the catbird seat in the budget and policymaking process, are just another vested interest with more concern for protecting their own programs and organizational inertia than promoting the larger common good.

Exhibit 2.3

Perceived Theory of Public Administration

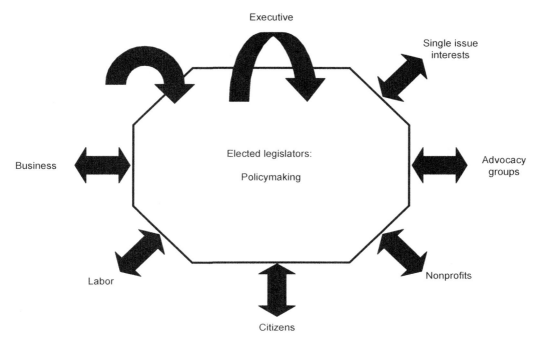

The Problematic Nature of Liberty

Despite the wide varieties of local forms of American government outlined in chapter 1, all of these systems rest on a shared set of democratic assumptions. These assumptions were put in place as part of the architectonic bargains that were struck by those who crafted the American constitutional system of governance in 1787. The same system has served as the template for designing American state and local systems of government. Even when there have been significant departures from the federal template (such as the **commission** or **council-manager forms of city government**), local governance debates remain grounded in the multiple goals that the U.S. Constitution is intended to serve. Consequently, the founding debates provide the clearest and best window for understanding the multiple and conflicting principles that are embedded in our complicated and multiple systems of local government. These principles have some important implications for the way we think about and practice public budgeting as a governance activity.

The founding of the American political system was an extraordinary and fortuitous achievement. Nowhere in the history of the world had a democratic republic been established and maintained over such a large and diverse territory as the United States. The framers of the republic were acutely aware of the unique moment in history when they gathered in Philadelphia in 1787 to reconsider ways of correcting defects in the Articles of Confederation. The Articles had proved extraordinarily weak during the Revolutionary War. The authority to raise taxes, the capacity to organize and supply armies, and the ability to respond quickly to external threats proved frighteningly difficult. As with the United Nations, the North Atlantic Treaty Organization (NATO), the United Nations (UN), and other loosely coupled confederations, it is difficult to act decisively when consent from nearly all members is required.

After the Revolutionary War, problems continued as states developed their own taxes on goods from other states and disagreed on the proper way to secure their borders from European encroachment. Despite dissatisfaction with the Articles of Confederation, participants in the Constitutional Convention knew that any attempt to correct those defects was an iffy undertaking at best. James Madison's *Notes of Debates in the Federal Convention of 1787* (Madison 1787/1987) document the attendees' concerns. Never in the history of humankind had a nation been able to protect the liberty of its citizens over such a large and diverse geographic base. In the convention hall, Benjamin Franklin remarked that he was uncertain whether the sun that appeared on the horizon in a large tapestry hanging on the front wall was rising or setting; he happily announced at the end of the convention that it was, indeed, rising.

The rising sun celebrated by the framers at the end of their work was a new government devoted to the preservation of individual liberty. The American system of government was founded on the principle that public life is secondary to the pursuit of one's personal choices in the private and social spheres. Most Americans live out this commitment by placing family, friendship, and economic well-being above civic responsibility. This libertarian interpretation of the Constitution emphasizes negative over positive freedom (Berlin 1969). "'Negative freedom' means freedom from interference, from being pushed around, restricted, locked up" (Held 1984, 124). The American system of government, according to this view, was not established to cultivate human excellence (either moral or intellectual), to advance the conditions of the rich and wellborn, or to promote equality of condition. All are permitted to pursue their goals in life because liberty is defined *negatively,* as the pursuit of individual interests (Diamond 1979, 45–49). As one commentator on the Constitution has observed, the founders solved the problem of establishing a working uniformity out of diversity by creating a "constitutional everyman"—a new kind of citizen—that served as the building block of the new political order.

> Citizenship is not a moral adventure or an educational experience. It is merely a legally defined bundle of rights and powers which the individual may use to defend and advance his interests. . . . The citizen is expected to disclose but a fraction of himself to the public gaze. . . . The construct of public equality serves as a mask behind which ones' inner self can hide from the probing, judging eyes of anonymous others. . . . The [public] space is kept as small as possible. Liberty, which expresses men's inequalities and diversities, resides within the [private sector]. The fundamental convention, then, is that all men shall be treated as equals in the public realm [in their legally defined role as citizens]. By assigning the principle of equality to one territory [i.e., equality under the law] and the principle of inequality to another, the constitutionalists thought that both could be preserved without conflict. (Schaar 1964, 887–888)

Schaar reminds us that American political systems are artificially constructed legal entities that have been created to preserve individual liberty from a variety of threats. To accomplish this purpose, individuals are left free to determine the course of their own lives with minimal obligations to government. This has some important consequences for local public budgeting. First, it helps explain why career public administrators frequently encounter difficulty engaging citizens in the business of government. Citizen are so preoccupied with the activities affecting their own economic well-being that it is difficult to get them involved in discussions and actions that affect the larger good of the community. The French historian Alexis de Tocqueville noted in his travels across America in the early 1830s, "It is difficult to force a man out of himself and get him to take an interest in the affairs of the whole state, for he has little understanding of the way in which the fate of the state can influence his own lot" (Tocqueville 1835–1840/2000, 511).

But local governments have an opportunity to turn the natural self-serving behavior of individuals toward the larger public good in ways that are not easily available to the state and national levels of government, where distance does not make the heart grow fonder. For example, Tocqueville argued that if a local government proposes to build a road through a person's private property, "he sees at once that this small public matter has a bearing on his greatest private interests, and there is no need to point out to him the close connection between his private profit and the general interest (Tocqueville 1835–1840/2000, 511).

Because individuals are better able to see the connection between their personal interest and the good of the community at the local level, they more readily join with others in a wide variety of voluntary activities that are directed at improving the larger good of the community. Repairing schools, cleaning parks, feeding the elderly, organizing neighborhood watch groups, and helping the homeless are all examples of the propensity of citizens to volunteer their time and money when they can see how it makes their own community a better place to live. Tocqueville was so immensely impressed by the vibrancy of voluntary associations, religious sects, and organized acts of self-help at the local level of government that he was moved to conclude that the "science of association is the mother of science; the progress of all the rest depends upon the progress it has made. . . . If men are to remain civilized or to become so, the art of associating together must grow and improve in the same ratio as [economic prosperity] is increased" (Tocqueville 1835–1840/2000, 118). Because this communitarian impulse emanated from the enlightened pursuit of one's own self-interest, Tocqueville dubbed this republican virtue "self-interest rightly understood," to distinguish it from the older aristocratic tradition that considered the virtue of public service an end in itself.

While the libertarian foundations of American government make it difficult to get individuals involved in local public budgeting, public officials have an opportunity to use the budgeting process as an enlightened self-interest hook to generate involvement. Such hooks occur frequently in the routine business of local government, whether in the form of zoning and building permits, increasing fees for services, the construction of public facilities, or transportation infrastructure improvement projects. All of these activities enlist the self-interest of the citizens, and, with proper management of the public education and outreach process by public officials, they provide opportunities to link the self-interest of citizens and organizations to the larger public interest of the community.

While the framers of the American constitution were in fundamental agreement with the libertarian foundations of the American political system summarized in the preceding paragraphs, they disagreed considerably on what most endangered liberty and, consequently, the conditions that needed to be put in place in order to secure liberty's long-term survival. By *framers,* we mean two groups of adversaries: the **Federalists**, who took the initiative in arguing for replacement of the Articles of Confederation, and the **Anti-Federalists**, who opposed the creation of a more consolidated national union. The framers' understanding of the preconditions for the survival of liberty was informed by their extensive reading of the historical success of democracies over the course of history. It was also influenced by their immediate experience in declaring independence from England and trying to make the new Declaration of Independence a reality both in terms of winning the war and in creating a successful system of self-government. These experiences served to highlight the four core values essential to the success of a regime of ordered liberty (Morgan, Green, Shinn, and Robinson 2013, 84–85):

- protection against the abuse of government authority;
- an energetic and competent government;
- protection against majority tyranny; and
- an engaged citizenry.

In the section that follows, we will show how these competing values emerged from the difference in beliefs between the Federalists and Anti-Federalists over what was needed most to ensure a well-functioning and long-lived system of democratic governance.

The Federalist/Anti-Federalist Debate: Implications for Local Public Budgeting

Disagreement over the priority that should be given to the core values enumerated above turns on answers to the following two questions: What is the role of government in society? and Who should have what kind of say in shaping this role? The Federalists and their major antagonists, the Anti-Federalists, answered these questions quite differently, but in doing so they established the framework for the ongoing debate over the purposes of a public budget and the role of administrators and nonprofit organizations in the budgeting process. Our exploration of this debate should be treated as a diagnostic tool for assessing how your local system of government uses the budgeting process to engage the support of the nonprofit and business community and how it functions with respect to the role of citizens and experts in the budgeting process. At each stage of analysis, ask yourself which model or which argument best explains the operation and function of your nonprofit or public service organization and its relation to the local public budgeting process. Ask how the government makes use of data, expertise, the business community, nonprofit organizations, and citizen engagement to structure the budgeting process to produce the final approved budget by the governing body. Our local communities change their priorities over time, and professional administrators move from one jurisdiction to another over the course of their careers. The democratic governance models we develop in our ensuing discussion can serve as a heuristic tool to help local administrators size up their local communities and determine the appropriate leadership roles they need to play within the governance process.

Local jurisdictions vary widely with respect to the role of citizens and nonprofit organizations in the public budgeting process. As we noted in chapter 1, the New England style of town government encourages more direct participation than is the case with the council-manager form of government. While considerable opportunities for citizen participation may exist in a council-manager arrangement, such participation is not formally required and is subject to the guidance and direction of the elected officials to whom the city manager reports. The commission and strong mayor forms of government are driven by political considerations in determining the kind and amount of citizen participation suitable in the formal budgeting process. Jurisdictions that have strong political parties are less inclined to provide for extensive citizen participation outside the formal political party channels than is the case for jurisdictions that require nonpartisan elections for office.

Nonprofit organizations that depend on public dollars to deliver services are vested in the outcome of local public budgeting processes. In many situations, nonprofit interests are expressed and constrained through the contracting processes. However, nonprofit service providers with extensive knowledge of community needs and organizational capacities can sometimes dominate local budget discussions (Berry and Arons 2003, chap. 5). Whether extensive citizen and nonprofit participation in the local budgeting process is better or worse in promoting the local public interest turns on one's theory of democratic governance.

The debates between the Federalists and Anti-Federalists have provided us with two distinct models for determining how much and what kind of participation is most appropriate for promoting the public good. They are the **procedural republican tradition**, a model that emphasizes the importance of structures, processes, technical expertise, professional experience, and formal rights to protect liberty, and the **civic republican tradition**, a model that emphasizes the importance of small face-to-face government and the reliance on nonprofit organizations and the business community (Kemmis 1990, chap. 2). We will elaborate more fully on each of these models in the sections to follow.

The Federalists: The Procedural Republic

The Federalists worried most about a weak government that did not have sufficient power and capacity to protect the liberty of citizens from majority tyranny and threats from abroad. They relied on two principal strategies for addressing these concerns. First, they argued for the creation of a strong central government that had the power and the capacity to regulate commerce, raise and support armies, and stand on an equal footing with other sovereign nations in the world. But the challenge was finding ways to structure the powers of government and the duties of the various offices so that government would remain attractive to the best and brightest, while simultaneously being safe from abuse by ambitious and self-serving politicians. The Federalists relied mainly on periodic elections, the specification of powers, and structural devices like the separation of powers and checks and balances. In doing so, however, they emphasized the importance of structuring the duties of public office so that "the interest of the man [is] . . . connected to the constitutional rights of the place" (Hamilton or Madison as Publius 1788, Federalist No. 51, quoted in Rossiter 1961). By this principle, they meant that the powers of any given office should not be too stingy, lest it discourage talented individuals from seeking public office and launching long-term projects that would advance the public good. Ambitious and long-term projects like the New Deal, the Fair Deal, the Great Society, and the New Frontier gave their founders a place of honor in history at the national level. There are examples of this principle at work in most local communities, which memorialize the contributions of their notable denizens by naming parks, schools, buildings, and other public artifacts to celebrate their community legacy. The Federalists were interested in finding ways of using this desire for honor or fame (as distinguished from a desire for immediate popularity) to become a powerful engine to promote the larger public good (Adair 1974; Hamilton 1788, Federalist No. 72, in Rossiter 1961).

The second key Federalist strategy for protecting liberty was their unique approach to addressing the problem of majority tyranny. In addition to relying on a system of separation of powers and checks and balances, they argued that the best way to prevent the dominant exercise of power by a tyrannical majority is to make certain that a wide array of social, economic, political, and religious opportunities exist for individuals to self-organize into diverse and competing groups; that way, no single group would gain control over another (1787 and 1788, Federalist Nos. 10 and 51, quoted in Rossiter 1961). Federalists worried that small, socially homogeneous systems of government might be less able to protect against the tyranny of the majority in the governing process than a large and more heterogeneous territory, which was better able to fragment opinion, multiply sectarian organizations, and balkanize the formation of interest groups (Hamilton 1787, Federalist Nos. 17 and 27, quoted in Rossiter 1961).

The Anti-Federalists: The Civic Republic

In contrast to the Federalists, the Anti-Federalists believed that liberty was endangered by a government that was too strong and by a socioeconomic order that would undermine the republican virtue necessary for democracy's survival. They believed that government was safe only when it was in the hands of ordinary citizens who did not pursue or hold office as a career. A powerful government that appealed to the ambitious would soon find itself victimized by the personal agendas of officeholders. The only safe government, according to the Anti-Federalists, was one that depended on those in "middling circumstances," who "are inclined by habit, and the company with whom they associate, to set bounds to their passions and appetites." The substantial yeomanry of the country was thought to be "more temperate, of better morals, and less ambition, than the great" (Storing 1981a, vol. 6, 158).

The Anti-Federalists believed that a large commercial republic of the kind envisioned by the

Federalists would undermine the republican virtues of moderation, vigilance, industry, thrift, and a generosity of spirit. Chief among the Anti-Federalists' worries was the idea that the energies of the people in a large commercial republic would be mobilized to increase trade and commerce in the service of what Patrick Henry—speaking in the Virginia ratifying convention—characterized as "grandeur, power and splendor," rather than in guarding their liberties. The republican virtues of those in "middling circumstances" (Storing 1981a, v, 214) fueled the vibrancy of volunteerism and resulted in the formation of a multitude of associations, which, as we pointed out in the introduction to this section, struck Tocqueville as one of the most remarkable features of American democracy.

The Federalists and Anti-Federalists leave us with two alternative visions of good governance, both of which have important implications for local public budgeting. These visions stem from a quite different understanding of what most endangers liberty and how these dangers can best be met. A summary of the differences appears in Exhibit 2.4.

The Federalists believed that you could not rely on an inherent sense of public duty to trigger citizen engagement or to ensure good behavior on the part of those who held positions of public trust. They planned for the worst in human behavior by designing a government based on checks and balances, one that would at least deter egregious abuses of power. But in so doing, they also wanted to appeal to the best in human motivations by providing public officials with sufficient powers and duties to make public service attractive to ambitious leaders—people who wanted to make a difference and leave a legacy for posterity. This is why, to this day, there is so much debate over the extent to which government jobs and initiatives should be hedged about with extensive oversight and elaborate rules of procedure. If these procedures become too arduous, they can discourage the best and brightest from devoting their careers to public service (Rohr 1981). But too little accountability can lead to self-dealing and other kinds of abuses. The Federalist tradition explains why local public budgeting debates are frequently focused on the proper mix of procedures to balance the need for dispatch, effectiveness, and efficiency on the one hand, with the need to provide for hearings, ensure notice and comment opportunities for citizens and clients, provide for public transparency, and honor multiple systems of accountability on the other.

While the Federalists shared a basic distrust of human nature, it was aligned with a belief in the importance of knowledge, skill, and extensive experience in government decision making and policy implementation. This was reflected in the way President George Washington staffed his first administration. He appointed public servants who possessed reputations of impeccable personal integrity, high levels of competence, and high standing in their local communities. The goal was to attract the best and brightest to public service, thereby adding "dignity and luster to our national character" (White 1948, 259). The Federalists would readily endorse budgeting systems that give a central role to individuals with extensive program, management, and organizational expertise.

The Anti-Federalists, as well, have left us with a legacy of public service that has served as a precedent for some important features of our modern-day approaches to public service. The civic republic tradition of the Anti-Federalists, with its emphasis on active citizenship, face-to-face communication, and reliance on the intelligence of ordinary people, provides significant norms for the exercise of **administrative discretion** in the public budgeting process. First, it means that career administrators may need to relegate technical expertise to a lower priority in favor of listening to and honoring the opinions of the uninformed, even when it does not result in efficient public policy outcomes. Transportation planners, for example, frequently find themselves facing this kind of dilemma when concerned citizens in a neighborhood insist on speed bumps, round-abouts, and other traffic-calming devices that interfere with the efficient flow of traffic and access by emergency vehicles, not to mention increase the costs of public service.

Second, the civic republic tradition requires more than simply listening and being responsive. It means engaging in collaborative decision making, where neither the problem nor the solution is presupposed at the outset of a process. There are numerous examples of this at the local levels of

Exhibit 2.4

How to Address the Multiple Threats to Individual Liberty

Sources of danger to liberty	Solutions	Citizenship and expertise implications
Arbitrary abuse of power by government officials: "The King George Problem" (Shared Federalist/Anti-Federalist priority)	• "Rule of Law" prophylactics such as the Bill of Rights • Separation of powers • Checks and balances • Federalism • Strong representative government and frequent elections • Limited and enumerated government powers	• Reliance on representational institutions by which citizens exercise control through periodic elections • Reliance on the "auxiliary precautions" of formal legal structures and processes, which reduce citizenship demands
Weak, incompetent, and fickle government: "The George Washington Problem" (Federalist priority)	• Strong executive branch • Reliance on experience and expertise • Separation of powers • Checks and balances • Structural incentives to encourage continuity in office and independent and informed judgment	• Creation of mediating structures that reduce dependence on highly active and knowledgeable citizenry (for example, Senate chosen by the states, court with life tenure, president elected by an electoral college with no term limits)
Majority Tyranny: "The Shays' Rebellion Problem" (Federalist priority)	• Structural checks and balances, both internally in the government and externally in the socioeconomic setting • Large commercial republic that would create a multiplicity of interests • Bill of Rights	• Reliance on a procedural democracy that places few demands on citizens except to pursue their own interests within a limited legal framework that protects rights
Disengaged citizens and loss of republican virtue: "The Bowling Alone Problem" (Anti-Federalist priority)	• Small, simple, and limited government • Large representative body composed of "those in middling circumstances" • Constraints on the "emergence of a large commercial republic"	• Reliance on a civic republic where small, local, and direct democracy is sufficient to address the major problems faced by citizens

government, where planners, educators, environmental experts, neighborhood officials, churches, and nonprofit service providers work with citizens to design collaborative solutions that do not fit a predetermined mold. Parent-led site councils in public schools and neighborhood community councils perhaps best exemplify this civic republic tradition at work.

Finally, the civic republic tradition emphasizes **coproduction** and delivery of public services (Levine and Fisher 1984). Community policing is a classic example of putting the principle of coproduction to work. This process enlists citizens in a joint effort by a public agency to define a given level and quality of service, and the citizens participate in the delivery of this service. In the case of community policing, this may take the form of neighborhood watch groups or community courts where citizens participate in adjudicating neighborhood-level disputes.

The civic republican tradition has implications not only for the way in which we view the coproduction and delivery of public services by citizens working in partnership with government but also for the role and function of nonprofit organizations. For example, watershed restoration projects have become an increasingly popular example of interorganizational and interjurisdictional coproduction. Citizens, businesses, and nonprofit organizations within a common geographic watershed identify common actions that can be taken by multiple stakeholder groups to preserve and protect the watershed from degradation, including such things as the use of pesticides, erosion control, grazing practices, irrigation use, and reforestation practices. In America's inner cities, the educational and social service needs of the community are frequently being met by securing interorganizational and interjurisdictional cooperation among nonprofit service providers, schools, courts, police, corrections, and parole/probation organizations. And in rural communities, the needs of the poor and elderly are being met on a daily basis by leveraging similar kinds of interorganizational and interjurisdictional cooperation among the voluntary sector, the business community, churches, and governmental agencies to coproduce the common good of the polity. To the extent that these common actions are successful, citizens and organizations across multiple sectors collectively join with career administrators to produce a public good that may reduce the need for harsh regulatory intervention by government agencies and provide services that would otherwise not exist. The goal of coproduction is not to replace administrators with volunteers but to link the professional expertise and accountability of career administrators with the local knowledge, organizational capacity, and attachment of citizens to produce a public good.

Together, the Federalists and Anti-Federalists leave us with two different traditions by which Americans judge the appropriate size of government and who can be most trusted to exercise political authority. The civic republic tradition of the Anti-Federalists emphasizes small government that has a face-to-face relationship with citizens who actively participate in the governing process to create a commonly shared sense of purpose and action. The procedural republic tradition of the Federalists emphasizes government taking the lead with experienced professionals who operate within a constrained system of accountability and role responsibility. This constrained system of checks and balances stresses adherence to formal rules, processes, and structures that create opportunities for access, a fair hearing, rule-bound decision-making processes, and the right to vote either directly or indirectly for those who make the decisions.

Exhibit 2.5 summarizes the chief characteristics of these two governance traditions. For the civic republic tradition, good governance is measured by the extent to which citizens and organizations in the community are willing and able to sit at a metaphorical public table and deliberate with others about what constitutes the public interest. This tradition assumes that citizens and organizations possess, or are willing to develop, the self-governing skills to contribute. For the procedural republic tradition, good governance is measured both by the extent to which interest groups, associations, and the formal processes of government are able to reflect the interests of the citizenry and by the extent to which the citizenry at large accept the outcomes, are tolerant of diverse differences of opinion, and defend the principles of procedural fairness. The burden of democratic governance in the procedural republic model is borne by formal institutions, expert career administrators, and knowledgeable, interested, expert citizens rather than by the citizenry at large.

The local public budgeting process provides a multitude of opportunities to see the consequences of the civic and procedural republic models in action. Some communities rely heavily on citizen participation and formal cooperation between government and the nonprofit and business sectors, while others do not. As noted earlier, the form of local government also makes a difference. Some local governments elect their governing bodies from districts in partisan elections and place the administrative functions under an elected mayor. These governing arrangements provide much greater opportunities for organized interest groups to influence budgeting outcomes than is the case for jurisdictions that elect their governing body in nonpartisan elections. The expectation is that the governing body will be working part-time with a full-time city manager in charge of preparing the budget and managing the daily operations of the jurisdiction. Such organizational

Exhibit 2.5

Good Governance Traditions

	Civic republic tradition	Procedural republic tradition
Origins	• Anti-Federalists • small republic agrarian tradition	• Federalists • interest group pluralism
Characteristics	• face-to-face communication • emphasis on substantive equality • emphasis on substantive agreement and consensus • community is socially constructed • emphasis on importance of place • emphasis on action, i.e., doing things together, rather than getting formal agreement • emphasis on duties as well as rights	• reliance on indirect representation • reliance on procedural equality • emphasis on voting and majority rule principle • community is a legal agreement • emphasis on procedural fairness with open access and right to participate • rule-of-law orientation • emphasis on rights over duties
Citizenship requirements	• high level of deliberative skills • development of relevant knowledge and expertise • personal participation • citizen ownership and control of decision	• voting • heavy reliance on interest group participation • opportunity for individuals to advise and counsel • heavy reliance on elected officials and career administrators
Legitimating criteria	• degree of participation • degree of citizen control • sense of ownership of both process and outcome	• due notice of important decisions and open access to decision making • opportunity for a "hearing" and right to be heard • procedural fairness in gathering and assessing information

arrangements rely heavily on the procedural republic tradition to reach agreement on a budget. Smaller local communities and those operating with elected commissioners who do not have a separate and quasi-independent full-time administrator make greater use of the civic republic tradition to reach agreement on a budget.

From the larger polity perspective, local government processes and procedures set the tone for relationships between the jurisdiction and the larger network of partners. The provisions and approaches in partnership agreements, service contracts, and intergovernmental agreements place requirements on both the local government and its partners. Governmental procedural requirements may indirectly set patterns and standards used by nongovernmental partners in the community. The budget process and its procedures are one aspect of these governmental requirements.

Whatever standard the government establishes in conducting relationships with its community partners can sometimes come into conflict with the standards and procedures used by those with whom it must do business. For example, small businesses and nonprofit partners have their own needs and set their own requirements, which may not fit easily with government protocols. When such conflicts occur, informal personal relationships often become the vehicle for reaching agreements and for moving the community forward (cf. Robinson 2004). Interpersonal and interorganizational relationships are the heart of the civic republican tradition. As part of the overall community polity, government, local businesses, and nonprofit administrators meet as agents of their organizations to manage and overcome procedural and dialogic challenges. These are opportunities for leadership on the part of all groups as they engage in the common goal of coproducing the larger community good.

Summary

For the founding generation, the preservation of liberty was problematic because the four biggest threats to democratic government could not be addressed with a single solution. (By way of review, those four dangers to liberty were the abuse of government authority, an incompetent government, tyranny of the majority, and a disengaged citizenry.) In fact, a solution to one of the threats might actually make the others worse. For example, creating a more consolidated government with greater executive power to protect against external threats and majority tyranny could potentially endanger the liberty of citizens in other ways—such as through internal abuses of power by governing officials or through limited civic engagement. Thus, from each of the four threats to liberty there emerged corresponding and rival correctives, which are aptly captured in the following beatitudes:

The Founding Beatitudes

Too much power begets usurpation, to which majority rule is a corrective;
Too much majority rule begets majority tyranny, to which separation of powers and checks and balances is a corrective;
Too much separation of powers and checks and balances begets incompetent government, to which unity at the center is a corrective;
Too much unity at the center begets usurpation, to which civic engagement is a corrective.
(Morgan, Green, Shinn, and Robinson 2013, 85)

THE POLITICAL ECONOMY OF PUBLIC BUDGETING: EXTENDING THE FEDERALIST/ANTI-FEDERALIST DEBATE

In chapter 1, we introduced what we described as the "mixed economy" (see Exhibit 2.6). This diagram is a simplified way of illustrating the fact that the libertarian foundations of the American political system create a complex nexus of institutional forms that include special districts, public agencies, market sector firms, and nonprofit organizations. We argued in chapter 1 that the interplay of these institutional forms determines the public good and that local governance and budgeting processes exert a decisive role in shaping how the entire network comes together to coproduce the public good.. How this process plays out depends on answers to the following two questions: (1) What is the proper role of government in society? and (2) What kind of expertise is needed to carry out this role? These two questions appear as the X and Y axes in Exhibit 2.7.[2] The axes produce four quadrants that represent different models of governance, all of which are reflected in each form of local government and the budgeting practices that it follows. In the ensuing sections of this chapter, we use these two fundamental questions to extend the Federalist/Anti-Federalist debates and to further elaborate our argument that local public budgeting is ultimately about one's theory of governance, not about numbers. We will draw on the American historical experience to illustrate the four models of democratic governance that have emerged from the Federalist/Anti-Federalist debates. In the process, we will also illustrate the significance of these models for shaping local public budgeting processes and outcomes.

Exhibit 2.6

Institutional Forms

		Scope of interests	
		Parochial	Common
How values are arbitrated	Political	Special district governments	General governments
	Market	For-profit private agencies and firms	Nonprofit organizations

"Who Should Govern?" Dimension (X-Axis)

The horizontal axis in Exhibit 2.7 (p. 71) summarizes the range of possible answers to the question, Who should govern? The left end of the axis represents those who believe that liberty is best protected by relying on governing experience and expertise. The right end of the axis represents those who believe that democracy is safest when decision making and policy implementation is placed directly in the hands of the people rather than with experts.

As we saw earlier in this chapter, the American Revolution celebrated the principle that government should be based on "We the People," which is memorialized in both the Declaration of Independence and the Preamble to the American Constitution. But this ode to the people was tempered by the Articles of Confederation experience of unsuccessfully trying to levy and collect taxes, raise and supply an army, and negotiate complicated relations with foreign nations without an experienced cadre of governing agents who could devote all their energies to their work. The issue of citizen versus expert-centered governance came into sharp focus in the Constitutional Convention as delegates debated the kind of government that was most needed to protect the liberty of the citizens from a variety of different dangers. The framers sought to have the best of both worlds. They believed that the establishment of three branches of government (i.e., the U.S. Senate, the Presidency, and the Supreme Court)—with different qualifications, terms of office, and modes of selection—could be used to attract those with more experience and give these individuals the independence to exercise judgment without fear of immediate retribution by voters at the polls. Tyranny could also be checked by relying on regular elections, the enumeration of government powers, a federal structure authority, a system of checks and balances, and a Bill of Rights. These formal legal provisions served as "auxiliary precautions" to the natural system of checks and balances that automatically operated in a large and diverse commercial republic to protect the citizens from having their liberty threatened by a tyrannical majority.

The American constitutional system of indirect democracy does not assume that everyone needs to spend considerable time and energy overseeing the work of their elected representatives. The majority of the founding generation believed that liberty could be secured from a multiplicity of dangers through a combination of regular elections and institutional checks and balances. The framers bet on Alexander Hamilton's assumption that the people's confidence in, and obedience to, a government "will commonly be proportioned to the goodness or badness of its administration" and that the federal institutions would on the whole produce better administration over time than their state and local counterparts (1787, Federalist Nos. 27 and 17, quoted in Rossiter 1961; see also Brinkley, Polsby, Sullivan, and Lewis 1997; Dahl 1989). This Federalist emphasis on expertise as the best security for preserving a regime of ordered liberty has been renewed repeatedly over the course of American history, first by the Progressive movement's emphasis on "scientific management" (for a description see Morgan, Green, Shinn, and Robinson 2013, 105–108) and the need for leaders to serve as moral exemplars for the masses. As we argued in chapter 1, the commission and council-manager systems of government were introduced because of the belief that more professional expertise was needed to make local systems of government work effectively and efficiently. This emphasis on using scientific principles to "make things work" was refueled again during the New Deal period and kept alive by both World War II and the expansion of the regulatory role of the government in the 1960s and 1970s, all of which required a growing cadre of trained experts who devoted their careers to public service (Morgan, Green, Shinn, and Robinson 2013, 109–118).

While the role of experts in making democracy work has grown over the course of American history, this trend has not necessarily come at the expense of those who share the Anti-Federalist and Jeffersonian view of a citizen-centered democracy. This view is represented by the right side of the X-axis in Exhibit 2.7. This side of the axis emphasizes the importance of decentralized government, with a focus on local face-to-face governance where people take personal responsibility for decision making and policy implementation rather than depending entirely on career experts to do the public's work (Box 1998). In its extreme form, this model is similar to direct democracy (in contrast to representative democracy), which is found in small geographic areas such as New England town meetings and local neighborhood associations, or is represented by coproduced public services in local government (i.e., community policing). The citizen-centered Jeffersonian vision has occasionally captured the hearts and minds of a national constituency and taken on the characteristics of a movement. This has occurred at several key points in American history, starting with the Jacksonian revolution in the 1830s, which introduced the principle of "rotation in office" as an antidote to rule by the rich and privileged elites. It resurfaced again in the 1890s during the Populist Era, as the initiative, referendum, recall, the "long ballot," civil service reform, regulatory control over corruption, and nonpartisan elections were popularized. During this period, the Pendleton Act was passed, creating a merit system for the appointment and promotion of career public servants. Reformers argued that such a system was needed to counter the corruption of the principle of "rotation in office," which had deteriorated into the spoils system that rewarded individuals for their loyalty to various kinds of ruling elites. The Jeffersonian model resurfaced once again as an important influence in structuring the implementation of President Johnson's antipoverty programs in the 1960s and more recently has been a galvanizing force for the antitax revolt in the West and the Tea Party movement in the 2010 congressional elections.[3]

The answer to the question, Who should govern? has shifted over the course of American history, much like a pendulum that shifts toward one end of the X-axis more than the other, but never to the exclusion of the claims represented by the countervailing antagonist. In this swing, the Federalist emphasis on the importance of experience and expertise has been the protagonist, with the Jeffersonian tradition constantly serving as the preeminent antagonist. As we will see in the next section, a similar story can be told of the answer to the second critical question that has shaped American governance traditions: What is the proper role of government in society?

Exhibit 2.7

Models of Local Democratic Governance

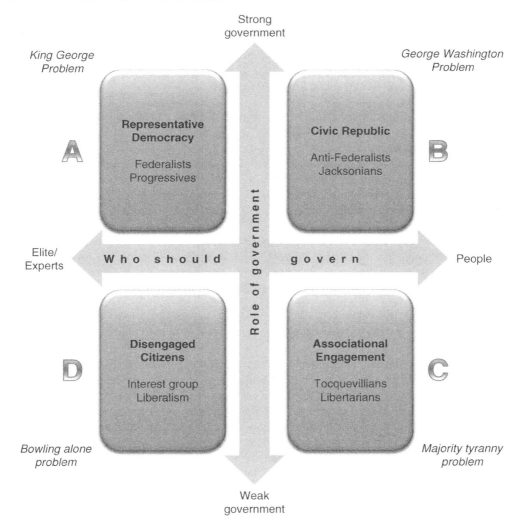

"What Is the Proper Role of Government?" Dimension (Y-Axis)

In Exhibit 2.7, the vertical Y-axis represents contending views regarding the proper role of government within American democracy. The upper end of the Y-axis represents the view that the government should be a proactive agent, which we have labeled the "strong government" role. The bottom end of the Y-axis represents the view that institutions other than the government should take an active part in the protection of individual liberty, with government playing a minimum role. We have labeled this the "weak government" role.

As noted earlier in this chapter, American democracy rests on the principle that the most important goal of government is to protect individual liberty. But this raises the question of which specific threats endanger liberty most: those from too little or too much government? The various answers to these questions have produced dynamic shifts in (1) the extent to which government is treated as a separate, but limited, actor within a larger system of market and civil society actors, and (2) the extent to which the market and civil society play a distinct and separate role in preserving individual liberty. In larger urban areas, the government plays a more limited role with respect to the operation of the polity as a whole than is the case with smaller and more rural communities, where government is the driving force that galvanizes and leverages the cooperative activity with the business and nonprofit sectors.

Framework for Governance Models: Four Quadrants

When the two dimensions in Exhibit 2.7 (Who should govern? and What is the proper role of government in society?) are graphed, four quadrants result. The upper left corner of the coordinate, labeled Quadrant A, represents the idea that "elite/experts should govern under strong government." The upper right corner of the coordinate, labeled Quadrant B, represents the idea that "people should govern under strong government." The lower right corner of the coordinate, labeled Quadrant C, represents the idea that "people should govern under weak government." And finally, the lower left corner of the coordinate, labeled Quadrant D, represents the idea that "elite/ experts should govern under weak government." To each of these quadrants, we have added the particular threat to individual liberty that the quadrant is seeking to address as discussed in our summary of the founding debates. In the following sections, we will explain (1) how the different political philosophies at play during the founding era represented each of these ideas, (2) what institutional problems each quadrant creates, and (3) the models of democratic governance that emerge from this debate.

Elite/Experts Govern Under Strong Government (Quadrant A)

The reign of King George III at the end of the colonial period represents the extreme case of elite/ experts governing under a strong government model. As described in the Declaration of Independence, this governing elite abused its power, resulting in oppression of the people. Reaction to this "King George Problem" spawned the Boston Tea Party and, later, preparations for battle against the British, calling for the creation of a new system that would check the abusive exercise of government power by domineering officialdom. As a consequence, the newly adopted state constitutions (with New York the exception) and the Articles of Confederation focused on limiting the power of the executive branch of government; these documents called for the creation of strong legislative authority in an effort to give more power to the people through indirect representation (Thach 1969). The result was a shift from the *elite/experts* end of the Who should govern? continuum toward the *citizen* end of the continuum.

However, in making a shift toward the *citizen* end of the continuum during the early days of the Revolutionary period, the states were assumed to be the primary governing agents through their systems of indirect rather than direct representation. The states were held together under a weak confederation model that embodied the procedural republic and representative democracy assumptions of the Federalist tradition.

People Govern Under Strong Government (Quadrant B)

The shift of power from the executive to the legislative branch of government was short-lived. The excitement of "giving all power to the people" soon foundered on the shoals of trying to raise and collect taxes, field and support an army, and conduct sensitive foreign relations under a citizen-centered system of government. Realizing that more power was needed at the executive level to solve the "George Washington Problem" resulted in the call for a Constitutional Convention to revise the Articles of Confederation, which produced a shift back toward a strong expert-centered government (see the middle of Quadrant A). But this shift was fought by the Anti-Federalist antagonists, who defended what has come to be called the civic republican model of democratic governance.

The Anti-Federalists had their first opportunity to put their beliefs into practice at the national level of government during the Jefferson and Jackson presidencies. Since most Anti-Federalist principles are more easily applied at local levels of government, these two presidential administrations provided an opportunity to test the applicability of the civic republic tradition in governing a wide expanse of territory, where citizen-centered approaches to rule from Washington, D.C. are difficult to implement. In both cases, Jefferson and Jackson exercised strong executive control, which seemed contradictory to their populist and "strict constructionist" legal principles. But in the case Andrew Jackson's veto of the National Bank and his introduction of the principle of "rotation in office," he defended the strong government model based on civic republican principles. These principles were published in the first issue of the *United States Magazine and Democratic Review*, a partisan journal devoted to the spread of the Jacksonian revolution (quoted in Rozwenc 1963, 19–25).

- "The best government is that which governs least. . . . Government should have as little as possible to do with the general business and interests of the people" (22, 23).
- "We have an abiding confidence in the virtue, intelligence, and full capacity for self-government, of the great mass of our people—our industrious, honest, manly, intelligent millions of freemen" (19).
- "The floating atoms will distribute and combine themselves, as we see in the beautiful natural process of crystallization, in a far more perfect and harmonious result than if government[s] undertake . . . to disturb . . . the process" (23).

Jackson's notion that the president, or executive branch of government, is a better voice for and representative of the people as a whole than the various branches of Congress laid the groundwork for the importance of the career civil service as the eyes and ears of the citizenry. These views were also embodied in the notion of a "representative bureaucracy" (Dolan and Rosenbloom 2003) and various citizen-centered strategies for the delivery of public services, particularly the coproduction of services (Levine and Fisher 1984).

People Govern Under Weak Government (Quadrant C)

Another important, long-standing governance tradition relies on the libertarian foundations of the American political system: It argues that citizens have the wisdom and decency to govern themselves—and that government should stay out of their way (Brinkley, Polsby, Sullivan, and Lewis 1997). The libertarian view relies on private social institutions and the market economy to protect individual liberty and maintain social order.

In his well-documented journey throughout the United States in the early 1830s, Tocqueville was struck by this libertarian quality of American life. "Americans of all ages, all conditions, all minds constantly unite. Not only do they have commercial and industrial associations in which all take part, but they also have a thousand other kinds: religious, moral, grave, futile, very general and very particular, immense and very small" (Tocqueville 1835–1840/2000, 489). The French writer and historian believed that this active associational life was due to "the extraordinary fragmentation of administrative power" (Tocqueville 1835–1840/2000, 494–495), which requires citizens to gather with others at the local level to meet their personal needs and solve common problems rather than rely on centralized governments at the state and national levels.

Tocqueville felt he was witnessing the formative stages of an entirely new social order—one that had never before existed in world history—where connections were formed when people took control of their own liberty, seemingly without any direct influence from a formal governing authority. Instead, the cohering forces of society seemed to be operating informally, as a result of the free association of individuals exercising their liberty to engage in commerce, practice their religion, and join with other like-minded individuals to share beliefs and advocate for causes within a rule-of-law system.

Models like this have gathered renewed support from many contemporary civic-minded libertarians who are advocating a return to the Tocquevillian ideal that is "egalitarian," "individualistic," "decentralized," "religious," "property loving," and "lightly governed" (Barone 1996). This ideal assumes that many of the functions performed by the government can be transferred to the multicolored cloth of voluntary associations and nonprofit associations.

Elites/Experts Govern Under Weak Government (Quadrant D)

As we have already noted, the procedural republic model of governance advocated by the Federalists relied on the combination of a formal system of checks and balances built into the Constitution and an informal system of interest groups operating in the social and economic spheres. This model requires that government play only a relatively small, but nonetheless critical, role in providing the infrastructure that "greases the skids" for the expansion and growth of civil society and the market economy. For example, a government grant may provide seed money to a nonprofit association for additional fundraising, or public funds may be used to leverage private funding, or vice versa.

Alexander Hamilton's "Report on Manufactures" (1791/1966) and his early efforts as secretary of the U.S. Treasury to create a system of public credit and debt management helped stabilize the young American economy and set it on a course for prosperous commercial and agricultural development. The regulation of the economy through the Federal Reserve Board's use of refined monetary policies to manipulate interest rates exemplifies the exercise of this "soft" and unobtrusive use of government power at work today. It is an approach consistent with the Federalist emphasis on the need to use expertise to create and build government infrastructure rather than relying on the latent civic capacity of citizens.

Various authors (e.g., John 1995; Lowi 1979; Skocpol 1997) have reminded us that this kind of facilitative role on the part of government has been important not only in the development of America's system of commerce but also in the robust development of associations. For example, John (1995) points out that during the 1830s and 1840s, the U.S. postal system was one of the biggest government operations in the United States. The institutional structure of the U.S. government and U.S. postal rules contributed both to the spread of a postal network and the resultant active use of information exchange among civic associations through mail and newspapers (Skocpol 1997).

This underlying reliance on government infrastructures by civic associations continued through the late nineteenth century and most of the twentieth century. Small local associations spread geographically and expanded their network in order to take advantage of "the opportunity to join together with like-minded others in crusades, associations, and parties that could make a difference—even at the level of the entire nation" (Skocpol 1997, 472). As the associations' networks expanded, their need to develop stronger ties with the extra-local government also grew. Unless they were purely local, many of these associations moved their headquarters to New York City and Washington, D.C., where their professional staff could work directly with government policymakers. Consequently, many civic associations became disassociated from the local citizens as the associational activities were taken over by the professional staff (i.e., the experts).

Professionalization of civic associations resulted in the rise of what has come to be called **interest group liberalism**.

Interest group liberalism is a system of powerful interest groups that are run by professional experts who have close working relationships with government officials at the legislative and executive levels of government. Sometimes called "the *iron triangle*, the system consists of key members of Congress who are responsible for funding and providing oversight for a particular program, a federal agency that administers the program, and the trade associations and lobbying groups that serve as the chief beneficiaries of the program. There is a common interest among these three sets of participants to construct solutions to problems that result in a weak role for government and *policy without the teeth of law* (Lowi 1979). This condition is represented in Quadrant D.

One of the implications of interest group liberalism is that ordinary citizens are not a part of this system of governance. Over time, citizens may become cynical and feel disenfranchised. Despite elections, the same groups of insiders end up being the real decision makers. As a result, citizens may start to feel that they can no longer "band together to get things done either through or in relationship to government" (Skocpol 1997, 472). When the frustration mounts to a boiling point, they may decide to form a movement to throw the rascals out. But a more likely result is that citizens decide to disengage from political and civic life. As Putnam (2000) and others note, between 1980 and 2000, American citizens significantly reduced their participation in political and civic organizations, opting instead to live in gated communities, became couch potatoes, and, metaphorically, "bowl alone" (Putnam 2000). Fearing that this condition will not naturally be reversed, a variety of individuals and groups have organized in the last decade to intentionally rebuild civil society (see Evans and Boyte 1992; Walzer 1992; Cohen and Arato 1992; Eberly 1994; Rebuilding Civil Society 1995; Schambra 1994; Sirianni 2009; Skocpol and Fiorina, 1999; Civic Practices Network 2013). Known as the civil society movement, the goal of participants is to foster the knowledge and skills needed for organizations and citizens to be good citizens.

Summary

The history of American democratic governance is a story of enduring uncertainty and disagreement about two questions: (1) Who should govern? and (2) What is the proper role of government in society? While the answers to these questions have changed over the course of American history, they have resulted in four different models that reflect the expectations of both citizens and leaders toward their governing institutions. The upper Quadrants, A and B, represent two models that establish strong norms in favor of active participation by citizens in political and civic life, with the *civic republic model* setting a higher standard than the *representative democracy model*. In terms of local public budgeting, quadrant A represents the reliance on government representatives and the expertise of professional career administrators to take the lead in setting budget priorities and deciding on the allocation of scarce resource. In Quadrant B, the shift away from executive-centered governance to a more citizen-centered approach is reflected in the coproduction of service delivery, greater reliance on nonprofit organizations for the delivery of services, and the use of citizen-centered approaches to help determine the allocation of scarce resources.

The lower Quadrants, C and D, represent two models that create weak norms in favor of citizen participation in the formal institutions of governance. For the *associational engagement model,* the norm is weak because the greatest source of security for individual liberty is believed to reside in associations and nonprofit organizations, not in government. From a local public budgeting point of view, this model relies on the goodwill of nonprofit associations and volunteerism to be the driving force in meeting the unmet needs of local citizens. For the *disengaged citizen model,* the participation norm is weak because people assume that the real decision-making power is in the hands of a small group of professional experts and insider elites. From a local public budgeting point of view, this model is the least intrusive and proactive of all of the other models. It presumes that if no organized group exists to advocate for a particular point of view, then government officials should not give it much priority or attention.

Quadrants A and D on the left-hand side of the exhibit set high standards for the role of experts in the governing process, but for different reasons. In Quadrant A, the role is high because of a dependence on elected representatives and career administrators who operate within constituted roles that are constrained by various accountability requirements. In Quadrant D, the role of experts is high because most citizens are disengaged, relying on organized key groups to advocate for their interests. At local levels of government where these interest groups may not be well organized or where the elected representatives are part-time and unpaid workers, the role of experts and career administrators becomes especially significant in setting budget priorities and in triaging the allocation of scarce resources among competing public needs.

A THEORY OF GOVERNANCE TO GROUND
LOCAL PUBLIC BUDGETING

In the previous section, we took two different paths to explore the founding generation's conclusion that democracy requires a careful balancing of competing democratic values. In the first path, we explored the debates between the Federalists and Anti-Federalists and abstracted two governing traditions that greatly shape our thinking about the role of citizens, experts, voluntary associations, and the business community in the public budgeting process. In the second path, we explored how these two governing traditions have combined to create four models of governance organized around the questions of Who should govern? and What is the proper role of government in society? Throughout our discussion, we have taken care to show how these governing models are reflected in the many forms of local government, how they influence local budgeting practices, and how they can be used as diagnostic tools to understand the community polity. In this final concluding section, we will summarize the major lesson from the founding debates that we will carry forward in subsequent chapters, especially those dealing with budget formats and the kind of information that is needed to make "good budget" decisions.

The first major lesson that we wish to carry forward is that local public budgeting is a political process that is grounded in a particular theory of democratic governance. The Federalist and Anti-Federalist debates framed this discussion exceptionally well by showing us what is needed most to preserve democratic liberty and, in the process, providing us with a range of answers to the two key questions regarding the role of government and the kind of expertise is needed to perform this role. Exhibit 2.8 provides a pictorial summary of what we call the **Democratic Balancewheel** model of governance, which we believe serves as the appropriate framework for local public budgeting. The model is value-centered rather than organized around the separation of powers and checks and balances that characterize state and federal systems of government. Still, the model is informed by the debates that produced America's unique federal system of democratic governance. For these reasons, we believe the Democratic Balancewheel theory is more applicable to the *fused power* systems of government that prevail at the local level of government. Public budgeting is perhaps the most important annual governing activity that puts our democratic theory to the test. And whatever form that theory takes—whether due to the particular type of local government in question, the configuration of relationships among the sectors, or the unique local history, values, and institutions in place—successful budgeting requires balancing competing democratic values. There is an important implication that follows from this conclusion and provides the foundation for the second lesson that we wish to carry forward from our discussion in this chapter.

If public budgeting is a political activity that requires balancing competing democratic values,

77

Exhibit 2.8 **The Democratic Balancewheel**

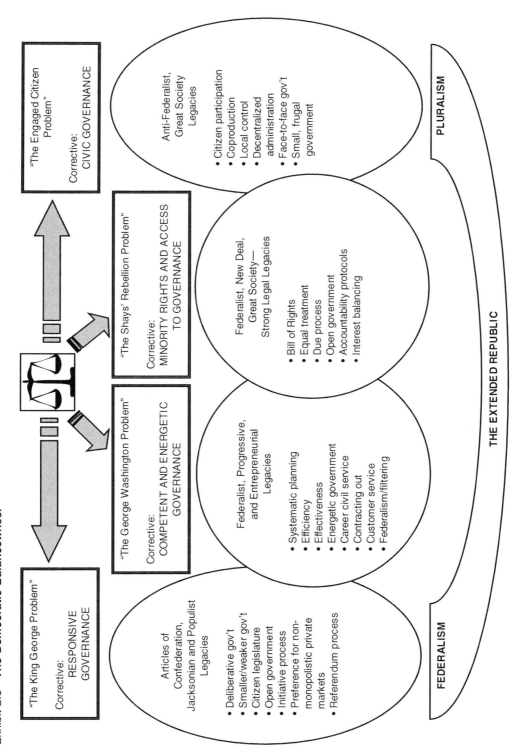

then those with official budget responsibility need to use the Democratic Balancewheel theory to help them understand the particular kind of balancing role they are playing in the budget development and approval process. Four leadership roles are embedded in the Democratic Balancewheel theory in Exhibit 2.8: (1) the Madisonian Interest Group Balancing role, (2) the Washingtonian Systematic Planning role, (3) the Hamiltonian Entrepreneurial role, and (4) the Jeffersonian Community Preserving role. A brief description of each of these roles will provide a framework that locates the particular type of role that government officials play in the public budgeting process and legitimates this role as a necessary part of making our local systems of democratic work.

The Madisonian Leadership Model: Administration as Interest Group Balancing

The interest group balancing model derives from James Madison's view that a multiplicity of interests in the economic and social spheres is the best check against tyranny of an overpowering majority. As Madison observed in *The Federalist Papers:* "The regulation of these various and interfering interests forms the principal task of modern legislation and involves the spirit of party and faction in the necessary and ordinary operations of government" (1787, Federalist No. 10, quoted in Rossiter 1961). The public manager shares responsibility for balancing these contending interests in the daily operations of the administration and in the budget development and implementation process. In jurisdictions that have part-time elected officials, administrators are expected to anticipate the reaction of various interests to policy and budget proposals and to arm the elected officials with the information they need to broker successful agreements. Better yet, the administrators will broker these agreements so that the elected officials are saved from having to use their limited time and capital to do so. Good administration under the interest group model consists of creating the circumstances for gathering together interests on an issue and then maintaining the discourse until common agreement and action are possible. Compromise and trade-offs are assumed to be central and morally necessary. How much of this work gets done by administrators versus elected officials depends on the form of government and expectations of the elected officials. In jurisdictions with full-time elected officials, and especially where elections are partisan, this interest-balancing work is done by the elected officials and their staff, but with the support of administrative staff and members of the leadership team.

The pluralist or interest group balancing model works best when interests are well developed, when these interests are securely attached to stable groups in larger society, and when the issues under discussion are well understood. This model is particularly effective in reconciling pragmatic differences; however, it is not well suited to dealing with strong ideological differences, or for optimizing the best use of resources, effectively achieving a planned set of objectives, or resolving problems that are fundamentally technical. Moreover, since the model starts with the status quo, it neglects interests that are poorly organized and underfunded; it is not always appropriate when planning for long-term needs; and it frequently results in inefficiencies through overlap and duplication of efforts and programs. At its worst, it stymies effectiveness and favors private interests over the public good.

The Washingtonian Leadership Model: Administration as Systematic Planning

The story of the near loss of George Washington's army at Valley Forge is the story of the failure of government to carry out its assigned work efficiently, effectively, and energetically. In short, it is a story of incompetent government—one not up to the task of achieving the goals it was assigned. Over time, the continued failure to deliver the goods is a recipe for the erosion of popular confidence and support. This is a message that has been repeated throughout history, including the recent call to "reinvent government" in order to make it perform more efficiently and effectively. Stripped of its adornments, the Washingtonian leadership model emphasizes the necessity of a powerful govern-ment to both protect and enhance democratic liberties. This is an argument used today to defend heightened restrictions on the rights of citizens in the name of protecting national security.

Having learned firsthand of the perils of inadequate government as commander-in-chief of the Continental Army, Washington incorporated a strategy of readiness, coordination, and responsive-ness in his role as the first U.S. president. The Washingtonian model highlights the importance of systematic planning, coordinated implementation with adequate resources, and the ability to act quickly and decisively. Alexander Hamilton's principle of "energy in the executive" required adequate unity of command, duration in office, competent powers, sufficient resources, and a cadre of experienced, knowledgeable officials—all of which characterized the Washington administra-tion. Washington's presiding leadership and sound judgment enabled subordinate colleagues such as Hamilton to develop plans and proposals and to help establish new institutions and practices that would begin to stabilize the new nation and set it on a course of commercial and agricultural prosperity. The Washington administration either bolstered or put in place the basic elements of a stable commercial economy, a sound defense, a basic communications system, and a revenue system, and in the process instilled broad public confidence in the viability of the new nation.

At the local level, this model is best represented by the council-manager form of government. The model works best when problems require systematic solutions, where elected officials do not want to oversee the complexity and detail of policy implementation, and when experienced and knowledgeable people are needed to address the problems that most members of the community accept as needing some kind of solution. It works less well in solving problems that are funda-mentally political in nature, or when the nature of the expertise needed to solve the problems is in dispute. For example, the model works much better at the local level when applied to choosing a new management information system or cleaning up a hazardous waste site than in ameliorating problems of racism, police violence, poverty, and economic inequality. Moreover, as early crit-ics passionately argued, the competent powers required for the model to work are double edged: While they can be used to advance the public good, they can be twisted just as easily for use in an oppressive manner. Information and expertise, for instance, can be used to obfuscate abuse and to overwhelm groups and organizations that do not have the analytic capacity to stand on an equal footing with government experts. This is a common problem at the local level in dealing with vari-ous land-use planning issues, such as zoning, permitting, and variances for building construction. Frequently, the weight of government expertise overwhelms the untutored opinion of citizens.

The Hamiltonian Leadership Model: Administration as Entrepreneurialism

Americans have a long-standing belief, dating back to the days of Alexander Hamilton's *Report on Manufactures* (1791/1966), that public service work can and should be run more like business. That is, agencies and organizations have purposes that can be expressed as goals toward which efficient and specific means may be prescribed. Furthermore, the entrepreneurial model assumes that public goals are well represented by individual interests. To the extent that this is true, the achievement of these goals is a matter of adhering to best management practices. Hamilton, for example, borrowed and improved upon best practices from Europe in fashioning the American financial system. His system of public credit and debt management helped stabilize the young American economy and set it on course for prosperous commercial and agricultural development.

Competition, choice, and measuring effectiveness by client satisfaction are the core values of the entrepreneurial model. Quasi-public/private institutions, contracting out for services, or delivering services through nonprofits are, at times, the most effective way for the public sector to achieve these values. Good administration under the entrepreneurial model is the work of the strategic apex of the organization: determining the goals, values, and principles that will guide organizational work, and then controlling the work based on market responses. The recent re-invention of government initiatives and the new public management movement embody these private market principles.

The Hamiltonian model, however, does not embrace a free market philosophy that emphasizes a strictly hands-off approach to the economy. Rather, Hamilton argued that a robust economy required robust governments with firm regulatory powers as well as economic stimulants to provide stable infrastructure and moderated business cycles. The government must aggressively regulate those markets deemed essential to our national interests, and it must counteract the self-destructive aspects of market behavior (Green 1993). We are reminded of these problems when contemplating recent abuses such as the 2007–2009 Wall Street meltdown, Countrywide Mortgage, Washington Mutual (WAMU), AIG Insurance, Bear Stearns, and the finance industry generally.

The Hamiltonian leadership model works best when goals are clear and stable, when societal goals are amenable to individual choice, and where institutions are well arranged to elicit market responses. The model is not well suited when society is required to act against individual interests, as is the case with racism, human trafficking, and violence. Nor does it work well when problems need attention long before self-interest will motivate any individual to action, as is the case with pollution, or when there are public benefits that no person can afford alone (such as those provided through public defense and public education). Moreover, natural monopolies make private competition highly inefficient, as is the case with public utilities.

While this model can enhance administrative efficiency and effectiveness, it also entails an inherent bias toward those who are rich, powerful, and possess expertise (especially combinations of private and public oligarchic interests). Such conditions can easily overwhelm other vital interests and threaten the viability of local communities and nonprofits. In doing so, the Hamiltonian leadership model can exacerbate the "engaged citizen problem" and thereby weaken the capacity for civic governance.

The Jeffersonian Leadership Model: Administration as Community Building

The Jeffersonian community building model embraces practices that support the civic republic tradition espoused by the Anti-Federalists. It places high value on living shared lives in a common place. To accomplish this goal, it requires face-to-face communication and assumes that differences among individuals and groups can be bridged through a web of long-standing relationships and mutual obligations. This assumption places considerable weight on facilitation, conflict resolution, and civic dialogue. For Jefferson, the ideal conditions supporting this model were found in the republican simplicity of rural, agrarian communities, where government remained close and familiar to the people. Civic governance is face-to-face governance. It is frugal and carefully limited in its scope of activity by a vigilant and engaged citizenry. Volunteerism pervades public life, and much of the community's administration is coproduced. Tenure in office is short and low paid. The role of public servants under this model is to gather people together, transform sharp differences of opinion into a common agenda, give voice to this agenda, and develop the necessary support over time to realize the common vision. It requires administrators to take seriously Tocqueville's injunction that they become experts in the "science of association," especially when economic improvements in the standard of living cultivate isolation and ever-greater independence of citizens from one another (Tocqueville 1835–1840/2000, 492).

The communitarian model works best when the groups and individuals involved have a history of working together through time and over tough issues. This model focuses on a stream of engagement over time, with concern for implications of past engagements on future work together. Individuals must be rooted in the community in such a way that they can be held accountable for what they say and do (McCullough 1991). Accordingly, this model is poorly suited to settings where the participants are transitory, where there is no sense of shared past or future, and where an issue is easily shifted to another venue or external authority. Thus, the conditions for the success of the communitarian model—with its emphasis on dialogue—stand in opposition to those found in the pluralist, interest group balancing model and the energetic and entrepreneurial models. Its inherent dangers lie in oppressive community majorities and weak institutions that can do little to resist them.

Summary

Exhibit 2.9 (on the next page) summarizes the characteristics of each leadership strategy in the Democratic Balancewheel models as discussed above. Each of the strategies plays an important role in ensuring the success of local public budgeting. In the chapters that follow, we will return to these strategies, showing how one becomes more important than another depending on the purposes one hopes to achieve in the budgeting process, the budgeting format that one selects to achieve these purposes, and the particular role that one has in the local public budging process.

We opened this chapter in search of a theory of governance that could structure the role responsibilities of administrators in the local public budgeting process and ground administrative action in legitimacy. The importance of discovering a theory that can address these dual goals is especially important in light of the conflicted understanding that most citizens have of administrative action, especially in local government. The structure and processes of most local governments do not fit neatly with the high school civics understanding that most citizens have about American government. Most local governments do not fit neatly with the federal notion of a system of separation of powers and checks and balances. A review of the U.S. Constitution and the founding debates pointed out important themes and models that can clarify the role of administrators in local government. The procedural and civic republican governance models, along with the four-quadrant local government model we developed in this chapter, provide an explanation and a set of diagnostic tools to guide administrators in both their internal roles within the organization as well as the external role government plays with other organizations in the larger community.

Equally important, we also believe the governance and leadership models we have presented in this chapter can be used to help those responsible for the local budgeting process assess the role that local government should play in partnership with local businesses, interest groups, and nonprofit organizations to coproduce the collective good of the community. Seeing the budgeting process as part of this larger role enables local leaders to use the Democratic Balancewheel as both an internal guide within their own organization and a guide for deciding what kind of budgeting role government should play in partnership with others who coproduce the public good.

STUDY QUESTIONS

1. What are the multiple problems of democratic governance the Federalists wished to solve in establishing the American system of governance? How did they resolve the complex trade-offs implied? What are the implications of their solution for the public budgeting process?

2. To what extent do you think there is a need for communities to remain as concerned with the problem of "majority tyranny" as were the Federalists? How, if at all, does this problem express itself within your local public budgeting process?

3. What does Publius mean in Federalist No. 51, when he claims that the American system of separation of powers and checks and balances relies on a "policy of supplying, by opposite and rival interests, the defect of better motives"? Give some examples of how this principle might be applied in your local public budgeting process to achieve successful budgetary outcomes.

Exhibit 2.9

Founding Era Administrative Leadership Strategies

	Washingtonian: Systematic Planning	Hamiltonian: Entrepreneurial	Jeffersonian: Community Preserving	Madisonian: Interest Balancing
Contribution to Preserving to Liberty	Ensures competent and effective government	Promotes innovation, creativity & adaptability to changing needs	Increases government responsiveness and checks abuses of authority	Checks majority tyranny
Central Values	Competence: order stability effectiveness energetic execution	Energy & Vitality: competition creativity innovation efficiency	Majority rule: popular control access responsiveness frugality & simplicity	Minority rights: • protection of property • freedom of speech, press and assembly • equal protection
Inherent Weaknesses	Abusive centralization, degradation of weaker local communities	Abusive combinations of private & public power	Oppressive majorities, weak governing institutions	Ascendance of private interests over public good

4. What dangers did the Anti-Federalists fear most about government? What correctives did they recommend for overcoming such dangers? How are their concerns reflected in the ways in which your local public budgeting process operates?

5. What are the consequences of the Anti-Federalist view for the role administrators play in the public budgeting process? How do these consequences compare with those of the Federalists?

6. Which of the four governance models presented in Exhibit 2.7 best represents your local public budgeting system? Into which quadrant(s) does your jurisdiction tend to fall?

7. How do the four leadership models presented in Exhibit 2.9 express themselves in your local public budgeting system? How are the roles (systematic planning, entrepreneurial, community building, interest group balancing) addressed, and who tends to ensure that they are carried out successfully?

NOTES

1. For this section, we are grateful for M.E. Sharpe's permission to draw extensively from the second edition of Morgan, Green, Shinn, and Robinson's *Foundations of Public Service* (2013, chaps. 4–6).

2. We are grateful for Information Age's permission to draw extensively from Nishishiba, Banyan, and Morgan, "Looking Back on the Founding: Civic Engagement Traditions in the United States," in *The State of Citizen Participation in America*, ed. Hindy Lauer Schachter and Kaifeng Yang (Charlotte, NC: Information Age, 2012), 27–36.

3. While the rhetoric of the antitax revolt and the Tea Party movement has been populist in tone, in practice the motivations of its members lack a consistent philosophy to put more power in the hands of citizens. For example a large contingent of Tea Party followers wants the government to use its centralized authority to limit liberty by (1) outlawing abortions, (2) more vigorously regulating immigration, and (3) imposing restrictions on citizens in the pursuit of antiterrorism. The call for a more active government contrasts with the classical American populist and libertarian concern for the abuse of government power. Edward Snowden's whistle-blowing exposure of the National Security Agency's collection of private information in the name of protecting citizens and the nation from terrorists is a better illustration of the populist and libertarian traditions at work than is the Tea Party movement.

3 | THE MULTIPLE PURPOSES OF PUBLIC BUDGETING

The chief financial officer (CFO) of a large urban school system was recently asked by the assistant superintendent for student achievement why she could not design a budgeting system that met all the requirements that managers throughout his organization were placing upon it. The school system's comptroller said she wanted a budget that was realistic enough for cash planning purposes. The director of personnel said he needed a budget that would reward employee performance. The assistant superintendent for operations told the CFO that he wanted a budget that would help him evaluate operating efficiency. The superintendent wanted a budget that could be used as the primary coordination device to harmonize all of the organization's activities. Finally, a consultant came in and told the superintendent that she ought to be using the budget as a tool for management development. Like the assistant superintendent for student achievement, the CFO rightly asked, "How can one budget be expected to do everything?"

We commonly assume that political parties, businesses, and most other human activities cannot succeed by being all things to all people, but that is not the case with public budgeting. The budgeting process is the operational heart of our many local systems of democratic governance and public-serving organizations. It is the focal point for the reconciliation of competing visions of the public good. The final **budget** that emerges from this process represents, for the time being, a working consensus of how best to allocate the tax revenues, charges for service, and philanthropic donations that have been collected with the promise of serving the larger public good. The budgeting process is the best forum to witness the reconciliation of these multiple and competing claims about what constitutes the public interest.

In every governmental jurisdiction and public service nonprofit, the development, adoption, implementation, and reconciliation of a budget reflects agreement over the proper balance to be struck among the following purposes served by the budgeting process:

- funding programs that are *responsive* to constituent wishes and client needs;
- funding programs that are *effective* in accomplishing their goals;
- funding programs that are *cost efficient*;
- *communicating* clearly to the multiple "attentive" publics; and
- using the budgeting to *plan, set, and coordinate policy priorities*.

Governmental jurisdictions add a sixth budget purpose: using the budget to ensure a *healthy economy*. Frequently, disagreements over the priority of these purposes are differences of opinion about using the budget to meet short-term versus long-term needs. For example, board members, elected officials, and program clients are usually much more concerned about the short-term impacts of a public budget than is the case for policy experts and program managers, who are more inclined to view the budget from a longer-term perspective. This is the case for both nonprofit and governmental entities. For those who have final responsibility for creating a balanced budget, the process is a *scarcity allocation problem*: How can we provide citizens and clientele with what they want and need using the revenue available? When viewed with this question in mind, the budgeting process is mainly a task of creating a working consensus that can survive through the next budgetary cycle. On the other hand, for many budget analysts, program managers, and administrators, the budget process provides an opportunity to improve the effectiveness and the efficiency of programs. The overall legitimacy of public-serving organizations and their ability to garner the ongoing support of the taxpayers, clients, customers, and donors may depend on how well participants in the budgeting process successfully balance these competing short- and long-term priorities. This is a tall, if not nearly impossible, order to meet successfully year after year.

The goal of this chapter is to explore these conflicting purposes in detail, with a special focus on how they are reflected in the budgeting process of preparing, adopting, and executing an annual or biennial **operating budget**. This chapter addresses each of the six purposes enumerated above in some detail, after an initial summary overview of the historical development of public budgeting and the impact of this history on the multiple purposes of a budget. In our discussion of each of the six purposes, we describe some important differences between local public budgeting and the budgeting undertaken by nonprofit organizations. We end the chapter with a summary discussion of how nonprofit organizations deal with the mix of competing purposes that surface during the budget development process.

We give special attention to nonprofit organizations in this chapter for two reasons. First, many public administration programs do not provide separate budgeting courses for nonprofit and public-sector-bound students. Most courses that offer such an option do not generally spend time emphasizing the differences between the two sectors and explaining why these differences are important in serving the public interest. Second, given the increased reliance by governmental entities on contracts and partnerships with nonprofit organizations to provide services, public administrators need to have a good understanding of the nature and purposes of the organizations over which they have oversight accountability for the expenditure of public funds.

Many of the purposes of a public budget are reflected in both the structure and the sequential order of the budget process itself. Even the analytic steps in budget preparation (chapter 5), and the formats and required informational content of the budget documents themselves (chapters 11–14) provide a means to reflect the purposes and goals of the budget. It is important to note that this structured process also serves to guide and condition the behavior of administrators, legislators, advocates, and other participants in the process (chapter 5). The challenge for budget practitioners is to design and structure budgeting activity and its products effectively to carry out the differing goals of these multiple participants in the process.

THE HISTORY OF PUBLIC BUDGETING AS A GUIDE TO BUDGET PURPOSES[1]

Historically, the evolution of local public budgeting processes has mirrored the national trend away from a legislative-driven model emphasizing constituent responsiveness and financial control and toward an executive-driven model emphasizing efficiency and effectiveness. The evolution of public budgeting has gone through the following three developmental stages, which we will discuss in detail in the sections that follow:

- *financial*, with an emphasis on spending control and accountability;
- *administrative*, with an emphasis on operational efficiency and effectiveness; and
- *policy development*, with an emphasis on strategic planning and policy coordination.

The antecedents of our present formalized and quite structured process of public budgeting emerged as one of many government reforms advocated by the Progressive movement at the turn of the twentieth century (Schick 1966, 1980). Prior to 1900, it was common for each agency or government commission to approach the legislature independently for funding. These conditions left the jurisdiction's executive or the president of the United States with only informal control and presented the legislature with an uncontrolled and uncoordinated flood of requests. A desire to ameliorate these problems laid the groundwork for the first major phase of budget reform.

The Need for Financial Control

The balkanized nature of the early budgeting process combined with several other factors to contribute to the development of a unified system of budgeting that was executive centered and focused on financial control. First, government was growing in both size and complexity. For some turn-of-the-century reformers (1890–1910), this growth demonstrated the need to curtail and control the size of government. For others, a more unified public budgeting process provided an opportunity to control graft and corruption, and to rectify the excesses of government spending. For still other reformers, the consolidation of fractured government commissions and agencies under strong executives marked a key step toward increasing government efficiency.

The development of what has come to be called the *executive budget* proved to be a ready-made solution to the multiple goals of controlling the size of government, preventing corruption, and increasing administrative efficiency. An executive budget simply required the chief executive officer of a jurisdiction to consolidate all agency spending requests into a single document that could be presented to the legislature. The 1921 Budget and Accounting Act required the president for the first time in the history of the United States to present such an executive budget to Congress each year. This set the stage for similar reforms to be put into place at the state and local levels of government. When these new centralized budgeting processes were combined with civil service and procurement reform, the primary tools were fully in place for increasing the efficiency and professionalism of modern government.

The turn-of-the-century reformers' goals of curtailment and control created the first and still primary justification for a unified public budget. To implement these purposes, accountants were hired and accounting practices were formalized. These practices emphasized the importance of clearly identifying costs and establishing routine protocols for controlling spending. Such a *control-centered* system resulted in what has come to be called the *object of expenditure* or the *line-item budget*. This system remains the primary tool used in public budgeting, as we will discuss in chapter 11.

The Administrative Need for Operational Efficiency and Effectiveness

By the end of the Great Depression and the beginning of World War II, a variety of civil service, purchasing, and budgeting reforms had created an increasingly professional government service. With spending control now institutionalized, the emphasis began to shift to a greater focus on the efficiency and the effectiveness of government operations. The idea of *performance budgeting* gradually emerged from these early 1940s concerns over how best to increase the efficiency and effectiveness of the administration of public programs. As this shift began to occur, public administrators became increasingly important members of agency budget staffs. The practice of presenting efficiency information in the budget documents raised the visibility of the all-important *performance* issues with legislators and executives.

The Need for Planning

During the 1960s, practitioners and academic researchers began emphasizing the importance of viewing budgeting as an integral part of long-range program and agency planning. Secretary of Defense Robert McNamara (in office 1961–1968) and his "whiz kids" from the Ford Motor Company set a very high standard of what careful planning could accomplish if systematically applied to public agencies (Schick 1966, 1973; see chap. 12 for a more detailed discussion of this development). The dominance of rational analysis and the practical availability of mainframe computers supported this shift to planning as a centrally important purpose for public budgeting. However, using the budget as a planning tool frequently conflicts with other priorities of agencies and professionals, who often feel that a more urgent use of the budgeting system is to deliver resources and services to clients, or to respond to legislative and political concerns. During this period of executive-centered planning, most members of the legislative branch of government expressed little interest in radical departures from program-focused budgeting and the baseline allocations forged in the budget agreements of previous years. As a result, the planning function of public budgeting was never fully adopted in practice.

Today's public budgets continue to reflect the learning and features of these earlier budget purposes. Line-item and performance budgeting are well institutionalized in structure, practice, and values. Over the years, public budgeting has come to serve other important purposes, especially in coordinating the related activities of agencies and in communicating to the various attentive publics.

PUBLIC BUDGETING AS A GOVERNING TOOL TO TEST POLITICAL RESPONSIVENESS

The budgeting process is an opportunity to test an organization's and jurisdiction's responsiveness to community desires. For nonprofits, the budgeting process tests responsiveness to a blend of community needs and donor/grantor priorities. For governments, the budgeting process assumes that what the community has supported in the past is likely to continue to be supported, incrementally more or incrementally less in the future. This has been the normal practice in most public budgeting processes. Only in the last few years has this incremental focus begun to shift in the face of unsustainable spending that the existing revenue base of many government jurisdictions cannot support. Nonprofit organizations also have traditionally budgeted in an incremental manner. Multiyear contracts and grants, annual renewable contracts and grants, continuing donor relationships, annual combined donation campaigns, and continuing community needs reinforce the incremental nature of nonprofit budgeting. The completion of major contracts and partnerships, and the commencement of new ones, may have the effect of forcing a reexamination of incremental budgets.

For government agencies, the budget process also presents an important political platform from which to make changes in both the selection of policy choices and the allocation of resources to support those choices. Almost all jurisdictions place responsibility on the **chief executive or administrative officer (CEO)** to prepare a balanced budget and to present it to the legislative body for review and adoption. The CEO's budget proposal provides an opportunity to array and prioritize all the functions and needs of the jurisdiction from a legislative and an executive perspective. In its final presentation, the executive budget represents a unified policy statement of the organization and the jurisdiction's services.

The opportunity to use the budget to make fundamental and important policy changes is especially important to elected officials and interest groups who seek to acquire the funding necessary to support programs important to their interests. The perspectives and needs of elected officials and interest groups may often conflict with the values and hopes of public administrators who need to weigh and adjust the competing program priorities. Understanding these contrasting perspectives is a useful key to understanding the budget process, which we will discuss in considerable detail in the next chapter.

Elected officials operating within the American representative system of government face a different set of performance evaluations than their administrative counterparts. Elected officials must respond to their constituents' needs and demonstrate a record of leadership. Even the most junior legislator must demonstrate an ability to control or use government to solve problems in the home district. Survival as an elected official rests on this ability. By contrast, civil service professionals rely more on agency and professional values to guide their sense of action and accomplishment. For example, program managers and direct service providers (social workers, police officers, civil engineers, foresters, and so on), as well as agency budget analysts are primarily committed to acquiring the resources necessary to maintain the continuity of program services to clients, not to delivering on promises to constituents. Sometimes, clients are constituents and vice versa, but there is a fundamental difference between "service delivery" to clients and "delivering the goods" to constituents. The former requires attention to issues of efficiency and effectiveness, while the latter is primarily a matter of responsiveness. The budget process provides recurring leadership opportunities to bridge and reconcile these competing perspectives.

Differing notions of appropriate budgetary goals must be viewed against the backdrop of a prevailing set of economic conditions. The implications of these conditions for budget choices become fully evident only with the compilation of an integrated budget. Good economic times generate strong revenues and provide a chance to strengthen the fiscal health of the budget. When acting in the midst of a recession, however, the CEO must curtail spending to match revenues. For all the hopes and promises of new programs and services, a downturn in the economy may make spending cuts and reductions a necessary order of the day, despite the promises made by elected officials during their campaigns.

Finally, a jurisdiction's or organization's budget process provides a means by which interest groups raise and debate issues. Nonprofit organizations can make a special contribution in this regard. Nonprofit service providers often have the clearest conception of community needs and the costs of services to meet those needs. As independent organizations, nonprofits can advocate for changes in service programs during local government budgeting processes. We give further attention to the nonprofit advocacy role in chapter 4.

Legislative proposals and votes on proposed funding levels create the necessity to set priorities and make choices among competing purposes. The budgeting process provides an important opportunity for citizens and interest groups to become involved in these priority-setting activities. Without this involvement, the budget process risks the loss of public trust and legitimacy. For major community nonprofits, the annual budgeting process provides an opportunity to revisit community priorities, community strategic visions, and community values. But unlike the open government budget process with its multiple internal controls and system of checks and balances, donors offering extraordinary-sized grants may in essence coerce nonprofits and their dependent partners into particular policy and program choices. For example, a major donor may want to establish a large endowment for a given target population that does not represent the greatest community need that the nonprofit is seeking to serve. Even those donors making small but consistent donations from year to year expect to see program outcomes that meet their particular vision of the community. The nonprofit budgeting process can provide a limited forum for a discussion on reconciling donor wishes with the organizational mission and community needs. A full discussion of these issues should contribute to an organizational strategic planning and visioning process.

PUBLIC BUDGETING AS FINANCIAL ACCOUNTABILITY

A second purpose of the budget process is to ensure financial accountability. This accountability is achieved in a variety of ways, including:

- limitations on spending through the use of accounting codes and regular monitoring of expenditures;
- statutory and/or constitutional limits on spending;
- ongoing legislative oversight;
- postexpenditure preparation of a comprehensive annual financial report (CAFR) and the conducting of audits at the close of the budget fiscal year or biennium;
- a legal requirement that the chief executive officer's proposed budget and the legislative adopted budget be balanced;
- a legal requirement that the legislative body enact a budget; and
- a requirement that the CEO comply with the expenditure obligations set forth in the adopted budget, rather than use discretion to implement other priorities.

Taken together, these accountability requirements ensure that elected officials will provide public documentation of how citizens' tax dollars are spent and that expenditures will not exceed the collected revenues.

Like the public sector, nonprofit organizations also use budget preparation and implementation to demonstrate financial accountability and to build donor and public trust. The wide variation in the purpose and size of nonprofits results in disparate capacities and resources for monitoring and demonstrating financial accountability. Small nonprofits may have little professional support and have few resources to bring to bear on financial issues, while larger nonprofits typically retain accounting and finance professionals, and recognize the need for a full set of financial controls to build public and donor support. In the past decade, new federal and state laws have revised the structures for demonstrating financial accountability for both nonprofit and for-profit organizations. The Sarbanes-Oxley Act of 2002 (SOX) was enacted into law in response to abuses and major financial scandals in the for-profit corporate sector. Though the act does not directly apply to nonprofits, concerns of legal liability and the expectations of board members from the private corporate sector have pushed many larger nonprofits to implement SOX compliance procedures. We give additional attention to nonprofit compliance with the Sarbanes-Oxley Act and other state laws in chapter 18.

The budget preparation and implementation processes provide the tools to demonstrate nonprofit integrity. Today, the extensive partnering between nonprofit organizations and government agencies through service contracting effectively blurs the boundary between the nonprofit and government sectors. Consequently, nonprofits and government are motivated to work more closely together to build donor and public trust through transparent accountability and performance standards.

PUBLIC BUDGETING AS MANAGERIAL ACCOUNTABILITY

Throughout this book, we emphasize the distinct perspective of those who manage programs and have the responsibility of making government and public service organizations work on a day-to-day basis. This has some important implications for the budget process. Program managers are uniquely situated to provide two kinds of information important to various stakeholders in the budget process. The first focuses on the best way to organize a coordinated response across organizational boundaries in the delivery of governmental services to the citizens. This role has become increasingly important as the public calls for a more responsive and accountable government that organizes and delivers its services with a common and coordinated sense of customer service.

Program managers are also equipped to provide another kind of information: data on enhancing productivity. With the spending information from repeated budget cycles, program managers have access to the information necessary for developing unit cost trends and other productivity measures. The growing public concern for productivity enhancement has increased the burden on managers to provide this kind of information to the decision makers in the budgeting process. For example, school board officials in a large metropolitan district might decide to allocate additional staffing to schools above a preexisting base level to close the achievement gap. Establishing a clear understanding of the expected student achievement results that these new positions would produce would be critical to gaining support for any additional resources. Similar kinds of productivity-based measures can be established for a wide range of public services.

Similarly, nonprofit organizations frequently find themselves needing to demonstrate performance and accomplishments. Grant and donor performance requirements often stipulate measurement and accomplishment criteria. The planning, programming, budgeting system (PPBS) and performance budgeting formats discussed in considerable detail in chapters 12 and 13 provide a means for non-profits to integrate donor performance requirements into an organization's annual budget.

PUBLIC BUDGETING AS A COMMUNICATIONS TOOL

The public budget process and its documents serve as a communications tool to a variety of audiences. The general public, issue advocates, and legislators all receive information from the budget process. Once the legislature adopts the budget and, if necessary, the executive signs it into law, agency administrators and staff members become information recipients. Each of these actors perceives the budget differently. A given budget format and its unique analytic emphasis may be especially helpful to one actor, but may be distinctly unhelpful, or hold little meaning or interest for others. For example, a budget showing high clientele satisfaction may make it more difficult for elected officials to reallocate scarce resources. Extensive performance information showing the inefficiency and/or ineffectiveness of a given program that has high levels of constituency support can pose the same problem for elected officials. This is a reminder that budget documents and other briefing materials must be informed by an understanding of the needs and expectations of the audiences they are intended to serve.

Agency department heads and directors face one of the most difficult budget communications challenges. They must prepare a budget request that persuades the CEO and the central budget office staff that the department and its programs are worthy of continued or increased funding and support. The departmental budget request must (1) demonstrate how well it is performing and using its resources; (2) justify and explain any proposed changes to programs, policies, and funding levels; and (3) explain how the department programs will implement the CEO's policy priorities. In short, department-level budget documents must communicate to the executive and the central budget office the current health and future needs of its programs.

After the central budget office compiles all the individual department budgets into a unified executive proposed budget, the primary audience for budget communication shifts from the CEO to the legislative body. The primary goal at this stage is to provide information to elected officials to support decision making and political outreach. At the state and federal levels of government, the congressional and legislative budget and appropriations committee staff analyzes the budget proposed by the governor or president and provides the legislative members with the necessary analysis and recommendations. However, local jurisdictions with part-time elected officials do not have this kind of staff support, and they must rely on the executive and central office budget staff to provide them with the information they need to make decisions on the proposed budget. This puts the budget staff in the challenging position of serving the executive and legislative branches of government, an issue we will discuss in detail in the next chapter.

One of the most difficult challenges for administrators in the budgeting process is to communicate an agency's intentions and performance record to the citizens and community. The budget process provides a routine mechanism for extending these messages, usually through an annual budget message from the chief executive to the governing body and citizens at large. The potential for building citizen trust in government departments or programs stretches beyond the formal budget process presentations to the city council, county commission, or board of directors. Communication on budget process events and outcomes includes attending face-to-face meetings and working informal contacts through neighborhood citizen participation groups, government-appointed citizen advisory groups, advocacy and client groups, community network partners, and contractors and grantees.

The media plays a major role in presenting budgets to the citizens of a jurisdiction. For that reason, those responsible for the budgeting process must have a keen eye for how the key activities in the budget processes and budget documents can be packaged and communicated online and through social media. Successful communication helps to build legitimacy for the programs, agencies, and departments—and more broadly for the governing entity.

PUBLIC BUDGETING AS AN OPPORTUNITY TO PLAN, SET, AND COORDINATE POLICY PRIORITIES

The budget process provides a platform for the selection of policy choices and for the allocation of resources to support those choices. The CEO's proposed budget sets the stage for this process by arraying and prioritizing all the functions and needs of the governmental entity. The compilation of the proposed budget also provides a means to coordinate service delivery across agencies and programs. A comprehensive response to complex social, environmental, and other problems often requires the expertise and services of several departmental units—and even external community partners and resources. A unified budget that brings together governmental, contractual, community, foundation, and nonprofit sources provides the basis for organizing a prioritized and coordinated response to these complex problems and needs. Finally, at the state level and in local government jurisdictions that have strong partisan political parties and a traditional separation of powers system, the proposed budget provides the foundation for the CEO's advocacy efforts during budget consideration by the legislative branch.

November elections often bring new strong mayors, county executives, or state governors into office. These newly elected officials must step instantly into the position of the organization's chief executive officer (CEO), often with little preparation or training. Depending on the start date of the jurisdiction's fiscal year (e.g., commonly January 1 or July 1) the newly elected CEO may or may not have the time or opportunity to revise or prepare a new proposed budget. Whether the people directly elect the executive or the executive serves at the pleasure of the legislative body, the promises made during an election campaign must be translated quickly into policies and programs. The campaign goals and visions must be transformed into legislation and directives that reorient administrative agencies to the goals of the newly elected officials—both executive and legislative (e.g., new council, commission, or board members). If the CEO is appointed (e.g., a city manager or district director), he or she becomes the immediate contact point for the all of the pressures placed upon newly elected officials by various constituency groups.

There are structural factors built into the process that require the CEO to exercise caution in using the budget to make quick and fundamental policy changes. The CEO's budget is reviewed and modified by the legislative body to meet the needs of the political leadership of that branch of government. Legislative bodies range from special district, corporate, and nonprofit boards of directors, to city councils and county commissions, to much larger state and federal legislatures. When the branches are divided along partisan lines, compromise is usually necessary to meet a twofold constitutional duty shared by the executive and legislative branches: (1) the CEO must present a balanced budget to the legislature, and (2) the legislative branch in all state and local jurisdictions is constitutionally required to enact a budget. In local jurisdictions with nonpartisan offices, these goals are easier to accomplish than is the case for jurisdictions that have divided branches of government and high levels of party partisanship.

Finally, and perhaps most important, there are economic reasons for a new executive to exercise caution in making significant changes to a budget that has been assembled by the outgoing executive. The implications of budget choices within a given economic milieu become fully evident only with the compilation of an integrated budget. As mentioned earlier, good economic times generate strong revenues and provide a chance to strengthen the fiscal health of the organization or jurisdiction's budget. But in times of economic slowdown or full-blown recession, the executive must limit spending to match revenues, regardless of earlier campaign promises.

PUBLIC BUDGETING AS AN INFLUENCE ON THE ECONOMY

The spending and taxing policies of public jurisdictions, regardless of size, have economic impacts. Of course, the federal government—with its $3.65 trillion budget in 2014, over 3 million civilian employees, and its capacity to deficit spend—has far more impact on the economy than a state like Oregon, with just under 60,000 employees, an appropriated budget of $28.44 billion for 2014, and a constitutional requirement to present a balanced budget. To provide additional perspective, a typical top five Fortune 500 company will generate $200–400 billion of annual gross revenue and have 350,000 employees. Most local jurisdictions have budgets that pale by comparison, yet they do affect their local economies.

State and local spending and taxing policy is important in attracting an expanding and qualified labor pool, and in competing for growing businesses whose incomes add to the jurisdiction's revenue stream (chapter 8). Federal matching dollars add to state and local economies, primarily through federal entitlement programs and transportation infrastructure. In turn, state grants complement county and local government spending, all of which spurs economy activity. In addition, local governments can use various tax incentives to encourage local economic development. These can include tax breaks on property and income, waiving various fees, and building needed infrastructure, just to mention some of the more commonly used development strategies.

Finally, government facilities and activities, which can include military installations, prisons, hydroelectric and reclamation facilities, national parks and natural resources, and research laboratories and facilities, can significantly affect local economies.

From a business economist's point of view, a jurisdiction's budget must:

1. Fund social service programs and contracts for those in need, thus increasing the demand for private-sector goods and services.
2. Fund the transfer of welfare benefits that redistribute income and provide entitlement payments, including Medicare, veterans' benefits, and Social Security.
3. Reflect tax policy that favorably affects business and individuals.
4. Reflect and fund the enforcement of commercial, transportation, land use, and environmental regulations that affect the business climate.
5. Fund education and other training programs that enhance the jurisdiction's human and economic resources.
6. Fund the direct and the contracted production of goods and services, such as the sale of state timber and other resources, higher education, the delivery of law enforcement and/or correctional services.
7. Fund routine purchases and capital projects that stimulate economic activity.
8. Serve to redistribute wealth across the jurisdiction's residents.
9. Fund economic development efforts to attract and help distribute economic activity within the jurisdiction.
10. Provide significant employment opportunities for citizens.

A final factor that influences the economic health of a community, but is usually taken for granted, is the overall integrity and competence of those who manage the budget and financial forecasting processes. If revenue and expenditure estimates are continually off the mark, and employees lose their jobs, negative signals are sent to the larger financial community. But when there is a structurally sound budget that matches recurring revenues with recurring expenses, lenders and financial analysts are encouraged to grant more favorable credit ratings and reduced interest rates to the jurisdiction. Structural soundness includes adequacy of resources to fund retirement programs, supplementary medical benefits for employees, Social Security, Medicare, and similar kinds of expenditures that can have a cumulative adverse impact over a multiyear period. Those preparing the budget have a responsibility to provide the public and elected officials with clear and honest projections that take into account these hidden or unforeseen cumulative costs of doing public business.

THE CONSEQUENCES OF MULTIPLE PURPOSES OF PUBLIC BUDGETS

The budgeting process for public service organizations and jurisdictions provides a necessary meeting ground for the many competing claims that are often in competition with increasingly shrinking resources. Exhibit 3.1 provides a summary of these enduring conflicts.

This list of purposes illustrates why public budgeting is the heart and soul of democratic governance. The process creates a necessary meeting ground for democratic claims that almost always are at odds. These claims include competing demands of interest groups, administrative concerns for operational efficiency and program effectiveness, leadership aspirations of elected officials, taxpayer discontent over excessive spending, citizen concerns for ever more responsiveness and accountability, and contending ideologies about the proper scope and limits of government's reach into the lives of its citizens.

While the periodic election process plays an important role in reconciling these competing claims, the budgeting process bears the reconciliation task on an annual basis. As we will see in the following chapters on the budgeting cycle and the actors responsible for making it work, the different sets of information needed from various experts at different stages of the process further complicate the task of producing an agreed-upon budget. This adds depth and complexity to each of the competing purposes we have discussed above. Despite the difficulty of the task, citizens commonly judge the success of their governmental entities and public service organizations by how well they accomplish this monumentally difficult budget-balancing task. This reinforces one of the major points we introduced in chapter 1: that public budgeting is more about successfully reconciling conflict than it is about managing numbers and technical expertise.

Two consequences result from the necessity of the budgeting process to generate a working consensus among conflicting priorities and competing purposes. The most obvious is the need for

---

Exhibit 3.1

Summary of Enduring Conflicts Regarding the Purpose of a Public Budget

A. What ends should the budget serve?
   1. Responsiveness to clientele interests
   2. Financial accountability
   3. Program effectiveness and efficiency
   4. Promoting a healthy economy
   5. Meeting the needs of those with little or no political influence

B. Who should decide?
   1. Experts and career professionals
   2. Elected officials
   3. Board members
   4. Citizens
   5. Clients

compromises among the competing policy priorities and political pressures. In most local jurisdictions with part-time elected officials, the city manager or executive mayor (the CEO) becomes the initial focal point for sorting, winnowing, and negotiating a working consensus. It is common for the manager, mayor, or CEO to informally test priorities with each member of the elected board before assembling the final budget and officially passing it on for debate and formal adoption. Most of the time, the local legislative body does not make significant changes to the CEO's proposed budget. When this is not the case, it reflects badly on the city manager, mayor, or CEO's ability to anticipate what the elected board will support. If this occurs with some frequency, the council members are likely to lose confidence in the executive. In the case of a city manager or CEO who works at the pleasure of the council, this puts their continued employment at risk. In jurisdictions with strong political parties and a federal-like separation of powers system, conflicts in the budgeting process get resolved more formally as part of the legislative budget compromise process. Legislative members of the executive's party serve as the executive's political advocates and agents in the legislative deliberation process, with the threat of an executive veto if the negotiation process does not proceed to the executive's satisfaction.

A second, less obvious consequence of the need for the budgeting process to produce a working consensus is that it helps explain why most local public budgets are often not tied very closely to systematic long-term plans. The frequency of elections, combined with the multiple purposes of the budgeting process that demand reconciliation from year to year, make it difficult to reach agreements that adhere closely to long-term strategic plans. Periods of economic uncertainty and instability exacerbate this difficulty. The amount of tax that will be collected and the demands for austerity by a vigilant public can quickly override carefully crafted longer-term strategic plans.

THE SPECIAL CHALLENGES OF NONPROFIT ORGANIZATIONS

We observed in chapter 1 (Exhibit 1.11) that nonprofits resemble special districts in that they have narrower missions than general-purpose governmental entities. However, they differ in that they rely on a volunteer/appointed policy board rather than on election processes to resolve differences. These similarities and differences have some important implications for managing the competing purposes of the budgeting process.

By virtue of their focus on providing service to narrow target populations, nonprofits have fewer competing programmatic purposes than is the case for general governmental entities—entities that must juggle the needs of transportation, parks, libraries, public safety, and multiple other purposes. For example, in the list of purposes summarized in Exhibit 3.1, the success of most nonprofit organizations has not been measured traditionally by the extent to which they promote a healthy economy, are responsive to a diverse array of citizens, or make efficient use of their resources. The primary measures of success have turned on whether the budget furthers the organization's mission, meets donor expectations, complies with law and regulation, and builds and sustains the organization's capacity.

Nonprofit board members have the responsibility of developing a budget and ensuring that it meets the four purposes referenced above. The variations in nonprofit budgeting processes reflect the very wide diversity in the size, complexity, and purposes of nonprofits themselves. Small nonprofits may follow an abbreviated budget process that summarizes and reduces expenses and revenues to a single page. In these small nonprofits, volunteer officers may receive little professional support. As nonprofits increase in size, the board and executive director may rely on, or perhaps retain, finance and accounting professionals to ensure quality and to generate confidence in the organization's budget and finances. This confidence is especially important for those nonprofits that rely heavily on external grants and contracts to fund their activities. Medium and large nonprofits, including **foundations** and **intermediary nonprofits**, typically have a **chief finance officer (CFO)** who is clearly responsible for both the finance and budgeting activities of the organization. In these and other larger nonprofit organizations, budgeting responds to a set of needs similar to those found in government:

- Funding programs to match community needs.
- Meeting donor expectations for performance, efficiency, and effectiveness.
- Demonstrating fiscal accountability, transparency, and stability.
- Meeting tax and corporation filing requirements.

The adoption of a budget for a nonprofit organization also frequently involves debate over how best to balance short-term operational and cash flow needs with longer-term strategic goals. For example, should the organization spend as much money as possible on direct services to its clients, or should it spend additional money on professional staff to build its fundraising, grant writing, and organizational capacity?

Over the past decade, the purposes of the nonprofit budgeting process have become significantly more complicated as a result of shrinking resources, greater dependence on government funding, and an expansion of government regulation. Since the mid-1980s, as noted in chapter 2, nonprofit organizations have become increasingly more dependent on government funding. This growing dependence has come with significantly increased federal and state standards for demonstrating financial and performance accountability for both nonprofit and for-profit organizations. The combination of dependence on government funding and increased oversight has made the budgeting process for many nonprofit organizations considerably more complex. In some cases, it has resulted in making compliance with government requirements a major preoccupation of the organization, which comes at the expense of program service to clients (Byrtek 2011).

In a series of studies undertaken by the Brookings Institution, researchers found that the "nonprofit sector survives because it has a self-exploiting workforce: wind it up and it will do more with less until it just runs out. But at some point, the spring must break" (Light 2004, 7). Due to pressures by government and private donors alike to work with extremely low indirect or administrative costs, "some nonprofits adhere to bare bones administrative budgets that actually jeopardize the organization's stability and hinder its ability to grow or respond to change" (48). This level of administrative support would cause the collapse of most businesses and public agencies. The Brookings study concluded with the publication of a monograph calling for government investment in nonprofit organizational capacity building (Light 2004). This conclusion reinforces our argument in chapter 1 that nonprofits in partnership with government enable local communities to function as polities. We will return to the issue of supporting and sizing community networks in the concluding chapter of this book.

STUDY QUESTIONS

1. What are the major purposes of the budgeting process in your organization?
2. How do these purposes compare with those of the federal budgeting process or other agencies for whom you have worked?
3. How do the priorities among various purposes of the budget align with different levels of the organizational structure and with the role responsibilities of those with decision-making authority?
4. In what ways, if any, are the purposes of the budgeting process in your agency in conflict? Illustrate with examples.
5. To what extent do you believe the conflicts among the various purposes of the budgeting process can be successfully resolved?

NOTE

1. This section provides a summary overview of budgeting formats and purposes. A more detailed discussion will be provided for each budgeting format in chapters 11–14.

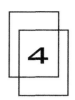

4

BUDGET ACTORS
CONFLICTING PERSPECTIVES

Politics can be viewed as the search for community, where community evolves in part from the capacity of governing institutions to resolve issues involving conflicting values. Political leadership is challenged to accomplish the public good through processes and institutions that foster both efficiency and inclusion. These structures and processes reflect as well as create shared values and goals, including consensus on the role of government in creating or shaping the good society.

(Donald Klinger, John Nalbandian, and Barbara Romzek 2002, 1)

The process of developing and adopting a budget is one of the best tests for determining "the capacity of governing institutions to resolve issues involving conflicting values" (Klinger, Nalbandian, and Romzek 2002, 1). This is because the budgeting process routinely places government agencies and programs in competition with one another for scarce resources. This competition results not only from program needs that exceed the existing revenue but, as we observed in the previous chapter, from the different purposes that a budget is expected to achieve. For example, the need to build up reserves to protect against the uncertainties of the economy comes at the expense of providing services to citizens. Or, the inability to pass a bond measure to support maintenance of facilities causes operating revenue to be spent on buildings rather than on services. In this chapter, we focus on a third reason for competition in the budget process: the role perspectives and responsibilities of the different participants in the budgeting process. As we will see, not all participants in the process measure their success by the same criteria.

There are two reasons it is important to have an appreciation for the multiple factors that create competition. First, a budget process is as much about building a consensus as it is about setting priorities and producing outcomes for which participants can be held accountable. To facilitate the generation of this consensus, it is important to know how the various roles of participants in the budgeting process play an important function in contributing to the larger public good. A second reason to understand the factors that produce competition is to gain an appreciation of the structural conditions that norm the budgeting process. These norms enable the participants to adjust their expectations to what the process can be reasonably expected to produce and what it cannot produce. For example, we will argue in chapters 10 and 12 on budget planning that it is unreasonable to use the budgeting process as the primary tool to set priorities. This task should be done outside the budgeting process in a separate strategic planning activity that precedes and sets the foundation for the budgeting cycle.

In this chapter, we develop an understanding of the roles of the various participants in the budgeting process in three stages. First, we discuss the major participants in the budgeting process and identify their respective role responsibilities. Second, we show how each of the various actors performs an important accountability role that taken together promotes the larger public interest. Third, despite the conflict that is inherently part of the budgeting process, we argue that the actors and the information they need to successfully perform their roles create a predictable dynamic within the public budgeting process at all levels of government. While our discussion focuses on local government budgeting, much of our argument in this chapter applies to all levels of governmental budgeting and to many contexts of nonprofit budgeting.

ROLE RESPONSIBILITIES OF THE BUDGET ACTORS

In the sections that follow, we discuss the perspectives and role responsibilities of each major participant in the local budgeting process. We begin with a summary overview of the roles played by various participants as the budget moves through very predictable steps in the planning process (see chapter 5 for a detailed discussion of this process).This is followed by a more detailed discussion of the specific role played by each of the major local budgeting actors, including administrators, elected officials, and nonprofit and intergovernmental partners. While we focus on local government, we also draw parallels and add some roles that are important at the state and federal levels of the budget process. We do so to draw comparisons and to point out implications for local governments and nonprofits that commonly rely on funds from the higher levels of government. Our discussion will cover the following sets of participants in the budgeting process:

- citizens as voters, taxpayers and clients;
- departments, divisions, and programs as requesters;
- polity governments and nonprofits as request partners;
- department heads and departmental budget staff;
- chief finance officer, organization **budget officer**, and the central budget office;
- the central office revenue and caseload forecasters;
- chief executive officer (CEO) (e.g., city **manager**, county executive, strong mayor, special district executive director);
- the local government **legislative body** (e.g., city council, county commission or board, special district board of directors);
- state legislatures and legislative committees;
- departments, divisions, and programs as implementers;
- polity governments and nonprofits as implementation partners; and
- financial officers and auditors.

Summary Overview

Budget decisions and products move from one set of actors to the next, building the agreement necessary to proceed through the process. Working through the budget process allows the various actors to use their role authority to pursue their specific goals. For most agency divisions and programs, the budget document is a tool to obtain critical resources in order to provide services to clients. For elected officials and the chief executive officer, policy priorities and the fiscal integrity of the budget over a multiyear period are the highest priorities. For elected council, commission, and board members, managing the role of government and meeting constituent needs may be the highest priorities. We will explore the importance and subtleties of these differences of perspective in the sections to follow.

In an added complexity, many actors find themselves playing several roles. For example, central budget office analysts in larger jurisdictions review department and program budget requests with an eye toward answering two different types of questions. First, does the budget request make good fiscal sense? The concern for fiscal integrity requires budget analysts to examine department/program budgets for both internal consistency and for historical patterns of change over time. Second and equally important is the concern that requests meet the jurisdiction's policy priorities. The budget submission process by departments is doubly important from a policy point of view. It is the point of greatest advantage by the chief executive officer over department and agency heads. In addition, the central budget office review process serves as the basis for all subsequent legislative reviews. In short, the analysis undertaken by the central administrative staff often sets the terms of discourse for all subsequent debate in the budget process.

Another example of multiple role players are the budget analysts who, after completing their program/departmental reviews, then work as a team with the chief executive officer to prepare an integrated *proposed* budget.[1] The proposed budget primarily includes an annual or biennial **operating budget** that covers organizational and program operations, but can also include a **capital budget** of proposed infrastructure projects. Ultimately, the proposed budget is submitted to the elected council or board for adoption. However, revenues and available resources are limited, and the act of integrating all of a jurisdiction's programs into a balanced budget can place some programs funded by general fund dollars into competition for resources. To gain resources, central office analysts must clearly and fully understand the status and needs of their programs, and then advocate for funding. We use the term *advocacy* here in a soft sense, rather than the hard sense normally attached to the meaning of the term for *interest group advocacy*. In advocating for resources, central budget analysts must explain and defend their budgets when presenting them to the executive officer for discussion and approval. In larger cities and counties and at the state and federal levels, the analyst is at first a critic and then an advocate. In smaller local jurisdictions and nonprofits, the chief executive officer is likely to do most of this work with the help of a finance director or assistant, but the dual role is still comparable. The responsible agent for the central budget preparation process first serves in an oversight role and then switches to an advocacy role.

Most local units of government that rely on a city manager or a commission form of government operate under a *fused power* model rather than a separation of powers system. Nevertheless, the city manager is still required to perform the dual role of advocating for programs while at the same time being sensitive to the fiscal constraint orientation of elected and **appointed board** members. Chief executive officers of nonprofit organizations similarly find themselves dealing with the dual role of advocacy and of ensuring overall fiscal integrity with their board of directors.

In the separated powers system of the state and federal budgeting processes, legislative appropriations or ways and means committees perform a dual role similar to that of executive branch budget analysts. Committee members first scrutinize the governor's or president's request, but then act as floor managers and advocates as spending bills move through the legislature. State governors also frequently find themselves serving in a dual role. They must be concerned simultaneously with developing a budget that balances with the available revenues, while also advocating strongly for programs that are important for achieving their policy priorities (Forsythe 2004). These dual roles are an artifact of the constitutional system of checks and balances, which encourages the advocacy of one's constitutional role responsibilities but, at the same time, requires that advocacy be tempered in order to acquire the support needed from other actors and government branches to coproduce the public good.

The budget process is structured to channel these political tensions and competition for resources into a set of final budget allocations. The department heads and program managers who report to and assist the executive officer in the development of a unified budget may have strong differences of opinion on needs and spending priorities. But once the executive of a local jurisdiction or a nonprofit organization has prepared an integrated budget for presentation to the elected body or board for formal adoption, all competition, tensions, and dissension will submerge behind a unified front. When a city manager decides on a budget request, the various departments and program directors are expected to join ranks in a unified front. Similarly, at the state and federal levels and in jurisdictions that have strong political parties, the differences between individual legislators are expected to give way to a unified party position. In short, the roles created by our system of separation of powers and checks and balances encourage a modicum of unity that usually tempers and mediates some of the competition and dissension inherent in the budgeting process. Exceptions to this unity reflect extraordinarily strong political pressures and a willingness to take political risks, which is a common condition we have increasingly seen at the federal level in the last several years.

Citizens as Voters, Taxpayers, and Clients

Citizens are the foundation of all levels of government in the United States. While some jurisdictions are more citizen centered than others (chapters 1 and 2), all forms of government require the support of citizens to generate the revenue and allocate the resources needed to fund the work of government. In most local jurisdictions, citizens can participate directly and personally in community decision making through some combination of voting, issue advocacy with elected officials, service on citizen boards and commissions, testifying before budget hearings and advisory committee meetings, supporting ballot initiatives and referenda, and offering comments during administrative rulemakings. To cover these different activities over the extended course of a budget or policy process, citizens often join into informal networks (Isett et al. 2011). Network members share information, provide mutual support, and ensure coverage at public meetings. Such **informal spontaneous networks** are expressions of citizen activism and **civil society**.

Even in jurisdictions that provide citizens with extensive opportunities to influence the budget-making process, the complexity and interconnected nature of modern public policy force most jurisdictions to rely heavily on formal processes that include indirect representation through elected boards/commissions/councils, agency rulemaking processes, and agency governing boards. In short, the development of public budgets in most local jurisdictions follows the requirements of complex, representative government.

As we pointed out in chapter 2, citizen fears of the power of uncontrolled government have followed our American governing systems since their birth. In western states, the ballot initiative and referendum systems allow a direct expression of the people on controversial issues. Citizens have used this process frequently to revise the legislative and constitutional provisions related to property tax collection and the passage of local bond measures. Budget process actors in many western states have had to integrate the mandates of the citizen initiative process into budget decisions and strategies. We will discuss the consequences of these developments in detail in chapter 7 as part of our discussion of the revenue generation strategies used by local governments.

For many taxpaying citizens, the delivery of government services represents a purchase of services and benefits. This model reduces citizenship to a customer service attitude of treating government as a simple business transaction. However, as we have argued in chapters 1 and 2, citizens are much more than customers and consumers of services. Citizens have a role in making public decisions and in implementing those decisions in neighborhoods and communities. Citizenship reflects a personal contribution to the community polity. Only where citizenship reaches beyond consumerism can government truly function as a trust relationship between citizen and the community. The budgeting process at the local level of government provides the best opportunity for administrators and elected officials to support citizens as they work to transcend the role of mere consumers of government services. Because local governments are the direct providers of the services that most affect the daily lives of the majority of citizens, local officials have a preferred advantage in exercising leadership that builds trust and legitimacy in democratic institutions. The budgeting process is perhaps the most critical activity where this opportunity is put to the test.

Departments, Divisions, and Programs as Requesters

Local government departments and their component divisions and programs provide the closest points of contact between the government and citizens. This is true even when local money comes from the state and federal governments. In most cases, local government frontline staffs administer this pass-through money to local programs. Based on staff experience and professional assessments, each program administrator determines the demand for its services. Program budget analysts match client demand with service delivery programs and requests for funding and resources. The division or program's budget proposal forwards this demand for resources to the higher levels of government. This process is similar to the one used by most nonprofit organizations, which depend on program managers for an accurate understanding of client needs in relationship to the available resources. The program managers and analysts have the most direct and detailed knowledge of client needs, their programs, and the effectiveness of their efforts. However, this relatively narrow view focuses the attention of the division or program analyst on resource expenditures and on the few revenue streams to which the program is tied.

For most practical purposes, program analysts in nonprofit organizations at the local level have little influence on funded and pass-through federal safety-net programs driven by formulaic allocations. The best the program analyst and local manager can do with these pass-through programs funded by state and federal agencies is to document the frequently growing gap between available revenue and client needs.

For programs funded through local revenue, program managers and their supporting analysts document the basic needs that they would like to see supported by the expenditure of public revenue. This work provides the *case statement* for the total amount of revenue that a jurisdiction or organization potentially needs to support the services it delivers. Since needs almost always exceed existing revenues, the collective work of the program managers and their budget analysts provides a snapshot of how significantly program budget requests must be reduced to achieve a balanced budget. As we will discuss in the next chapter on the budget cycle, the central budget office establishes the guidelines for departments and programs in the preparation of their budget requests. For example, if the central budget office knows that program demands are likely to exceed the general fund by an average of 10 percent per year, the budget office may require that program managers submit two budget options: one that funds programs to meet the expected need, and one that is 10 percent below the amount funded the previous year.

Programs are commonly organized into larger units that share a common programmatic purpose. For example, several different types of mental health and addiction programs may be lumped together into a mental health program budget. The same kind of program integration commonly occurs for public health, juvenile justice, corrections, environmental programs, and the like. In turn, these subprograms are organized into departments. For example, a county executive and commission might organize the mental and public health programs into a department of community health, and the juvenile justice and corrections programs might be organized into a department of community justice. Regardless of how the programs are arrayed into larger programmatic units, they share a common characteristic in the budgeting process. Almost without exception, the program and subprogram structure perspectives reflect the support of the constituencies and clients they serve. In this important sense, program managers are advocates in the budget process for their constituencies and clients. While central administrative control limits the direct appearance of program staff before the legislative body, client groups and citizens provide a powerful voice to convey support for each set of program and subprogram needs.

Polity Governments and Community Nonprofits as Request Partners

Local governments do not govern, operate, or budget in isolation from other governments and community nonprofits, as we recognized in chapter 1. Local governments of all types operate in polity networks of other governmental, for-profit, and nonprofit community and regional partners (O'Toole 1997, 2006; Isett et al. 2011; Provan and Kenis 2007; Provan and Milward 2001; Milward and Provan 2000).

To gain efficiencies and to save money, local governments often participate in **intergovernmental agreements (IGA)** with other regional and local-level governments (**interlocal agreements**) (LeRoux, Brandenburger, and Pandey 2010; LeRoux and Carr 2007; e.g., City of Sammamish,

WA 2012b). These arrangements include city to city, city to county, city to special district, and special district to county relationships, all of which are typically formalized in a two-party agreement between the governments. However, where a large local government agency such as a county sheriff or transportation department provides similar services to several cities or towns, a multiparty service network arises. These types of agreements can provide the full array of local governmental services, among them wastewater collection and treatment, transit service, port and economic development services, fire and emergency medical services (EMS), library services, and public safety and police services. Another interlocal relationship occurs when a city or county government relates to a central regional council of governments or government (e.g., Puget Sound Regional Council in Washington State; Metro regional government near Portland, Oregon). These multiorganizational networks are often structured around a primary **lead organization** or an independent **network administrative organization (NAO)**. Provan and Kenis (2007) have identified such centralized types of networks as lead-organization and network administrative–organization (NAO-led) governed networks. Other intergovernmental agreements link local governments vertically to state or federal agencies.

Entering into an intergovernmental agreement increases each government's interests and responsibilities in its partner government's budgeting process and decisions. For example, a decision by a small city to purchase fire and emergency medical services (EMS) from an adjacent larger jurisdiction opens mutual concern with the other partner's revenues, budget decisions, and issues of joint program performance. The jurisdiction providing the services remains concerned that revenues and political support will continue unabated from the purchasing jurisdiction's. The purchasing jurisdiction, whose citizens use the provided services, remains concerned with the program performance, effective customer service, and responsiveness of the provider partner.

Much like the program staff analysts we described in the section above, the staff and managers from the providing governmental partner have a close and comprehensive understanding of service needs and field conditions. This information needs to be communicated to both the purchasing and provider governments for use in their budgeting processes. A truthful portrayal of service demand that explains new needs, changing conditions, and gaps in service helps elected officials and executives understand the need for action through the budget process. Truthful information also prepares elected officials and executives for meetings with clients and constituents who may have frustrations with poor performance, want additional services, or oppose changes to existing programs. However, the intergovernmental partnership arrangement can open awkward concerns of partner ethical conflict of interest. Overly aggressive advocacy for intergovernmental programs in the budget process may raise citizen suspicions and cause skepticism about whether an intergovernmental partnership is the most economical and effective means to deliver the service.

Other polity networks are structured as procurement and business relationships. In some instances, the relationship is clearly defined by procurement rules and contract provisions from the purchasing government or major nonprofit (LeRoux 2007; Cooper 2003). These are often two-party contract or **grant** for services agreements. In other instances, the provider partner involves a third-party subcontractor or grantee to complete the specified work. This opens a two-party relationship to the uncertainty of network performance, because the subcontractor may also have obligations to other purchasing governments or nonprofits producing the same types of services but by different procedures or to different standards.

Beyond a simple, two-party, single-service procurement relationship, many **partnership contracts** cover the delivery of entire programs of multiple, integrated professional services. These complex extended-duration public-private partnerships, often with loosely specified program outcomes, require partners to share authority, technical expertise, and risk in a multilevel relationship. Ensuring performance in these complex partnerships is especially challenging because professional discretion is involved with both partners in service delivery and outcome definition (Forrer, Kee, Newcomer, and Boyer 2010; Lawther 2003; Cooper 2003).

Local governments often partner with nonprofit community foundations, private family foundations, regional federated intermediary organizations (e.g., United Way, Catholic Charities, and other religiously affiliated organizations), and service provider nonprofits to comprehensively address community needs through ongoing programs or special initiatives. Nonprofit community foundations and federated intermediaries typically have critical knowledge of donor resources, policy needs, and governance opportunities that can support and enhance local government efforts and resources (Frumkin 2010). In these instances of multiorganizational collaboration, the structures and enforcement mechanisms of government procurement contracts give way to looser agreements and promises resting on a common vision and good intentions. Provan and Kenis (2007) identify **participant-governed networks** as those with decentralized authority and a relatively equal balance of power between network partners. While several organizations in the network may have greater capacity, resources, or political position, no single organization takes the lead as the primary resource provider or administrator for the network. Instead, network partners contribute resources and staff time to the network and its common goal, and network governance is achieved through dialogue and joint agreement. Effectively fulfilling a partnership agreement requires that the partners meet their responsibilities to deliver resources and to perform as agreed. As illustrated in our teaching case for Part I, the heightened interdependence of community partners increases nonprofit concerns with the local government revenue situation and budgeting decisions. Participation and advocacy throughout the local government budgeting process provides an important avenue of joint governance for nonprofit members of the polity network. However, the relationship behaviors between local governments on the one hand and community foundations and major nonprofits on the other may often reflect political motivations rather than client or professional considerations. For example, a jurisdiction that is the home of a major corporate foundation may be reluctant to use its political capital to secure funding from the foundation for a joint undertaking with other jurisdictions for fear of undermining support for its own jurisdictional-specific priorities. Awareness of these kinds of political motivations among all network members is especially important in participant-governed networks' member relationships, which are typically grounded in high levels of interpersonal trust (Provan and Kenis 2007).

The type and structure of a polity network will partially define how its members participate in network-level budgeting (Robinson and Morgan 2014). Informal-spontaneous networks and participant-governed networks will tend to rely on dialogue and consent among most or all partners to develop network positions on resource needs, policies, and program performance. A joint review of each partner's contribution of money and in-kind donations, staff time, and leadership provides a starting point for determining total network resources. Network members may need to reconcile and manage the differences between network-level needs and requests and their own organizational budget priorities. In contrast, if the local government is the dominant funder, the lead organization, *and* the service provider in the network, its policies, administrative protocols, and budget decisions define the operating environment for its contractors, grantees, and partners. Local government organizations acting as network leads or NAOs must demonstrate an awareness of their larger role and recognize the implications of their decisions outside of their organizational boundaries.

Like their government program–level counterparts, the leadership, supervisors, and staff of service delivery nonprofits have firsthand knowledge of client situations, available resources, and program effectiveness. This is critical information for government, intermediary nonprofit, and foundation analysts trying to construct and refine annual budget requests. Government and nonprofit contract and grant administrators should routinely forward this and other performance information back to their budget department analysts. As budget actors, nonprofit service delivery partners typically demonstrate a client-centered, professional perspective similar to that of government departments and programs.

In addition to providing services, many social service nonprofits define their role as actively advocating for citizens in need. The annual government budget process provides a forum in which nonprofits may raise social justice issues and advocate on behalf of their clients. As independent organizations, nonprofits hold important rights to free speech and advocacy. The public participation workshops and public hearings in the annual budget process provide opportunities for nonprofits to explain community needs, advocate for programs, and demonstrate the successes of effective service delivery.

In many communities, local government departments have partnered to such a degree that their program capacity has become severely limited (Milward and Provan 2000). This capacity often is shifted to community or regional nonprofits. Overly aggressive advocacy by strong nonprofits may overshadow government program and department recommendations for funding and program targets (Berry and Arons 2003). Excessive advocacy or political pressure in the budget process by nonprofits, especially those in contractual partnerships with local governments, may be interpreted by the public as unethical or self-serving.[2]

Department Heads and Departmental Budget Staff

In most local jurisdictions—cities, towns, counties, and special districts—departmental requests are the primary components of a proposed budget that the chief executive officer assembles and presents to the legislative body. These departmental budgets are produced through an internal process that requires the consolidation of the various subunits (i.e., divisions, offices, and program-level budgets) into aggregated requests. The departmental structures help to integrate individual divisions and programs into a seamless provision of services to clients. The departmental budget provides a primary tool to support this integration, and the department head administrators are responsible for this consolidation process. A similar process occurs at the state and federal levels, where cabinet-level department budget officers consolidate the requests from agencies, agency departments, programs, and multiple field offices.

The department budget officer and the department budget staff lead the integration process. The budget officer is responsible for matching expected resource levels with requests from program managers and field supervisors for funds, personnel, contracting authority, and capital purchases. This matching must be aligned within resource constraints and the chief executive officer's policy priorities (chapter 10). In cases where the chief executive officer serves at the pleasure of the elected body or board (as is the case with most city managers and many nonprofit executive directors), these policy priorities reflect the previous work the chief executive officer has done both formally and informally with members of the body or board. Examples of a CEO's formal work with the body or the board include priority setting and strategic planning sessions that occur prior to the start of the formal budget process. Informal work can take the form of one-on-one meetings with each member of the elected body or board making the final decision on the chief executive's proposed budget submission.

The department budget officer and staff analysts play a critical role in winnowing the program- and advocacy-centered requests that are advanced from below. After review, selection, and refinement by the department head, the analysts integrate the short list into a requested budget that aligns with the policy priorities and financial constraints set forth in the CEO's budget instructions and guidance message at the beginning of the budget process. This "winnowing role" places the department budget analysts in frequent tension between serving client needs and adhering to the fiscal limitations created by the CEO's policy priorities. In contrast to program-level analysts who respond to client and staff needs, department budget staff are subjected to the policy agenda set by the department heads appointed by the chief executive officer. Understanding the need to keep citizen, clients, and interest groups informed of budget developments, some departments develop formal and informal advisory groups and public involvement processes to explain budget and funding changes. These involvement opportunities also allow departments the chance to gather citizen and client advice on how best to narrow program spending requests to align with available resources.

Chief Finance Officer, Organization Budget Officer, and the Central Budget Office

The preparation of the chief executive officer's proposed budget proceeds under the direction of the chief executive's staff and the director of the central budget office. Depending on the executive officer's preference and the organization's structure, the chief financial officer (CFO), the finance department director, or the organization budget officer can serve as the budget office director. The staffing and capacity of the central budget office varies from a dedicated, highly professional, knowledgeable, and nonpolitical staff to a single town clerk who performs budget duties in addition to other finance and administration tasks. Whatever the size, the central budget office staff assists the chief executive in the preparation of the proposed budget and serves as a critical bridge between the nonpartisan administrative units of the jurisdiction and the more political and partisan members of the legislative body. The central budget office provides a framework and structure to ensure that the chief executive can successfully balance the trade-offs between the fiscal constraints of the jurisdiction/organization on the one hand and the political aspirations of elected officials and board members to fund their personal priorities on the other.

Following the chief executive officer's policy priorities and fiscal and economic constraints, the central budget office aggregates all budget requests from the various departments and units of the local jurisdiction. The central budget office exerts its influence early in the budget process with the release of its budget instructions and guidelines (chapter 10). These instructions set the activity schedule, the analysis standards, the procedures, and formats that department and program analysts will follow in their budget preparation efforts. Once the departments submit their budget requests, the central budget office analysts examine the requests and place them in context with the CEO's priorities and available resources. Budget aggregation by the central budget office serves, at least temporarily, to resolve interdepartmental and agency conflicts and competition for resources.

With the aggregation of the funding requests into a single document, the broad fiscal impacts of the proposed budget can be recognized and analyzed (chapter 15). The structural balance between estimated continuing revenues and proposed continuing expenditures becomes a central analytic element at this stage of the budget process. Integration also allows the initial development of the political strategies and tactics necessary to gain the support of the legislative body elected or appointed for its adoption. As the budget is integrated and concerns for political and fiscal viability increase, individual program demands and client needs tend to become less of a priority focus.

As demonstrated in the teaching case introducing Part I, a chief finance officer, a finance director, or an organization budget officer can lead the central budget office. These senior administrators may report to the CEO, but they have substantial independent clout in the budget process, and they usually hold sufficient stature to have a direct relationship with the elected officials or board of directors. The teaching case demonstrates that this relationship is often built on solid, consistent technical performance rather than on political strength. Finance officers, finance directors, and organization budget officers frequently find themselves negotiating their mutual relationship boundaries with the executive and the board.

Revenue and Service Demand Forecasters

Estimating and predicting future revenues for the coming fiscal year is the most politically significant undertaking in the budget process because it sets the expectations for the degree to which expenditures will have to be cut or increased to reach a balanced budget. If the forecast is too low, programs will be cut unnecessarily and employees will be laid off. If the forecast is too high, programs may be expanded prematurely with the need to reverse course toward the middle or end of the budget year. Forecasting for the pending fiscal year reflects the recent and immediate changing health of the local, regional, and state economy that supports the community's tax bases. Forecasters also often develop long-term forecasts (6–10 years) that predict revenues based on the capacity and anticipated growth trends of the local and regional economy. These forecasts set realistic expectations on future revenues and help to ensure the underlying structural balance of the government or organization budget (chapter 7).

In large cities and counties, dedicated revenue sources (licenses and permits, dedicated taxes like gas tax, user fees, grants) are forecast by department experts, not central budget staff. Central staff typically deal with nondedicated taxes (property, sales, and—where used—income and wage) and other general revenues like franchise fees and interest earnings. In smaller jurisdictions, central budget office analysts may perform all forecasts in consultation with the department heads and department analysts. As budget actors, forecasters approach their task from a technical perspective tempered with sound professional judgment.

At the federal level and in many states, a work group within the central budget office collects data and performs the technical analysis to build revenue forecasts. A governor's council of economic advisors or a professional advisory group of academic economists, corporation economists, and business representatives review and critique the budget office's technical forecasts. This external review step provides a means to gain experiential and obscure information and to accept public concerns and criticisms in the form of professional advice and debate. Effective use of an economic council or professional review group assists in the building of an accepted technical foundation for subsequent legislative debates. Using a review group can also help to remove charges of political influence in the forecasting process.

In keeping with the need to ensure technical validity and control political influence, some states have established service demand or caseload forecast councils. Technical analysis units in the various state agencies typically perform the initial caseload demand analyses for K–12 student counts, university student counts, corrections and prison counts, and other social service caseloads. Such caseloads define the program levels and revenue needs in a proposed budget. These units also provide effective technical capacity, but a service demand forecast council allows outside experts the chance to publicly review and critique the forecast estimates for changing field conditions and methodological quality.

The Chief Executive Officer (CEO)

Unique among all the budget actors, the chief executive officer is involved throughout the entire budget process. The intensity of this involvement, whether direct or indirect, varies with the agency and the stage of the budget process. In larger jurisdictions (including large cities and counties) and in large nonprofits, the central budget office or a designated staff person may serve as the proxy for the chief executive's involvement in the budget development process. In smaller jurisdictions and in most small- and medium-sized nonprofit organizations, the process is coordinated directly by the CEO or by the person in charge of the budget or finance office.

If the CEO of a local jurisdiction is an elected official (e.g., strong mayor configuration) rather than a career administrator, then he or she becomes the visible target for lobbying efforts by a variety of interest groups and citizen coalitions. These groups expect the executive to use the budgeting process to deliver on commitments and policy priorities about which they care deeply. Unlike legislators from a specific district, the elected executive must develop broad community support. In the end, the chief executive must balance the policy desires of particular constituent groups against the political losses of refusing to support their claims. The executive may decide to forego the support of specific groups who make costly demands but do not provide compensating political benefits. Local governments tend to establish a variety of citizen advisory boards, committees, and commissions to gain recommendations on issues and policy. Some of these boards contribute more than advisory roles. Local planning commissions and development permit review boards frequently have rule interpretation and adjudication authority. Resolutions and recommendations on policy and budget matters adopted by these boards may not always carry the force of law, but they still stand as important statements that carry political weight with the chief executive officer. The citizen **appointed commissions** and boards described in Exhibit 4.1 add another twist to the budget puzzle for governors in states with populist, decentralized governance arrangements. Governors, too, may need to weigh board and commission recommendations against the need to meet fiscal constraints. Adverse political reactions may result if recommendations are not followed or if communication and explanations between the citizen board and the governor falter.

In addition to balancing political considerations, the chief executive officer must assure the fiscal integrity of the budget. At the local and state levels, this may include meeting constitutional requirements for preparing a balanced budget in which proposed spending matches anticipated revenues. These conditions usually put the chief executive in the position of limiting desired spending increases by constituent groups, department heads, and service provider network partners. This is one of the inevitable consequences of creating an integrated budget—one that has to take into account the realities of the economy and the revenue it can generate.

When the chief executive serves at the pleasure of the legislative body, as is frequently the case at the local level of government and almost always the case in nonprofit organizations, there is much less explicit advocacy. Rather, the executive's role is more facilitative in nature and focused on the council or board's policy priorities, the impact of the budget on the fiscal health of the jurisdiction, and the performance of the organization. In the end, whether appointed or elected, the executive's proposed budget will reflect a balancing act that combines political considerations with the fiscal and economic conditions. This balance constrains the framework and parameters for negotiation on budget decisions.

An important role for both appointed and elected executives in the budget process is an assessment of the impact of any mandatory requirements that have resulted from the passage of recent federal or state legislation, citizen initiatives, or judicial rulings. These mandates include compliance with such federal environmental, homeland security, disabilities, and education requirements. Statutory requirements such as these add to the budget negotiation framework and parameters. The executive must work through and negotiate the meaning and implications of these requirements with both the staff and elected officials. Nonprofit executives may need to consider these same statutes because their funding and program requirements can affect grant and contract performance requirements.

Once the CEO's proposed budget has been developed and presented to the legislative body, he must execute a political strategy to assure its passage (Forsythe 2004). This is the case whether the chief executive is elected or appointed. Of course, the dynamics of the strategy are seriously altered by the kind and amount of independence the executive has from the legislative body (chapter 15). For example, in many states, the governor may have line-item veto authority, which means she can disapprove specific provisions of the budget passed by the state legislature without endangering approval of the budget as a whole. While an elected chief executive may need to trade the funding of her policy initiatives with the legislature's priorities, the underlying fiscal integrity of the budget remains a primary concern. Local government executives who serve at the pleasure of the legislative body do not enjoy the kind of independence experienced by most governors.

The adoption of a budget by local government is a legislative action that makes the budget document law. Once the city or town council, county commission, special district board, or other

Exhibit 4.1

Appointed Boards and Commissions

The states and federal governments frequently make use of executive **appointed boards and commissions**. Some states have adapted the local government commission system (chapter 1) to include the oversight of executive departments and agencies (Morgan 2005). Members of these governing boards and commissions are nominated by the governor and confirmed by the state senate. As defined by statute, board and commission members may represent the general public or specific constituent interests affected by the department. In contrast to an advisory or regulatory role, these commissions often hold the authority to appoint the related department executive, to promulgate applicable policy and regulations, and to oversee the finances and budget of the related department. State board and commission examples may include transportation and highways, state parks, liquor control, lottery, forestry, fish and wildlife, higher education, and K–12 education. While service on these boards and commissions is distanced from partisan politics, their members owe a political debt to the chief executive who appointed them.

At the federal level, the Federal Energy Regulatory Commission (FERC), the Federal Trade Commission (FTC), and the Food and Drug Administration (FDA) are examples of the commission approach to governance. The president nominates five to nine members with U.S. Senate confirmation to a specified term to provide governance oversight of a limited range of activities. These activities are specified by statute and bounded by a body of case law and court precedents. The major difference from the local government commission system discussed in chapter 1 is that the members of regulatory commissions are appointed, not elected, and their role combines legislative, executive, and judicial functions. Federal commissions oversee the setting of rates for utilities and for public transportation, the licensing of use of public communication airways, the establishment of rules for "fair competition," the regulation of the money supply and the economy, and measures ensuring food and drug safety. In addition to setting policies governing such issues, commissions implement the policies and adjudicate cases that are brought by aggrieved parties.

The members of state and federal boards and commissions generally have some degree of expertise or interest in the substantive area of the related department. However, this level of knowledge may be minimal. Board and commission members commonly have limited backgrounds in public finance or in the jurisdiction's budget process; rather, they provide a lay, public perspective on department budget construction and finances. The department budget and finance staff must make a special effort to educate and clearly communicate with the citizen appointees of the department's board or commission. Like the division and program analysts, the board and commission members have a relatively narrow fiscal view limited to department expenditures and specific sources of revenue.

By statute, board and commission members may be in a position to raise fees for services and other revenues to cover department expenses. This authority to generate funds is critical to the development of a balanced budget request. However, increased fees may adversely affect the citizens and constituent groups served by the department. After consideration and review, the board or commission must ratify the department's proposed budget and fee rates. After ratification by the board or commission, the agency submits its budget to the chief executive's central budget office for consolidation into the integrated chief executive's budget.

The commission system significantly undermines the ability of the executive branch to present a unified budget to the legislative body for debate and approval. The extensive use of citizen boards and commissions dilutes executive power by forcing the executive to realign the priorities of the separate commissions with the unifying priorities of the official proposed budget. Local governments do not make extensive use of the commission form of government. To do so would further confound their ability to create a shared sense of the common good.

government legislative body has formally adopted the budget, the CEO and the organization leadership are responsible for its faithful execution. This includes being bound by the budget spending limits. The executive must ensure that the organization keeps overall spending within the legislatively adopted limits. Any significant changes in funding reallocation may require legislative approval by the council or board (chapter 17). Each state and local governing body has legal requirements that determine the amount of discretion the chief executive has to transfer funds between programs and fund accounts. Even when legal requirements for reallocation approval are not needed, it is common practice for the executive and the chief financial officer of the jurisdiction to keep members of the council or board fully informed of any major changes from the formally adopted budget. The faithful execution of the budget is one of the major factors shaping the goodwill and future cooperative relationship between the two branches of government.

In contrast, nonprofit organization budgets do not have the force of law. A budget adopted by the nonprofit governing board is a working plan and forecast for the coming fiscal year. As a private entity, the nonprofit may change its budget at any time. While this flexibility reduces compliance pressure on the nonprofit executive, the public announcement of the annual budget and its funding of grants, contracts, and agreements with external partners creates pressure to stick with the original adopted budget provisions and limits. For this reason, the nonprofit budget and its executive performance requirements resemble those of a government organization more than that of a private corporation. Executive performance in meeting and complying with budget provisions may become a major factor in determining continued employment and executive contract renewal.

The Local Government Legislative Body

Reflecting the wide variety of local governments and state statutes, local legislative bodies go by a variety of names: city or town council; county commission, board, or court; town selectmen; special district board of directors. Whatever the name, local governing bodies are citizen legislatures composed of members who come from all walks of life. While legislators bring political expertise and the expertise of a personal profession, most are not legislative or public finance specialists. Many local elected officials and most nonprofit board members are part-time and unpaid workers, which means they rely heavily on the central budget office staff to frame the issues, provide background briefings, and supply enough analytic and long-term financial information for decision-making purposes. This organizational structure contrasts sharply with the systems that operate at the state and national levels of government.

Whether part-time or full-time, most elected officials choose to run for office because they have programmatic priorities or issues they would like to see addressed. Without a record of at least some success in delivering on the promises made during the heat of an election campaign, a candidate's chances for reelection are slim. It is common practice for legislators at all levels of government to avoid blame for policy and performance failures while taking credit for successes. Senior career administrators must recognize this simple truth and do all they can to boost the reputations of elected officials in the eyes of the citizens they serve. One of the most successful county managers known by the authors of this book served as county administrator for 18 years in the fastest growing county in the state of Oregon. Upon retirement, the county commission renamed the county's administration building in his honor, which is a very rare occurrence indeed. When asked about the secret to his success, he said you have to realize *and accept* that a big part of your responsibility is doing 85 percent of the work that needs to be done by elected officials—but in a way that enables *them* to take the credit. The tenure of career city managers and directors of nonprofit organizations is similarly determined by the extent to which they succeed in accomplishing this simple goal.

Local government jurisdictions and nonprofit organizations are spared the complexity and, thus, much of the conflict that is characteristic of the state and federal budgetary process. Still, it is common for city council, commission, or board members to develop expertise on revenue and budget issues, with newly elected members relying on the old hands members with expertise for technical and procedural information. Because of this mutual dependence, it is important for council, committee, and board members to be aware of the concerns of their fellow members and to keep them fully informed on budget issues throughout the process. If communication is not maintained, the formal budget hearing and adoption process can become unnecessarily contentious and complex. The rule of thumb is that no one should be surprised by a budget or revenue issue during the budget adoption process. If fellow council or board members fail to communicate well, it falls to the executive and the budget/finance staff to provide background briefings on budget and revenue issues. This is the safest course for a local executive to follow when dealing with part-time and unpaid members of the legislative body.

Legislatures and Legislative Committees

As we have mentioned previously, state governments and the federal government rely on the strong separation of branches as defined in their constitutions. These structural arrangements and the political pressures that accompany legislative service help to define the roles and behavior of elected officials. Understanding the basic legislative committee structure, the legislative process, and the pressures that fall on legislators brings some clarity to their behavior as budget process actors.

Legislative Structure and Process Helps Define Roles and Behavior

With the exception of Nebraska, which has a single unicameral legislative branch, state legislatures are divided into a house of representatives (or assembly) and a senate. Each house or senate in turn is divided into a system of committees. The membership of each committee reflects the balance of majority and minority party membership in each house. Legislative success rests on "learning to count," which means gathering dependable support from a sufficient number of committee members to win votes by a majority or a specified rule. One group of committees—the authorizing committees—has substantive authority for reviewing proposed bills in various policy areas. Another set of committees typically has authority for budgeting and appropriating funds to support state programs. While the two sets of committees work together, and their membership may overlap, tensions often appear between the authorizing committee and the budgeting and appropriations committees. The reason for these tensions is reflected in the different purposes of the two committees.

A legislature's authorizing committees are structured to cover the full array of policy and governance issues. Typically, legislative bodies establish committees dealing with human services, natural resources, agriculture, commerce, transportation, energy, public safety, economic development, education, consumer protection, food and drug administration, just to mention some of the more common areas. These committees have responsibility for reviewing proposed bills in their respective areas of expertise, holding hearings to gather information, preparing legislation, and moving their proposed legislation through floor debates to acceptance by the full body.

A legislature's budget and appropriations committees tend to be set up in loose parallel with the authorizing committees. Budget and appropriations committees are divided into subcommittees with expertise in a particular program and issue area. For example, natural resource and social service authorizing committees that provide oversight of these policy domains will have parallel natural resource and social service appropriations subcommittees to provide budget oversight and the approval of expenditures.

A budget committee typically responds to the governor's proposed budget by holding hearings and preparing a budget framework for the entire state government. A revenue or ways and means committee may review the taxes, fees, and other revenues in the budget. An appropriations committee then works within the budgetary framework to allocate funds to the different state programs for spending in the upcoming fiscal year. Agreement on a budget package may mean resolving turf and policy issues among the relevant authorizing committees and appropriations subcommittees in both the house and senate.

Reflecting their position, these spending and revenue-focused committee members commonly develop a level of expertise regarding agency budgets under their purview. However, without professional backgrounds in public budgeting and finance, members of the committee are forced to rely heavily on the information provided by the legislative fiscal and revenue office analysts for any detailed technical understanding. If the legislative body does not have its own source of analysis upon which to rely, it is then dependent on the information provided by the budget and finance office within the executive branch.

Members of appropriations and revenue-centered committees play three roles in the legislative phase of the budget process. First, committee members closely scrutinize agency funding requests and provide routine oversight on agency spending and performance. Second, committee members must forge the agreement to pass and to protect a spending and revenue package. This agreement must include the concerns of the majority leadership, the concerns of the minority, and in some instances the needs of the chief executive. The committee members also need to address the concerns of interested factions of legislators in building a bill and obtaining the necessary agreement to get it passed. The tensions between program and client needs, along with efforts to limit government through fiscal restraint, are often at the center of debate among competing legislative factions.

Finally, revenue and appropriations committees perform a third role by having their members act as floor managers and advocates for the passage of the appropriations bill that will fund the agencies under their charge. In this capacity, committee members work to gather the votes necessary to pass the committee's bill on the floor of the house and senate. As a key to building support, the appropriations/revenue chairs serve as a contact point for legislators as they request funding for special projects in home districts. This control of resources gives the chairs great power in sustaining support for revenue and appropriations bills.

The combination of dual legislative branches, multiple committee systems, partisanship, and the separation of the **authorization** of new legislation from the **appropriation** of money to fund programs fosters factions, disagreement, and tensions within the legislative process. An added dimension is that the passage of the annual/biennial budget is the largest single issue faced by a legislative body and a required legislative action. If a legislature fails to develop and adopt a budget, the state or federal government will shut down at the end of the fiscal year. The need to pass a large number of appropriations bills (or a few very large omnibus bills) each year provides legislators with an opportunity to "make a statement," to "take a stand," and to secure funding for programs of special importance to them personally or to their home district.

Reaching agreement on a budget may be especially difficult when the chief executive and the majority party in the legislature are of different political parties. To prevent a government shutdown, the majority party leadership must steer the session toward the final adoption of several appropriations bills. For example, in the U.S. House of Representatives, the Rules Committee reflects the needs and strategy of the Speaker of the House and the majority party. To exert this authority, the Rules Committee defines the procedural rules for debate and passage for each bill brought before the full House. The rules for consideration of appropriations bills may be especially restrictive to prevent extensive amendments and to ease passage.

Pressures of Legislative Service

State and federal legislators face the continuing task of raising election campaign funds and of running for election. This type of pressure is especially intense on representatives with two-year terms and slightly less so for senators with four- or six-year terms. The pressures of the election cycle condition the behavior of legislators collectively and individually during legislative sessions. For members of Congress, the ongoing need to raise funds for one's own campaigns, and to assist other legislators with their campaigns, is especially strong. Living in the shadow of constant fundraising and campaigning keeps legislators keenly sensitive to home issues, party priorities, and the expectations of important advocacy groups. All legislators, regardless of party ideology, must demonstrate responsiveness to these types of political demands.

The difficulty of building legislative agreement at the state and national levels and the incredible complexity of most public policy issues leave legislators with a very challenging and unappreciated task. For most legislators, developing the necessary legislative skills and mastering the policy and budget knowledge for one or more issue areas requires a long learning process over several legislative sessions. Term limits have blocked this extended learning process in many states and local jurisdictions (National Conference of State Legislatures 2011a). Term limits also have become the common practice for nonprofit boards and academic institutions (Association of Governing Boards of Universities and Colleges 2013).

Term limits may prevent the domination by an old guard of power brokers, but there are a number of adverse consequences that go along with their implementation. First, there is a resulting loss of expertise in leadership knowledge, and in negotiating and process management skills. Second, policy expertise and institutional memory get lost. Without a permanent staff to sustain experience, the accumulated knowledge and power of the legislature may slowly slip to the more permanent agencies and to the private advocacy lobby.

Agencies, Departments, Divisions, and Programs as Budget Implementers

Upon legislative or board adoption of the executive's proposed budget, departments and program staffs turn to program implementation and service delivery. These tasks identify and respond to the implications of the adopted budget on program structure, staffing, organization structure, contracting authority, service delivery, and policy. The legislative body may provide only a terse sentence or two of program guidance in a budget ordinance. It falls to the chief executive officer, the department heads, program leads, technical specialists, and even line supervisors to translate those terse program legislative comments and a funding level in the budget ordinance into an effective program. In smaller cities, towns, counties, and special districts, it is often the administrative memos, directives, and conversations between the chief executive and his or her department heads that provide the opportunities for interpreting the intent of the legislative body and for developing an action plan to implement program spending. In these circumstances, administration is direct, interpersonal, and often informal.

In large cities and counties, however, more formal expressions of intent are commonly relied upon to give meaning to the final budget passed by the legislative body. In addition to the formal budget document, these may include budget notes and the records of discussion and expressions of intent by individual board members in casting their votes on the budget. These expressions of intention may be complemented by formally adopted board goals, priorities, operational plans, oversight processes and other protocols for maintaining administrative accountability to board intentions. Nevertheless, administrators may still find themselves needing to interpret budget directions. External and political pressures sometimes cloud efforts to interpret and apply the newly adopted budget even further, and formal policy statements from the executive may be needed to communicate a uniform understanding of program and performance intent. Within the budget implementation guidelines provided by the chief executive, department and program administrators may modify programs, adjust staffing, reform staff behavior, implement new procedures, arrange new grants and contracts, set up new information and financial systems, and involve other agencies, nonprofits, and the public to meet the new spending direction.

In this implementation mode, administrators need financial information that can measure the expenditure of appropriated funds over the budget cycle. Detailed management-oriented information is also needed to measure program outcomes and efficiency. Unfortunately, agency managers and administrators may have little understanding or appreciation of the usefulness of such numerical outcome and efficiency measures. In a further complexity, program service delivery often involves the multiparty arrangements discussed above, including contracts and grants for services, comprehensive and extended contractual partnerships, intergovernmental agreements, and networked partnerships. Administrators need the management and reporting tools to track partner accomplishment and performance information across organizational boundaries.

At the state and federal levels, the task of interpreting and understanding legislative intent in budget and appropriations documents often becomes much more challenging. Because of the strong separation of the executive and legislative branches, state and federal administrators must reconcile the executive's agenda and authority with legislative direction, as well as with the administrative requirements of efficient and effective program and service delivery. These tensions can become especially challenging when the governor or president is from one political party and the legislative majorities in the legislature or Congress are from another. The implementation of an appropriations act and the guidance in the legislative report that accompanies it may quickly become a task of adroit positioning between competing political demands and administrative effectiveness.

Polity Government and Nonprofit Partners as Implementers

Adoption of a new budget by a local government also sets in motion a response process among contractors, grantees, partner governments, and community nonprofits. These partners are highly dependent on the funding, administrative guidance, and policy decisions embedded in the newly adopted budget ordinance. The executives, finance directors, program leads, and analysts with partner organizations begin by assessing the expenditure levels, program guidance, and policy statements in the budget ordinance and its accompanying guidance. Initial assessments give an indication of continued funding and program policies or of potential changes in program levels and performance requirements. Additional information on program continuation or changes appears after the local government organization executive and staff interprets the budget ordinance and develops an action plan for its implementation. Local government contract and grant administrators, along with midlevel government program coordinators, play a critical role in explaining to partners the implications brought by the new budget.

Based on the provisions and implications of the newly adopted budget, partner organizations face the decision of continuing with the current intergovernmental, contract, grant, or partner relationship, or seeking to change it. Changes in funding levels or performance requirements may indicate that the partner can no longer meet performance requirements or retain the integrity of its organization. Program, performance, or policy changes in the local government budget may come into conflict with the partner's organizational mission and values, capacity, or donor intentions. The partner's board of directors must review the new budget and its implications and determine whether to proceed with the partnership or network membership. In many instances, a new local government budget will bring sufficient funds and few, if any, policy changes. Partner board review may be a nonevent.

If the local government is a member of a network of providers, its budget decisions may ripple back, thus affecting the other network partners. In a participant-governed network, all network members would engage in joint dialogue to assess the implications of the funding levels and policy changes adopted by local governments, major nonprofit intermediaries, and other major donors. On the other hand, if the local government serves as the lead organization and primary donor in the network, it would likely have contractual or other administrative mechanisms for more direct control on program size and partner performance.

Finance Officers and Auditors

As the government departments, programs, and agency divisions turn to implementing the new budget direction, the need for management-oriented financial information becomes greatest. Government finance officers, business managers, and town clerks play an important role in this phase of the budget process. In contrast to the earlier planning and program development stages of budgeting, the dual goals of control and delivery of services drives this phase of the budget process. The control orientation is twofold: (1) it focuses on the proper legal use of appropriated funds and resources; and (2) it emphasizes the measurement of the effectiveness and efficiency with which program administrators meet their statutory directives.

At the department, division, and agency levels, financial controls work to ensure that program spending occurs at the intended levels. Control measures also monitor the rate of spending over the fiscal year or biennium, as well as prevent agency overspending at the end of the budget period. Disbursement ceilings, quarterly allocations, and variance reporting provide the tools for these forms of spending control (see chapter 17).

At the division and program levels, cost accounting and other management-oriented tools help to increase the effective and efficient use of appropriated funds. In this role, financial analysts frequently design objective measures that can provide supervisors and managers with short-term and medium-term perspectives on program outcomes and productivity. Aggregated into a longer-term perspective, this same information provides a basis for performance reporting and program planning in budget development. For example, a program manager with longitudinal historical information on various measures of program performance can assemble a long-term strategic plan for the development and allocation of program resources. There is wide variation among agencies in their systematic use of this kind of information for ongoing managerial purposes. In chapter 13, we will discuss in greater detail how performance measurement can be undertaken in ways that tie it more closely to program planning and budgeting.

Sufficient and accurate financial and program information is necessary to support external audits and investigations of agency activities. Audits and investigations can serve a useful purpose for the agency. In some cases, investigations can publicly demonstrate a need for increases in program resources, staff, and funding. In other circumstances, audits and investigations can build legitimacy and public confidence in an agency or program. Although often regarded as intrusive and stressful, audits and investigations are an important complement to the oversight of department activities and programs by elected officials and boards of directors.

As professionals, agency finance officers ground their work in the standards of professional practice. For example, auditors follow the standards established by the Auditing Standards Board (ASB), which serves as the senior technical committee designated by the American Institute of Certified Public Accountants (AICPA) to issue auditing, attestation, and quality control standards. Governmental financial officers follow the standards established by the Government Accounting Standards Board (GASB). Private professional associations establish many of the standards governing financial management issues. Consequently, one of the challenges for those working for government and nonprofit agencies is to place financial analysis into a larger context—one where technical, managerial, and legislative tasks may well place greater priority on values other than those emphasized by the national accounting and financial professions. For example, auditors may want to have all of the funds balanced on a quarterly basis, which serves the ends of financial control but is hardly realistic for government and nonprofit programs that are self-funded or that rely largely on donations booked near the end of the calendar year. These tensions between external professional standards and what makes sense for clients or for managerial purposes add another important dimension to the competing values that must be reconciled as part of the budget development and implementation process.

BUDGET ACTOR ROLE CONFLICTS: IMPLICATIONS FOR DEMOCRATIC GOVERNANCE

The conflicting perspectives of budget actors summarized in the previous section result from different professional expectations of "what counts for success." For example, financial analysts, accountants, and public administrators reflect the traditions and standards of their professions. These standards filter, focus, and constrain their work products. In contrast, elected officials must meet the needs of the voters and of their constituents and, in the process, demonstrate legislative success. Those responsible for managing an organization with the goal of delivering high performance have yet another set of interests that are not always in alignment with the priorities of finance/budget professionals and elected officials. Out of these competing purposes, elected officials—supported by the staff and professional career administrators—forge the larger public interest.

Despite their differences in purpose, elected officials, managers, and financial professionals actually pursue a common goal. All perform an oversight and control function over the bureaucracy by being responsible for different kinds of accountability. The elected officials are accountable for being responsive to the needs and wants of the citizens. Managers are accountable for the efficient and effective delivery of program services. Finance professionals are accountable for maintaining the fiscal integrity of government operations. Together, these oversight roles, while often viewed with suspicion by administrative leaders who want to build an organizational culture of trust, contribute to the generation of trust and build legitimacy in the bureaucracy. Financial and performance audits conducted by external, independent auditors may provide some assurance of expected performance to members of the public who don't share the program's organizational or professional cultures, or who do not personally use the services but must nonetheless pay for them through taxes and fees.

In keeping with these different role responsibilities, the analytic capabilities and information needs of each budget actor group varies considerably. For example, those preparing budget requests at the individual program level are primarily concerned about the programmatic consequences of the budget and the ability to meet client needs. However, building this base requires a strong analytic capability and the ability to organize large amounts of detailed information. Reworked into larger and more integrated programmatic formats, this same information may be very useful for program managers, for other financial analysts, and for auditors.

In contrast to the focus of program managers on client needs, chief executives and legislators serve as generalists in the budget process. Elected officials prefer aggregate data with limited detail. This is because they are accountable for the context and the larger political implications related to budget proposals rather than for the actual value of the numbers themselves. To provide the most help for elected officials and other generalists, financial analysts must be able to drastically simplify their findings into clear concepts and a few key numbers. As elected officials examine the proposed budget, fiscal concerns over the size and role of government often begin to emerge. In many instances, concerns over the size and role of government in the market economy may conflict with programmatic goals. For example, an elected official may favor unfettered competi-

Exhibit 4.2

Purposes of a Public Budget

Purpose	Kinds of information necessary	Who cares and kinds of needed expertise
1. To implement rational plans	Information on mission, goals, objectives	Department heads; program planners, who have both operational and client-based knowledge.
2. To allocate scarce resources	Very little, if allocation uses existing base and "fair share" formula	Chief executive; legislators; citizens, clients, and program managers
3. To promote efficiency and effectiveness	Considerable performance information regarding efficiency and effectiveness	Chief executive; legislators; citizens, clients, and program managers
4. To achieve accountability		
a. Monetary/financial	Detailed tracking and control systems	Accountants/auditors
b. Effectiveness	Performance information regarding achievement goals	Managers at all levels of the organization
c. Efficiency	Cost-benefit information	Economists, program managers
d. Political	Political forums that require career administrators to justify actions	Elected officials
5. To create commonly shared organizational and community values	Value differences of participants and a process for reconciling	Citizens and stakeholders, elected officials
6. To regulate the economy	Constructs that serve as surrogates for a healthy economy such as unemployment, housing starts, inflation rate, etc.	Economists, citizens, politicians
7. To redistribute wealth	Income and wealth distribution information among socioeconomic classes	Citizens, elected officials, economists

tion in the private marketplace but choose the programmatic protection of a particular industry important to his/her constituent base.

With such a variety of professional backgrounds and process goals at play in the budgeting process, along with the adversarial nature of the process itself, it is not surprising that tensions and misunderstandings arise among the various actors. However, because this conflict occurs within a deliberately crafted structure of authority, some of it is tempered by role expectations that are understood and widely accepted. For example, the legislative perspective will differ from that of the program manager and the chief executive, both of whom are expected to be responsive to different clientele and constituency influences. Likewise, department heads assume that their program managers will ask for more funding than is budgetary possible. In turn, program managers assume that their requests for funding are likely to be cut. The same analogous set of expectations is repeated as the budget moves from one set of actors to another, up through the bureaucratic chain, and then to the legislative body for deliberation and approval.

Exhibit 4.2 summarizes the multiple purposes and actors that are part of the public budgeting process. It uses the information from chapter 3 on the purposes of a public budget to show how these purposes align with the roles of the various actors in the budgeting process and the kinds of information they need to carry out their respective roles.

By matching the kind of information needed with the expertise required, one acquires a greater appreciation for the multiple sources of complexity and conflict that are inherent in almost all public budgeting. One also acquires a better understanding of how each of the roles plays an important accountability function that contributes to the larger public good. The budgeting process carries the primary burden for successfully managing this complexity and conflict, probably more so than any other activity that the government undertakes. In fact, we frequently judge the success of our government in general by how well it accomplishes this monumentally difficult budget-balancing task. In the next chapter, we will further examine how the rules of engagement that routinize and norm the budgeting process temper the potential for conflict, thus reducing tensions and increasing the possibility for agreement.

STUDY QUESTIONS

1. Consider the standards and practices that count for success among the various participants in the budget process for an organization or jurisdiction of your choosing. How many distinct actors can you identify? How do the standards for measuring the success of each actor compare? Use the blank form in Exhibit 4.3 that follows to record your observations.

2. What are the most common conflicts that predictably arise during the budgeting process? What factors most contribute to the successful resolution of these conflicts?

3. Consider the most recent budget analysis or audit with which you have been involved. How would you repackage the analysis results for a member of a council, a board of directors, or a legislative appropriations/ budget/ revenue or ways and means committee? Consider how you might recast your findings in order to be as clear and precise as you can.

4. In a situation involving several competing program needs, consider how you might allocate funding among these programs. What technical tools would you rely upon to make your allocation? Think about how a member of a city council or legislature might make the same allocation. How might pressure from interest groups, constituents, and the legislature influence the legislator's allocation?

5. What are some useful strategies for reducing conflict between elected officials and program administrators during the budget allocation process?

6. What types of financial analysis might support program managers during the program-spending phase of the budget process? How might you demonstrate the value and uses of such analytic products to a skeptical manager?

Exhibit 4.3

Budget Actors Exercise: Contrasting Roles and Perspectives

Budget process actor	Clientele representation (directly or implicitly represents)	Substantive orientation: fiscal or programmatic	Career orientation: professional or political
Budget Preparation			
Programs, divisions, departments as requestors			
Polity network nonprofits and partner governments as requestors			
Department and agency heads			
Chief finance officer, budget officer, and the central budget office			
Revenue forecasters and caseload forecasters			
Preparation and Release of Proposed Budget			
Chief executive officer (CEO): e.g., city manager, county executive, district or nonprofit executive, state governor			
Budget Adoption			
Local government legislative body: e.g., city council, town council, county commission, district board of directors			
State legislature: program authorizing committees			

Exhibit 4.3 *(continued)*

Budget process actor	Clientele representation (directly or implicitly represents)	Substantive orientation: fiscal or programmatic	Career orientation: professional or political
State legislature: budget, appropriations, revenue, ways and means committees			
Budget Implementation			
Programs, divisions, and departments as implementers			
Polity network nonprofits and partner governments as implementers			
Finance officers, clerks, business managers as budget implementers			
Agency internal financial analysts and auditors; external auditors			

NOTES

1. Wide variation of state laws results in variation in local government budget processes and terminology. We use the term *proposed budget* here as typical of an organization-level, balanced operating budget that reflects the executive's agenda and recommendations, and is ready for delivery to the legislative body for consideration and adoption. Other terms with similar usage include *executive proposed budget, executive recommended budget, approved budget,* and in some instances, *preliminary budget.* Chapter 5 on budget cycles provides additional discussion.

2. For this argument we draw on material from "Local Government as Polity Leadership: Implications for New Public Governance" (in Morgan and Cook, 2014, chap. 12).

5

THE BUDGET CYCLE
CHARACTERISTICS AND CONSEQUENCES

As the seasons change from hot to cold
And I watch the leaves change their clothes
From green, to brown, from red to gold
They never seem to change their souls.
They remain humble even as they grow old. . . .
(Sharonda D. Chery 2009)

When I tread,
in secret, untrodden snow
with Winter
I shuffle, beside the low sun,
through crisp, golden chestnut leaves
of Autumn
and dance with daisies
in the wild meadow
of Summer.
(Sally Plumb 2010)

The budgeting process can best be viewed as a series of seasons, with characteristic patterns of activities and behaviors that occur in each phase of budget development, adoption, and implementation. The budget development and **budget adoption** seasons demand especially high energy and focus from participants. During these phases of the budget process, participants expend an abundance of activity on gathering, analyzing, organizing, and presenting information. As in spring, there is a lot of dust in the air, and preparations are being made for planting. Under these pressing circumstances, the time allotted to complete budgeting-related activities is never enough to meet deadlines. This is not only because the preparation and adoption season is short, but also because many participants must keep up with other duties that are not directly connected with their seasonal budget responsibilities. As spring gives way summer and the extended period of budget implementation, participants become more relaxed. The close of the budget year and the post-budget audit seasons resemble fall and winter, where the heat of budget preparation gives way to taking stock of the budget harvest and its implications for the next seasonal round of activity.

In this chapter, we explore the distinctive characteristics of the budgeting seasons and the behavioral consequences for participants. An understanding of these seasonal dimensions of public budgeting is important in helping us establish realistic expectations of what the public budgeting process can and cannot bear. We also intend to provide readers with a greater understanding of and appreciation for the important role that the budgeting process plays in guiding and regulating the behavior of participants. This process, known as *norming,* helps reduce potential conflict among budget actors and facilitate agreement among various programs and units within the organization.

The primary purpose of the budget process at all levels of government is to produce sufficient agreement to obtain approval of a balanced budget. An effective budget process plays a critical role in reducing the complexity and potential conflict inherent in the procedure. Part of this complexity and conflict arises from the multiple purposes that a budget seeks to achieve. You will recall that in chapter 3, we identified the following, often conflicting, purposes of a public budget:

1. building and maintaining financial control;
2. allocating scarce resources;
3. program coordination;
4. improving program efficiency and effectiveness;
5. communication;
6. protection of the organization's fiscal condition;
7. influencing the economy;
8. a political opportunity for elected officials to exercise leadership;
9. building trust and legitimacy in government agencies and programs.

The political purposes of the budget captured by the last two purposes in the list are especially important. The budget process provides elected leaders with an opportunity to demonstrate leadership of the public organization by setting new priorities for existing government programs and by demonstrating the accomplishment of campaign goals. The process also provides one of the most important means for building public confidence in government organizations, in public revenue strategies, and in the very practice of budgeting. In fact, many argue that the transparency, openness, and fairness of the budget process may be more important than the resulting substantive allocations and appropriations (Global Movement for Budget Transparency, Accountability and Participation 2014; OECD *Best Practices for Budget Transparency* 2014). With so much at stake, participants need to emerge from the process with the will to work cooperatively with each other on future issues.

In addition to the complexity and conflict produced by the multiple purposes of a public budget, the conflicting perspectives among the many budget actors create additional layers of uncertainty and difficulty. We argued earlier in this book that these competing purposes and perspectives are largely the product of the structures and processes we have deliberately constructed to achieve the multiple goals of our various systems of democratic governance. The structural complexity of federalism, separation of powers, and checks and balances reflect as well as contribute to the inherent conflict and complexity that is part of public budgeting. A clear, predictable, and agreed-upon process helps to temper this potential conflict, thereby facilitating the achievement of sufficient agreement to gain formal approval and public acceptance of the budget. The routine predictability of the budgeting process both norms the behavior of the participants and provides an opportunity for agreements and differences of opinion to be aired and carried forward—presumably with sufficient goodwill intact—so that productive policy and budget debates continue in the future.

To summarize our basic argument in this chapter, the public budgeting process must be designed and organized to support what is fundamentally a political process. The roles of elected officials, administrators, interest group advocates, and citizens must be coordinated in order to produce the political agreements necessary to pass and adopt a budget. The more contentious the issues, the greater burden there is on those responsible for the process to build in features that ameliorate conflict. As we will argue in this chapter, the most common techniques that are used to reduce conflict are the principles of **base budget** and **fair share**. *Base* simply means that those who have budget responsibility start with the assumption that last year's budget will serve as the starting point for building next year's budget. *Fair share* means that any large departures from the previous year as a result of dramatic changes in revenues and the overall operation of the economy will be shared "fairly" among participants in the budgeting process. Together these two principles provide "norming rules" that significantly constrain the behavior of participants in the process, reduce the scope of potentially contested issues, and provide a path forward for resolving the allocation of scarce resources.

The statutory requirement of each local government to produce and adopt a balanced budget prior to the beginning of the next **fiscal year** or **biennium** provides an additional incentive that facilitates budget agreement. Failure to meet this requirement results in the loss of authorization for spending, which requires government operations to cease functioning. Most local governments adopt a budget without the kind of political gamesmanship and posturing that is often evident at the federal congressional and some state levels of government. Few elected or administrative officials at the local level are willing to take responsibility for shutting down government programs crucial to the public good.

The budget process of nonprofit organizations shares similar goals and characteristics with local governments. Nonprofits, like government, need a process that ensures technical soundness, facilitates political agreement, builds internal acceptance, and enhances the confidence of external stakeholders and funders. But there are also some important differences between nonprofit and local government budget processes, which we explore in more detail later in the chapter.

This chapter is organized around the following six goals of any successful local public budgeting process:

1. Organize the activities of participants through a schedule that produces approval of a final budget.
2. Create a process that aligns with the scale and needs of the jurisdiction.
3. Respond to the needs and goals of participants.
4. Ensure technical proficiency.
5. Respond to changing conditions.
6. Coordinate budget development with the resource allocation of polity partners.

HOW WELL DOES THE BUDGET PROCESS ORGANIZE ACTIVITIES OF PARTICIPANTS?

All public budgeting processes must guide and coordinate a diverse set of participants toward a final budget agreement that can provide resources and policy direction to agency and organization administrators. These goals are accomplished by ensuring adequate opportunities for chief executives, legislators, agencies, governing boards and appointed commissions, interest groups, and the general public to influence the development of the budget spending allocations and policy directives. A stable, well-publicized process schedule is a critical tool for organizing and negotiating the development of this necessary political agreement.

A stable schedule also (1) provides sufficient lead time for technical preparation of the budget by the various governmental units and programs, and (2) norms the expectations of what is needed by whom and at what time, thus easing the movement of the budget through the six phases of the process.

Budget Process Phases: An Overview

State statutes and regulations define the local government budgeting process and requirements in each state, but local governments often use ordinances to make refinements to the state established process. Despite local variations, all budget processes are divided into the following six phases (see GFOA 1998).

- Executive budget planning
- Preparation of agency, program, or organization requests
- Budget compilation and executive proposal
- Legislative review and adoption
- Departmental and agency implementation
- Audit, reconciliation, and feedback

These six phases recognize a sequential order of events centered on the fiscal year or fiscal biennium. Each process phase triggers a season of work and behavior among budget actors. Unlike the fluid and circular nature of many policy processes, budget processes tend to follow a linear calendar of steps with work product deadlines, and requirements for executive and legislative actions. State regulations often define the exact schedule and dates for task and activity completion. These highly prescriptive processes help to build momentum, contain conflict, and push the actors and the budget process to a timely closure. Each phase of the process builds on the outcomes of earlier phases to produce the needed technical and policy actions and to build public confidence in the budget process and final resource allocations.

Larger jurisdictions typically take a formal approach to the process with strong separation of the executive and legislative roles. Smaller cities, towns, and special districts often use a more collegial process that involves department staff, executives, and elected officials in the planning and development of a proposed budget. Nonprofit organizations use the same basic phases if in modified or attenuated form. Wide acceptance of the standard budget process provides citizens, issue advocates, elected officials, and administrators with a quick understanding of expected events and opportunities for participation at various stages of the process.

Exhibit 5.1 presents a representative budget process for a small city or town. (The budget process for a small- or medium-sized special district would look similar.) Typically, it takes about four months to prepare and adopt a budget. Exhibit 5.1 shows both the months elapsed and the budget phases. It depicts a January 1 to December 31 fiscal year, but the schedule and stages are applicable to other fiscal year starting dates, including July 1 to June 30.

Description of Process Phases

The first step in the budget preparation process is executive planning. As we describe in greater detail in chapter 10, budget planning has become an executive-centered activity. The executive takes the initiative in preparing an organization-wide schedule that establishes responsibilities, work products, and due dates for completing a series of activities by the executive, department heads, chief finance officer or clerk, and the elected officials (GFOA 1998). The executive planning phase also sets forth the economic assumptions and policy guidelines/priorities to be used by participants in submitting their **budget requests**. Many local governments distill the executive phase of the process into a set of budget instructions that give detailed guidelines to the department, program, and central budget office analysts on how to prepare the budget documents. Chapter 10 presents an extended discussion of the budget planning phase.

The second process phase (see Exhibit 5.1) calls on each major department and program to follow the budget instructions and to prepare a comprehensive budget request for the coming fiscal year. This is a season of intense, focused work for the department staff analysts. The department directors and analysts work closely with the town clerk or city finance officer to craft a realistic request that responds to both political agendas and programmatic needs. A department budget request reflects long-term and recent revenue forecasts, workload forecasts, labor agreements and personnel costs, and requests for policy changes. The schedule in Exhibit 5.1 allows one month for the department to prepare its budget request; in reality, however, the department will begin

Exhibit 5.1

Example Small City and Town Budget Schedule (Hypothetical One-Year Fiscal Year January 1–December 31)

Month	Budget Phase	Activity
August	**Budget Planning**	→ Coordination between executive (city manager or mayor) and finance officer or clerk on budget instructions and economic environment.
		→ Optional council, executive, and department head/staff budget meeting. Status update reports, strategic planning, and priority setting.
September	**Prepare Department Requests**	→ Clerk makes budget call to department heads and offices to prepare program requests. Requests include estimates of revenues and costs.
		→ Requests and estimates filed with clerk by end of month.
October (1st wk)	**Executive Proposal and Approval**	→ Requests and estimates presented to executive mayor, city manager (CEO/executive officer). Clerk under direction from CEO makes modifications and consults with departments and programs.
		→ Executive officer presents a balanced preliminary budget to council or board with revenue estimates and any proposed changes to revenues.
October (2nd–4th wk)		→ In some states, council or board holds hearings on revenues, especially on any increases in taxes or fees. Council or board may take several weeks but adopts or rejects changes to tax levies and fee rate schedules.
November (1st wk)		→ Executive prepares a budget message to cover the preliminary (proposed) budget; presents both budget message and budget to the legislative council or board.
November (2nd wk)	**Budget Adoption**	→ Clerk publishes advanced public notice of preliminary (proposed) budget for prescribed announcement period; clerk publishes public hearing dates.
		→ Copies of preliminary (proposed) budget available to public or posted on web.

(continued)

Exhibit 5.1 *(continued)*

Month	Budget Phase	Activity
November (3rd wk)		→ Council or board holds hearings on revenue and spending estimates, and on program requests and estimates; may call department and program heads to testify; may make revisions to preliminary (proposed) budget.
December (1st wk)		→ Final public hearing on proposed budget.
December (2nd wk)		→ Council or board adopts budget.
December (3rd–4th wk)		→ Clerk submits copies of adopted budget finances and certification of tax levies with state officials.
January (1st)	**Budget Implementation**	→ **Fiscal year begins.** Based on adopted budget, staff allocates funds and begins to implement program and spending in budget.
December (31st)		→ Fiscal year ends, all authorized spending activity completed.
January (2nd wk) of year following fiscal year	**Audit and Feedback**	→ Fiscal year closing expenses and revenues booked; audits begin.

Source: Modified to a generalized process from Municipal Research and Services Center (MRSC) 2013.

collecting information on program needs and the analysts will be doing the deep analysis to build the request over the previous summer months. The department budget preparation will come together into a final product in late September. In chapters 11 through 14, we provide a detailed discussion of how departments complete phase two of the budget process for each of the four major types of budget formats currently in use.

In the third phase of the budget process, the clerk [1] or finance officer receives the department requests. After reviewing the requests in detail and consulting with the chief executive officer (CEO), the clerk integrates the separate requests into a consolidated **preliminary budget**. This budget displays all existing and proposed sources and levels of revenue, all proposed expenditures, and all the internal transfers and internal service charges between the different departments and programs. At this point, some states require the public announcement of the proposed preliminary budget for the public review and adoption of any tax and revenue increases necessary to fund it. Review of revenues can include increases or changes to property, sales, or income tax levels, or to fee and charge rate schedules.

Once the revenue levels have been adopted, the clerk consults with the CEO, adjusts expenditure levels as needed to match revenues, and finalizes the preliminary budget document.[2] Because of their decision-making authority and direct control of the process, CEOs make their requests for funding and policy changes through the preliminary budget document. The final preliminary budget may also be known as a **proposed budget**.

In the fourth budget phase, the legislative body—the city or town council, the district board of directors, or the township board—receives the preliminary or proposed budget. The town clerk or finance officer publishes an announcement that a budget is available and that a public process of hearings will be undertaken prior to formal adoption of the budget by the legislative body. For elected officials and issue advocates, this often is a season of reconsidering needs and choices, responding to constituent pleas, building political agreements, and diligent monitoring and nursing of the budget package into law. For town clerks and department analysts, though, this is a season of hurried, last-minute council or board demands for more information and revised analyses.

As the elected legislative body approaches adoption of a final budget, it is common for its members to review the budget in detail and ask department heads and program leads to provide public testimony. The council or board also holds a series of public hearings to take public concerns and comments on the budget. Considering comments and concerns from the hearings, the council or board members may make revisions to the preliminary or proposed budget by vote. The town clerk or the finance officer helps to ensure the technical integrity of any changes to the budget. The legislative body then votes to adopt the budget by ordinance or resolution. The budget must be adopted well in advance of the first date of the pending fiscal year, which is prescribed in state regulation. In the Exhibit 5.1 example, the city council must adopt the budget by the second week of December in order for the budget to be ready for implementation by January 1, which begins the new fiscal year. The adopted budget takes the form of an ordinance or resolution passed by the town, city, or district. Any future changes in excess of dollar limits specified in the jurisdiction's financial policies must be made using the ordinance process. The final step in the budget adoption phase is to submit copies of the adopted budget and supporting forms to the appropriate state officials.

Once the budget is adopted, the executive, the clerk or finance officer, and the departments move to phase five of the budget process: implementation. This stage includes allocating the budgeted funds to the various departments and programs, and scheduling allotments of funding for release over the fiscal year. Once the budgeted funds have been allotted, the department and program staff make expenditures following defined procurement regulations and rules. The procurement regulations and rules assure that an electronic or paper trail is available to verify the purpose, date, and amount of spending. In addition to making expenditures, the jurisdiction receives and logs revenues from each of the sources it draws on to fund public activities. Using various accounting and tracking systems, the clerk or finance officer prepares regular reports matching actual spending and receipt of revenues against the adopted budget. These regular reports enable the CEO and department heads to monitor their "real time" cash flow. Should conditions change radically, the executive may request that the council or board consider and adopt an amendment to the adopted budget (chapter 17).

Once the fiscal year or biennium closes, the budget process moves into its final phase (chapter 18). In this, the sixth phase of the process, auditors review spending levels and patterns for appropriate outlay and identify opportunities to increase organizational performance. The audit results typically feed into a **Comprehensive annual financial report (CAFR)**. Audit information also informs the budget planning discussions and the department budget request preparation for the pending fiscal year.

The local budget process is largely executive driven. In a variation, where a CEO elects to delegate authority, the chief financial officer (CFO) or town clerk may exert a dominant control throughout the budget process. Chief financial officers often play a strong guiding role in nonprofit budgeting. Whether through the executive or the finance director, this centralized control demonstrates the competent and energetic governance tradition (chapter 2)—a tradition that embraces systematic planning and the values of government efficiency, effectiveness, and entrepreneurship. The need for timely adoption of a budget prior to the beginning of the next fiscal year, along with requirements for precise financial analysis and auditing, reinforce executive and finance officer dominance of the budget process. Statutory attention to competent and energetic governance may obscure the need to consider the other governance traditions of civic governance, responsive governance, and attentiveness to the needs of minority target populations. Effectively involving and integrating the public into various activities associated with the budget process (i.e., issue framing, priority setting, alternative exploration and decision making) may help to build public confidence in the budget process. Simonsen and Robbins (2000) argue for greater public involvement in budget processes and provide a series of case examples to illustrate ways of accomplishing this goal. However, most citizen involvement in local budget processes is confined to statutorily defined structures in the form of citizen budget committees, a limited number of citizen listening sessions, and formal public hearings.

HOW DOES THE BUDGET PROCESS ALIGN WITH THE SCALE AND NEEDS OF THE JURISDICTION?

While the budget process is marked by some common characteristics that are uniform across jurisdictions, there are important variations that reflect the scale and needs of particular governmental entities. Large cities, county governments, and special districts have a much more complex and extended budget process than is the case for smaller jurisdictions. These larger jurisdictions may take up to 10 or 11 months to prepare and adopt their budget. Still more complex, state governments begin preparation and adoption of an annual or biennial budget up to 18 months ahead of actual implementation. The large numbers of state operating departments, programs, and boards, not to mention the sheer magnitude of dollars spent by state agencies, demand an extended lead time; still, these larger governments follow the same basic budget process phases as smaller jurisdictions.

The size and value of the revenues and program expenses—and the greater likelihood of oversight and public scrutiny in larger governments—require staff who are highly trained and skilled in various types of financial and technical analysis. Large cities and counties typically have the resources to hire budget specialists to produce the required budget documents. The CFO for a large city or county normally manages a small staff of budget analysts. In some counties, deputy county administrators serve as the budget analysts.

Large City and County Processes Provide Greater Opportunities for Public Influence

Exhibit 5.2 displays the flow and relationships of a representative large city budget process. This process, which is more involved, takes about nine months of preparation and adoption time. A large county government would follow a similar path. In this example, the fiscal year begins on January 1 and ends on December 31. For a large city government, the strong mayor, finance officer, and city council are the primary actors. In a county government, the elected county executive or board chair, or the appointed county executive would serve in the executive officer role. The county commission or council would act in the legislative role.

The large city budget process begins with a budget planning stage in late February or early March. This phase includes close communication between the mayor and the finance officer over the budget instructions, the budget schedule, political agendas, the revenue situation, the economic backdrop, and any audit results from the previous years. Preliminary instructions are communicated to city department heads and their analysts by mid-March. Based on the instructions, the department budget analysts quickly begin to prepare the department budget request.

At about the same time in early March, the mayor, council members, the department heads, and department managers hold public listening sessions to gather citizen concerns and recommendations for the budget. The city office of neighborhoods may serve as the venue for systematically reaching all neighborhoods and parts of the city. Advocacy contact between citizens and city

Exhibit 5.2

Example Large City Budget Schedule (Hypothetical One-Year Fiscal Year
January 1–December 31)

Month	Budget Phase	Activity
February	**Budget Planning**	→ Coordination between mayor (or executive) and finance officer on budget instructions, schedule, policy, issue agenda, revenues, economic environment, and audit results.
		→ Finance officer provides budget preliminary instructions and schedule to department and programs.
March	**Prepare Department Requests**	→ Departments hold neighborhood listening sessions to hear public concerns.
March–April		→ Central budget office prepares revenue forecasts.
April		→ Finance officer transmits final budget instructions to departments.
April–May		→ Departments provide central budget office a preview of proposed service levels and requested changes to current adopted budget.
May/June–mid-July		→ Departments prepare operating requests, program modifications, and capital improvement program proposals.
May–June		→ Mayor's office and central budget office provide feedback on departments' preparations.
Late July–August	**Executive Proposal and Approval**	→ Central budget office and mayor's office review department operating requests and capital improvement proposals (CIP).
August–September		→ Mayor's office makes final decisions on spending and policy. Government-wide proposed budget and CIP document produced.
September		→ Mayor presents proposed budget request and CIP program to city council.
September–early October	**Budget Adoption**	→ Central budget office and departments prepare oral presentations for city council on revenues and proposed expenditures.
October–November		→ City council takes testimony from central budget office and department heads. Council reviews proposed budget request, CIP program, and revenue changes in detail.
		→ City council holds public hearings on proposed budget request, revenue changes, and CIP program.

(continued)

Exhibit 5.2 *(continued)*

Month	Budget Phase	Activity
October–November		→ City council proposes and makes revisions to proposed budget request, revenue changes, and CIP program.
Mid-November		→ Final public hearing on proposed budget, revenue changes, and CIP.
Late November		→ Council adopts budget, revenue levels, and CIP.
Late December		→ Finance officer submits copies of budget, CIP, and certification of tax levies to state officials.
January (1st)	**Budget Implementation**	→ **New fiscal year begins.**
Early to mid-January		→ Center budget office and finance staff makes allotments and sets position controls, accounting controls, and encumbrances to control spending.
January to December of fiscal year (12 months)		→ City staff spends funds to implement programs and to make capital investments.
Monthly or quarterly		→ Finance office provides monthly or quarterly revenue status reports and department expenditure reports.
As Needed		→ As necessary, mayor proposes and city council adopts amendments, supplements, or rescissions to the adopted budget. Any adopted changes are recorded in an engrossed budget.
December (31st)		→ Fiscal year ends, all revenues logged, and authorized spending activity completed.
January of year following fiscal year	**Audit and Feedback**	→ Finance office and external auditors review financial compliance. Begin preparation of comprehensive annual financial report (CAFR). Performance audits opened. Preliminary feedback developed for pending budget request.
June of year following fiscal year		→ Release of CAFR.

Sources: City of Bellevue, WA 2005; City of Seattle, WA 2006, p. 10. See also Revised Code of Washington Chapter 35.32A.

officials is especially effective at this early stage of the budget process, before technical analysis and political agreements have limited flexibility to accommodate new spending requests or adjustments to existing programs. Toward late March, the analysts in the city finance office prepare detailed forecasts of taxes, fees, and intergovernmental revenues to support preparation of the budget requests of the department analysts.

By early April, the department budget analysts and program leads have begun the preparation of expenditure requests. Analysts closely follow the budget instructions provided by the central budget office and consult closely with the department heads and program managers to assure accurate estimates and to gain internal support for the requested program. Requested changes to program spending levels and spending policies are highlighted for later inspection. A separate request for capital improvements to facilities and for major equipment purchases is also developed.

The preparation of the department request phase of the budget process is largely closed to the public. Allowing analysts to work in a closed environment lets them concentrate on technical aspects of the budget and develop the broadest array of pre-decisional materials possible for final review and approval by the CEO. At this time, citizens and advocates may have some success influencing the department heads with respect to a particular program. Citizens may also have fruitful discussions with the mayor and council members at this fairly early point in the budget process. As departmental requests are prepared, department analysts consult regularly with their colleagues in the central finance office to ensure compliance with instructions, to confirm that proposed program spending matches forecast revenues, and to guarantee conformity with the political goals of the council and chief executive. Completion of the department requests marks an important milestone, since it creates expectations and starts to mobilize vested interests external to the organization as well as potential alliances within the organization.

In late July and early August, the central finance office requests all departments to submit their final budget proposals and begins the process of compiling the many department submissions into an integrated budget for mayoral approval. Typically, the finance office staff members each take responsibility for a detailed review of one or more departments/programs. This allows staff members to build up familiarity and expertise within a program area. This familiarity increases with each year, which over time allows for deeper analysis and better understanding of program needs. The central finance office staff carefully reviews the proposed funding levels and program changes in the department request, verifies the assumptions of program demand and needs, and checks expenditure levels against revenue forecasts. After reviewing the requests, finance office staff members identify any available funding that could support program increases or changes. Staff members then advocate among each other and with the executive to allocate any extra resources. Following mayoral review and approval of all requests and changes, the finance office staff assembles the budget into the mayor's proposed budget. The proposed budget may also be known as the executive's **approved, recommended,** or **requested budget**. These latter terms reflect the perspective and strong influence of the executive officer in this part of the budget process. Again, this phase of the budget process is closed to public review and comment. Assembly of the proposed budget is a pre-decisional process: The closed process allows the staff to focus on building a technically accurate and balanced budget. Once completed, the proposed budget clearly identifies key issues that need to be addressed by the council, explains how all available revenues will be used, and details the allocation of resources to the various programs. The development of the proposed budget provides an opportunity for the chief executive to frame the debate for budget consideration by the council or commission. The complexity and size of large city (and county) budgets prevents elected councillors and the public from fully understanding the numerous budget decisions made by the executive and the finance office staff. In the sample schedule in Exhibit 5.2, the mayor releases his budget to the public and legislative council in September. This gives the city council about two months to review and adopt a final budget.

The budget adoption phase begins in late September–early October. Here, the city council reviews the executive's proposed budget request and moves through a public review and decision process to adopt the budget by ordinance. Depending on the institutional arrangement, the council may have some staff analysts assist with the legislative review. In many jurisdictions, however, the part-time council is on its own or must rely on the finance office staff for explanation and further analysis. The council announces a schedule of hearings to review revenue forecasts, take testimony from department and program heads, and consider public comment and recommendations. After taking testimony, the council members may propose changes to the budget. These changes are typically incremental adjustments to the mayor's proposal. After weighing commentary on any proposed changes, the council adopts the necessary revenue levies and fee rate structures to fund the budget and then, by ordinance, adopts the budget. The definitions in the executive budget and the complexity of the budget limit the depth of changes the council is likely to make. The public has an opportunity to comment and to make recommendations to the council formally in testimony and through informal contacts, but input at this point may be largely pro forma. Efforts to make changes to the budget require substantial political agreement and energy. The city council must formally adopt the budget to allow a sufficient lead time for administrative processing before the fiscal year begins. A council would complete work on a budget in early to mid-December—two or three weeks before the start of the fiscal year.

In the example in Exhibit 5.2, the fiscal year begins on January 1. The central finance office allocates funds as directed in the budget. Policy decisions on how to spend funds and how to hire staff are turned into guidance documents to organization managers. The departments and programs then spend funds over the fiscal year. Tax and fee revenues are collected, and intergovernmental revenues are received. Both spending schedules and revenue forecasts are compared against actual levels to determine variances, and adjustments are made as necessary. In the example in Exhibit 5.2, all spending must be completed by December 31 at the close of the fiscal year. The audit and reconciliation phase of the process then begins. This phase typically runs until the finance office staff and external auditors complete all audits and produce a CAFR.

The representative large city or county budget process that we have just described spans more than two years of elapsed time. This requires staff to prepare next year's requests while simultaneously monitoring the spending for the current fiscal year. The auditors are also examining the previous year's books while those responsible for answering their questions are deep into budget implementation for the current fiscal year. Exhibit 5.3 diagrams the overlap in budget years and the different activities being carried out across **budget cycles**. Exhibit 5.3 also demonstrates the cyclical flow and timing of events as seasons of the budget cycle.

State Government Budget Process

Like local governments, state governments follow a budget process with the major phases of planning, preparation, executive request, adoption, implementation, and audit. But in general, state governments are at least an order of magnitude larger than most local governments. Mid-sized and larger counties, large cities, and very large port and special districts develop general fund budgets on the scale of hundreds of millions of dollars in annual spending. States typically adopt total general fund spending in the billions of dollars. The size of state government organizations and the diversity of programs add a level of complexity to the budget process not experienced by most local governments. This size and complexity reflects the states' important role in the U.S. federal system as program delivery agents and as major recipients of federal intergovernmental revenues. State governments also must rely on an extended, formal legislative process to complete the adoption of appropriation and revenue bills. The formal legislative process must respond to the concerns of a state's diverse population and its needs. The legislative process allows for greater political influence and the chance that a budget will be delayed or not adopted in time for the fiscal year. In most instances, however, budget adoption is "must pass" legislation that attracts orphan issues and allows for complex grand bargains of legislative agreement in the waning hours of the budget process.

State governments are similar to local governments in an important aspect. Virtually all state governments must balance their annual or biennial budget. The exact form and timing of the bal-

133

Exhibit 5.3

Large City Overlapping Budget Cycles

	1st Qtr	2nd Qtr	3rd Qtr	4th Qtr	1st Qtr	2nd Qtr	3rd Qtr	4th Qtr	1st Qtr	2nd Qtr	3rd Qtr	4th Qtr	1st Qtr
FY1	FY1 Implementation				Audit and CAFR								
FY2	Planning and Prep		Adoption	FY2 Implementation				Audit and CAFR					
FY3					Planning and Prep	Adoption	FY3 Implementation					Audit	

Note: CAFR = Comprehensive Annual Financial Report.

ance varies with state law. Some states require the governor to submit a balanced budget. Other states require the legislature to adopt a balanced budget. While state spending, employment, and procurement all influence the regional economy, balanced budget requirements limit the states' capacity to serve as economic stimulus agents.

States vary in their fiscal period and budget structure. Most states rely on a one-year fiscal year, but several states budget and spend over a biennium (Exhibit 5.4). The biennial fiscal period is a product of state constitutional requirements and a holdover of the traditional practice of convening a legislative session every two years. Careful allotments and financial controls meter state spending over the full two-year period, but revenue shortfalls toward the middle and end of the second year of the biennium can be especially crippling because all appropriated funds have been spent and the legislature is often out of session.

In most states, the budget preparation and adoption process requires at least nine months of lead time. Revenue forecasts to support budget preparation are often produced and updated quarterly. The timing of the budget planning and preparation phases responds to the opening of the state legislative session. The session in turn responds to the beginning of the state's fiscal year. We will discuss implications of the start date of a state's fiscal year later in this chapter.

Exhibit 5.4

State Annual and Biennial Budgeting Table

Annual Budgets	Biennial Budgets
Alabama	**Biennial Budgets Adopted Once Every Two Years**
Alaska	North Dakota
Arizona	Oregon
Arkansas	Washington
California	Wyoming (odd-year adoption)
Colorado	**Biennial Budgets Adopted Annually**
Delaware	Connecticut
Florida	Hawaii
Georgia	Indiana
Idaho	Kentucky (odd-year adoption)
Illinois	Maine
Iowa	Minnesota
Kansas	Montana
Louisiana	Nebraska
Maryland	Nevada
Massachusetts	New Hampshire
Michigan	North Carolina
Mississippi	Ohio
Missouri	Texas
New Jersey	Virginia
New Mexico	Wisconsin
New York	
Oklahoma	
Pennsylvania	
Rhode Island	
South Carolina	
South Dakota	
Tennessee	
Utah	
Vermont	
West Virginia	

Source: Adapted from National Conference of State Legislatures (NCSL) 2008.

State governments follow a budget schedule that is similar to the one summarized in Exhibit 5.5. The budget planning phase begins in March, with the state governor meeting with her staff and the head of the central budget office (Forsythe 2004). As in local government, the budget planning phases establish the basic rules to be followed by departments and programs in submitting their budget requests, including the formats for presenting the budget, the budget production schedule, the governor's budget priorities, the economic and policy backdrop, and the revenue parameters under which the departments will prepare their requests. By late April, the central budget office releases budget instructions to all state departments, agencies, programs, and commissions. Release of the budget instructions begins the budget preparation season and gears up the organization for an annual exercise. Early citizen and advocacy contacts with department executives and program leads may be fruitful at this beginning stage of the budget process.

The budget staff in each state department agency and program works closely with their agency executive and program managers over May, June, and July to craft a spending request. The department or agency may hold public listening sessions around the state to gather client and advocate recommendations. The department then carefully assesses forecasts of caseload demand, any need for program changes, and any needed changes in law and policy as it prepares its request. Updated quarterly revenue forecasts appear in June, which helps to frame the request with new information. Analysts rely heavily on information from the prior budget year to build their proposed budget request. This use of templates and updates saves time, guides staff energies, and presents the governor and legislature with familiar presentations formats (see especially chapter 11 on line-item budgeting). The departments complete their requests by early August and file them with the central budget office according to a delivery schedule. As in local governments, the department and agency budget preparation phase is closed to public review and comment.

From August to October, the central budget office staff reviews the department and agency requests and then, under the governor's oversight, develops a combined **operating budget**. Depending on state law and practice, the budget office may produce a separate capital spending request, or include the capital request as part of the department or agency request. The central budget office staff works closely with department executives and analysts to verify numbers and to test possible funding levels and organizational arrangements. The central budget office staff also ensures that the governor's agenda is thoroughly represented in the various programs, and—perhaps most important—that the budget balances. Final decisions on funding levels, policy choices, staffing, and major procurement are left to the governor and her personal staff, but department executives may be able to appeal any final decisions to the governor. The governor normally releases her budget request to the general public in early December. This is in advance of the legislative session that begins in January of the following year.

The governor's budget request is formally presented to the legislature shortly after it convenes in January. In most states, the governor's request is a strong statement of executive power, and this sets up an interbranch check and balance between the executive and legislative branches. This formal check and balance contrasts with the more informal and collegial relationships of local government budgeting.

Each state follows a variation of the federal legislative model. Administrators must learn the legislative procedures and practices of the respective branches of their state legislature. All states, except for unicameral Nebraska, follow the bicameral structure of a house of representatives (or an assembly of delegates) and a senate. Typically, legislative policy committees must first authorize a program and its overall spending levels. **Appropriations** or **budget committees** then address legislation on annual spending. **Ways and means** or **revenue committees** handle tax and revenue policy. In some states, the transportation authorizing committees have jurisdiction over transportation capital projects. In another variation, the house and senate may assign joint committees to prepare the appropriations and overall budget.

Exhibit 5.5

Example State Government Budget Schedule (Hypothetical One-Year Fiscal Year July 1–June 30)

Month	Budget Phase	Activity
March	**Budget Planning**	→ Coordination between governor, governor's staff, head of central budget office on budget instructions, budget schedule, policy, agenda, revenues, economic environment, and audit results.
March		→ Quarterly revenue forecast provides initial resource levels.
April to mid-May		→ Central budget office issues budget instructions, budget schedule, and revenue context.
May–July	**Prepare Agency and Department Requests**	→ Agencies and departments prepare budget requests. Agencies and departments may have public listening sessions across the state.
June		→ Quarterly revenue update.
August		→ Agencies and departments submit budget requests and policy change requests to central budget office.
August–October	**Prepare Governor's Budget**	→ Central budget office staff reviews agency and department requests, and assembles an integrated state budget.
September		→ Quarterly revenue forecast updates revenue assumptions, forecasts, and program levels.
November		→ Governor and governor's staff work closely with central budget office to set final spending, program levels, and policy. Final communication and appeals between governor's office and agencies and departments.
December		→ Quarterly revenue forecast update.
Mid-December		→ Public release of governor's budget request. Printing and posting of summary documents.
January	**Legislative Budget Adoption**	→ State legislature convenes. Receipt of governor's budget request. Budget begins the legislative process.
January–March		→ Legislative committee process. Appropriations, ways and means committees consider the governor's request and provide oversight of current agency spending. Transportation committees may consider capital infrastructure requests. Committees take testimony from agency and department heads. Committees take public testimony.
March		→ Quarterly revenue forecast update supplies most recent data to legislators.

Exhibit 5.5 *(continued)*

Month	Budget Phase	Activity
April–May		→ State House and State Senate reach agreement on budget package. Floor action on overall budget and appropriation bills. Governor may have a supporting role in building agreement.
June		→ State legislature passes appropriations bills. Governor signs bills into law.
July (1st)	**Budget Implementation**	→ New fiscal year begins.
July to mid-August		→ Center budget office and finance staff make allocations and allotments to agencies and departments, set position controls, accounting controls, and encumbrances to control spending.
July to June of fiscal year (12 months)		→ Agencies and departments spend funds to adopted levels to implement program.
Monthly or quarterly		→ State treasurer or finance office provides quarterly revenue status reports to agencies, departments, legislative committees, and central budget office.
June (30th)		→ Fiscal year ends, all revenues logged, and authorized spending activity completed. Legislature and governor complete work on appropriations for next fiscal year.
July of year following fiscal year	**Audit and Feedback**	→ State auditor, agency and department auditors, and external auditors begin review of fiscal year financial records.

Legislators use the legislative committee process to conduct a careful examination of the governor's funding and policy requests for each state agency and program. In February and March, the appropriations committees conduct oversight of the current year's spending and levels of program demand. In addition to taking testimony from the department executives, the committees typically hear from the public and from interest group advocates. March brings an updated revenue forecast that refines the resource levels for appropriations. By late March, the leadership in both houses has begun to coalesce on a budget and spending deal. However, final action on appropriations bills may not come for another month. But, as the appropriations and revenue committees make reports back to the full body, the contours of revenue and spending start to come into focus. The governor may play an overt or behind-the-scenes role in nudging a spending bill toward completion (Forsythe 2004).

Ideally, by May, both houses of the legislature have agreed to appropriations bills and sent the legislation to the governor for a signature. In addition to the funding levels specified in legislation, the legislature may add spending policy guidance to the department and agency executives. Unlike the federal system, with its "all or nothing" presidential veto, many states allow a governor to use a line-item veto to reject selected portions of a spending bill. The line-item veto gives a governor even more power relative to the legislative branch. In our representative schedule in Exhibit 5.5, the legislature must complete work on all appropriations bills by early June. This allows time for the governor to act on the legislation before the fiscal year or biennium begins on July 1.

Once the fiscal year begins and the appropriations bills have been signed into statute, the central budget office and the state finance office begin to allocate and allot funds to the departments. Then, the spending process commences. While effective cash management ensures that the departments continue to run smoothly from one fiscal year to the next, it takes time to process funds out to the various departments, agencies, and programs; thus, local governments and nonprofits may face a lag time of one to two months from the beginning of the fiscal year to the availability of funds for new grants and contracts. Over the fiscal year, departments, agencies, and programs spend their allotted funds. Quarterly or monthly status reports indicate areas of over- or under-spending by programs. Revenue performance is also tracked, and spending is adjusted as necessary. It is especially important to note that most spending must be completed by the close of the fiscal year. Unspent funds typically revert to the state treasury; however, legislatures may allow outlays to continue into the subsequent fiscal year. The close of the fiscal year opens the audit and review phase of the budget cycle. Audits are used by the central budget office and the legislature as future budgets are built and adopted.

Federal Government Budget Process

In this section we provide a brief overview of the federal budget process mainly to illustrate the contrast with most local budgeting processes. The federal budget dwarfs even the largest of state budgets. If state government budgets are several orders of magnitude larger than local budgets, the federal government budget is several orders of magnitude larger than state government budgets. The total federal government budget is tallied in trillions of dollars, with many individual federal agencies spending hundreds of millions or billions of dollars annually. The massive federal budget reflects the full scale of the U.S. economy, extensive military and security programs, Social Security, Medicare, and other large welfare programs. Changes in federal spending or policy can have an almost immediate impact on hundreds of thousands of citizens and benefit recipients.

The U.S. Constitution requires that all money bills originate in the House of Representatives, thus giving this branch a preferred position among equals in the federal budgeting process. But because of the complexity and size of the U.S. budget, both the House and the U.S. Senate are organized similarly to deal with complicated budgetary issues. Most issue advocates, federal agency analysts, and congressional staffers focus on a small set of agencies or program areas in which they develop expertise. Experienced nonprofit, local, and state government administrators tap into this expert network to learn of pending changes to agency and program funding and policy. The National Association of Counties (NACo), the National League of Cities (NLC), and the National Conference of State Legislatures (NCSL) provide communication points into the expert network. Congressional staffers from your state delegation may also offer effective assistance.

The federal budget process follows the six main phases we have described above: planning, preparation of agency requests, executive budget and request, review and adoption, implementation, and audit. However, each phase takes longer, involves a more extensive network of national, regional, and local offices, and involves decisions over larger sums of funds. The preparation and adoption of a budget and spending authority for a new fiscal year takes up to 21 months. In the federal budget process, the president relies on the director of the **Office of Management and Budget (OMB)** as the chief budget officer. Highly skilled technical budget analysts who are guided from above by several layers of presidential political appointees staff the OMB organization. The OMB assures the technical integrity of the budget request and ensures federal agency compliance with the president's political and policy agenda.

Congress provides a check on the president's budget request. After receiving the president's request in late January, it uses its legislative processes to review the request, adopt a budget, and appropriate spending authority for the new fiscal year. Congress relies on the

Congressional Budget Office (CBO) to provide independent estimates on the president's budget request and on any proposed budget and spending legislation. The CBO, like the OMB, is staffed by very experienced analysts and assiduously strives to maintain partisan independence in its analytic work.

Completing the legislative process to adopt a budget, appropriate funds, and reconcile spending in nine months' time is extremely challenging. House and Senate Appropriations subcommittee chairs are typically seasoned legislators who can present and move bills through the committee and floor debate processes, but even with such expertise, the process often breaks down because of political agendas and diverse beliefs over the role and size of federal spending. In recent years, Congress has failed to pass many of the 12 annual discretionary and military appropriations bills. Exhibit 5.6 presents a very terse summary of the federal budget process timeline. For more refined information on the federal budget process, consult TheCapitol.Net (2009), Schick (2007), and Collender (1996).

The federal process provides several opportunities for citizens to gain information on budget decisions. The release of the president's budget request in late January is the first and best of these opportunities. Inclusion of a funding request for a program provides recognition and a base level of funding upon which to build in the congressional adoption process. The president's proposed budget provides detailed program-level information and comparisons to current and previous years' spending.

Exhibit 5.6

Federal Budget Timeline for Fiscal Year 2014

Budget phase and activities	Calendar date
Budget Planning	
Budget instructions developed by Office of Management and Budget (OMB).	December 2011 through January 2012
Preparation of Agency Requests	
Agency receives budget instructions from OMB. Agency regional and field offices prepare requests. Completed requests transmitted back to national headquarters. Review by agency budget office, agency executive, and cabinet secretary.	April 2012 through August 2012
Compilation of President's Budget Request	
All agency requests submitted to OMB. OMB reviews, aligns with revenues, ensures compliance with agenda, compiles the president's budget request.	September 2012 through December 2012
Congressional Budget and Adoption of Appropriation Bills	
Congress receives the president's budget request and adopts a budget. House and Senate each review presidential request, develop and pass appropriations bills, conference on differences. Presidential acceptance or veto.	January 2013 through September 2013
Implementation of FY 2014	
Allocation and allotment of budget authority to departments and agencies. Outlay and spending of funds to meet program objectives. Quarterly reporting. All outlays completed by September 30, unless carryover allowed.	FY 2014 runs October 1, 2013 through September 30, 2014
Audit and Review	
Internal financial audits, external audits, Government Accountability Office (GAO) reviews.	October 2014 into 2015

In the congressional legislative process, there are three additional opportunities for citizens to obtain information on possible future funding levels. The House of Representatives and Senate appropriations committees are broken into 12 subcommittees. Each subcommittee has jurisdiction over the discretionary appropriations for a defined group of programs. Subcommittee jurisdictions include: agriculture and food; commerce, justice, and science; defense operations; defense construction and veterans affairs; energy and water development; financial services and general government; homeland security; labor, health, human services, and education; the State Department and international affairs; transportation, housing, and urban development; natural resources and environment; and the federal legislative branch. After reviewing the president's request for the program area, taking testimony, and preparing an appropriations bill, each subcommittee will pass out and report a bill providing budget (expenditure) authority and policy guidance for its program area. The House and Senate subcommittee bills and subcommittee policy reports are the second and third critical sources of information on potential future funding levels for programs and agencies. The levels of funding provided in the two subcommittee policy reports typically bracket the range of possible program funding for the coming fiscal year.

The House subcommittees act first, preparing their bills and moving them through the full appropriations committee, the House Rules Committee, and then to the House floor for an adoption vote. The Senate subcommittees then follow and do their work, and through the Senate majority leader report a bill to the Senate floor for passage. Ideally, representatives from both the House and the Senate come together in a conference committee to reach agreement on a common bill for final passage. The conference committee report and conference bill are a fourth and final information point for funding levels and policy guidance. The conference committee report and final bill contain the final funding levels for the fiscal year unless vetoed by the president.

Overlap and Inconsistent Timing Across Levels of Government

The extended lengths of the state, federal, and large local government budget processes result in overlaps between the different levels of government. Exhibit 5.7 demonstrates this overlap for a representative county government, state government, and the federal government.

The exhibit includes two federal cycles to demonstrate the overlap more clearly. Both the county government and the state government represented in Exhibit 5.7 begin their fiscal years on July 1. This common start date presents budgeting challenges for county governments because they must adopt a final budget without knowing the exact funding levels for revenues coming out of the state legislature. An ongoing, incomplete legislative process causes county and other local government officials to budget in likely ranges of intergovernmental revenues. Additionally, once the legislature and the governor adopt a budget, it may take several weeks for the state agency bureaucracy to allocate the new funding and deliver it to local governments.

Similar budget cycle overlaps plague the federal-to-state relationship and the federal-to-local relationship. For example, in Exhibit 5.7, state legislators are in session in the first and second quarters of the calendar year (January through June) and have knowledge of funding levels in ongoing federal cycle I implementation. But state budgeting for the coming fiscal year rests on funding levels from the newer federal cycle II, and Congress is in the middle of the legislative process for this cycle. State budget analysts and legislators can only use funding proposals in the president's budget request and in the appropriations subcommittee reports as indicators of final federal funding for the coming fiscal year. County and other local governments on this schedule have the same difficulty. Potential funding level information is important to state governments because they receive on average nearly 40 percent of their revenue from intergovernmental transfers from the federal government.

Several states have adjusted their fiscal years to try to compensate for the budget process

Exhibit 5.7

Overlapping County, State, and Federal Budget Cycles (July 1 to June 30 State and County Fiscal Year)

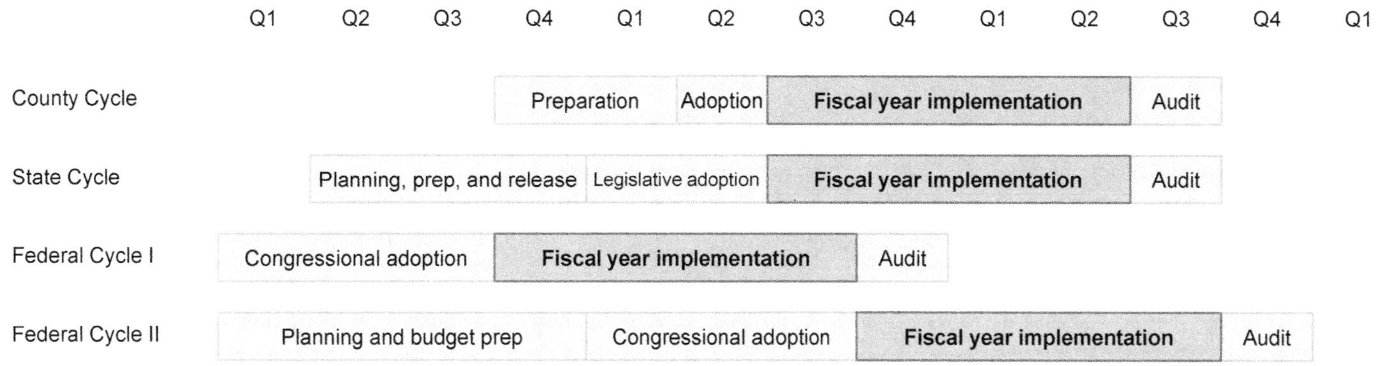

overlaps, but many remain stuck in asynchronous confusion. The majority of state and local jurisdictions in the United States are on a fiscal year that begins July 1 and ends June 30, but there are exceptions to this general practice. The states of Alabama, Michigan, and the District of Columbia have a fiscal year that begins in October, which coincides with the federal process. Texas has a fiscal year that begins on September 1, and New York's fiscal year begins on April 1 (NCSL 2008). Local governments are even more varied in their fiscal year timing. In Washington state, cities, towns, districts, and other local governments begin their fiscal year on January 1, but counties begin on July 1. In other states, all local government fiscal years begin July 1. School district fiscal years may begin on September 1 to coincide with the academic year. In the end, administrators must know and fully understand the implications of the fiscal year dates and budget process calendars in their states.

We close this section with a summary of the key factors that influence the kind of budget process a given government jurisdiction needs to develop in order to align funding with its needs. The left-hand column of Exhibit 5.8 lists some of the key conditions that must be considered in any budget process. Small special districts that provide a single service and obtain most of their revenue from a single source have relatively low levels of complexity with respect to contested issues, political partisanship, multiple structures of authority, legal responsibility, and scale of operation. As one moves horizontally across the columns in Exhibit 5.8, all of these factors grow both in their degree of complexity and mutual influence. One of the ironies illustrated by Exhibit 5.8 is that the American rule-of-law system places very high demands on even local levels of government to conduct processes that serve multiple purposes. In managing the public treasury, financial resources, etc., local governments must respond to public expectations for legal and political accountability including separation of powers, checks and balances, federalism, responsiveness, and local control. Furthermore, political accountability must be tempered with respect for professional technical standards and expertise. This is an important reminder when constructing a budget process that is well aligned in meeting the particular needs of a given governmental entity.

Exhibit 5.8

Comparison of Budget Processes

	Small cities, counties, and nonprofits	Large cities, counties, and nonprofits	States	Federal government
Problem/issue complexity	Low-Medium	Medium-High	High	Very high
Political conflict	Low-Medium	Medium-High	High	Very high
Structural complexity	Low-Medium	Medium-High	High	Very high
Legal complexity	Medium	High	High	High
Scale of responsibility	Low-Medium	Low-Medium	High	Very high

HOW WELL DOES THE BUDGET PROCESS RESPOND TO THE NEEDS AND GOALS OF PROCESS PARTICIPANTS?

All the budget processes we have summarized in the previous sections serve to organize budget actors into a predictable flow of sequential activities. A repeating process sets an internal work schedule for the budget actors, fosters legal compliance with budget regulations, and provides the public with expected work products, opportunities for participation, and closure of the process itself. But other political processes interact with the budget process. The electoral process often conditions the budget process and injects uncertainty into it. Additionally, the budget process generates social and psychological behaviors in the budget actors. These behaviors are critical to the successful completion of the budget process. In the sections that follow, we review several of the behaviors that increase predictability and certainty in the budget process.

The Electoral Processes Tempers the Budget Process

Clearly, public budgeting processes interact with other political and legislative processes. For example, election cycles and electoral politics may have a strong influence on the budget process. This influence becomes more pronounced every two or four years during the campaign and election for the president, state governors, and local officeholders. Campaign issues and candidate commitments may transform quickly into budget initiatives by those running for office. A newly elected president, governor, or local chief executive never fully owns his first-year budget. This is especially true for states and jurisdictions with a January 1 or July 1 fiscal period start date for the budget year. Typically, the first-year budget has been prepared by the central budget office under the direction of the preceding administration. The newly elected official has limited time to make marginal adjustments and to incorporate agenda items. For example, in states that have a July 1–June 30 budget cycle, the newly elected governor might have until February 1 following his election to complete and deliver a budget request to the legislature. This contrasts with nonelection years, in which the governor would present a budget request by December 1—before the legislature convenes.

At the county and local levels of government, the effect of election cycles may be more moderated. Membership terms on city councils and on county commissions are staggered to assure continuity on policy and budget decisions, and in most western states local elections are nonpartisan. However, elections in cities with a strong mayor form of government may have an especially strong influence on budget cycles falling in campaign years.

The Budget Process Builds Confidence and Trust Among Participants

Interest groups, clients, government employees, and elected officials all enter the budget process with the chance of gaining resources and opportunities, but also with the fear and chance that resources may be lost or severely restricted by allocation choices. There are several ways in which the budget process helps to temper these fears and potential for conflict.

First, the defined steps in the budget cycle impose some order, predictability, and certainty, however much uncertainty and potential for conflict there may be in the larger budget environment. Detailed budget instructions, a public schedule of activities and due dates, defined financial analysis and reporting formats, oversight hearings, public listening sessions/hearings, public notice and comment opportunities, organizational expectations and rules, and the norms of professional practices all provide routinized compliance structures that help to manage the uncertainty and risk in the budget process (cf. Robinson 2004). The degree of confidence actors have in each step of the process conditions their confidence in later process experiences. If confidence is lacking at a given stage of the process by one or more of the budget actors, the regulatory detail and linear flow of the budgeting process provide critical evaluation points against which budget actors can hold their peers accountable. These accountability points help the actors manage distrust and build confidence in each other and in the budget process (cf. Kass 2001).

A second set of factors that contribute to building confidence and trust in the budget process are professional relationships. Exhibits 5.1, 5.2, and 5.5 point out the many intra-organizational, interpersonal, and intergroup relationships embedded in local budgeting processes. Process regulations and position descriptions may define the structure, contours, and intent of a relationship between budget actors, but how a professional uses personal skills and values to build and maintain that relationship is critical to process success. Trustworthy relationships between and among the budget actors are mandatory for managing the risk and uncertainty of the budget process. Interestingly, trustworthiness is not defined by whether someone supports or opposes your actions or point of view. It is defined by consistency and dependability. A trustworthy budget actor consistently supports or consistently opposes another actor or interest group. The consistency of support or opposition provides certainty around which other actors can work. This certainty ultimately facilitates the successful completion of the budget process. Similarly, professionals in the process demonstrate their trustworthiness through consistent prudential judgment, effective communication, and reciprocity in understanding other actors.

The public budget process has a third set of structural attributes that help manage its inherent uncertainty and risk. Budget preparation and adoption is an annual or biennial activity. The repetitive cycles of the budget process year after year allow budget actors, advocates, and citizens to learn about each other and to build a history of shared process experiences—that, through time, condition the mutual expectations of participants for future budget cycles (cf. Robinson 2004). These unwritten rules enable the budget actors to work together even when they encounter unexpected difficulties along the way, because they have had the experience of working successfully together in the past. Consistent experiences with these unwritten structures allow actors to build confidence in the process and trust in each other.

Finally, the legal requirement to adopt a budget by a specific date norms the expectations of actors in ways that temper the risk and uncertainty that is an inherent part of the process. The threat of closing down a local government on the first day of a new fiscal year is too large a political risk for almost all budget actors. The requirement to complete the budget process on time effectively pushes budget actors toward process closure. Timely closure of the budget process sends a signal to the larger tax-paying public of a functioning government that can perform for the public good. This positive signal, however, can be undercut by the "rush to closure," which comes at the expense of sound technical data and adequate time to address the concerns of affected parties. Like all successful governance work, budgeting is a matter of balancing competing needs and priorities.

Budget process structure, trustworthy relationships, familiarity through repetition, and timely process closure all build a sense of confidence and trust in a budget process and its outcomes. Confidence and trust, in turn, lead to a public perception of fairness and justice in government, revenue collection, and the use of public resources. The opportunities for **public involvement** and the checks and balances embedded in the process help to ensure a fair budget process. Government employees, unions, government partners, interest group advocates, and citizens may tolerate a less-than-expected or less-than-satisfactory share of budget resources if they have confidence that the budget process itself is impartial and was conducted fairly (Rawls 2001; Thibaut and Walker 1975). In instances where the budget process is defined by state regulation in ways that limit process fairness, local administrators may need to exercise their discretion to add other public activities, offer new analyses, and provide more opportunities for citizen, client, nonprofit partner, and advocate involvement in the budget process.

The Budget Process Creates Behavioral Norms

The disciplined ordering of the various stages of the budget process both reflects as well creates some predictable behavior norms. For example, there is the norm that what you spent last year, absent significant changes, is the starting point for estimating what you will need next year. If there are significant changes, there is the norm of assuming that everyone will do "their fair share" in helping to balance the budget. Together, these norms create the principles of **base budget** and fair share, which tend to foster incremental changes from year to year in agency and department budgets. As a result of frequently relying on these two principles, some students of the public budgeting process have tagged the public-sector process with the label **incrementalism** (Wildavsky 1984, 1992). In Part III of this text, we discuss incrementalism in greater detail, including various efforts to overcome the tendency for public agencies to continue what they have been doing in the past without much reexamination. In the meantime, it is important to understand the forces inherent in the very nature of putting a budget together—forces that predispose participants to take an incremental approach and make alternative approaches sometimes difficult to implement.

Base Budget

All agencies, programs, and participants in the budgeting process begin with a presumption that they will be able to obtain support for an existing base of services without providing extensive analysis and justification. What constitutes the base may change from one jurisdiction to the next and from one year to another. In some cases, the base may be fixed at some reduced percentage of last year's authorized budget. In other cases, the base may be what was authorized last year, increased by some inflationary factor (i.e., 3 percent). The existence of some kind of base from which to operate greatly simplifies what has to be examined with care and what will serve as the primary focus of debate. (For purposes of the exercises associated with this text, we provide a very clear definition of *base budget* in chapter 11).

Fair Share

A second important shortcut that reduces conflict and the need for extensive analysis in the budgeting process is the norm of *fair share*. Whenever expenditure requests exceed available resources and cuts have to be made, what criteria should be used in funding some programs over others? This question can be answered by gathering plenty of data and analyzing it extensively—two steps that are not always possible within the tight time frame of a budget cycle. The use of the principle of fair share, like the notion of base, provides a norm that is easy to apply and implement. Usually, fair share is operationalized by asking for across-the-board cuts from all departments and programs, sometimes even from enterprise fund (user charge) agencies that are not supported by general fund revenues. When you hear requests being made for a fixed percentage cut in budget requests, you know that the principle of fair share is being used without an extensive analysis of data. Reliance on the principles of a base budget and of fair share results in a process that produces only incremental changes from year to year.

Incrementalism

There are several ways that the incremental features of the budget process surface during the budging cycle (for a good description of the expression of these incremental features of the budget process at the federal level, see Wildavsky 1984, chap. 2). First, as already noted, most requests begin with an assumption that everyone will ask for a little more this year than last year. Second, there is an assumption that there are likely to be cuts in the original request, but these will normally be small. Both of the first two assumptions about a relatively fixed base with small departures from year to year grow out of and reinforce a third source of incrementalism: the desire to keep past political agreements intact (see chapter 11). In subsequent chapters, especially chapters 12 and 13, we will discuss various alternatives to incrementalism, including priority setting as a way to encourage agencies to sort and order the most essential budgetary priorities to be funded. While incremental decision making purposefully narrows options, the approach has several positive attributes. One advantage is that the principles of fair share and base make it easier for participants in the budgeting process to simplify complexity, avoid potentially difficult conflict, and complete the budgeting process in a timely fashion. Equally important, the process can be completed with enough goodwill for the participants to engage one another in a civil fashion in the next cycle, which is always just around the corner. Building from current political agreements speeds the development of future agreement. The incremental approach also provides continuity to budget decision making and to the routine funding for each agency. And incremental decisions provide stability in another manner. When one or two programs among many in an agency receive relatively large adjustments, incremental decisions at the larger agency level help to maintain the relative structure and balance among the remaining programs within the agency as well as balance from one agency to another.

Modifications to the Budget Process

The budget process for local jurisdictions reflects the laws and regulations of the state from which the local jurisdiction receives its governing authority. Budget actors engaging in local budget processes must comply with all aspects of state law. Failure to do so could result in legal liability to the jurisdiction and to the government employee. Beyond legal compliance, local budget actors perceive the state budget and revenue laws as objectively firm. Budget steps must be executed on time, and a budget must be delivered in time for the new fiscal year. Only the state legislature can change the state local budget and finance statutes, and only the responsible state agency can modify regulations and official guidance promulgated from those statutes. State legislative and administrative changes quickly affect hundreds of county and local budget processes. The only recourse to address any adverse consequences of state control is to advocate for change in the legal requirements through the state association of counties, state association of cities, or association of special districts. Petitions for statutory changes would be handled through the state legislative process, and administrative changes to state regulations would follow a formal administrative process of notice and comment.

While state law grounds the local budget process in a defined structure, local jurisdictions may go beyond the minimum requirements—especially if the changes would enhance the process and better meet local needs and conditions. For example, if a city manager wants to and can effectively employ a citizen budget committee, this can be accomplished by adopting an ordinance that formally changes the city's budget process, adding steps for convening, managing, and using a budget committee throughout the process. Such a change would normally precede the upcoming budget cycle and be adopted by a vote of the council. Deciding when to go beyond the minimal budgeting requirements established by state law requires local administrators to have a deep knowledge of the authority they have been granted and an understanding of how best to align their administrative discretion as interpreters and refiners of state law with the ultimate goal of meeting pressing local needs. The executive budget instructions to staff, developed to guide preparation of the department and program requests provide, a powerful administrative tool for implementing local discretion and for creating a process responsive to local political and polity needs.

State legislatures and U.S. Congress may change their own budgeting procedures by passing laws and by legislative agreement. Process revisions have been successful in some cases, and in other cases have produced poor results. For example, in the early 1990s, congressional leadership met with the George H.W. Bush administration and struck an agreement to balance annual federal deficit spending. The agreement was incorporated into law with a revised version of the Gramm-Rudman-Hollings Budget Act of 1985 (Collender 1996).[3,4] Over the next decade, Congress constrained annual spending and generated an annual surplus at the close of the Clinton administration. More recent experiences with federal budgeting and appropriations have pointed to the severe limitations of the federal budget process (Schick 2007, Meyers and Joyce 2005).

HOW WELL DOES THE BUDGET PROCESS MEET
THE TEST OF TECHNICAL INTEGRITY?

While the primary purpose behind a public budgeting process is to organize political forces, the process must also support the technical analysis needs of producing a balanced budget. At its most fundamental level, the budget process must clearly and fully demonstrate that revenues will match with expenses over the short term of the next fiscal year and that the jurisdiction will maintain a structural balance over the long term. The technical analysis supporting a public budget must fully disclose all of the procedural, economic, organizational, and political assumptions used in assembling the budget.

Whenever the integrity of this technical analysis is called into question, citizens will challenge the legitimacy of the budget, the budget process, administrators, and ultimately the elected officials. A lack of technical integrity will also become evident to the financial community to whom the government must demonstrate ongoing creditworthiness. The public budgeting process at both the state and local levels must provide sufficient and accurate technical information to support investment decisions.

The technical aspects of budgeting are especially critical in the preparation of the department, program, and agency requests. In this early phase of the budget process, technical analysis must fully and accurately describe the public demand for services as well as the resources needed to meet those demands. Careful crafting by budget and program analysts helps to ensure accurate information and a comprehensive picture of needs and available resources.

During the adoption phase of the budget process, the rush to political agreement must not subvert the technical integrity of the budget under development. Arbitrary adjustments to incremental baselines, redefinition and recombination of line-items, and the use of revenue gimmicks challenge the integrity of the budget process and the final budget it produces. In addition to following announced budget schedules and meeting applicable regulations, the culture of the legislature or local government must allow sufficient time for budget analysts and staff to develop realistic and accurate analyses that can fully support political intentions and agreements. At the local government level, technical standards defined in state law and regulation, and set by the Government Finance Officers Association (GFOA) provide standards for technical integrity and clarity of budget development and presentation.

HOW WELL DOES THE BUDGET PROCESS
RESPOND TO CHANGING CONDITIONS?

The public budgeting process does not end with the legislative adoption of a new budget. Once adopted, agency administrators and program directors must allocate and program the appropriated funds and resources into workable programs. Administrators must also interpret and prioritize the policy directions that have accompanied the appropriations. Agency administrators may need to reconcile funding shortfalls or excesses as set by the legislature with other private- and public-sector funding.

Even with the best program planning and forecasting, economic and business conditions change. Over the course of the fiscal year or biennium, expected tax and fee revenues may fall short or may exceed forecasts in a revenue windfall. Changing economic conditions and policy changes may lead to unexpected changes in client demand and service needs. In most local jurisdictions, state governments, and at the federal level, departments and agencies may reprogram or change the spending purposes of appropriated funds up to a certain ceiling without legislative, council, or board oversight. However, once this threshold has been reached, legislative action is required for changes in spending purpose. Amendments to the previously adopted budget in the form of legislative ordinances allow the jurisdiction to respond to changing conditions. Specific actions of budget amendments include rescission or the taking back of funds, reprogramming or the redirecting of spending authority, or the supplemental addition of funds. Chapter 17 provides additional information on budget amendment procedures.

HOW WELL DOES THE BUDGET PROCESS COORDINATE WITH POLITY PARTNERS?

Local governments sit in context with an array of nonprofit and for-profit service delivery, resource, and policy partners. Governments typically sit as primary nodes of the partner network because of their substantial resources and policy authority. The government budget process and its outcomes (1) define when and under what constraints public funds reach nonprofit and for-profit community partners, and (2) authorize the funding of intergovernmental agreements between governments for service delivery. But local governments are not the only major resource providers to community networks. Foundations and nonprofit federated intermediaries provide substantial resources to a community. These organizations convene their own budget processes and make their own resource allocation decisions. Effective community governance requires an awareness of each organization's budget cycle in terms of preparation, decision making, resource delivery, and project implementation. Because of its open and publicly defined nature, the government budgeting process may act as a foundation for community decision making. To better understand these relationships, we first review budget processes in nonprofit organizations and then examine how government budget processes set the timing and schedules for partner nonprofits.

Government versus Nonprofit Budgeting: Some Important Process Differences

Like local governments, medium and large nonprofit organizations tie their budgeting to their financial fiscal year, which often does not coincide with the calendar year or the government fiscal year. Also, because of their competitive quasi-private sector status, the nonprofit budget process can be partially or fully closed to the public. To build credibility with the community, major federated intermediaries and other larger service providers open their processes to the public as much as possible. Another important difference is how nonprofits use budgets. The budget of a nonprofit organization does not carry the force of law; it is more of a strategic and operational guide than a true mandate. Even with these differences, for the major nonprofit organizations, the budget process follows the familiar steps of planning, request preparation, compilation and presentation, adoption, implementation, and audit. (Dropkin, Halpin, and La Touche [2007] recommend extended budget planning and budget request preparation phases for large nonprofit organizations.) Nonprofit organizations typically budget on a one-year fiscal period to comply with tax and reporting requirements. The audit phase following budget implementation results in annual financial statements for the organization. The organization's chief financial officer plays a major role in all phases of the budget process and may exert substantial control over the process and budget outcomes. The CFO convenes and leads the planning phase, prepares instructions, sets revenue and service demand forecasts, and coordinates the unit and program staff to prepare their requests. The CFO and her staff continually consult and coordinate with the unit and program analysts. As in the government process, the unit and program requests are consolidated into a unified budget in consultation with the executive officer. The CEO and the CFO present the request to the board. After review, the board may make changes to the proposed budget but then adopts a final budget. The adopted budget is then distributed throughout the organization.

Any effort by the public to influence the nonprofit budget must come through personal contact with the unit and program heads, the executive, and especially with members of the board of directors. For foundations, contact with program officers may offer another means to communicate needs and recommendations. Service providers, clients, government representatives, and citizens must advocate on an interpersonal level to make changes to most nonprofit budgets. If approached adroitly, government and interest group representatives may be able to make presentations to the organization board on particular needs or issues.

Challenges of Overlapping Budget Cycles and Coordination

Hundreds of nonprofit, for-profit, and governmental organizations contract with or partner with state and local governments to implement public programs and to deliver services. All of these dependent governments and service providers are affected by budget process timing. Much as local governments are off cycle relative to the federal budget process, the local government budget cycle is often out of time with nonprofit fiscal years. This inconsistent timing makes it difficult for community foundations, federated intermediaries, and other nonprofits to budget for and to contribute matching funds for government programs. Administrators in both sectors must recognize these timing differences and plan accordingly.

Governments must appropriate funds through an adopted budget to fund contracts and partnerships, and the budget must contain sufficient funds to support the program at the desired level. Once the fiscal year begins, it takes time to distribute funds and to make payments to contractors and partners. Effective cash management by local governments helps to ensure that ongoing contracts and programs operate continuously from one fiscal year to the next (chapter 17). However, new programs and new contracts may face delay until new funds become available. Also keep in mind that the close of the government fiscal year may condition contract closure and program completion. Unless given authority to carry over spending, most government programs must spend all resources by the close of the fiscal year. This spending requirement may require contractors and partners to expend their allotment of funds by that same fiscal year deadline. Nonprofits and partners entering into a government contract should clarify the spending timeline and conditions. Nonprofits and partners working with governments late in the fiscal year or biennium may find that government administrators have little flexibility in timing the use of their resources. When this occurs, funds may have already been spent down to a minimal planned level, with limited flexibility until the beginning of the next fiscal year. Government administrators are normally reluctant to start new fiscal commitments for shared expenses on joint programs late in the fiscal year.

Even with asynchronous budget processes, the well-defined, public timeline of the government budgeting process sets a foundation for all members of a community polity. All organizations in the polity network know the government's budget timeline and can plan accordingly. Through their budget cycles and spending policies, governments provide an important structure to polity governance, operational planning, and service delivery.

SUMMARY OF BUDGET PROCESS
CHARACTERISTICS AND IMPLICATIONS

At the beginning of this chapter we posed the following question: what are the consequences of the budgeting process on the actors? The well-defined phases and the repeated cycling of the budget process give those inside the process a sense of seasonal activity. The seasonality brings a familiarity and a certainty that helps build budget actor and citizen confidence in the budget process and its outcome. In addition, the public budgeting process is structured to ensure a technically sound budget and to respond to changing external conditions. While strictly governed by state law, most local jurisdictions have some discretionary authority to make changes in the process to meet local needs. In its most encompassing impact, the government budgeting process provides a calendar and a structure that serves as the foundation for local polity governance. The legal requirements for resource availability and for completion of spending provide a schedule around which foundations and other community nonprofits can coordinate. The government budgeting process is much more than an internal work schedule: It helps to structure community polity governance.

STUDY QUESTIONS

1. What are the major steps or stages in your agency's budget process?
2. What is the importance of a formalized budget cycle for your agency/program?
3. What are the major characteristics of the budget cycle? What, in your view, explains the difference between federal, state, and local budget cycles?
4. What changes would you recommend in your local government budgeting cycle and why?
5. To what extent do you believe there should be greater public involvement in your local government budgeting process? Why? How would you propose to accomplish greater involvement? To what extent would this compromise the efficiency and closure of the process?
6. What is the significance of the state legislative budget timetable for your agency? The federal budget timetable?
7. To what extent does your agency rely on the principles of *fair share* and *base* in assembling and finalizing its budget request? What effect, if any, does this have on participants in the process?
8. For the major foundations and federated intermediary nonprofits in your community, identify the fiscal year start and end dates and the budget process calendars. How do these calendars synchronize with local governments? The state budget cycle?
9. How open are the major foundations and federated intermediary nonprofits to public review of their budgets and operational plans?
10. How do the small and medium service provider nonprofits in your community respond to the local government budgeting process?
11. To what extent does your local government/agency coordinate budget development with other private, government, and nonprofit service providers in the community? What improvements could be made with greater coordination? What would greater coordination accomplish?

NOTES

1. The title of the person responsible for assembling the budget various by the size and kind of jurisdiction. For example, some jurisdictions place this responsibility in a single budget and finance office. Others separate budget and finance duties, with a separate person or office that is in charge of providing staff support for budget development and oversight. Small jurisdictions often place this responsibility in the hands of the clerk. Because this is the most common practice for the majority of the nearly 89,500 local governments, we use the term clerk throughout most of our discussion in this section.

2. The order of process steps and terminology vary by state law and local refinement. A "preliminary" budget is typically an initial working version of a budget that identifies the desired expenditures and the revenues needed to cover them. In Washington State, a formal step by the council or special district board midway in the budget process publicly ratifies the tax levies needed to fund the preliminary budget spending. Other states do not have the mid process formal revenue ratification step and move directly to an executive proposed, approved, recommended or requested budget. Tax levies are then reviewed by the legislative body as part of adoption of the proposed executive budget.

3. *Balanced Budget and Emergency Deficit Control Act of 1985,* Public Law 99–177, title II, U.S. Statutes at Large 99 (1985): 1038, codified at U.S. Code 2 § 900, commonly known as "Gramm-Rudman-Hollings" or "GRH."

4. *Budget Enforcement Act of 1990,* Public Law 101–508, title XIII, U.S. Statutes at Large 104 (1990): 1388–573, codified as amended in 2 U.S.C. and 15 U.S.C. §1022.

PART II

REVENUES AND BUDGETING

COMMISSIONERS REQUEST RECOMMENDATIONS ON A PUBLIC SAFETY SERVICES LEVY

CASE NARRATIVE

County finance director and budget officer Elizabeth Brown worked down through her list of meetings scheduled for the next two days. It was a steady stream of government and community representatives all focused on the subject of a possible public safety services property tax measure for the November ballot. A week ago at the last board meeting, the Upper Cascadia County Board of Commissioners had requested that the county executive officer make a recommendation in two weeks on whether to place a new property tax levy before the voters. Such a request would ask county voters to pay additional property taxes to support an enhanced public safety program above the service level supported by the permanent base levy.

Director Brown was delegated the task of preparing an action memo on the levy issue. She must complete her final draft of a memo by this Friday in order to allow time for discussion and redrafting by the county executive officer before presentation to the commissioners. Fortunately, she knows this issue well. Before becoming the county finance director and budget officer, Director Brown had been the lead budget analyst for the county's public safety programs. In this role, she reviewed in detail the annual budget requests from the sheriff's department, corrections, the prosecuting district attorney, and youth and juvenile services departments. After assisting the departments in budget preparation and submission, she would assist the county executive officer in deciding what budget recommendations to make to the board of commissioners. This previous work made her quite familiar with the budget needs and activities of the public safety departments.

The last six months weren't easy. At the previous general election, the county voters had rejected the renewal of an expiring public safety services tax levy. Adoption of the renewal levy seemed a safe bet because it simply would have replaced the previous five-year levy, thus resulting in no increase in taxes for county residents. There were few changes in the services covered or the costs in the renewal measure, and there was very little indication by voters and citizens that they were unhappy with the overall performance of the public safety department or with the specific package of services that would be provided by the levy.

Like the expired levy, the defeated renewal levy would have provided additional operating revenues above the level in the permanently adopted base levy over a five-year period. County voters had twice readily accepted such local option supplemental levies. Based on broad public support, rapid population growth, growing community needs, and inflation, Upper Cascadia County elected officials and county administrators had enhanced public safety programs to provide for higher-level and more comprehensive services. The renewal levy rejected by the voters would have maintained the enhanced service level at a cost of $0.42 per $1,000 assessed property value, or about $85 annually for the average home in the county.

In total, the renewal levy would have provided $17.2 million annually to fund a wide variety of public safety services. These services and programs included:

- Opening a mothballed pod in the county jail and fully operating the jail facility ($1.66 million, 14.5 FTEs [full-time equivalents])
- Providing probation oversight services for all released felons and sex offenders ($1.06 million)
- Providing effective transitional support, counseling, substance abuse treatments, and job training for released jail inmates ($550,000)
- Operating the county work-release center at full capacity ($1.2 million, total probation and release supervision FTEs = 30.0)
- Upgrading the county 911–emergency communications center ($125,000)
- Funding four emergency shelters for domestic violence victims ($610,000)
- Enhancing sheriff patrols and services, including traffic enforcement and offender transportation from local jurisdictions to the county jail ($4.7 million)
- Providing full staffing for special enforcement and interagency teams for gangs and narcotics; and for special investigative teams for major crimes, fraud and identify theft, and auto theft ($1.7 million, total sheriff's office patrol, enforcement, and investigations FTEs = 55.0)
- Funding prosecution services by the district attorney, along with child advocacy and victims assistance ($1.25 million, 17.0 FTEs)
- Establishing new youth and juvenile services, including a shelter for homeless/runaway youth, reimbursing the costs for secure detention ($840,000, 5.0 FTEs)
- Levy administration and departmental administration ($1.2 million)

The rejected renewal levy would have provided 19 percent of the expected revenues for the county sheriff's department, 15 percent of the expected revenues for the county corrections department, and 30 percent of the revenues for the prosecuting district attorney and its victims' assistance and witness programs. The levy also would have supported 12 percent of the county youth and juvenile services department. County information pamphlets and voters' pamphlet arguments for the levy clearly explained the detailed list of services. The actual wording on the ballot, however, simply asked voters if they wished to impose the additional $0.42 per $1,000 assessed value rate for public safety services.

Adequately funding public safety programs had been a challenge for the county. The sheriff's, corrections, and youth and juvenile services departments, and the office of the district attorney provided governmental services that involved citizens' and victims' civil rights. By intent and design, these programs did not generate substantial revenues. State law mandated the county to operate a jail and a local corrections program and to provide a number of other public safety–related services. State reimbursements, however, typically left gaps in program coverage and fell short of meeting the full cost of the mandated services.

The Upper Cascadia County public safety departments have always relied heavily on the county general fund—a large, primary account that accepts retail sales tax, general property tax, and other nondesignated tax revenues. Expenditures from the general fund may support any program or activity authorized by law. Because the public safety departments have limited capacity to generate revenues and provide mandated local governmental services, they are supported as necessary from the general fund. This puts the public safety departments in competition with each other and with other general fund–reliant departments. The county board of commissioners determines the allocation of general fund monies through the annual budget process. The general fund allocations have never fully met the needs of the growing county.

To ensure an enhanced level of public safety services and to reduce general fund dependency, the county had turned to five-year, local option, supplemental property tax levies. Property tax revenue generated by the local option levy was channeled to a dedicated fund account separate from the general fund. This dedicated fund segregated the public safety levy revenues and allowed for full transparency in their use. Public safety programs benefited all county residents individually and collectively. A broadly applied tax provided an appropriate tool to fund public safety services as a public good that benefited the entire community.

Everyone from the commissioners to the community leaders expected the public safety services measure to pass. But stacked up against two other major levy requests—one by the local fire and rescue district and the other by a major school district—the public safety proposal seemed to fall to third preference on the ballot. The recent strong downturn in the regional economy likely contributed to voter rejection of the renewal levy as well. A spate of employee layoffs from local businesses, high unemployment, and a depressed local housing market raised issues in voters' minds over priorities—and cast doubt on their willingness to commit to five years of extra payments to the government.

Once the voters rejected the levy renewal, the county and its departments, contractors, and partners had to carefully review and downsize all aspects of the public safety and judicial programs. These reductions didn't just affect the county staff. Nonprofit partners under contract with the county also had to downsize their programs and lay off staff. Community nonprofits not tied to the county were left to respond to the holes left in the domestic violence and inmate release programs.

The negative consequences of reduction in services and downsizing became more evident in the months following the failure of the renewal levy. Part of the commissioners' charge to the county executive and Director Brown was to assess the service situation and any consequences. In an effort to gather firsthand data on which to base her recommendations, Director Brown asked to meet with several of the affected groups and community leaders. The meetings on her calendar over the next two days were the response to those requests. At 9:00 A.M. on Tuesday, she would meet with county public safety officials: the county sheriff, the prosecuting attorney, the corrections director, and the youth and juvenile services director. Later that day, she'd meet with community leaders and advocates: youth services leaders, domestic violence victims' advocates, work release and parole partners, and social service leaders. A meeting with the police chiefs of the three cities and towns in the county was scheduled for Wednesday morning, followed by lunch with the county communications director and an early afternoon meeting with the finance directors of the library, flood control, parks and recreation, and community college districts. Late Wednesday afternoon, she would wrap things up with a reflection and debrief session with the county executive officer.

In the half hour before her first meeting, Director Brown sketched out a series of questions on her legal pad to help structure and guide the meetings to come. What kind of impact did the nonrenewal have on each leader or group? Had each department or group been able to continue to function at a reduced level, or were there growing gaps in some areas of service delivery? Were organizations facing permanent changes and capacity reductions because of the loss of funds? And, going forward, was each leader supportive of placing another levy request on the ballot? Did the leaders think voters would be more accepting of a downsized request? What should she recommend to the county commissioners in her memo? She had just finished compiling her list when her administrative assistant appeared at her door and reported that the county sheriff and prosecuting attorney had arrived and were waiting in the nearby conference room.

The county sheriff, prosecuting district attorney, corrections director, and youth and juvenile services director lumbered into the room and settled into their chairs near the head of the table. Director Brown asked the sheriff how things were going. He replied that his staff was managing and that most of the cuts resulting from the failed renewal had been put into place. The gang, major crimes, and drug and alcohol task groups had been combined under a single task force lieutenant, and the staff of special teams detectives had been cut in half for a reduction of 8.0 FTEs. Several of the deputies cut had been reassigned to the patrol division, but four had been put on on-call reserve status. Fortunately, emergency service response times remained within published standards. The prosecuting attorney added that he had been forced to reduce three junior attorneys to half time for a 1.5 FTE reduction and that the caseload backlog was beginning to grow. The child advocacy and victims' assistance programs received a basic level of state support, but both programs had been pared back to the basic level at a loss of 0.5 FTE each. The district attorney had asked the state department of justice if any additional state money was available, but he had yet to receive a reply. The domestic abuse programs remained intact, but funding had been reduced to the lowest level allowed under their contracts and agreements.

The corrections director concurred and reported that his jail staff had been cut back by 4.0 FTEs, and that he had been able to obtain some discounted commissary foodstuffs under a state purchasing piggyback. However, he would begin working next month with the sheriff, the prosecuting attorney, and the presiding district court judge to begin early release and home monitoring of 25 low-level offenders. The youth and juvenile services director reported that plans for a new youth homeless/runaway shelter had stalled due to lack of funds.

Looking ahead, all four officials argued forcefully that the rejected renewal levy would have covered very basic safety and justice services. The voters had paid for these same services in two previous public safety levies. They unanimously recommended that the commissioners place a levy referendum on the coming November ballot. They argued that the levy should fully fund public safety services programs at a levy millage of $0.42 per $1,000 of assessed value. All four officials also recommended adding a second levy question that asked voters to add the $0.42 millage to the permanent property tax base levy. Making the public service supplemental levy part of the permanent tax base levy would prevent the uncertainty of voter approval and save considerable election costs, public education costs, and administrative time every five years.

More meetings followed. On Tuesday afternoon, Director Brown received word that the community partner agency heads had appeared and settled into the conference room, coffee cups in hand. The renewal failure had especially devastating consequences for one of the domestic violence shelter and hotline contract nonprofit partners. The shelter director reported that she had cut back her two professional staffers to half time; the cutbacks had dropped the organization's staffing from 3.0 to 2.0 FTEs. In the past, the shelter staff had provided training for new volunteers and hotline responders three times a year. Training would now be provided annually, which would likely discourage many volunteers from applying. The shelter had subcontracted for security services to keep endangered women and their families safe from malicious attacks. With the funding reductions, the shelter would now need to rely on sheriff's deputies to prevent unwanted visitors and to enforce restraining orders. Community donations, however, continued to keep the shelter pantry filled, and volunteers were doing an amazing job staffing the hotline and operating the shelter. Still, volunteer efforts would only go so far. If funding didn't appear soon, the shelter organization would have to reevaluate its commitment as a county partner.

The local community foundation director was more focused on asking questions than on giving a status report. Was the county going to go forward with a November levy referendum? Would the county propose a full levy of $0.42 per $1,000 assessed value or a smaller reduced levy that might be more acceptable to the voters? Would the levy include funding for youth delinquency prevention programs and for drug and alcohol treatment programs for parolees? The director explained that his organization would begin to prepare its own annual budget in the next month, and it needed to fully understand the situation in order to prepare alternative budget scenarios. Furthermore, if a new November levy failed and reduced county program levels became the new norm, the foundation would have to rethink its priorities and would likely need to shift funds and contracts. Last-minute shifts would be especially disruptive to the foundation's contractors and partner agencies.

That wrapped up Tuesday's meetings. On Wednesday morning at 10:00 A.M., the local city and town police chiefs appeared for their session with Director Brown. They reported that their programs were absorbing some of the impacts of the renewal failure. Local police officers were supporting county sheriff deputies on patrol, on the interagency regional SWAT team (special weapons and tactics team), and on major traffic accident reconstruction teams. All city police officers were state-certified law enforcement officers, so providing backup was not an impossible issue. But city police officers were wasting valuable patrol time having to drive arrested suspects and intoxicated drivers across the county to the county jail. The loss of county transportation services to move offenders in custody from local police stations to the county jail carried a high burden in officer time. The police chiefs reiterated that the county should request a $0.42 per $1,000 public safety services levy in November.

Lunch with the county communications director, a sympathetic insider, proved a pleasant break for Director Brown. The communications director was apologetic. He had just come on board shortly before the voters had rejected the renewal referendum last year. His communications efforts had been limited and really hadn't carried the message to the community. Now, after seven months on the job, he was ready to move forward on a campaign for the November ballot. He explained that he had a much better sense of the services covered, his media contacts, the views of community thought leaders, and the socioeconomic makeup of the community. Elizabeth appreciated her colleague's support. The communications director, the county itself, and the county administrators could supply only factual information on the levy during a campaign. They were prohibited by law from spending taxpayer money on lobbying activities; however, the communications director could be proactive in delivering neutral information, especially in informing residents of the implications of the service-level reductions resulting from the failure to renew the tax levy. Active advocacy and campaigning for a public safety services levy would have to come from the county commissioners and sheriff as elected officials, as well as from community leaders. The communications director reminded Director Brown that the county economy was still fragile after the recent economic downturn: Overall regional employment trends remained weak.

At 1:30 P.M., Director Brown's peers and colleagues from the regional library, parks and recreation, flood control, and local community college districts were standing ready for their scheduled meeting. Mostly accountants and analysts, the finance directors focused on the numbers. They were especially concerned about any proposal to make a new public safety renewal levy part of the permanent property tax levy base. Just days earlier, the state supreme court had upheld a new state property tax limitation law. As one mechanism to constrain property taxes, the limitation law established a general government category tax rate cap of $5.50 per $1,000 of assessed property value. Adding a public safety services levy would likely result in a combined property tax rate that would exceed the new limitation rate cap. Should the combined tax rate from all governmental districts in the county exceed the limitation rate cap of $5.50 per $1,000 value, each government's tax rate would need to be proportionately reduced or *compressed* until the combined rate complied with the cap. The finance directors noted that adding a public safety levy rate of over $0.37 per $1,000 assessed value to the permanent tax rate base would exceed the limitation rate cap. To prevent impinging on the other governments in the county, the finance directors recommended that the county commissioners package a public safety services levy as a nonpermanent supplemental local option levy of five years' duration.

The community college finance director then mentioned that student enrollment was at record levels and that the college facilities were maxed out. The economic downturn had encouraged many unemployed and part-time workers to return to school for supplemental skills training. Traditional-aged undergraduate students that might have gone to state universities were now living at home and attending the community college because of its lower tuition and fees. Any increase in state support for community colleges appeared very limited because of the legislature's emphasis on K–12 educational funding. The community college district planned to put two levy proposals on the ballot in November: one for supplemental operations and maintenance funds, and another for facilities and capital improvements. The finance director from the parks and recreation district also indicated that his district was considering placing a capital levy on the November ballot. To encourage voter adoption of all levies, the finance directors recommended that the county scale back the public safety request to a reduced rate of $0.35 per $1,000 value. Director Brown indicated that she fully understood the numbers and appreciated her peers' situations.

After the meeting, the director returned to her office and closed her door. She needed to summarize her notes and gather basic ideas prior to her debrief session with the county executive. Difficult as it had been, departments and agencies had been surviving the recent cutbacks. But several sorely needed programs had been severely reduced. The public safety agencies wanted a full levy to recover their program levels and make them permanent. They might need to settle for a reduced supplemental levy. A permanent $0.42 per $1,000 levy would definitely affect partner governments under the new state limitation rate cap. There would be political fallout if the other local governments in the county had to face a compression of their tax rates. County voters had always been supportive of public safety levies, but with the weak economy, voters might be opposed to generous funding even for public safety programs. Director Brown proceeded to sketch a series of options.

CASE ANALYSIS

In this case, you have shadowed Finance Director Elizabeth Brown through two days of meetings with a range of officials affected by a possible decision to put a public safety services levy on the November ballot. A boundary spanning and coordination role such as this is typical of mid-level managers who have considerable discretion to transform information from numerous sources into meaningful decision-making options for the county leadership team, especially the county executive and the commissioners. As a journeyman financial expert with a good grasp of program costs, Director Brown has considerable influence over the tax rate proposed by the commissioners. More subtly, how she frames the issue in her memo, what information she highlights, and how she portrays the different action alternatives all demonstrate her judgment and leadership.

Director Brown must now organize her findings. Her thinking will need to take into account the following concerns: (1) assuring funding for county services; (2) legal compliance with the new state property tax limitation; (3) maintaining good relations with intergovernmental partners; (4) retaining the trust of county contractors and community partners; and 5) the uncertainties and consequences of placing an additional tax on county residents and businesses during a period of economic uncertainty.

As county finance director, Elizabeth Brown has a full understanding of state regulations and procedures governing the levy referendum process. As the Upper Cascadia County budget officer, she is one of several county administrators responsible for county compliance with budget process procedural deadlines. Meeting those procedural deadlines will require a prompt decision by the commissioners: The filing deadline for the November ballot is only four weeks away. Any proposal for a public safety services levy must be vetted and adopted by the commissioners as a resolution. Adopting any board resolution takes time and must include the opportunity for citizens to express their views on what the elected officials should do.

Review and answer the following questions as you consider and discuss this case:

- How would you summarize for the commissioners the impacts and department adjustments resulting from the failed renewal levy?
- How would you characterize the views of other local taxing entities on the county's levy option possibilities?

- What options do you see available to the board of commissioners? If a community college operations levy, a community college facilities levy, and a parks and recreation levy all appeared on the November ballot, how should the county best size and package a public safety levy? Should the county propose a public safety levy at all? Should the county enter into conversations with these other taxing entities to stage and coordinate their levy requests over two to three years?
- How will the new state property tax levy limit constrain your thoughts on a solution?
- What political issues will the commissioners need to address? What recommendations can Director Brown give the commissioners relative to relationships with community partners and the community polity?
- Suppose the voters failed to adopt a new public safety services levy: What might be the implications of their vote?
- Faced with limited tax revenues, should some public safety services be shifted to a fee for services basis? With what implications?

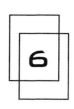

6

OBTAINING
GOVERNMENTAL
REVENUES

The effects of Prop 13 [California's Proposition 13] have been felt most strongly, though, in local politics. Before the Jarvis-Gann measure, local agencies and their boards had dual duties. They decided how much to spend on public services, and they set the property tax rate needed to supply that money. . . .

Without the power to tax, local governments were less of an immediate threat to local pocketbooks. It was no longer necessary for business and taxpayer groups to watch them so carefully. And so leaders of business groups began a retreat from local service.

(Joe Mathews and Mark Paul 2010, 54–55)

The Upper Cascadia County public safety teaching case points out the challenges of obtaining revenues to fully fund this fictional county's public safety programs. The rejection of a renewal **levy** by county voters at the last election sparked a chain of events with large, small, near-term, and long-term consequences. Faced with a pending reduction in revenues, the county's finance director, Elizabeth Brown, the department analysts and directors, and the county executive implemented thoughtful but broad reductions in services and programs. County administrators have followed the expressed directions of the voters and trimmed programs and services. From the teaching case, we can infer that a few public safety services, such as the sheriff's patrols and emergency call response, will remain as before, but many other important services concerning inmate release, reentry, and retraining; domestic abuse response; criminal prosecution; and youth and juvenile services will either close or fall to a reduced level. With the immediate program reductions in place, county administrators must now figure out the best way to reestablish and rebuild funding for the public safety function.

All local governments face the challenge of securing and blending revenue sources to support their programs, operations, and capital investments. **Taxes**, charges and fees, fines and penalties, **intergovernmental revenues**, nongovernmental grants, and borrowed funds provide the primary revenues for local governments. Based on these sources, local governments strive to develop a diversified, consistent, durable, and resilient resource base from which to fund their programs. The active design and management of a revenue system requires attention to the policy intention and regulatory structure of the system, and to its implementation and operation (Mikesell 2005, 99). Not only must local governments design a diversified, sustainable, and publicly acceptable revenue portfolio, but they must implement their revenue system in a fair and open manner. The Upper Cascadia County teaching case demonstrates that while government revenues often seem somewhat "guaranteed," voters may exercise unexpected choices. Proactive entrepreneurial efforts are necessary to develop and maintain revenue flows for governmental programs. Administrators have a critical leadership role in educating elected officials and the public on the need for revenue development activities, on the value citizens receive for the revenue, and on the technical aspects of effective revenue system design and implementation.

To explain this challenge fully, this chapter opens with an overview of the sources and types of revenues used by county, city, and special district local governments. This includes a discussion of taxation, **charges for service** and **fees for service**, intergovernmental revenues, and other governmental resources. Intergovernmental grants and reimbursements typically do not fully cover the local government costs of meeting state and federal requirements. Based on this imbalance, the chapter touches on the challenges of unfunded and underfunded mandates. It then discusses the differences among state government revenue sources and local government sources, including how different sizes and types of local government rely on different blends and sources of governmental revenues in their attempts to develop a sturdy revenue base. The chapter explores this variability and provides a summary of the tax and revenue burden state and local governments place on citizens in the different states.

The relative importance and balance of the different revenue collections has changed over time. The 1970s brought a major reduction in the importance of local **property taxes** due to property tax limitation initiatives that were spawned by California's Proposition 13. Between 1980 and 2003, however, changes in the balance of revenue sources were less dramatic (Mikesell 2005). Property tax, individual income tax, and utility and liquor sales tax receipts have declined slightly in importance. Local option sales taxes, along with charges and fees for service receipts, rose to replace some of the lost property and income tax revenues. This chapter closes by considering the continuing impacts of the financial downturn and recession of 2007–2009 on the balance of future local government revenues.

SOURCES OF LOCAL GOVERNMENT REVENUES[1]

State statutes and regulations provide local governments with the authority to raise and collect revenues in order to carry out their legally authorized missions. In the United States, local governments stand as a third quasi-independent government alongside the federal and state levels because of their delegated authority to independently raise revenues. Acting within the structures and constraints set by state laws, local governments access and use revenues from a variety of sources to fund their programs and activities. The blend of revenues tapped by each local government reflects state statutes, the health of the local economy, and the local political culture and citizen attitudes toward government and taxation. As the chapter's introductory epigraph explains, taxation motivates citizens to take an active interest in local community governance. Without effective taxation authority, California's local governments lost business leaders as active members of their local polities. Business leaders with their backgrounds in finance should provide a critical oversight to local government finance and revenue decisions. This expertise was lost in California with the passage of Proposition 13, which shifted many revenue generation decisions away from local governments to the state capitol in Sacramento.

The rationale behind the American Revolution presents a stark contrast to the loss of citizen interest in local tax and revenue issues. The British imposition of the Stamp Act and other mercantile duties on the American colonies without their representation in Parliament resulted in a loss of American confidence in government efforts to raise revenues. The failure of the British government to hear and respond to colonists' pleas and expectations fueled the war for independence. A functioning tax and revenue system requires involvement both by citizens and by government institutions to clarify needs, set expectations, and ensure transparency in decision making.

State taxation and revenue structures vary widely from one state to another. Each state's constitution, statutes, administrative regulations, manuals and handbooks, judicial precedents, and traditions combine to define the framework within which local governments in the state may raise revenues. The state framework in turn shapes the kind of financial and revenue relationship that local governments have with respect to their parent state. Local revenue authority illustrates and expresses the principle of federalism that is extended downward from the national government through the states and finally to local jurisdictions. In keeping with the American decentralized model of federalism, states typically do not micro-manage the financial decisions of local governments, but they do exert control on local revenue generation in a variety of ways. State laws and regulations authorize local government to collect tax and fee revenues. State laws and regulations also may (1) limit tax rates, (2) cap the total potential collection or **tax levy**, (3) define property valuation practices, and (4) define the procedures by which a local government considers and imposes a tax or changes rates for charges and fees. State manuals and regulations define the formats and reporting that structure revenue collection procedures for local governing jurisdictions. On a more subtle level, state reimbursements, matching funds, and grants motivate local governments to adopt preferred programs and adhere to required procedures (Henkels 2005, 205 and 221). As the Upper Cascadia County public safety services teaching case demonstrates, state laws define procedures for placing property tax proposals before the voters, and state courts determine the constitutionality of revenue generating strategies, especially property tax rate limitations.

Ideally, different sources of revenue will blend to provide a diversified, stable flow of resources to a local government. A diversified revenue base reflects a roughly equal proportional balance of different tax revenues (Carroll, Eger, and Marlowe 2003; Carroll 2009; Carroll and Johnson 2010). Diversification also applies to the balance of tax and nontax revenues and to the balance of different intergovernmental revenues sources (Carroll, Eger, and Marlowe 2003). An effective balance of revenue sources enhances the prospects for stability over time. This stability is important for sustaining organizational competence and capacity and developing program activities that effectively address community needs. Under a diversified balance of revenues, a temporary increase in one source of revenue can help to offset a cyclical or temporary decline in another source. For example, during a period of economic downturn, individual and business income taxes quickly fall, reflecting a contracting economy. In contrast, property taxes fall at a slower rate because of the lag time that delays the application of lower assessments to all properties in the district. State property tax limitations also have the effect of dampening fluctuations in property values.

The complexity and variability of the impact of the economy means that local governments need to develop a revenue mixture that consistently generates the funds needed to support existing services. A diverse portfolio of taxes may also increase taxpayer equity by extending several different levies to all groups of citizens and types of economic activity. For example, a retail sales tax will capture revenues from tourists and out-of-state visitors who do not own property or earn income in the state. The following sections introduce the different forms of local government revenues and summarize their strengths and weaknesses. The overview deals first with tax revenues that require ballot initiatives or legislative action for their adoption. In importance, these sources include taxes, charges and fees for service, and fines and penalties. The overview then turns to revenue forms that require administrative action for acquisition. These include the major category of intergovernmental revenues, as well as those generated through the financial system.

Revenue Source: Taxes

Taxes provide the primary revenue source for most governments, but as we've just described, levying and collecting taxes quickly raises concerns among citizens. Taxation has equity benefits that other revenue raising techniques lack. An understanding of why governments levy taxes and how they seek to generate fairness and equity in a tax system is critical to its public acceptance. To build this understanding, we turn next to a discussion of some basic tax theory and then to a discussion of tax system equity and fairness.

Why Tax? The Economic Intent of Taxation

The purpose of a **tax** is to fully recover costs from all possible citizens who could benefit from a good or service. A broad-based tax with effective collection spreads the tax burden and lowers each citizen's proportional share (Mikesell 2005). Taxation also accommodates variation in citizen demand for a service. Communities and local governments do not know exactly how much each citizen desires a particular public service, but a broadly and consistently applied tax assures program cost recovery and prevents free riders from taking advantage of the services without paying for them (Browning and Browning 1992; Irvin and Carr 2005).

Taxes are especially effective in covering the costs of public goods and nonmarket governmental services. Once a **public good** is made available to all citizens, it is difficult to limit access to the good or service: the delivered benefit is not exclusive to a particular citizen. It is also very difficult to assign a specific cost for a public good to each taxpayer. For example, when a community decides that a local library is a community good, it becomes difficult to fund the library operation solely out of user fees. The library becomes a public benefit (public good) for all and a community amenity, whether a citizen chooses to use it or not. It is better to fund the library out of taxes that everyone pays. Familiar public goods provided by most local governments include clean and affordable water, sewers, a well-maintained street and transportation system, a broadly educated citizenry, a safe community, national defense, scenery, and a clean environment.

Some governmental services produce **nonmarket goods and services**. Such services cannot be valued, or are purposely not valued, through market transactions. To value such services in the market (1) would place a monetary value on inalienable rights of citizenship, (2) might actually jeopardize constitutional protections, or (3) could, perhaps, raise questions of ethical conflict of interest. Nonmarket governmental services include (but are not limited to) elections management, property tax assessment, criminal procedures and issues, and matters involving civil rights. Again, a broadly based, equitable tax allows the community to provide these nonmarket services to all of its citizens.

As a public finance tool, a tax recovers an increment of value from one of three economic bases: wealth, consumption, or income. As examples, property taxes capture a percentage of the value of the accumulated wealth of individuals and corporations. **Retail sale taxes**, **use taxes**, motor fuel taxes, and **excise taxes** all tax the value of consumption at the point of sale to the consumer. Individual income taxes capture a portion of the value of income generated by residents who live in the jurisdiction or of workers who work in the jurisdiction but live outside its boundaries.

Most states rely on some blend of tax revenue from property, income, and **sales taxes**. Where a state does not impose an income tax or a sales tax, it must make up the foregone revenue through some other type of tax. Not imposing a particular type of tax might be advantageous to certain types of businesses, which can lead to increased private investment and job growth. As examples, a deferral of property taxes and a favorable corporate income tax treatment of large and costly manufacturing equipment may encourage equipment-dependent businesses to settle in a particular state. Alternatively, favorable treatment of capital gains revenues on income taxes may support personal small businesses and entrepreneurs seeking to capture value in their companies. Understanding the tax environment imposed by a state requires a comprehensive understanding of how the different taxes integrate to create a total tax burden on property owners, businesses, and citizens. We examine the relative tax burdens among the different states later in the chapter.

Tax Acceptance and Fairness

The tax transaction asks individual and corporate taxpayers to pay a cost in return for a set of benefits of roughly comparable value. For most taxpayers, the combination of direct personal benefits and indirect community benefits must roughly equal or exceed the taxes paid. Each citizen's preference of the exact balance of K–12 schools, police protection, fire protection, public works, parks and recreation, libraries, or social services is never fully known. Communities and local governments don't know exactly how much each citizen desires, or doesn't desire, a particular public service (see the discussion of Anthony Downs's theory of relative ignorance in chapter 1). Statistical indicators, user counts, demographic information, and public opinion surveys give an indication of a community's aggregate demand for different services. State law may require counties or cities to provide a minimal volume and quality of a particular service irrespective of citizen preferences. In practice, local government programs represent a bundle of transactions that cover an array of services and an array of service delivery approaches. An individual taxpayer might prefer more or less of a particular service, or delivery of a service in a certain manner. A citizen might prefer more funding for public safety, prefer less to fund mail-in or electronic voting, and be satisfied with contracted fire protection services. Voters may find a particular program or service to be unnecessary, wasteful, and even philosophically repugnant, but they are forced to pay into the service because it is part of a larger bundle. Thus, to gain broad coverage of all beneficiaries and low per citizen costs, taxes are compulsory on members of the community to a greater or lesser degree. Economist Charles Tiebout (1956) argues that, if citizens are freed from constraints such as property ownership or employment requirements, they will move into or out of a community to match the level and blend of public services that they desire and can afford. This selective shopping behavior often becomes evident when new residents move into a metropolitan region and have a choice of residing in one of several school districts and numerous local jurisdictions. However, national technical and professional standards, state and regional codes, and citizen expectations have led to a surprisingly uniform selection and quality of local government services.

The broad, compulsory coverage of effective taxation contrasts with the somewhat voluntary nature of charges and fees for services. In a charge or fee for services transaction, a citizen chooses to pay for the government service consumed. For some citizens, a fee is preferable to a tax because it theoretically recognizes the economic liberty of the citizen purchaser. But the charge for services transaction for government services is not a simple two-party exchange. Most governmental services generate not only the purchased benefits to the individual, but also public benefits to the community as a whole. In paying a charge, the purchaser is in effect paying for a share of the community's public benefit generated by the service. Funding government services through taxes shifts the cost of community benefits back onto all taxpayers.

Each community must find a balance between services supported by taxes, those supported by fees, and those that are left to citizen responsibility. As examples, citizens in extremely high wealth communities find less need to fund local public libraries because, through personal wealth, they have access to all necessary books and media sources. Similarly, citizens in wealthy gated communities may not prefer a full level of police and public safety protection because the community association provides its own private security services. Parents with religious preferences may prefer to homeschool their children in lieu of using secular local public schools. Parents who practice homeschooling may be reluctant to support taxes for the local school district.

Those who are suspicious of taxation often perceive no direct benefit from a particular government service or investment. For example, a citizen may rarely, if ever, use a road or bridge on the far side of a county and thus feels no ownership or responsibility to pay for its upkeep or replacement. Similarly, citizens from the urban center of the county may feel indifferent about roads in a rural part of the county. One of the challenges faced by public service leaders is to educate the public to see and value the whole. This holistic perspective is necessary in order for a community to agree to tax itself for the betterment of all citizens. A set of uniform, broadly applied taxes both reflects and helps to generate the sense of a commonwealth across the entire community (Fischel 2000, 26). Implicit in this governance agreement is that most citizens and businesses will use only a portion of the full spread of government services. Each citizen will use some level of services, and other citizens may provide a subsidy to cover the costs. Broad-based taxation provides the means to share costs, to build economies of scale, and to efficiently and effectively deliver services.

As we observed in chapter 1, voters tend to have a limited or short-term perspective on tax initiatives. Anthony Downs (1960) argues that this perspective results in a limited understanding of government services and the benefits they generate. Voters evaluate the types and mixes of services proposed for enactment and then support the candidate or party that appears to provide the greatest total benefit. In reality, Downs argues, voters are often ignorant of the benefits received, the timing of when benefits are delivered, or the downstream implications of a particular bundle of services. Voters lack perfect and complete knowledge because gaining knowledge is extremely time consuming and labor intensive. Moreover, the full array of government services is extraordinarily broad and complex. Many public services deliver benefits in the distant future or in unexpected places. Applied to the real world, voters are consumers and are used to the immediate benefit of private market goods: fast food, instant downloads, and information at a click. Much government spending takes the form of investments for prevention or of incremental spending on an issue or problem. And with this kind of gradual spending over time, voters often fail to realize the full array or the delayed benefits they are receiving. Instead, they focus solely on the immediate costs in taxes and payments to government. They see these upfront payments as a lost opportunity for spending on private goods with a more immediate or recognizable near-term benefit (Downs 1960, 551). According to Downs, even the most knowledgeable citizens vote using partial or imperfect knowledge (544). The cumulative result of voter ignorance is budgets that are smaller than they otherwise would be if citizens had full knowledge of what benefits their tax dollars were producing.

Downs's general argument about why democracy produces smaller budgets than what the benefits would justify is tempered by our highly decentralized system of local government. Land-use economist William Fischel (2000, 37 and 39) argues that unlike the large national and state governments, local governments are geographically bounded and identifiable. Fischel finds that homeowners behave more like corporate stockholders. Most homeowners work to maximize the value of their property individually and collectively as a community by purchasing services for themselves and for the community. Fischel argues that homeowners and certainly homebuyers have a strong understanding of local schools, neighborhood quality, city services, and the quality of the community. At the local level, government services are more evident and defined: a local parks district might build a pool, recreation center, and athletic fields using a 30-year bond for funding. Citizens can see the facility under construction, use the facility, and understand where their money has gone and what it supports.

The degree of remoteness and uncertainty is often less obvious in local government services. However, even at the local level, voters rarely understand the full array of services provided by a county, large city, township, or special district governments. Part of this lack of awareness is because governments, especially local governments, strive to be as unobtrusive as possible in the lives of citizens. Similarly, voters typically do not keep track of which special district or local government provides which service to the community. Voters also may not fully appreciate the complexity or remote benefits of education, social services, recreation, urban renewal, or community development services. In the end, most voters are partially or preponderantly ignorant of their local governments. Accepting taxation for future or obscure benefits remains a challenging decision.

Even if voters had perfect information on both taxes and services, they would still tend to underfund public goods. This is because when you fill up your own shopping cart at the supermarket, you are paying for exactly what you want. But a pluralistic system guarantees that no one will be exactly happy with the collection of items in the public goods shopping cart; there will always be a dearth of some things and too much of others. The cartload of public goods and services is never worth to us (as individuals) what it costs.

The voter decision to accept a new tax also reflects a set of expectations related to the fairness or justice in the structure and burden of the tax. Expectations of fairness include both procedural fairness and allocative fairness (Rawls 1999, 2001; Thibaut and Walker 1975). These expectations express themselves in at least four ways. First, voters expect that the procedures used to adopt a tax or fee increase will be fair. Most citizens expect to vote on any measure that changes or imposes new taxes. Citizens also want to present their concerns over a proposed tax to their elected representatives. Procedural fairness requires that citizen have an opportunity to voice their opinions, concerns, and frustrations.

Second, voters expect their allocated tax burden will be the same as that carried by their peers in similar circumstance. This notion is defined as **horizontal equity** in the tax structure. Voters also expect **vertical equity** in tax burden. Some voters feel that all payers—high or low income, high wealth or low wealth—should carry a uniform burden. This is known as a **proportional tax structure** or *flat tax*. Policy choices may ask those citizens and businesses with greater wealth or income capacity to pay proportionately more than others may. This would give the tax burden a **progressive structure**, with a heavier burden on those with a greater ability to pay because of greater wealth or higher income. A tax that places a relatively heavy burden on those with lower resources is termed **regressive structure**. Sales taxes and motor fuels taxes are considered regressive—since low-income individuals and families must purchase gasoline and food, they therefore must pay a larger proportion of their total income or wealth in order to do so.

Third, voters need assurances that peer compliance with a tax is at a high level and is consistent. Visible and effective tax enforcement reinforces the fairness of universal compliance. Fourth, voters expect fairness in the administration and in the application of the tax rules to their personal circumstance. Technically competent, experienced, and unbiased assessors, and prompt, courteous, and accessible review of appeals by a county board of equalization, reinforce taxpayer perceptions of fairness in local property tax procedures. Clear instructions and well-defined procedures help citizens and businesses comply with, and have confidence in, a tax. Similarly, if the state department of revenue audits one's tax returns, one expects fair procedures, oversight of the revenue agent, and fairness in any settlement.

Fear of being caught and enforcement deterrence may provide an effective compliance motivator for some taxpayers. A strong enforcement program raises the costs and the consequences of cheating (Andreoni, Erard, and Feinstein 1998, 851). Strong and consistent enforcement demonstrates that tax cheats will be caught and that the opportunity to underpay, or not to pay, is very rare. At the local government level, property taxes and sales taxes are largely imposed and enforced through well-designed systems. While performance varies across local governments, annual property tax delinquencies typically range between 2 and 5 percent (e.g., Waldhart and Reschovsky 2012; Johnson 2011), with an exceptionally low rate of 0.59 percent in Arlington County, Virginia, in 2011 (McCaffrey 2011). The property tax delinquency rate recognizes that counties will not receive the full amount of expected revenue. Where permitted by state regulation, counties may increase the property tax rate in order to compensate for this expected loss in revenue (Johnson 2011).

Most taxpayers, however, possess a sense of moral obligation to support the community (cf. Bellah et al. 1985). Taxation is a trust reliance relationship between taxpayer and government (Scholz 1998, 135). Accepting a tax is a risk on the part of the voter that the government is trustworthy and will perform as promised into the future. In the reverse, a government hopes that taxpayers will be trustworthy and will make prompt and full payments. The more taxpayers perform in making payments, the less effort and expense is required to ensure compliance. Both taxpayer and government must see each other as trustworthy, dependable, and embracing the interest of the other party. Trustworthiness on the part of the citizen is expressed as a duty to contribute to the community. Performance of duty in turn leads to the emotions and behaviors of trust reliance that in turn leads to compliance.

The willingness of citizens to accept and to pay taxes reflects a complex personal psychology that includes deeply held political values, a sense of the community, the need for services, concerns over the fairness of the tax, pressures from the media and current events, individual finances, the limitations of the current economy, and hopes for and perceptions of the future. The taxation transaction is almost always much more complicated than a mere cold rational exchange.

To gain broad acceptance, citizens must view the combined state and local tax system as fair, equitable, and efficient (Bartle 2003; NCSL 2007b). State and local government tax policies should strive for a tax system that has stability, certainty, and sufficient yield; low administration and compliance costs; and a diversified balance of revenue sources (Carroll, Eger, and Marlowe 2003). From an economic perspective, taxes should be efficient with minimal distortion to the larger economy, and a state and local tax system must recognize and be responsive to interstate and global competition. No combination of state and local tax policy will score perfectly on all of these criteria, and poor implementation by state agencies and local governments can weaken effective tax system design and policy. Quality tax administration by local governments is critical to meeting citizen expectations of fairness and equity. To understand what makes up a local revenue system, we turn next to explain the different types of taxes.

Local Taxes

Property taxes provide the predominant source of revenues for counties, cities, and special district governments. Additionally, a small set of cities and counties collect income taxes or **wage taxes** (also called **payroll taxes**) from individuals. Most states collect an individual income tax, and most collect a retail sales tax and use taxes. In many states, a portion of the sales tax revenues collected by the state are returned to county and city governments. States also collect taxes from corporations, although nationwide this revenue source has gotten proportionately smaller over recent decades (Mikesell 2005). Whether local or state imposed, tax revenues form a primary and critical source of local government financial resources. We review each of these forms of taxation in detail below.

Property Taxes. Many local governments and some state governments impose **property taxes** on the wealth of their residents and corporations. State laws and regulations authorize the collection of a local property tax and define the structure, features, and requirements of the local property tax system. In many states, the actual property value assessment and revenue collection is delegated to county governments. To implement a property tax, county governments must assess the value of the property owned by each resident or corporation in the jurisdiction. For individuals, the county typically assesses the value of real property and real estate, and sometimes personal property, including automobiles, boats and trailers, and financial securities. For businesses, the assessment often covers facilities, equipment, inventory, corporate office furniture, and furnishings. Once an assessed value has been determined, a percentage tax rate is then applied to the value to determine the tax due. County governments collect taxes for themselves, for all the other local governments in the county, and sometimes for the state government.

Property taxes impose a uniform percentage burden across all levels of taxpayer wealth. Taxpayers with high property wealth will pay more tax because of higher property values and property attributes. The applied tax rate, however, will be uniformly the same for all property owners. Property tax burdens especially affect retirees and others who hold wealth in their property, but who have lost the cash income needed to pay the annual tax. State tax codes often provide an alternative assessment or delayed payment scheme for senior retirees. These adjustments inject a degree of progressivity into the uniform tax burden.

The concept of a uniform rate–based assessment on property values first appeared in the American colonies. In Revolutionary America, taxes were often more heavily enforced on the poor than on the rich. In New York, where political concessions were needed to build support for the war of independence, tax enforcement fell heavily on the wealthy. The concept of an ad valorem, or value-based, uniform tax was proposed and debated as a means to equalize tax collections across rich and poor citizens (Fisher 1997). Congress established the first federal property tax to finance the War of 1812. This was a temporary and successful tax. Throughout the Jacksonian period, a uniform ad valorem tax was seen as an instrument of tax limitation, and uniformity clauses were included in 34 state constitutions between 1834 and 1896 (Fisher 1997). Throughout the nineteenth century, administration of property taxes became much more difficult. The property assessment included land and real estate, but also personal property and intangible business assets. Valuing mobile property and complex businesses became difficult. The adoption of the federal income tax with the passage of the Sixteenth Amendment in 1913 gave the federal government a more responsive and elastic means to capture economic growth, but the property tax remained the primary form of taxation for states and local governments until the Great Depression, when the income tax and retail sales taxes increased in importance.

Property taxes are the least popular form of tax. Part of this dislike reflects the large lump sums billed by counties rather than billing in smaller amounts on a more frequent basis. Recent research indicates that dividing large biannual tax payments into several smaller billings, or requiring routine tax payments through **escrow accounts**, may help to prevent tax delinquency, increase revenues to governments, and reduce home foreclosures (Waldhart and Reschovsky 2012; Anderson and Dokko 2009). Another source of dissatisfaction with the property tax reflects the difficulty of reaching an accurate, up-to-date assessment of property value. Typically, a county assessor has responsibility for implementing the property tax system and for collecting the taxes due. The assessor may be elected or appointed, depending on state law and county charter. A staff of professional assessors and analysts work under direction of the county assessor. The task of the staff is to: regularly visit every piece of property in the county; assess and estimate the value of the property; apply the appropriate tax rate to the assessed property value; respond to any protest of the assessment; produce the tax bills and notify the property owner; collect any tax due; and follow up on delinquent payments. In extreme cases, the county may seize and then sell properties with delinquent taxes. We will further discuss the mechanics of the property tax system and the effects of property tax limitations in chapter 7.

Retail Sales Use and Excise Taxes. **Retail sales taxes** and **use taxes** are percentage assessments at the point of retail sale on the value of items purchased by the consumer. The merchant or seller typically remits retail sales taxes to the state, while the purchaser pays use taxes directly to the state. Residents of a state with a retail sales tax are supposed to declare and pay tax on all purchases made outside the state but used within the home state. Many residents fail to pay use taxes on out-of-state purchases, often out of ignorance, and the cost of enforcement precludes states from enforcing collections on lesser value items. Because of the difficulty of enforcing *use taxes,* states tend to focus their enforcement activities on high value items that require licenses such as motor vehicles, boats, and trailers. For example, a state might assesses a use tax on the value of purchased motor vehicles at the time of licensing. The tax revenues are dedicated to cover the cost of the vehicle's use of the state's road infrastructure.

State statutes and regulations establish the authority and the structure for collecting retail and use taxes at all levels of government. All but five states—Alaska, Delaware, Montana, New

Hampshire, and Oregon—levy a state general retail sales tax. Thirty-five states allow local governments the option of implementing a sales tax (e.g., local option sales tax) (Edwards 2006, 17; Krane, Ebdon, and Bartle 2004, 524). These states typically set a maximum authorized local tax rate and delegate the authority to local governments to adopt a tax rate up to the maximum authorized level. The local tax increment is then added to the state's own sales tax rate to obtain a total tax rate charged to the consumer. The state department of revenue records and publishes the retail sales tax rates for all taxing jurisdictions in the state. The department of revenue also enforces the tax and collects the sales tax revenue. All businesses making taxable sales compute the prescribed percentage of the value of each sale. At the end of the month, quarter, or year, the retailer submits the collected revenues to the state department of revenue. Sales tax revenues are often submitted at the same time as any estimated corporate income tax to ease the reporting burden. The state department of revenue then returns the appropriate portion of the collections to the county or city. In four states (Alabama, Arizona, Colorado, and Louisiana), retailers submit the local portion of tax collections directly to the local governments (NCSL 2007a). The burden of collecting the sales tax falls to retailers, but with effective state auditing and electronic systems, sales tax enforcement is quite high.

The local use of the retail sales tax responded to the declining state and local property tax revenues, tax delinquencies, and widespread property foreclosures of the Great Depression. Mississippi levied the first state sales tax in 1930, and New York City levied the first local level sales tax in 1934 (Edwards 2006). The retail sales tax originated when state economies were fixed in brick-and-mortar stores with a defined retail point of sale. The service sector was a relatively small portion of the total economy and was a costly sector from which to collect revenues. Doctors, attorneys, and accountants resisted the imposition of taxes on their services. The massive growth of the service sector as a portion of the U.S. economy over the last half of the twentieth century has challenged the effectiveness of the traditional retail sales tax. Three states (Hawaii, New Mexico, and South Dakota) have comprehensively integrated services into their sales tax programs (Edwards 2006, 21). Other states have tried to expand taxes on services with mixed results. Finally, collecting taxes on the barter and exchange sphere of the economy—encompassing domestic help, swap meets, farmers markets, garage sales, and the like—remains difficult.

In an extension of consumption taxation throughout an economy, Canada, Australia, New Zealand, the members of European Union, and many other countries impose a national **value-added tax (VAT)**. This type of tax is imposed on the increased value of a product at each purchase or value point between material and component suppliers, manufacturers, distributors and wholesalers, retailer, and consumer in the production chain. VATs may be imposed on goods and services. Value-added taxes are not commonly imposed in the U.S., however, they have been proposed as an element of comprehensive reform of state tax codes. The imposition of a VAT results in relatively efficient collection from businesses, but the full extent of the taxation is largely obscured from the end consumer's perspective.

There have always been sales tax evaders who travel to adjacent states without a sales tax, make purchases, and then fail to declare and pay taxes on the value of the purchases brought home. However, out-of-state telephone retail sales and, more recently, the explosion in online sales have driven deep holes into the coverage and effectiveness of state sales taxes. The U.S. Supreme Court decisions in *National Bellas Hess* (1967) and *Quill* (1992)[2] denied states the authority to require the collection of sales tax revenues by other states, unless the retailer had a nexus in the state of sale. A nexus has been understood as some form of physical presence—a facility, staff, or contractor. Recently, one major online retailer has purposefully closed facilities and discontinued contracts and internet relationships with online advertising affiliates to prevent a nexus in all but a few critical states. These actions have not prevented legal and legislative actions against the retailer by cash-strapped states wanting to collect internet sales taxes (Weintraub 2011; Metz 2011; Martinez

2010, 2011). This is a developing area of case law. Researchers Bruce, Fox, and Luna (2009; Bruce and Fox 2004) project that uncollected national and locale-commerce sales tax revenues in the 46 sales tax states and the District of Columbia would reach $11.4 billion annually by 2012.

In the *Quill* decision, the Supreme Court specifically left room for Congress to act on the sales tax issue under the commerce clause of the Constitution. In May 2013, the U.S. Senate passed a measure that would allow states to enforce sales tax collection on online purchases. At publication, the House of Representatives had yet to act on the bill. Since the *Quill* decision in 1992, 24 sales tax states have passed consistent state legislation and joined the Streamlined Sales Tax system in which cooperating states collect and remit balances to the state in which the consumer resides (Streamlined Sales Tax Project 2005, 2011).

In addition to general retail sales and use taxes, states collect **excise taxes** on specific goods and services, or authorize the local jurisdiction to collect an excise tax. An excise is placed on a particular product on a per-unit basis rather than on the value of the sale transaction as a percentage (ad valorem). The excise is usually on a narrow range of specific products, and the business is expected to recoup the cost of the tax when the product is sold to the consumer. Though these taxes generate a smaller amount of revenue than the property or general sales tax, they are important supplemental sources of revenue for local governments. Excise taxes on liquor and tobacco sales, and hospitality taxes on lodging, restaurants, and rental car services are examples of this type of specialized tax. Taxes on motor fuels, gasoline, and diesel fuel represent another type of sales tax dedicated to specific program purposes. Motor fuel taxes are established by the state, but revenues are commonly shared with county and other local governments for road maintenance and construction.

From the consumer's perspective, the full impact of the general retail sales tax burden is obscured. A consumer's total sales tax burden is dispersed over hundreds of purchases throughout a tax year. Where taxpayers can deduct state sales taxes from federal or other state income taxes, a taxpayer might sum up an annual sales tax figure, but for many consumers the total sales tax burden is never totaled up and made evident. Nonetheless, sales taxes have a high level of public acceptance (Edwards 2006, 17).

Retails sales, use, and excise taxes are generally perceived as regressive taxes. When assessed on all types of sales, these taxes affect low-income taxpayers most heavily. These taxpayers have the least available disposable income to cover costs beyond mandatory purchases of food, drugs, and medical care. For this reason, many states exempt the collection of sales taxes on some combination of food, drugs, and other selected staples. This helps to make the effects of sales taxes more flat or progressive.

Income Tax. Most people understand income taxes from their experience with the annual personal federal and state income tax returns they file on April 15. However, seven states have no state individual income tax: Alaska, Florida, Nevada, South Dakota, Texas, Washington, and Wyoming (Braybrooks, Ruiz, and Accetta 2011). For states with an individual income tax, 15 states authorize a local option wage or individual income tax for use by local governments (Edwards 2006, 30). Local governments usually implement **wage taxes** on wages and salaries and compensation. Local **income taxes** cover wages, salaries, interest and dividend income, and other forms of income. These taxes may be implemented locally or through the state income tax system. The local wage or income tax is widely used in Indiana, Kentucky, Maryland, Michigan, Ohio, and Pennsylvania (Braybrooks, Ruiz, and Accetta 2011).

The federal government established the income tax with the Sixteenth Amendment in 1913. But with the substantial decline in property values and property tax revenues in the Great Depression, local governments also turned to the income tax as a new form of revenue (Carroll 2009; Fisher 1997). Philadelphia, Pennsylvania, began assessing a wage tax in 1938. The city continues to assess a personal wage tax on salaries, wages, and compensation earned by nonresidents working in the city, and on city residents working anywhere (City of Philadelphia 2014). Philadelphia also imposes a personal income tax on unearned income, interest, dividends, royalties, and certain rents on residents to support local schools. Cities in Ohio widely levied income taxes starting in the 1940s. By the 1960s, Michigan cities, Maryland counties and the city of Baltimore, and New York City all levied a local income tax (Edwards 2006, 30). Other governments have used an income tax on a selective basis to meet specific needs (e.g., Multnomah County, OR 2003–2005 to support public schools) (Multnomah County, OR 2014).

The federal income tax and most state taxes set graduated tax rates tied to income brackets. Tax filers with greater income typically pay at a higher rate. Numerous deductions, exemptions, and adjustments customize the tax burden for each filer and help to ensure horizontal equity across all filers of similar circumstance. In general, income taxes are understood as progressive because of the increasing tax rate for higher bracket filers. But, the Philadelphia example described above is a flat tax, with all filers assessed the same rate. The actual task of implementing an income tax falls on employers and businesses, which must withhold a portion of wages and benefits to meet tax requirements and then must submit the withholdings on a routine basis. Computerized payroll and recordkeeping has eased this burden. Self-employed residents must often submit estimated taxes on a quarterly basis over the course of a tax year.

Compared to property and sales taxes, income taxes are especially sensitive to changes and swings in the regional and national economies. A rising, growing economy brings in an increasing amount of income tax revenue, while a declining economy results in less revenue. Sales and property taxes provide complementary sources of revenue that can dampen the volatility of the income tax.

Taxes on Businesses and Corporations. Small businesses and corporations provide the economic engine that brings wealth to communities. Local governments in turn tax this wealth to provide the public goods and services that support businesses and employee satisfaction. Local governments provide the infrastructure, public safety, K–12 schools and community colleges, and quality of life amenities that sustain business operations, attract and retain talented employees, and attract new businesses. State-level tax codes, however, largely define the tax structure businesses face. Similar to personal taxes, governments typically tax the property, income, and purchases and consumption of businesses. Unless prohibited by state law, local governments may place additional taxes on businesses in their communities.

Small businesses and corporations take a wide variety of forms reflecting their purpose, multistate or global structure, facilities and equipment needs, staffing, and capital requirements. Legally, small businesses include sole proprietorships, partnerships, and associations. Larger businesses are often chartered as corporations. Developing a fair tax structure that can respond to the wide variation in business types is especially difficult. For example, the features of a state tax code that gives favorable treatment and reduced assessment to large capital investments in equipment and facilities may not be especially helpful to creative firms developing software or advertising. The tax code in each state presents opportunities and disincentives to different types of business forms and ventures. As we will discuss further in chapter 8, business taxes are one of many factors that business owners and management take into consideration when deciding where to locate.

The state tax code in each state defines the property wealth held by businesses that may be taxed by local governments. In most states, businesses pay property taxes on some combination of real estate, equipment, and office furnishings. The local assessor makes valuation determinations and generates tax billing as would be done for individual taxpayers. In some states, assessors from the state department of revenue assess the value of large capital equipment, industrial facilities, or utilities that cross county boundaries. Such central assessment of high value properties helps to ensure knowledgeable, accurate, consistent assessment. Property taxes on commercial equipment and industrial facilities can generate hundreds of thousands of dollars of property tax revenues annually to counties and cities. Industrial and light manufacturing facilities are critical to the establishment of a diversified local property tax base.

The state tax code also defines any income taxes or business and occupation (B&O) receipts tax that apply to businesses. Mikesell (2005) explains that state corporate income taxes continue to decline as a revenue source. This trend is reinforced by business legal structures that pass profits from the corporate entity to its individual owners. This transfer of wealth tends to lower corporate tax liability. An array of tax breaks granted by states to businesses to encourage economic development (chapter 8) also work to lower state corporate tax revenues. Some states have imposed a minimum tax on corporate receipts irrespective of a business's annual profit or loss. This has led to a debate over whether government spending should rise and fall with the cycles of the economy, or whether government revenues should be stabilized at a minimal level over good and bad years to provide services when they are most needed in economic downturns. A corporate minimum tax or a tax on gross receipts would support the latter viewpoint.

Many states assess a corporate income tax on corporate net earnings. Similar to the personal income tax, corporate earnings are typically adjusted for capital losses, depreciation of capital investments, spending on research and development, and for other incentives prior to computation of taxes due. Other states and jurisdictions assess business net taxable income or net profit at a prescribed rate (City of Philadelphia 2014).

In Washington State, a business and occupation (B&O) tax on business gross receipts makes a contribution similar to a corporate income tax. The state level B&O tax applies to all forms of businesses with annual gross receipts over about $12,000. Part of the B&O tax rate assessed on a business reflects a local government share of the total tax rate. West Virginia once imposed a statewide B&O tax, but now only local jurisdictions may apply this tax.

Revenue Source: Charges and Fees for Service

Charges and **fees for service** are a growing source of revenues for many local governments. They are imposed to cover the direct and related costs of providing a specific service. A fee approach works especially well when a local government can clearly define both the service provided and the purchasing customer group. In contrast to taxes, charges and fees for service cannot be used to fund general government services; fees are funds dedicated to support the activities and services for which they were collected. Charges and fees cover the specific costs of a wide variety of local government services including:

- monthly residential water and sewer charges;
- electric and plumbing code permitting and inspection fees;
- local swimming pool and golf course access fees;
- utility franchise and right-of-way access fees (Henkels 2005, 222);
- development planning and permitting fees; and
- community college tuition and building use fees.

Utility franchise fees can provide a substantial and major source of revenues for cities and towns, though these too should be used only for the reason for which they were collected. In the past, this restriction has been liberally interpreted by local franchising governments as other revenue sources have declined or been limited. Although infrequently used, jurisdictions can also apply charges and fees to nonprofit organizations that are normally shielded by state tax codes from most local taxes (Dugan 2010). Such a loss in property taxes and business revenue has provided justification for some jurisdictions to seek ways of recovering this foregone revenue.

Closely related to charges and fees for service, local governments grant a variety of **permits and licenses**. The cost of the permit or license allows the citizen or client to undertake, at the citizen's discretion, an activity regulated by the government. Permit and license rates are typically set to recover the cost of processing the application, recording and documentation, and any enforcement actions taken to ensure compliance with requirements. County governments issue familiar permits and licenses, including marriage licenses, pet ownership licenses, food handler licenses, and restaurant sanitation licenses. Many counties and cities require some form of a business license from all enterprises operating within the jurisdiction, though this is generally not as a revenue-generating action, but as a regulatory process. **Permit and license revenues** typically contribute a minor share of the total revenues generated by a local government.

A revenue approach that relies on charges and fees for service allows a local government to recognize a specific set of public needs and to tailor a service response. For example, homeowners wishing to make substantial changes to their dwelling must pay a fee to obtain a building permit, and then allow any plumbing, electrical, or structural inspection for compliance with city or county building codes. Fees for service respond to the needs of groups of citizens for specific public services by isolating the cost burden to those who consume the service. In our example, only homeowners voluntarily undertaking remodeling and construction projects are subject to the permit fee. The transparent and isolated linkage between fee and service delivery can sometimes help instill public confidence in a government's ability to efficiently and effectively deliver the needed service in the same manner as the private sector. However, packaging many government services as simple transactions overlooks the broad public benefits generated by widespread compliance with regulations. In the case of construction and remodeling permits and code inspections, consistent compliance to high specifications over all construction results in reduced fire danger and reduced service costs related to fires, and lower homeowner and business insurance costs.

The transaction aspect of charges and fees stands in contrast to the public benefit aspects of tax-funded public spending. While some taxes support a narrowly defined, prescribed program or service (e.g., building a community library or a public safety levy in the teaching case example), tax revenues most often support spending on general government programs. Tax revenues can cover the cost of service delivery, but they also cover the cost of positive economies of public goods that accrue to the community through government programs. For example, K–12 schools could be run on a fee-based or voucher approach that would charge parents directly for the education of their children, much as private schools charge their students tuition and fees. In contrast, a tax-based approach to education covers the cost of educating children but also allows employers and the community to recognize that an educated population has broad economic and community benefits. A well-educated workforce allows a community to compete in the national and global environment for employers and facilities. Imposition of a tax often recognizes the public benefit from a service or investment. By contrast, imposing a fee can obviate any sense of paying for the larger public benefit. Imposing a fee tends to stratify those paying the fee as a separate group within the community. Supplementing charge and fee revenues with tax-generated funds helps to remind citizens that fee-based services generate a larger public benefit that deserves full community support.

Charges and fees for service are making an increasingly important contribution to funding local government services. With tax limitations capping increases in property tax revenues, and rising uncertainty surrounding state and federal intergovernmental revenues, charges and fees present local government with a way to cover program costs; furthermore, in a market-style feedback, a steady flow of fee revenue also indicates that citizens or clients desire a program. Under the fee approach, however, citizens often feel nickeled and dimed with innumerable small charges. But because of their greater transparency and transaction focus, voters typically are more accepting of fee increases than of general tax increases. From a larger perspective, charges and fees for service and taxation are complementary approaches to funding government services. Each community must find the balance between these two approaches in order to fund public services adequately.

Local governments have the option of setting charges and fees at varying levels of cost recovery. Governmental agencies and social service nonprofits may establish fees on a sliding scale that allows a larger number of low-income clients to receive services, and to enhance their sense of self-worth and dignity by contributing to some portion of the service cost. This approach provides a level of subsidy to those clients most in need. However, in most cases, governments set fees to recover the full cost of providing the particular service. A break-even analysis of the costs of delivering a given quantity of services allows governments and nonprofits to set this cost recovery level. For example, county and city development planning, permitting, and construction inspection programs often use a full cost recovery approach. The downside of this approach is volatility in program staffing. In a rapidly falling construction market, fee revenues fall and government staff must be either temporarily furloughed or permanently laid off. In a rapid growth market, county and city governments must rush to hire and train examiners and inspectors.

To gain full cost recovery, local governments and especially special districts may charge out-of-district residents a supplemental fee above in-district rates. For instance, parks and recreation districts may charge out-of-district residents a surcharge for classes, for participation in athletic leagues, and for the use of swimming pools and gym facilities. This out-of-district surcharge recognizes that in-district residents have paid taxes to cover a portion of program costs and that the services were designed specifically for the population within the local government jurisdiction.

Cost recovery–based charges and fees require that the government have a full understanding of the service costs involved. Effective cost recovery requires moving beyond rates based on the average costs of service delivery. Gaining such an understanding requires comprehensive data collection to support effective performance measurement and cost analysis. In-depth cost analysis allows a local government to identify high-cost clients and to monetize the extra costs of providing services to their more complex or extensive set of needs. Beyond cost recovery, local governments may purposefully set charges and fees to generate a profit. Some local governments provide selected services on a for-profit basis. For example, a city might manage its golf course, ice rink, or recreational facilities on a for-profit basis and use any net profit to subsidize other city services.

The procedure for setting the rates for charges and fees typically requires a public process and action by the county board of commissioners or judges, city councillors, or district board of directors. Public utility rates for electricity, water, sewer, storm water, and public transportation affect broad numbers of people and, as a result, may draw public scrutiny during a rate-setting procedure.

Where governments use charges and fees for service as a revenue source, accounting regulations may require the establishment of an enterprise fund accounting framework. This framework separates the fee revenue stream from other revenues and activities. For example, cities often establish separate enterprise funds for water, sewer, storm drainage, and electricity utility services. Enterprise fund accounting is especially useful when fee revenue is used to pay off capital construction bonds, when the law requires the use of fees rather than taxes as a revenue source, and when policy requires the use of fees (Johnson and Bean 1999). This issue will be examined more fully in our discussion of accounting funds in chapter 9.

Many local government jurisdictions impose a *systems development fee* or *systems development charge* on any new residential or business development and construction. This fee covers the cost of the utility and service system infrastructure needed to support the new development. Funded infrastructure includes water and sewer lines, drainage, roads and traffic management infrastructure, and sometimes parks and recreation and schools. The fee can be used only to support the construction of new facilities, not for routine maintenance. Transportation development charges provide a similar source of revenue for road and traffic infrastructure development. As a comparable revenue source, some states impose a real estate excise tax (REET) on the value of real estate sales to accomplish infrastructure development outcomes. Revenues from both the systems development fees and real estate excise taxes are highly dependent on development and construction activity and on the strength of the local economy. Laws and regulations may require tracking both of these forms of revenue separately from other revenues.

The service development charge is often assessed on a per-residence or per-office basis without regard for the inherent value of the unit. For example, a county might assess a fee of about $12,000 per house. This reliance on a per-unit rather than a per-value approach subjects the jurisdiction to criticism that the fee is regressive and places a relatively heavier burden on lower income homebuyers. Extensive use of the systems development fee could also shift an unfair share of infrastructure development costs away from the general public and onto first-time homebuyers, new residents, and new businesses of the county or city (Chandler 2006). Real estate excise taxes are subject to similar criticisms of heavily loading costs onto real estate purchasers. This criticism has grown as local jurisdictions struggle to find ways of replacing water, sewer, and transportation infrastructures that are rapidly failing.

Counties and cities also impose utility access fees. These fees allow private utilities access to residences and businesses over public streets and rights of ways. Payment of these fees allows nongovernmental telephone, electricity, natural gas, and water and sewer providers the privilege of placing cables and pipes underneath city or county streets. Counties and cities set these fees not only to encourage the development of infrastructure services but also to cover the costs of maintaining and repaving roads and streets.

Counties and cities allow businesses the privilege of serving their residents under business franchise agreements. These fees often generate substantial revenues for local jurisdictions. Such agreements allow utilities access to county or city residents for a prescribed fee. Cable television and internet fiber, natural gas piping, and water and wastewater utilities may fall under the franchise fee arrangement.

In addition to the major charges and fees discussed above, counties and cities charge fees to cover the cost of numerous other activities. Public safety and corrections functions attempt to recover fees from inmates who move through the justice system. Parks and recreation departments work to recover operating costs through entry and facilities use fees. Annual business licenses, sign permits, and pet licenses bring in fee revenues as well.

Special districts make extensive use of charges and fees for service to cover their program and operating costs. The dedicated purposes of special districts reinforce their specified mission and enterprise nature. Charges and fees for services complement and reinforce this transparency. As examples, cargo handling and tonnage fees, passenger use fees, and facility rental fees imposed by a port or airport district may comprise the major source of revenue for the district. Public hospitals charge patients fees for services, medicines and supplies, and for facilities maintenance. Similarly, tuition charges and building and student fees comprise a major source of revenue for community college districts. As with city and county governments, special districts must set rates for charges and fees in such a manner as to recover costs, but not to prevent access by citizens and clients. For example, parks and recreation districts must make strong efforts to cover costs, but they must ensure that citizens of all income levels can afford and have access to district services.

Revenue Source: Fines and Forfeitures

Fines and forfeitures typically constitute a very small portion of a local jurisdiction's revenues. These revenues represent an individual's or business's compensation to the community for criminal infractions, tax noncompliance, or failure to meet program requirements. These revenues include proceeds from property tax liens and forfeitures, penalties for traffic and parking violations as adjudicated by a court of law, penalties on late payments, and library charges for late and lost materials. Skepticism about the fairness of local law enforcement's use of fines as revenues has long clouded public confidence in this form of revenue.

Gross failure to pay property taxes generates an unfortunate source of revenue for county governments. However, the sale of tax delinquent properties allows the transfer of the property to new owners who can pay the required taxes and who can stabilize or increase the economic value of the property—all for the public good of the community. The procedures used by county governments to recover delinquent taxes by tax foreclosure (Whatcom County 2010), forfeiture (Itasca County 2011), and property sales follow state rules and regulations. The exact procedures vary among the different states. However, the process typically requires multiple notifications to the property owner, elapsed time for an owner response, and an auction of the property to gain the highest possible value. County governments sell forfeited properties to recover the back taxes, interest, and costs on which liens have been executed. In Minnesota, the state and county reviews forfeited properties and may retain selected properties for inclusion in the state- and county-owned natural resource lands (cf. Itasca County 2011).

Revenue Source: Sale of Assets

Many local governments own clear title to land and sub-surface mineral rights within their boundaries. Ownership of these lands (as public property) may have resulted from tax delinquencies and forfeitures, and from subsequent decisions by state and county governments to retain rather than sell the land parcels (Itasca County 2011). Governments often manage their lands and natural resources to produce revenue by routinely selling timber, forage, oil, or natural gas. Governments also generate rental income by franchising the operation of government-owned lakefronts, recreation areas, campgrounds, and other recreation facilities.

Revenue Source: Intergovernmental

Intergovernmental revenues reflect the principles of federalism and local autonomy that are built into the U.S. and state constitutions. Governments at any level—federal, state, or local—may independently raise revenues and may, within their authority, transfer or grant revenues to other levels of government to further the public good. From a budgeting perspective, revenues transferred from one governmental entity to another governmental entity on the same or on a different level are categorized as intergovernmental revenues. Intergovernmental revenues are roughly structured in the following forms:

- Direct grants or payments for the performance of a specific service or defined program of services under a voluntary intergovernmental agreement or a contract.
- Reimbursement payments to another level of government to offset the costs of providing statutorily delegated or mandated programs and services, allocated by formula, lump sum, or entitlement.
- Revenue sharing between one level of government and another.[3]

State governments are the largest source of intergovernmental revenues for local governments. These revenues range from the direct return of shared tax collections to reimbursements granted for the operation of specific programs or services. Federal transfers typically provide an important but smaller source of intergovernmental revenues for cities, towns, and special districts. Federal funds often become the final source of several complementary revenues for a project, thus making it achievable. Local governments must carefully document intergovernmental revenues both for legal and financial compliance purposes, and to enhance transparency and public trust.

Direct Grants and Payments

Direct grants and payments for services are voluntary exchanges between governments. These types of grants and payments often exchange the performance of services for payment. For example, a small city might purchase law enforcement services from the local county sheriff's department. The purchase would be structured under an intergovernmental agreement, similar to a contract that would specify the services provided, staffing and performance criteria, and payment amounts and schedules. The city would make regular payments, and the county sheriff's office would register those payments as intergovernmental revenues. Programs to make intergovernmental grants may be structured on a competitive or noncompetitive basis, but the final decision to enter into agreement is voluntary. Federal grants in this category would typically include project grants, cooperative agreements, and direct federal payments for a specific use of local services (CFDA 2011, 10). For example, the U.S. Department of Justice offers grants on a competitive basis to local police departments to increase officer staffing or to support the purchase of specific equipment. To receive the funds, the local government would need to perform as specified in the grant agreement, and may need to commit a contribution of local matching funds over a defined schedule.

Program Cost Reimbursements

Intergovernmental reimbursement payments provide resources to local governments in compensation for the provision of program services as specified in a given statute. The transfer of revenue along with accompanying policy, program guidance, and spending controls expresses federalism in government structure. Here, federal and state governments use local governments as agents to implement their policies and programs. Statutes may mandate local government involvement, but the transfer of revenues typically becomes the largest incentive for local governments to participate in, and to comply with, the intentions of federal and state policies. Restrictions and constraints on the use and spending of transferred revenues reinforce the federal delegation of intention.

State and federal governments provide the sources of these payments. Reimbursement payments may be allocated as a grant of defined amount that covers a package of services and time span (block grant), apportioned on a per capita basis, apportioned by formula, or apportioned based on the number of entitled recipients. Statute, regulations, and program policies define how the grants are allocated as well as the standards for local performance. For example, a state department of corrections may provide a grant to a local county to establish and operate a county jail and corrections program based on the number of inmates participating in the program.

Similarly, states often make grants to local school districts based on the number of pupils served or under a formula that considers pupils served, labor costs, location, and other factors. This formula-based approach helps to equalize the K–12 educational resources and quality across the state and generate relative equity among school districts or counties. The larger issue of what exactly constitutes a fair share in equalization is left as a policy question for the legislature. Equalization of resources often results in a substantial subsidy of revenues flowing from the wealthier urban and suburban regions of a state to poorer communities.

The amount of intergovernmental revenues granted to local governments frequently fails to meet the full cost of providing the services mandated or prescribed by law. Local governments are then left with an **unfunded mandate**. We give greater attention to the unfunded mandate problem later in this chapter.

Revenue Sharing

Revenue sharing allows the federal or state governments to transfer or *share* revenues with local governments. Shared tax revenues and some federal entitlement programs fall into this category of revenues. Revenue sharing arrangements typically place loose or minimal restrictions on how the receiving local government can use the transferred funds. In most states, the state department of revenue acts as a fiduciary agent collecting retail sales taxes, use fees, corporate taxes, and liquor and cigarette taxes, and returning the prescribed proportion back to counties and cities. The proportion of tax returned back to the local government is an example of revenue sharing. Federal revenue sharing with counties is authorized under several programs, including the Payment in Lieu of Taxes (PILT) program and other sharing programs based on federal agency sales of natural resources. We provide additional discussion on federal land and resource-related payments in chapter 8.

Maintenance of Effort Requirements

Many reimbursements and direct grants require the local government or school district to match a federal or state contribution at a proportional rate, or to cover a specified share of costs over the life of a grant. These specifications are known as **maintenance of effort** requirements. For example, a federal Department of Justice grant might require an increasing local contribution to cover the cost of hiring a new police officer over the three-year life of a grant. Typically, grant agreements contain triggers and penalties for noncompliance with performance requirements or matching funding levels. Most of these provisions are financially onerous by design. Critically, to receive funds through a matching arrangement, local governments must appropriate and spend funds. In times of tight budgets and limited local resources, administrators must take a leadership role to ensure that both elected officials and the general public are educated on the need for the local government to allocate and spend money in order to receive money. Ensuring the availability of local matching funds is challenging when budgets are tight and other needs are pressing. In many grant programs, local governments and school districts must further demonstrate to the federal or state agency that they will make a commitment and will maintain appropriations of matching funds over the full life of the grant.

State Sourced Intergovernmental Revenues

State governments provide a wide variety of intergovernmental revenue streams to their counties, cities, towns, and special districts. As mentioned, state intergovernmental revenues are structured and packaged in a variety of forms, ranging from one-time grants and reimbursement for contracted services, to partial or full reimbursement for provision of state-mandated duties, to the fiduciary collection and sharing of tax revenues. Each state structures its intergovernmental revenues differently. Counties in Alaska, Massachusetts, Michigan, North Carolina, Oregon, Tennessee, and Virginia receive over one-quarter of their annual revenues from state intergovernmental aid. In contrast, counties in Delaware, Maine, New Hampshire, and Vermont receive less than 1 percent of their revenues in state intergovernmental revenues (Bartle 2003). This partially reflects the much-reduced role of county governments in the New England states (U.S. Census Bureau 2007b, see chap. 1). State governments often act in a fiduciary capacity to efficiently collect tax revenues and then return a prescribed portion of these entitlement revenues to local counties. These collected revenues include retail sales and use taxes, liquor excise taxes, liquor profit share, beer and wine excise tax, cigarette taxes, timber severance and natural resource use taxes, as well as motor vehicle and highway fund shares. A portion of state **lottery revenues** may be shared with county governments. Depending on state law, cities and towns may also receive a share of some of these entitlement tax and revenue streams. Counties may receive state grants as reimbursement for the provision of services to its residents. Under this type of contractual or partnership arrangement, the state is purchasing program delivery services from local governments. Mental health services, services to the elderly, veterans' services, and other services may be structured under a grant for service model.

Federally Sourced Intergovernmental Revenues

A large number of federal programs and revenues provide intergovernmental revenues to local governments (NACo 2011a). In contrast to state governments, the federal government does not act in a fiduciary tax collection and distribution role. However, the federal government does provide funds to help reimburse county governments for federal lands and facilities within county boundaries (chapter 8). Numerous other programs provide federal support to county governments, cities, and local communities. Community development block grants (CDBG) and the HOME Investment Partnerships Program from the U.S. Department of Housing and Urban Development provide a critical source of federal funds to counties and cities for community development and housing. U.S. Department of Justice public safety programs provide matching funds through competitive grants to counties and cities. These funds allow local governments to hire law enforcement officers and to purchase equipment and software on a cost share basis. U.S. Department of Homeland Security grants are also available to cities and local governments for emergency management and security preparedness. Other federal departments provide grants to local governments for transportation infrastructure and transportation planning, conservation, environmental infrastructure, missing children and law enforcement, and education assistance. The Catalogue of Federal Domestic Assistance (CFDA, www.cfda.gov) provides an entry point for identifying federal intergovernmental grant resources.

Unfunded Mandates

Shortfalls in intergovernmental revenues renew the long-standing debate over unfunded mandates. An **unfunded mandate** is a statutory or regulatory responsibility or duty from a higher level of government delegated to another government without providing sufficient funding to allow compliance and implementation (Osbourn 1995; NCSL 2013 Unfunded Mandates Reform Act of 1995). The National Conference of State Legislatures (NCSL) applies a broader definition that recognizes an unfunded mandate any time a federal decision requires a state or local government to spend funds (NCSL 2013). NCSL sees any spending requirement by state or local governments as a cost shift from the federal level. Unfunded mandates are evidence of the challenges and realities of federalism and the delegation of authority across levels of government. State and local governments are asked by the federal government to become instruments of program implementation, but they are frequently left with insufficient funding and regulatory burdens that make their participation difficult and costly. The NCSL estimates that U.S. Congress has shifted over $131 billion in costs from FY 2004 to 2008 to states (NCSL 2010b). Federal unfunded mandates on states and local governments take a variety of the following forms (NCSL 2013):

- direct federal orders without sufficient funding to pay for their implementation;
- burdensome conditions on grant assistance;
- cross sanctions and redirection penalties that imperil grant funding in order to regulate and preempt a state's actions in both related and unrelated programmatic areas;
- amendments to the tax code that impose direct compliance costs on states and restrict state revenues;
- overly prescriptive regulatory procedures that move beyond the scope of congressional intent;
- incomplete and vague definitions that cause ambiguity; and
- perceived or actual intrusion on state sovereignty.

The Unfunded Mandates Reform Act of 1995 (UMRA, P.L. 104–4) gave formal recognition to the unfunded mandates problem. The act (1) requires that Congress perform a financial analysis to determine the impact of legislation on states, local governments, tribes, and the private sector; and (2) establishes congressional procedures to prevent the creation of an unfunded mandate. UMRA also establishes similar checks on the regulatory process. However, UMRA allows the federal government many loopholes for major entitlement programs, emergency assistance, national security, emergency legislation, constitutional rights of individuals, prohibition of discrimination, and accounting and auditing requirements (Osbourn 1995). For example, the Medicaid, child support, and Title 4E foster care and adoption assistance programs are open-ended entitlements without a cap on federal funding or state administrative costs or matching obligations (NCSL 2013). Given these many exemptions and a limited availability of federal funds, unfunded mandates will continue into the future. Faced with similar revenue shortages and federal performance requirements, state governments too are not immune from creating unfunded mandates for local governments.

The NCSL and the National Association of Counties (NACo) have long advocated against unfunded mandates (cf. NCSL 2014, 2013; Whitley 2010). Local governments should actively communicate and advocate with their legislators at the federal and state levels to prevent the imposition of unfunded mandates. But in situations where intergovernmental revenues are chronically insufficient to accomplish needed program outcomes, local governments should also make a policy decision to develop new sources of revenue to cover shortfalls.

Intergovernmental Revenues Are Vulnerable to Reduction

In most states, intergovernmental payments have been a consistent and durable revenue source for state and local governments (Carroll, Eger, and Marlowe 2003, 1500–01). However, these payments are authorized by statute, and the legislature or governing body that created the statute can modify it as the situation demands. The economic downturn of 2007–2009 curtailed economic growth, which led to a major reduction in income and sales tax revenues to state governments. In 2009 and 2010, this reduction was somewhat blunted by the American Recovery and Reinvestment Act of 2009 (ARRA, "Recovery Act"), which included a variety of intergovernmental revenue shared with states and local governments. The Recovery Act helped many states bridge to a new reality of reduced revenues, but since its conclusion, states must balance their budgets without this major federal supplement. Facing reduced revenues and requirements to produce balanced budgets, state governments have carefully examined all expenditures, including intergovernmental entitlements and grants to local governments. These state intergovernmental payments are now in jeopardy of reduction or elimination (cf. Hannah-Jones 2011). Efforts by Congress to balance the federal budget and to eliminate deficit spending will leave federal intergovernmental transfers to state and local governments in jeopardy for years to come. Local governments should actively advocate in their state legislatures and in Congress to protect and to ensure full funding of programs that authorize and fund intergovernmental transfers (e.g., NACo; NCSL). Beyond advocacy, where intergovernmental revenues are chronically short or are permanently eliminated, local governments must make a policy decision to diversify and to develop new sources of revenues to support community needs, or face the prospect of cutting services.

Revenue Source: Borrowing and Debt Instruments

State statutes grant local governments the authority to borrow money and to use that money as revenue for short- and long-term purposes. The debt instruments used by local governments include several major forms. Many local governments have established lines of credit for short-term needs. Like a line of credit on a residential home, a line of credit provides a local government with the potential to borrow up to a specified level of funds quickly at a preset rate. Local governments may also borrow funds using short-term notes or bank loans. These are often used to cover cash flow needs, especially in paying operating expenses during the short period of time when quarterly or semi-annual tax bills from citizens and businesses have not been collected (see chapter 17 on cash flow management). These loans are called **warrants** because the local government guarantees the payment of the loan from the taxes it will receive. Continuously relying on short-term notes to cover routine operations and maintenance expenses indicates that a jurisdiction is living well beyond its revenue means and is in jeopardy of defaulting.

For longer-term borrowing to cover capital projects and capital purchases, local governments often sell bonds to investors. Local governments typically place a ballot measure before voters to propose a capital project, to agree to borrowing to fund the project, and to establish a special tax assessment. Governments use the dedicated tax revenues to make regular payments to pay off the borrowed principal and interest, much like a home mortgage. We take an extensive look a long-term debt instruments and capital purchases in chapter 16.

Revenue Source: Gifts and Donations

Gifts and donations make up a very small but growing source of local government revenues (Irvin and Carr 2005). The contribution of gifts to the larger revenue picture is largely a function of how aggressively government administrators work to develop philanthropic sources and to assure transparency in use of the donations. Rather than take gifts and donations directly, many local governments have established quasi-independent nonprofit organizations to accept and to coordinate public donations. *Friends* groups or *foundations* widely support community libraries, parks and recreation programs, and other local government programs (Irvin and Carr 2005, 41). Chapter 8 provides additional discussion on **governmental and public foundations**, including their revenue sources. Philanthropy theorists argue that government-provided services will displace and extinguish philanthropy to nonprofit organizations supplying the same service. However, Weisbrod (1977) argues that citizens will provide donations to government organizations to provide service levels above the median level of voter provision. For example, citizens with school-age children may contribute heavily to their local public school or school district education foundation to assure classroom or extracurricular resources above the level provided by a community property tax.

Revenue Source: Opening Fund Balance Forward

A public budget allocates revenues and resources to particular programs and allows the spending to accomplish program tasks. However, governments may purposely leave some money unspent in a program's account or fund. Some resources in a fund are purposefully reserved for specific purchases or for pending program expenses. Other resources are left to cover anticipated end-of-year expenses and fiscal year close out (chapters 17 and 18). An increment of resources simply may not have been spent at the close of the fiscal year. Any unreserved resources in an account or fund at the close of the fiscal year may be available for spending in the coming fiscal year. These unspent resources often accumulate in a fund or account and are termed the **opening fund balance**. The level of the opening fund balance tends to increase in a growing economy when tax and fee revenue exceeds forecasts and budgeted spending. Opening fund balances may provide substantial resources to supplement tax, fee, intergovernmental, and other revenues. Budget policy in some jurisdictions may encourage keeping a large opening fund balance as a quasi-reserve fund. The unspent opening fund balance may be used as a reserve cushion against short-term cash flow problems, as a response to unexpected increases in service demand, or as resources to backfill revenue shortfalls due to economic downturns. We will provide a more detailed discussion of accounting funds and opening fund balances in chapter 9.

Exhibit 6.1

Local Governmental Revenues by Source, 2009, for All U.S. Local Governments

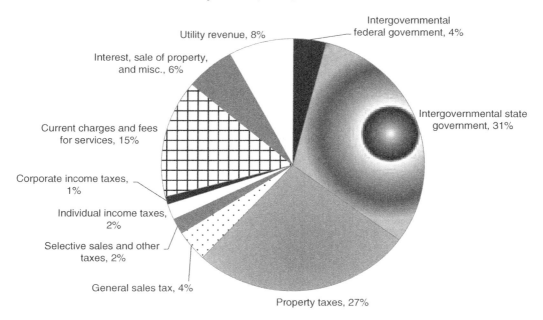

Source: U.S. Census Bureau, 2009. Table 1: State and Local Government Finances by Level of Government by State.

REVENUE BLENDS TO SUPPORT LOCAL GOVERNMENTS

The regional economic activity and the accumulated wealth in the community form a base from which to generate the continuing revenue to fund government operations and capital projects. Property taxes, sales taxes, charges and fees for service, and intergovernmental revenues provide a solid, continuing financial base for most local governments (Edwards 2006). Continuing revenues provide the base on which to size a government's organization and procurement. Exhibit 6.1 displays an estimate of the relative share of the major sources of local governmental revenues for all U.S. local governments in 2009. The exact balance of the different continuing revenue sources used by a local government will vary with the fiscal year. Economic cycles of growth and recession will cause an ebb and flow in sales, income, and business tax revenues.

The wide variation in size, state tax regulations, and purpose causes an individual local government to deviate from the national averages in Exhibit 6.1. State property tax limitations may lessen the contribution of property taxes as a revenue source. State law may or may not authorize a jurisdiction to impose a retail sales tax or an individual income tax. Enterprise revenues from water and electricity utility sales, recreation facilities, or transit district fares may contribute an identifiable and substantial share of a government's total revenues. The size and stability of enterprise revenues, as well as policy decisions on how to use enterprise profits to subsidize other governmental functions, determines the continuing revenue base on which to size an organization and its procurement.

Revenues related to one-time activities and to one-time short duration revenues serve to supplement and complement a local jurisdiction's continuing sources of funding. The flow of borrowed revenues from bonds and financial notes often will follow the start-up, construction, completion, and lifespan of capital construction projects. Grant revenues from the federal and state governments will increase intergovernmental revenues over the lifecycle of the grant. Some grants provide local governments with continuing revenues on a permanent basis, while other short-term grants last for only one to several years. Administrators and elected officials should recognize that short-term, one-time grants from public and private sources provide only a supplement to continuous revenues or **recurring revenues**. The revenue balance that supports a jurisdiction adjusts over time, but increasing the diversity of both recurring and one-time sources of revenue should stand as a strategic goal (NCSL 2007b; Krane, Ebdon, and Bartle 2004).

Examples of Local Revenue Sources

The following set of exhibits (6.2 to 6.6) presents representative examples of the balance of revenues used by local governments of different sizes and types. These exhibits demonstrate the ongoing importance of property taxes and charges and fees for most local governments. Charges and fees are especially important for special district governments.

Large- and mega-sized urban/suburban counties are some of the largest full service governments in the country. Exhibit 6.2 demonstrates revenues for one such county government. This county contains 1.9 million residents, including one city of 600,000 residents and two cities of about 100,000. For 2010, the total budget from all funds was about $4 billion. Even with its mega size, the county government is heavily reliant on property and sales taxes, and on charges and fees for services. Local intergovernmental revenues add to the total county revenues. For example, small

Exhibit 6.2

Large- and Mega-Sized Urban/Suburban County Revenues by Source, 2009: All Funds

Total revenues, $4.07 billion; Total population, 1.91 million

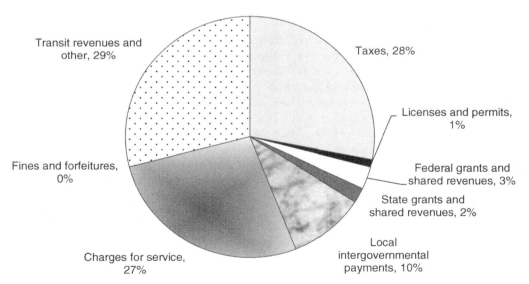

Source: King County, WA 2009, B-11. For clarity, all federal grants and revenues, including Recovery Act funds, were combined into a single federal category. All state funds were combined into a single category, and all local intergovernmental revenues and grants were combined. King County operates a very large transit system that accounts for a large portion of the "transit revenues and other" wedge.

Exhibit 6.3

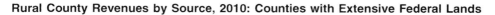

Rural County Revenues by Source, 2010: Counties with Extensive Federal Lands

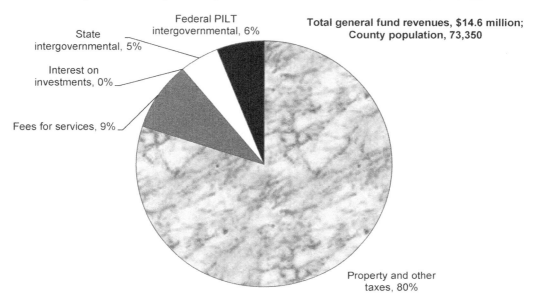

Source: Umatilla County, OR 2010, General Fund 101, pp. 16–17. Umatilla County has elected to take federal Payment in Lieu of Taxes (PILT) payments to compensate for lost property tax revenues on federal lands in the county.

cities in counties often contract with the county sheriff under an interlocal, intergovernmental agreement for law enforcement patrol and investigative services. Large counties may also operate an extensive transit system and wastewater and sewer facilities on an enterprise basis. These enterprise functions result in substantial utility and transit revenues, all segregated to support the operations of the particular service.

In contrast to a mega urban/suburban county, Exhibit 6.3 represents a western state rural county with a small population and an extensive acreage of nonassessed federal public lands. While the geographic size of the county is quite large, the county government is very small, serving a population of about 73,000 citizens with a limited economic base. Again, property taxes provide the primary source of revenue for this county government, while charges and fees for services provide a smaller portion of the total. Interestingly, the direct federal PILT reimbursement payments provide about the same proportion of federal intergovernmental revenues as in the much larger mega county just described above.

Exhibit 6.4 demonstrates the revenue balance for a representative small city with a population of about 16,500. Property taxes generate about one-third of the total revenues, and charges for service generate about 40 percent—a little bit more than in the mega-county example. Retail sales and use taxes generate a small but important source of revenue for this city. The state actually collects this tax from local merchants and then reimburses the city and the local county according to authorized percentages. Licenses and permits, as well as fines and forfeitures, each contribute a small portion of the total revenues.

Townships in the mid-Atlantic and central states provide local services to suburban and rural residents. Larger townships (first class in Pennsylvania) typically surround large cities and serve suburban areas. Smaller townships (second class) are smaller in capacity but provide similar lo-

Exhibit 6.4

Small City and Town Revenues by Source, 2010: All Funds

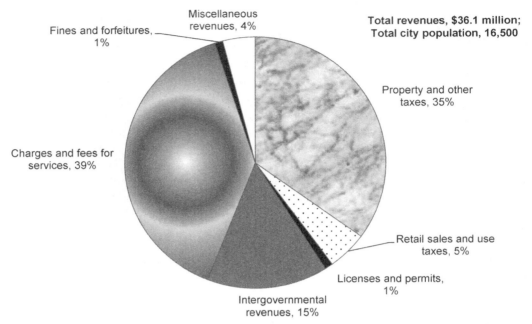

**Total revenues, $36.1 million;
Total city population, 16,500**

Source: Revenue proportions for this example small city are drawn from the *City of Camas, Washington, Budget 2010.* Camas operates proprietary storm drainage, city sanitary and water-sewer programs that generate extensive charges for service revenue. City of Camas 2009.

cal government services to suburban and rural residents. Exhibit 6.5 demonstrates revenues for a representative small township that serves about 3,800 residents. The exhibit covers general fund revenues and six other dedicated special fund revenues. The exhibit indicates that the township relies on real estate property taxes, but it also depends heavily on wage- and services-based income taxes. The township collects no sales tax revenues. The township receives intergovernmental revenues from the state and other local governments, but none from the federal government.

The township example in Exhibit 6.5 and the small city example in Exhibit 6.4 demonstrate useful comparisons. Taxes provide a major source of revenue for both jurisdictions (40 percent in the city and 66 percent in the township). The township, however, collects very few charges and fees for services; instead, taxes and permit revenues cover most service costs. The small city uses the nomenclature of charges and fees (about 40 percent) to include revenues from its enterprise funds and services to individual users. Interestingly, the combination of taxes, license and permit revenues, and fee revenues in both jurisdictions totals about 80 percent of all revenues collected. Intergovernmental revenues provide about the same percentage of revenues to both jurisdictions (about 15 percent) with little federal contribution.

In contrast to the general-purpose county and city governments, Exhibit 6.6 demonstrates a medium port district with a marine shipping program. The district operates enterprise functions loading and unloading a variety of bulk commodities, containers, large manufactured equipment, and passengers, and renting land and property to businesses. The enterprise functions bring in the majority of the district's revenues. Marine terminal fees are an especially important source of revenue. The district also receives property tax income that funds a set of nonenterprise governmental

Exhibit 6.5

Small Township Revenues by Source, 2012: All Funds

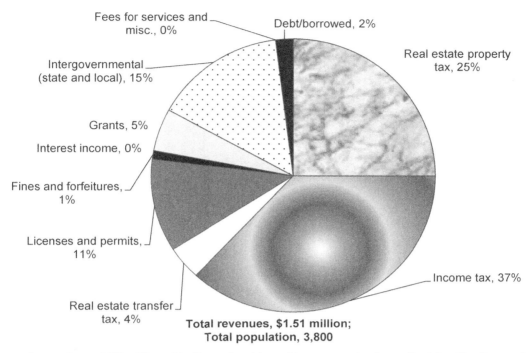

Fees for services and misc., 0%

Debt/borrowed, 2%

Real estate property tax, 25%

Intergovernmental (state and local), 15%

Grants, 5%

Interest income, 0%

Fines and forfeitures, 1%

Licenses and permits, 11%

Income tax, 37%

Real estate transfer tax, 4%

**Total revenues, $1.51 million;
Total population, 3,800**

Source: Lower Milford Township (Pennsylvania) provides an example of a smaller (class 2), often-rural township government. Lower Milford Township 2011.

functions. These governmental functions provide general government services, facilities planning and environmental services, and economic development services similar to a county government. This district is located in a state with general and local retail sales and use taxes, but the district receives no sales tax revenue. Any federal revenues would come from specific grants.

Our focus here is local government revenue sources. There are important differences between local and state revenues, as explained in Exhibit 6.7 on page 189.

Relative Revenue Burdens

The collective structure of law, regulations, and tax program implementation combine to create the revenue burden carried by the residents and businesses of each state. Exhibit 6.8 provides the relative ranking of the per capita revenue burden by state based on state and local revenue collections. Revenue sources include property taxes, general sales taxes, motor fuels taxes, alcoholic beverage taxes, tobacco taxes, individual income taxes, corporate income taxes, and charges and fees collected. A ranking based on a total of all revenues is included on the right side of the table. The exhibit computes its rankings on a per capita basis that standardizes the revenues for comparison across states. However, several states with apparent high burdens (like Alaska, Wyoming, and North Dakota) receive their high rankings because of **severance taxes** on petroleum, natural gas, and coal extraction. To imply that each citizen of these states bears a full revenue burden is

Exhibit 6.6

Special District Revenues by Source, 2010: Medium-Capacity Marine Port District

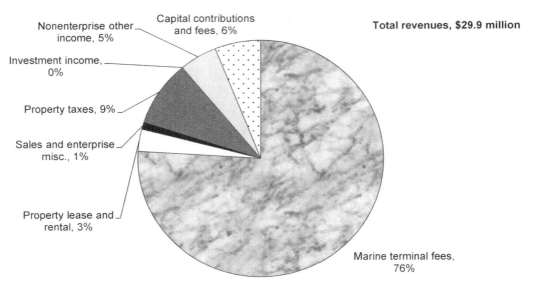

Total revenues, $29.9 million

Nonenterprise other income, 5%

Capital contributions and fees, 6%

Investment income, 0%

Property taxes, 9%

Sales and enterprise misc., 1%

Property lease and rental, 3%

Marine terminal fees, 76%

Source: Port of Longview (Washington) provides the data for this representative port special district. Port of Longview 2010, 4.

incorrect (Braybrooks, Ruiz, and Accetta 2011). Operating a state government requires a basic fixed cost of program and funds, thus small population (fewer than a million residents) states may generate high per capita burdens relative to most states. Alaska, Wyoming, Vermont, Delaware, North and South Dakota, Montana, and even the District of Columbia have high burdens, in part because of their comparatively small populations.

Exhibit 6.8 demonstrates the relative revenue burden between states, and also how states balance individual tax, corporate tax, and charges and fee revenues into a total package. The exhibit demonstrates a set of high revenue states with relatively heavy burdens: the District of Columbia, New Jersey, New York, Connecticut, and Hawaii. Another group demonstrates relatively low total revenues collected per capita: South Dakota, Tennessee, and Arizona. Other states demonstrate a balancing of revenue sources with heavy reliance on one or two preferred revenue sources. Wyoming relies heavy on property taxes and general sales taxes, along with charges and fees, but has no personal or corporate income tax. Washington State has high general sales and business gross receipts taxes, and high charges and fees for service, but no individual income tax. Hawaii has a high general sales tax that captures tourist spending, but a very low corporate income tax. In contrast, Maryland and Oregon rely heavily on individual income taxes. Oregon has no general sales tax, and Maryland has a relatively low general sales tax and low charges and fees. In general, the New England states rely heavily on property taxes. Massachusetts, New Hampshire, and Vermont have very high property taxes, as well as strong corporate income taxes, but low or no general sales tax. The District of Columbia, Connecticut, and Rhode Island assess very high property taxes, but collect very low fee revenues. South Carolina and Iowa assess relatively light property, general sales, and income taxes, but rely heavily on charges and fees. As these configurations illustrate, states may collect little or no revenue from a particular source, but then diversify their revenues from all other available sources.

Exhibit 6.7

State Governments Revenue Sources Are Different

In contrast to local governments, state governments rely on a slightly different set of revenue sources (Braybrooks, Ruiz, and Accetta 2011). Although in limited use by local governments, 43 states and the District of Columbia impose an individual income tax that generates substantial revenues to state and district coffers. All but four states impose a corporate income tax that provides a smaller, but nevertheless important, source of revenue. Retail sales, gross receipts, use taxes, and excise taxes are another major category of revenues. Tobacco and liquor taxes, along with liquor sales profits, provide important sources of excise tax revenue. Thirty-six states have authorized a state property tax. Michigan, Vermont, and Washington impose a state property tax to fund K–12 education statewide (Braybrooks, Ruiz, and Accetta 2011, 5). A state level property tax for K–12 provides one means of equalizing school funding across a state. Inheritance and estate taxes provide a typically minor but politically sensitive source of revenue. Severance taxes on the extraction of petroleum, natural gas, and hard rock minerals, or on the harvest of timber, provide a substantial source of revenue for several states. State-owned lands and utility rights of way generate rental revenue.

Unique to the state level, many state governments operate a lottery. Lottery profits provide a steady source of unencumbered nontax general revenue. Lottery dollars may be earmarked for a particular program or purpose, or used as annual revenues to pay off bonds. Local governments may receive a pass-through of lottery funds, but most lottery revenues remain at the state level.

In contrast to the relatively limited contribution of federal intergovernmental funds at the local government level, federal transfers provide a major source of revenues at the state level for a broad array of programs. A listing of some of the major federal intergovernmental programs follows (Federal Funds Information for States [FFIS] 2011). Federal transfers for nutrition, social service, and child care programs are substantial. These transfer funds include: Women, Infants, and Children (WIC) and Supplemental Nutrition Assistance (SNAP); Temporary Assistance to Needy Families (TANF) annual block grant; Child Care and Development block grants; Child Welfare funds; Social Services Block Grants; Head Start early childhood learning funds; and Low-Income Home Energy Assistance funds. Federal funds support major health programs as well: Medicaid administration and Medicaid provider reimbursement for qualifying low-income citizens; Children's Health Insurance Program; Mental Health Services block grant; and the Substance Abuse block grant. Many of these programs require a state percentage match for each federal dollar, or the maintenance of state spending effort. The unemployment insurance program in each state is jointly funded by federal and state payroll taxes but administered as a federal trust fund with payments to states. Federal dollars support programs for adult and youth worker training and for dislocated worker assistance. Federal funding provides critical support to state and local housing programs. The HOME investment partnership program, the Section 8 Rent Subsidy programs, the Community Development Block Grants (CDBG), the Community Services Block Grant, and housing for the elderly draw on federal funds. Federal Homeland Security funds support grants to states and to local governments for security, emergency response, and emergency preparedness. Department of Justice programs fund the Community Oriented Policing Services (COPS) and policing grants to local sheriff and police departments, the Violence Against Women program, and the Juvenile Accountability block grant. Federal transportation dollars provide substantial resources for airport, highway, and mass transit facility construction. Federal environmental funds support energy weatherization and clean drinking water programs.

The National Conference of State Legislatures (NCSL) provides extensive coverage of state fiscal situations and the status of federal revenue programs (access NCSL at http://www.ncsl.org). Efforts to reduce the federal spending deficit will very likely reduce federal transfers to the states in the coming years.

Exhibit 6.8

Rankings of Per Capita Tax Burden for Selected Major Tax and Charges Categories by State, Including the District of Columbia, with U.S. National Average, 2008–2009

State	Property tax ranking	General sales tax ranking	Motor fuels tax ranking	Alcoholic beverage tax ranking	Tobacco tax ranking	Individual income tax ranking	Corporate income tax ranking	Charges and fees ranking	All taxes and charges ranking
Alabama	52	32	24	2	40	39	29	5	44
Alaska	11	48	52	1	3	—	1	3	1
Arizona	34	10	30	38	30	43	33	50	50
Arkansas	51	9	11	23	29	32	23	43	48
California	16	20	48	43	45	9	7	11	10
Colorado	26	18	31	45	35	22	43	10	24
Connecticut	3	27	21	31	11	5	22	51	6
Delaware	45	—	28	21	2	12	8	7	15
District of Columbia	1	5	51	42	25	2	2	52	3
Florida	14	13	6	11	47	—	31	13	27
Georgia	36	25	47	12	48	31	41	37	45
Hawaii	37	3	35	6	22	18	45	15	8
Idaho	42	36	19	48	41	33	35	18	49
Illinois	10	31	26	22	28	34	17	46	21
Indiana	33	22	32	46	16	24	20	25	32
Iowa	24	26	17	50	17	20	37	4	16
Kansas	21	16	13	5	37	19	18	12	17
Kentucky	48	43	14	15	32	17	24	36	46
Louisiana	47	4	23	30	42	36	16	29	28
Maine	12	39	7	32	5	15	28	49	26
Maryland	29	42	29	49	20	3	19	44	13
Massachusetts	9	45	44	35	10	4	5	32	9
Michigan	17	28	45	28	6	37	42	17	30
Minnesota	22	30	18	25	15	7	13	22	12
Mississippi	43	17	15	27	44	41	26	8	40
Missouri	39	33	37	47	51	28	46	41	47
Montana	25	—	3	13	9	30	11	40	39
Nebraska	18	21	8	24	38	23	27	21	22
Nevada	23	12	20	29	36	—	—	31	31

191

New Hampshire	4	—	43	40	1	44	4	47	34
New Jersey	2	24	50	33	12	8	6	33	5
New Mexico	49	6	46	18	50	42	39	42	43
New York	6	11	49	34	19	1	3	20	4
North Carolina	40	34	9	8	46	16	32	23	38
North Dakota	31	15	1	36	39	40	10	9	7
Ohio	32	35	12	41	14	11	47	28	29
Oklahoma	50	19	40	16	21	35	34	26	42
Oregon	30	—	42	51	23	6	40	16	35
Pennsylvania	27	40	10	14	18	13	15	38	25
Rhode Island	8	38	38	37	4	21	30	48	19
South Carolina	38	41	41	9	52	38	48	2	33
South Dakota	35	8	16	20	13	—	44	45	51
Tennessee	44	7	25	4	33	45	21	34	52
Texas	15	14	34	10	26	—	—	39	41
Utah	41	29	27	26	49	27	36	14	36
Vermont	7	47	22	7	8	26	14	30	11
Virginia	19	46	39	17	43	10	38	19	23
Washington	28	2	4	3	24	—	—	6	14
West Virginia	46	44	2	44	27	29	9	35	37
Wisconsin	13	37	5	39	7	14	25	27	18
Wyoming	5	1	36	52	34	—	—	1	2
United States Nat. Avg.	20	23	33	19	31	25	12	24	20

Source: Original data from U.S. Census Bureau 2009. Tax data are as of 2008–2009 from Excel tables 09sslstab1a.xls and 09sslstab1b.xls. Population estimates are from U.S. Census Bureau 2012a. Authors' compilation.

Changing Balance and Relative Importance of Local Revenue Sources

The relative importance of the various revenue sources used by local government has evolved over the decades. The effects of the 2007–2009 economic downturn will have a continuing impact on this evolution. Property taxes once provided nearly all local government revenues. Property taxes remain especially important as a source of revenue in the New England states, but they have become less important in the southern and southwestern states. At the beginning of the twentieth century, property taxes supplied 82 percent of all local government revenues (Bartle 2003). Property tax revolts in California and in other states in the 1970s caused a precipitous decline in this share (Mikesell 2005, 112); tax and expenditure limitations are now in place in 43 states (Edwards 2006, 3). In the 1990s, the decline in property tax revenue moderated, but by 1999 the property tax share of revenue had fallen to about 37 percent. Exhibit 6.1 confirms that this share continued to fall to about 27 percent by 2009. In an unintended political consequence, tax and expenditure limitations have often centralized local control over property taxes and revenues to the state level. In 30 states, state payments to local school districts for K–12 education have replaced some of the lost property tax revenues (Bartle 2003, 28). Some of the increase in centralized state school funding may be attributable to efforts to equalize education funding across rich and poor school districts (Edwards 2006, 4; Krane, Ebdon, and Bartle 2004, 524).

The relative contribution of federal intergovernmental payments to local governments has also evolved over the recent decades (Krane, Ebdon, and Bartle 2004, 515; Edwards 2006, 2). Federal payments to local governments reached a high in the 1960s and 1970s with the Johnson administration's Great Society programs and the Nixon administration's revenue sharing block grant and environmental infrastructure programs. The Housing and Community Development Act of 1974 began the Community Development Block Grant (CDBG) program during this period. This era of generous federal resources also brought spending flexibility and program responsibility to local governments. But by the late 1970s, Congress began to increase regulatory mandates on states and local governments and the supporting federal funding began to decline. This set up a wave of unfunded program requirements and mandates, many of which continue to today. By the early 1980s, the Reagan administration aggressively reduced the federal revenue programs to state and local governments. Exhibit 6.1 demonstrates that in recent years federal intergovernmental grants have become an increasingly smaller source of revenue for most local governments. Perhaps the major exception to this trend was an increase in federal funds to local governments for homeland security after the 9/11 attacks in 2001.

The recent extensive federal spending on economic recovery, dysfunctional federal budgeting and appropriations (Meyers and Joyce 2005; Joyce 2005), and a substantial federal deficit and debt have increased calls for a balanced federal budget and stronger federal spending controls (National Commission on Fiscal Responsibility and Reform [NCFR&R] 2010; Ryan 2011; Obama 2011). Recent political action has pointed toward continued pressure to constrain federal spending. Over the longer term, state and local governments will likely need to adjust to a reduced level of federal support.

State aid to local governments increased into the 1980s, but then shifted to a decline. At the same time, states devolved substantial additional functions, responsibilities, and administrative capacities to local governments, including land-use planning, regional planning, and economic development. These new administrative capacities and procedures exceeded the basic authorities granted under home rule charters (Krane, Ebdon, and Bartle 2004, 527). State intergovernmental transfers continue to provide extremely important entitlement and shared tax revenues to county and city governments, even though these transfers often do not meet the levels needed to cover local program costs.

The decreasing contribution of property tax revenues, and of state and federal intergovernmental revenues, set the backdrop for the wild events of the economic downturn of 2007–2009. At the completion of this text in 2014, the effects of the downturn lingered, affecting local government revenues and borrowing in many communities. Unemployment rates remain high in many communities, even as housing values have stabilized and housing construction has begun to recover. In the face of constrained property tax revenues and limited federal and state intergovernmental transfers, local governments will need to identify sustainable levels of revenue and size spending accordingly; seek out and develop new sources of continuing and one-time revenues, explore jurisdictional consolidations and sharing of service delivery responsibilities, and possibly shed services to other organizations better situated to obtain and concentrate the necessary revenues. This situation reinforces the need for local governments and government administrators to take an energetic, entrepreneurial approach to diversifying revenue sources. It also illustrates that issues of revenue are tied together with larger issues of governance, including building community capacity and resiliency in the provision of services by community partners.

CONCLUSION: LEADERSHIP CHALLENGE TO RAISE AND STABILIZE REVENUES

The hypothetical Upper Cascadia County teaching case with which we began this chapter presents a scenario of voter disapproval and subsequent efforts by the finance director, Elizabeth Brown, and other officials to rebuild a revenue base for public safety programs. Upper Cascadia County and all other local governments strive for a tax and revenue system that can efficiently generate a reliable and stable flow of revenues in the face of changing economic conditions. Elected and appointed county treasurers, assessors, and clerks are the key to fair and cost-effective implementation of property tax and revenue systems. A diversified balance of tax, fee, intergovernmental, and other revenues is critical to such revenue stability and reliability. From the viewpoint of citizens and businesses, a tax system must be fair and equitable in design and implementation. Local government officials have limited control over the elements and equity in their parent state's tax structure and policy, but these officials make a major difference in how the state structure is interpreted and applied to local taxpayers. Local government officials have choices as to when and how to exercise the taxing authority delegated from the state. They can also set local property tax rates and choose when to exercise local options for sales and income taxes. Each of these choices calls for effective political and administrative leadership.

Against the challenges of public frustrations and suspicions, community traditions, staff relations, economic backdrop, and the state revenue structure, the task of administrators and elected leaders is (1) to lead the community to recognize its needs, and (2) to gain the agreement to accept taxation and other revenues. Administrators are in a unique position to take the leadership role to explain needs, nurture and clarify a vision of the future, answer concerns, admit to the costs, demonstrate benefits, and deliver the services as expected.

STUDY QUESTIONS

1. Consider the county, township, or city in which you live or work. Compare its sources and balance of revenues to the graphs in the chapter. Which revenue sources are, or are not, present? What community preference and policy choices explain or drive the balance of revenue sources?

2. In your jurisdiction, how have local government revenues changed since the economic downturn that began in 2007? Is your community faced with extensive residential property foreclosures? How have local property values affected property tax revenues?

3. In your jurisdiction, what analysis and public process are used to set the fee rates for services (e.g., permitting, construction inspections, health inspections, utility franchise, and utility service, including water, sewer, or electricity)? Are these fees set for partial or total cost recovery? Is it just to set a fee for partial cost recovery? Can you identify a fee that is set to generate a profit?

4. If you work for a governmental or nonprofit organization, how do you set the fee rates for the services that you provide? What analysis and policy process do you use to set fee rates? Are your customers, board, and donors supportive of your fee structure?

5. The chapter describes the wide variety of intergovernmental revenues shared between state and local governments. Obtain a schedule of state revenues shared with local governments in your state. Which are the most important intergovernmental revenues? If your state has a lottery, is a portion of the lottery profits returned to counties or local governments?

6. Can you identify a partial or major unfunded mandate imposed on your local government by a state or federal program? Examine the mandate from all perspectives. Is it fair for the state or federal government to impose a requirement on a local need or condition with insufficient resources?

NOTES

1. We draw on the material in chapter 10 of Morgan, Green, Shinn, and Robinson, *Foundations of Public Service*, 2d ed. (Armonk, NY: M.E. Sharpe, 2013) for the preparation of this chapter.

2. See *Quill Corp. v. North Dakota*, 504 U.S. 298 (1992) and *National Bellas Hess, Inc. v. Department of Revenue*, 386 U.S. 753 (1976).

3. King County, Washington, follows a similar breakout: entitlements, shared revenues, and grants for services. See King County, 2009, *2010 Executive Proposed Budget Book,* Economic and Revenue Forecast, B-11.

FORECASTING GOVERNMENTAL REVENUES

TECHNIQUES AND LIMITATIONS
WITH THE ASSISTANCE OF DREW S. BARDEN*

Performance by another that entails consistency, competence, and reliability is likely to enhance greatly the likelihood of the development of a relationship of trust.

(Valerie Braithwaite 1998, 52)

State statutes and local ordinances define the sources and types of revenues potentially available to local governments, but to build a budget, governments must have some idea of the accessibility, amount, flow, and timing of those revenues over a fiscal year or biennium. Developing **forecasts** or best estimates of the expected revenues for the coming year is a critical step in the budget process. The forecast level of revenues, plus interfund transfers and any funds brought forward from previous years, define the resources available to fund expenditures. The amount of available resources defines the potential size, capacity, and mix of government services for the coming budget year. Revenue forecasts also help to define the political environment faced by elected officials, interest group advocates, nonprofit foundations, service providers, and other budget actors. An understanding of pending government finances and program potential allows community nonprofits, foundations, and network providers to develop complementary and supplemental programs. Revenue forecasts also help to assure debt service payments and the potential for future capital investments. In sum, revenue forecasts form the foundation for the local government budget and for many polity-level governance decisions by community leaders.

Long-term revenue forecasts provide important information to support **financial forecasts** and strategic financial plans (chapter 10). These extended forecasts of three or more years reflect assumptions about the local and regional economies, employer behavior, community wealth, and state and federal support for intergovernmental revenues. Matched with extended forecasts of future program expenditures and service caseloads, these long-term revenue forecasts help to ensure the ongoing structural balance of the local government budget (chapter 15). The long-term revenue forecasts also provide trends against which to context short-term budget-cycle forecasts.

Effective revenue forecasting is as much a professional art as it is a technical procedure. Underneath the rigor of mathematical and statistical techniques, revenue forecasts rest on a series of assumptions about demographic changes, future business behaviors, and evolving economic conditions. Regional, state, national, and even global economic conditions affect local businesses and their decisions to expand or to reduce capacity. For example, the decisions by local property owners to develop agricultural land into new housing and commercial facilities would typically

---

*Drew Barden, PhD, retired economist for the City of Portland, Oregon, provided the initial approach and content for this chapter.

reflect favorable economic conditions, available developers, other business plans, and often, personal decisions of retirement or career change. In the same way, family decisions to build a new home, or to renovate and expand an existing home, reflect personal savings, family circumstances, and job security. Homebuilding and remodeling decisions ultimately affect government building permit revenues and property tax assessments. The cumulative effect of these small individual decisions across a community provides critical information to forecasters as they generate budget-cycle and long-term revenue estimates.

With so much uncertainty folded into forecasts, analysts and forecasters must strive for both technical accuracy and for credibility with forecast users. This uncertainty applies to both budget-cycle forecasts and long-term forecasts, but the need to understand the near-term revenue situation for budget development and adoption especially sharpens credibility concerns with the budget-cycle forecasts. Revenue forecasts must be sufficiently certain to support public statements and decisions by elected officials, executive administrators, nonprofit partners, and other community leaders. A forecaster's ability to communicate and to explain is as important as the technical skill needed to model data into forecast estimates. True credibility is built year after year with accurate forecasts and effective explanations. We address the importance of confidence and organizational relationships in the first part of this chapter.

Effective forecasters and analysts bring a full toolbox of approaches and techniques to the revenue forecasting task. The techniques range in sophistication from educated estimation, to spreadsheet deterministic models, to averaging and trending techniques, to highly complex statistical regression and systems models. Mathematical break-even analysis techniques are particularly important for forecasting revenues from fees, charges, and rates for services. Each technique brings its own assumptions, limitations, and strengths. The quality of a forecast reflects the forecaster's skill at making valid assumptions, applying the appropriate models to the available data, and selecting a forecast from among a range of options. The second part of this chapter provides an overview of the major forecasting techniques and details their application.

Property taxes provide a major source of revenue for many local governments. The details of the property tax assessment and computation vary by state, but the basic system relies on the accurate assessment of all property in the jurisdiction, computation of tax owed, and collection of the tax. After explaining the property tax system in detail, the chapter summarizes a common technique used to forecast property tax revenues.

Revenue forecasts by local governments reflect the structures and requirements embedded in the parent state **tax** system. Statutory limitations on property tax revenues and government expenditures, also known as **tax and expenditure limitations** (**TELs**) affect the revenues available to local governments to support programs. Accurate property tax revenue forecasts must consider any tax limitations in the state tax code. This chapter closes with an overview of the main types of property tax limitations and a discussion of the effect of limitations on revenue and the viability of local governments over the medium and long terms.

REVENUE FORECASTING TO BUILD CREDIBILITY

Revenue forecasting forms the foundation of the public budget. The identification of the types, availability, and timing of revenues dictates the levels of spending possible in a budget. Over-estimating expected revenues results in midyear program cuts and dashed expectations. Under-estimating revenues leads to a scaled-back budget that leaves public needs underserved; it also leads to the embarrassment of excess revenues, charges of overtaxation, and the political task of explaining how a jurisdiction will constructively use the unexpected windfall. How to build accurate forecasts and gain the confidence of budget actors in those forecasts is the forecaster's primary task.

Revenue Forecasts Support the Budget Process

Revenue forecasts contribute to the budget process at several critical points. Depending on the size of the local government and the budget process calendar, the activities of budget preparation adds a five- to ten-month lead time before a budget is actually adopted and executed. A **budget-cycle revenue forecast** must accurately cover the entire budget preparation time frame and carry through the final months of the fiscal year or biennium with the best possible estimates. Revenue forecast updates, often on a quarterly basis, provide the means to keep the initial round of forecasts updated over the months or years of budget preparation and execution. A review of the forecast accuracy from the previous fiscal year may often provide additional information on assumptions and analytic model effectiveness. The quarterly revenue forecast updates may trigger a revision and rework of agency program spending requests. Rather than a linear flow, the budget process becomes circular as new information from each subsequent forecast update is reviewed, considered, and adjusted into the proposed budget.

On the technical level, the budget-cycle forecast estimates provide critical revenue levels to the department-level analysts beginning to schedule out potential programs for the budget year. Restrictions may limit the use of some funds in place of others, and certain funds may not be available until partway through the budget year. The programming of revenues, purchases, and work activities during the budget preparation phase sorts out such timing conflicts. Periodic updates and refinements to revenue forecasts help the department analysts develop the most likely scenarios for potential programs and service levels. Analysts in the central budget office and executives refining budget allocations and program levels also benefit from the most recent revenue forecast updates. Budget-cycle revenue forecasts also help community issue advocates explain the changing economic realities to their membership and clients.

Long-term revenue forecasts (three or more years' time frame) prepared as part of the organization's financial forecasts and financial strategic plan provide a backdrop and context to the budget-cycle revenue forecasts and updates. The long-term forecasts reflect durable trends and assumptions about the local and regional demographics, business operations, and regional and state economic capacity, state and federal fiscal, monetary and revenue sharing policy, accumulated community wealth, and revenue generation potential. In contrast, the budget-cycle revenue forecasts help the budget actors understand the implications of recent and ongoing changes in economic conditions. The combination of strategic context and current detail helps executives (CEOs) and elected officials adjust their political agendas and budget decisions to both the limits and to the full potential of regional economic capacity and wealth.

Budget-cycle revenue forecasts become especially critical following release of a proposed budget by the CEO to the council, commission, or board. A decision by the CEO not to raise additional revenues sets a cap on program size and composition for the coming fiscal year. Any request for increased taxes must be presented to the council, commission, or board for hearing and adoption before any subsequent adoption of the full budget. Recent and accurate revenue forecasts form the basis for the political decisions of whether to raise additional revenues or to rely on current taxation levels. Once the budget is adopted and execution begun, revenue forecasters continue to supply refined estimates over the fiscal year. Program analysts can then adjust service delivery capacity as needed. Revised revenue forecasts also help community groups and advocates understand potential changes to government programs.

Thus, the main task of the forecast group is to generate a set of numerical estimates that work. These estimates norm budget process deliberations and get the budget and the agency through the immediate fiscal year or biennium without program cutbacks. Optimistic revenue estimates for the current years should not result in reduced revenues in future years. Overly aggressive front-loading of revenue estimates only leads to reduced service levels and dashed expectations in future years. Long-term forecasts provide a larger context for making adjustments to program size and composition. The close of the fiscal year provides an opportunity for forecasters to review their approaches, techniques, and judgment against actual events and changes in the economy.

Building Budget Actor Trust in Revenue Forecasts

Elected officials, program administrators, community leaders, issue advocates, program clients, and citizens all bring different priorities and needs to the local government budget process (chapters 3 and 4). Executive administrators use the forecasts to help set priorities in a consolidated all-funds budget and to structure discussions with the legislative body (e.g., council, commission, or board) (see chapter 15). Elected officials use the forecasts to set political strategy and tactics and to set expectations with constituents, community leaders, and interest groups. Revenue forecasts help set the resource context for the community services network, for intermediary nonprofits, and for community foundations. The forecasts also help advocacy group leaders set expectations and define the limits of what is politically possible to their members and clients. Program managers, contractors, and nonprofit partners may use the forecasts to program resources and to guide hiring decisions. Revenue forecasts set the framework for labor negotiations between unions and governments (see first teaching case in Part IV). Investors and financial rating agencies review revenue forecasts as part of risk assessment in the offer and purchase of public bonds and other debt instruments. In sum, revenue forecasts are applied both inside and outside of the budget process, in both the short and long term.

As described in chapter 4, the different budget actors bring different perceptions, values, and understandings of taxes and public finance to the budget process. These differences apply to revenue forecasting as well. A consensus reconciling all of these different needs and perspectives is unlikely, but it is important that the budget process actors enter into the debate with some agreement on the rules of the game. Agreement in advance, on the size of the estimated revenues and resources available for programs is one major rule that can help contain subsequent budget debates.

Revenue estimation and forecasting relies heavily on quantitative, statistical, and economic techniques, but sophisticated techniques are only one part of building trust in the forecasting process and its estimates. The techniques for assembling revenue estimates are partly science and partly artful judgment. This is true whether the forecast is developed by a clerk in a small city finance department, a central budget office staff analyst, a contracted expert consultant, or a small staff of economists and forecasters working for a large city or county government. The techniques that feel familiar and solid to the revenue forecaster may easily appear as a mysterious "black box" to the general public and to elected officials. Revenue forecasters must make a special effort to translate their approaches and processes into terms that are easily understood and trusted by the various actors and publics who get involved in the budget process. Along the way, program managers, peer reviewers, central budget office analysts, and interest group analysts will bring higher levels of sophistication to their critique of revenue forecasts. Forecasters must be ready to respond to these many different forms and levels of oversight.

The art of forecasting reflects the application of judgment in: (1) the selection of forecasting techniques and tools, (2) the evaluation and selection of assumptions, and (3) the selection of forecast results to bring political agreement. The selection of forecasting tools and techniques reflects the importance of the revenue source, the time available, the data available to support a forecast, and the variation in the data. We will summarize the data needs, application, and sophistication of the different techniques later on in this chapter. Each technique will yield a slightly different revenue estimate. An **estimate** is the numerical prediction of revenue generated under specific assumptions and by a given technique. Where a simpler, more easily understood technique provides acceptable results, building credibility may call for its selection and use.

The evaluation and selection of assumptions comes in the interpretation of law and regulation, and in the assumptions that structure an estimate analysis. Assumptions also flow from an understanding of the political and economic context in which the forecast is developed and used. The forecaster's sense of context, understanding of the larger economy and revenue situation, and intuition support his or her selection of an estimate.

In the end, the final selection of a revenue forecast should come from a range of potential alternative estimates. Technically sound, unbiased analysis stands as the foundation of credibility. Sound analysis develops a truthful picture of the revenue situation for better or for worse. Selecting the most conservative estimate may underestimate revenues. Selecting estimates that are more conservative also opens the estimates to political scrutiny and mistrust. Erring in the opposite direction of overly optimistic revenue may lead to uncomfortable belt-tightening later in the fiscal year. The most useful estimate may be the *most likely* estimate. The most likely, or baseline, revenue estimates are neither optimistic nor pessimistic. Ideally, the actual collected revenues come in at, or slightly above, the most likely estimate. Most likely estimates may, in fact, be slightly pessimistic.

Several additional principles help to inform the judgment of forecasters and analysts in the estimation and selection of revenue estimates.

- A forecast needs to be reproducible—that is, generated with a systematic and coherent set of underlying assumptions and conditions. The same initial conditions and assumptions should always produce the same results.
- The new forecast should always be compared to the old forecast so that elected officials and managers can see how and why resource estimates have changed. For all but the newest revenue sources, a previous forecast should always exist. The previous forecast might be the second-year estimate of last year's long-term forecast.
- All revenue estimates need to be rationally developed out of history; this is particularly true for an estimate for a new revenue source.
- Initial conditions are extremely important. Next year's forecast needs to be continuously conditioned by both the current year and by history. Any forecast should be accompanied by a history, estimates for the current year, and a multiyear resource forecast.
- Forecast results must be presented in a coherent document that clearly conveys the estimates to elected officials and managers. The forecaster needs to develop a core set of tables, text discussion, and graphics that appear in regular format, even as the content changes. Many jurisdictions establish a formal **revenue manual** to catalog the detail that supports each forecast.

This last point stresses the need for analysts and forecasters to effectively explain and communicate their forecast results, assumptions, limitations, and processes. In the heat of debate, elected officials will often leave the assumptions and limitations behind as confusing details. Briefing materials should take this behavior into account and package assumptions and limitations in concise, easily presented concepts. In communicating the results and details of a revenue forecast, "less may be more."

Qualities of a Credible Forecast

Developing accurate revenue forecasts that closely match actual revenue collections is a technical challenge. As mentioned, forecasters must rely on data and cues from past and current conditions to forecast revenue collections up to a fiscal year or even 24 months (biennium) into the future. Hundreds of variables across numerous business sectors can influence forecasting assumptions, decisions, and estimates. Local population growth, demographics and age profiles, employment rates, investment and employment decisions by major local employers, state government spending and policy decisions, and local economic conditions provide the primary set of variables for forecasts. National-level economic and monetary decisions by the Federal Reserve, national and regional economic performance, and the performance of the major financial trading markets may add more variables to the forecast dataset. Forecasters often face the challenge of limited, nonexistent, or inconsistent data, and data may need adjustment for seasonal factors or for changing economic conditions. In the end, the forecast estimates rarely match the actual revenue collections exactly. Consistent success in generating forecasts that nearly match collections enhances forecaster credibility with decision makers and users. Acceptable deviations reflect the particular techniques involved, as well as the importance and contribution of the revenue sources to the jurisdiction. Major deviations and repeated large deviations between forecasts and actual revenue collections are cause for a loss of forecaster credibility.

A credible forecast uses quality data and correctly applies the appropriate mathematical, statistical, or economic techniques. Once an effective forecast model is established, analysts should try to continue to use the same technique as long as possible. The continued use of the same technique year after year builds familiarity and acceptance in elected officials and in the public. Widely used systems and widely accepted techniques add to their confidence. Any deviation from commonly used methods will need explanation and justification. Consistency with Federal Reserve forecasts and commentary, published statistics on regional labor, commerce and housing surveys, census and demographic statistics, and university research publications are also important.

At the state government level, revenue forecasts can have substantial impacts on state budgets and agency service levels. This tends to generate public concern and political interest in the forecast quality. To respond to this interest, governors and legislatures may convene a peer review process to review both quarterly and long-term forecasts. A peer review process typically involves a mix of academic economists, corporate and independent economists, and local and regional business analysts. One panel may review the selection of technical methods and mathematical models, while a second panel may review the recent economic situation and any assumptions underlying the forecasts. The findings of the peer review panel provide critique, explanation, and, ideally, ratification of the forecast. A full peer review process is applicable only to state governments and to the largest city and county local governments, but scaled-down reviews and the endorsement of expert consultants can help to add critical credibility to any forecast team and its work.

Managing the Revenue Forecast Team

Revenue forecasters face the professional challenge of blending technical methods into an environment of political pressures. Forecasters must be ready to fully display their approaches, methods, assumptions, and estimates to skeptical elected officials, community activists, and the public. In many jurisdictions, the budget process allows public hearing or formal work session agenda time for a formal recitation and oversight. A successful performance during oversight sessions sets the cornerstone for building credibility in the forecaster's work. Executive administrators, central budget office analysts, and program managers also cast a critical eye on forecasts. Once these actors are satisfied and won over, they can act as trusted messengers to key community opinion leaders, stakeholders, advocacy groups, and interested citizens. Beyond the basic task of building credibility, forecasters often face increased political pressure to find additional revenue. Requests by executives and elected officials may cause forecasters to go back and review their assumptions of economic conditions and their selection of the most likely revenue estimates. Here, forecasters face the decision to support a marginally more optimistic revenue forecast, or to hold firm with a more pessimistic—but more likely—forecast. Chief executive officers, finance directors, chief finance officers (CFOs), and staff directors need to provide the political support necessary to allow forecasters to present unbiased, truthful estimates of the revenue picture. Doing so will support the forecasters' credibility and build support for the budget as a governance outcome.

During the budget preparation season, revenue forecasters live in a world of process deadlines, last-minute requests, and intense overwhelming workloads. Even in the smallest jurisdiction, there are too many revenue sources and too little time and money to be equally thorough and systematic in making an estimate for each revenue source. However, each revenue source represents a different level of importance to the overall revenue picture. Revenue forecasters must concentrate their time and attention on those revenue sources with the greatest contribution and impact to the budget. Primary sources of revenue such as property taxes, income taxes, retail sales taxes, and major charges and fees require the greatest attention and the greatest rigor in forecasting techniques. If the collection and distribution of property taxes and retail sales tax revenue is centralized at the county or state level, the central authority may contract with expert consultants or professional organizations for forecasting services. Local governments may purchase forecasts on a fee subscription basis. More minor sources of revenue, especially those with little variation from year-to-year, deserve adequate but limited attention. Forecasters should not spend extensive time or effort developing complex techniques on very minor revenue sources with little historical data or annual variation. Time pressures reinforce the need to prioritize a forecaster's attention. Limited time and data may force an analyst to make a "quick and dirty" forecast. In some cases, these quick but knowledgeable estimates will provide sufficient information for decision makers. Here, the relative or magnitude difference in estimates may be much more important than the absolute level of the estimates.

Analysts and economists work to develop accurate, defensible forecasts within the constraints of revenue importance, time, and money. Elected officials, especially in large cities, counties, and in state legislatures, face a much different reality as political actors, and their behaviors respond to a different set of needs and discomforts. An elected official may request a review of a forecast analysis to ensure its validity. Requesting a review may be a way of signaling the reality of exceptionally low revenues to themselves, to disbelieving colleagues, and to constituency groups.

The availability of quality data is a critical requirement for effective forecasting. Ideally, datasets contain sufficient points to support statistical analysis; oftentimes, however, this is not the case. In many instances, the collected dataset covers only a few recent years, has gaps, or reflects changing conditions that render early years inconsistent or incomparable with later years. Gathering the data necessary for statistical and trending analysis takes time and money. Organization effort and commitment are required to gather the cost information, performance measures, and output measures that fill out forecasting datasets. Support from program managers, staff directors, and other administrators helps assure that forecasters have the data they need to make the case to elected officials and to the public.

OVERVIEW OF REVENUE ESTIMATION TECHNIQUES

Revenue forecasting is the analytic process of using data from the past with contextual assumptions to develop expected revenue estimates for future fiscal years, budget periods, or strategic planning time periods. A forecast is made up of a series of annual or periodic estimates. **Estimates** are the numerical result of an analysis process. For most forecasts, the levels of revenue generated in the past are seen as indicative of future revenue levels, and revenue forecasts are specifically designed to compute future estimates that exceed the time range of the dataset. This approach contrasts with most statistical procedures with assumptions that limit predictions to within the time range and variation of the dataset.

Forecasters gather the best data they can and make the best assumptions they can, but in the end, forecasts are a best guess of future revenue levels. The future is uncertain, and unexpected events of varying intensity disrupt and challenge the familiarity of past experience. Changing economic conditions may quickly stretch beyond the experience and performance of the most complete dataset. For example, few analysts and observers could have foreseen the extreme financial conditions caused by the economic downturn of 2007–2009. By fall of 2008, real estate values became highly uncertain, consumer spending was colored with caution, and the returns from financial investments failed to produce expected returns. These extreme conditions resulted in data points that strongly deviated from historic data trends. Forecasting property, income, and sales tax revenue for 2009 and 2010 became especially difficult.

Commonly used revenue forecasting techniques include:

- Educated estimation
- Deterministic spreadsheets
- Break-even analysis
- Different forms of averaging
- Trending methods
- Linear regression analysis
- Systems and models of regression equations

We provide explanations and examples of several of these techniques on the textbook webpage. Each of these forecasting techniques responds to particular types of data, assumptions, and legal and economic situations. The above list, however, loosely orders the techniques by increasing statistical power and data requirements. The trending, regression, and other statistical techniques require the use of an electronic statistical analysis package. Graduate-level coursework in analytic methods typically provides the theory and background for using these types of forecasts. While using a high-powered technique may offer professional satisfaction, we caution analysts to keep things simple. A simpler model may give satisfactory results and be much easier to explain to elected officials, senior administrators, and the public.

Local governments typically rely on dozens of different revenue sources. State statutes and regulations, along with local ordinances, authorize many of these sources, including taxes, intergovernmental revenues, charges and fees for services, and fines and penalties. These laws define the revenue authorization, define which citizen or business group is subject to taxation, define the rates and rate caps that local governments may levy, and prescribe how the revenue may be used. It then becomes incumbent on each local government to identify those sources that it is authorized to use. The major forms of revenues are familiar and easy to identify—property taxes, retail sales taxes, or major state intergovernmental payments. Minor, less familiar authorizations for special purpose taxes may require detailed research for their identification and use. Each source of revenue deserves some level of forecast, and each forecast generates numerous assumptions, estimates, and supporting details. A revenue manual provides a central repository in which a local government can organize and document its revenue sources. All revenue sources should be described in a standard format that results in consistent information for each source. The entry for each revenue source should include the following information (e.g., Clark County, WA, Auditor's Office 1999; Municipal Research and Services Center, WA 2009):

- a definition/description of the type of tax, charge, or revenue source;
- the statutory authorization allowing collection or use with details to the budget fund level;
- the mechanisms to assess and collect the revenue;
- the revenue limitations that apply to the tax or source;
- a description of the methodology for calculating revenue;

- an assessment of the stability and adequacy of the revenue;
- a categorization of recurring or nonrecurring (one-time) revenue (GFOA 2013b);
- the accounting details, including relationships to budget fund, budget line-item, or accounting codes;
- the model(s) used to forecast the revenue including assumptions, model description and statistical or mathematical methods, key constants and parameters, and confidence intervals and sensitivity analyses;
- a list of demographic, economic, political, and policy factors that can affect model estimates;
- the limitations behind the forecast;
- a revenue history for each source, with the actual annual collections for the past five or more years;
- a comparison of the actual annual collections with the forecast estimates for the past five or more years;
- any helpful notes and hints for analysis and explanation.

A well-maintained revenue manual provides a basis for public explanations and confidence building.

Educated Estimation

Educated estimation may provide the most appropriate estimation technique for minor revenue sources. The approach is especially applicable when revenues vary little from year to year, and when the forecaster is knowledgeable of the history and context for the source. In developing an educated estimate, a forecaster considers recent revenue levels and any changes that would affect the revenue stream. Changes affecting the future revenue stream might include demographic trends, revisions to the state or federal tax regulations, changes in tax or fee enforcement, or economic cycles. In another appropriate application, the forecaster may have knowledge of a one-time, isolated spike in a normally stable flow of revenues. An analyst may be forced into educated estimation when historical data are very limited or unavailable. Forecasters using educated estimation should be extremely careful about documenting their assumptions. Accumulating estimates with comparable assumptions through time allows the development of a rudimentary dataset. This dataset can ultimately be used to support the forecasting of future estimates with more refined techniques.

Deterministic Spreadsheets

Property taxes and other taxes with defined regulatory structure often present clear relationships that forecasters can effectively model with deterministic forecasting. Deterministic models are simply a string of equations with known coefficient values that model the assessment and valuation of a particular tax or fee. These models lack the variable nature of stochastic (random), statistical models, but their step-by-step linked equations lend themselves to electronic spreadsheet modeling. We explain how to apply a deterministic model to property tax revenue forecasting in the next section of this chapter.

Break-Even Analysis

Break-even analysis provides an analytic basis for determining fees and charges for service, and for rate-setting actions by local governments. Break-even analysis also applies to the determination of fees for licenses and permits, franchise access fees, tolls, and utility rates. Council, commission, or board actions on fees and rates serve not only to set consumer charges but also, in aggregate, to determine the level of total revenues generated by the program annually. Forecasts of aggregate revenue levels determine whether the program recovers its costs, or whether it will need a subsidy to meet program objectives.

Effective rate-setting actions and the accompanying cost analysis should reflect the full and true costs of providing the particular service, including all direct and indirect costs for operations and maintenance, administrative overhead, and charges for the use of capital facilities (GFOA 1996). For analysis purposes, analysts categorize costs as *fixed, incremental/step,* or *variable.* **Fixed costs** typically cover program capital investments and the costs that occur at any service level—administrative facilities, basic staff, communications, and information systems. In general, the more customers the department or program serves, the lower the per client share of the fixed costs.

Incremental or **step costs** and **variable costs** reflect costs that increase or decrease as the level of output rises or falls. Incremental/step costs reflect a level of cost tied to a defined range of service output. They are often linked to facility or machinery capacity. Suppose, for example, that a small program uses a single 7-passenger van, then grows to a 15-passenger van, then three 15-passenger vans, but at some point grows to need one or more large buses. Incremental costs would reflect each cost level to purchase and operate the needed vehicles. Variable costs directly increase or decrease as client citizens or businesses purchase more or less of a good or service. Variable consumption can be closely metered, as for electricity from a public utility district or water consumption from a city water utility.

The relative contribution of the fixed, incremental, and variable cost components to a charge or fee rate schedule varies by policy decision. Governments and nonprofits may structure rates to include more cost in the fixed cost portion of the rate. This approach, in essence, designates a larger basic fee with relatively small increments of variable cost. Other contrasting fee structures place less weight on the fixed fee portion and proportionally more cost in a graduated schedule of incremental steps for higher consumption or higher service attention.

Categorizing costs as fixed, incremental/step, or variable allows analysts to compute the cost for each unit of service produced by a program. With an understanding of the unit cost of a service, and how the per unit cost rate changes over different levels of output, analysts can develop estimates of total program cost at varying levels of output. With estimates of total program cost, analysts can then estimate program expenditures, or the charge and fee revenues, needed to operate the program at a given level of service delivery over the coming fiscal year. Cost management and performance analysis techniques similar to those described in chapter 13 provide the techniques to develop the refined per unit cost information needed for a detailed break-even analysis.

Break-even analysis forecasting techniques have wide application in commercial businesses, nonprofits, and governments (Ullmann 1976; Dropkin, Halpin, and La Touche 2007; Gainer and Moyer 2005, 296–297; Chen, Forsythe, Weikart, and Williams 2009). In a very simple break-even analysis, all the costs necessary to produce the service for a single category of client are totaled into a total cost amount. Actual expenditures from the previous fiscal year provide the data to determine total program costs. To cover costs, the jurisdiction or nonprofit must collect an equal total amount of revenue—the total revenue. Governments often know the number of customers they serve. For example, a city water delivery system serves a known number of residential and commercial customers. Knowing the total cost (equal to the total revenue) and the number of output units, the analyst can compute a per customer charge. More advanced break-even analyses break customers into categories of users, break costs into different categories, and determine rate schedules that increase with increasing consumption of water or electricity.

For some services, local governments and especially nonprofits may be able to increase the number of customers as a means to increase revenues. This also allows a greater amortization or sharing of the fixed and incremental costs. A detailed break-even analysis would also identify classes of customers or clients and would consider the relative costs of providing services to each class. Effective cost management would monetize, or place a value on, the extra program capacity and service attention required for high-cost users (e.g., Winthrop and Herr 2009; Cordes and Winthrop 2008). Once a detailed, unbiased analysis is completed, the jurisdiction's legislative body (council, commission, or board of directors) can turn to the social justice issues of how to subsidize particular classes of clients. The council, commission, or board may decide to impose a surcharge for high-impact users, a full cost recovery rate, or a partial rate for subsidized cost recovery (GFOA 1996). Council or board members may decide to forego full cost recovery in order to ensure service to certain groups of low-income or disadvantaged citizens as part of meeting larger goals of fairness and broad public good. The issues of cost allocation, high-cost clients, full cost recovery, and subsidy allocation are also very relevant to nonprofit executives and board members. For many small social service nonprofits, a sliding scale fee structure allocates cost discounts based on a client's ability to pay. To further explore these issues, we provide an exercise on break-even analysis and rate setting on the textbook webpage.

Different Forms of Averaging

When a dataset of historical revenue information shows a steady visible trend, or shows a constant explained variation, averaging may provide the most appropriate forecasting tool. As with educated estimation, averaging is appropriate for relatively minor revenue streams. In developing a forecast using averaging, an analyst should consider any changes in the legal, economic, demographic, or organizational environment that could produce changes in past trends or introduce new variation into the forecast estimate.

A forecaster using revenue averaging can follow several strategies. Where no trend appears in the data, the familiar arithmetic average of all available past per period revenue levels is normally used. If a simple trend appears in the historic revenue data, a prior moving or *rolling* average that uses only the most recent two, three, or four rolling data points may provide an effective estimate (Berman 2007). However, computing an estimate using two, three, or four rolling data points may result in a prediction above or below the trend in the data. The analyst needs to exercise judgment in selecting the number of data points to include in the rolling average estimate. Some local jurisdictions use averaging to forecast the catch-all category of Miscellaneous Revenues.

Trending Methods

Where historical data of past actual revenues and the forecast estimates for those revenues are available, a trending technique such as exponential smoothing may provide the most appropriate forecast estimate (cf. Ullman 1976; Chen, Forsythe, Weikart, and Williams 2009). If wide variation appears in the actual revenues, a trend becomes difficult to identify and the technique has limited effectiveness. The technique is appropriate for data with limited variation and without spikes.

The trending technique of exponential smoothing estimates the future revenue for the next year based on a relationship between the actual revenues for past years and their comparable forecast estimates. A weighting factor between 0 and 1 sets the relative balance between the actual and forecast estimates in the future prediction. While computer packages can perform the calculations to select the weighting factor and to make the estimations of future revenues, the analyst must carefully review the weighting factor selection. Too low a weighting factor dampens the effect of the actual revenues, while too high a factor limits the value of past estimates. Local jurisdictions may rely on trending techniques to forecast telephone utility license fees and state revenue sharing for cigarettes and alcoholic beverages.

Linear Regression Analysis

Linear regression analysis is commonly applied in a two-step procedure to develop revenue forecasts. This technique uses historical data to first build a mathematical relationship between past revenue levels and one or more economic, social, or demographic explanatory factors. The regression relationship is expressed as a mathematical equation. A regression dataset usually pairs the level of actual revenue collections with numerical data on each explanatory factor. Each explanatory factor serves as an independent variable in the regression equation. The data are often collected on an annual, quarterly, or monthly basis. In the second step of the procedure, forecasters use the computed regression relationship to estimate expected future revenue levels. Using linear regression techniques to forecast future revenues assumes that the conditions affecting the explanatory factors and their relationship to revenue generation remain unchanged from the past.

In contrast to the relatively simple data requirements of the previous techniques, linear regression has more comprehensive data needs. Gathering the wide variety of data measures and indicators from which to select out a final set of explanatory factors is often an expensive and a long-term process. Buying datasets from economic research firms, consulting firms, or universities sometimes provides an alternative to the data collection process. Once the data are available, building a refined regression model to estimate revenues requires professional abilities and a computerized statistical package. As with other forecasting techniques, the amount of time and resources invested in a regression estimation effort should be proportional to the importance of the revenue source. Even with a long-term, comprehensive dataset and a high level of talent, regression models may generate a revenue estimate of only limited quality. Typically, when this occurs, a critical explanatory factor has not been identified or is missing from the regression equation.

As an example, a large city government uses a regression equation model to forecast annual revenues from business licenses. This revenue source is too large and important to rely on trending or averaging techniques. It is also highly affected by the business cycle and the national economy. After an analysis and selection of explanatory variables, the final regression equation contains three variables to explain revenues: the annual unemployment rate for the metropolitan area, national corporate profits, and the license revenues from the preceding year. In another example, regression models have been developed to forecast lottery ticket sales and the future revenues from a new lottery game. Important explanatory factors that affect lottery ticket sales and revenue include variables that a state lottery board can control and other factors related to seasonality. Variables controlled by the lottery board include promotions, advertising campaigns, game changes, and accounting changes. Seasonal variables can include week of the month, month or season of the year, and holidays.

Linear regression techniques offer analysts a set of highly flexible tools for computing revenue estimates. For difficult forecasting situations, advance regression techniques may prove helpful. These advanced techniques include nonlinear regression and variable transformations. Obtain professional guidance when considering the use of these advanced techniques.

Systems and Models of Regression Equations

As revenue sources grow in terms of absolute size and contribution, the application of more complex forecasting techniques may become justified. In an increasing step in forecasting complexity, several linear regression equations may be linked together into a system to forecast a revenue stream. State government forecasters, forecasting teams in the very largest county and city governments, and expert consultants use these complex techniques to forecast personal and corporate income taxes. At this advanced level, complex models of linked regression equations are used to describe a state's entire economy. This type of forecasting incorporates key information from regional and national economic conditions as well as from recent state-level tax collections. Using these advanced techniques requires credibility with elected officials and the public. Without clear presentations, constant communication, and an open, peer-reviewed process, public trust in revenue forecasts may bottom out.

Effectively interpreting the estimates from a complex system requires considering both the estimates generated and the variation or *error* that surrounds the estimates. Typically, the error that surrounds an estimate is the uncertainty of the statistical, mathematical, and random sampling procedures used in the estimation process. It provides a range of probability and a quality context for the estimate. The error may originate from several sources: (1) a variety of structural assumptions built into the system of equations; (2) the interaction of several statistical estimates and regression equations; and (3) the variation in the data used to run the model. In the case of estimates generated from a single linear regression model, statistics from the regression calculation will provide error and quality measurements. But in systems of several regression equations and in larger complex systems, **sensitivity analysis** procedures are used to develop a range of possible revenue estimates under different data conditions and structural assumptions. For example, one state presents a "low," a "likely," and a "high" set of estimates for its quarterly update revenue forecasts. Professional review of both forecast estimates and any sensitivity or error analysis is critical to ensuring public trust in the forecasting effort. Analysts should always exercise special caution when using large and complex forecasting systems. Statistical models can capture only a portion of the real world and its many variables. Changes in the economy or in external conditions outside the range of the data or the models in the system may render computed estimates inappropriate and unusable. The forecasting system should be used as a tool, not as an absolute predictor of future revenues.

Selecting a Revenue Estimate

We have just outlined the major methods for forecasting current year and future year revenues. Each technique has data needs and brings strengths and weaknesses for a forecast estimate. Selecting the appropriate technique, making the appropriate assumptions, and selecting the most appropriate estimate are left to the forecaster's professional judgment. The use of judgment is really the art of the revenue forecast.

The wide range of techniques from the simple to the complex reminds us that a remote rural town clerk can make effective revenue forecast estimates that are fully adequate to the setting. To develop a high-quality calculation, forecasters may apply several techniques to develop a set of comparable estimates. For example, averaging techniques, trending, and simple linear regression may all be used to develop estimates of future retail sales tax revenues. The forecasting feature in commercial accounting software offers another option for generating revenue estimates. Review of the estimates developed by the different models—but using the same data—points out their relative differences. One technique may generate a higher level of future annual revenues, while another technique may generate a lower level of revenues. One technique may generate a gentler, smoother model of the historical data and of future estimates. Another model may generate a more volatile model that closely tracks historical variation. One regression model may have a very good **statistical fit** or match to the historical data, but then grow wildly to unrealistic future estimates beyond the first year or two. Another regression model may fit well, but then sink to unrealistically low levels. An effective estimate will have both good statistical fit to the data and a realistic fit to expected future economic and business circumstances for the budget year.

Selecting a forecast model with both good statistical and realistic fit to economic capacity and conditions is especially important for long-term forecasts of three or more years. This is because unrealistic increases or decreases in the mathematical and statistical estimates often appear more strongly in the out-years of the forecast. Additionally, the statistical error or the statistical quality of the estimates becomes poorer in the out-years of a long-term forecast. One approach to managing the statistical error of long-term revenue forecasts is to develop and select a baseline forecast set on a preferred combination of statistical and realistic fits. Analysts then apply the sensitivity analysis procedure described above to learn how the **baseline forecast** behaves under varying assumptions and data inputs (Swanson 2008). This approach would typically generate a range of "low," "likely," and "high" revenue forecasts. With the context of a range of forecast scenarios, analysts and planners can increase the tolerance of financial forecasts and financial plans to changes in economic conditions.

PROPERTY TAX MECHANICS AND REVENUE FORECASTS

As we described in the previous chapter, property (or ad valorem, [value-based]) taxes are the most important form of local government revenue. While some jurisdictions rely heavily on income taxes or other forms of revenue, some form of property tax almost always contributes to the mix of local government revenues. A full understanding of the property tax system and its mechanics is critical for revenue forecasting and for budget development.

Valuation Forms the Basis of the Property Tax

In many states, a popularly elected county assessor holds responsibility for implementing the property tax system and for collecting property taxes. In other states, an appointed administrator serves in the role. A staff of professional assessors and analysts works under the direction of the assessor. The task of the staff is to: regularly visit every piece of property in the county; assess and estimate the value of the property; apply the appropriate tax rate to the assessed property value; produce the tax bills and notify the property owner; collect any tax due; and follow up on delinquent payments. As mentioned in the previous chapter, the county may seize and then sell properties with delinquent taxes.

Establishing a timely, accurate, and fair assessed value for each property is the most difficult aspect of the property tax system. While most property owners accept their assessments, concerned owners may want clarification, and skeptical owners may want to challenge the assessment. State law and county governments establish an administrative **appeals** process under which property owners may appeal their assessments (cf. Washington County, OR 2011; and Washington State Department of Revenue 2010). The process typically begins with a hearing before a county **board of property tax appeals** or **board of equalization**. The initial appeals procedures are often informal in nature to support citizen initiative. Should the county appeals process fail to bring a property owner satisfaction, state-level review procedures or judicial review are available. The varied background and varied skill levels of assessors and the decentralized location of assessors in remote county offices have sometimes led to inconsistent and inaccurate **appraisals**. Professional organizations (IAAO 2011) and strong training have helped to improve assessment quality. However, state regulations may reserve high value and unique industrial properties for skilled state revenue agency assessors.

Typically, the county assessor provides tax assessment and revenue collection services for the county government and for all of the other governments and special service districts within the county. These related governments and programs include: cities, towns, and townships; school districts; regional transportation and port districts; special service districts for fire, insect control, flood control, and hospitals; and state government levies. A local government or district may impose one or several tax levies. Thus, any particular piece of property in the county falls into a number of overlapping taxing levies as established by several of these governments.

Visualize the overlapping taxing districts as a stack of layers or pancakes. Geographic information systems (GIS) effectively capture this stacking and overlapping arrangement. A **tax code area** is a portion of the county where the combination of overlapping **tax districts** is the same. A large county may have more than 100 tax code areas, and a smaller jurisdiction or district likely has several, as demonstrated in Exhibit 7.1. The left column in Exhibit 7.1 demonstrates a hypothetical array of levies imposing taxes on a single piece of property in tax code area 110002. The levies fall into several types:

- general or current services fund for operating and maintenance expenses (e.g., City of Upper Cascadia and Upper Cascadia County general funds, Upper Cascadia school district M&O general fund, port general fund);
- operations and maintenance funds for specific programs (e.g., school equalization, mental health, mosquito control, EMS);
- levies for specific equipment, capital purchases, or construction (schools capital project fund, schools vehicle transportation [buses]);
- bonded debt service levies for construction and capital purchases (schools debt service, port bonds, and library, parks, and recreation).

Exhibit 7.1

Property Tax Rate Detail for Tax Code Area 110002 (rate on $1,000 assessed valuation)

Governmental entity/levy	Total
Schools	
Schools General Fund Maint. and Ops.	2.38025
Schools Capital Projects Fund (Levy)	0.21873
Schools Debt Service (Bonds)	2.19842
Schools Vehicle Transportation (Levy)	0.08863
State and County	
State School Equalization (state)	2.47115
Upper Cascadia County General Fund	1.34063
Mental Health	0.01250
Developmental Disabilities	0.01250
Mosquito Control	0.00842
Soldiers/Sailors Fund (state)	0.00874
Conservation Futures Fund (state)	0.06250
City (City of Upper Cascadia)	
City of Upper Cascadia General Fund	3.36833
Emergency Medical Services (Levy)	0.23368
Park/Recreation Bond	0.14296
Library Bond	0.15281
Port District (Port of Upper Cascadia)	
Port General	0.26700
Port Bonds	0.16826
Cemetery (District #1)	0.02106
Fire District	n/a
Library	n/a
County Road Fund	n/a
Total Rate	13.15657
Total Assessed Property Value	$76,010,000

Tax code area 110002 lies within an incorporated city boundary. The services provided by the City of Upper Cascadia include fire and police, planning and development, road maintenance, library operations, and park operations. Library and park facilities are constructed under separate levies to cover capital bonds. In contrast, county residents living outside the city in an unincorporated area do not receive this enhanced level of services. Residents in unincorporated areas would contribute to the county road fund under a countywide **levy**, and they would pay separate levies for a fire district and a library district if they had voted to tax themselves for these services (bottom of Exhibit 7.1). Where cities, towns, and townships do not provide a particular service, residents may vote to establish a special service district funded by a **tax levy**. Such a levy would appear as a tax district listed in Exhibit 7.1. Notice also that the school district imposes four different levies for operations, for capital facilities projects, for debt service, and for school bus purchases.

Exhibit 7.1 includes several state property tax levies. In this state, the county serves as the assessment and collection agent for the state government. The state school equalization levy is substantial, at $2.47115 per $1,000 assessed value. The state collects the levy and uses the revenue to help equalize school funding across rich and poor districts. The state has also imposed several small statewide initiatives for veterans' support and conservation futures. Some states may not have state-level assessments.

The county assessor establishes an assessed value for each piece of eligible property in the county. Residential property is typically assessed on the value of the land and the permanent structures. Commercial property assessment may include land, facilities, equipment, inventory, and furnishings. In many states, the assessed value directly reflects the full fair market value of the property. In other states, the value may be reduced by a fixed dollar exemption, by a percentage reduction, or by a rollback to the values of a starting year. The assessed value or its adjusted substitute determines the value variable of the property tax computation. The imposed burden of the property tax is expressed as the *millage,* or dollar amount levied on $1,000 of assessed property value. This is the property tax **millage rate**.

To compute the tax for an individual residential property owner, apply the following formula:

$$\text{Property Tax} = (\text{Property Assessed Value}) \times (\text{Total Dollar Rate}/1{,}000) \qquad (7.1)$$

Suppose our City of Upper Cascadia homeowner owns a house and property assessed at $200,000. Using the total millage rate from the bottom of Exhibit 7.1, the total annual property tax owed would be calculated as:

$$\text{Property Tax} = (\$200{,}000) \times (13.15657/1{,}000) \qquad (7.2)$$
$$\text{Property Tax} = \$2{,}631 \qquad (7.3)$$

While a homeowner is most concerned about his or her individual tax burden, governmental entities are most interested in estimating the total potential tax levy or revenue generated from their tax base. To develop this total potential revenue, the county assessor must compute the tax revenue from each tax code area within the jurisdiction and sum these components into a total revenue figure. Exhibit 7.2 lists all the property tax code areas that fall within the Upper Cascadia city limits.

The assessed value column typically includes the values of taxable real property—multifamily residential, single-family residential, commercial, industrial—and business equipment, inventory, and furnishings. Tax code area 115000 likely contains major industrial and commercial facilities generating an assessed value exceeding $2 billion. The assessor omits any exempted properties such as churches, most government buildings and facilities, and public schools. Note that the

Exhibit 7.2

City of Upper Cascadia Potential Property Tax Revenues, 2008, by Source Tax Code Areas (general fund levy for regular maintenance and operations)

Area	Assessed value	Millage	Potential tax revenue
110002	$76,010,000	3.36833	$256,027
110031	$17,402,283	3.36833	$58,617
112032	$351,673,333	3.36833	$1,184,552
115000	$2,602,234,511	3.36833	$8,765,185
Total Levy	$3,047,320,127	3.36833	$10,264,380

uniform tax millage rate of $3.36833 per $1,000 valuation applies in the four different tax areas that fall within the city boundaries. The combined revenue generated from each of the tax areas within a jurisdiction's boundary is the total levy:

$$\text{Total Tax Levy} = (\text{Total Assessed Property Value}) \times (\text{Dollar Rate}/1,000) \tag{7.4}$$

Following through on our example, for the City of Upper Cascadia, the total tax levy from all tax areas in the city is:

$$\text{Total Tax Levy} = (\$3,047,320,127) \times (3.36833/1,000) \tag{7.5}$$
$$\text{Total Tax Levy} = \$10,264,380 \tag{7.6}$$

Forecasts of the total tax levy provide a base for budget construction for a jurisdiction. However, a few taxpayers fail to make their payments in a timely manner. Taxpayer delinquencies are an inevitable occurrence, and analysts routinely apply a 2 to 5 percent reduction to the estimated total revenues (e.g., Waldhart and Reschovsky 2012; Johnson 2011). The delinquency-adjusted total levy becomes the revenue estimate used in budget construction.

Property Tax System Dynamics

The basic property tax relationship described in Equation 7.1 has implications for the property owners in a community and its local governments. The assessed values of properties can change for several reasons, but local governments need a continuing flow of revenues. The property tax formula responds to these changes (Franklin 2010).

The property tax formula applies to all eligible land and property in a tax code area. The assessed value of each property is multiplied by the total rate, and each property contributes its share of the total revenues collected by the county. In our homeowner example (see Equations 7.1, 7.2, and 7.3), the homeowner paid $2,631 annually. If all the homes in the tax area were identical, each homeowner would pay the same $2,631. Each home would be assessed at $200,000, and the tax rate for each property would total $13.15657 per thousand dollars of value. Suppose also that Upper Cascadia Library District proposes an annual operating budget of $1 million. Each of the 380 homes and properties in the community would contribute $2,631 for an equal share of the levy needed to meet the $1 million proposed budget.

In the real world, however, the local real estate market fluctuates with economic growth or contraction. The $200,000 market value of each house and property will fall with a sustained contraction in the local economy. Yet, local government continues to need $1 million annually to cover service costs. Thus, if the assessed values drop, the tax rate must be increased to compensate and to assure delivery of $1 million. Similarly, if property valuations increase in a growing economy and the assessed value of a home increases, the tax rate will decrease slightly to deliver only $1 million to local governments. It is important to recognize that value and rate, as a mathematical product function, compensate in changing conditions to assure $1 million to local government. If the assessed values of all of the houses in the community are equal, and the tax rate is equal, each homeowner's share of the total tax levy will be equal.

More realistically, some homeowners make investments to their homes—remodel kitchens or bathrooms, add landscaping, and construct major additions. These investments increase the value of those particular homes and their assessed value relative to other homes in the community— say to a home value of $220,000. Similarly, other homeowners perform minimal maintenance, and their houses decay. The assessed value of these homes will fall relative to the others—say to $180,000. But, many homes will continue near the average assessed value of $200,000. The tax rate applied to all properties is the same—13.15657. Thus, houses with above average assessed values will pay a larger tax, and those of lesser value will pay a lesser tax. In the end, however, the averaged property values of all 380 properties and the standard tax rate must produce the $1 million needed by local government. New construction and improvements to homes and property add new value to the tax code area. This increased value serves to spread the tax burden and to reduce the tax rate on the existing property owners to generate our hypothetical $1 million of revenues, though not at a one-for-one dollar value, since new construction requires additional schools, public safety, and other governmental services and facilities.

Grasping these dynamics aids our understanding of how property tax limitations have their effect. Controls on any part of the property tax equation affect the flow of revenue to local governments. We summarize these effects and property tax limitations in the last part of the chapter below.

Forecasting Property Tax Revenues

Detailed property assessments provide a rich database for forecasting annual property tax revenues. Property taxes are also grounded in a highly structured regulatory procedure. A deterministic spreadsheet model can effectively integrate these features into an effective revenue forecasting model. Forecasters develop a model for each code tax area within a jurisdiction (Exhibit 7.2). The combined forecasts from all tax code areas would provide a revenue forecast for the city, county, or special district.

As we summarized above, a deterministic model is simply a set of linked equations. Typically, the total assessed value for the tax code area is entered into the model. Estimates of the value of new construction are added to the total assessed value. If the assessed value is assumed equal to the fair market value, the model might adjust for broad changes in real estate valuation. If the model is applied in a **budget-driven state** that allows the jurisdiction to set a budget level and then raise funds, the model would input the needed level of total revenue. The model would then compute the tax rate for the coming fiscal year. Alternatively, in **rate-driven states**, the defined tax rate would be applied against the assessed values to compute the total available revenue. Forecasters can add tax limitations restrictions on assessed values, tax rates, or total levies as necessary. Once the model computes values, rates, and levies for the coming year, the same procedures can be used to forecast the successive year. The model can be cycled as needed to compute forecasts for the out-years.

PROPERTY TAX LIMITATIONS AND LIMITATION EFFECTS

Tax limitations and related expenditure limitations (**tax and expenditure limitations**, or **TELs**) to control tax burdens and the size of government have recently been imposed in most states (U.S.

Advisory Commission on Intergovernmental Relations [ACIR] 1995). Of these TELs, limitations on property taxes have been especially common. But property tax limitations have been imposed almost as long as the property tax has been used. The first round of limitations appeared in the 1880s and coincided with local home rule efforts. More recently, the current round of limitations began in the late 1970s and 1980s. Many of these limitations remain in statute and in force. In some states, multiple citizen initiatives have resulted in an accumulation of statutes and a confusing combination of controls. The actual impacts of the combined limitations often produce unexpected consequences as the economic conditions change.

Restricting the flow of property tax revenues requires placing restrictions on one or several components of the property tax equation (Equation 7.4). As a basis for this discussion, we reproduce the jurisdiction-level version of the basic property tax equation here:

$$\text{Total Tax Levy} = (\text{Total Assessed Property Value}) \times (\text{Total Dollar Rate}/1{,}000) \qquad (7.4)$$

In this equation, the *total tax levy* represents the combined revenues from all tax code areas within the jurisdiction, while the *total assessed property value* covers all the eligible property in the jurisdiction. The dollar rate divided by 1,000 is the *millage rate* adopted by the voters and adjusted or capped in conformance with state law.

A catalogue of tax and expenditure limitations (TELs) reveals six methods for controlling property tax revenues (ACIR 1995; Mullins and Joyce 1996):

1. Overall Property Tax Rate Limitation

This limitation mechanism covers aggregate total tax rate faced by a property owner in a particular tax code area. The dollar rate of $13.15657 per thousand dollars of assessed valuation for our City of Upper Cascadia homeowner is such an aggregated (Exhibit 7.1) tax rate. An overall rate limitation would cap or reduce this aggregate total rate.

2. Specific Property Tax Rate Limitations

This type of limitation caps or reduces specific rates individually, or by a class of rates. For example, a state may place a category rate cap on the school operations and maintenance rate, or on the general government rate, which combines all city, county, and special district governments. Some states allow the voters to lift a state-set rate cap through a ballot referendum (cf. Maher and Skidmore 2009). Super-majority requirements for measure acceptance may be even more restrictive than a simple majority vote.

3. Property Tax Levy Limit

This limitation caps the total tax levy generated (left side of Equation 7.4). Levy limits set a cap on the rate the levy may grow from year to year. The cap is sometimes linked to the rate of inflation and population growth. For example, Initiative 747 in Washington State in 2007 capped the total levy limit at a 1 percent per year increase for most local jurisdictions. Voters may lift the levy cap by ballot referendum.

4. Limits on Assessment Increases

This restriction controls increases in the assessed value of property. Many states embrace the assessed value as fair market value and place no restriction on the total assessed property value component in Equation 7.4. Limitation controls in these states use rate and total levy limits to achieve revenue control. But many other states place controls on the assessed value of property. These controls include exempting a portion of the assessed value from tax, rolling back the value of property to a prescribed starting year, or limiting the growth of assessed value by a prescribed annual percentage. The exemption of a portion of value is used by many states. Some states use taxpayer age-based categories to provide tax relief to senior property owners (NCSL 2002). In contrast, California's Proposition 13, adopted in 1978, set values at 1975 levels and placed a maximum 2 percent annual growth rate on values for property held continuously since the imposition of the initiative (McCaffery and Bowman 1978).

5. General Revenue or General Expenditure Limit

This restriction steps outside the property tax equation and places limits on all revenue received by a jurisdiction. Similarly, a general expenditure limit places a cap on total spending by the jurisdiction. This type of restriction is often proposed at the state level to constrain state general fund spending (e.g., State of Colorado, Taxpayer Bill of Rights of 1992 [TABOR]; Martell and Teske 2007).

6. Full Disclosure or Truth in Taxation Requirements

This approach may focus on changes to the property tax, but also may step outside the property tax equation to include other types of taxes. This type of control requires governments to fully explain why tax increases are occurring, and may require public discussion and a formal vote before a tax increase. However, a public vote to raise taxes supersedes any information or discussion. This is a relatively weak tax limitation measure, but it may help to increase the quality and uniformity of assessments (Cornia and Walters 2005). Utah (Cornia and Walters 2005) and Florida have used this type of control (Riley and Colby 1991, 95).

The TEL statutes, regulations, and voter initiatives in a state may use one or several of these restrictions. Some features may be especially binding, and others not especially effective. A limitation on only one part of the property tax equation (see Equation 7.4) leaves room for minor adjustments in other factors. For example, a rollback restriction on appraised value may be circumvented by a marginal tax rate increase. While a limitation on one factor in Equation 7.4 may reduce a resident's tax bill and the revenue flow to local government, effective constraints on two of the three factors in the equation are required to ensure tax relief. State law may allow specific exemptions from the limitations, and in the end, administrators must dig through and thoroughly understand the details and exemptions of their state's property tax system. Oftentimes, the various caps and limitations adopted by a state are "stacked" on each other. The entire tax process then becomes arcane and hard for the average citizen to follow, thereby lowering the trust of the citizenry in the system.

Changing economic conditions and changes in real estate assessed values may make the TEL more or less binding. A boom of economic growth, along with new building and facility construction, may inflate assessed property values in the short term. The increase in value may allow a burst of revenues that hides the long-term effect of a limitation. A burgeoning growing economy in the 1990s obscured the ultimate effect of the Colorado Taxpayer Bill of Rights (TABOR) limitation until the early 2000s, when the economy changed. At that point, the TABOR generated a severe reduction in public services (Center for Budget and Policy Priorities [CBPP] 2013; Martell and Teske 2007). However, in Oregon, a property tax limitation from the late 1990s had aggressively adjusted assessed property values to below market rates. During the recent economic downturn, these adjusted property values remained relatively constant even as real market values declined steeply, and taxpayers grumbled that the adjusted values should also decline. The divergence and dampened fluctuations in adjusted assessed values helped to hold property tax revenues to a stable level over the downturn. Public education helped to remind taxpayers of the benefits, and burdens, of the tax limitation over a full economic cycle.

Imposing a tax rate cap as a property tax limitation may bring unintended consequences. A tax rate limitation imposes a cap on the tax millage rate, but also brings up the issue of how the community should prioritize the component array of services funded under the cap. Exhibit 7.1 demonstrates the many services funded out of the aggregate $13.15657 per thousand dollars assessed value tax rate. As the combined rate is capped and reduced, the question becomes, Which services should take the largest reduction? Each state resolves this issue differently. Some states apply a uniform reduction that *compresses* all rates equally. Other states reserve priority funding to senior districts, and then let junior districts take the *suppression* or prorated rate reductions to bring the aggregate junior district rate under the prescribed limit. Junior districts might include single service special districts for flood control, cemetery, library, parks and recreation, or mosquito control. If all junior district rates are reduced to zero, senior district rates are then prorated. Such a division makes sense on paper until circumstances demand full services from a junior flood or fire district. Compression, versus suppression and proration, demonstrate two different approaches for reducing district tax rates to meet statutory limits with a final goal of ensuring compliance with a rate cap.

Limitations that modify or roll back and adjust assessed valuations of property may also generate unwanted consequences. Application of an assessed value modification begins at a date specified in the ballot referendum, statute, or regulation. Property assessments on existing property are then constrained into the future, often with a limited percentage annual value increase. In actuality, real estate and property values for entire neighborhoods may escalate steeply after the implementation date specified in the limitation, but this value increase may not be recognized in a modified assessment. In contrast, new growth may be valued at its full market value and carries a higher tax burden. Limitations on assessed value can quickly set up two classes of property owners and a shift in tax burden to new growth and recently arrived residents and businesses (Martens 2011; McCaffery and Bowman 1978, 534). Efforts to limit property taxes can quickly challenge taxpayers' perceptions of fairness and horizontal equity.

The implications of TELS extend beyond the mechanics of the property tax equation. Property tax limitations can generate unintended shifts in funding, along with shifts in political power and control. Mullins and Joyce (1996) in a nationwide analysis of TELs reported numerous unexpected consequences resulted from limitations. In general, TELs increased the centralization of government authority to the state level, lessened local responsiveness, increased the use of nontax revenue (charges and fees) by local governments, and lessened government's ability to respond to the needs of dependent populations (Mullins and Joyce 76). Mullins and Joyce note that after tax limitations, the overall size of government doesn't increase, but state government expenditure decisions become much more important. State government funds have had a tendency to backfill the loss of revenues caused by local level limitations. With greater funding authority shifted to the state level, local governments may become less responsive to local needs and preferences. Mullins and Joyce conclude that the centralization caused by TELs conflicts with free market public choice advocates' preference for local control of government and taxation. With state governments under fiscal pressure following the economic downturn of 2007–2009, little revenue often remained to backfill local government property tax revenue losses.

To the positive, the capping of local property taxes and the centralization of funding to the state government can have an effect of equalizing school funding across the rich and poor school districts (Oregon Legislative Revenue Office 1999).[1] To the negative, McCaffery and Bowman (1978, 535) describe how California's Proposition 13 threatened to undo the California legislature's response to the *Serrano v. Priest* (1971, 1976, 1977) California Supreme Court decision that requires school finance restructuring in the interest of greater equalization of expenditures across school districts.

Voters and legislatures enact TELs at the state level as amendments to the state constitution or as statutes. In either case, a TEL represents a major part of the institutional structure that defines local government finance and revenue collection. Adoption of a TEL is both a mechanical manifestation of tax containment and a symbolic statement of a desire to limit a particular form of tax or of government in general. Public opinion polling and campaign literature may provide explanations behind citizen adoption of a TEL, but once enacted into law, local government administrators must implement the TEL structure.

To enact a TEL, local administrators and elected officials must fully follow state regulations generated by the limitation statute, interpret any previous limitations for a collective effect, and design an organization and policy to best implement the limitation. The limitation singly, or in combination with earlier restrictions, may severely reduce local property tax revenues. As the teaching case at the start of this section demonstrated, administrators and the community must truthfully adjust staffing, policy, program delivery mechanisms, and program service levels to match revenue reductions. If the impact of the TEL is delayed and subtle, administrators must take on the difficult task of communicating its potential impacts to elected leaders and citizens. Long-term revenue forecasts and strategic financial plans are the principal tools for describing an impending budget structural imbalance and its implications on service delivery and on the jurisdiction's creditworthiness.

Administrators and elected officials must know their community and understand how the TEL should fit against local policy and values. Once a TEL is imposed, administrators must ask themselves: What is the TEL limitation trying to tell me, my government, and my elected officials? A review of the community culture may reveal that a small minority of taxpayers are explicitly concerned with excessive or unfair taxes, or with an unconstrained government presence. On the other hand, a major portion of community taxpayers may be messaging a fear that government is too big relative to community resources, is too complex, is espousing and supporting values different from those of the community, or is not providing comparable worth of services. Outreach and an adjustment of services may be in order. But, where political support and community values message otherwise, administrators should recognize and honor community calls for government response and services. In many states, the taxing district residents may challenge a tax rate cap or levy limit by a ballot initiative (Maher and Skidmore 2009). In a nearly offensive response, local governments and special districts in Washington State have offered voters the option of lifting a tax levy cap, and then in a second ballot question establishing a permanent tax rate to fund a specified service. Where tax limits cannot be lifted, administrators may need to identify alternate sources of revenue to respond to community needs. Nontax charges and fees for service may provide such a locally controlled revenue source. Alternatively, administrators may need to look to the nonprofit sector as a source of resources and program support.

REVENUE FORECASTING SUMMARY

Forecast revenues set the foundation for the public budget and its allocation of resources to prioritized needs and programs. Generating revenue forecasts is a blend of science and art. Forecasters must have strong skills in statistical and mathematical methods as well as a good handle on economic conditions and their effects on local businesses. Forecasters also need a strong sense of professional judgment in the selection of assumptions and in the selection of forecast estimates from an array of choices. Most important, forecasters must not only generate forecasts but also effectively communicate their methods and professional choices to elected officials, community leaders, interest advocates, and the public. Every forecast becomes an opportunity for building confidence in professional workmanship and in the larger budget process. Effective forecasting should also demonstrate the effects of tax limitations on local governments. A truthful picture of the short- and long-term effects of limitations builds credibility with taxpayers. A truthful revenue picture allows government leaders to return to voters with a request for additional funds to meet increased community needs.

STUDY QUESTIONS

1. Take the role of a fiscal analyst in a large port or airport special district government. The executive director and finance officer have asked you to take charge of all revenue forecasting to support the annual budget process. List the primary sources of revenue for your district. What technique would you use to forecast future revenues from each source? What data would you need to support a forecast, and how long would it take to collect?

2. Again, as a special district fiscal analyst, what priority would you give to each revenue source? How would you prioritize time and resources in developing revenue forecasts? Which sources would require substantial effort with regression modeling? Which other sources could use educated estimation?

3. What qualities and standards would you want in a revenue forecast? How would these qualities build public confidence in your work and in the budget process? Should your forecast assumptions necessarily match those used by the adjacent county in their forecasts? Explain?

4. Most forecasting approaches use historical data adjusted by current and near-term conditions to forecast future revenues. The economic downturn of 2007–2009 injected such uncertainty into the financial and real estate markets that the trends in historical data provided little help for the 2009 and 2010 revenue forecasts. For example, once robust county revenues from building permit fees and development service charges fell to near zero in hard-hit states. What approaches and data would you use to develop forecasts for building permit fees and development charges estimates under conditions of drastic economic and employment uncertainty?

5. Review your local government, special district, or nonprofit organization and identify a major fee charged for services. Which user or customer group in the community carries the burden of this fee? Should this fee be reauthorized as a tax broadly borne by all citizens? Is the fee structured for partial or full cost recovery, or for profit generation? Analyze the cost structure of the fee and identify the base charge, incremental charges, fixed costs, step costs, and variable costs and explain their integration into a total fee.

5. On the textbook website at www.pdx.edu/cps/budget-book, exercise 7.1 Revenue Forecasting: Property Tax provides an opportunity to forecast property tax revenues using a simplified deterministic spreadsheet model. To practice forecasting retail sales tax revenues with a simplified trendline model, work exercise 7.2 Revenue Forecasting: Retail Sales Tax.

6. Research property tax limitations in your state or in an adjacent state. How do the limitations restrict or affect the assessed value, tax rate, or total levy of residential homeowners? How has the limitation shifted tax burden among groups of taxpayers? Has the limitation system created favored treatment among certain groups of homeowners?

7. How have property tax limitations affected the revenue available to local governments in your state? Consider both immediate and long-term revenue consequences. Has major business, real estate, or residential development delayed the impact of property tax limitations in your area? Have depressed economic conditions delayed the effect of limitations? What larger political implications have the limitations caused?

NOTE

1. For additional information on state-level school equalization of funds, see Melissa Beard, Heather Moss, Isabel Munoz-Colon, and Sarah Reyneveld, *A Reference Guide of Six States: K–12 Funding Formulas in Colorado, Kentucky, Maryland, Massachusetts, North Carolina, and Oregon* (Olympia, WA: Washington Learns, Office of Financial Management, and Office of Superintendent of Public Instruction, August 2006), www.washingtonlearns.wa.gov/materials/SixStateStudyREALFinal.pdf (accessed May 16, 2011).

8 POLITY REVENUES AND GOVERNANCE DECISIONS

In May 2007, libraries in Josephine County [southern Oregon] were closed due to lack of funding. In September 2007, community members formed Josephine County Libraries Inc. (JCLI), a nongovernmental, nonprofit organization dedicated to reopening and operating the libraries in the county.

(Dawn Marie Gaid 2009, 56)

Oregon Statute: 307.130
Sunset Date: None
Year Enacted: 1854

Property owned or being purchased by literary, benevolent, charitable organizations or scientific institutions is exempt from property taxation. To qualify, the organization or institution must:

- *Be a nonprofit corporation,*
- *Provide a charitable gift to the public without expectation of payment, and*
- *Occupy and use the property in a manner that furthers the organization's charitable purpose.*

2009–10 Assessed Value of Property Exempted: $4.3 billion
2009–11 (biennial) Revenue Impact: $116,300,000 Loss [Loss of tax revenue]
2009–11 (biennial) Revenue Impact: $24,200,000 Shift [Tax burden shifted to other payers]

(State of Oregon 2010, 280) [explanations added]

Each local government sits in context with its **polity** network of nonprofit service providers, related governments, for-profit providers, advocacy groups, and citizens. A Greek term for the *form* or *constitution* of an organized unit of governance, *polity* emphasizes the organic interrelated social, economic, cultural, and political components of a community that combine to form its distinct identity and character. Just as local governments must develop and maintain sources of governmental revenue, nonprofit members of the surrounding polity network must also raise and maintain revenue flows. Nonprofit-sector revenues are similar to governmental revenues (chapter 6)—but with important differences. Charges and reimbursements for services form the primary revenue base for many nonprofits, including large education and health services providers. Membership dues help to cover the program costs of member service and public interest nonprofits. Most nonprofits engage in some form of donor development and fundraising, and an understanding of the motivations of charitable and philanthropic donors is critical to successful fundraising. Additionally, many nonprofits rely on the revenue from government grants and contracts to fund programs. In appropriate circumstances, nonprofits rely on commercial credit markets to borrow funds.

The need to develop revenues for all members of a community polity network forces local government and nonprofit organization leaders to consider a larger view that transcends economic-sector boundaries. From this broader integrated perspective, leaders can understand that the polity relies on a single common pool of resources. How a community or region generates resources from the different economic sectors defines how it uses the mixed economy to solve complex issues of the public good. This chapter explores how communities have taken on this task of multisector resource development and allocation.

The Upper Cascadia County public safety services levy teaching case points to the issue of revenue generation by polity members in different economic sectors. In that hypothetical case, the community foundation representative seeks to understand the possible size and scope of social service programs the county government intends to support so his organization can develop a program response to assure continued services to the community. Local governments will use the taxation and charges for services to raise their share of revenues, while the nonprofit sector must use fundraising and other techniques to tap other sources and forms of community wealth. This chapter explores such a complementary approach and encourages administrators, elected officials, and financial analysts to define and manage resources and revenues at the community and regional levels.

The policy decisions of how to develop wealth and revenue generation capacity in a community can raise difficult questions of fairness. A healthy commercial sector of businesses is critical to revenue generation for government and for **charitable giving**. Tax relief to businesses provides an important economic development tool that can attract and retain key businesses in a jurisdiction, but the decision to give a tax break to a business places an additional burden on all other taxpayers. Exempted and noncollected tax revenues reduce the governmental funds available to fund programs and grants/contracts in the nonprofit sector. How a community and its polity decide to balance business development and long-term revenue generation against the immediate needs for social services, education, and other requirements is a major policy question. The last section of the chapter explores some of these trade-offs and dilemmas.

To discuss these issues, this chapter begins with a very brief overview of nonprofit-sector revenue trends. It then turns to a discussion of nonprofit organization–level revenues, including charges for services, grants and contracts, fundraising and donor development, enterprise revenues, and credit-based income. Charitable and philanthropic giving form major revenue sources for many nonprofits, and the chapter examines the donor intentions behind using these forms of giving. This leads to a discussion of recent trends and changes in fundraising such as ethical behavior and professionalism in donor development and fundraising. A look at the process of blending government-sector and nonprofit-sector resources follows, demonstrating an understanding of polity network–level resources. This discussion includes an approach for assessing network resources. The chapter then takes on the policy issues of granting tax relief to increase justice in the community and for economic development to grow revenue bases for taxation and giving.

HISTORICAL TRENDS IN NONPROFIT REVENUES

Federal policy and spending decisions condition the amount and type of intergovernmental revenue that reaches state government and local communities. A very brief historical review provides context for our discussions on nonprofit revenues and polity financial resources. In the 1960s and 1970s, funding from the federal and state governments provided a substantial share of social welfare resources used by nonprofit organizations (Salamon 2012, chap. 5). This support fell steeply in the mid-1980s with the Reagan administration, but then later rebounded in the 1990s, especially in the areas of health care (Froelich 2001, 183). The entitlement and consumer choice–driven bases of the federal Medicare and Medicaid programs have led to increasing and continuing revenues to nonprofit and for-profit health care service providers. Additionally, a number of social services have been recategorized as health programs, which fall under the Medicare and Medicaid revenue streams (Salamon 2012, 100). The federal welfare reform act of the mid-1990s block-granted payments to states, but with a strong economy and falling caseloads, surplus monies often became available. This unexpected combination of conditions marginally increased federal and state social service resources. These federal health and social welfare policies and revenues helped to sustain nonprofit-sector revenues and employment over the late 1990s and through the two years of economic downturn from 2007 to 2009 (Salamon, Sokolowski, and Geller 2012). The American Recovery and Reinvestment Act of 2009 (ARRA) provided funds to state and local governments for a variety of recovery and capital investment programs. ARRA funds helped to sustain the flow of funds for social service and workforce development nonprofit grants and contracts into 2010. However, the expiration of the ARRA, a drastic reduction in state tax revenues, constraints on state intergovernmental funds shared with local governments, and reduced property tax revenues led to deep cuts in government employment in the post-downturn period (Pew Center on the States 2012a; Baden 2011). Reduced state and local government resources also led to fewer and smaller grants and contracts to social service providers (VanderHart 2010; Hannah-Jones 2011). Although conditions varied by state and regional economies, reduced government funding often resulted in service nonprofit closures and consolidations.

For nonprofit organizations outside of health care and related services, the economic downturn of 2007–2009 was especially challenging, particularly for nonprofit organizations heavily dependent on philanthropy and charitable gift income. The downturn resulted in a severe hit to private wealth and charitable donations (Salamon 2012, 204). This adversely limited revenues to arts and cultural nonprofit organizations. In response, nonprofits increased charges for services and enterprise revenues, providing some offset to the drop in philanthropic donations. Recent (2012–2013) improvements in the financial and investment markets have generated some improvement in donor resources.

NONPROFIT ORGANIZATION RESOURCES

Unlike the coerced nature of tax revenues that fund governments, nonprofits must raise funds in a competitive marketplace. Without a steady and sufficient stream of revenues, program delivery will grow inconsistent, and client and donor confidence in the organization will waiver. No matter how needed a service or how honorable a mission, nonprofit action and service delivery rests on a foundation of revenues. Resource development is a critical and ongoing task for almost all nonprofit organizations. From a leadership perspective, obtaining sufficient funding requires both short-term opportunistic and broad-picture strategic behaviors. Nonprofit fundraising often takes place in a competitive environment, with organizations vying for a share of too few resources, not unlike the jump ball in a basketball game where players jostle for possession.

Nonprofit organizations typically strive to build a revenue base from diverse sources (Froelich 2001). Relying on an array of revenue sources allows the organization to better withstand changing economic conditions such as a major loss of revenue, an unexpected increase in service demand, or an abrupt change in mission. Most nonprofits rely on an evolving blend of revenue sources. Grants and contracts begin, run their course, and then end; major donations allow for specified program development but then expire; annual fundraising events have strong and weak years; and the ebb and flow of financial market conditions the availability of donor resources. Nonprofit executives, chief financial officers or finance directors, and resource development directors must constantly work across a spread of sources to ensure a steady flow of resources to meet the organization's ongoing expenses and program costs. In the end, organizations size their organization structure, staffing, and programs to match the available resources, and sometimes must adjust the organizational mission to subordinate it to a particular funding source.

Most nonprofit scholars and consultants recommend that nonprofit organizations undertake a comprehensive strategic planning process to guide development of a mission, organization program goals, and financial goals (Bryson 2005, 182; Jackson 2007; see also chapter 10 of this book). A financial strategic plan including an analysis of the fundraising environment is a critical element of a broader organizational strategic plan. The essential elements of a fundraising environmental analysis include:

- the evaluation of the threats and opportunities in the revenue environment;
- the identification of current and potential revenue sources;
- a recognition of donor perceptions of the organization;
- a recognition of donors' sense of confidence in the organization;
- an identification of trends in giving and the fundraising behavior of similar organizations; and
- the level of resources needed by the organization to deliver its current and potential programs.

Jackson (2007, 120) explains that a nonprofit must develop a solid donor base and a solid revenue stream in order to effectively engage and build confidence in new and larger donors. Additionally, a nonprofit's strategic plan must clarify mission priorities and the sources of resources that it will accept to support those priorities. An effective strategic plan also encourages a small nonprofit to think of itself as a larger, successful organization (Jackson, 162).

As we will describe further in chapter 10 on financial forecasting and planning, strategic plans are helpful guides, but a nonprofit organization must effectively operationalize and implement its plan. Operational plans, often known as business plans, provide the critical bridge needed to translate strategy into actions and outcomes. Operational plans should include a detailed schedule of all current and potential revenues. A comprehensive revenue schedule should include (for all revenues), the source, type, beginning and ending availability; access restrictions; speculative or certainty of availability; sequential timing; and reporting requirements (see Dropkin, Halpin, and La Touche 2007, 21 and 70). Alternative scenarios of revenue combinations and availability schedules should also be considered. Where sufficient data is available and valid assumptions can be developed, analysts should develop mid- to long-term forecasts for continuing sources of revenue. Where multiyear government and foundation contracts allow annual cost adjustments for inflation, revenue forecasts should be adjusted as well. Once forecasts are developed, an organization should look back and compare projected versus actual performance. Nonprofit organization revenue forecasts will typically include the following broad categories of revenues: charges and reimbursements for services; grants and service contracts; charitable and philanthropic gifts; investment income; enterprise funds; and borrowing from commercial credit sources. These operational planning procedures parallel those we describe for governmental organizations in chapters 10 and 12 of this book.

Charges and Reimbursement for Services

Charges for services (fees for service) and reimbursement for services provide an important revenue foundation for many educational, health care, arts and culture, recreation and sports, and social service nonprofits. As examples, private religious-affiliated primary and secondary (K–12) schools and academies charge students tuition. Nonprofit hospitals and medical groups charge fees for their services. Theater, opera, and orchestral organizations sell tickets by seasonal subscription packages or individually by event. Other charges and fees for services include sports league operating fees and organization annual membership dues. Private universities and colleges charge students tuition and fees to cover the majority of operating costs. Such charges provided almost 77 percent of all revenues collected by nonprofit universities and colleges in 2009 (Salamon 2012, 150).

Charges and fees based on production costs provide a means for organizations to recover costs in total or in part. The mechanics of rate determination and cost recovery are the same as those used to determine governmental fees in chapter 7. Organizations initially set rates for charges and fees to fully recover all direct program costs and indirect administrative costs for the volume of services produced. Nonprofit organizations, however, operate in a competitive marketplace. Their program charges and fees must be competitive with their peer providers, or the value added to a service by a nonprofit must justify its added expense over the governmental-sector alternative. For example, a religiously affiliated private elementary school must have competitive prices with other nearby private schools, especially those of the same religious denomination. Additionally, parents must see sufficient added value in educational quality or cultural training to justify paying substantial private school tuition as compared to the lower costs associated with a local public elementary school. While nonprofit organizations always face the need to recover costs, organization missions may specifically provide for services to disadvantaged populations. Here, the organization may purposefully charge reduced rates to needy clients, and proportionately raise charges on other paying clients to ensure total cost coverage.

Nonprofit organizations often receive reimbursement income for services that have been rendered. For example, nonprofit hospitals accept Medicare, Medicaid, and state health plan reimbursements for patient services. Here, the reimbursement rates set by governmental programs or private insurance define the revenues earned per patient or procedure. Once reimbursement rates are determined, nonprofit providers can forecast annual caseloads and then determine expectations of total future reimbursement revenues. For many hospitals, reimbursement income amounts to a substantial portion of the total organizational income. Thus, federal and state administrative and legislative policy- and rate-setting decisions have far-reaching effects on both nonprofit and for-profit providers. Restricting reimbursement rates is one method of limiting governmental program costs and expenditures.

Grants and Service Contracts

Grants and service contracts are a major subcategory of charges and reimbursement for services. This revenue source is of such importance that it merits separate discussion. **Grants** and **contracts for services** are agreements between a service provider and a purchasing government, an **intermediary nonprofit**, a foundation, or a commercial corporation to purchase services (see LeRoux 2007; Ott 2001, chap. 7; Cooper 2003). The two terms, *grant* and *service contract,* are used somewhat interchangeably, but a grant often implies a request for work that involves substantial professional judgment and discretion in work accomplishment. A foundation, intermediary, or other private purchaser may offer a grant without executing a competitive procurement process. Governments, however, typically must use open, competitive procurement procedures to purchase program and professional services. The criteria for competitively evaluating vendor bids or proposals usually considers (1) the professional qualifications and work capacity of the proposing organization, (2) its past performance on similar tasks, (3) its proposed package of services, (4) the quality and quantity of services in its proposed package, and (5) its cost to accomplish the work. The bid or proposal with the highest scores on the selection criteria is selected to perform the desired work. The grant or contract agreement spells out the tasks to be accomplished, the work completion schedule and performance requirements, the resource and staff contribution from each party, a reimbursement amount and payment schedule, the audit and reporting requirements, and the dissolution and other administrative provisions. The reimbursement to the provider may be structured on a scheduled basis to coincide with task completion, on a quarterly basis for ongoing services, or as a lump sum total payment.

To ensure a continuous flow of grant or service contract revenues, nonprofit administrators must dedicate staff time and resources to identifying and researching project opportunities and procurement applications. Preparing proposals, responding to solicitations and procurement procedures, preparing bid and proposal documents, and following through on legal, administrative, and project details involves a major amount of staff time and resources. Proposals and bids require high-quality content and readability, and they must be delivered on time and in the correct format. Even with the best of efforts, many of the proposals submitted by an organization will not result in a winning bid or obtaining a grant award. Organizational leadership must strategically target potential funders, carefully manage the preparation efforts, and evaluate the cumulative rejection ratio as part of the larger effort to obtain revenues for the organization. Administrators must carefully balance the resources diverted to grant and bid preparation relative to more effective uses in other revenue development tasks or in program delivery.

Fundraising for Charitable and Philanthropic Gifts

Charitable and philanthropic gifts provide an important source of revenue for many nonprofit organizations. In many organizations, charitable and philanthropic revenues complement other revenues from charges for services, reimbursements, and grants and contracts. Organizations face competition in their efforts to obtain charitable and philanthropic donations. Small-scale charitable donors and large-scale philanthropic donors have choices, and they can easily contribute to a vast array of organizations. Donors also have the very real option of not contributing at all.

Successful resource development requires organizational commitment and investment. Donor research, fundraising events, and campaign planning, event and campaign implementation, long-term contact information management, development of an Internet presence, and sustaining personal donor relationships takes considerable staff time and effort. In smaller nonprofits, the chief executive officer, board members, and staff directors all contribute to the fundraising effort. Recognizing its importance, larger nonprofits typically dedicate an executive-level position with full support staff to the fundraising and development tasks. Additionally, the chief executive officer spends a substantial amount of his or her time in fundraising activities. Fundraising initiatives are often recognized and managed as proactive business development activities that bring little short-term benefit. Building a donor relationship to fruition may take years, while yielding marginal or substantial results in the process. Nonprofit budgets rarely cover the full cost of fundraising activities. In the short-term, funds allocated to fundraising and resource development reduce the funds available for mission and service operations, but failure to develop resources threatens the life of the organization.

The size, purpose, and mission of different organizations distinguish and differentiate their fundraising strategies and sources.

Small Member-Benefit Groups

Citizen-led service organizations, youth groups, and religious organizations typically generate revenues on a small volume and from familiar sources. Youth groups sell candy, popcorn, and holiday decorations; hold barbeque and meal fundraisers; organize raffles; and sell services or entertainment. Churches and religious organizations collect membership dues and tithes. Gifts, memberships, and grants as cash contributions; noncash contributions; donated services; and donated facilities and equipment may also contribute to the revenue streams for small-scale nonprofit and local religious organizations.

Federated Intermediary Nonprofits

Regional community chest organizations and other combined campaigns, known as **federated intermediary nonprofits** (Salamon 1992; Frumkin 2010) typically raise large volumes of revenues

POLITY REVENUES AND GOVERNANCE DECISIONS 225

through a network of donors often tied to a parent organization or geographic community. Federated intermediaries may solicit funds to support their own programs and administrative needs, or they may raise funds on behalf of other organizations. Federated intermediary nonprofits that use access across many employers to raise funds include regional United Way chapters and combined national campaigns for federal government agencies. Fundraising by religion-sponsored and religiously affiliated federated organizations relies on donations from individual members and from member churches, synagogues, and branches. Examples of familiar religious-affiliated intermediaries include Catholic Charities, Lutheran Community Services, and the Jewish Community Center Association (Gelles 2001). Federated intermediaries also raise funds through grants and bequests, endowment income, donated services, fees for service, special events income, rental income, and other sources. From the money raised, federated intermediaries then act as donor organizations by giving substantial grants and contracts to other nonprofits and even to government agencies.

Federated intermediary fundraising campaigns tend to give a face to the entire community and its needs. Through this shift in scale to the community, federated organizations can provide a structure for community coordination and planning. General, **unspecified giving** to a federated intermediary provides a flexible resource that the organization can prioritize and allocate to meet administrative costs, polity network administrative costs, or a broad array of community needs.

Public Community Foundations

Foundations are another form of intermediary nonprofit. Public **community foundations** gather donations and other resources from numerous individuals in the community. The foundation staff assesses community needs, provides grants to service providers to accomplish services, and then evaluates provider performance and community progress. A board of directors with broad representation of business, civic, government, and religious leaders typically guides community foundations from the community. Like federated intermediary nonprofits, community foundations can represent the community as a whole and work to respond to its issues. Community foundations use a variety of fundraising campaigns to build donations, and we give further attention to foundations and their donor motivations in the next section.

Major Service Delivery Nonprofits

Major service delivery nonprofits have sufficient organizational capacity to both deliver services and to act as an intermediary donor to other service providers. These organizations include nonprofit schools, colleges, universities, hospitals, public broadcasting organizations, and community service organizations such as the YMCA and YWCA. These medium to large nonprofits typically have well-developed fundraising and donor development capacities. While they often raise donations from the community at large, many of these organizations draw on their extensive donor bases of clients, members, or alumni. The emotional connection that donors hold for an organization triggers continuing and often substantial donations. Defined donor lists allow these organizations to repeatedly contact donors through preferred message channels and for specific requests. These strong contacts lead to extended relationships that may result in multiple gifts over a donor's lifetime. Donor development activities include holding special events, direct mail contact and newsletters, interpersonal meetings, and online contacts through social media. Donors may contribute gifts as single or multiple donations or as a bequest from their estates at their death. Community action organizations (CAOs) rely on donations and fundraising activities for a portion of their revenues, but as Exhibit 8.1 relates, these organizations also receive funding from federal government grants. In many ways, these federal grants are comparable to the intergovernmental revenues received by local governments as we discussed in chapter 6.

Exhibit 8.1

Community Action Organizations (CAO) Rely Extensively on Government Funding

Over 1,000 community action agencies nationwide serve as important antipoverty service delivery and coordination agents in rural and urban communities. Community action organizations are blended private and public nonprofit organizations established under the Economic Opportunity Act of 1964 as part of the Johnson administration's War on Poverty. Each organization has a board of directors containing members from various walks of life: at least one-third being low-income members; one-third public officials; and one-third from the private sector, which includes businesses, faith organizations, charities, and civic organizations. Under strong local control, community action organizations select and tailor emergency services, food and nutrition programs, child care, counseling, information and referral services, and other family support programs to meet local needs. About 54 percent of community action agencies serve rural areas; 36 percent serve both rural and urban; and 10 percent service urban areas (Community Action Partnership 2012; Washington State Community Action Partnership 2013). Community action agencies are important service providers and actors in community and rural polities. In addition to delivering their own programs, community action agencies complement the efforts of local governments, state government agencies, community foundations, and federated intermediaries in a polity network.

In contrast to most foundations and federated intermediaries that rely heavily on charitable and philanthropic giving, community action agencies rely heavily on state and local government funding. In this reliance, community action organizations typically provide the local service delivery for federal child care, Head Start early childhood education, job readiness and training, and weatherization/energy subsidy programs. The federal Community Services Block Grant (CSBG) provides a foundational source of funding for community action agencies. Appropriations for FY 2013 provided about $635 million in funding to the states, the District of Columbia, and Puerto Rico and the other U.S. territories (Spar 2013). The states then provided grants to the local community action organizations and to other qualified service providers. Ninety percent of the federal grant must reach the local organizations for service delivery. Five percent may be used for administration, and the remaining 5 percent may support state-initiated projects to eliminate poverty. The funds must support programs targeted toward low-income residents. Community action organizations receive funds under federal grant and contract guidelines, and they must be responsive to federal audit requirements and procedures. Grants from other federal programs supplement the CSBG funding.

Forecasting the potential revenues for community action programs requires close attention to the annual budget and appropriations debates in Washington, DC. Analysts can follow the proposed funding levels in the president's budget request, and then follow the appropriated funding levels adopted by the House of Representatives and the Senate. Close attention to the committee reports and tables prepared by the appropriations subcommittees for the federal Departments of Education, Energy, Health and Human Services, and Housing and Urban Development indicates the range of likely funding for the coming fiscal year. The national Community Action Partnership provides information on emerging appropriations and policy issues related to these agencies.

Source: Community Action Partnership 2012.

Investment Income

Nonprofit organizations collect and invest resources for investment income and equity growth. These resources may come to the organization as donations of land and real estate, financial securities, or cash. Should an organization receive or accumulate a substantial level of investment assets, it may establish an **endowment** from which to draw an annual flow of interest and investment income while leaving the principal intact. Under any arrangement, the organization's board should establish investment goals and objectives, investment policies, and risk management policies to guide the staff or financial professionals. Based on its policies, the organization may keep donated securities that complement its investment objectives, while it may sell other donations that do not comply and then invest the proceeds into more desirable investments. Nonprofits often hold a portfolio of long-term investments in land and real estate, as well as in financial instruments including bonds, stocks, and investment funds. Larger nonprofit organizations and foundations may accumulate cash from donations and routine operations. These resources are available for safe, short-term investments as part of a cash management policy (see chapter 17).

Enterprise Activities

For charitable public service organizations, the revenues and profits from a commercial or enterprise activity such as food services, gift stores, or gym memberships can provide an independent revenue stream to complement the typical nonprofit revenue streams from charges for services, grants, contracts, and donations. Nonprofit public service organizations are allowed by tax regulations to operate for-profit businesses as long as the proceeds are not distributed back to the organization shareholders and owners. These commercial-style, revenue-generating activities have become increasingly popular under the name of **social entrepreneurism** (Young 2001; Weisbrod 2001; Massarsky 2005). Revenues from enterprise activities usually provide a revenue stream that is unrelated to the other sources of revenue used by the organization. Donors, clients, and the public often raise concerns that commercial activities by nonprofits will divert the organization's mission and activities away from its intended public service functions.

Credit-Based Revenues

Nonprofit organizations also tap the credit markets for revenues, especially to fund capital purchases. On a small scale, churches, synagogues, other local religious organizations, and other local nonprofit chapters take out mortgages to finance buildings and other infrastructure. Pledges based on the wealth and income of the organization membership typically drive the size of the building effort (chapter 16, Exhibit 16.1). On a larger scale, private nonprofit hospitals, colleges and universities, museums, and libraries often tap the municipal bond markets or sell a **certificate of participation (COP)** to obtain funds for major building, infrastructure, and equipment investments. The institution normally identifies future revenues such as patient fees or student tuition as a stream of dependable revenue that will cover the debt principal and interest payments over a period of several decades. In the case of a COP, the physical project is the collateral for the note. State governments use their creditworthiness to give major private institutions access to low-interest debt through the municipal bond markets (National Association of Health and Educational Facilities Finance Authorities 2008).

DONOR INTENTIONS IN CHARITABLE AND PHILANTHROPIC GIVING

Charitable giving allows individuals, corporations, and other organizational entities to donate funds to public service "religious, charitable, and educational" nonprofit organizations with tax benefits (Salamon 2012, 36). Voluntary charitable giving enables citizens and businesses to respond to community needs without the perceived taint of government coercion. For many donors, the choice and voluntary aspect of giving exercises a form of personal economic liberty. Charitable giving in the United States totaled almost $291 billion in 2010. Individuals were responsible for over $211 billion of this total—about 73 percent (Giving USA Foundation 2011). An estimated 65 percent of all U.S. households donate to charities (National Philanthropic Trust 2012; Morningstar 2007).

Direct, small-scale, charitable giving allows individuals, young and old, to support their local religious organizations, local youth groups and sports leagues, human and social service groups, arts organizations, and local schools. Direct giving may respond to donor personal initiative, fundraising events, direct mail solicitations, or annual campaigns. Though effective, small-scale charitable giving often fails to provide sufficient resources over a sustained period to make a substantial difference in meeting community needs and complex social problems. Furthermore, most small-scale charitable donors make a contribution trusting that the receiving organization will effectively deliver services to those in need as promised (Frumkin 2010, 34–37). Arrillaga-Andreessen (2012, 81–84) recommends in-depth research of the recipient organization before making a direct charitable contribution.

Large-scale, strategic **philanthropic giving** allows donor involvement and emotional satisfaction and can often provide a more effective response to public needs. Strategic philanthropy can include a planned program of giving that sets goals, sets a strategy to achieve those goals, defines metrics to measure goal attainment and achievement of success, and requires the assessment of returns on the philanthropic investment (Arrillaga-Andreessen 2012, 283). Effective philanthropic gifts should have the capacity to enable individuals and communities to make transformative changes in their well-being. Philanthropic giving also has the potential to locate and support social innovations, to restore equity in society, to enhance pluralism in society, and to counteract the perceived overarching influence of government. Philanthropy responds to the donor's needs for self-actualization and emotional satisfaction as well (Frumkin 2010, 3–4).

The motivations behind philanthropic giving are complex. At one extreme, donors may give instrumentally to respond to community priorities and needs, but with minimal thought to personal emotional satisfaction or involvement in the project. On the opposite extreme, donors may give with strong attention to their own emotional needs, perceptions, values, and agendas, but without sufficient attention to understanding community needs and priorities. Frumkin (2010, 45) argues that effective philanthropy balances the motivations of instrumentality and expressivism. From the public's perspective, philanthropic donations are also a public statement of legitimacy for the receiving organization and its mission (Froelich 2001, 183).

Philanthropy raises multiple concerns of legitimacy (Frumkin 2010, 5–9). While a donor may wish to give funds to a particular cause, the receiving community or group may question the legitimacy of a wealthy donor interpreting public needs, defining public policies, and implementing public solutions through a personal agenda, or seeking to meet personal emotional needs. Frumkin argues that effective philanthropy must evaluate the effectiveness of the giving program and its strategy, the program's mechanisms for financial and performance accountability, and the legitimacy of donor motive and strategy.

Philanthropic donors often struggle to understand community needs and priorities. Recent government budgets provide one indication of public needs and values in the community. Patterns of giving by federated intermediary organizations and community foundations can provide a second source of information about relative public needs. These local government budgets can indicate areas of strong community investment and resource gaps.

Effective and accountable giving requires some form of legal and financial structure to receive resources, select projects, distribute funds, and monitor effectiveness. Family trusts, private foundations, corporate foundations, community foundations, Internet foundations, and donor-advised funds provide mechanisms to meet these needs. Effective giving selects the appropriate structure to meet the donor's and the recipient's needs (Frumkin 2010, 129–156; Arrillaga-Andreessen 2012, 90, 264–265). Quasi-public, government-sponsored private foundations represent a blending of the private, corporate, and community foundation models. Because of their concentrated resources and social ties, trusts and foundations of all types are important constitutive members of a local community or regional polity.

Private Personal and Family Trusts

Family **trusts** are legal structures commonly used by middle-income and high-wealth families to transfer wealth to successive generations on the death of an individual. The trust structure presents a mechanism to manage resources, to designate and make gifts, and to receive a variety of tax advantages. Bequests from personal estates often provide individuals and families with an opportunity to step above routine small-scale charity to make substantial charitable donations. Donations from personal and family trusts typically express the values and wishes of the individual or the family. Charitable giving by bequests totaled about $23 billion in 2010, or about 8 percent of all contributions (Giving USA Foundation 2011).

Private Family and Independent Foundations

Private foundations established by families or individuals usually rely on the interest income generated by their investment endowments (Salamon 1992; Boris 2001) to fund projects or to meet goals. Once a substantial endowment is developed with sufficient revenue generation to achieve its goals, the private foundation becomes relatively insulated from the need to raise funds (Frumkin, 129–156). This makes foundations unusual among organizations in the nonprofit sector. A board of directors controls a private foundation, which may or may not have a professional staff. **Family foundations** are typically private foundations with family members as the board of directors. The Gates Foundation, the Ford Foundation, the Getty Trust, the Robert Wood Johnson Foundation, the W.K. Kellogg Foundation, the David and Lucile Packard Foundation, the Lilly Endowment, and the Pew Charitable Trusts represent some of the largest and most widely known family foundations (Salamon 2012, 48). As generations pass, members of the named family may have diminishing involvement in the foundation, leaving its management to an independent board of directors.

Corporate Foundations

Businesses and corporations may establish a private **corporate foundation** to further their interests and presence in a community. A corporate foundation may have an endowment but also may rely on transfers of corporate revenues to sustain philanthropic giving. Corporate foundation giving can provide major grants for community purposes, but with the strategic purpose of furthering the organization's presence in the community.

Community Foundations

A **community foundation** (Salamon 1992, 18; Boris 2001) is a **public foundation** that focuses and limits giving to a defined community or region. Tax regulations require community foundations to have broad public participation from many donors and broad participation in their governance. The coordination and consolidation of wealth from many contributors then allows the foundation to address major community needs not covered by government programs. Community foundations may have an endowment or may raise funds for direct distribution. Alternatively, a group of citizens may establish an **independent foundation** to complement government programs. For example, parents, teachers, and community leaders may establish a community fund to support local schools. Community foundations may employ a professional staff to assess community needs, propose policies and strategies, distribute funds, and evaluate program effectiveness. To receive grants, nonprofits in the community follow procedures and typically make proposals to the community foundation. Based on their policies, strategic plans, and giving priorities, community foundations can have a substantial impact on service program design and implementation. The major federated intermediary nonprofits are closely related in design and mission to community foundations.

Governmental Foundations

Governments and government agencies establish allied nonprofit **governmental foundations** to support and augment their missions. These quasi-public foundations typically blend attributes of a corporate and community foundation. As examples, at the national level, U.S. Congress has established governmental foundations to support federal agencies. Locally, a school district, its parents, and its teachers may establish a foundation to raise supplemental funds for schools and extracurricular activities. The boards of governmental foundations may include a blend of public officials and private citizens. Governmental foundations provide a means for government agencies to accept private donations without having to send the donations along to its general fund. Governmental foundations may be authorized to establish and grow an endowment. Because they receive both public and private monies, governmental foundations are quasi-public organizations, and maintaining accountability over governmental foundations is challenging. Governmental financial and policy controls become limited because private funds and nongovernmental individuals contribute to the foundation. These nongovernmental donors influence policy and affect service delivery.

Donor-Advised and Gift Funds

Donor-advised funds or **gift funds** (Frumkin 2010, 148; Arrillaga-Andreessen 2012, 78–79) provide an alternative to personal trusts and private foundations for individual philanthropic giving. These funds, established by financial services companies, provide an efficient giving pathway for investors. The investor-donors typically provide their own research into charities and community needs; the funds verify tax-exempt status of recipient organizations, make payments, and keep records of donations. The donor provides any research and strategic direction to focus the giving. Donor-advised funds are similar to federated intermediaries in that they act to collect funds and then distribute them to designated organizations, but they are quite opposite in terms of professional strategy, program evaluation, and oversight. Donor-advised funds distributed about $7 billion in 2011 (National Philanthropic Trust 2012).

Donor Motivations and Behavior

The particular choice of philanthropic method—trust, foundation, donor-advised fund, and so on—reflects the donor's many needs. These include the need for personal satisfaction, the need for personal involvement and control, responsiveness to financial and legal concerns, the type of service delivered, and the administrative costs. However, donor restrictions on charitable and philanthropic gifts may have downsides for nonprofit administration and effective program response. This includes limiting fund use to a specific, designated purpose, or limiting use to a specified period (Dropkin, Halpin, and La Touche 2007, 22).

Many donors prefer to specify the cause or activity for which their funds will be used, but the specified donations given to a particular activity or service may not match with the reality of service needs. A specified donation may bring emotional satisfaction to the donor for responding to an immediate identified need, but a specified donation cannot be used to address the underlying structural and long-term issues causing the problem; nor can it be transferred to address an even more pressing need. Unfortunately, a donor's future giving is often dependent on demonstrated successful performance on the immediate "band-aid" response. Donor-specified giving may indicate a desire to meet an advertised need, but it may also indicate a lack of confidence in the nonprofit's judgment and a desire to control performance to prevent the waste of resources. High levels of program performance become difficult when problems are complex, with significant factors beyond the reach of the nonprofit and its programs. Generous, one-time donations to a specific program may allow a needed increase in programs and staff, but without continued support from donors, programs must reduce capacity when the funds run out. Clear messages during fundraising, along with communication between the nonprofit leadership and the donor, can help to define common understanding of the need situation and of nonprofit performance expectations. Where a community issue or problem remains, and donor resources are insufficient or intermittent, nonprofit administrators need to turn to their polity network peers to find additional resources.

The acceptance of large donations, large foundation grants, or major governmental contracts has the potential of diverting a nonprofit's core mission from previously planned strategic directions. Major donors often expect a nonprofit to conform to their perceptions, expectations, objectives, and values. Nonprofits must carefully balance the sources and diversity of their revenues with control of their organizational mission (Froelich 2001, 190). Some donors have ethical objections to charging fees for services and to using entrepreneurial and business activities to generate enterprise revenues. Enterprise revenues may be perceived as undermining the altruistic values of the nonprofit organization. Based on their strategic plans and predetermined financial policies, nonprofit boards and executives must carefully assess the relative benefits and liabilities of accepting different revenue opportunities.

Finally, in addition to effective program performance, knowledgeable donors demand effective financial management by grant recipients. Jackson (2007) argues that trustworthy nonprofits develop strategic plans that include strong financial controls and risk management systems. These attributes become marketing points that can reassure and encourage donors. The acceptance of a grant or contract by a nonprofit may require the modification of systems and procedures for financial record keeping, performance measurement, reporting, and audit systems. Full compliance with reporting and audit requirements may be a critical criterion for grant renewal.

TRANSITIONS IN FUNDRAISING

Nonprofit administrators face the challenge of working in real time to ensure sufficient revenues for their organizations while at the same time adapting to a fast-changing world. Two areas of change—Internet- and web-based fundraising and the rise of professional fundraising practitioners—deserve special attention because of their widespread and deep implications.

Technological Transformation of Fundraising

Nonprofit fundraising and donor development techniques have evolved tremendously over the last two decades. Much of this transformation has been propelled by the revolution in computer technology, social media, and information management. In the past, fundraising relied on direct mail solicitation, telephone marketing, and print advertising. While these methods remain in use, the Internet and social media systems have steadily replaced the traditional solicitation techniques. However, multiple interpersonal contacts and sustained relationships form the basis for most large charitable and philanthropic gifts. Building the relationship between the donor and the foundation or nonprofit requires repeated contacts in person, by mail, or electronically. The administrative tasks of donor identification and development have also been transformed. Paper records and staff work have been replaced by electronic databases that can efficiently recall, sort, and identify the most appropriate donors. However, the maintenance of up-to-date donor records and information remains an important, continuing task.

To effectively raise funds by online means, nonprofit organizations must establish and maintain a presence on the Internet (Arrillaga-Andreessen, chapter 2). This presence includes maintaining a web homepage for the organization, establishing webpages and links on social media systems, recording and posting videos and podcasts, hosting and maintaining blogs, and working to boost traffic to the organization's site (Genn 2009). Online newsletters and emails provide another avenue of communication to organization members and potential donors. Additionally, organization websites must have a mechanism for collecting and processing donations. This usually requires a webpage that can accept credit card information, a service that can process credit card information, and a merchant services account with a bank or third party provider (Genn 2009, 133). However, small nonprofit organizations may not find it worth the effort and cost to accept online donations, and webpages with instructions for telephone or postal contacts may provide an effective alternative.

Direct appeal to donors via the Internet is a growing phenomenon. The global reach of the Internet can bring awareness of needs and service organizations to donors from outside the local community and region, which can help to expand the resource base available to local nonprofits. The Internet has also allowed donors to take an active role in building support for issues and organizations (Arrillaga-Andreessen 2012, 45). However, extensive and large donations by distant donors can raise legitimacy issues of external control over local decisions. The Internet provides donors with a powerful tool for research into issues, specific nonprofit organizations and their performance, and social activists engaged in their interests. Nonprofit organizations need to respond to the information needs of potential donors by ensuring that program performance, budget, and financial information are available for online review.

In recent years, **directed giving** through the Internet has begun to compete with and even replace unspecified giving to major intermediaries and nonprofits. In directed giving, donors specify the exact use of their gift to particular organizations on a master list. Internet websites allow business and corporate employees to direct donations to a desired organization without intermediary support. Electronic directed giving obviates the need for a fundraising campaign and the expense of involving an intermediary organization. However, directed giving bypasses the professional judgment important to strategic fund allocation and the monitoring of program performance that effective intermediaries provide (Arrillaga-Andreessen, 57–58). While e–philanthropy may expand donor flexibility and offer an increased sense of personal liberty, bypassing the regional intermediaries may weaken governance and accountability structures in the community polity. Note that this loss of community capacity is of little importance to corporate benefits managers who simply desire an efficient, responsive employee donation procedure.

Growing Professionalism in Fundraising

The complexities of diverse revenue sources, changing fundraising techniques and tools, donor activism, and changing client and member needs demonstrate the need for the services of professional fundraisers and donor development experts. Fundraising and donor development has gained increasing professional status in recent decades. Tempel (2010) and Greenfield (2002) provide detailed overviews of fundraising techniques and strategies. Grant writing and proposal development have also become a refined professional art.

While not constrained by regulations to the same degree as their government colleagues, nonprofit administrators must also work within a structured set of practices and roles as they raise revenues for their organizations (Gelles 2001; Jeavons 2001; cf. The Giving Institute; cf. Association of Fundraising Professionals).[1] Transparency, integrity, and conformance with professional practices provide part of the trust and confidence necessary for a donor to voluntarily commit resources to an organization. An organization must effectively perform and fulfill the donor's wishes and intentions in order to encourage future support. Unsolicited reviews by state regulators and independent third-party evaluators provide public scrutiny on administrative costs and organization performance.

Many states require the registration of nonprofit organizations to prevent fraud and to increase the financial and performance information available to donors (Jackson 2007, 24). Nonprofits must be in full compliance with state incorporation and registration requirements, state tax reporting requirements, and federal tax and reporting requirements if they are to be fully successful in their fundraising activities. Independent professional fundraisers who contract with nonprofits may also need to register in some states.

COMMUNITY-LEVEL RESOURCES: FINANCING THE POLITY

Extensive contracting and grants making, widespread comprehensive public-private partnerships of extended duration, and the rise of quasi-public governmental foundations have blurred the once bright line between the governmental and nonprofit sectors. A polity network with discretely separate actors is now integrated contractually, financially, by policy, and by opportunistic arrangements. This blurring has forced a recasting of the public revenue framework. Increasingly, governmental, charitable, philanthropic, and bond and credit revenue sources define the resource base that sustains the community polity and its network of public service organizations. The polity revenue base is the most complete and integrated local public budgeting perspective.

Full understanding of the polity revenue base requires shifting from an organization-centered perspective to the broader community, metropolitan area, or rural substate region perspective. This is a shift to a broader social and economic scale. In an urban and suburban context, the polity revenue base might approximate the metropolitan area's land-use planning or urban growth boundary. In rural areas, the polity revenue base may be centered on the nearest city or town that acts as a social, commercial, or political center (cf. Kemmis 1995). The physical boundary of a rural polity might stretch from the city or town center across miles of sparsely inhabited ranch, farm, or forest lands. In both urban and rural contexts, a polity revenue base integrates revenues from the governmental, charitable and philanthropic, and commercial sectors to generate combined revenues to meet local and regional needs. This chapter's opening epigraph reinforces the flexible nature of public service revenues and delivery mechanisms.

A polity-level focus also shifts attention to the network of organizations within the region or community (see chapters 1 and 4). Typical networked organizations include county and other local governments, special district governments, state and federal government agencies, **quasi-governmental foundations**, community and major personal foundations, corporate foundations, federated intermediary nonprofits, nonprofit service providers, service groups and other citizen associations, and religious groups. The perception of a network as a holistic entity shifts the focus from the activities, needs, and survival of an individual nonprofit or organization to consideration of the population of resources, assets, and service providers available to the region (McKnight and Kretzmann 1996; Perrow 1986, 192–200). For major donors and governmental agencies, the issues of how to link community needs and clients with the most responsive, effective, and efficient service provider and funding source becomes the critical budgeting and procurement challenge.

Recognition of the presence and importance of the regional or community polity network forces local governments, federated nonprofits, and local foundations to pay attention to the revenue sources and usage across the network. A formal polity-level assessment of resources helps to identify where governmental revenues are available and where they are limited. Similarly, an assessment can demonstrate where charitable and philanthropic donations may exceed or fall short of community needs. Resource planning helps to prevent community overspending and underspending, and it allows complementary funding for programs and initiatives. A comprehensive, polity-level revenue assessment tracks the trends of resource flows from all sectors of the economy over the forecast period. A comprehensive assessment might follow the proportional contribution from different sources, the certainty and dependability of sources, any dedicated purpose restrictions on resource availability, and constraints on the future availability of resources. Past revenue trends form the basis for forecasts of future revenues. Based on past giving, an assessment develops an expected base level of small-scale charitable and large gift philanthropy in the community given certain economic conditions. Exceptionally large philanthropic gifts would be recognized as more sporadic in appearance. For instance, one polity-level revenue analysis for social services aligned government-sector revenue trends with revenue trends from the nonprofit and for-profit sectors. The analysis concluded that the governmental sector was failing to provide its share of resources relative to the other sectors (United Way of the Columbia-Willamette [UWCW] 2008).

Major intermediary nonprofits, local governments, or government agencies acting as network lead organizations may be in the best position to develop and maintain a polity-level revenue analysis. Networks administered by a formal, independent network administrative organization (NAO) would rely on that organization for a network-level assessment of member contributions. Alternatively, a nonprofit dedicated to community planning and analysis or analytic talent from local universities could be contracted to provide revenue and needs analyses. This latter approach might be more acceptable to members of participant-governed networks featuring decentralized structures with high-trust member relationships (Provan and Kenis 2007; Isett et al. 2011). At a minimum, local government analysts should look beyond their own organizational revenue picture and consider the availability and potential of other revenues in the polity. Elected officials and government administrators need to see government revenues and programs against the larger community resources (McKnight and Kretzmann 1996). Polity-level revenue assessments allow governments to identify and respond to the limits of their peer community foundations and federated intermediaries. Similarly, a polity assessment allows nonprofits to monitor governmental finances and public support for tax, fee, and intergovernmental revenues.

Especially difficult, complex, and resistant community problems often require the development of special community initiatives both to raise revenues and to target resources over a defined, extended period. For example, several metropolitan regions have developed 10-year initiatives to eliminate homelessness (cf. United Way of King County [UWKC] 2010, 2011; and United Way of the Columbia-Willamette [UWCW] 2008). Special initiatives serve to focus attention and channel sustained resources to the root causes of a social problem or community need. The special initiative label can focus charitable and philanthropic donors on the issue and provide opportunities for donors to **leverage** or combine donations to a critical level for effective programming (Frumkin 2010, 61). A local government or major foundation may make an initial **seed donation** to spark support for the initiative. Other donors may make their own donations based on the initial donor commitment. Careful planning to support an initiative encourages governments and nonprofits to develop integrated goals, objectives, and operating plans to address the problem. Success in planning helps to demonstrate the effectiveness of the combined multisector approach. This success in turn generates added donor confidence in the effort. Detailed assessments and concise demonstrations of program success encourage donors to fulfill their commitments and to provide additional resources when needed. Even with the best-developed community plans and initiatives, philanthropic donors have perceptions of community needs and how best to approach solutions. A donor's approach may not match the size or complexity of the issue, and there may be more technically and administratively effective approaches available.

Administrators raising funds at the community or polity level must consider the constraints and limitations faced by their peers in other sectors of the polity network. Effective fundraising in the polity context requires recognition of the regulatory and organizational constraints faced by each network member. Government organizations face a constrained context of detailed and specific regulations related to raising taxes, setting fees and charges, and accepting intergovernmental revenues. Government administrators may have limited discretion in how government funds may be applied to meet community needs. The philanthropic fundraising and development context is constrained differently. Nonprofit organizations and foundations engaged in fundraising must comply with state regulations and IRS requirements. Professional ethics and best practices serve to guide the behavior of fundraising and development professionals. Restrictions placed by the donor or granting foundation on philanthropic gifts may serve to limit their use and availability. The competitive context of the nonprofit sector defines the policies and behavior of these organizations. While most nonprofits have adopted a wide level of transparency in an attempt to build donor support, antitrust compliance requires a minimal level of independent decision making and often competitive behavior. This behavior may seem disconcerting to a government administrator accustomed to extreme openness and high levels of public scrutiny. Nonprofit organizations must carefully balance their behavior and policies between public openness and competitive behavior.

A comprehensive perspective on the polity and its revenue sources opens a series of important mission and financial policy issues of how best to integrate public and private resources. These are financial policy issues that governments and major nonprofit organizations typically address at the organizational level (see chapter 10); however, these policies often have implications for the organization's community or network partners. For example, should a local government provide a base level of funding across all youth, substance abuse, elderly, veterans, and housing programs, or should local government provide funds to supplement only private and nonprofit resources? The relative contribution of any major contributor to the polity provider network will condition the response and behavior of all other members of the network. The level of government funding can condition the response from the nonprofit sector, but a major reduction of resources from a major community foundation can affect the response by other nonprofits and government. If severe economic conditions force a major drop in philanthropic giving and a reduction in intermediary and foundation grants, should governments step up to fill part of the gap with tax revenues? Another policy issue asks how government should behave as a major community donor. Should government have the authority to take the lead in providing the initial "seed" grant donation against which private donors can leverage their funds? Understanding how state agencies and local government revenues and resources fit in context with other resources in the community is an important step in community or polity budgeting.

The economic downturn of 2007–2009 demonstrated the implication of these types of financial questions. The loss of revenues from foundation and philanthropic sources and from declining government contracts placed severe pressure on nonprofit service providers in many communities. Long-standing nonprofit organizations were forced to close facilities, stop service delivery, lay off staff, reorganize, and consolidate their remaining capacity to a smaller, more sustainable level. Nonprofit organizations serving as partners and subcontractors to larger nonprofit organizations were affected in turn. The closure or retrenchment of nonprofits across a community raised issues of how the community as a polity would deliver needed services. Forecasts of local government revenues and program support can raise the issue of whether the community needs to raise new revenues or to adjust program capacity. Major nonprofit intermediaries, community foundations, and major nonprofit service providers can contribute information to this discussion, but each may have to make independent decisions on costs and service levels to comply with federal antitrust laws.

TAX RELIEF FOR SOCIAL JUSTICE AND ECONOMIC GROWTH

The polity revenue base integrates government tax revenues with private wealth and income to support a service delivery network that serves a metropolitan area or rural region. Revenue-related decisions made in one sector of the network often have ramifications on other network actors. Local voters and their governments make the decisions to adopt or to increase a tax, but within the structure of state law and regulation, local governments can also make the decision to not collect and to forego tax revenue. Not collecting tax revenues limits the resources available to meet immediate program needs, but the reprieve from taxes may encourage citizen or business behavior with long-term benefits to the community and its polity. Decisions to forego tax revenues are polity-level choices sometimes decided by voters, but often made by elected officials and government administrators through regulatory actions.

The policy decision to forego and not collect authorized tax revenue is known as a **tax expenditure**. In not collecting tax revenue from a particular source or group, all other contributors to the tax base must step up to meet community needs. The uncollected tax burden is *shifted* to the remaining taxpayers, and the government in essence gives an appropriation of funds to the tax expenditure recipient. Tax expenditures carry a pejorative label due to their misuse and inappropriate adoption in legislatures; however, tax expenditures provide important tools to increase the fairness of the tax regulations and to accomplish desired community objectives. A major group of tax expenditures are designed and adopted to support the production of public goods and to support community goals and values. Nonprofit and governmental organizations are major beneficiaries of these tax expenditures. Local governments also use tax expenditures to attract businesses and to sustain a tax and wealth base. In this type of application, a county, city, or special district government may reduce, defer, or forgive annual property taxes for a specified period for new businesses or for major expansions of existing businesses.

Exactly how far and to what degree a local government should go to build a diversified and sustainable tax base is a policy question for the polity that reflects community values and economic vision. A community must have a strong economy to generate the resources for good works. Intentional policy and program choices by state and local governments can help to encourage development of a diverse revenue base with sustainable yield.

Perhaps most important, state and local governments must have a clear understanding of the revenue foregone to support each tax expenditure. A clear presentation of this information explains the intent and public value behind each exemption and gives transparency to the reasons and risks behind it.

Tax Expenditures to Promote Community Goals and Social Justice

Tax expenditures to support nonprofit organizations and government can cost state and local governments millions of dollars annually in lost tax revenue. The state tax code and its expenditures provide most of these tax breaks. Local government policy supplements the larger state code. Tax expenditures in the form of exemptions can take three levels: full exemption, partial exemption, and special assessment. Exemptions may be permanent or may last for a specified period. Administrators must carefully consult their state tax code to understand where and how exemptions apply.

Nonprofit organizations benefit from tax expenditures in numerous and far-reaching ways. The largest and most evident are exemptions from local property tax for religious and nonprofit facilities, along with exemptions from retail sales and use taxes. Taxes on property owned by charitable and religious organizations for day care facilities, schools and academies, student housing, senior centers, museums, and private parklands are all typically exempt. Property leased by charitable and religious organizations may also be exempted, as may retail stores operated by charitable organizations (see epigraph at the beginning of this chapter).

Tax exemptions for government-owned lands and facilities also support public benefits and community social justice. Housing authority rental units receive a full property tax exemption, low-income housing may receive a partial exemption, and newly constructed low-income housing may receive an extended exemption. State and federal facilities, including public community colleges and universities, dormitories, and parking garages, are usually all exempted from local property tax. The land under public streets, roads, and highways, called rights of way, is likewise exempt from property taxation. Federal agency property and Native American property on reservations are also typically exempted from local property taxes. When all of these exemptions are aggregated, one begins to appreciate the growing constraints on local revenue generation and the need to take a polity-centered focus to revenue development. In many instances, nonprofit organizations and government agencies will make a voluntary annual contribution to local governments to compensate for a portion of the lost property tax revenue.

To compensate local governments for lost revenues due to federal land ownership within county boundaries, the federal government established tax reimbursement programs as early as 1908. The most widespread federal compensation program is the payment in lieu of taxes (PILT) program, which pays local counties on a per capita and acreage basis. Other federal programs provided substantial revenue sharing to county governments based on a *percentage* share of federal timber, recreation, mineral, and other resource sales receipts. Under the Secure Rural Schools and Community Self-Determination Act of 2008, counties with substantial acreages of U.S. National Forest (USFS) and U.S. Bureau of Land Management (BLM) natural resource lands could elect to receive transitional federal payments based on historic payment levels.[2] Due to its transitional nature, the Secure Rural Schools Act expired in 2012 with a substantial reduction in federal revenues to these rural counties. A drastic reduction in county road maintenance, K–12 education, and general fund public safety, health, and library services has followed the loss of federal revenues (Gaid 2009; see epigraph). Recent federal legislation in 2013 restored payments to rural schools and counties for an additional year (U.S. Forest Service 2014).

Senior and low-income homeowner deferrals on property taxes represent another widely offered tax expenditure (NCSL 2002). These expenditures are typically adopted into state law but are largely implemented and have their effect at the local government level. Under these programs, a qualifying senior or low-income resident typically receives an exemption for a portion of the home's value, or a deferral of all or a portion of the annual property tax bill until he or she dies or sells the property. For each year of exemption or deferral, the state government pays the taxes that are due and places a lien on the property for the value of the tax. Local governments do not incur a loss of revenue, but the state government must forego the opportunity cost of the reimbursement funds and take the risk that the future property value at sale will cover the value of deferred taxes.

Tax expenditures and their related tax exemptions provide key incentives for citizens and businesses to support and participate in nonprofit programs. Many exemptions give behind-the-scenes support that clients never see. On the other hand, as Exhibit 8.2 details, tax exemptions may provide a critical tool to build personal dignity and economic justice in the community.

Tax Expenditures to Promote the Community Economy and Wealth

Targeted tax exemptions are a widely used tool for local and regional economic development. Economic development activities are focused to attract new businesses and to retain and grow businesses already in the community. Local governments and economic special districts develop incentive packages with several forms of tax relief, permit fee reductions, and favorable zoning

---

Exhibit 8.2

Partial Tax Exemption for Affordable Housing

A partial tax exemption for residential property owners is one tool that the Portland Housing Bureau (PHB) of Portland, Oregon, is using to restore blighted areas of the city and to bring social justice to home ownership. The 10-Year Limited Tax Exemption program encourages contractors to build new homes in all neighborhoods of the city. The PHB continues taxation of the land at the normal adjusted assessed value, but grants the new homeowners a 10-year exemption on the value of the dwelling. The program is aimed at encouraging home ownership for low- and middle-income buyers. To qualify, the builder must apply for the program before beginning construction. Also, the home must be priced for $291,000 or less and the buyer must have an income of $69,400 or less for a family of four. The purchaser must remain in the house for the full 10-year period. After that, full taxes resume on the house. Minority group purchasers make up more than half the buyers of these new houses. Active participation by minorities meets city goals of building diversity in homeownership. The program also helps to renew the city's housing stock by replacing distressed, deteriorating, and unsafe housing with new construction (Behrs 2011). Statewide for the 2013–2015 biennium, the tax expenditure for the program was $8.5 million. About 2,100 houses in the city of Portland and in surrounding Multnomah County, Oregon, are involved in the program (State of Oregon 2012, 296–297; City of Portland, Oregon 2014).

---

and permitting policies. Targeted tax exemptions allow a community or region to effectively compete for new businesses at the state, national, and international levels. Successful economic development generates economic activity that in turn stabilizes and grows the business property, residential property, retail sales, and income tax bases. An increased philanthropic donor base also results. However, in the short term, tax exemptions reduce the flow of tax revenues that may be needed to attend to community problems and needs. Excessive tax expenditures may reduce the flow of revenues needed for other business support activities, including roads and transportation, utilities, planning and permitting, and the schools, colleges and universities needed for workforce development. The decision to grant an economic development and incentive package must balance the tax benefits granted to the recipient business with the loss of revenues and the shift of burden to other taxpayers. The decisions to grant tax expenditures as part of an economic development package are polity-level governance decisions. A polity must decide how it values and supports business and economic growth relative to its other needs and service demands.

Incentive packages with tax expenditures represent a risk for both government and business. For government, an incentive package is a calculated trade-off: business property tax and corporate tax revenues foregone today with the expectation of enhanced personal wealth, enhanced taxes and fee revenues, and economic activity in the future. Local governments have no ownership and only indirect control of businesses in the community, and government actions and investments may or may not generate the desired response of business activity and success. Similarly, for business, committing to settle and to build a facility in a community opens a risk that the jurisdiction will successfully provide the promised tax treatment, transportation and utility infrastructure, labor and worker availability, worker education and quality, community amenities and facilities, and sense of quality of life. The business decision to settle in a community assumes that the package of incentive and support features remains competitive and more favorable than in other states or regions. (*The Oregonian* Editorial Board 2010a).

Local governments—especially counties, cities, towns, port districts or authorities, and redevelopment districts—can play a key role in setting an environment to sustain and attract businesses.

Many local governments establish an economic development staff group or department to develop policies and programs to support business. Business decisions to locate in a community often reflect a complex blend of factors (Center for Economic Development 2012), and a community's attitudes toward business are of primary importance. Community attitudes include regulatory environment, fiscal climate of taxes and fees, and a perception of community support of business. Other factors include distance to customers, cost of property, and financial incentives.

The decisions to establish and offer tax expenditures for economic development reflect a combination of state and local government policies. Any local option to grant tax exemptions must be authorized in the larger state tax code. Incentive packages and offers to attract businesses reflect a combination of state and local law and policy, and state and local decisions to offer a particular set of incentives (NCSL 2002, 25–29). Incentive packages may be targeted to small businesses with just a few employees or to large multinational corporations. Incentive packages granted to large corporations may be worth hundreds of millions of dollars over the life of a manufacturing or research facility. In this latter situation, a major portion of the economy of a region and its business and personal wealth may rest on the presence and viability of one or two corporations. In these instances, state support for the economic development is critical.

Tax expenditures granted to business take a variety of forms. These include exemptions and reductions in property taxes; relief from taxes on business inventory and finished goods; and relief from sales, use, and other taxes over a specified period. Property tax relief may be offered as a complete exemption from assessment, a deduction of value on an assessment, or as an abatement or reduction in the tax rate (NCSL 2002, 27; Center for Economic Development 2012). Property tax relief can apply to land, buildings, manufacturing equipment, and business personal goods and furnishings. Tax relief can also apply to inventories and finished goods awaiting shipment (NCSL 2002, 25; Center for Economic Development 2012). Other tax expenditures offered to businesses include relief from retail sales and use taxes, favorable equipment depreciation schedules on income taxes, and credits for worker retraining, worker training, and job creation. Tax relief typically expires after a specified period and rates return to full tax burden. At the point of expiration, both government and the business must review the incentive package for renewal, modification, or discontinuance. The blend of tax types and rates in a package can encourage or discourage particular sizes and types of businesses. Reduced property taxes and favorable depreciation schedules are especially effective for businesses with large capital investments in facilities and equipment. Reduced personal income taxes and moderate capital gains taxes are especially helpful for entrepreneurs and small businesses.

If state law allows, state and local governments may establish **enterprise zones** to focus and stimulate economic development in a depressed area. The specific requirements for an enterprise zone vary, but they often include extremely high and sustained unemployment and a major loss of business activity. Businesses coming into an enterprise zone typically receive some form of tax relief for an extended period. In return, a new business must employ a specified number of workers at a certain pay level, make a facility investment, and establish a permanent presence. In lieu of tax payments, the business may make specified compensatory payment for services provided by the local government. As in any contract, the agreement must be implemented, supported, and monitored by both parties. Effective monitoring causes both the community and the business to perform up to standards. Where companies fail to meet standards, local governments may actuate claw-back provisions to recover damages (Babwin 2010). The period leading up to the expiration of an exemption agreement allows the community and local governments to review the provisions and its success. Reevaluation allows the community to reconsider if the balance between lost tax revenues and immediate program needs on the one hand, and an enhanced economy and tax base on the other, supports community goals and values.

Tax increment financing (TIF) provides another commonly used tool for local governments to remove *blight* and to accomplish urban redevelopment. Forty-eight states allow some form of tax increment financing.[3] This public funding tool typically requires a city or county to establish a renewal tax district, which usually has a finite lifespan during which redevelopment occurs. The property tax base in the district is then frozen at a beginning point in time. Any increase in property tax value after the starting point generates tax revenues that are redirected to a district improvement fund rather than to the city, county, school, or other revenue recipients. The directed funds may be spent directly on improvements but more typically are used as a revenue stream to make payments for bonds. Because all the other taxing districts that overlap the renewal district are affected by the redirection of the increased revenues, all districts must support the renewal district establishment. Gaining political support for the redirection of revenues is often the major challenge to acceptance of a TIF district. The renewal district expires when all projects are completed and all expenses and bonds are fully paid off. Upon expiration of the district, the flow of tax revenues returns to the permanent underlying county, city, or special district taxing districts.

The key assumption with TIF is that the property values in the renewal district will increase sufficiently over time to pay off any improvement expenses or bond principal and interest. Renewal districts are typically designed to hold debt (bonds or loans), which allows projects to be funded up front and the debt service to be spread out over future years. Key renewal investments may change the site sufficiently and successfully attract additional investment. Property tax values may increase new tax revenues in sufficient quantity to cover all bond payments. This is often, but not always, the case. Tax increment financing arrangements are not without risk. If the property values in the renewal district do not rise, or if the flow of anticipated revenues fails to meet expectations, revenues may not be available to make investments or to make timely debt payments. Local governments rely on several mechanisms to help ensure timely debt payments. These include state agency review and financial backing (e.g., Pennsylvania TIF Guarantee Program; State of Pennsylvania Department of Community & Economic Development 2013), establishment of cash reserve funds, and obtaining tax revenue interruption insurance. Financial ratings agencies also routinely review the financial health of the renewal district and its revenue stream. Where the revenue stream fails, the district defaults and the parent local government may become liable for debt payments, since the debt was originally secured with the full faith and credit of the parent local government.

Several authors point out a number of shortcomings with TIF. Kerth and Baxandall (2011) note that the TIF process often lacks transparency and accountability. Government administrators may hold wide discretion in how redirected tax revenues are used, and uses may be largely unrelated to redevelopment efforts (O'Toole 2011). O'Toole (2011) further argues that favoritism may occur in the selection of contractors and redevelopment projects. Dye and Merriman (2006) question the assumed increase in property values and counsel caution and care in using tax increment financing. TIF is an important tool for improving community infrastructures and for attracting new businesses. However, local governments must rely on conservative financial assumptions, place strong controls on redevelopment projects, and ensure transparency of the TIF process and performance. The decision to adopt a renewal district and a TIF program may require a citizen ballot initiative and adoption. Effective political and administrative leadership are an absolute requirement in order to establish a successful TIF renewal district.

Summary

Targeted tax exemptions provide polities with important tools for revenue base development, for supporting the nonprofit sector, and for enhancing justice in the community. Certainty and stability in exemptions are critical to support investment decisions by businesses and nonprofits. An exemption must be in place for a period sufficient to allow its financial payoff to occur. The expiration of an exemption, enterprise zone, or economic renewal district provides an important period for a community to reconsider the trade-off of meeting immediate needs or of making long-term investments that could build the community into the future.

ADMINISTRATIVE LEADERSHIP TO BUILD PUBLIC REVENUES

Developing revenues for local governments has always been a responsibility of government administrators and elected officials. The blurring of lines between the economic sectors of the community reinforces the notion that the polity revenue base supports an interdependent network of government, nonprofits, and for-profit organizations. Both government and nonprofit administrators must proactively work to build a diverse, robust revenue base to support the service delivery network. Public administrators can step into this challenge, use their professional discretion, and make a tremendous difference for their organization, their community, and their polity. Administrators bring important technical expertise, communication skills, and the political understanding necessary to build community support for revenue enhancement initiatives.

STUDY QUESTIONS

1. Select a nonprofit organization with which you are familiar. Does the organization have a strategic plan? An operational business plan? How does the plan assess current and potential revenue sources, describe and structure a fundraising and donor development program, and set policy for the selection and rejection of grants and offers of revenue? How does the organization balance governmental revenues, revenue from small-scale charitable giving, revenue from large philanthropic grants, and fees for services and enterprise revenues?

2. For a familiar functional service area or issue, map out the revenue sources supporting the community or regional polity. Include any state government sources, local government tax and fee sources, regional intermediary federated nonprofits, state-level foundations, community foundations, corporate foundations, major family and charitable trusts, service delivery nonprofits, and commercial service providers.

3. Consider your own personal charitable giving. What factors cause you to give to a cause or organization? Do other donors have the same or different motivations and concerns? Do you consider a nonprofit's ratio of administrative expenses to total donations an important factor that conditions giving?

4. Imagine that you received a major inheritance of $2 million. How would you structure a program of philanthropic giving? Consider your own emotional satisfaction, how you might complement government spending or lack thereof, how to develop a strategic focus of giving over time, how to leverage your gifts with other providers, and the selection of a legal structure such as a trust, community foundation, or donor-advised fund.

5. For one branch of social service programs (e.g., low-income health care, youth, elderly, homeless, child care, etc.) map the polity network of governmental and nonprofit organizations. Does any nonprofit, foundation, intermediary group, or local university research group in your network take responsibility for development of a comprehensive polity-level assessment and forecast of revenues and grants? If you were in charge of such a research group, how would you structure an analysis and forecast of revenues?

6. Position yourself as the finance director for a medium to large nonprofit serving youth and the elderly. The organization operates extensive child care, after-school care, child summer camps, and senior center operations. What analysis process and policies do

you use to set fees for service rates? Are your donors and board supportive of your fee structure?

7. Consider your community. List at least five tax exemptions provided to governments and nonprofits in your community. For each exemption, to whom is the tax burden shifted?

8. Review the commercial and industrial base in your polity. What economic development programs have the state, local governments, and business groups established? Has government granted any property tax exemptions or abatements to attract or retain business? Describe the risks to governments and to businesses of a tax relief program for business development.

9. Does your state allow the establishment of enterprise zone or tax increment financing districts? Describe the major risks inherent with each of these programs. How would you explain the complexities and risks of tax increment financing to voters considering a ballot initiative?

NOTES

1. Websites for these organizations are as follows: The Giving Institute (www.givingusa.org/) and Association of Fundraising Professionals (AFP; www.afpnet.org/) (both accessed on March 16, 2014).

2. Citations for these three federal statutes are as follows:

- 25 Percent Fund Act of 1908, P.L. 60–136, 25 Stat. 260, shares 25 percent of federal national forest timber sale revenues with local counties for county schools and local road maintenance.
- Payment in Lieu of Taxes Act of 1976 (PILT), 31 U.S.C. 1601–1607, substituted by the Money and Finance Act of 1982 chapter 69, P.L. 97–258, Stat. 1031, 31 U.S.C. 6901–6904. PILT provides federal compensatory payments based on federal land area and population to counties, boroughs, and parishes; cities and districts certified as independently providing local government services; the District of Columbia; Puerto Rico; and other U.S. territories. PILT funds may be used for any governmental purpose.
- Secure Rural Schools and Community Self-Determination Act of 2000 (SRS), P.L. 106–393, provided counties with declining 25 Percent Funds and Bureau of Land Management O&C County payments with transition funds. The SRS act was reauthorized for four additional years 2008–2011 in P.L. 110–343.

These federal payments have been extremely important during the economic downturn for western state rural counties with double-digit unemployment. Consult the National Association of Counties, "Legislation and Policy," at www.naco.org/legislation, or the U.S. Forest Service. "Secure Rural School and Community Self-Determination Act of 2000," at https://fsplaces.fs.fed.us/fsfiles/unit/r4/payments_to_states.nsf for additional information on these programs. On the 2013 reauthorization, see the U.S. Forest Service April 4, 2014 press release at www.fs.fed.us/news/2014/releases/04/rural-schools-payments.shtml (accessed on May 10, 2014).

3. For additional information on tax increment financing (TIF) districts, see the Council of Development Finance Agencies (CDFA) and the International Council of Shopping Centers (ICSC), *Tax Increment Finance Best Practices Reference Guide* (Columbus, OH: CDFA, November 2007).

9 | BUDGET FUNDS ORGANIZE THE PUBLIC BUDGET

We've got to hand it to [the mayor] when it comes to invention. His proposed diversion of $20 million in the city sewer's budget to start building bicycle boulevards around town offers a fresh look at public finance. . . . More than $15 million of that money was "saved" by the city's Bureau of Environmental Services from capital projects turning out not to cost as much as projected. . . . Bureau of Environmental Services aimed that money at other needy projects. Stuck holding the bag in this transaction are those who pay handsomely to flush toilets, run showers—and withstand blinding rate increases.

(*The Oregonian* Editorial Board 2010b)

Public revenues come from a multitude of sources: water and sewer user fees, property taxes, retail sales and use taxes, fines and penalties, charges for services, and intergovernmental revenues. In providing these revenues, taxpayers and fee payers trust in the integrity of government to use revenues for the advertised, intended purposes. Breaking this commitment causes taxpayers and ratepayers to rethink their support for government and its requests for needed resources. The failure of the Cascadia County public safety services levy in Part II's case study demonstrated the challenge of building taxpayer confidence that tax revenue will be used wisely and for its intended purpose. If county officials were to abruptly and seemingly arbitrarily divert public safety revenues to fund construction of a new county building, taxpayers would quickly balk at any future levy renewal. Transparency in how government revenues are collected, organized, and spent is essential to maintaining public confidence in the tax and revenue systems. The mechanisms and procedures of accounting provide a critical tool for ensuring this transparency. This chapter offers a very brief and selective overview of the public-sector accounting techniques that support public-sector revenues and spending.

Accounting procedures, practices, and standards are professional controls that provide uniform financial analysis and reporting conventions for all governments and nonprofits. The **Governmental Accounting Standards Board (GASB)** sets the standards for state and local governments, the Federal Accounting Standards Advisory Board (FASAB) provides guidance for the federal government and its agencies, and the Financial Accounting Standards Board (FASB) provides standards for accounting for nonprofit organizations.

Accounting standards are a powerful set of procedural controls that limit and guide the behavior and practices of financial and administrative professionals. Auditors annually verify organizational compliance with standards. To meet audit level performance standards, administrators and staff must collect sufficient and prescribed information on budgets and financial transactions; follow established standards, practices, and analysis; demonstrate sound judgment; and make the required reports for audit compliance. This text summarizes the contribution of financial reporting and audits to local budgeting in chapter 18. Additionally, the national Government Finance Officers Association (GFOA) has established criteria under its voluntary Distinguished Budget Presentation Awards program detailing the content and analyses expected of an effective local government budget. Many state governments supplement the national professional standards with regulatory standards for local government budget presentation. These state standards have the strength of adding consistency in budget formatting, analysis, and reporting across all local governments within a state. This makes legislative and public oversight easier. However, the highly prescriptive nature of regulations can stifle new, more effective approaches to budgeting and performance management. All these standards and regulations limit and guide administrators, clerks, business officers, staff analysts, and elected officials in budget preparation and execution. But no matter how tightly a standard or regulation is prescribed, there is an opportunity for professional interpretation and discretion. Such judgments—and their ethical applications—contribute important elements of compliance with accounting procedures and standards.

As described in chapter 6, taxes, fees and charges, fines and penalties, sales of property, and intergovernmental sources all generate governmental revenues. Accounting techniques provide a means to organize these financial resources and to monitor their flow and use through financial systems. Accounting techniques provide transparency to all levels of the organization. For example, accounting practices and standards are designed to respond to the situation described in this chapter's opening epigraph—sewer-related revenues collected for one purpose are segregated from other spending—and accounting structures signal when such segregation is broken.

We begin our accounting overview by focusing on governmental accounting. First, the chapter defines and explains accounting funds, their function, nomenclature, and account definitions. This discussion includes distinctions between general funds and special purpose funds. Second, the chapter discusses the different accounting methods that are used and examines their impact on presenting government financial information to the public. Third, we contrast governmental accounting practices and standards with nonprofit standards. This very brief and limited overview will help students understand the differences in the structure and function of governmental and nonprofit budget documents. The overview will also help students understand the rationale and formatting used in the different budget expenditure formats in Part III of this book. For more advanced treatments, we encourage students to consult texts specific to governmental and nonprofit accounting and budgeting (cf. Granof and Khumawala 2011; Finkler 2010; Copley 2008; Gross, McCarthy, and Shelmon 2005; Farris 2009; or Dropkin, Halpin, and La Touche 2007).

ACCOUNTING FUNDS: RESERVOIRS AND FLOWS

A **fund** is a budgeting and accounting concept and analysis structure that segregates a set of financial transactions for a defined purpose or program. A fund may support a single program, activity, or organizational department, or it may cover several of each as in the case of a local government's **general fund (GF)**. **Revenues** from taxes, charges, and other sources are deposited into the fund and tracked by accounting transactions. Once revenues have been entered into the fund, they become **resources** available to fund programs. At the beginning of a new fiscal year or biennium, there may be some resources already in the fund. These resources are known as the **opening fund balance**. **Expenditures** or **expenses** flow out of the fund by transactions to make payments for goods and services. At the end of the fiscal year, any remaining unspent or *unobligated* resources are denoted as an **ending fund balance**. Equation 9.1 must **balance** at the beginning and at the close of the fiscal year. At any given moment in the fiscal year, the equation will likely not balance because of the varying ebb and flow of revenues and expenses:

$$\text{Opening Balance} + \text{Revenues} = \text{Expenditures} + \text{Ending Balance} \qquad (9.1)$$

On an illustrative level, an **accounting fund** is like a picnic drink jug. Water or juice is poured in the large opening at the top, and drinks are dispensed out the spout to each person's cup at the picnic. This is akin to tax, fee, and intergovernmental revenues pouring into the fund, with a controlled flow of resources out of the fund to pay for specific expenditures tied to a particular program. There may be leftover juice in the jug before the picnic begins. This corresponds to the opening balance in the fund. Adding new juice (revenues) to the old makes more total juice (resources) available. By the end of the picnic, the jug may be empty, or it may be left with a little juice in the jug that would be available for the next day. Alternatively, it may have been a cool, cloudy day—one in which folks did not drink much. In this situation, there may be quite a bit of leftover juice in the jug—very much worth saving and using the next day.

Accounting funds are similar. A program may spend all its funds for a fiscal year and empty the fund. In other instances, the programs do not completely spend all resources, or a program may purposely reserve some resources for a specific purpose. This leaves a positive ending fund balance in the fund, a portion of which may be available in the next fiscal year as an opening balance. The intentional reserve left in a fund may be substantial, but portions of the fund reserves may be reserved, **restricted**, or **encumbered** for specific purposes such as pending debt service, capital project payments, or an operating reserve per state requirements. The unrestricted portion of the reserve would be available as resources for the coming fiscal year or biennium. It is important to note that the level of the unrestricted general fund balance is one measure of the financial health of a local government or organization. A sufficient unrestricted general fund balance should be large enough to cover expenses between major revenue deposits (e.g., annual or biannual property tax collections), and to cover unexpected expenses and revenue shortfalls (Brown 2012). We discuss the issue of fund cash flows and balances in greater detail in chapter 17.

Because funds must balance at the end of the fiscal year, they establish control over the resources expended by a program or set of programs. Most government budgets are designed to control at the fund or departmental level. Spending restrictions limit the rate and total amount of spending by administrators. Any spending above the defined level requires the permission of the executive (CEO) or legislative body. Accounting controls can be focused downward to the level of individual programs and activities. This refined level of accounting can help improve productivity and cost analysis.

Funds Link Budgeting and Accounting

Budget funds catalog the expected revenues and the resources available over the fiscal year and match them with an anticipated allocation of resources to particular programs and activities for spending. Budget funds must show a balance of revenues and expenditures at the time a budget is adopted in order to comply with laws requiring balanced budgets and to prevent deficit spending. Correspondingly, **accounting funds** track the actual accumulation of revenue and expenditure transactions over the fiscal year. Tax, fee, and other revenues are deposited, and payments for services and goods are expended by individual transactions. The accumulation of these expenditure and resources transactions over the fiscal year produce the *accounting fund balance*, which often varies from the budget fund totals approved at the beginning of the budget year.

An important class of financial transactions allows a program or activity to purchase services from other programs and branches within the same organization. These **internal charges for services** result in the **transfer** of funds from the purchasing program to the unit providing the service. Usually these transfers are based on the *cost of service principle*, which simply means that the customer is only charged the cost of providing the service. **Interfund transfers** are commonly used for the internal purchase of central administrative services such as human resources, legal counsel, financial services, motor pool, and telecommunications and information technology. Like an economic public good, once a service is provided for one program, the remaining unused capacity can benefit all the other programs in the organization. These interfund purchases and transfers add to the fund expenditure levels, but they are not assessed against a fund's cash revenues.

Once a government budget is formally adopted by ordinance, budget funds remain as the resource allocation and spending definitions, but the accounting funds become the actual structures for tracking the individual and accumulated revenue and expenditure transactions.

Governmental accounting follows a set of conventions and practices that distinguish it from nonprofit and private-sector accounting. One of these differences is that governmental accounting establishes multiple funds to segregate revenues sources and spending purposes. This allows governments to demonstrate transparency in finances and to encourage citizen confidence in government operations. A small local city government, town, or township might have 10 or more funds to segregate and organize revenues and spending for different programs. A large county or city may have over 100 such funds. A government budget document may include a **chart of accounts** table that will list all funds by code number and use. A single fund, or multiple funds, may resource a program or department within a local government. The use of multiple funds contrasts with nonprofit- and for-profit-sector accounting, which tends to consolidate programs and activities into fewer funds.

States vary in their degree of prescription regarding the number and use of coding systems for budget funds and transactions. New York (cf. Chen, Forsythe, Weikart, and Williams 2009, 153–156) and Washington State have well-developed systems for local government budgeting, accounting, and reporting. The codes detailed in these systems define the expenditure and revenue items used in **line-item** and **object code budgeting**. The Washington State BARS system includes procedures and a uniform chart of accounts that apply to all local governments in the state. Administrators, elected officials, and citizens can rely on this uniform system to quickly understand a new situation in budget construction, review, or adoption. The Washington State system (Washington State BARS Manual 2013, Part 1, chaps. 1, 3–4) codes all financial transactions using a 16-digit code. This code breaks into a nine-digit organization number prefix and a seven-digit account number suffix as demonstrated in Exhibit 9.1.

The first field of three characters indicates the fund coding. This is a combination of state definition of the first digit code, along with two local fund numbers. The first digit codes indicate the purpose of the fund. These fund purposes and their codes are listed out and explained in the next section. The second and third fields are left to local discretion but provide room for indicating performance budgeting or other program objectives (field 2, e.g., 001) and for organizational departmental or program identification codes (field 3, e.g., 242). The fourth field of the 16 digits is the *prime* that determines if a fund is a budget fund, an accounting revenue fund, or an accounting expenditure fund. This fourth field links budget funds and budgeting directly to accounting funds for recording revenues and spending transactions. Field five defines the basic revenue source or type of purchase. Fields six and seven then prescribe the exact source and type of revenue, or the exact type and purpose for the expenditure. Codes for fields five, six, and seven are flexible enough to exactly describe the source of tax or fee revenue, the activity and circumstances that generated it, or the type of federal grant or payment as defined by the Catalog of Federal Domestic Assistance (CFDA). Similarly, the expenditure category codes are well developed and able to describe any local government activity and its details.

The Washington State BARS system reinforces the importance of state regulations as a refinement to national accounting standards and practices. Administrators must learn and follow the systems and practices used in their state in order to meet audit requirements and to build public confidence in the jurisdiction's budget and financial products.

Budget Fund Designations

The establishment, definition, and linkages between funds create the internal skeleton of a government's budget and accounting system. Budget funds serve a variety of purposes. The most

Exhibit 9.1

Example State Budget and Recording System (BARS) Coding

Washington State Budget and Reporting System (BARS)
Fund and Transaction Coding Format

P = code set by BARS manual (state)
L = code set by local government

BARS codes use 16 digits broken into seven fields
with a 9-digit prefix and a 7-digit suffix.

PREFIX (9)			SUFFIX (7)			
1	**2**	**3**	**4**	**5**	**6**	**7**
PLL	LLL	LLL	P	PP	PP	PP
Fund field	Local objective	Local dept.	Prime	BASUB	Element	Object

Example: Local County Corrections Department

103	001	242	3 2 5	31	99	99

31 → Basic spending category code / Or basic revenue source code

3 2 5 →
2 budget prime
3 revenue prime
5 expenditure prime

Source: Adapted and applied from the Washington State BARS Manual 2013, Section 1.1.2.

widely used and frequently the largest fund, as the name suggests, is a government's general fund, which receives all revenues not assigned to other funds established by the jurisdiction. These revenues commonly include general property taxes; retail sales and use tax revenues; any income or wage taxes; unrestricted fees, fines, and penalties; and unrestricted intergovernmental grants. The jurisdiction may expend general funds for any purpose authorized by law. Resources in a general fund are also known as **discretionary funds** because of the broad flexibility allowed in their use. In some states and jurisdictions, the general fund or its counterpart is known as the **current expense fund**. A local government general fund is similar to a nonprofit's operating fund or **current unrestricted fund** (Finkler 2010, 469). The general fund is typically the largest fund used by a local government, and it supports a variety of programs, especially those with governmental functions such as the elected council, commission or board, elections, and public safety. These governmental services bring in relatively little in departmental revenues. General funds are most often used to cover program operating expenses and maintenance (O&M), but may be used to cover capital expenses.

In contrast to the discretionary nature of a general fund, other budget funds that support government programs are more limited in the revenues they may receive, or the expenses they may pay. Funds may receive dedicated revenues from one or several specific sources—these are called **dedicated revenue funds**. As the epigraph at the beginning of this chapter demonstrates, dedicated revenues may be used only to cover specific programs or expenditures; the establishment of a separate fund serves to keep these funds out of the general fund and away from other dedicated revenues. Programs or departments may generate revenues through fees and charges for services, penalties and fines, and grants from outside sources. These revenues are credited to the earning program or department as **departmental revenues**. Some departmental revenues may be dedicated to a particular program and set of expenses. For example, a program may receive a grant, in which case grant revenues would be dedicated to the particular funded service.

Budget funds are typically designated and numbered by category according to purpose and revenue source (e.g., Washington State BARS Manual 2013). Funds supporting governmental activities (**governmental funds**) include:

- *General Funds, Current Expense (Codes 000–099, typically 001):* discretionary funds, which may support any authorized purpose. Receives general property tax, sales tax, income tax, fee, and shared intergovernmental revenues.
- *Special Revenue Funds (100–199):* legally restricted revenue sources or dedicated revenues. For example: property taxes from a specific levy for specified services, motor fuels tax revenue dedicated to road construction and reconstruction, or systems development fees dedicated to infrastructure planning, development, and construction.
- *Debt Service Funds (200–299):* revenues collected to repay debt instruments such as bonds and loans as part of program operation. For example, rental revenues to pay off low-income housing construction loans.
- *Capital Project Funds (300–399):* revenues collected to repay debt instruments tied to capital projects. These monies are restricted to facility construction and acquisition.
- *Permanent Funds (700–799):* a fund with a balance sufficient to generate interest income, which may be used for a defined purpose. The principle amount in the fund remains at a prescribed level permanently.

A second group of funds supports government business operations. These funds are commonly called **proprietary funds**:

- *Enterprise Funds (400s):* revenues and expenses of self-supporting business operations including public utilities: sewer, water, electricity, or steam.

- *Internal Services Funds (500s):* the internal purchase of services by one program or department of a government from another program or department. For example, internal purchases of central services (i.e., human resources, legal advice, accounting, purchasing, etc.), information technology, motor pool and vehicle services, equipment use and rental; and financial funds: workers' compensation, unemployment compensation, self-insurance services. Internal service funds record the cashless transfer of value between departments and program within a government. The dollar value of these interdepartmental purchases may be substantial, and when added to cash-based expenditures, total organizational spending often seems to exceed total revenues.

A third group of funds is established on behalf of specific groups or individuals. These are known as trust and agency funds. **Trust and agency funds** (600s) are investment trust funds, pension and employee benefit trust funds, private purpose trust funds, and agency funds. Interagency contributions for task groups, interagency coalitions, task forces, and claims clearing funds are also in this category. For school districts and local schools, student activity and club accounts are kept separately and numbered as trust and agency funds.

Under this system, fund codes include three digits. The first digit of the three indicates the type and purpose of the fund per the above categories; the second and third digits reflect local numbering of the fund. For example, a special revenue budget fund would display the forecasted budgeted level of revenue raised from a supplemental public safety levy. The fund code would be between 100 and 199, but the county may have several dedicated revenue budget funds, so the supplemental public safety fund might be designated 103 for the county's third special revenue fund. The corresponding accounting funds (again code 103, but with different prime indicators as an accounting fund) would catalog the actual transactions to receive all property tax revenues collected for the fund, and all expenditures made to pay for public safety activities.

Fund Type Reflects Source of Resources

Local government programs and organizational departments may be supported by the general fund or by a combination of general fund and other dedicated funds. Programs and departments that are fully or heavily supported by a jurisdiction's general fund are known as general fund programs. Partially supported programs or departments blend general funds and dedicated departmental revenues. For example, a county health department might use general funds to cover the coroner and public health epidemiology functions, but rely on fees from restaurant and sanitary inspections to generate dedicated departmental revenues to cover that portion of its program. Programs and departments that receive little or no general fund resources must rely on their own departmental revenues, dedicated tax and fee revenues, or specified intergovernmental revenues. These programs are known as **self-supported** programs because of their lack of reliance on the general fund.

Exhibit 9.2 demonstrates how five hypothetical county government departments rely to varying degrees on the county general fund. The chart also shows the variety of revenue sources that fund county government programs. The Assessment and Taxation (A&T) Department and the Public Health Department are partially reliant on the county general fund. In this county, the general fund is numbered 001. In partially reliant and **general fund departments**, internally generated departmental revenues—whether large or small—combine with a supplement from the county general fund to set the level of department expenditures. For example, the A&T department generates 74 percent of its income from departmental revenues and receives a general fund supplement for 26 percent of its total spending. Similarly, Public Health receives 82 percent of its funding from license and permit revenues, intergovernmental revenues, and charges for service, but then receives a general fund supplement to cover 18 percent of its expenses. The size of the general fund supplement determines the total resources available to the department, and the total available resources in turn set the total departmental expenditures for the fiscal year (100 percent expenditures equal 100 percent of resources). Reliance on the county general fund exposes these departments to executive and commissioner decisions over general fund allocation. As part of a final budget, the commissioners could increase or decrease the general fund supplement for either department and thus quickly change the size of its programs.

The bottom line of Exhibit 9.2 indicates the fund beginning balance, but these entries are crossed out in the chart for the general fund departments. The county fund has a beginning fund balance brought forward from the previous year; however, the general fund serves all county departments, and no single department has control of the beginning fund resources. The beginning fund balance for the general fund is managed at the county government level, and its resources are reserved or allocated by political decision as part of the department supplements.

In contrast to the general fund departments, the Building Services Department, which conducts plumbing and electrical system inspections on new construction, the Mental Health Department, and the Housing Department are all nongeneral fund departments. These departments are nearly entirely reliant on departmental revenues and are self-supported. The Building Services Department (Exhibit 9.2) runs what might be termed an entrepreneurial shop by generating 72 percent of its revenues from license/permit fees and charges for services. The department has accumulated a substantial 27 percent beginning fund balance in its dedicated revenue fund numbered 108. Together, revenues and beginning fund balance set the total resource level and thus the total expenditure level for the department's program (100 percent expenditures equal 100 percent resources). Exhibit 9.2 indicates that the Mental Health Department receives 93 percent of its revenues from intergovernmental revenues, 1 percent from charges for service, 2 percent from miscellaneous transfers, and 1 percent through an interfund transfer from the general fund. The Mental Health Department is funded from revenue fund 135, indicating that this is a special revenue fund of dedicated revenues—in this case, state government reimbursements. The department does have access to the beginning balance in fund 135, which supplies 3 percent of the department's resources. Departmental revenues (97 percent) and the beginning fund balance (3 percent) set the total size of the Mental Health Department's expenditures. The Housing Department presents a very similar pattern, with intergovernmental revenues providing 43 percent, miscellaneous revenues (rental fees and purchase revenues) providing 56 percent, and a very small general fund transfer. The Housing Department has spent all resources in prior years and does not bring forward any beginning fund balance (0 percent). Finally, the General Fund Supplement line at the bottom of Exhibit 9.2 is crossed out for these three departments. While this indicates a lack of a general fund supplement, it does not imply a lack of executive or commissioner oversight. The county executive and commissioners review the blend and total level of department revenues and projected department expenditures as part of budget construction, review, and adoption. The commissioners exert control over access to the beginning fund balances as they would over the general fund supplement for the A&T and Public Health departments.

Exhibit 9.2 demonstrates departments funded from a single budget fund, e.g., the Building Services Department is totally funded from fund 108, and even though the Public Health Department receives revenues from many sources, it is described as a general fund (001) department because of its supplement. Single fund dependence makes for straightforward examples that can clearly display revenue components and fund balances. In practice, local government departments may be funded from one, two, or several revenue funds, resulting in a more complex flow and mix of resources.

Exhibit 9.2

Example Comparison of Fund Sources, Expenditures, and Supplement for Hypothetical County Government

Comparison of Fund Revenue Sources and General Fund Supplement for a Single Fiscal Year

	Assessment & Tax Department (A&T) Revenue Fund: 001 Percent of Department Total Resources	Building Services Department Revenue Fund: 108 Percent of Department Total Resources	Mental Health Department Revenue Fund: 135 Percent of Department Total Resources	Housing Department Revenue Fund: 270 Percent of Department Total Resources	Public Health Department Revenue Fund: 001 Percent of Department Total Resources
Departmental Revenue Sources					
Licenses and Permits	2	41	0	0	28
Intergovernmental Revenues	22	0	93	43	33
Charges and Fees for Services	47	31	1	0	17
Fines and Penalties	2	0	0	0	0
Miscellaneous Revenues	0	1	1	56	4
Transfers from Other Funds (Code)	0	0	(001) 1	(001) 1	0
Interfund Revenues	1	0	1	0	0
Department Total Revenues	74	73	97	100	82
Department Total Expenditures	100	100	100	100	100
Department Total Resources	100	100	100	100	100
General Fund Supplement	26	XX	XX	XX	18
Fund Beginning Balance	XX	27	3	0	XX

ACCOUNTING BASES: PERSPECTIVES TO DEFINE INFORMATION

The accounting profession and accounting standards have adopted several analytic methods—that are called **bases** (singular, **basis**)—to measure the timing of the revenue and spending transactions that affect fund balances. While these bases are formally promulgated as professional standards, they are widely recognized outside the accounting profession. This widespread support helps to increase the credibility of accounting systems with the public. As with any analytic perspective, a particular accounting method will have strengths and weaknesses. Inappropriately using one method in place of another can obscure the full impact and implications of a decision or situation. Administrators, elected officials, and the public must question financial professionals as to whether a particular method is the most appropriate for the situation. For tracking operating funds, local governments often rely on the modified accrual basis, but for full understanding, we need to describe the cash basis and the full accrual basis. The following paragraphs provide very brief summaries of these bases, and we encourage students and practitioners to consult government accounting texts, standards, or regulations for extended descriptions.

Cash Basis Accounting

As the name implies, **cash basis** accounting focuses on the flow of cash money in transactions through a fund. Transactions include (1) the deposit of revenues into a fund, and (2) payments out of the fund. Transactions are recorded on the accounting ledger on the day the revenues are received and when payments are made. The exclusive focus on cash is helpful for understanding the current status of the fund, but the cash basis is very limiting. A homeowner's tax payment may be months overdue, but cash accounting would record the payment as revenue only on the date of deposit. Similarly, under cash accounting, a government might purchase office supplies in one month, but record the payment for those supplies only on the date of payment, more than a month later.

Full Accrual Accounting Basis

The **full accrual basis** focuses on (1) when the revenue is due (earned), and (2) when the benefit of an expense is consumed or received. This puts the focus on the actual use or benefit of the purchase rather than on the cash usage. Full accrual accounting of revenues would recognize that many property owners will pay their bills on time (cash), but that a few will not. Full accrual basis would recognize delinquent bills as *receivables,* that is, revenue that is due and will ultimately be received. This revenue will eventually be received and is therefore counted as an available resource in the fund balance. On the spending side, accrual accounting focuses on the actual use of a purchase rather than the up-front cash used for payment. For example, a county government might purchase a pickup truck for its roads department. The department uses the truck over a lifespan of six years to a specified mileage limit before its disposal. Full accrual accounting would register the cost of the truck in annual increments spread over the six-year lifespan. Full accrual accounting is effective in representing long-term capital projects and long-term capital revenues. For example, a local port district invests in a dock and cargo crane facility. Full accrual accounting would recognize that the benefits of dock and crane would be spread over a 30-year lifetime. Expenses would be allocated over the 30-year period; similarly, revenues will be received over the same 30-year lifespan. Accrual accounting would not place the emphasis on the up-front current year cost of the dock and crane as would cash accounting.

Modified Accrual Accounting Basis

Neither of the previous bases is especially helpful to local governments, which for transparency and political reasons must focus on the short-term period of the fiscal year or biennium. To budget and plan, governments must be able to recognize revenues expected during the fiscal year, and must plan for expected expenses during the same period. The **modified accrual basis** provides a remedy to these needs. Modified accrual accounting recognizes a revenue when it is measurable and available. That is, the revenue is expected in cash form in the normal course of operations in the fiscal year. For example, property tax revenue is due from a homeowner in cash payment according to a two-payment schedule over the fiscal year. Knowing this, under semi-accrual accounting, the government prepares a fiscal-year budget on the expectation that the tax revenue will be paid on time. Modified accrual accounting allows governments to demonstrate the revenues that are expected to be available in the annual budget. On the expense side, this type of accounting recognizes that a bill is due when received, but it also recognizes that the government must have the resources available to pay it. Modified accrual accounting renames expenses *expenditures* and logs an expenditure paid when the bill is due and the cash is available to make payment.

Modified accrual accounting is good for supporting the short-term perspective of a fiscal year or biennial budget. The modified accrual basis does not do well describing major capital, infrastructure, or multiple-year purchases. Modified accrual recognizes a major capital purchase as a single expenditure. Any borrowed revenues from bonds would be recognized as revenues because these would be expected at some point over the fiscal year, but these revenues may partially or fully cover the purchased asset. Recording the full cost of major capital and infrastructure purchases in a single year would cause the fund balance to vary widely with expenses rising by millions in one year and then falling by millions in the next. For this reason, local governments typically split off their capital programs into a separate budget that is structured under the full accrual basis (chapter 16).

Following state regulations and accounting standards, local governments typically employ different accounting bases for different purposes. For example, a large county of about 350,000 uses modified accrual accounting and budgeting for its governmental funds, including its general fund, special revenue funds, debt service funds, and capital project funds. The county has a separate capital projects and infrastructure budget. For proprietary funds, including **enterprise funds** and internal service funds, the county uses full accrual accounting and budgeting (Clark County, WA 2010, 91). Proprietary enterprise funds cover county sewer, wastewater treatment system operations, and facilities costs. Budget documents and year-end consolidated financial statements (known as a **Comprehensive Annual Financial Report**, or **CAFR**) will typically explain which basis a government uses for the different parts of its budget and accounting (see chapter 18). In most instances, the government staff selects the accounting framework to meet professional standards and to provide the reader with the greatest explanation and clarity of the situation. Readers should always review this decision and question the implications of the selection.

The detailed system of accounting described above gives the impression that such systems ensure high levels of transparency and financial accountability. However, this impression can also be quite misleading. There are numerous instances where accounting techniques have been used to obfuscate the true financial condition of governments (Anthony 1985). The Governmental Accounting Standards Board (GASB) was convened in 1984 to address many of these shortcomings in transparency and accountability. A continual effort to revise and improve accounting standards and practices has resulted in increasingly accurate portrayals of a local government's finances. We review some of these practices in chapter 18 on financial auditing and performance review.

NONPROFIT ACCOUNTING DIFFERENCES

Nonprofit organizations come in a broad array of sizes and purposes, and the accounting and budgeting systems that support them vary widely. Nonprofit budgets and accounting range in complexity from, say, the highly complex activity cost–centered systems used by nonprofit hospitals for high performance, to a simple spreadsheet accounting ledger used by a local climbing club. Even with many differences, the accounting fund concept provides a common base for both organizations. Like local governments, large nonprofit organizations establish many funds to separate programs, cost centers, revenue sources, and capital investments that result in complex budgets and financial reports. However, the climbing club's spreadsheet that logs in member dues, payments for meals, equipment, gasoline for trips, guest speaker visits, and building rent is also an accounting fund that must balance at year's end.

The climbing club's spreadsheet represents a simple general fund. Because the club's spreadsheet includes revenues from all sources without restrictions, and the club can spend the funds on any purpose, the spreadsheet represents a **current unrestricted fund**. A current unrestricted fund is a general fund that supports the daily operations of the organization. More complex nonprofit organizations, including hospitals, schools, foundations, and service providers, denote a general fund, operating fund, or unrestricted fund.

Like local governments, nonprofits receive grants, donations, and other monies with restrictions on how and when the money may be spent. Nonprofits typically establish separate accounting funds for internal tracking purposes, to demonstrate compliance with donor wishes, and to comply with grant and contract requirements. Federal and other foundation grants usually require a separate tracking and accounting of resources. A **restricted fund** established for a specific purpose, grant, or contract keeps the restricted monies separate from general funds. Nonprofit accounting uses segregated funds for internal use but loosens the definition of restrictions to allow the consolidation of funds for external reporting (Finkler 2010, 428). Funds that contain segregated revenues may be available in the current period, but they may have donor restrictions limiting their use to a specific program or purpose. These are denoted *current restricted funds*. They are available in the current period, but there are extensive restrictions on their use; a segregated accounting fund provides a means to separate these resources and their transactions from the organization's general fund. Nonprofits also establish separate accounting funds for endowment resources that allow the release of monies at specified points in the future. These funds are denoted as *long-term restricted funds* because of their delayed release. *Permanently restricted funds* prevent access to the principle in a fund but allow the organization access to the annual growth of and interest on the principle. For example, the members of a local church, synagogue, or community foundation with an endowment are strictly prohibited from spending the fund principal, but may size a service program based on the annual interest generated by the endowment. Nonprofit accounting often uses accounting funds to segregate revenues according to future availability. Recognizing the temporal aspect of revenues is a useful concept that is often overlooked by governments that use a semi-accrual basis. Semi-accrual accounting places the focus on the short term of the fiscal year. While this reflects the budget process and political realities of a one- or two-year budget, it obscures the limits on resources into the medium-term out-years.

The short example shown in Exhibit 9.3 demonstrates how effective categorization of resources can help administrators and elected officials understand a revenue situation and explain it to a confused public. A major city school district was faced with reduced revenues, a falling student population, and an aging, expensive infrastructure.[1] The school board's inclination was to move through the annual proposed budget, cut across the board, and spend down its reserves. A newly hired budget officer advised against this broad approach. Traditionally, the district had organized its budget funds based on programs and departments, but drawing on her accounting skills, the

Exhibit 9.3

Example of Resource Categorization by Access Restrictions
(hypothetical large school district)

Fund type	Flexible funds		Inflexible funds			
Expense type	Flexible current unrestricted	Flexible grants	Revenue	Mandated	Contractual	Total
Totals	92,000,000	40,000,000	68,300,000	93,000,000	158,700,000	452,000,000

budget officer proposed breaking the district's expenses into funds based on flexibility and board control of the expense. Flexibility reflected accessibility and time restrictions. The expense categories from her presentation chart are shown in Exhibit 9.3.

The *flexible funds* columns represent current expenses over which the board has control. *Flexible expenses* are covered by current unrestricted or general funds. Cuts here would have an immediate effect of reducing expenses. *Flexible grant* expenses can be cut, but are covered by nontax or fee revenues. Cutting these funds would unnecessarily reduce revenues, resources, and program levels. Flexible funds account for 29 percent of total expenses. In contrast, the *inflexible funds* columns represent expenses with restrictions, about 71 percent of district expenses. The *revenue* column represents expenses needed to obtain revenues. These include the matching funds needed to obtain federal funds and the **maintenance of effort** spending levels necessary to demonstrate good faith commitments to partner governments. The revenue column reiterated to the board that the district must spend dollars to receive dollars. Cutting expenses here cuts off important and substantial sources of revenues. The *mandated* column represents the expenses required by state and federal regulations. Compliance with these expenses prevents legal liability from the state, federal government, or parents. The *contractual* column indicates that personnel costs for teachers, staff, and administrators are a major expense for the district, and that labor contracts lock the district into a set of expenses for a three- to five-year period. Contract requirements prevent any reductions to these labor expenses in the near to midterm. These expenses are reflective of mid- to long-term restricted funds. Based on this breakout, the board began to understand that they have relatively little control—at least in the near term—over 70 percent of the budget. Cutting parts of the flexible expenses will help balance the budget on the margins, but not in a substantial way. Recategorizing expenses into flexibility-based categories was an important tool for clarifying the situation and the board's decisions.

As in governmental accounting, nonprofits have a choice of accounting basis. Nonprofits use either a cash flow basis or an accrual basis. The local climbing club spreadsheet reflects a cash flow basis of accounting. It records, on the date of payment, the donations and member dues in, and it records payments out for expenses. However, the **generally accepted accounting principles (GAAP)** that guide nonprofit financial reporting require reports on an accrual basis. Thus, larger nonprofit organizations—hospitals, universities, schools, foundations, and service providers—all follow accrual accounting procedures to allow development of year's end financial statements and external audit compliance. Larger organizations also may use a standard chart of accounts that classifies and codes revenues and expense transactions according to a unified system (Chen, Forsythe, Weikart, and Williams 2009, 7; National Center for Charitable Statistics 2009). The unified system allows universal understanding by administrators, board members, auditors, and the public for transactions between nonprofits.

HOW ACCOUNTING CONCEPTS HELP TO CLARIFY BUDGET OPTIONS AND BUILD PUBLIC CONFIDENCE

Accounting standards and procedures provide powerful tools to enhance transparency, accountability, managerial control, and decision making. Budget and accounting funds stand at the heart of these standards because they segregate and organize resources and expenditures into identifiable quantities. The requirement that funds must balance at the close of the fiscal year sets restrictions and controls on elected officials, the executive, and the organization's staff. These controls are the key to accountability, and to building taxpayer and donor confidence in government and nonprofit organizations.

For all their positive benefits, accounting standards and procedures can confuse and obfuscate. Arbitrary transfers between accounting funds can distort the true status of a government's finances, and obsession by elected officials or the public over compliance with a certain accounting detail can quickly divert attention from more important issues. Public organizations face legal requirements to follow professionally defined accounting procedures to manage their finances, but administrators should question finance officers and financial advisors as to the appropriateness and effectiveness of the accounting procedures used to portray their organizations.

STUDY QUESTIONS

1. How does the governmental or nonprofit organization for which you work structure its budget into funds? Alternatively, explore your local county, city or town, or township government. How does this organization define its general fund, current expense, or unrestricted fund? How many special purpose funds does it define? Why? Review the chart of accounts for the organization to gain insight into its budget design and fund structure.
2. Access and work exercise 9.1 Budget Funds Segregate Revenues on the textbook website at www.pdx.edu/cps/budget-book. The exercise results produce a table similar to Exhibit 9.1. To what degree does the county general fund contribute resources to general funds departments? Compare the county general fund proportions in departments dependent on special revenue funds or other dedicated revenue sources. How does the beginning fund balance contribute to the resources for special fund departments?
3. What state laws and regulations define accounting bases and procedures for your county, parish, or borough government? Does the state mandate the use of a standardized fund and account coding system by all local governments in your state?
4. Why should a local port district, or any other local government, use an accrual accounting basis to describe capital and infrastructure expenses?
5. Examine your state's budget structure. How does your state define its general fund, and how does it segregate federal funds and other sources of revenue?

NOTE

1. This example drawn and adapted from a class presentation by Linda Sebring, CPA, Budget Manager for the Seattle Public Schools, in Winter 2006.

10 BUDGET PLANNING
PREPARING THE ORGANIZATION
AND COMMUNITY TO BUDGET

Prior Planning Prevents Poor Performance (5Ps).

(U.S. Army Adage)

Political rationality is the fundamental kind of reason, because it deals with the preservation and improvement of decision structures, and decision structures are the source of all decisions. . . . There can be no conflict between political rationality and . . . economic rationality, because the solution of political problems makes possible an attack on any other problem. . . . In a political decision . . . action is never based on the merits of a proposal, but always on who makes it and who opposes it. . . . Compromise is always a rational procedure, even when the compromise is between a good and a bad proposal.

(Paul Diesing 1982, 198, 203–204, 232)

Planning has become an increasingly important activity for the success of public budgeting for at least two reasons. First, increased demands on shrinking public resources has made planning a critical strategy for setting priorities, achieving the greatest efficiency with existing resources, and demonstrating effectiveness in the allocation of public resources. Second, in addition to these good business reasons for planning, there are some good political reasons as well. It is often the case that planning is used as a way of tempering the influence of politics on the allocation of scarce public resources. A planning approach to budgeting carries the impression that the budget has been prepared based on the collection of lots of data, the creation of rationally based criteria for the assessment of budgeting alternatives, and the selection of programs based on some kind of evaluation. In contrast, a political approach to budgeting carries the impression that the budget is primarily the result of deference to political preferences and constituencies. As we have argued throughout this book, there is always some degree of ongoing tension between the planning and political dimensions of public budgeting. How much and when do we budget to a plan? How much and when do we budget based mainly on the mobilization of and response to political interests? These are the central questions that we will explore in this chapter as we discuss the various kinds of planning associated with the public budgeting process.

At the federal government level, and to a somewhat lesser degree at the state level, budgets are highly political. Most observers of these processes assume that the president's or governor's budget plan is based on political preferences and the lobbying priorities of various interest groups more than it is based on the outcomes of a carefully crafted data-gathering, assessment, and planning process. Plans developed in highly charged political contexts are frequently seen as rationales to justify political preferences rather than plans that guide and determine political preferences. There are several reasons why this commonly held view does not apply as much to local public budgeting. First, the requirement that local budgets must be balanced means that considerable amounts of information have to be gathered by different groups of experts in the budget preparation process. For example, those in charge of the capital infrastructure and the long-term financial capacity of the local jurisdiction are expected to know the existing and near-future streams of revenue and expenditures that are needed to maintain the fiscal and physical well-being of the jurisdiction. This is hard to accomplish without some kind of financial plan and capital facilities plan (see chapter 16 on capital budgeting).

A second reason that planning is more essential at the local level than at the federal and state levels is the formal accountability and reporting requirements. These requirements are in place as a result of state laws and professional standards governing financial reporting and auditing for local government jurisdictions. For example, local governments conform to financial planning and reporting guidelines recommended by a variety of professional associations, including the Association of Government Accountants, the Government Finance Officers Association, the Auditing Standards Board of the American Institute of Certified Public Accountants, the Governmental Accounting Standards Board (GASB) and other professional associations and standards. We will discuss the roles that these groups play in the budget planning process in subsequent sections of this chapter.

A third reason that planning is more essential at the local level is the proximity of citizens to the process of collecting revenues and allocating expenditures. Citizens in local communities are much more inclined to exercise close oversight of decisions over taxes, fees, and other revenues, as the Upper Cascadia County public safety services levy case at the beginning of Part II demonstrates. This intensity of local oversight is much greater than at the state and federal levels of government.

Finally, planning is more important at the local level because of the need for part-time elected officials to rely on a larger framework of information for making decisions that connect the past, present, and future. The preparation of various kinds of plans by administrators serves to meet this need.

Organizations undertake many different types of planning. Consider the following list of activities to which the word *planning* can be attached:

- Strategic
- Financial
- Program
- Systems
- Budget
- Capital
- Operations
- Revenue
- Stakeholder
- Community

The above list is not exhaustive and can be suborganized into a variety of different superordinate planning-related categories. You probably can think of types of planning that have not been captured in the list, and you may have your own preferred way of organizing the list into simpler categories.

In this chapter, we will use the framework we developed in chapter 3 to organize our discussion of the role that planning plays in the various aspects of the budgeting process. You will recall that we argued that our local systems of democratic government mirror in important ways the goals and purposes of our state and federal governments. While local jurisdictions vary widely in the source of their legal authority and in the structures of their governing arrangements, all share a common desire to meet the sometimes conflicting expectations of our democratic rule-of-law system: responsiveness to citizens, the efficient and effective administration of the business of government, protecting the rights of citizens, and honoring the unique polity characteristics

Exhibit 10.1

Local Democratic Governance Framework

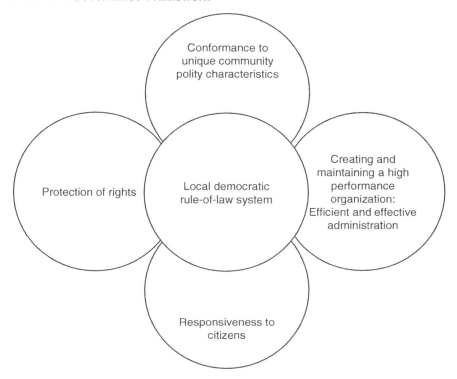

of the geographic community being served. Exhibit 10.1 provides a simplified summary of the governance model we developed in chapter 3.

At the center of Exhibit 10.1 is the local system of democratic governance that has been put in place to meet the expectations of citizens, whether it be a strong or weak mayor system, a council-manager form of government, or a commission system, and whether it be a county, city, special district, borough, or some other kind of governing body. Regardless of form and regardless of structure, all systems are expected to undertake the preparation and approval of a budget that is responsive to the concerns of citizens, makes efficient and effective use of public resources, honors the rights of all citizens, and takes into account the unique polity characteristics of the local community. Deliberate planning to incorporate these values into the preparation and approval of the budget are critical to building trust and legitimacy in our systems of local government.

Drawing from Exhibit 10.1, we will organize our discussion of planning into the following three major categories around which we will divide the remaining sections of this chapter: organizational, political, and polity. Exhibit 10.2 summarizes the types of activities that fall into the various categories we are using for purposes of our discussion in this chapter.

The category of organization-centered planning in Exhibit 10.2 includes all of the budget, finance, staffing, program, and operational planning that are necessary to create and maintain high-performing organizations. This category constitutes the largest set of planning activities, which is reflected in the disproportionate attention we devote in this chapter to various types of organizational planning that support an effective and efficient public budgeting process. The reason

Exhibit 10.2

Types of Budget-Related Planning

Organization-Centered Planning
- Budget process planning: Resource allocation, data information flow and systems
- Financial information, plans, and policies
- Operational information, plans, and policies
- Bringing it all together
  - The central role of the executive in the budgeting process
  - The budget instruction manual

Political Planning
- Anticipating the priorities of elected officials
- Citizen engagement

Polity Planning
- Jurisdictional strategic planning
- Community strategic planning: Network mapping and facilitation
- The role of elected officials in polity budgeting

this category is so large is because the budget preparation, approval, and implementation process is an integrative activity: It draws together multiple organizational functions, each of which is performed by career professionals whose expertise is essential for collecting the appropriate data and analyzing its meaning and relevance for the budget process.

Political planning in Exhibit 10.2 refers to all of the activities that are needed to prepare citizens and elected officials for the discussion and approval of the local budget. These activities include process design, public outreach, priority setting, oversight, and review. Polity planning, a unique theme of this text, has to do with all of the activities related to the network of community partners, nonprofits, and civic organizations that contribute resources to the achievement of the public good. The public budget planning process can be used to mediate conflicts among community and network partners, temper the adverse impact of service reductions on target populations, and leverage the resources of partners to serve the greatest benefit of the community.

ORGANIZATIONAL PLANNING TO MEET EFFICIENCY AND EFFECTIVENESS EXPECTATIONS

In this section, we will organize our discussion around the following three major types of planning that need to be successfully completed prior to the start of the budget process: budget process planning, financial planning, and operational (program) planning. We will follow this with a discussion of how the executive in charge of the budgeting process melds all of these planning activities together into an integrated framework for successfully completing the budget development process.

Budget Process Planning

It is essential that all participants in the budget process described in chapter 4 have what they need to work successfully to produce an approved budget quickly. As we have pointed out in our discussion of the budget cycle in chapter 5, there is a very short amount of time to collect, analyze, discuss, and make final decisions. This work would be impossible without extensive planning long before the budget process begins. For example, infrastructure replacement and maintenance plans, demand/satisfaction information from customers, and staffing plans all have to be in place prior to the start of the budgeting process. An overall budget process plan is needed to stage and norm the budget preparation process and the roles of each of the essential participants.

The budget process plan is frequently called the **budget instructions** or **guidelines**. It is prepared by the central budget office in coordination with the chief executive officer (CEO). The goal of the document is to prepare the various parts of the organization to carry out their respective budget preparations and approval obligations within a prescribed time frame. Budget instructions ensure that analysts and administrators throughout the organization hold the same assumptions about the general revenue condition, uniformly understand predetermined financial policies and priorities, clearly address and respond to important community and political issues, and understand the schedules and due dates for completing the various stages of the process. From an analytic perspective, the budgeting instructions define a *conceptual framework* of assumptions, procedures, data selection, information displays, and issue focus. The budget instruction document is written primarily for the professional administrators, budget and financial analysts, forecasters, and program managers. Together, these professionals take responsibility for capturing all of the relevant information related to organization systems and staff capacity, **financial policies**, operational policies, **strategic plans**, strategic long-term **financial forecasts**, executive agendas, **budget-cycle revenue forecasts**, citizen recommendations, and community needs. This overall planning-related body of information conditions the preparation of public budgets and their adoption. The CEO of the organization uses the budget preparation document to prepare the organization, elected officials, and the community for the budgeting exercise that is about to unfold.

Preparing the Organization: Allocating Resources to Budgeting

While budgeting is a routine and basic exercise for governmental and nonprofit organizations, it is an organizational function that requires its own allocation of staff and resources. In most local government organizations, the staff and resources devoted to the preparation of the budget are shared with, or totally diverted from, service delivery or other functions for a large portion of the year. Budgeting draws heavily on the central office finance staff and on the department and program analysts and finance staff, but also touches the department and program leaders, the strategic planning staff, and the public involvement staff. Ensuring sufficient and available resources from all of these participants is critical to the success of budget preparation and can't be assumed without a plan.

Viewed from the perspective of a work activity, preparation of the budget requires administrators to dedicate organizational resources to accomplish a series of scheduled tasks. One aspect of scheduling is in the design of the budget process itself; another relates to ensuring and organizing the staff and expertise needed for budgeting (Christensen, McElravy, and Miranda 2003, 15–16). Responsibility for both process planning and resource allocation falls to the executive, line managers, and program managers throughout the organization.

Budget process design allows the CEO, the chief financial officer (CFO), the budget officer, and other senior leaders to adjust workloads within limits established by state regulations and guidance. Sufficient time must be incorporated into the schedule for departmental request preparation, central budget office review and construction, and legislative adoption. In the past, budget document preparation and formatting took a substantial part of central office time. Today, electronic systems can reduce the preparation time, which allows analysts more time to focus on planning, evaluation, and decision support analysis (Christensen, McElravy, and Miranda 2003, 17).

As we pointed out in chapters 4 and 5, work during the request preparation phase of the budget cycle initially falls most heavily on the program and department budget analysts and leaders. With the submission of the program and department proposals to the central budget office, central office staff becomes fully engaged and operates in an emergency response mode. Both department staff and central office staff remain fully engaged through the preparation and release of the executive's proposed budget and then remain on tap to answer requests from elected officials for explanations, additional information, and analysis of alternatives. Adoption of the budget brings a slight reduction in workload, although central office and department staff have tasks related to the setting up of appropriations in the accounting system, routine reporting of spending and revenue flows, managing cash flow, and preparing a year-end budgetary status report.

In larger governments, the central budget office staff may be largely dedicated to budget tasks. In slack periods, central office staff may work on forecasting, performance analysis, or other financial issues. But in smaller governments and special districts, the finance officer with several accountants and account clerks support not just budgeting but accounting functions, financial reporting and audits, procurement, and investments.

Budget analysts in the departments and programs may have a formal earmark on their time to support the budget process. More often, however, staff time is informally allocated to budgeting among many other analysis, finance, or performance measurement tasks. This is especially true in smaller governments and special districts where a department manager serves as program leader, operational manager, and budget analyst. Whether by formal allocation or informal time management, the chief executive and leadership team must assure that department managers, program managers, and staff analysts are available and can devote sufficient attention to the budget preparation process. Refinement of the budget process activities and deadlines provides the senior leadership and the budget officer a chance to review workload demands. This includes balancing the workload and staff expertise between the department and central office levels.

In recent years, reduced revenues have often forced reductions in financial office staffing. This is because finance and budgeting are frequently treated as overhead functions that do not directly contribute to service delivery and therefore are considered *safe* reductions. But annual budgets must be completed on time and to state specifications. Cuts in the finance and budgeting functions simply transfer work back to the department and program analysts, which in turn comes at the expense of program and service delivery. These considerations are important factors that need to be taken into account in the budget preparation planning process.

While budgeting is often perceived as a managerial task handled by the executive, elected officials also hold some degree of responsibility for the process. Elected officials must highlight and stress the importance of the budget process to their elected colleagues, the executive, the organization's leadership team, and the public. Elected officials support the budget process by advocating for sufficient expertise, staff time, and information systems, and by ensuring budget quality through oversight of the budget process and the organization's budget function.

Preparing the Organization: Data Information Flow and Systems

A budget and its analysis are only as good as the quality and completeness of the underlying data. Chief financial officers and department directors hold especially critical roles ensuring the availability and quality of the information necessary for budget preparation. These lead actors have responsibility for building and maintaining the interdepartmental relationships and organizational systems that support the budgeting activities. With these relationships and systems in place, staff-level budget analysts can then make informal contacts to speed the exchange of financial, performance, and resource information that supports budget preparation. Effective leadership and clear performance expectations can improve these cross-department relationships. Take, for example, the task of maintaining updated and accurate human resource information. Both the CFO and the human resource department director have ultimate responsibility for ensuring that part-time and full-time position and salary information is current and available for budget development. Other preparations ensure that the budgeting process integrates with other financial, cost analysis, performance management, personnel, and strategic planning systems.

The selection, design, and purchase of software to support the budget process represent a set of major choices that defines how budget preparation and decision making will occur. Information systems support the analytic, computational, and reporting activities during the budget process, while also defining staff and budget actor behavior. Restrictions on information access and on deadlines for loading and processing information help to define behavior. Thus, information systems contribute to and affect both the administrative framework and the analytic conceptual framework that supports budgeting.

Budgeting information systems range in complexity from a series of linked electronic spreadsheets, to commercial relational database financial systems, to corporate performance management (CPM) software (Kavanagh et al. 2006, 10).[1] Many smaller jurisdictions and smaller nonprofits rely on electronic spreadsheets or on increasingly powerful small business accounting software (Kavanagh and Ruggini 2006). Medium and large governments, however, typically invest in larger, more costly, relational financial systems or CPM software. Relational database systems were developed for commercial corporate use in the 1990s and early 2000s to allow online transaction processing (Kavanagh et al. 2006, 16). These systems represented an improvement in their effort to integrate information and reporting from the finance, payroll, and human resources functions. However, the budgeting software modules were often designed as a subsystem or module of the larger, integrated system (Kavanagh and Ruggini 2006), which—even with custom refinements— failed in many cases to respond to a government's unique needs and circumstances. Governments were often encouraged to change their budgeting and financial process to conform to the system requirements rather than customize the system to the unique needs of the organization. Budgets organized by program goals and objectives (chapter 12) or by performance analysis (chapter 13) faced challenges in accessing and organizing useful information (Kavanagh and Ruggini 2006, 9).

Recent advances in computing technology and software have transformed finance and budget information systems. The aforementioned CPM software links data from finance, payroll, and human resources systems, but CPM systems are designed for maximum accessibility and flexibility in data use rather than for processing speed. When fully implemented, most CPM systems have the capacity to support budgeting, planning, and forecasting; support activity-based costing and management, which is important in cost and performance analysis; and provide performance scorecards and dashboards (Kavanagh and Ruggini 2006). CPM systems allow many different users and analysts to access and format data to their specific needs rather than relying on standardized applications and reports. Additionally, the flexibility of a CPM system allows the organization to respond to changes in the budget process. For example, if elected officials prefer some additional analysis of options during consideration of the executive's proposed budget, the system can respond to that need. The flexibility in CPM allows analysts to more quickly respond to unique information and analysis requests (Kavanagh and Ruggini 2006).

The flexibility of CPM systems is both an advantage and disadvantage (Kavanagh and Ruggini 2006). The high degree of flexibility allows the CPM system to connect with databases maintained in different parts of the organization. CPM systems also allow analysts to access and extract data for custom-designed analyses and reports. However, for routine budget process applications, analysts must first build a base model in the CPM system that describes the organization's budgeting situation—its funds, internal financial relationships, financial transactions, human resources hours and costs, production and performance costs, planning goals and objectives, and other information. Because the building of this initial model can be challenging, time consuming, and costly, most jurisdictions continue to rely on more narrowly focused budget software or on homegrown spreadsheet and database applications for budget development and reporting tasks.

Purchasing any financial records and budgeting software system requires careful planning, needs assessment, procurement, installation, and implementation (Garson 2006). Large financial systems and CPM systems are costly to develop and maintain. In addition, they integrate so deeply into and across the organization that system procurement becomes a major project involving the information technology (IT), procurement, finance and budgeting, and operating department staffs. For these reasons, IT systems development and maintenance need to be budgeted as part of the capital planning activity we describe in greater detail in chapter 16, and organizations should include IT system needs, upgrades, and replacement as an integral part of their strategic planning process. Procurement planning and needs assessment are critical phases of the IT procurement process. This phase determines the products available from vendors, defines the organization's needs, and sets the criteria against which potential systems will be evaluated. Governments typically hire consultants to guide and support this early phase of procurement. Procurement of IT systems often follows a proposal, evaluation, and negotiation process. Entering into a major IT procurement sets up a fluid partnership between the contractor and the government. Performance is based on structured goals and timelines, but the complexity and importance of IT systems demands the mutual exchange of expertise, skills, information, and trust. Contract administration and enforcement usually falls to a partnership model rather than to the enforcement model of a sealed bid procurement.[2]

Financial Information, Plans, and Policies

Previous chapters have outlined the many forms and sources of revenues that support local governments (See chapters 6 to 8). Those chapters also discussed the primary methods for revenue forecasting and noted that analysts must regularly update their short-term **budget-cycle revenue** forecasts to ensure the best possible estimates of future revenue levels in an adopted budget. Most forecast updates represent incremental and minor changes along relatively stable economic trends. However, as the economic downturn of 2008 demonstrates, radical and fundamental changes can occur that reset long-standing trends. Biannual and quarterly revenue forecast updates provide fresh information to guide department and central office budget analysts as they prepare proposed budgets. The same information also helps the chief executive and elected officials understand the revenue reality in which they must make budget decisions.

Some of the most important pieces of financial planning information are the long-term financial forecast for each major budget fund, including the general fund, all enterprise funds, and major special revenue funds. A financial forecast projects all of the different types of revenues that contribute to the fund: program expenditures, client demand needs, multiyear expense obligations, and capital credit needs and revenues three to ten years into the future. When aggregated, the forecasts provide a major element of the jurisdiction's **strategic financial plan**. Without such a plan, participants in the budgeting process may be oblivious to the consequences of having to pay debt obligations out of the operating budget or to fund wage and benefit increases 10 years into the future. We discuss such a plan in greater detail in the last section of this chapter on polity budgeting.

Accurate and timely budget-cycle revenue forecasts and long-term revenue and financial forecasts are essential components of successful budget preparation, but the financial policies of the organization play an equally important role. When we speak of **financial policies**, we have in mind the following categories of information and answers to the questions these categories raise.

- *Revenue Stabilization Reserve Funds:* How will the jurisdiction establish reserve and stabilization funds for catastrophic emergencies, operational reserves for unexpected service needs, liquidity reserves to ensure sufficient cash flow, and capital reserves to allow for the replacement of capital equipment, information technology, and infrastructure (Clark County, WA 2004, 22)? What percentage level of total revenues will be maintained in the general fund as a contingency for unexpected expenses? What level will be maintained in other major dedicated funds?

- *Fees and Charges:* How will the jurisdiction set the rates for user fees and charges? How will the rates recover total costs, direct costs, and indirect overhead costs? How often will the jurisdiction revisit and review the rates? Are the rates excessively burdensome on residents?
- *Debt Issuance and Management:* How will the jurisdiction use, or not use, long-term debt to finance ongoing operations? How will the jurisdiction balance the use of revenue bonds with general obligation bonds? How will issued debt match with the service life of the financed capital equipment or infrastructure?
- *Debt Level and Capacity:* How will the jurisdiction comply with any state restrictions on local government debt loads? How will the jurisdiction protect its bond rating to ensure the lowest possible cost of current and future borrowed funds, and how much debt can the jurisdiction issue as a percentage of the general revenues?
- *Use of One-Time Revenues:* How will the jurisdiction use one-time revenues? How will one-time revenues match with one-time expenses? How will ongoing revenues match with ongoing, continuing expenses? If a grant funds new positions, how will the jurisdiction continue to fund those positions into the future after the grant expires?
- *Balancing the Operating Budget:* Define that the budget process provides the only forum for assessing, granting, and amending spending requests. If state law, state regulation, local ordinance, or local policy requires adoption of a balanced budget, how will the jurisdiction define "balanced" and achieve compliance? How will the jurisdiction use the beginning fund balance in the general fund and in other major funds? How will the jurisdiction define and manage carryforward balances, encumbered funds, or reserved monies? How will it handle ongoing appropriations that cross fiscal years? How will it incentivize departments to save money?
- *Revenue and Revenue Diversification:* How will the jurisdiction collect taxes? How will the jurisdiction take on intergovernmental grants that require local government matching contributions?
- *Contingency Planning:* How will the jurisdiction ensure the presence of a sufficient **contingency reserve fund**? How will the jurisdiction prioritize services (e.g., mandated, essential, discretionary, or support) and programs for major cutbacks or for growth? How will the jurisdiction apply incremental cuts, major program cuts, across-the-board cuts, or develop and implement new revenue sources? How will the jurisdiction reduce services under conditions of major financial and revenue uncertainty, including reducing services to state minimal levels (Washington County, OR 2000, 327–328)?
- *Financial Forecasting:* How will the jurisdiction conduct financial forecasting of revenues and expenses for each budget fund into the midterm? Depending on the fund and type of program, forecasts may extend for three, five, or ten years. Enterprise funds and capital improvement funds may require a 10-year forecast to ensure structural balance.
- *Capital Improvement Plan:* How will the jurisdiction develop a separate capital improvement plan over a midterm period (five or more years) showing the capital equipment and infrastructure inventory, replacement and rebuilding needs, funding sources, and potential operating costs and maintenance costs. How will the jurisdiction balance pay-as-you-go financing with debt financing, and how will it conduct financial planning to develop funding sources to meet capital needs?

Operational Information, Plans, and Policies

Operational-level information, plans, policies, audits, and studies play an essential role in norming the budget preparation process and in providing the information necessary to create an approved budget. The types of information that are included under the heading "Operational Information,

Plans, and Policies" (Exhibit 10.2 above) include multiyear business plans; program operations, maintenance, and expansion plans; budget and programming analysis; performance evaluation studies; and customer and stakeholder satisfaction surveys. For example, a parks manager who has tracked the costs, the customer participation, and satisfaction rates in last year's summer programs has a reliable basis upon which to assemble a summer program for the coming year. Without this planning information, budget requests become unreliable and, over time, undermine the credibility of the park manager. In fact, credibility in itself may become a surrogate for a carefully crafted plan. Once planning credibility has been established through repeated budget cycles, this credibility may be used by political and administrative superiors in the process as a substitute for the plan (Wildavsky 1988, 105–109). But once that credibility is called into question, it may take several years of recovery to regain the lost trust. And this process of recovery may entail engaging in ever more detailed planning than is necessary to produce credible and reliable information. The point to be made here is that plans are not only important for the program information they yield but also for the trust that is built among stakeholders, clients, fellow administrators, and elected officials.

Reports of current-year program spending rates and the performance of the current year's budget provide near real-time information that can inform construction of next year's budget request. Semiannual, quarterly, or even monthly status variance reports for revenue collection, service demand levels, spending rates, and program performance provide new information to refine forecasts and budget assumptions. Status and variance reporting (see chapter 17 for a complete discussion) compares the actually experienced levels of revenues, costs, and performance to the expectations in the current year's budget. These reports test the accuracy of the current year's budget projections and provide an indication of changing conditions that will require adjustment in the coming fiscal year's budget. Similarly, information from certified financial statements and audit reports adds retrospective information that can increase budget accuracy and program effectiveness.

The preparation of mid-tier operational plans, often called *business plans* or *operating plans,* are important for the budget preparation process. These plans align resources with the strategic plan goals and identify means-end relationships between resources inputs and program outcomes (Rivenbark 2003, 23; for examples, see chapter 12). Means-end relationships establish the basis for performance measurement and performance-based management at the middle and lower levels of the organization. The strategies and decisions made in supplemental strategic subplans for finance, cost management, information technology, office space, organization infrastructure, and capital improvement inform and support operational planning. Often neglected or shortchanged, midlevel operational planning or programming often is one of the most challenging tasks of planning. This is because it is difficult to relate ends and means over an extended period of time when you do not have control over the conditions for success. For example, a park manager may not be able to set forth a business plan for the next three years because he or she does not know the impact of a proposed park levy, of summer programming for a variety of community organizations, or of the opening of a new Boys and Girls club, or any number of other unknowns. Without such information, it becomes difficult for the park manager to prepare a budget that responds to strategic goals and to the resource programming needs outlined in the operational plan. We devote considerable attention to the interface of strategic plans with operational program goals and objectives in chapter 12 in our discussion of planning, programming, budgeting system (PPBS) format.

In addition to the importance of operational-level plans for informing the preparation of the current budget, operational-level policies may be important for managerial and program design reasons. For example, design policies provide guidance on the development and expansion of services and programs (see GFOA 2000, Practice 5.1). These policies include guidance on whether to contract or partner with nonprofit and commercial external partners; whether to develop an intergovernmental agreement with other government agencies; whether to use a public-private competition process, which pits government organizations against private-sector vendors; or whether to perform the activity with in-house staff and organization. If the service is provided in-house, organization staffing, training, and leadership must be developed. In short, the preparation of a budget for existing programs may entail a much larger process of analysis that explores various options against a prescribed set of protocols.

Procurement policies provide another example of the importance of undertaking extensive planning prior to the preparation of a local public budget. Procuring the delivery of public service from external partners, either public or private, may frequently require adherence to a combination of procurement procedures, existing contract requirements, or partnership agreements. Take, for example, a contract agreement between a county government and a nonprofit mental health provider. This contract may fully specify the services the county will provide, as well as those that the contractor or partner will contribute. The agreement may also specify and define shared resource contributions—how the government costs of personal services and materials will be calculated and limitations on changes that can be made from one budget cycle to another. Contracts may be negotiated over an extended period that limits any significant changes being made from one budget year to the next. For large jurisdictions, the annual aggregate payment liability for purchases, service contracts, intergovernmental agreements, and capital construction contracts may be in the hundreds of millions of dollars. In the very smallest local jurisdictions, administrators and elected officials can likely keep track of the major ongoing contracts mentally; in medium and smaller jurisdictions, however, the aggregate value of contracts adds up, and one or several major contracts may account for a large portion of the jurisdiction's spending. One researcher (Rubin 2006) suggests that jurisdictions explicitly list and report the details of their major contracts as part of their annual budget. These details could include (1) the duration of the contract or agreement, (2) the scope and activities planned for the contract, (3) how much revenue is expected from the contract and when, (4) the fees required for payment and when, and (5) how the fees would change over the life of the contract (Rubin 2006, 9).

Bringing It All Together: Executive Leadership

Planning is an inherently executive activity. This was an early lesson that the framers of the American Constitution learned from their experience with the Articles of Confederation. While the Articles were well structured to facilitate debate on issues of grave importance to the new nation, the deliberative assembly could not create the plans needed to collect the taxes, to buy needed supplies for the army, and to deliver the needed supplies on time and within budget. To correct these defects, representatives from the various states called for a new Constitutional Convention, leading ultimately to a document that created more unity and energy in the executive function (Thach 1969). In this section, we will discuss the role of the local government chief executive officer (CEO) in the budget planning process, particularly in preparing the organization for producing a balanced budget that obtains board approval within the time specified by law.

Planning Is an Executive Function: Implications for Control over the Budget Process

Our discussion so far in this chapter dealing with prebudget planning has important implications for executive control over the budget process. Public budgeting was largely a legislative-centered process until the passage of the Budget Accounting and Control Act in 1921. This act required the president for the first time to present a unified budget to Congress for discussion and approval. The growth in the number and complexity of government functions has increased the need for executive planning and made control of the budget preparation process necessarily an executive function. This is also the case in state and local governments, as well as in nonprofit organizations, where the practice of relying on part-time elected officials and board members has further increased the need for executive control.

Planning and budgeting have become so central to the success of local governments that executives are commonly hired because of their vision and future plans for an organization and its constituents. While always subservient to the elected board, appointed local city managers and city administrators play a central but muted role in establishing the agenda that guides the organization, elected officials, and the community. Control of the budget process is fundamental to playing this muted role; it requires a marriage of the needs of the organization with the political needs of the community as reflected through and by members of the elected **legislative body**. The preparation of the budget by the executive is the core governance activity that integrates the political and organizational needs of the community.

To be successful, governors, strong city mayors, and other elected and appointed governmental chief executive officers, must act before the budget cycle begins by appointing key actors in the process, including the chief financial officer, the budget officer, and key members of the central budget office staff (Forsythe 2004, 4–8). In large governments, the executive's deputy or chief of staff may take on these tasks. By taking an early leadership role, the executive can direct the CFO or the budget officer to set financial policies and assumptions, define analytical requirements and perspectives, and set preparation requirements that are informed by executive and board priorities.

Preparation requirements include the selection and use of budget formats, fund structures, and accounting perspectives (chapter 9); proposed policy changes; and preliminary funding levels and staff allocations. Additionally, executive requests to department and program directors for department-level budget alternatives and program-level scenarios can reinforce the executive budget and its political agenda.

And so it becomes clear that local government executives have extensive power in the budget development process. In fact, some argue that this power may be excessive and come at the expense of the deliberative side of the governance process. This was the concern at the federal level, which prompted the passage of the federal 1974 Budget and Impoundment Control Act. As we reviewed in chapter 1, this act strengthened the ability of the legislative branch to undertake its own analysis by establishing the Congressional Budget Office. It put in place some constraints on the executive and created a process that would enable Congress to approve a balanced budget. While the act failed in its "balanced budget" aspirations, it did strengthen the deliberative side of the budgeting process by creating a new budget committee in both houses of Congress. These committees serve as deliberative forums that enable participants to focus on the budget as a whole, with particular attention to the interrelationship between expenditures and revenues.

Compared to the national and state levels of government, the power of local government executives to use the budget process to drive personal political and organizational agendas would appear to be much greater. Part-time boards and small organizations put the executive at the center of almost every activity of any significance, but there are a variety of constraints that limit executive control of the budget.

First, one needs to consider the differences among the various types of government we discussed in chapter 1. As we pointed out, a strong mayor system that allows the mayor to appoint his or her own budget director has more control than a weak mayor who works within a city manager system. A city manager who has a part-time elected board has more control than a city manager with a full-time board. The chief executive of a nonprofit organization governed by a voluntary board may have the most control of all.

But for all the best hopes of expressing their agendas, regardless of the form of government, executives face the constraints of policies, economic conditions, and strategic financial forecasts

(Forsythe 2004, 14). Together these constitute a second set of constraining conditions. A third set of constraints is the weight of history. Elected and appointed executives may be able to selectively ignore or interpret the strategic plans developed by prior administrations, but this may require violating previous commitments made to constituent groups, organizational managers, stakeholder groups, and citizens. Shifting these previously established expectations may be time consuming and politically difficult. As we will discuss further in the next section dealing with the establishment of political priorities and in chapter 12 on the planning, programming, budgeting system (PPBS), it may be easier for executives to initiate changes through their own strategic planning process.

A fourth set of factors that constrain the executive's ability to use the budgeting process to initiate major changes is the larger political forces at work within a given community. Other elected council, committee, or board members have their own agendas for the organization, and these agendas may conflict or align with that of the executive. In urban and suburban mega counties and cities, the county commission or city council as a legislative branch may provide a formal check on the executive's actions. Here, the executive must either build support for or defend, the agenda in his or her proposed budget. In smaller jurisdictions, collegial agreement between the executive and the council may result in a joint agenda that guides annual budgeting. Nonprofit organizations often follow the collegiality of this latter pattern. No matter what the political dynamic, the executive and the legislative body must compromise differences sufficient to obtain majority approval of the budget in time to meet regulatory deadlines.

A fifth set of constraints on executive control of the budget are the administrative functions and organizational priorities of professional career administrators who have been hired and promoted because of their competence in successfully carrying out their organizational functions. The political and organizational agendas of executives may create tensions with these professionals. As we pointed out in chapter 4 on budget actors, career administrators have a different role in the budget process and measure success by different criteria. Career administrators typically respond to programmatic needs for resources and staff, unmet or partially met community and client needs, resources for administrative improvements, infrastructure needs, and concerns over the strength and health of the government institution. Professional administrators also bring concerns over technical competence in budget preparation and decision making. Administrators provide a reality check of the executive agenda based on standing policies, previously adopted strategic plans, long-term financial forecasts, and economic cycles and conditions. In the end, however, both administrators and the executive must ensure that the budget process concludes on time with the adoption of a technically complete and accurate annual budget.

The Role of the Executive in Nonprofit Budget Process Planning

Much of what we have discussed in the preceding section on the role of the executive in local public budgeting applies to nonprofit organizations as well. Even more than is the case with local government jurisdictions, the nonprofit chief executive is more singularly in charge of setting budget priorities and controlling the budget process to achieve board approval and, more important, to gain the renewed confidence of the board in both the organization and the CEO's leadership. Since the two are so integrally connected, it is even more important that the budget process be designed to minimize conflict both within the organization and between the organization and outside stakeholders. But the nonprofit CEO faces special challenges in the budget planning process, three of which we will discuss in greater detail in the sections that follow: These challenges are (1) determining the level of participation in the process, (2) balancing the conflict between budget preparation demands and direct service delivery, and (3) deciding how much of a role to play in the organization's strategic and operational plans.

Conflict Between Executive Control and Extensive Participation. We have pointed out in our previous discussion of nonprofit budgeting that it is common for the CEO to prepare the budget with a few members of the leadership team. This process is undertaken with an eye toward the chief priorities of the organization that have been established by some kind of governing board strategic planning process. But how these goals are realized through program delivery is often a mystery to the voluntary board members, who have been recruited because of their fundraising capacity rather than for their expertise in program or managerial issues. Under these circumstances, it is easy for the CEO to assemble a budget without necessarily involving frontline staff or second-level program managers in the process—especially if there is a high potential that programs and staff may have to be cut, reconfigured, or reorganized because of revenue shortfalls. With a donor-centered board, the degree to which these expense-oriented strategies will need to be used may not be known until very late in the budget process. This contrasts sharply with the government budgeting process, where the revenue stream is known early on and is unlikely to change very much during the budget construction process. For these reasons, there may be a strong incentive to limit the participation of staff in the planning process so as not to create expectations that limit flexibility later on in the budgeting process.

Conflict Between Planning and Service Delivery. Financial policies, strategic and operational business plans, and extended financial forecasts provide a framework that guides and supports nonprofit budget development. The extent and form of these policies, however, varies considerably with the size and mission of the organization. Large consolidated intermediary nonprofits or community foundations need fully developed policies, plans, information systems, and staff resources. Liability risk, annual tax reporting, and accountability reporting (Jackson 2007; e.g., Sarbanes-Oxley Act [SOX] reporting) reinforce the need for fully developed financial policies and information systems. These well-developed systems, while taking time away from service delivery, are nevertheless important to an effective annual budgeting process (Farris 2009, 123).

Small and micro-nonprofits need plans and policies appropriate to their size and complexity. Smaller nonprofits frequently review the policies used for large organizations and adopt reduced or less complex versions appropriate to their situation. The various kinds of plans discussed in the previous sections for governments can also be used as a template to help nonprofit organizations decide how much detailed planning policy development needs to be done in advance of the budgeting process. One of the ways of benchmarking the adequacy of the existing budget-related plans is to ask the following kinds of questions:

- How does the organization handle credit for routine purchases and debt for major equipment and capital investments?
- How does the organization conduct procurement and purchasing?
- How does the organization use one-time revenues, diversify its revenues, and manage its sinking and savings funds?
- How does the organization respond to contingencies, including an abrupt cut or growth in revenues?

In the absence of plans and policies covering any one of these issues, a simple statement of intention would begin the development of a policy. A review by the organization's certified accountant or attorney would provide further development of a policy. Adoption of a policy framework would require board approval.

The Nonprofit Executive's Role in the Creation of Strategic and Operational Plans. As with governments, strategic and operational planning are important exercises for both large and smaller nonprofits. These activities depend almost entirely on the initiative of the CEO, who may feel constrained by time and resources to initiate the development of such plans. Unlike government organizations, there are few external pressures on a nonprofit organization to have these plans in place. But a strategic plan allows the organization to identify its mission, vision, goals, and objectives, and to conduct an environmental SWOT (strength, weaknesses, opportunities, and threats) analysis that helps align it with its customers and its current and future environments. There is a robust body of literature that provides nonprofit CEOs the help needed to undertake strategic planning and process implementation (Bryson 1995, 2001). These resources also provide nonprofit CEO's with a range of choices that enable them to integrate strategic planning with nonprofit accounting (Finkler 2010, 30–31), with budgeting (Farris 2009, 123–130), or with the development of a financial plan (Reason 2005).

A financial strategic plan is especially important for most nonprofit organizations, which are vulnerable to large and sudden fluctuations in revenue streams. Such a plan considers the flow and sources of revenues, as well as the flow of expenses over an extended time frame of at least five years. A financial strategic plan sets the boundaries of the current revenue and financial realities but also identifies areas for new fundraising and development to meet emerging needs. It helps to ensure that resources will be available to meet those future needs. Jackson (2007) calls for enfolding a risk management and accountability reporting framework into the nonprofit strategic planning task. Risk management strategy includes donor relationships and reporting of fundraising. She applies her concepts to both large and small nonprofits. Completed strategic mission and financial plans provide a context for the development of operational business plans and an annual budget.

Organization Budget Instructions Make the Budgeting Process Real

The budgeting conceptual framework for a governmental or nonprofit organization reflects its policies, plans, strategic financial forecasts, near-term revenue and economic forecasts, and executive direction. All of this information must be articulated and communicated to the organizational leadership and the staff analysts. A set of detailed **budget instructions** or **guidelines** provides the means for the executive to transmit this information succinctly, and to direct and control the budget process. The release and transmittal of the budget instructions by the CEO or the CFO indicates the close of the budget process planning phase and the opening of budget request preparation phase by the departments and programs. The transmittal also signals the kickoff of the budget as an official organizational work activity that is expected to produce a product within a certain time. A budget kickoff meeting brings together the executive, the CFO, the central budget office staff, and the department analysts in an information and training session. Together, the budget instructions and the kickoff meeting provide the uniform standards and role definitions that support decentralized budget preparation in the different divisions and programs of an organization. Constituent groups, unions, neighborhood groups, and the general public focus their attention on the formal initiation of the budget development process and the opportunities it provides for future public involvement.

Budget instructions pull together both executive direction and the myriad of technical assumptions and details that support budget development by the departments and programs. It is commonly the case that the annual budget instructions represent incremental adjustments to the previous year's instruction booklet, thus providing stability to the budget process. From a technical perspective, the instructions (1) reframe policy decisions into a budgeting context; (2) define the provisions and rates in labor contracts as assumptions for personnel costs; (3) provide updated fund balances, including available and reserved resources; (4) define the budget formats and data templates to be used; (5) define analysis procedures; (6) specify the financial and accounting standards; and

Exhibit 10.3

Budget Instructions Checklist (Representative Example)

____   Table of contents
____   Transmittal letter with executive direction to staff
____   Budget activity schedule and due dates
____   General policies and guidelines, integration with other plans and policies
____   Data entry procedures
____   Data for personnel wage and benefits computations
____   Key FTE hour and rate definitions
____   Updated chart of accounting/budget funds with opening balances and any encumbrances
____   Procedures for new positions and for policy change requests
____   Instructions on direct and indirect charges
____   User fee and charges update
____   Current year midyear review results, quarterly/monthly variance results, audit results
____   Strategic and operational plans implications
____   Strategic financial plan extended forecast constraints
____   Economic conditions and revenue forecast implications
____   Information systems directions and data entry forms
____   Requests for capital expenditures and vehicle purchase
____   Budget analysis baseline computations
____   Definition of budget formats and analyses
____   Executive-requested scenarios for program reduction or changes
____   Department and program assignments to central budget office staff members

(7) provide detail on the information system and its data needs. Budget instructions also describe the current and projected economic conditions and the expected economic impacts on current and future revenue collections. The budget instructions embed the executive's agenda by requiring certain analysis procedures, data displays, and analysis scenarios. Critically important, the instructions provide a detailed production calendar with completion dates and budget cycle events. This calendar, in essence, structures the time and defines the professional lives of the budget analysts and the central budget office for the next four to nine months. Exhibit 10.3 provides a content list for a representative set of local government budget instructions.

Following the budget instructions and the budget calendar, the department and program staff analysts and leadership begin to prepare their budget requests for the coming fiscal year. We discuss additional important steps in the budget preparation process in the next two sections of this chapter.

While preparing the organization to budget consumes most of the CEO's time, it is not necessarily the most important part of the process. Equally important is the preparation of the elected officials and the larger community to participate successfully in the budget process. We will discuss these two functions in the remainder of this chapter as well.

POLITICAL PLANNING

One of the central themes of this book is that budgeting is an integral part of the political process of a given community. This is especially the case at the local level, where elected officials and citizens are likely to express their strongest views of what should be done during the budget process. For that reason, it is not sufficient that the CEO prepare a budget that meets all of the technical requirements of being balanced and providing accurate and timely information to decision makers; additionally, the CEO must prepare the elected officials (city councillors, commissioners, and district board members) and citizens in a given jurisdiction to participate knowledgeably in the budget development and approval process.

The Role of Elected Officials: Anticipating and Coordinating Multiple Political Agendas

While elected strong city mayors, elected county executive commissioners, and state governors have a direct role in budget preparation, most elected officials play an indirect or marginal role. As we noted earlier, budget preparation is normally delegated to the CEO and a small support staff. In small jurisdictions, this might include the budget director working closely with the city manager or mayor. But CEOs face peril if they fail to include elected officials in the thick of the budget preparation process. The president and state governors need to anticipate the kind of support their budget proposals will receive. This is even more important in the case of local levels of government. Without anticipating the political priorities of elected officials and incorporating them into the executive's proposed budget, the budget adoption process may be characterized by time-consuming debate, politically costly amendments, and public frustration and confusion.

In small jurisdictions with a part-time legislative body, elected officials often do not understand or appreciate many of the technical and legal aspects of preparing a balanced budget. These requirements may sometimes conflict with the agendas and hopes of newly elected officials, who have not experienced the procedures and dynamics of a full budget cycle. Helping elected officials understand revenue and financial realities requires clear, well-packaged explanations, including details on the revenue situation, grant and matching fund requirements, labor agreements and other long-term spending obligations, budget fund and accounting structures, state reserve requirements, and payment obligations for borrowed funds. Early involvement of elected officials in the budget process gives administrators a chance to explain the requirements of a technically sound budget and how these requirements might limit political expectations.

In addition to the need to involve elected officials in the planning process to avoid subsequent disagreements that may imperil the budget approval process, there are many positive reasons for the CEO to use the budget planning process to connect with city council members, county commissioners, township selectmen, and special district board members. Primary among these reasons is gaining a sense of their concerns and strategically focusing their efforts in support of the budget development process.

First, elected officials are a major set of the eyes and ears of the government organization. As government and community leaders, elected officials reflect and respond to the intentions and emotions of the community, shape and define issues, provide substantive information, and help to build trust and legitimacy in the budget process and its decisions. Elected officials are especially important in communicating to citizens and the business community when significant adjustments need to be made to the budget because of changing fiscal realities.

Elected officials can also help support the budget process by ensuring that organizational resources, technical capacity, and information systems are available when needed. Additionally, they can play a critical role in the design of public involvement procedures (Creighton 1992, 44). Elected officials are generally concerned that the process is designed to address citizen concerns, handle complaints, and respond effectively to the desire for information.

Finally, elected officials play important outreach roles to the service provider network that delivers local government programs. Elected officials who have been briefed on the financial situation and who have been involved with budget decisions are in a position to credibly explain the rationale behind decisions to partners and community advocates. In their outreach role, they often become aware of the resource constraints and relationship challenges among organizations within the community. This knowledge and set of relationships can be an important asset to the CEO and budget staff as they seek to identify and consolidate resources from many sources in support of networked service provision.

Nonprofit board members play roles very similar to those of elected officials. As an organization's outreach and listening experts, they are in a perfect position to explore client and community needs and explain the limitations or opportunities in the nonprofit's revenue situation. Nonprofit board members become important communication ambassadors to the community when funding shortfalls or major program changes occur. They have critical oversight responsibilities over the executive, the staff function, and the budget process, much like those outlined above for elected officials. Additionally, nonprofit board members work to build credibility for the organization and its decisions on strategy, policy, and program delivery.

To summarize, in lieu of second-guessing how the budget preparation process can best be designed to address the concerns of elected officials, it is wise for CEOs to involve these officials in the design of the process at the very beginning. This involvement helps to reinforce the legitimacy of the budget process and its decisions. There are a variety of techniques the CEO can use to collect important information on the priorities of elected officials—and to do so in ways that norm the process. These include holding personal meetings, planning retreats, and informational outreach meetings with the community. Exhibit 10.4 provides an example of the use of a prebudget planning retreat to collect the necessary information from elected officials that the CEO may want prior to the preparation of the budget for formal review and approval by board members. Retreats are especially useful for small jurisdictions with part-time board members and a full-time CEO. This process is also useful for nonprofit CEOs who want to prepare their governing board for budget decisions that may not be routine.

The Role of Citizens and Public Involvement in the Budget Process

Preparing the community to participate in the annual budgeting process is another political role that the CEO must anticipate and manage well. This task is in addition to the CEO's role in anticipating the priorities of elected officials and producing a technically well-prepared budget. **Public involvement** in the budget process generates several benefits (Marois, Amsler, Keidan, and Speers 2010): It (1) helps to keep the public informed of central issues and opportunities to participate in the process; (2) provides citizens, groups, and businesses with a more complete picture of the financial and budgeting situation governments are addressing; (3) clarifies the funding and benefit trade-offs faced by government; (4) provides a communications channel for government to receive concerns and recommendations from the community and, in the process, it (5) builds substantive legitimacy in the final adopted budget, not to mention meeting all of the legal requirements that might be in place for participation (Marois, Amsler, Keidan, and Speers 2010, 38).

Building legitimacy for—and acceptance of—an annual budget requires an accurate and honest assessment of community social capital and political opinions. If the government and its community partners have had to make unpopular decisions in previous years, public confidence in the government may be uncertain or shaken. This lack of confidence may sometimes be the result of factors over which local officials had little control, such as the loss of a major business, loss of state or federal funds, or the consolidation of major nonprofit service providers into a new entity. Such events place administrators and elected officials in the position of having to repair and restore community social capital and confidence in the government organization before full support for a budget can be obtained. Rebuilding confidence and building support for a budget

Exhibit 10.4

Informal Briefing Sessions, Strategic Planning, and Budget Retreats Prepare Town Elected Officials for the Annual Budget Process: A Hypothetical Case

Elections for town council, mayor, and other local government offices add a layer of uncertainty and confusion to annual budget process planning and preparation efforts. The fictional town of Upper Cascadia has learned to use informal briefing sessions during the election campaign season to educate candidates and the community on the budget situation and upcoming decisions. The briefing sessions complement the town's use of an annual budget retreat to prepare elected officials for the upcoming budget process.

Upper Cascadia is an incorporated town located on the far edge of a large metropolitan area. The town's economy is supported by farming, agriculture support, and logging, and by serving as a bedroom community for the neighboring metropolitan area. Upper Cascadia has a population of about 1,500 residents. The town's small size and rural character provide a sense of place that attracts and holds many of its residents. Property taxes are low relative to adjacent larger cities, which have extensive industrial properties and a higher level of suburban and urban services.

The town operates under a weak mayor, council-manager form of government with five town council members and a mayor. Council members serve four-year terms. Elections for town council occur every two years in November with two or three council seats coming open each election. The mayor's seat comes open every other election for a four-year cycle. Having three positions open during each election tends to bring out many candidates and the potential for strong turnover of council membership after each election. The town manager grew to understand that educating council candidates in advance improved council effectiveness.

Upper Cascadia's recent election and budget preparation experiences are instructive. The campaigns for town council and mayor began in earnest in July. Shortly thereafter, in late August and early September, the town manager scheduled a series of informal briefing sessions for the candidates. During the meetings, the town manager and other key staff members explained the organization of the town government and the services it provided. Part of the presentation reviewed the town's current operating budget. Besides transferring information, the briefings enabled the candidates to speak effectively during the campaign about what each one planned to do if elected. Additionally, the briefings let the citizenry become aware of important issues facing the town and its administration. As an enduring benefit, holding briefings also enabled newly elected council members to join the town council with a reasonable understanding of the town's financial situation. The candidates brought a fresh perspective on citizen concerns and needs to the town manager and staff. November saw the reelection of one incumbent and the election of two new members to the council.

The town manager and the staff proceeded to work individually with the new council members to further bring them up to speed on town programs and finances. The town manager, mayor, and other council members also worked with their new colleagues to educate them on the recently completed strategic planning effort. The effort had taken two years to complete, involved a facilitator, and was highly inclusive to gain citizen support. The planning process had assessed the community's situation and then sought advice on the appropriate actions the town government should take to respond to issues. Contributions from other nongovernmental organizations and stakeholders were also explored. The resulting 10-year strategic plan included a mission, vision, and goals for the town government and for the community. The strategic perspective of the plan provided an overall umbrella strategy with guidelines for land-use planning, zoning, and economic development. While the new plan and its planning exercises had helped to focus the community, the plan results were too general for annual budgeting. To bridge this gap, the town council and manager agreed to convene a budget retreat for the council.

(continued)

Exhibit 10.4 *(continued)*

Fiscal years in this state run from July 1 to June 30. Accordingly, the town of Upper Cascadia must prepare and adopt a budget in early June in time for the beginning of the new fiscal year. To start the budget process and to meet the June deadline, the town council scheduled a budget retreat as soon as possible in mid-January. For the two new council members, this was an on-the-job training experience. The town manager and mayor hoped that the results of the retreat would build unified support for the drafting of a proposed budget. Scheduling the retreat very early in the budget process was also important. Obtaining agreement on goals and priorities would allow their full expression in the budget document, and the early surfacing of council member and citizen concerns also would help in building political support for the budget.

Upper Cascadia's retreat was conducted as an open public meeting, per state law. Any interested citizen or media representatives could attend. The council chose to meet on two consecutive evenings from 5:00 P.M. to 9:00 P.M. To maintain an air of informality and to build collegiality, the retreat was held in a large conference room at the town library. This was within the town limits, but away from the formality of the council chambers. Light refreshments were served to keep the participants' energy up.

The council and town manager organized the first night's session around a series of presentations by the staff directors of the different town departments. Key town staff members also attended, contributing valuable explanations on technical issues, status reports, as well as staff responses to citizen concerns and complaints. As part-time, uncompensated elected officials, the council members typically did not contemplate town operations to the degree that the town staff does on a daily basis. After summarizing their program and activities, each director presented updated detailed information on key issues and the financial situation. The presentations provided the elected officials with a way to respond to citizen concerns and to explain the rationale behind town decisions and actions. The town council has a policy of listening and responding to suggestions from citizens in attendance; toward evening's end, the council held a short formal session to take questions from several citizens who had attended but were not actually part of the retreat.

Upper Cascadia's council used the second evening retreat session to address goals and issues for the coming year. Building from the new strategic plan, the council members listed issues and then developed a series of goals to respond to each. The goals were then consolidated using a winnowing process to leave a set of prioritized goals for the coming fiscal year. The town manager and budget officer used those goals to guide budget preparation talks with town staff. Having the key town staff members in attendance allowed them to understand the nuances of the prioritized goals. The budget officer could then reflect these nuances in the budget instructions/guidance document, and the department directors and staff members could use their understanding of the subtleties that distinguished the various goals to inform their everyday operations in the coming fiscal year.

Sources: This hypothetical case reflects the experiences of the City of Banks, Oregon. See City of Banks webpage at www.cityofbanks.org. The case also reflects the professional experiences of one of the authors, James A. Hough (personal recollection, October 14, 2012).

requires extensive outreach to citizens, businesses, advocacy groups, other governments, and other groups in the community. The trust-building process may require the involvement of the jurisdiction's public affairs office or neighborhood participation staff to assist with gathering demographic data, undertaking surveys, and organizing outreach meetings (cf. Creighton 1992, 47–49). This is a reminder that the mobilization of expertise and outreach work during the public budgeting process is why we have argued throughout this book—that budgeting is not instrumental work but a constitutive activity essential to building democratic trust and legitimacy.

Flexibility is crucial in the application of required laws governing public participation in the budget preparation process. Consideration of and adaptation to the unique needs and expectations of local communities is essential for success (Simonsen and Robbins 2000, 4–5; Creighton 1992, 50; Ebdon and Franklin 2006). A community with an activist tradition may require more and deeper opportunities for involvement than a community that accepts a more passive oversight of the annual budget through representative governance. The degree of involvement may also reflect the extent of changes and the degree of impact in a new budget. Major changes to funding and program levels sometimes require additional public involvement in budget-related decisions (Simonsen and Robbins 2000, 45). To summarize, those in charge of managing public participation during the budget process need to consider different approaches and combinations of approaches (Marois, Amsler, Keidan, and Speers 2010, 3, 36; Simonsen and Robbins 2000, 40) of the kind listed below:

1. Relationships with neighborhood councils and citizen involvement organizations
2. Education and outreach
3. Surveys
4. Advisory committees
5. Workshops
6. Deliberative forums

Education and outreach efforts rely on a variety of communication tools to broadly reach community members. These tools are important for explaining the budgeting process, for explaining the revenue and expense needs of the governing jurisdiction, and for explaining constraints on decisions. Statistically representative citizen surveys and focus group forums provide tools for collecting broad public opinions and concerns (Simonsen and Robbins 2000, 22–23). These techniques are the same as those used in public administration and social science research. The methodologies, assumptions, and limitations discussed in administrative research design courses apply to the use of these techniques in budgeting process public involvement.

Budget committees are officially appointed groups of citizens that review government actions on budget preparation and decision making. Budget committees are a required part of the local government budget process in some states (e.g., Oregon), but in other states their use is optional. Citizen juries and panels (Simonsen and Robbins 2000, 26) provide a similar, if less formal, venue for citizen involvement.

Standing neighborhood councils or citizen participation organizations (CPOs) provide additional channels to conduct outreach and to generate citizen awareness and interest. These groups provide established meeting forums and communication pathways. Such groups are typically knowledgeable of their membership base and of the best way of making effective contact. Though often poorly attended, routine council and CPO meetings also provide an excellent opportunity for face-to-face education and outreach, and for conducting workshops and deliberative forums.

Budget committees, juries, and panels are typically small groups of citizens. Their small size may limit their ability to provide representative coverage of the full community. On the positive side, however, their small size helps them to speed education on issues, to narrow points of disagreement, and to reach timely agreement on recommendations. Workshops, budget balancing, and deliberation exercises provide participants with hands-on opportunities to become involved while personally confronting the funding allocation trade-offs under constraints of limited revenues. These in-person sessions serve to clarify financial and revenues situations and the trade-offs necessary to reach a balanced budget.

To gain and effectively use public input, administrators must take the time to listen and embrace recommendations early in the budget process (Ebdon and Franklin 2006, 439–440). For example, some jurisdictions conduct neighborhood listening sessions around the city prior to beginning the budget preparation process. Many jurisdictions make use of web pages and social media networks to communicate and receive information related to the budget development and approval process. Sometimes, departments and programs that provide the services directly to citizens may be the best choice to serve as the primary agents of involvement early on in the process, since they have the most convenient venues for contact with neighborhood councils, local government citizen committees, business groups, civic and citizen groups, issue advocates, major nonprofits, and service network partners.

Major changes in the revenue environment may trigger the need to undertake extensive outreach by the organization leadership. This may require repeated contact with both internal and external community constituencies. In-person forums can be a critical tool for communicating and building acceptance with internal staff who face layoffs and with citizens and clients who face reduced service. However, administrators must set honest expectations regarding citizen input and the parameters within which citizens can influence decision makers and final budget decisions. For example, in Exhibit 10.5 below, we provide an example of extensive use of citizen participation, but the parameters are clear. No amount of participation will change the need to make serious budget cuts unless voters adopt a proposed supplemental property tax levy.

POLITY PLANNING

In this final section of the chapter, we focus on a new type of planning that we believe will become more important in the future, as local jurisdictions seek to maximize the use of increasingly scarce public resources. In chapter 1, we introduced the concept of *polity leadership or governance* to describe how the collective assets of the public, private, and nonprofit sectors are enlisted at the local level to coproduce the public good. Currently, these contributions are uncoordinated and largely unknown to the multiple silent partners. We argue that one of the steering roles that government can play is to actively identify these contributions and to facilitate conversations about the collective consequences and the implications for the participants. For example, if several churches or nonprofit groups are operating soup kitchens for the homeless on Monday, Wednesday, and Friday, would practices change if this information were shared? If toy drives at Christmas are conducted by 10 different businesses, and clothing drives are conducted by six churches and nonprofit organizations, how well are these activities meeting the collective needs of the community? Could these needs be better met through coordination? Such questions are what we have in mind when we speak of polity planning. In this final section, we will discuss two ways in which local governments can play a role in this kind of planning. The first is for the jurisdiction to have a clear long-term understanding of its financial condition and a strategic plan that sets forth what government can and cannot do going into the future. The second is to facilitate the development of a community-wide strategic plan that sets out community goals and strategies that will be used by the government, the business community, and nonprofit and voluntary associations to meet these goals.

Strategic Planning

Strategic planning is a common way of taking a more comprehensive and long-term view of how well the mission and goals of a given organization or community are aligned with the larger and changing contextual environment (Rivenbark 2003). A strategic planning exercise results in a vision of a future state of the community and the organization, establishes specific goals, and builds strategies to attain those goals. Citizen and constituent group participation is critical to getting the goals and strategies right and to gaining public support for the plan. The extended perspective in strategic plans helps to provide context, continuity, and stability to the annual budget process and to daily program-delivery activities. Strategic plans can be prepared by any unit within an

Exhibit 10.5

A Large Suburban School District Explains Major Revenue and Program Cuts

For the 2012–2013 fiscal year, a large suburban school district had to make a $40 million cut (about 12 percent) to its operating budget, staff, and programs. Faced with falling state support, the district proposed a ballot measure to increase the property tax levy for schools in 2011 to generate about $14 million. The voters rejected this measure because of a weak economy and a sense that the teachers and government employees needed to carry their fair share of economic reductions. District property tax revenues were expected to remain level for the coming year. The school district had developed an extensive public outreach program of seminar teaching sessions to explain the cuts and to gather public opinion on how to allocate them. School principals served as teaching seminar conveners.

The district is the third largest in the state of Oregon, serving almost 38,600 students. It operates 33 elementary schools, 8 junior high/middle schools, 5 high schools, and 24 option schools and programs. The district expanded its enrollment by 11 percent over the past decade and, prior to the cuts outlined in this story, employed about 4,250 teachers and staff. Like most local governments, school districts in the state use property taxes to fund school operations and capital purchases. The district also collects fees for specific activities, but this is a relatively minor source of revenue.

A major portion of the district's funding comes from the state (58 percent). This support level fell from about $7,000 per student to about $6,000 per student since 2006–2007. Property taxes are the second largest revenue source (37 percent). Faced with a revenue shortage since 2010, the district cut heavily into central office staff positions, used federal one-time funds, and raised student fees. This helped to forestall major cuts to local schools and teachers, but such steps proved inadequate to cover a major revenue shortfall for the following fiscal year.

For the fiscal year beginning July 1, 2013, the district needed to propose and adopt a balanced budget. The basic figures in the table below outline the situation:

Anticipated Revenue and Expenditures (Establishing a Balanced Budget)

Operating fund	Millions of $
Beginning Fund Balance Opening	9.8
Revenues	288.6
Expenditures for Current Program	330.0
Closing Fund Balance 3% Contingency	9.0
Balance	−40.6

To balance the budget, the district had to cut its program size by 12 percent, or $40.6 million—the equivalent of about 300 teaching and staff positions. The cuts would result in major increases in class size and raise the student to teacher ratio from 24.5 to 1 to just over 30 to 1. Many popular arts, band, and after-school programs were eliminated entirely or severely reduced at all schools. The magnitude of the cuts was a major shock to teachers, staff, and to the community.

To explain the gravity and implications of this situation, the school district conducted its usual budget process and outreach, but then took several additional steps. The routine procedures included using a budget committee of citizens and elected officials to oversee the budgeting process, along with public hearings held at each of the five high schools during the budget adoption process. Additional actions extended public outreach on the cuts. The district superintendent conducted a campaign of personal and electronic video

(continued)

Exhibit 10.5 *(continued)*

appearances to explain the situation and alternatives. The district finance office developed a budget-balancing simulation game, and district leadership, including the school principals, convened over 100 sessions for parents, teachers, staff, and students in order to explain the depth and implications of the reductions. The simulation exercise provided an opportunity to begin a grieving and staff adjustment process that laid off most teachers with fewer than six years experience and reassigned many teachers with midlevel seniority between schools according to union bumping rights policies.

Sources: For documentation of this case, see Owen 2012; consult the Beaverton, Oregon, School District website (www.beaverton.k12.or.us/); see also Beaverton School District 2012b and Beaverton School District 2012a (participant-observation notes recorded by author Kent S. Robinson from Highland Park Middle School teaching session on March 6, 2012) and Beaverton School District's basic statistics www.beaverton.k12.or.us./about/quick/facts.

organization, but in this chapter we will focus our discussion on the value of a strategic plan for the local unit of government.

Jurisdictional Strategic Planning

Bryson (2001), and Lampel and Mintzberg (1999) identify multiple approaches to strategic planning, but the most widely used by public organizations is called the *design school* approach. This approach inventories the strengths and weaknesses of the organization and the threats and opportunities in the surrounding environment (SWOT), and searches for a fit between the organization and its environment. From this analysis, planners and organization leaders devise a future state for the organization and strategies to attain that state. Strategies reflect both the constraints and opportunities of the environment. The Government Finance Officers Association (GFOA 2005) recommends the development of a strategic plan prior to budgeting, with specific attention to each of the following steps:

1. Initiate the Strategic Planning Process
2. Prepare a Mission Statement
3. Assess Environmental Factors (SWOT)
4. Identify Critical Issues
5. Agree on a Small Number of Broad Goals
6. Develop Strategies to Achieve the Broad Goals
7. Create an Action Plan
8. Develop Measureable Objectives
9. Incorporate Performance Measures
10. Obtain Approval of the Plan
11. Implement the Plan
12. Monitor Progress
13. Reassess the Strategic Plan

GFOA (2005) argues that a plan should help the jurisdiction bridge the gap between current conditions, needs and priorities, and a desired future vision of the jurisdiction and the community. This includes the development of an organizational mission for the local government and a series of broad, timeless goals. A plan should recognize the constraints and opportunities of currently available resources, but the lack of immediate resources should not prevent consideration of a desired future vision.

Financial Strategic Plans

Strategic plans respond to the external environment and issue reality faced by a government. **Financial strategic plans** examine the extended financial reality of revenue availability and expense obligations faced by a government. A financial strategic plan works to align current and future financial capacity with long-term service goals (GFOA 2008), which leads to sustainable spending and sustainable programs. To gain this perspective, financial plans include long-term financial forecasts that project all the different types of revenues, demand needs and expenditures, multiyear expense obligations, and capital credit needs and revenues three to ten years into the future. This is a longer period than the one- to two-year forecasts used for budget-cycle revenue forecasting. The mathematical and statistical techniques used for both forecasts are the same, but the time frame is longer for the financial plan (chapter 7). Conditions evolve and change over the extended forecast period, and periodic revisions are an important step in forecast maintenance (chapter 17). Long-term financial forecasts provide participants in the budget process with research-based, thoughtful sideboards on annual budget development and decision making.

A financial strategic plan is an analysis product separate and independent from the annual budget process. An effective financial plan evaluates the financial status at the level of the unified government and at the accounting/budget fund level. A jurisdiction's general fund, each enterprise fund, all other major funds, and all major capital investment programs should be examined individually in the plan. Through the extended analysis of revenue and expenditure streams, financial plans help to reduce financial risk. An understanding of the available future revenues also allows a jurisdiction to determine its borrowing limits as a percent of general fund revenues, which in turn sets the level of potential capital investment. To obtain the greatest benefit, a financial strategic plan should clearly describe the time horizon and scope of the plan, the frequency of plan update, and an action path for communicating and making visible the plan results (GFOA 2008). Building forecast scenarios of different conditions and revenue levels provides a means to compound and parse the effects of different economic and political conditions. A **baseline forecast** or baseline scenario demonstrates the extension of current conditions into the future and provides a comparison point. Each alternative revenue and expense forecast describes possible changes to the baseline conditions and assumptions. All scenarios should be rerun with conditions and assumptions varied by prescribed amounts to develop a **sensitivity analysis** of high, medium, and low intensity conditions (chapter 7).

A financial strategic plan identifies and evaluates the key factors that can change the level of expected future revenues (GFOA 1999). From one perspective, a financial strategic plan indicates limits on available and potential revenues, which in turn set limits on potential expenditures. The same limits, however, may identify a strong need for services and a need to raise revenues from alternate sources. The strategies developed in the strategic financial plan provide the vision and goals to access and raise these new revenues (e.g., Tualatin Hills Park and Recreation District 2013).

The accrued wealth and the economic realities and potential of a region or community ultimately define the resources available to local governments in future years. Assumptions of population growth, business growth and activity, and overall regional economic activity provide a basis for **long-term revenue forecasts**. Tax revenue forecasts recognize the potential and limitations of the current tax and revenue bases, along with the potential improvement or degradation of those bases over the longer term. The implications of any tax limitation policies are also reflected. Forecasts of user fees and charges include setting schedules for evaluating and resetting rates (chapter 7), as well as for identifying and evaluating factors and conditions that could affect fee and charge levels over the forecast period. The plan should identify possible changes in the political and fiscal environment at the state and federal level that could affect the level of intergovernmental revenues. State-level initiatives to maintain a balanced budget and federal initiatives to balance the federal budget will likely constrain intergovernmental payments to county and local government in future years. A comprehensive revenue forecast will identify and analyze the uncertainty facing each revenue source.

The forecasts in a strategic financial plan also identify and evaluate future expenditure commitments and resource demands. As with revenues, expenditure forecasts analyze the unified jurisdiction, each major accounting/budget fund, and, if used, performance costs centers. Expenditure commitments include: personnel/personal services expenses under multiyear union contracts; expenditures and rate increases scheduled under major multiyear purchases, major service contracts, and partnerships; and changes in client and customer service demand levels. Labor agreements often determine numerous variables that set policies and determine future costs and expenditures. These variables include wage rates, overtime triggers, weekly and annual hours worked, health care benefits, and retirement benefits. Expenditure forecasts must include federal benefit contributions, and the expected cost of retirement contributions to state retirement plans, local retirement trust funds, or employee benefit plans. Modeling future required contributions to state employee retirement funds is especially difficult because uncertainty in the financial markets changes the value and payout potential of state **public employee retirement system (PERS)** trust funds (chapter 15). The underfunded condition of state pension plans may often leave local governments, special districts, and school districts liable for any immediate payout shortfall. Annual budgets must respond to this shortfall because state retirement funds often have contractual relationships with their retiree members.

Resource demands reflect future community needs and the size of the program needed in response. The number of users provides a primary indicator of staff and expenditures for many service programs. For example, a small hospital district might track patient use hours by procedure and service delivered to develop forecasts of future costs. Local K–12 school districts track the number of total students, the number of low-income students for subsidized meals, and the number of special education students to develop a forecast of federal intergovernmental grant revenues. State and county corrections departments track population, crime, and inmate levels as the basis of determining demand trends. Social service agencies track the number of seniors, children, low-income families, and veterans to determine future program and expenditure levels.[3]

To summarize, the strategic financial plan and its extended financial forecasts provide a community-informed perspective to the budgeting conceptual framework. The forecasts provide a reality check for elected officials, administrators, organization staff, community partners, and the public as to levels of potential resources under specific revenue combinations. Because of their forecast limits, strategic financial plans should be prepared, publicly vetted, and adopted well before their use in the annual budgeting process.

Facilitation and Planning for the Community Polity Network

Multiple local governments, multiple state agencies, federally funded community action agencies, nonprofit community foundations, nonprofit consolidated intermediaries, religious institutions, and major service delivery nonprofits all contribute resources to the community and its service network. Much like budget process planning and preparation for an organization, community network members need to be involved with the budgeting and planning processes used by their local government partners. Similarly, local governments need to be aware of and respond to the budgeting and planning processes conducted by other network members whose decisions can have an impact on the larger network. The executive, elected official, and board member outreach techniques discussed earlier can be used to build such awareness.

Facilitating Network Budgeting

Each organization in a network brings its own budget process steps, budget process timing, spending decisions, administrative requirements and controls, success criteria, and claims on the larger network. Budget process planning by local governments and major nonprofit organizations provides an opportunity to recognize and accommodate the many policies and processes used by the network members. Lead organizations within a network of service providers realize that their organizational budget preparation and budget decisions have effects on formal and informal network partners and on the decisions of other major organizations in the network. For example, a decision by a major community intermediary organization to end the uncoordinated funding of homeless shelters has implications for the other organizations that have been providing clothing and employment support, not to mention the city and county governments that may have been providing direct financial subsidies. Ensuring the early and effective representation of network service delivery partners is a critical element of public involvement in budgeting.

Legal mandates, organizational policies, and contractual provisions may provide some guidance on what should be taken into account by organizational leaders participating in the network, but these factors may often undervalue networks that are built over time through interpersonal and interorganizational relationships of trust. There are two kinds of trust that need to be taken into account in undertaking polity-level budgeting: first, the trust between organizations in the network; second, trust in the network as a whole (Provan and Lemaire 2012). These two kinds of trust require government and other network lead organizations to communicate with partner organizations on budgeting issues and to demonstrate leadership on the funding levels and performance of the full network. Take, for example, running a typical network soccer program in a suburban community. The local parks and recreation special district may operate a youth soccer league with 40-plus teams (cf. Fong 2012; Tualatin Hills Park and Recreation District 2013). The district is currently contributing numerous athletic fields for games and practices, and the local school district has dedicated numerous fields and specified times to youth soccer and to other sports leagues. A soccer league nonprofit organization with minimal professional staff organizes the players into teams and trains the volunteer coaches, but another organization trains, certifies, and supplies youth and adult paid referees for the games. Parents pay an activity fee to the soccer league organization that helps the league recover costs. The youth soccer league is but one mininetwork the district uses to deliver youth sports to the community. In addition to soccer, the district sponsors and coordinates mini-networks for youth football, baseball, softball, basketball, and other adult sports leagues. The combined network of youth and adult sports providers is substantial and complex. How to assure sufficient information flow and response for the annual budget process is a leadership challenge. The concerns and funding changes of an annual public budgeting process may not need to reach every youth sports family in the community, but even incremental changes must reach each league organization and the school district.

Preparing a network to participate in the annual public budgeting process requires reflection on its membership, structure, and relationships (Provan and Milward 2001). Effective interorganizational communication within a network requires establishing and maintaining intermember relationships on multiple levels. With multiple levels open, service delivery supervisors, department directors, executives, finance directors, elected officials, and board members can all communicate budget process messages, policies, and decisions to their respective counterparts in other member organizations (Provan and Lemaire 2012, 643). The tangible resources in a network, such as funding, are typically controlled by a small number of major actors (Provan and Huang 2012). These network actors and partners become critical contacts in the annual budget outreach process. How the network members and partners govern themselves, however, reflects the level of trust between network members, the number of network participants, the degree of goal consensus among members, and external demands for network performance and competence.

We have previously described three forms of networks with sustained governance and service delivery capacity (Provan and Kenis 2007, 234–236). In participant-governed networks, all the member organizations, large and small, contribute to network governance and decision making and to managing relationships internal and external to the network. Governance includes service needs assessment, resource assessment, resource allocation, and network-level budgeting, all of which are typically done collectively by the network partners. In networks with authority and control centralized in one or two lead organizations or in an independent network administrative organization (NAO), the lead network member has the legitimacy and resources to define and execute a leadership role in matters of financial policies, strategy, and budgeting. The network lead organization or NAO provides and coordinates resources, sets financial policies and reporting rules, reviews performance and compliance, and may determine the contractual and partnership relationships between network members. Working with a participant-governed network requires consistent outreach among all network members to build trust (Provan and Kenis 2007, 241). In lead-organization and NAO-structured networks, the members may develop and use trust relationships; more often, however, members in these networks rely on structured relationships and formal administrative procedures (Robinson and Morgan 2014). In the case of the local parks and recreation district and its athletic leagues, the district may take the role of the lead organization. Several factors reinforce this lead role in that it has the ultimate responsibility for delivering a wide variety of recreation programs to the community, has taxing authority to deliver such programs, and has the authority to grant the use and scheduling of its facilities. The sports league organizations, however, have power in the network because of their fee revenue and their ability to motivate large numbers of volunteers. The parks and recreation district likely serves as the lead organization in the network but works collegially with the leagues in a partnership arrangement. To support effective involvement in the annual budget process, the parks and recreation district must ensure that its network members know the flow of the budget process and its important dates, and that they are kept apprised of major changes in policy, partnership arrangements, facilities arrangements, and program funding levels.

Network lead organizations and NAOs steer their networks through financial policies and practices and through their strategic planning. Intermediary nonprofits, for example, may establish principles defining how the lead organization will provide resources and services to the community, as illustrated in Exhibit 10.6.

The principles in Exhibit 10.6 indicate that this United Way chapter prioritizes its funding around three criteria: meeting people's basic needs; ending homelessness; and getting all children ready to succeed in school (United Way of King County [UWKC] 2011). But these criteria are guided by a combination of other considerations that include the opinion of its donors and other participants in the network of service providers. In a cutback environment, the United Way chapter will not make across-the-board reductions in its funding levels but will use a strategic approach to reduce funding and programs. It is important to note that the chapter will take into account changes in the funding levels provided by public-sector governments and by other nonprofit funders; the organization might, under certain conditions, react to policies and decision made by other organizations and not follow its own self-determined strategic directions. The responsibility to consider the responses of other network participants illustrates how the United Way chapter plays the role of a network lead organization with regard to total community funding for a particular service or program.

Local governments may also take on the role of network lead. When this occurs, it is common

---

Exhibit 10.6

United Way of King County Funding Principles

United Way of King County

The following principles will be used for making funding decisions beginning July 2011.

<u>United Way of King County Funding Principles</u>:

Overall guiding principle: Proposals should be consistent with our mission of *bringing caring people together to give, volunteer, and take action to help people in need and solve our community's toughest challenges.*

1. United Way of King County investments are guided by our donors. As stewards of donor dollars, we match our investments in the community with donor intent.

2. United Way prioritizes three bodies of work: meeting people's basic needs, ending homelessness and getting all children ready to succeed in school.

3. United Way prioritizes support for services to the most vulnerable and underserved people in our community, for example, very low-income families with young children, people experiencing long-term homelessness, older adults struggling to meet basic needs.

4. United Way prioritizes funding for services and programs that address racial disparities. We are intentional about funding organizations that deliver effective, culturally competent services that work to reduce racial disparities.

5. United Way prioritizes support for programs, services and strategies where our investment and involvement leverages other funds, is part of a larger partnership or plays an integral role in the human services system.

6. United Way of King County serves all of King County and we balance funding support across the county as needs arise.

7. United Way considers the impact of funding shifts from the public sector as well as other nonprofit agencies—to the extent that it affects our ability to accomplish our identified goals—when making our funding decisions.

8. United Way funds high-performing agencies. Where there are low-performing or noncompliant agencies, funding will be affected. This can be based on outcome successes, or reporting compliance, material deficiencies or other willful non-compliance.

Additional information for grant applicants:

•   *United Way grants are for amounts of $30,000 or greater. Any exceptions to this guideline will be specified in individual Strategy and Investment Plans.*

•   *United Way sets our grantmaking budget each year based on donor contributions. When and if there is a change in the amount of money available to grant from one year to the next (either positive or negative), <u>United Way will not make across the board adjustments in our investments</u>. Instead United Way will make strategic decisions based on our funding principles.*

Approved by CBC October 2010

Source: United Way of King County (UWKC) 2011. Used with permission. You can also find the funding principles for UWKC (Washington) at www.uwkc.org/ by entering "funding principles" into the website's search bar.

for local governments to decide that they will not backfill reductions in funding to the network. For example, if intergovernmental funds for mental health and drug abuse treatment programs are reduced by the state or federal government, county leaders may set a policy of not using county general fund monies to backfill the gap left by these reductions (e.g., Tims 2011, April 16). It is important for network members to know the assumptions governing the participation of all network providers.

The previous parks and recreation district example demonstrates a well-developed network with substantial resources. But in rural areas, network size and capacity may be limited. Local governments, state agencies, and lead nonprofits may have limited choice in service partners and contractors. Additionally, the available network members may have limited capacity to undertake comprehensive planning or analysis tasks. Under such constrained conditions, policies, plans, and network lead organization behavior must adapt to meet the limits of a partial network.

Community-wide Strategic Planning

The most encompassing type of network governance system is a community-wide strategic plan. Such a plan contains the key elements listed earlier in our discussion of a strategic plan. But instead of focusing on an organization as the unit of analysis, the community strategic plan inventories the strengths and weaknesses of the community as a whole, along with the threats and opportunities in the surrounding environment (SWOT). From this analysis, participants in the process devise a future state for the community and strategies to attain that state. These strategies capture the contributions that will be made by local government bodies, by the private-market sector, and by nonprofit organizations and the voluntary sector. Such plans may commit or ask government to contribute resources and actions toward community goals, in which case the local government budget becomes the tool for providing resources and implementing plan agreements.

Community-wide strategic plans may be the product of a government planning process, or they may follow development of an extended community initiative. Typically, community foundations, lead nonprofit intermediaries, churches, and business organizations work with local governments to develop community plans and initiatives. For example, many communities have developed long-term initiatives and strategies to end homelessness. Initiatives not only set strategies for responding to the need and conditions in a given area but also set expectations for funding contributions over the plan period. Funding levels may not be binding, but they mark a commitment by all of the organizations in the community network. Community plans and agreements provide a set of external expectations to which all signatory organizations are expected to fully respond.

The Role of Elected Officials in Polity Planning and Budgeting

Elected officials can play a key role in successful polity-level planning and budgeting. Knowledgeable and well-briefed elected leaders are in a position to credibly explain decisions that will have an important impact on service delivery partners and contractors. In their outreach role, elected officials often become aware of the larger funding and resource situation in the community. In their role as community leaders and budget process actors, elected officials can help form alliances with other community leaders and use these alliance to identify and consolidate resources from many sources in support of the community-wide polity plan.

SUMMARY

In this chapter, we have focused on the importance of planning as a necessary prelude to successful budgeting. From a departmental, organizational, jurisdictional, and community-wide perspective, considerable planning needs to be undertaken by numerous experts (finance forecasters, auditors, accountants, program managers, capital planners, etc.) in order for public revenues to be effectively and successfully allocated. This allocation process is the point of integration where various kinds of expertise and plans are linked to the needs of the community and to the political preference of citizens, elected officials, and community service providers.

Over the past several decades, the various kinds of organizational, operational, and strategic planning we have discussed in this chapter have increased in significance: Tax limitations and a declining economy continue to constrain revenues and increase the call for allocations that provide taxpayers with the "biggest bang for the buck." We are confident that planning and renewed interest in budget formats will become increasingly more important for those responsible for budgeting at the local levels of government.

As resource constraints at the federal and state levels of government result in tax increases for different population groups and cuts in entitlement programs, local jurisdictions will face increasing pressures to use revenue strategies that leverage resources from community partners and neighboring local jurisdictions. In some cases, these pressures will push communities to create more special service districts that transfer expenses from the general fund to a special levy that funds a target service (i.e., library, parks, special police patrol, fire, water, sewer, street lighting, and so on). Adding new service districts will only add to the urgency for planning and coordination. Some metropolitan areas in the United States already contain as many as 300 governing jurisdictions, hundreds of service providers, and hundreds of businesses that donate funds and volunteer time to the community. What these organizations collectively add up to in terms of aligning resources with the larger needs of the community is not well known in most communities. Whether planning is driven by the need to coordinate resources across an increasingly balkanized community landscape, or whether it is driven by the need to preserve essential government functions, we are confident that planning will continue to carry more weight at the local government level.

We are also confident that there will be renewed interest in budgeting formats as local jurisdictions are pressured by a vigilant citizenry to demonstrate that tax revenues and fees are being used to maximum advantage. In the ensuing chapters, we will turn to an exploration of the four major formats currently in use. Each format was developed at a specific point in time to solve a very practical set of political and administrative problems—problems that resulted from giving too much power and influence to some members of the community at the expense of other democratic priorities. The history of budgeting formats is much like the rest of the history of public budgeting. It is one of balancing the competing goals that need to be equally and successfully met in order to preserve our multiple systems of democratic government.

STUDY QUESTIONS

1. What procedures does your governmental or nonprofit organization use to compile and adopt financial, budgeting, and procurement policies? How do these policies integrate into the budgeting process?
2. Has your organization completed a strategic plan? What is its cycle for updates?
3. What is your organizational mission and goals? How do they guide and focus the annual budgeting process?
4. Does your organization conduct long-term (three to ten years') financial forecasting of revenues, long-term spending commitments, caseloads, and expected expenditures? If not, what resources and commitments would be needed to prepare such forecasts? Attempt an exercise of a simplified version of financial forecasting at the textbook website at www.pdx.edu/cps/budget-book.

5. How does the chief executive of your organization enfold his or her political or administrative agenda into the budget process?
6. Consider the partnerships and networks to which your organization belongs. How would you provide leadership to involve these partners in your organization's budgeting process?
7. What computer software does your organization use for budget preparation? Have you received training in this system? Do you feel that this system is sufficient to support routine budget preparation? To support on-request, specialized analysis?
8. Review a set of budget preparation instructions for your organization. Do these instructions provide a sufficient conceptual framework to structure and guide budget analysis and decision making? Does the preparation calendar provide sufficient time for the staff to respond to and complete each phase of the budget process?
9. How does your organization involve citizens and the public in the budget development and decision process? Does the local political culture and tradition enhance or restrict this participation?
10. How does your organization balance the input of community leaders and organization advocates with citizen and neighborhood input? How does your organization build legitimacy for the budget process and its decisions?

NOTES

1. Spreadsheet programs rely on widely available office productivity software that is an inexpensive, routine investment. Virtually all analysts and public administrators are trained in spreadsheet use, and the spreadsheet layout is familiar to private business professionals and to the public. The widespread use and familiarity of spreadsheets allows expedited training in data entry, routine budget analysis tasks, and custom analysis procedures. Spreadsheets, however, were designed as an individual productivity tool (Kavanagh et al. 2006, 10); still, budget development and assembly requires an organizational collaborative process of reviews by multiple parties. Complex and linked spreadsheets are difficult to secure and transfer safely among staff and administrators. Spreadsheets are also limited in their ability to manage text and to produce extended pages of budget detail. Furthermore, they tend to lack advanced statistical procedures to support revenue and expense forecasting (Kavanagh and Ruggini 2006).

Larger budgeting and financial systems present the only real alternative for medium and large governments. These larger systems were first developed for corporate use, and early adaptions of such systems to public-sector use often resulted in well-publicized failures (Beal and Prabhakar 2011). Beal and Prabhakar (298–301) note that system vendors and designers failed to fully appreciate the role of the public budget in defining organizational spending; the importance of the extended budget process, incremental budgeting, numerous and variable revenue sources, and the use of separate capital budgets; and the need for budget controls to manage spending over the course of the fiscal year. Nor did vendors understand the unique financial, political, organizational, and budget process needs of public-sector budgeting. By 2010, vendors had begun to respond to public-sector needs and to develop more effective software (Beal and Prabhakar 2011, 296).

2. Following the development and installation of a new system, several steps are required to assure that it will be useful and dependable. First, the new system must undergo extensive testing to validate its processes and outputs. This may require running both the existing system and the new system in parallel for the testing period. Second, system implementation is a major procurement step. This step involves introducing the new system to the organization, training the staff in its use, debugging and resolving errors and shortcomings, and building staff confidence in the system and its capabilities. An effective IT procurement contract must include time and attention to these needs from both the vendor and the government. Full implementation of a new finance and budgeting system may take several years and budget cycles. Elected officials can help this procurement and installation process by ensuring political support, consistent funding, and strategic project oversight. Continuity from elected officials across election cycles is especially important.

3. For a well-developed state-level example, see the Washington State Caseload Forecast Council at www.cfc.wa.gov.

PART III

EXPENDITURE FORMATS FOR DECISION AND CONTROL

A NEW MAYOR MANDATES PERFORMANCE-BASED BUDGETING

CASE NARRATIVE

The newly elected mayor of the City of Upper Cascadia was holding his first formal press conference after campaigning on a platform to "make government more efficient." Now, three weeks after the November election, everyone was anxious to hear what the new mayor had in mind, especially the career administrators who had heard this kind of campaign sloganeering repeatedly over the past several decades. The mayor would assume his new role in January, but he had already gathered a transition staff that was making plans to "hit the ground running," and had received a promise of complete support from the outgoing term-limited mayor to make the transition as smooth as possible.

There were a couple of highlights of the press conference that had important implications for those involved with the budgeting process and its decisions. First, the mayor announced the creation of a blue ribbon Advisory Committee on Performance Innovations, consisting of prominent community and business leaders who would serve as a sounding board for innovative ideas that could improve government performance. Second, the mayor announced the appointment of Spiro Augustine as his director of budget and finance. A former chief of finance for one of the largest regional health organizations, Augustine had developed a national reputation for successfully introducing performance-based assessment approaches into health care organizations—and the payoffs in increased efficiency, reduced costs, and improved effectiveness were remarkable. For example, he had saved his organization millions of dollars by evaluating administrative transaction costs, which resulted in the elimination of unnecessary steps in the patient billing and tracking processes. He had undertaken an analysis of insurance billing practices, discovering new ways of tracking, billing, and collecting payments in a more timely fashion. In addition, he had introduced a patient-centered assessment process that reduced the number of unnecessary medical procedures and cut costs without having negative consequences on patient health.

The social service advocates in the press conference audience grimaced in fear as the mayor introduced the new budget director. Social services for youth, the elderly, and the disadvantaged and disabled residents of the city never penciled out well on a strict cost versus benefit basis. The inability to demonstrate the intangibles of social service outcomes would surely cause the elimination of entire social service programs in favor of city programs with easily measurable outputs. Aggressive performance budgeting would likely result in lower contract payment rates for the same level of service outputs. City contractors delivering social services were already running on slim margins after six years of declining budgets. The advocates whispered among themselves that they would oppose the performance budgeting initiative and sandbag it to death in the city council and bureaucracy.

What caught the attention of those responsible for the city's budgeting process was Augustine's announcement that after consulting with the Advisory Committee on Performance

Innovations, he was introducing performance-based budgeting for the first time in the city of Upper Cascadia. In the weeks ahead, he would be meeting with department heads to discuss a strategy for having such a system in place to develop the budget for the next fiscal year. It was now late November, and the process of building the budget for approval for the next fiscal year would begin in January, with the requirement that the city of have a council-approved budget by June 30 (only six months after assuming office). Director Augustine announced that he would appoint an internal steering committee consisting of one representative from each of the five major general fund city departments, one representative from an enterprise fund department (either water or sewer), and two representatives appointed by the mayor but recommended by the more than 16 active neighborhood associations in the city. Augustine would serve as the chair of the steering committee.

Those who were responsible for preparing the city's budget at the department and program levels were unclear what the implications of Augustine's announcement might be for their work over the next six months. There were four issue areas that gave them pause: First, how would this new approach work alongside the current system that relied on line-item, object code budgeting that was tied to decision packages? State law required line-item based budgeting and financial reporting. Any new performance based budgeting system would have to crosswalk back to the old line-item object codes.

It had been common practice over the past several years for departments to be given a total revenue target that almost always was less than what was needed to fund programs at their current service level. So the central budget office directed departments to cut their base budgets by a fixed percent and then requested them to build their budgets back up to the current service level with discrete decision packages that had costs identified by line-items (i.e., personnel, materials and supplies, capital outlay, etc.). This modified zero-base approach had kept the budget within the constraints of resources but had also introduced some discretion for the department directors and elected council members to make certain choices on the reallocation of resources to better align with their policy priorities. But the truth of the matter was that this discretion constituted less than 10 percent of the total budget: The directive from the central budget office had been to cut back department and program base budgets from the current fiscal year by 6 to 8 percent and then add back decision packages to bring the programs and departments back up to 100 percent of the current base budget. The problem with this approach is that it did not include inflationary cost increases (e.g., medical insurance, retirement premiums, union wage agreements, fuel costs, and the like). Because the city had been using the principle of base budget rather than the principle of current service level budget, there had been a consistent absolute decline in service levels for most departments across the city for at least six years. This approach had led to some positive cost-saving results. Several departments and programs had reconfigured their organization structure and turned to contracted service delivery to lower their operating costs. But multiyear revenue forecasts assumed a continuous, slow decline in revenues, while operational plans called for maintaining the same level of service output. This imbalance implied shrinking programs in future years. Department budget analysts and program managers could only envision performance budgeting as a tool for program reduction and elimination.

A second set of questions gave the steering committee pause. How could a performance approach be applied in an evenhanded fashion across the wide variety of services provided by the city and to the quite different circumstances faced by the various departments and programs? Overall, 20 percent of Upper Cascadia's budget comes from nondiscretionary sources, which includes grants and donations; contract revenues; interagency service agreements and purchases from another city bureau; revenues from services provided to the public for which there is a charge or fee; and internal service charges, which recover from other funds the cost of services provided by central administrative bureaus. Some units like water, sewer, and the planning department are entirely dependent on fee for service. These departments are held to a strict cost-of-service standard that requires them to justify their fees by carefully tracking and documenting the cost of delivering the service. Electrical, plumbing, and other inspection services are handled in this way, as are the charges to customers for water and sewer services. Performance metrics are already in place and benchmarked against similar services offered by comparable units of government around the United States. There are other departments, like transportation and social service programs, that rely on pass-through grants and allocations based on formulas and performance metrics that are a necessary part of the grant application and reporting process. Still other departments are relying increasingly on contracting out for services, which have performance and accountability standards built into the contracting process. Performance metrics on building safety, accounting and financial practices, auditing, and similar kinds of professional-centered work is governed by national professional associations to which the city deferred as the seal of approval for ensuring compliance with credible and acceptable performance standards.

In addition to the performance metrics that are currently in place, Upper Cascadia's independently elected auditor undertakes an annual Services Efforts and Accomplishments Report (chapter 18) that compares the performance of the fire, police, parks, transportation, water, and sewer bureaus on the basis of 5 to 7 measures. All in all, performance measurement in Upper Cascadia is a patchwork of different systems and standards that, taken together, seem to be working in maintaining accountability.

Third, the investment in data collection, information technology, and software needed to support a new performance budgeting initiative was unclear. The current budgeting software used line-item object codes at the program level as the unit of analysis. The object codes served as the basis of budget computations and accounting fund balances. In contrast, true performance budgeting would require activity centered costs as the unit of budget analysis. Activity centered costs would result in refined cost information more specific than simple average unit costs. The data needed for true performance budgeting was unavailable and would take time and money to gather and accrue. Procuring and installing costly new budgeting software would take additional time. The inadequacy of the current budgeting software raised the issue of whether cost analysis and performance management should be a system separate from the annual budgeting system. Steering committee discussions suggested that a new cost and performance management system should contribute to, but should not necessarily replace, the current budgeting system.

Finally, there was a question of how this new performance initiative would align with the city's commission structure of governance. The commission form unites the legislative and executive functions, rather than separating them into distinctly independent governing bodies. It does so by providing for mayoral appointment of city councilors to oversee a portfolio of bureaus, much like a parliamentary system in which cabinet ministers are appointed from parliament by the prime minister to provide executive oversight of the functional operations of the government. In Upper Cascadia, commissioners run for office without such portfolios, which are assigned by the mayor after their election. The appointment power of the mayor under the city charter to make bureau assignments is supplemented by the power to prepare and present the annual budget to the commission for adoption. In theory, these two powers are significant and distinguish Upper Cascadia's commission form of government from other commission systems, where these powers do not exist at the mayoral level. In practice, however, the dynamics of individually elected commissioners requires the mayor to gingerly exercise his special legal powers over the budget and bureau assignments in order to ensure the three votes needed to support his agenda. The need to maintain a voting majority makes the relationship among the commissioners an ongoing dance that depends not only on the personality of the commissioners but on the background music in the dancehall. The mayor, the four commissioners, and the auditor comprise the city's six elected officials. The mayor and the four commissioners together make up the city council, all of whom have an equal vote. All officials are elected at large on a nonpartisan basis and serve four-year terms. Elections are staggered, with the mayor and commissioners numbered 1 and 4 elected one year, and the auditor and commissioners numbered 2 and 3 elected two years later. The staggered election schedule avoids a complete change of elected officials in any one year, except under unusual circumstances.

It is common practice during Upper Cascadia's annual budget deliberations for the mayor to reclaim administrative oversight authority over all the bureaus, thus leaving the four commissioners without any executive responsibilities. During this process, the commission functions mainly as a deliberative body, with the exception of the mayor, who holds all of the executive functions but only 20 percent of the deliberative control. This practice during the annual budget process is believed to encourage commissioners to act in the larger interest of the city as a whole, rather than merely serving as advocates for their respective bureaus. Since the mayor can redistribute bureau responsibilities differently after the budget process has been completed, the mayor's power during the budget process can be singularly important. But there have been instances over Upper Cascadia's recent history in which the potential power of the mayor has been nullified by three members of the council who have formed an alliance to take control of the budget process, thus altering the priorities and the processes put forth by the mayor.

An important change was made to Upper Cascadia's structure of government in 2000, when the council passed an ordinance creating the position of chief administrative officer (CAO). The CAO reports to the mayor and has statutory authority over the Office of Management and Finance. This statutory power has enhanced the mayor's ability to develop a unified approach to budget planning and execution. In addition to the disproportionate executive authority exercised by the mayor through the CAO during the budget process, the mayor retains the right to oversee all of the administrative operations that are executive in nature (e.g., government relations, human resource management, planning, emergency management), as well as the police and economic development bureaus.

Misinformation, uncertainty, and a degree of fear over the four issue areas made performance accountability and budgeting considerably problematic for the mayor, Director Augustine, and the city council. Over the months following the press conference, the internal steering committee of department heads met on a weekly basis and narrowed the issues down to the following three questions, over which there was considerable disagreement.

Issue 1

Performance accountability should not be a central goal of the budgeting process. This confuses the purpose of the budgeting process with the purpose of a performance management system. The purpose of the budget process is to allocate scarce resources in the most equitable and peaceful manner possible. The existing system has met this test very well, weathering continual declines in resources while still maintaining high levels of employee morale and acceptable levels of service. Upper Cascadia already has multiple systems of accountability in place, both internally and externally, to ensure that the city is managing its resources efficiently, effectively, and responsively. Using this argument, department heads and program managers made two arguments. First, performance budgeting should be used only in those cases where there are no existing performance accountability standards in place. Second, performance measurement should be viewed as a management issue, not the basis upon which to allocate the budget. Managers always need good performance systems, and the management structure of the organization—not the budget system—should be used to ensure management accountability.

Director Augustine listened with care but found these arguments all too familiar. He had heard the same story from managers in the health care system over the course of his career. He knew from his experience that management performance systems are driven by human resource principles and legal requirements, which have never been sufficient to focus attention on the allocation of scarce resources to achieve the highest benefit. He believed that "managers do what you measure," and tended to discount the idea that a management system "measures what managers do." He knew there was an underlying philosophical difference that no amount of argument was likely to change.

Issue 2

The second set of questions identified by the internal steering committee focused on the strategy for implementing performance-based budgeting. There was general agreement that such a system could not be put into place for all departments and used as the basis for budget development by the June 30 start to the next fiscal year. Some members argued that the system should be phased in over a three-year period by having approximately one-third of the departments convert to the system each year for the next three years. They argued that the first group of departments making the transition should be those with well-developed performance metrics already in place. These departments and programs would just need to focus on connecting their existing metrics to the budget allocation process. Others argued that this was not as easy as it seemed, even for the departments and programs that had well-developed performance measures. For example, while there was much transactional performance information (e.g., number of road miles paved, the response time to 911 calls, the satisfaction of citizens with various kinds of services, the amount of infrastructure considered up to standard, etc.), these measures were not easily usable for budget allocation purposes. For instance, just because 911 calls are up doesn't mean that more money should be allocated to the emergency call system in the next fiscal year. In the first place, we don't know why calls are up, and, even if we did, we do not know if allocating more money to 911 is a better investment of public resources than allocating funds to bring parks and recreation infrastructure up to standard.

All of these issues raised the more fundamental question of what performance measures are supposed to contribute to budget allocation. How are the purposes of budget-related performance measures different from other performance measures? These concerns led many on the steering committee to argue that if performance budgeting is to be adopted, it requires a three-year period of implementation: one year to develop appropriate measures, a second year to test their adequacy and appropriateness, and a third year to tie the measures to the budget allocation process.

Again, Director Augustine listened with care in an attempt to understand which of the alternative strategies made the most sense. In his experience, performance measurement preparation and its use ultimately depend on the knowledge of program managers at the operating level of the organization. Not one of these managers was represented at the table, so he was not confident that he was getting access to the sources of information that counted most to help him understand the best strategy for implementing his initiative.

Issue 3

A third set of questions surrounding performance-based budgeting was the use of measures to penalize programs and their managers for things outside their control. For example, performance can decline because of external conditions in the economy, the diversion of resources to address stakeholder concerns, or taking advantage of a window of opportunity to partner with other jurisdictions—all of which slows down a "management-by-objective" driven process that achieves high levels of performance. What incentives do managers have to participate in a long-term and time-consuming process of developing a performance-based budgeting system for their work unit when they are already overstressed and understaffed?

> Director Augustine knew the value of sincerity and patience when facing an audience threatened by a potential alteration to the status quo. This certainly seemed to be the case in his work with members of the steering committee. Leaders were ultimately unwilling to commit themselves to getting ownership of the process at the level where it was needed in the organization—at the program operational level. In his previous experience, this ownership had been accomplished by using promotions and bonuses to recognize and reward innovative achievements of individual managers who were willing to take the initiative and to use their discretion to "make things happen." But the director knew that reliance on such incentives was not easily accomplished in the public sector. And he also knew that the commission form of government provided many opportunities to use process to "stonewall" and delay implementation of certain initiatives. For these reasons, Director Augustine had deliberately used the neighborhood associations as the vehicle for getting ownership in the performance-based budging initiative at the grassroots level. He believed that this strategy could be used to bring program managers on board. From his experience, he knew that performance budgeting is most successful when managers at the operating level of the organization see how it can be used to strengthen their political base with their clients, customers, and stakeholders. This was his ultimate goal.

After another month of weekly internal steering committee meetings, Director Augustine received a phone call from the mayor. The social service advocates had gained the support of three city councilors who were threatening to kill the performance budgeting initiative. The mayor wanted Augustine to meet with the advocates within the week. Somehow, he and the mayor would need to assuage the advocates' fears, and Augustine would need to demonstrate clearly and convincingly how performance accountability and performance budgeting could result in better service to the city's disadvantaged residents. The director would need to demonstrate that performance budgeting would support a viable network of nonprofit service providers and volunteer partners. Augustine had to turn the advocates around or the initiative and the mayor's vision would die. He cleared a workspace on his desk and began to organize his presentation for the meeting.

CASE ANALYSIS

This case illustrates a common debate that is held periodically by local government jurisdictions regarding what kind of budgeting formats are best suited to achieve their goals. As we observed in chapter 3, the purposes of the public budgeting process are numerous and include:

- Effectiveness: Successfully achieving policy/program goals and objectives
- Efficiency: Achieving a high benefit to cost ratio in the use of public resources
- Economic development: Stimulating the local economy
- Responsiveness: Building and maintaining political support
- Equity and fairness: Providing services and programs to those in need
- Political consensus: Producing a budget that citizens can "live with"
- Community governance: Communicating and linking with community providers and partners

These purposes can never be achieved equally through the budgeting process. The process nevertheless becomes an annual focal point for bringing these contested purposes together with the goal of reaching sufficient agreement so that the debate can continue with goodwill into the future. The choice of a budget format becomes an important part of this debate, since it creates the decision rules and "what counts for evidence" in deciding how to allocate public resources.

In this case, you witness these contested purposes: department directors who want to protect their already overburdened staff and organizational capacity from initiatives that may require lots of time and resources but also may produce an uncertain end, change agents who want to create the space for innovation and to stir the imagination to use this space for more productive ways of "doing the public's business," advocacy groups who are fearful of change and of losing the meager resources they currently receive, elected officials who want to find ways of building the trust and confidence of citizens in their systems of government, and career administrators who want to maximize the allocation of resources in a scarce resource environment to provide the most essential public service in the most effective manner possible. These competing purposes come into contention within the context of a specific structure of governance and local history that shapes what is possible.

The new finance director, Spiro Augustine, must find his way through these multiple and competing goals of the budgeting process—and do so in ways that take into account the structure of government and the expectations of local institutions. The director must use his knowledge of these issues to craft a way forward that will assuage the worst fears of his opponents and enlist the support of his most enthusiastic supporters. What would you recommend to accomplish these goals? As you ponder your recommendation, consider the following questions:

- What arguments and commitments should Director Augustine make to alleviate the social service advocates' concerns?
- In what ways do you think the governance structure should affect Director Augustine's strategy to develop and implement a performance-based budgeting system? What particular characteristics of the system are especially important to take into consideration in the development of his strategy?
- What weight should Director Augustine place on the concerns of the department heads who are serving on the internal steering committee? What control (both direct and indirect) does he have over them?
- How should the director use the mayor's blue ribbon committee to support his efforts?
- How might the director use the neighborhood associations to support his efforts?
- To what extent should the director separate his concern for developing a performance-based governance system from the budgeting process? How much should he shift the weight of his performance concerns from the budgeting system to the management system?
- What kind of phased approach would you recommend for implementing a performance-based budgeting system?
- What does a performance-based budgeting system achieve that can't be achieved by other budgeting formats such as line-item budgeting (expenditure controls), program budgeting (effectiveness), and zero-base budgeting (innovation)?

PART III INTRODUCTION

EXPENDITURE FORMATS FOR DECISION AND CONTROL

For the forms of budgeting, let fools contest,
That which is best administered is best.

(Morgan and Robinson 2000, 58)

In a democratic society, the division of resources between the public and private sectors
is roughly determined by the desires of the electorate. But because it is such a complex
and time-consuming task to acquire adequate political information, the electorate is
chronically ignorant. . . . This ignorance causes governments to enact budgets smaller
than the ones they would enact if the electorate possessed complete information. . . . The
resulting misallocation of resources becomes more and more serious as the economy
grows more complex.

(Anthony Downs 1960, 76)

To paraphrase an old line from the poet Alexander Pope, one might argue that budget formats themselves, like the various forms of government, are less important than how well they are administered. But an important difference exists between budgeting formats and the forms of government: Formats not only establish the structural rules by which the budgeting process is carried out (the decision rules) but also create the standards by which success is measured (rules of evidence). Because budgeting formats create both decision rules and rules of evidence, it is hard to separate the form from the content.

When we speak of budgeting formats, we are talking about the conceptual perspective taken on the budget task and issues, the kinds of questions that are asked during the process, the way in which budgeting information is structured, and the kind of information that is required to justify budget requests. These issues extend the discussion developed in chapter 10. Budget format selection and implementation contribute a major element of the conceptual framework that supports a budget. For purposes of discussion in Part III of this book, we will focus on line-item budgeting, program budgeting (planning, programming, budgeting system [PPBS]), performance budgeting, and zero-base budgeting (ZBB) as distinctly separate formats. In practice, most governmental jurisdictions make use of several of these formats as part of their process. Most nonprofit organizations rely heavily on line-item budgeting, reflecting private-sector accounting practices and tax reporting requirements. However, government contracting requirements are pulling many service delivery nonprofits toward performance measurement, cost reporting, and ultimately performance budgeting. And increasingly, constrained resources are pulling all levels of government in the same direction.

Historically, the evolution of public budgeting formats is the story of ongoing efforts "to speak truth to power" (Wildavsky 1979a). Aaron Wildavsky argued that the development of new budget formats reflects a common and persistent attempt to discipline the forces of interest group politics by subjecting them to the systematic gathering and analysis of information (1979). The goal of this disciplined analysis is to raise questions that normally do not get asked when interest groups lobby for allocation of money to support their favorite activities. As examples: Are we spending the taxpayers' money efficiently? What are we accomplishing with the money we are spending? Should we be spending the taxpayers' money on different programs that do a better job of promoting the public interest? These are the central questions that performance, program, and zero-base budgeting formats respectively seek to raise and answer. In short, budgeting formats should be viewed as a way of structuring the conversations during the budget-making process to encourage participants to address the "right questions." Our review of these budgeting formats will focus on how information is collected, organized, and used to answer the different "right questions" that people believe should be addressed during the budget development and decision processes.

Because budgeting formats are about information collection and communication to all of the participants and stakeholders in the budgeting process, they play an important role in educating citizens, clients, donors, and customers, and in building trust and maintaining legitimacy. Formats provide an opportunity to directly address the problem identified by Anthony Downs in the introductory quotation to this section. Because citizens lack knowledge of what is in the budget and what purposes the money is accomplishing, they end up supporting a smaller budget than would be the case if they had greater knowledge. Mastering the informational and educational opportunities offered by each budget format helps participants to systematically overcome this problem.

As you review the origins, purposes, strengths, and weaknesses of various budget formats in the chapters that follow, it is worth keeping in mind the three central questions that have been raised earlier in chapters 3 through 5:

1. How do the different budgeting formats define and reinforce the purposes of the public budget (chapter 3)?
2. How do the different budget formats define and reinforce the roles given to various actors in the budgeting process (chapter 4)?
3. How well does each format deal with the uncertainties, ambiguity, and the potentials for conflict that are inherent in the budgeting cycle (chapter 5)?

BUDGET FORMATS AND PURPOSES

As we observed in chapter 3, the budget process seeks to reconcile a multiple set of purposes. The process is partly a matter of collecting good technical information and using it to make data-based decisions that succeed in balancing expenditures with available resources. It is also a matter of (1) making the best use of existing resources to achieve a set of strategic goals to promote the public good in the community and polity; (2) mobilizing political influence and using it to pressure decision makers to address citizen and societal needs; and (3) influencing economic growth and the kinds of development deemed to be in the best interest of the community. How do we strike a balance in the public budgeting process among all of these purposes? How do we balance the need for high levels of technical expertise and the need for public responsiveness and accountability? Budgeting formats play a central if not decisive role in answering these two questions.

BUDGET FORMATS AND ROLE RESPONSIBILITIES

As we observed in chapter 4, budget decisions and products move from one set of actors to the next, building the agreement necessary to proceed through the next stage of the process. Participants at each stage have an opportunity to use their authority to pursue the goals that are important to their assigned role. For most agency divisions and programs, the budget process provides the opportunity to obtain the critical resources necessary to provide services to clients. For CEOs, CFOs, and their central budget office and management divisions, policy priorities and the fiscal integrity of the organization or jurisdiction's budget are of the highest priority. For council and board members and elected legislators, managing the strategic role of the organization and meeting constituent needs are the highest priorities.

As we noted in chapter 4, many actors find themselves playing several roles. For example, budget analysts in the central budget office of larger jurisdictions and organizations review unit budget requests with two questions in mind. First, does the budget request make good fiscal sense? The concern for fiscal integrity requires budget analysts to critically examine unit budgets for both internal consistency and historical patterns of change over time. Second, and equally important, is the concern that the request meets the chief executive's policy priorities. The budget requests by unit and program managers are especially important from a policy point of view. The review of these budget requests by the central budget office is the point of greatest leverage from which the chief executive office can obtain policy compliance from agency and program heads. Once the executive's review is complete, the budget office analyst then defends the unit and program requests as elements of the executive's proposed budget to the legislative body. The analyst first plays the role of critic and then turns to play the role of advocate. The budget format defines how and what the analyst emphasizes in his or her critical review and advocacy.

The roles of various participants in the budget process require different kinds of information, thus making some budget formats more valuable than others. For example, those preparing budget requests at the individual program level are focused primarily on meeting clients' needs and demonstrating results. Those in the middle of the organization responsible for managing multiple programs are interested in information that helps them decide how to allocate scare resources. For these participants, efficiency and effectiveness information may be more important than client satisfaction, the number of clients served and/or unmet needs, which tend to be the focus of those providing direct service. At the top of the organization, central office administrators want information that helps them address concerns that citizen advisory board members and elected officials may have, which frequently take the form of success or failure stories told from the perspective of the client, voter, or constituent. And these CEOs also may want information that demonstrates to taxpayers and donors that they are getting a very good return on their investment. Financial and procurement administrators who have responsibility for monitoring spending rates and authority want detailed information by amount and kinds of spending. These differences in the kinds of information vital to performing the various roles in the budgeting process make it difficult for a single format to satisfy everyone's needs. That is why in practice many organizations use a combination of formats. As you read the following chapters in this section, keep this in mind and ask yourself, Which combination of formats are needed to serve my organization or to serve the roles of the various participants in the budgeting process?

BUDGET FORMATS AND UNCERTAINTY, AMBIGUITY, AND POTENTIAL FOR CONFLICT

We explained in chapter 5, while the budget process provides a relatively predictable flow of events, uncertainty exists throughout the process. This uncertainty often translates into seemingly unpredictable or inexplicable behavior by the actors at various stages of the process. At a technical level, uncertainty surrounds the state of the economy and the potential generation of the revenues that support budget spending. Uncertainty also surrounds the actual needs of constituents and program recipients. Political pressure from the legislative leadership, constituents, and interest groups introduces uncertainty into the behavior of legislators. Tense relationships at the state level between the governor and the legislature may introduce an additional element of uncertainty into the development and adoption of an annual or biennial budget. For nonprofits, there is the constant uncertainty of knowing they have more needs to meet than revenue, that contracts may be reduced or not renewed, and that donors may not come through to make up the differences between expenditures and needed income.

One of the consequences of this conflict, uncertainty, and ambiguity for the process as a whole is that it predisposes the participants to *satisfice* (i.e., to make sufficient allocation decisions that minimally meet multiple requests or needs), to focus on small changes from year to year, and to emphasize dollars rather than programs or performance because dollars can be divided in more finite ways than can programs or performance. These pressures for greater flexibility increase as one moves up through the budget process and outward toward constituency interests and elected officials. For example, since elected officials frequently experience multiple and conflicting pressures, they are more inclined to want as much discretion as possible in dividing up the budgetary pie. This contrasts with a more performance- and program-based focus of career administrators and the target clientele they serve. The central budget office is caught in the middle, usually with the need to find ways of cutting back on agency and department requests in order to present a balanced budget for review by the legislative body or board of directors. In short, conditions of uncertainty, conflict, and ambiguity create a common motivation to preserve maximum discretionary authority at each level of the process. Program managers want discretion to adjust programs and service levels to best meet clientele needs; central budget office managers want discretion to adjust the budget to achieve the maximum policy priorities of the chief executive; and legislators want discretion to adjust the budget to meet constituency interests. As you read each of the chapters on budget formats, keep this concern for discretion in mind and ask which combination of formats best meets these varying needs.

The democratic balancewheel model outlined in chapter 2 serves as the central framework for this section on budget formats. Career administrators play a critical role in balancing the competing claims of efficiency, effectiveness, equity, fiscal accountability—in short, all of the claims about what is in the public interest that come into play during the budgeting process. As we shall see in the chapters that follow, public budgeting formats are not about esoteric techniques, knowledge, and numerical calculations. As we argue throughout the book, public budgeting is really about how to balance competing democratic values and the appropriate amalgam of participation, expertise, and decision-making processes in order to best achieve the larger public interest. We hope to demonstrate this point once again in our discussion of budget formats.

11 LINE-ITEM (OBJECT CODE) BUDGETING

Putting objectives first, alternatives second and choices third is inefficient as a method of calculation, ineffective in relating thought to action and inappropriate as a design for learning. . . . The [line-item] approach is more efficient for resolving conflicts . . . because . . . it does not require its practitioners to discover all or most possible conflicts and to work out answers to problems that may never materialize.

(Aaron Wildavsky 1979b, v, 166–167.)

Line-item budgeting presents little useful information to decision makers on the functions and activities of organizational units. Because this budget presents proposed expenditure amounts only by category, the justifications for such expenditures are not explicit and are often not intuitive. In addition, it may invite micromanagement by administrators and governing boards as they attempt to manage operations with little or no performance information.

(National Center for Educational Research 2009)

The **line-item budget** is the most widely used of all budget formats. It is used even when other formats have been put into place to correct for its deficiencies. It is celebrated, as Wildavsky observes, for its flexibility in allocating scarce resources and for its ability to quickly adapt to changing circumstances. It is also highly valued for its capacity to facilitate one of the major purposes of democratic governance—namely, to resolve conflict peacefully. But it is simultaneously criticized for continuing with the status quo without any supporting justification and neglecting questions of efficiency, effectiveness, and reexamination of budget priorities. In this chapter, we will see why both points of view are correct and demonstrate the conflicting needs that successful democratic government must strive to accommodate.

Line-item budgeting is technically known as **object code** or **expenditure code budgeting**. A typical example of a line-item schedule for a county department of assessment and taxation is provided in Exhibit 11.1.

The example illustrates clearly how line-item budgeting breaks expenditures down into major categories that include personnel/personal services, materials and supplies, capital outlay, and interfund/interdepartmental expenditures. Within each of these major categories, expenditures are further broken down into as many refined object codes as a jurisdiction wishes or is allowed to create under local budgeting law or organizational rules. Each separate budget unit within the organization is also assigned a unit identifier number (e.g., Exhibit 11.1 top, 161 code for the Assessment and Taxation Department). Subordinate units are nested within their parent units, but the units at all levels use the same object codes. This allows the aggregation of expenditures from subordinate units into a total level for the parent unit. The object code categories remain consistent throughout the organization and the jurisdiction, thus ensuring uniformity of practices and the ability to quickly see by the code number what part of the organization to charge each expense that is incurred. To further ensure this uniformity and consistency in accounting practices, the organization or jurisdiction maintains a master list of object code numbers and definitions

Exhibit 11.1

Example County Line-Item Budget Worksheet

Upper Cascadia County
Line-Item Budget Worksheet
Organization Unit—Expenditure

161   ASSESSMENT & TAXATION

Object Code	Description	FY1 Actual	FY2 Actual	FY3 Actual	FY4 Actual	FY5 Adopted	FY6 Requested
	Personnel (Personal) Services						
51105	Wages and salaries	$3,565,656	$3,561,447	$3,692,131	$3,866,152	$4,187,195	
51110	Temporary salaries	$164,327	$174,625	$116,446	$229,667	$150,622	
51115	Overtime and other pay	$28,843	$26,861	$21,696	$35,764	$113,680	
51125	FICA	$285,205	$285,478	$290,498	$313,846	$330,929	
51130	Workers compensation	$30,505	$34,099	$47,461	$45,941	$47,515	
51135	Employer paid work day tax	$2,781	$2,697	$2,626	$2,611	$2,935	
51140	PERS contribution	$421,613	$466,875	$390,590	$586,355	$675,005	
51141	PERS reserve	$0	$111,628	$219,505	$581	$0	
51150	Health insurance	$622,564	$649,759	$793,040	$783,232	$884,976	
51155	Life and long-term disability insurance	$10,551	$4,702	$4,694	$4,854	$5,449	
51160	Unemployment insurance	$8,876	$7,720	$8,258	$18,939	$18,933	
51165	Metro Transit District employee tax	$21,006	$21,099	$21,752	$23,764	$27,391	
51175	Automobile allowance	$4,296	$4,331	$3,621	$6,212	$0	
51180	Other employee allowances	$1,305	$1,310	$1,160	$57	$1,482	
51199	Miscellaneous personal services	$1,045	$0	$0	$0	$184,540	
	Personnel Services Total	$5,168,573	$5,352,631	$5,613,478	$5,917,975	$6,630,652	
	Materials and Supplies						
51205	Supplies—office, general	$21,710	$25,917	$14,277	$17,146	$37,397	
51210	Supplies—general	$0	$0	$1,945	$0	$0	
51220	Supplies—food	$0	$282	$0	$0	$0	
51270	Postage and freight	$44,986	$44,586	$44,435	$44,662	$63,670	
51275	Books, subscriptions, and publications	$7,916	$9,574	$10,017	$10,487	$12,568	
51280	**Services—contract, government**	$16,440	$17,644	$18,271	$52,849	$59,897	
51285	**Services—professional services**	$67,644	$57,409	$62,431	$64,446	$79,430	
51295	Advertising and public notice	$1,814	$1,293	$1,563	$1,440	$4,200	

Code		Col1	Col2	Col3	Col4	Col5
51300	Printing and duplicating	$30,304	$45,416	$29,756	$40,335	$184,058
51310	Utilities	$1,685	$168	$0	$0	$0
51320	Repair & maint. services—general	$8,564	$11,798	$5,348	$7,868	$41,977
51340	Lease and rentals—space	$8,568	$2,142	$0	$0	$603
51345	Lease and rentals—equipment	$0	$0	$0	$0	$0
51350	Dues and membership	$685	$843	$1,618	$2,197	$2,025
51355	Training and education	$11,439	$8,515	$11,006	$14,461	$28,580
51360	Travel expense	$5,050	$5,063	$7,245	$14,770	$34,774
51365	Private mileage	$41,576	$39,474	$39,181	$42,523	$53,879
51460	Office supplies—**Internal**	$21,121	$25,941	$24,376	$26,089	$28,891
51465	Postage and freight—**Internal**	$154,261	$118,766	$110,127	$117,936	$139,185
51470	Mail messenger services—**Internal**	$16,576	$17,292	$18,422	$20,102	$19,392
51475	Printing—**Internal**	$12,569	$11,963	$9,542	$7,841	$18,366
51480	Photocopy machine—**Internal**	$15,286	$15,896	$15,230	$13,807	$17,047
51495	Telephone monthly—**Internal**	$26,013	$29,952	$27,533	$24,270	$23,287
51500	Telephone long-distance—**Internal**	$1,039	$0	$0	$0	$0
51505	Telecom equipment install—**Internal**	$1,028	$210	$0	$382	$0
51510	Telecom Cellular Air Time—**Internal**	$375	$354	$172	$0	$0
51520	Facilities charges—**Internal**	$5,454	($4,878)	$4,287	$4,323	$4,315
51525	Fleet—**Internal** (noncapital)	$4,915	$4,206	$3,342	$4,527	$5,842
51555	Inventory issued default account	$0	$0	$0	$1,637	$0
	Materials and Supplies Total	$527,018	$489,544	$426,359	$505,787	$833,726
	Capital Outlay					
57115	Machinery and equipment	$0	$0	$0	$6,120	$46,000
57120	Vehicles	$0	$17,129	$61,466	$346	$0
57155	Computer equipment	$0	$21,634	$0	$99,962	$0
	Capital Outlay Total	$0	$38,763	$61,466	$106,428	$46,000
	Other Expenses					
52005	Bank service charge	$60	$800	$0	$144	$2,780
	Other Expenses Total	$60	$800	$0	$144	$2,780
	Interfund (Interdepartmental) Expenses					
53040	Facilities	$5,674	$2,129	$151	$0	$560
53055	General charges	($4)	$0	$0	$0	$165
53505	General charges—other	$4	$5,727	$221	$153	$0
53530	ITS charges	$0	$0	$0	$0	$0
	Interfund (Interdepartmental) Expenses Total	$5,674	$7,856	$372	$153	$725
161	**ASSESSMENT & TAXATION TOTAL**	$5,701,325	$5,889,594	$6,133,495	$6,559,080	$7,541,485

Exhibit 11.2

Example Department Budget Detail

Professional Class	Position Title/Grade	FTEs
375	Cartographic and Recording Manager	1.0
373	Senior Cartographer	1.0
372	Cartographer II	4.0
371	Senior Administrative Specialist	4.0
358	Director	1.0
357	Appraisal Division Manager	1.0
356	Administrative Division Manager	1.0
355	Tax Collection Supervisor	1.0
354	Appraisal Supervisor	3.0
353	Appraisal Data Analyst	1.0
352	Senior Appraiser	3.0
351	Appraiser II	24.0
350	Appraiser I	0.0
349	Appraisal Assistant	1.0
348	Personal Property Tax Collector	1.0
053	GIS Specialist	1.0
028	Senior Management Analyst	0.5
026	Management Analyst	1.0
011	Delivery Clerk	1.0
010	Data Control Coordinator	1.0
009	Data Entry Operator	1.0
008	Support Unit Supervisor	2.0
005	Accounting Assistant II	5.0
002	Administrative Specialist II	22.5
	Permanent FTEs	82.0

Note: FTE = Full-time equivalent.

of which expenses should be included within each code and subcode classification. Where applicable, object codes apply and extend the state mandated budget fund and account definitions and nomenclatures (chapter 9).

Personnel services expenses make up the largest expenditure (or expense) category for most government and nonprofit service delivery organizations. The **personnel/personal services category** of object codes represents the complex details of a department or program's employees, including the number of employees, their professional series and grade levels, the blend of permanent and temporary employees, and the **full-time equivalents (FTEs)** allocated by position and in total to a department or program. Exhibit 11.2 above details the positions and FTEs that correspond to the departmental funding for the Assessment and Tax Department in Exhibit 11.1.

The **materials and supplies category (M&S)** of expenses (Exhibit 11.1) lists the consumable supplies, the program delivery services, and the administrative services needed to operate the department or program. Many of these purchases are from *external* providers. Funding for **contracts for services**, grants, and intergovernmental agreements are included in this category of expenditures. In Exhibit 11.1, left column bolded object codes 51280 and 51285 cover competitive service contracts, grants, and intergovernmental agreements, professional service contracts. These seemingly minor and buried line items can provide the funding for a substantial portion of program service delivery capacity. These codes fund ongoing contracts and agreements, the start-up of new contracts, and the closure of completed contracts. Such expenditures can add up to a major portion of the departmental budget. This is especially the case in organizational units where contracting out and new public management (NPM) strategies have been extensively employed.

In this particular jurisdiction, the materials and supplies category also includes a series of line-items showing the *internal* purchase of facilities and administrative services from other departments in the county government (Exhibit 11.1 M&S category bolded "internal" labels). These line-items are termed **internal charges for services**, or **internal service charges**. Each department purchases these services from a central services budget fund or directly from a fund attached to the providing department. For example, the police department purchases vehicle assembly and maintenance services from a central fleet management budget fund that supports the city motor pool department. The central finance office determines the rules and policies for allocating these common administrative expenses across all departments in the county organization. Allocation may be based on simple percentages or on a refined set of service use and need criteria. Placing the internal charges for service inside the M&S category highlights their presence as program costs. Other jurisdictions prefer to categorize internal charges for service as interfund or interdepartmental purchases. This highlights the internal exchange nature of these charges. We provide additional explanation and detail on internal charges for service and their allocation in chapter 15.

The **capital outlay category** includes the expenses for durable equipment (extended service life of more than one fiscal year) used by a department or program. This includes motor vehicles, furniture, and computer equipment, among other expenses. However, the label *capital outlay* has a specific meaning in the line-item context. Most governments have a separate budget, called a **capital budget**, to deal with the long-term funding, purchase, construction, rebuilding, and replacement of buildings, facilities, major pieces of equipment, and other major assets (chapter 16). Capital expenses for these major investments are not included in what is called the **operating budget**, which is the focus of our discussion in this section on budgeting formats. But there is a need to take into account normal expenditures to maintain rather than to replace existing equipment and infrastructure. This may include painting buildings, supporting service maintenance agreements, and replacing worn parts. Expenditures that fall into the maintenance category are considered capital outlay and are included in the operating budget. You can think of the difference between capital investments and capital outlay as the difference between replacing your car and doing regular maintenance. If you depreciate your car on an annual basis and put the money in an account that accumulates with the goal of replacement within 10 years, you are doing capital budgeting for an investment. On the other hand, if you do annual maintenance, you are making capital outlays.

Finally, the **interfund/interdepartmental category** of expenses funds the purchase of services from other branches of the organization. Expenditures in the interfund category often represent purchases that directly support service delivery by the receiving department or program. For example, the Assessment and Tax (A&T) Department may maintain the county geographic information system (GIS) to support its assessment function, but it also may sell GIS services to the land-use planning program, the transportation planning and construction program, and the building permits program. These purchasing programs would budget funds in an interfund object code to make payment to A&T for GIS services. As we mentioned earlier, many jurisdictions also include allocated internal charges for central administrative services in this category of expenditures.

The columns in Exhibit 11.1 are also typical of a local government line-item display. The expenditure object codes and the expenditure descriptions are on the left. The actual spending levels for each line-item in the previous four fiscal years (FY) counting from the earliest to the most recent are in the center (FY1 to FY4). The FY5 Adopted column reflects the current year's spending levels and the current budget adopted into law by the council, committee, or board. The values in this column may not be identical to the budget originally approved by the council or board just prior to the beginning of the fiscal year. Rather, this column reflects the current law, which includes all amendments made by the legislative body (council, committee, or board) to the original approved budget. The adopted budget is the appropriation that the organization is currently using as its benchmark for spending limits and control. Finally, the empty column on the far right, titled FY6 Requested, will hold the yet-to-be determined estimates for the coming budget year. Departmental and program budget analysts and the department leadership have the task of filling in an expected spending level for FY6 for each object code as they prepare the department's **budget request** for the next budgeting cycle.

ORIGINS AND PURPOSE

Line-item budgeting was first introduced as part of the early twentieth-century reforms to reduce political corruption. By creating detailed object codes for specific classes, or even for individual items of expenditure, public money could be tracked more easily from the point of appropriation by a legislative body to the point of expenditure by an administrative agency. Budgeting by object code makes it more difficult for money intended for a bridge improvement project to be diverted to build a community center or to undertake projects that benefit specific neighborhoods or target populations without specific legislative authorization. This was a common practice by George Washington Plunkett and other machine bosses in charge of Tammany Hall in New York, as well as in other political machines in the Midwest and the Northeast before the turn of the century. They diverted public funds from legislated purposes in ways that built political loyalty among the new immigrant classes streaming to the United States to pursue better economic opportunities.

The main purpose of line-item budgeting is to ensure high levels of financial accountability. Object code tables prepared at the project level or cost center level isolate spending for that function. The spending levels in the object code table are one-year totals that may mask variation in production costs and in the timing of expenses. Thus, object code spending levels are insufficient as measures of performance or as instruments for cost analysis. Nonetheless, project-level and cost center–level line-item budgets provide management control over cash flow at a refined level. As we described, line-item budgets for subordinate units can be aggregated by object code into a line-item budget for a parent unit such as a department or a major government function. Project and cost center line-item budgets are also segregated by budget fund and compared to budgeted revenues. This aggregation by fund allows management control at the budget fund level, which is typically a state regulatory and professional accounting requirement. A jurisdiction's line-item budgets for its general fund, all other major revenue funds, and all enterprise funds form the basis for the year-end financial reporting (chapter 18).

But extensive controls over line-item categories can stifle administrative discretion and the ability to make adjustments under adverse circumstances that no amount of planning can anticipate. Whether it is overtime pay to deal with a storm emergency or a broken piece of equipment, budget managers need the freedom to exercise their discretion without having to call the legislative body into session for approval. For this reason, most organizations permit the transfer of funds *within* the large categories of personnel/personal services, materials and supplies, and capital outlay, typically designating an upper limit on the amount of money that can be freely transferred among subcategories without legislative action by the city council, commission, or board (chapter 17). Some organizations provide for managerial discretion to transfer funds across broad categories, thus empowering administrators to manage the budget, not simply to exercise budget control. Organizations built on a culture of mistrust give specific limited authority within the budgeting chain of command for the approval of expenditures. This central control eliminates an incentive for financial accountability on the part of operating managers.

The financial control focus of line-item budgeting has particularly important consequences for nonprofit organizations that are required to demonstrate financial accountability for the grants and contracts they receive from government and foundations. Line-item budgeting applied to separately identifiable budget funds allows organizations to demonstrate to their contract administrators and auditors that they have adequate financial controls in place. We describe examples of such oversight in chapter 18. While recipient organizations must demonstrate fiscal accountability for all the funds they spend, they also must report and demonstrate programmatic outcomes and results. These additional requirements lead most organizations to establish accounting and performance tracking systems, and to hire qualified fiscal and budget personnel, all of which adds administrative costs that come at the expense of direct service delivery to clients.

Because of its high value in promoting financial accountability, line-item budgeting has become the most durable and commonly used budget format throughout the public sector. In fact, one can hardly imagine public budgeting without it. Line-item budgeting is almost always superimposed or used alongside all other budgeting formats. This practice frequently creates some obvious tensions, since the purpose, information, and expertise needed to carry out line-item budgeting is different than what is needed to carry out program, performance, and zero-base budgeting. These tensions sometimes result in one format dominating the budget, or dual or multiple budgeting systems that are not necessarily integrated into a single system. For example, a parks manager who is responsible for multiple summer programs may need to establish separate **program budgets** in order to ensure that each program is self-supporting, but this information may not be tracked by the jurisdiction's centralized budgeting system, which is designed to support line-item budgeting.

CHARACTERISTICS OF LINE-ITEM BUDGETING: BASE, INCREMENTALISM, AND FAIR SHARE

We mentioned in chapter 5 that there are three characteristics of the budgeting cycle, each of which has been associated with line-item budgeting. First, the budgeting process starts with the assumption of an existing **base budget**, which is defined as the amount needed to fund the current level of services being provided by the organization or jurisdiction. Second, participants in the budgeting process assume there will be only incremental change up or down (**incremental budgeting/ incrementalism**), depending on the revenue estimations for the coming budget cycle. If there is to be more than an incremental change, there is a presumption that participants will abide by the principle of **fair share** in making cuts or in enjoying the bounties of any increases beyond what is needed to accommodate inflationary increases to maintain current levels of service. Why do many administrators associate these core characteristics of the budgeting process with line-item budgeting? We answer this question in the sections that follow.

Base Budget

Line-item budgeting collects historical information by object code. This accumulated information can then be used without much analysis to make budget projections for the coming year. Analysts simply look at the patterns of spending by category and, using workload estimates, determine with a high degree of accuracy how much money the organization will need for the next year, adjusted for inflation. Most agencies do not experience dramatic changes from year to year in service demands, and most of the costs of providing public service are tied up in personnel costs, including salaries, health benefits, retirement, and unemployment insurance. These personnel-related costs constitute 75–85 percent of a typical public agency budget, and are often restrained on a multiyear basis by union-negotiated labor contracts. The multiyear provisions reinforce the notion that the previous year's spending levels will serve as the benchmark for the coming fiscal year. Existing multiyear service contracts, grants, partnerships, and extended intergovernmental agreements for services also add continuity to future spending levels (Wanat 1978, 120).

It is reasonable for most agencies to assume that the legal authority they have been given to provide public services is not going to be removed by the authorizing body during the budget development and approval process. Based on historical experience, this is a very safe assumption. Managers put their budgets together with the fully rational assumption that program and service levels will continue with small adjustments up or down. The line-item budget format enables information to be gathered and easily transformed into a request that supports and reinforces this assumption. This reinforces the belief in an existing **base budget**. A base budget contains the resources and inputs needed to continue program content and service delivery at the current year's level. The base budget reflects the most recent version of the adopted budget, which may include amendments of funding increases or decreases to the original budget adopted by the legislative body before the beginning of the fiscal year.[1] However, the adopted budget may contain one-time revenues and projects that apply only to the current fiscal year. To reflect a base budget, these one-time revenues and program costs must be subtracted out of the updated adopted budget. For example, a local fire department may receive a grant from the Federal Emergency Management Agency (FEMA) to hire four new firefighters. The grant provisions may not require a commitment from the city that it will continue to fund the new positions after the grant expires. The grant could be seen as one-time funds in that the positions will end when the grant funding ends. To compute a base budget, the grant revenues and the related FTEs would be removed from the adopted budget. On the other hand, if the city makes a policy and revenue commitment to fund the new firefighter positions permanently, then the base budget would increase to include the new positions. The base budget reflects the revenues and expenses for continuing programs and for continuing administrative costs at the level of service reflected in the most recent adopted budget. It is important to note that the base budget reflects only the minimally necessary costs to accomplish department or program operations. Necessary costs reflect mandatory legal requirements and the foundational costs of operations. Improvement costs to gain efficiencies or new programs that may be needed by the community are *not* included as part of the base budget (Riley and Colby 1991, 61).

Incrementalism

There are several ways the incremental features of the budget process surface during the budget cycle. First, as already noted, most requests begin with an assumption that everyone will request a little more this year than they did last year to accommodate inflation, built-in cost inflators from union contracts, and cost drivers in the economy like health insurance and fuel costs. Second, there is an assumption that there are likely to be cuts in the original request, but normally these will be small. These two assumptions about a relatively fixed base with small departures from year to year grow out of and reinforce a third source of incrementalism: the desire to keep past political agreements intact. Once you achieve agreement among various constituency and clientele groups outside the organization and various career administrators and elected officials within the organization, it is difficult to renegotiate these agreements afresh each budgeting cycle. Line-item budgeting is viewed as a major contributing factor to this incremental characteristic of public budgeting (Wanat 1978, 114; Wildavsky 1978).

Fair Share

A third important principle of line-item budgeting is the assumption that if cuts have to be made, or increases allotted, then everyone should share the pain or gain as equally as possible: each program receives its *fair share*. After all, the legislative body in almost all cases has given each agency the legal authority to deliver services without ranking which ones are more important than others. Once a program has been authorized, there is little guidance provided by the board or legislative body about the priority ranking among the existing programs that are being funded. And when such rankings have to be made to balance the budget in a given year, traditionally there has been little reason for budget managers to assume that this ranking will fundamentally alter the assumption in future years that the majority of programs have an equal standing with the authorizing body. Exceptions to this general rule occur when the governing board engages in a priority-ranking exercise that provides managers with policy guidance (see chapter 14 for a discussion of "priority-based budgeting"). In the absence of such guidance, budget and program managers assume that reductions in funding will abide by the fair share principle.

Usually, the norm of fair share is applied by asking for across-the-board cuts from all departments and programs, sometimes even from enterprise fund agencies (chapter 9) that aren't supported by general fund revenues (such as property taxes, income taxes, and some fees). When you hear requests being made for an across-the-board cut in budget requests, you know that the principle of fair share is being used rather than relying on extensive analysis. Reliance on the principles of a base budget and fair share results in a process that produces only incremental changes from year to year.

LINE-ITEM BEHAVIOR AND TECHNIQUES

Line-item budgeting norms the behavior of participants in favor of expecting that the present world of budgeting will continue into the future with only marginal changes. This future includes maintaining labor agreements, service contract and agreement provisions, statutory authorizations, and relative constancy of public need and client demands. Under these conditions, there is little discretion to start or grow new programs or to reconfigure existing programs. The incremental aspects of line-item budgeting respond to the realities of a limited decision space and scarce resources. More than a computation procedure, line-item budgeting generates a set of attitudes and behaviors (Wanat 1978, 128–129; Riley and Colby 1991, 29).

With annual repetition, building and updating a line-item budget often becomes a "rule of thumb" procedure. Administrators with long organizational tenure and extensive experience with a budget system may simply increase the line-item category subtotals (personnel services, materials and supplies, capital outlay, interfund/interdepartmental) by a preferred percentage to quickly generate a budget request. Once an administrator or analyst develops a successful line-item budget and budgeting approach, it becomes a template for use in coming years. Using the previous year's budget as a template maintains limits on the decision space and reduces the amount of detailed analysis needed to produce expenditure estimates. These characteristics and behaviors make line-item budget construction relatively efficient. As long as there are no major changes to cost structure, client demand, or program configuration, using the previous year's budget as the basis for the next year's request can be both efficient and reasonably accurate.

Continuing Costs Drive Incremental Change

For analysts and administrators who have limited familiarity with an organization and its budget system, adjustments at the line-item level form the basis of budget construction. With much of the budget decision-making space confined, analysts follow a predictable pattern of cost estimation to construct a line-item budget request for the pending fiscal year. The line-item schedule in Exhibit 11.1 defines a typical base of expenses needed to operate a county department or program. To generate a FY6 Request (blank column on the far right), analysts must develop expected expenditure levels for each object code. Subtotals are also developed for each major cost category of personnel/personal services, materials and supplies, capital outlay, and interfund/interdepartmental spending. The expected expenditures are then summed into a department-level or program-level request. Expected expenditures are then compared to the current FY5 Adopted level to define the request as a total percentage increase (or decrease) over the current year's adopted budget level.

Exhibit 11.3 presents an extract of Exhibit 11.1 with the previous fiscal years' actual expenditures deleted to highlight the current year FY5 Adopted budget and the incremental changes (center column) needed to develop an FY6 Request.

The far right column in Exhibit 11.3 provides terse notes describing the contract, payment requirement, or data source that determines the percentage adjustment for each object code. To develop a line-item request, analysts build from the current law FY5 Adopted level. This is the last legal budget reported to the public and to state authorities. Analysts take an incremental approach to estimating personnel services salary and wage expenses based on labor contract provisions (Riley and Colby 1991, 29). Second, analysts do the same thing for employee health and retirement benefits. These incremental changes may be based on contracts between the jurisdiction and insurance carriers and brokers, retirement trust funds, or state retirement fund agencies (**public employee retirement system [PERS]**). In recent years, these uncontrolled expenses have increased substantially—often at rates far exceeding annual inflation (chapter 15). Other employee costs are incrementally changed based on labor contracts or regional inflation rates. Third, following directions in the CEO's budget instructions, analysts may or may not apply an explicit inflation increment and cost adjustments to all other object codes to continue the existing level of services (e.g., 2 percent in Exhibit 11.3). The exception to this blanket adjustment is the cost adjustment for service contracts, grants, partnership agreements, and intergovernmental agreements. Contracts and agreements may include payment escalation clauses that define any year-to-year adjustments. Analysts would set expense levels to meet these requirements. Fourth, analysts consider any size and capacity changes to the department or program operations. Expenses are adjusted on a proportional basis to add or close capacity. Finally, analysts consider any new programs or productivity improvements. Using percent changes reinforces the line-item analytic approach and further illustrates the incremental behavior that is associated with line-item budgeting.

Electronic spreadsheets (Chen, Forsythe, Weikart, and Williams 2009) and relational budgeting software have greatly eased the task of projecting expenses for personnel/personal services. These electronic packages can be used to provide a total projected expenditure for each personnel service object code for the coming year. Spreadsheet systems allow departmental analysts to project a given year's personnel services budget once they know the incremental drivers, such as cost of living or contractual increases, grade-step increases for service time, grade-level increases, hazard and overtime pay expenses, vacation and leave expenses, required salary-based contributions to retirement, unemployment insurance contributions, and costs for life, disability, health, and dental insurance. With relational software packages, personnel expense projections are often centrally computed with summary values returned to the department analyst. Thinking and working in terms of summary totals reinforces the incremental nature of line-item budgeting.

The example in Exhibit 11.3 also includes several discretionary expenditures for expanded programs, among them a new interagency agreement (see contracting costs for object code 51280) and capital outlay expenses for a new vehicle and for software and hardware upgrades (see object codes 57120 and 57155, respectively). The need for each of these discretionary expenses would be fully explained and justified as part of the department's budget submission. The request in Exhibit 11.3, however, basically intends to maintain the current level of programs and service delivery for Assessment and Taxation. While there may be employee turnover due to retirements, resignations, and replacements, the FY6 Requested budget expects to maintain the current staffing and personnel expense levels. Any discretionary requests to increase staff would be reflected in identifiable increases in the personnel/personal services cost category and would be justified in new position requests to the executive, the board, or the council.

Analysts and administrators are aware that the percentage rate increment or dollar adjustment they request will be compared by the central budget office staff to the levels requested by their

Exhibit 11.3

Example County Line-Item Increments and Request Computation

Upper Cascadia County
Line-Item FY6 Increments and Request Computation
Organization Unit—Expenditure

161   ASSESSMENT & TAXATION

Object Code	Description	FY5 Adopted	FY6 Percent Increment	FY6 Requested	Notes/Rate
	Personnel (Personal) Services				
51105	Wages and salaries	$4,187,195	2.5	$4,291,875	Labor Contract Provision
51110	Temporary salaries	$150,622	2.5	$154,388	Labor Contract Provision
51115	Overtime and other pay	$113,680	2.5	$116,522	Labor Contract Provision
51125	FICA	$330,929	3.0	$340,857	Federal Gov't Rate
51130	Workers compensation	$47,515	3.0	$48,940	State Insurance Pool Rate
51135	Employer paid work day tax	$2,935	3.0	$3,023	State Dept of Revenue Rate
51140	PERS contribution	$675,005	6.0	$715,505	State PERS Rate
51141	PERS reserve	$0	0.0	$0	Unused
51150	Health insurance	$884,976	8.0	$955,774	Insurance Broker Rate
51155	Life and long-term disability insurance	$5,449	3.0	$5,612	State Insurance Pool Rate
51160	Unemployment insurance	$18,933	3.0	$19,501	State Insurance Pool Rate
51165	Metro Transit District employee tax	$27,391	3.0	$28,213	Regional Transit Dist Rate
51175	Automobile allowance	$0	0.0	$0	Unused
51180	Other employee allowances	$1,482	2.0	$1,512	Inflation
51199	Miscellaneous personal services	$184,540	2.0	$188,231	Inflation
	Personnel (Personal) Services Total	$6,630,652	3.6	$6,869,953	**3.6% category increase**
	Materials and Supplies				
51205	Supplies—office, general	$37,397	2.0	$38,145	Inflation
51210	Supplies—general	$1,945	2.0	$1,984	Inflation
51220	Supplies—food	$0	2.0	$0	Unused
51270	Postage and freight	$63,670	2.0	$64,943	Inflation
51275	Books, subscriptions, and publications	$12,568	2.0	$12,819	Inflation
51280	Services—contract, government	$59,897	6.0	$63,491	Contract Esc Terms/New Contract
51285	Services—professional services	$79,430	4.0	$82,607	Contract Escalator Terms
51295	Advertising and public notice	$4,200	2.0	$4,284	Inflation

(continued)

Exhibit 11.3 (continued)

161 ASSESSMENT & TAXATION

51300	Printing and duplicating	$184,058	2.0	$187,739	Inflation
51310	Utilities	$0	2.0	$0	Unused
51320	Repair & maint services—general	$41,977	2.0	$42,817	Inflation
51340	Lease and rentals—space	$603	2.0	$615	Inflation
51345	Lease and rentals—equipment	$0	2.0	$0	Unused
51350	Dues and membership	$2,025	2.0	$2,066	Inflation
51355	Training and education	$28,580	2.0	$29,152	Inflation
51360	Travel expense	$34,774	2.0	$35,469	Inflation
51365	Private mileage	$53,879	2.0	$54,957	Inflation
51460	Office supplies—Internal	$28,891	2.0	$29,469	Internal Service Charge Rate
51465	Postage and freight—Internal	$139,185	2.0	$141,969	Internal Service Charge Rate
51470	Mail messenger services—Internal	$19,392	2.0	$19,780	Internal Service Charge Rate
51475	Printing—Internal	$18,366	2.0	$18,733	Internal Service Charge Rate
51480	Photocopy machine—Internal	$17,047	2.0	$17,388	Internal Service Charge Rate
51495	Telephone monthly—Internal	$0	2.0	$0	Unused Int. Service Charge Rate
51500	Telephone long-distance—Internal	$0	2.0	$0	Unused Int. Service Charge Rate
51505	Telecom equipment install—Internal	$0	2.0	$0	Unused Int. Service Charge Rate
51510	Telecom Cellular Air Time—Internal	$0	2.0	$0	Unused Int. Service Charge Rate
51520	Facilities charges—Internal	$0	2.0	$0	Unused Int. Service Charge Rate
51525	Fleet—Internal (noncapital)	$5,842	2.0	$5,959	Internal Service Charge Rate
51555	Inventory issued default account	$0	2.0	$0	Unused
	Materials and Supplies Total	$833,726	2.5	$854,385	2.5% category increase
	Capital Outlay				
57115	Machinery and equipment	$46,000	-100.0	$0	None in FY6
57120	Vehicles	$0	—*	$22,000	Vehicle Replacement per Policy
57155	Computer equipment	$0	—*	$5,000	Scheduled Upgrades per Policy
	Capital Outlay Total	$46,000	-41.3	$27,000	-41% category increase
	Other Expenses				
52005	Bank Service Charge	$2,780	2.0	$2,836	Inflation
	Other Expenses Total	$2,780	2.0	$2,836	2% category increase
	Interfund (Interdepartmental) Expenses				
53040	Facilities	$560	3.0	$577	Budget Instruction Internal Rate
53055	General charges	$165	3.0	$170	Budget Instruction Internal Rate
53505	General charges—other	$0	3.0	$0	Budget Instruction Internal Rate
53530	ITS charges	$0	3.0	$0	Budget Instruction Internal Rate
	Interfund (Interdepartmental) Expenses Total	$725	3.0	$747	3% category increase
161	**ASSESSMENT & TAXATION TOTAL**	$7,513,883	3.2	$7,754,920	3.2% departmental increase

Note: A percentage increase is inapplicable on occasional or one-time capital outlay purchases, especially with no purchases ($0) in the FY5 Adopted Budget.

314

peers. Any requested adjustment will typically comply with the fair share test of relatively equal gain and pain. Comparison also serves to check and limit the size of any requested increase.

Historical Trend Information Contributes to Incremental Budget Development

Recent spending patterns can add another reason for an incremental approach to line-item budgeting. Historical types of information often take three forms: (1) recent year-to-year percentage changes in expenditures by object code; (2) sufficiency of the current year's adopted expenditure level; and (3) a current year's rates of spending as an indicator of changing needs and conditions. As context demands, analysts and program administrators may use one or several of these sources of information to supplement the basic line-item procedure described above. We provide detailed examples and details of line-item adjustments on the text website (www.pdx.edu/cps/budget-book). Recognizing and incorporating historical expenditure trends reinforces the incremental aspects of line-item budgeting. Using trend indicators steers analysts away from comprehensive cost analysis or from asking if spending supports organizational goals and objectives.

Using the first form of historical data, analysts can use several methods for computing percentage changes between years. Analysts can calculate an *average change* occurring for each object code and category total using available data from previous fiscal years. Alternatively, analysts can compute the *percentage change* from one year to the next and use that to make their projections. Depending on current circumstances, one approach or both may be useful in informing a new budget estimate.

In the second form of data, the original FY5 Adopted budget and its object code spending levels represented the best estimate of future spending at the time of its official adoption. Depending on the elapsed time into the fiscal year, this was likely six or more months ago. A thoughtful look back over the fiscal year to date may indicate that conditions have changed, or that conditions have been stable. In the latter case, an analyst or administrator may conclude that the adopted budget levels are still relevant, and that they could serve as expenditure levels for the coming fiscal year.

If, on the other hand, the look back shows that conditions have changed, analysts can consider a third form of historical data—the rate of current year spending—as a guide to what will be needed in the next fiscal year. Based on the number of accumulated months of spending information, analysts multiply the line-item values by the appropriate multiplier to obtain a full-year projection of spending. The full-year spending levels give an indication as to the need to increase or decrease spending in a budget request. The danger in using this approach is that spending for a program or department may be highly seasonal, with the bulk of expenses concentrated in one part of the fiscal year (for example, a county medical clinic with an intense cold and flu season, or a state forestry department with a costly summer wildfire season). Spending to the reported date may not reflect the true annual spending needs of the department or program. But, taking these seasonal variations into account, analysts compare the FY5 full-year projected levels to the FY5 Adopted levels to identify consistency or divergence. Divergence typically indicates rapidly changing conditions that will inform the requested levels for upcoming FY6. A variation on this projection method involves making a separate projection for spending in the remaining months of the fiscal year and then adding this amount to the year-to-date amount. Good budget analysts use judgment as to which technique to use for each line. A simple extrapolation works fine for smaller amounts or for line-items that do not see much month-to-month variation.

Exhibit 11.4 offers a line-item budgeting exercise to illustrate the line-item budget methodology.

Current Service Baseline Makes Assumptions Explicit

Using percentage change increments may provide an efficient and even reasoned basis for a line-item budget request, but central budget office analysts, budget committee citizen members, council

---

Exhibit 11.4

Exercise: The Line-Item Budgeting Methodology

Using the book website (www.pdx.edu./cps/budget-book), select a line-item budget schedule for a city, county, or special district department or program. As a practice exercise, use an electronic spreadsheet to develop a requested budget for the coming fiscal year. Identify the most recent version of the adopted budget and use that as a base for your computation. Exhibit 11.3 provides a template for your work sheet. Proceed line-item by line-item. First, develop a percentage incremental adjustment. Consider the following expense multipliers.

Labor contract salary and wage escalators	2.5 percent
Health, dental, and other insurance benefits	6.0 percent
PERS or local retirement trust fund contributions	7.0 percent
Service contract and intergovernmental agreement expenses	3.5 percent
Inflation multiplier	2.0 percent
Interfund, interdepartmental, and internal charges for services	2.5 percent

   If your sample budget schedule contains actual spending levels from previous fiscal years, use any useful historic information to adjust your line-by-line incremental adjustments. Changes in spending across previous years may indicate trends of growth or reduction. Work line-by-line and reconsider your incremental adjustments in light of historic information. When you've completed your line-by-line adjustments, multiply the incremental adjustment by the adopted budget level to compute a dollar request level. Do this for each line-item. Sum the line-items by major cost category: personnel (personal) services, materials and supplies, capital outlay, and interfund/interdepartmental. Sum all line-items into a total dollar request for the full department or program. Finally, express the total dollar request as a percentage change from the current year's adopted level total.

---

and board members, and the public will demand explanations for the procedures and assumptions behind a request. The line-item methods we have just described provide a macro-explanation by documenting what is required to continue the base program and the funding adjustments for program increases or decreases in a single percent increment (e.g., 3.2 percent on the bottom line of Exhibit 11.3). But there is a more explicit approach that increases transparency by separately detailing the adjustments needed to continue the base budget at the same program and productivity levels over the next fiscal year or biennium. This approach is called the **current service baseline (CSB)**, which separates the base budget and its adjustments from changes in program size, content, or productivity. The procedural steps for building a current service baseline would be included in the organization's budget preparation instruction/guidelines. The following is an example of what these instructions might look like (Riley and Colby 1991, 61).

- *Current year's budget.* Begin with the current year's adopted budget levels (e.g., FY5 Adopted column in Exhibit 11.3). In separate spreadsheet columns add the following information:
- *Amendments and modifications.* If not already included in the adopted budget, add in any legislatively adopted budget amendments and modifications to the adopted budget levels for all affected object codes. This includes any additions through supplemental appropriations, or subtractions from any rescissions of unneeded or unused funds. These adjustments are in dollar amounts as detailed in adoption ordinances.
- *Deduct one-time nonrecurring expenses* so they do not appear in the permanent base (see chapter 15).

- *Annexations and population changes.* Recognize any change in the jurisdiction's population, especially those caused by annexation of new territory and population. Proportionately increase or decrease program spending levels and FTEs to maintain service levels on a uniform per capita basis.
- *Cost multipliers.* In separate spreadsheet columns, determine percentage multipliers for each of the following expense adjustments and apply the multipliers to the appropriate object codes:
  - *Employee benefits administrative changes.* Add in the effects of any organization-wide changes to retirement or insurance programs (e.g., administrative changes, shifting from a local retirement plan to a state PERS system, or changing from one insurance broker/carrier to another). In many cases, these are systemic changes that are intended to be cost neutral. These changes may be in dollar amounts or in a percentage rate adjustment.
  - *Employee grade and wage step increases.* Increase current employee salary and wages based on current labor contract provisions for grade level, seniority, and time in grade-step increases.
  - *Employee wage and benefit contract provisions.* Adjust current employee salaries and wage rates according to existing or expected labor contract provisions.
  - *Employee benefit provisions.* Health care costs and retirement benefits costs often escalate much faster than other expenses, and local governments may need to make supplemental payments to state PERS or other retirement funds to ensure solvency (object codes need to reflect these increased costs); for current employees, adjust object codes for higher rate increases of employee health and dental benefits, and for an increased rate or lump sum contribution to retirement funds.
- *Adjust existing service contract, grant, and partnership expenditures.* For all existing multiyear service contracts, grants, partnerships, and intergovernmental agreements, increment appropriate object codes per contract inflation adjustments. Make rate adjustments to continue existing levels of contract administration and partnering.
- *Adjust part-year service contract, grant, and partnership expenditures.* For contracts, grants, and agreements adopted in the previous fiscal year, adjust any part-year expense levels to full-year levels. Remove any part-year expenses for contracts, grants, and agreements that closed in the previous year.
- *Continue installment purchases* per procurement contract provisions.
- *Continue any debt installment* payments.
- *Include any capital equipment* and information technology replacement purchases needed to maintain current service levels.
- *Adjust interdepartmental and internal charges for service purchase rates.* Adjust the expenditures for interdepartmental purchases from other governmental departments and programs based on revised overhead rates in the budget instructions/guidelines.
- *Annualization of new program start-up costs.* New programs may have been adopted and new facilities may have been opened in the previous year. Part-year start-up and operating costs may have been included in the previous year's budget. Continued operations require a full year of expenses. Adjust all affected object codes as needed.
- *Adjust all remaining expenditures by inflation rate.* As directed in budget guidelines, adjust all other materials and supplies, along with capital outlay object codes, by the regional or metropolitan area's commercial inflation multipliers (e.g., Federal Reserve publications). On rare occasions, no adjustment or a deflation of costs may be appropriate. This may result from a lack of inflationary increases or a belief that substitution works as well in government spending as it does in other sectors of the economy when costs are increasing.

Inflators like the Consumer Price Index (CPI) tend to overinflate budgets because they don't recognize the motivation to find cheaper substitutes to reduce costs or keep them from rising.
- *Define and apply any productivity enhancements that could increase efficiency and lower costs.* Clearly identify any up-front expenditures necessary to achieve these efficiencies and any expected lower costs.

For transparency purposes, analysts establish separate spreadsheet columns that break out the effects of each of the above bulleted factors on the current year's adopted budget object codes. For summary reading, the effects of all factors are aggregated into a combined adjustment to the FY5 current year adopted budget. This adjusted budget is the current service baseline budget for FY6. Once the baseline is computed, program increases or decreases and other deviations from the current service baseline can then be presented separately and compared to the current service baseline as budget alternatives.

Critically, the executive, elected officials, and constituent group advocates must fully understand the components and assumptions implicit in any current service baseline computation. The current service baseline provides an inflation adjusted package that keeps service at current levels, but in effect also provides an increase in absolute program funding. As the teaching case for Part III describes, in times of limited revenue, governments and private-sector organizations often budget without recognition of inflation and contract rate adjustments. This approach of not recognizing inflation and cost changes serves to marginally reduce the funds available for program delivery on an annual basis. Critics of budget baselines and current service budgets remind administrators to fully disclose the methodology and components for baseline computations, and to educate elected officials, the media, interest group leaders, and the public as to the need for and effect of current service baselines.

With the current service baseline level developed and displayed separately, analysts at the request of program, department, and board leaders can then develop budget alternatives that make specific proposed adjustments and changes to department and program funding for the coming fiscal year. The proposed changes may reveal revisions to only a few object codes, or they may require the development of a full object code schedule that signals an alternate budget scenario for the program or department. Modifications to the current service baseline can reflect: (1) the executive agenda; (2) changing conditions in the community that result in the need for more or fewer services; (3) new program start-ups and staffing; (4) new intergovernmental policies and requirements; (5) increased operational expenses tied to the opening of new capital facilities; or (6) the commencement or completion of service contracts, grants, partnerships, or intergovernmental agreements. Updated forecasts of client usage and service demand levels provide a rationale for program increase alternatives. Proposed decreases from the current service baseline levels may reflect program obsolescence, declining client demand, or a decision by senior leaders to reprioritize. Based on direction and changing conditions, budget analysts work with their department and program leaders to develop line-item schedules that form the foundation of a requested budget for the coming fiscal year.

Even with more analysis and with extensive attention to expense and rate adjustments, the current service baseline suffers from the same weakness as the incremental behavior of line-item budgeting. Adjustments to compute a current service baseline are largely developed using percentage and proportional changes to existing expense levels and cost rates. No attention is given to whether the organization or program is spending on the right things, and no attention is given to productivity or performance. A current service baseline assumes that the current program is appropriate for the coming year, and that any changes to the program appropriately build from the current organization and program configuration.

ADVANTAGES AND DISADVANTAGES OF LINE-ITEM BUDGETING

As we noted earlier in the section on the incremental characteristics of line-item budgeting, not much programmatic or managerial expertise is needed to successfully carry out object code budgeting. In fact, this is its chief advantage. As we have suggested in our discussion of the chief characteristics of object code budgeting, you do not need to know how pencils are going to be used in order to budget for pencils. If you used 100 pencils last year and your overall workload and FTEs haven't changed much, you can with some degree of confidence assume that you will need enough money with inflation to buy 100 pencils next year. This example illustrates both the strengths and weaknesses of line-item budgeting. On the one hand, you can assume that what you have been doing will likely continue being done next year, with some exceptions on the margin. You can then concentrate your limited time and energy on analyzing and planning these marginal changes. This reduces complexity and allows the budget to be assembled without endless hours of analysis, pouring over reams of spreadsheet information, planning, and spending hours in meetings with others in reexamine everything that is currently being done.

In addition to the efficiency in putting a budget together, line-item budgeting reduces conflict. It lets sleeping dogs lie. Whenever managers and employees are asked to reexamine what is currently being done, they normally become defensive. At the point where this examination begins to create priorities for organizational funding, conflict internally and externally begins to rise exponentially. With line-item budgeting, when there are more requests than resources available, the budget can be brought into balance by cutting dollars, usually by relying on formulas like across-the-board cuts or some similar notion of fair share. By shifting the universe of discourse to dollars and away from programs and activities, budget balancing obscures the impact of cuts on services, thereby reducing conflict in the budgeting process. Dollars can be cut and divided in far more ways and in much smaller increments than is the case with programs. In short, line-item budgeting and its reliance on formulas like *base* and *fair share* tend to keep the conflict and complexity in the budgeting process within manageable bounds. The format, according to Wildavsky, "does not require its practitioners to discover all or most possible conflicts and to work out answers to problems that may never materialize. It permits each participant to go his own way until he discovers that the activities of others interfere. Efforts can then be devoted to overcoming the difficulties that do exist" (1979b, 166–167).

Another advantage is that line-item budgeting is quite flexible. It can exist alongside other budgeting formats without requiring extensive changes in existing subcodes. You simply have to rearrange the subcodes into programs (program budgeting), decision packages (zero-base budgeting), or performance units (performance budgeting) to accommodate purposes that go beyond interest in financial accountability. In addition, you can make changes in the budget during the year by simply transferring dollars from one part of the organization to another without having to spend time determining how all of the pieces fit together into a coherent and integrated whole. The line-item budget avoids the "matching suit of clothes problem," where the parts cannot be easily separated and worn separately without destroying the integrity of the larger whole (Wildavsky 1978).

The aforementioned advantages of object code budgeting are mirror images of its chief defects. Because line-item budgeting can proceed without knowing the purposes or accomplishments of expenditures, questions regarding efficiency, effectiveness, and future priorities aren't systematically addressed. While there is nothing in line-item budgeting that prevents these issues from being examined, the format itself does not require it. In fact, in order to justify requests for increased expenditures, it is a common practice under line-item budgeting formats to incorporate a wide variety of quantitative information such as workload measures, activity indicators, etc. But the inclusion of such information is not inherently necessary to line-item budgeting and usually raises questions about the larger purposes these measures are intended to serve.

The incremental nature of line-item budgeting also makes it difficult to respond to major changes in community needs. The funding levels of the past may be completely inadequate to address major new needs, and inertial spending on existing programs may continue programs of lesser value that could be discontinued and the money reprogrammed to address higher priorities. Adopting a percentage change in funding levels for the coming year hides the increases or decreases needed to respond to major changes in demand or community needs.

Over the past several decades, the budgeting process has emphasized efficiency, effectiveness, and priority-setting approaches that supplement the system's basic reliance on the line-item format. The goal of these supplementary approaches is to avoid the line-item critics' concern that object code budgeting perpetuates a status quo approach that gives an advantage to constituency groups whose interests are reflected in the existing base, while woefully neglecting public needs and priorities that currently lack political support. In addition, because the purposes/goals of expenditures are not clearly articulated, reliance solely on line-item budgeting contributes to an overlap and duplication of effort—the very inefficiencies that have become the prime targets of the reinvention of government movement (Osborne and Gaebler 1992; Osborne and Hutchinson 2004). Supplementing the line-item budgeting process with this additional information on efficiency and effectiveness does not, however, mean that an additional format has been adopted and is systematically being used to achieve a new set of goals. This will become clearer when we discuss these alternative budgeting formats in the chapters that follow.

A final criticism of line-item budgeting relates to the flexibility of transferring dollars from one set of activities to another within the limits allowed by the rules governing line-item categories. With loose rules and weak oversight, significant program changes can occur under the radar, without anyone really knowing what has occurred. Natchez and Bupp's study of the Atomic Energy Commission (the predecessor agency to the federal Nuclear Regulatory Commission) over a 15-year period demonstrated that priority funding shifted significantly among 24 programs, 12 of which prospered, 8 of which did not, and 4 of which held their own in the period from 1958 to 1972 (Natchez and Bupp 1973, 961). While funding remained relatively stable, showing incremental growth between 1958 through 1972, the changes in prioritization undertaken by "the program director and the operating-level bureaucrats" effectively shifted the agency mission from supporting research on the production and peaceful uses of nuclear energy to research on nuclear weapons and high energy physics (Natchez and Bupp 1973, 963). In short, line-item budgeting—if used as the exclusive budget format over a long period of time—hides the significant policy consequences that remain hidden behind relatively stable dollar amounts.

CONCLUSION

Line-item budgeting continues as the mainstay of public budgeting techniques. It offers many strengths: financial controls and a linkage to financial control systems, minimal data needs, ease of use, relative fairness between competing departments and programs, the maintenance of political peace within the organization, and regulatory compliance. But the simplicity and expense-centered focus of the line-item format leave it with glaring weaknesses. A line-item budget details where money will be spent, but it never explains what the funds will buy or how spending will improve the public welfare. In the next chapter, we turn to a budget format and analysis framework that can answer some of these questions.

STUDY QUESTIONS

The textbook website (www.pdx.edu/cps/budget-book) provides extensive budget data and organizational information for several public service agencies. This information may be helpful in answering one or several of the following study questions. The information and data can also be used to complete the line-item budget exercise described earlier in this chapter.

1. Drawing on your experience in completing the line-item budget exercise as well as your professional or volunteer experiences, what were the most difficult obstacles to the formulation of a line-item budget for your department or organization. What strategies would you use in overcoming these obstacles?
2. What kind of information is required to undertake line-item budgeting? Who possesses this information?
3. In what ways is the information provided by a line-item budget useful to a program manager? A department head? The central budget office? Elected/appointed members of a policy/legislative board? Clients? Citizens?
4. In developing a line-item budget, what strategies would you follow if you were a program manager? A department head? The central budget office? Elected/appointed members of a policy/legislative board? Clients? Citizens?
5. Explain why line-item budgeting is associated with the phenomenon of incrementalism.
6. What is meant by the terms *base budget*, *current service level,* and *fair share*? How are these principles related to line-item or object code budgeting?
7. Does your organization develop and use a current service baseline? What assumptions are included in the baseline computation? Does using a current service baseline appear to help or confuse budget discussions and decision making? (If you have yet to work with a government or nonprofit organization, go online (www.pdx.edu/cps/budget-book) and complete work exercise 11.2 Line-item Baseline and Packages; then reconsider this question).

NOTE

1. The Washington State budgeting system formally recognizes the amendments and adjustments to the adopted budget by computing a *current law budget* as the foundation for budget construction.

12 PLANNING, PROGRAMMING, BUDGETING SYSTEM (PPBS) FORMAT

Program budgeting (PPB) is planning oriented; its main goal is to rationalize policy making by providing (1) data on the costs and benefits of alternative ways of attaining proposed public objectives, and (2) output measurements to facilitate the effective attainment of chosen objectives.

(Allen Schick 1966, 250–251; 1980, 56)

Putting objectives first, alternatives second and choices third is inefficient as a method of calculation, ineffective in relating thought to action and inappropriate as a design for learning. . . . The [line-item] approach is more efficient for resolving conflicts . . . because . . . it does not require its practitioners to discover all or most possible conflicts and to work out answers to problems that may never materialize.

(Aaron \Wildavsky 1979b, v, 166–167)

Program budgeting, including the *Planning, Program, Budgeting System (PPBS)*[1] seeks to increase the effective use of public resources by budgeting to clearly defined objectives. It broadens the line-item (object code) format's preoccupation with expenditure control to a concern for programmatic accountability for results. It is hailed by advocates as a great advance in expanding the values that need to be taken into account in promoting the public interest. But it is also severely criticized by critics who argue that it consumes large amounts of time and resources to carry out, and that it empowers career administrators to use large amounts of discretionary power to "cook up" programs in response to problems that are not supported by strong political constituencies (Wildavsky 1979b, 167). Finally, by configuring expenditure allocations into sets of programmatic activities that have clearly identifiable outcomes, program budgeting tends to exacerbate political conflict among those who benefit or are disadvantaged by these outcomes during times of budget cuts. In this chapter, we will show why both the proponents and opponents of program budgeting are correct, and in doing so, demonstrate the conflicting objectives that democratic government needs to accommodate.

ORIGINS AND PURPOSE OF PROGRAM BUDGETING

Program budgets organize expenditures around the **activities** performed by an agency or program to meet defined **objectives**. It focuses the attention of managers on the results achieved by the expenditure of public funds, not on attempts to control all of the individual expenditures needed to accomplish a given set of activities. Controlling the amount of money spent on personnel, materials, and supplies does not necessarily produce effective outcomes. For example, we can control the amount of money spent by a contractor to build a new house, but doing so will not ensure that the house is well built or meets the standards in the architect's drawings.

Program budgeting has been advocated by local government reformers for nearly a hundred years. In fact, it was first advocated by the New York City Bureau of Municipal Research in 1917. The bureau argued that public budgets should include "all the details of the work plans and specifications of cost of work" (quoted in Schick 1980, 52). Program budgeting, as we know it today, gained popularity as a distinct budgeting innovation in the 1960s under the moniker planning, programming, budgeting system (PPBS). Robert McNamara, as secretary of defense, brought PPBS with him from the Ford Motor Company, where, as company president, he had introduced the system to significantly improve the company's performance.

In his role in the Kennedy and Johnson administrations, Secretary McNamara used PPBS to help settle the competition among the various armed services for costly missile defense systems, extended range bombers, nuclear submarines, and upgraded conventional forces. At the height of the Cold War with the Soviet Union, how was a secretary of defense to manage this kind of escalating and competing demand for more military weaponry by each of the separate services? The massive size of the Department of Defense budget and the contrasting cultures of the different services challenged any attempt to bring order to the department's budget. Added to the interservice strife, congressional pressure to protect the "home-town" benefits of military spending made it difficult to rationally prioritize military expenditures. Further compounding the challenge, the development and procurement of a major weapons system was (and remains) a multiyear process that touched off a cascade of fiscal commitments lasting far beyond the initial fiscal year. Initial research and development of a weapons system led to expenses for prototype development and testing, procurement, manufacturing, use in the field, repair and maintenance, rebuilding and upgrading, and retirement. The useful life of a weapons system often lasted several decades, and budgeting needed to recognize the full, long-term implications and commitments of its procurement.

The Department of Defense budgeting system presented McNamara with a final challenge. The budget was structured around intermediate activities such as maintenance and supply, and around object code line-items, but not around final objectives, goals, or outcomes. The budgeting structure conflicted with the operational decision making used by military leaders (Lyden and Lindenberg 1983). There was no way to identify and contain duplicative or unnecessary programs, and terminating ineffective programs was extremely difficult. To counteract the politics, and to identify priorities and best allocate resources, McNamara needed a **strategic plan**. Such a plan would clarify department needs and priorities, and it would provide a rational basis for decision making that could help fend off political pressures.

Budgeting to a strategic plan is not a new idea. Alexander Hamilton, in his 1791 "Report on Manufactures," established a precedent for "budgeting to a plan" (Hamilton 1791/1966). Hamilton, in his role as secretary of the U.S. Treasury, presented an elaborate, well-argued, and well-documented long-term plan to Congress as the cornerstone of his strategy for obtaining members' support for public funding of the U.S. financial and transportation infrastructure.

Plans and planning are the essence of program budgeting (Novick 1992; U.S. Department of Defense 1984/2003). Budgets may carry a program budget label, but unless there is a *concrete plan that connects program expenditures to a set of objectives, which in turn are connected to goals, a true program budget does not exist.* Many agencies organize their budget into functional categories or sets of activities that may carry the *program* label. But without knowing the plan behind these functional categories and programmatic activities, it is difficult to tell what purposes the object code line-item categories composing the larger set of program activities are intended to serve. That was the problem McNamara's PPBS system was intended to solve: the need to budget to a plan and then to link that plan systematically to programs to create a three-legged stool that integrated: (1) planning, (2) programming, and (3) budgeting. If these three organizational activities were successfully linked, a manager would be able create an integrated budgeting *system,* thus the use of the phrase **planning, programming, budgeting system (PPBS)**.

EXAMPLE OF PPBS: COMMUNITY CORRECTIONS

The example in Exhibit 12.1 presents a simplified application of PPBS for one department in a larger county government organization. This hypothetical county community corrections department provides probation and parole services to adult offenders following incarceration, and administers home and community monitoring for offenders. The example illustrates how a mission statement and goals established through a strategic planning process are causally and hierarchically linked to the achievement of a concrete set of objectives that have specified budgetary consequences. The instrumental nature of this linkage process cannot be accomplished without careful and time-consuming planning. In practice, describing the full department's activities would require 8 to 12 goals, each with a set of subordinate objectives.

Exhibit 12.1

Cascade County Community Corrections Department PPBS* Example

Mission: To provide safe and productive incarceration for citizens who have been sentenced to prison or released on parole.

Goal 1: To rehabilitate clients on parole and probation so they can return as productive members of society.

FY2 Requested Expenditure

1. **Objective 1.1**	To increase FY2 employment references of clients by 10% more than FY1 levels with no budget increase over what was allocated for these activities in FY1.	$_____
Activity	Direct service delivery activities, staff positions, FTEs assigned, procurement, and contracts.	
Activity	Indirect and administrative support activities.	
2. **Objective 1.2**	To double total mental health consultations experienced by clients in FY2 compared to FY1 at a cost of 1.0 FTE Mental Health Nurse.	$_____
Activity	Direct service delivery activities, staff positions, FTEs assigned, procurement, and contracts.	
Activity	Indirect and administrative support activities.	
3. **Objective 1.3**	To limit FY2 parole and probation violations to 15% of Corrections clientele by introducing a bracelet monitoring program at a cost that does not exceed the total budget allocation expended in FY1 for parole and probation monitoring.	$_____
Activity	Direct service delivery activities, staff positions, FTEs assigned, procurement, and contracts.	
Activity	Indirect and administrative support activities.	

Note: PPBS = Planning, Programming, Budgeting System.

The preceding example illustrates the planning steps of successful PPBS budgeting: creating a mission statement, setting goals, establishing objectives, determining the activities that need to be undertaken to achieve the objectives, and attaching a total cost of producing each objective. Objective level costs can then be aggregated to the goal and departmental levels. The integrated combination of plan intentions, resources, staffing, procurement, activities, and an expected cost is known loosely as a **budget package, decision package**, or simply a **package**. A package is one alternative for funding a goal or objective. Depending on the context and budget instructions, a package may cover funding for an entire department, a program, or just a portion of a program.

The PPBS hierarchy of mission, goals, and objectives builds out and gives structure to the strategic and operational planning concepts we discussed earlier in chapter 10. When measures of workload, effectiveness, or efficiency are included and considered in the selection of objectives and their service delivery activities (see chapter 13), we have a complete PPBS system. Including performance and expenditure information in PPBS lets analysts and decision makers consider the relative efficiency and effectiveness of different budget packages in meeting plan objectives. We will address the measurement element in the next chapter on performance budgeting. But in the sections that follow in this chapter, we will discuss each of the core elements that make up the PPBS approach to budgeting.

KEY ELEMENTS OF PROGRAM BUDGETING

PPBS is composed of the following four key elements organized into a hierarchical structure that clearly links means to ends: mission, goals, objectives, and activities. This structure aligns with the planning structure of many organizations and with the budget planning framework described in chapter 10. The mission statement is the product of the strategic planning level of the organization; goals specify how the strategic plan will be transformed into operational level sets of activities; objectives further specify how these sets of activities will take concrete form in the organization's operational and business plans; and activities specify the tactical work that frontline workers will undertake to implement the mission, goals, and objectives. PPBS is flexible, however, and additional levels of subgoals or subobjectives may be added between the original four levels to accommodate greater organization size or special initiatives.

PPBS Element 1: Mission Statement

When someone says, "I'm on a mission," we usually assume that the person is devoting all of her emotional, physical, and intellectual energy in the pursuit of a single-minded purpose. Similarly, when an organization sets forth its official mission, the single-minded focus is narrowed down to a concise statement of the worthwhile purpose that justifies its existence. Accordingly, mission statements describe what you do, whom you serve, and the values that guide the work of your organization. The goal of a mission statement is to let people inside and outside of the organization know what it is trying to accomplish and how it will do it.

There are different uses and types of mission statements. Some organizations use their mission statement as a publicity tool for marketing and fundraising; others publish their mission statements in annual reports meant to be read by investors, donors, clients, and stakeholders; still others create mission statements that serve as a compass for leadership decisions and as a galvanizing force for employees. It is important to have a clear sense of the various audiences intended to be served by a mission statement before putting words to paper. A good mission statement answers three questions: (1) Why do you exist? (2) Whom do you serve? and (3) What values guide the work of your organization? Sometimes these multiple needs are divided up into three separate documents. A **vision statement** provides clarity about what success looks like. A **beliefs and values statement** sets forth the values that guide the work of the organization, and a **mission statement** focuses on the purposes that the organization hopes to achieve. All of these can be collapsed into one statement, but this usually requires three or four sentences, not just one. Together, these statements describe and define a "brand" of what makes the organization distinctive among its neighbors, peers, and competitors. The appearance of key descriptive words and the priority of their placement in these statements signals how an organization hopes to perform for its constituents and for the community. Following are some examples of mission statements. Determine whether you think the mission statement is sufficient to stand alone or needs to be accompanied by a vision statement and by a beliefs and values statement.

Mission Statement Example 1

"The Self-Start Program, a broad-based collaborative community initiative, assists low-income mothers and their children to help themselves complete their education and achieve economic self-sufficiency through empowerment skills, access to affordable housing, child development services, health care, support services, and meaningful employment. Self-Start mothers and children develop positive self-esteem and clarify the values on which to build a successful life" (based on Executive Women International [EWI], Minneapolis, MN 2007).

Mission Statement Example 2

"The American Society of Public Administration's (ASPA) mission is to be the leading public service organization that:

- Advances the art, science, teaching, and practice of public and nonprofit administration.
- Promotes the value of joining and elevating the public service profession.
- Builds bridges among all who pursue public purposes.
- Provides networking and professional development opportunities to those committed to public service values.
- Achieves innovative solutions to the challenges of governance" (ASPA 2013).

Mission Statement Example 3

State Department of Public Safety

Mission: To protect human life and property by enforcing state laws, deterring criminal activity, ensuring highway and public safety, and providing vital scientific, technical, and operational support to other criminal justice agencies.

Vision: To be a national model in providing ethical, effective, efficient, and customer-oriented state-level law enforcement services (Arizona Department of Public Safety 2013).

These examples illustrate the all-encompassing, strategic function that a mission statement serves for all of the subunits operating within the larger structure of organizational authority. For that reason, programs and suborganizational units commonly adopt the mission, values, and statement of beliefs that have been developed for the organization as a whole. In such cases, the burden of developing subordinate goals, objectives, and workload measures falls on each of the subprogram units within a department or agency.

PPBS Element 2: Formulating Goals

Formulating goals and objectives is not an intuitively self-evident process, especially because we commonly use the two terms interchangeably. But in PPBS, goals and objectives have a hierarchical and causal relationship with one another. *Goals define a destination, and objectives tell us how we are going to get there.* In that sense, objectives are efficient causes, which, when systematically linked, produce the goal. If our goal is to build a rock wall, the objectives tell us the concrete steps that we will take, the expertise and people we will need, and the amount of time and the resources needed to complete the wall. The key to success in creating goals and objectives is the clarity and certainty we have as to *exactly how* an objective is going to cause the achievement of the stated goal. If the relationship between the objectives and the goal is uncertain, fuzzy, or unknown, then we aren't ready to include the objective within a PPBS plan. If we end up not being able to create objectives that have this kind of causal clarity and certainty, then it may be time to reconsider the goal statement, which itself may be unachievable, too ambitious, or outside the orbit of organizational control. For example, a public safety goal of "reducing the fear of crime" may not be a goal that makes much sense within the context of a given community because the fear of crime is an artifact of external forces and socioeconomic conditions over which the police have little control. A border town that has high numbers of drug gang killings may not be something that local law enforcement officials can control without lots of outside help and, even with the reduction in the number of drug- and gang-related killings, the fear of crime by residents may not be changed. In short, what is the objective data that provides the rationale for the choice of a given goal, and what is the objective data that supports the choice of a given objective as the best way to achieve this goal? These questions remind us that the goal- and objective-setting process is not just an intellectual exercise; it is a data-gathering and analysis exercise. This will become clearer as we elaborate more fully on the formulation of goals in this section and the formulation of objectives in the section to follow.

A **goal** is a statement of purpose directed toward an identified community need. A good goal statement has the following characteristics:

1. It expresses an important value to be sought.
2. It includes adjectival wording that defines a service approach.
3. It is related to an important community need.
4. It is timeless in terms of when it will be accomplished.
5. It helps to achieve the organizational mission.
6. It is capable of being achieved by the establishment of clear objectives.

Examine each of the following examples of goal statements in terms of the six criteria set forth above. What would you add, if anything, to strengthen each statement?

- Operate and maintain the sewage treatment facility in a dependable, safe, and efficient fashion such that the discharged effluent meets state and federal standards, protects the environment, (i.e., receiving streams), and safeguards the public health. (Wastewater Treatment)
- Manage the traffic system in order to reduce accidents, congestion, and negative environmental impacts. (Traffic Engineering)
- Assist the legislative body and agencies by the provision of timely, accurate, and relevant information for use in the development, implementation, and evaluation of state policies; assist agencies utilizing such information; recommend budgetary and managerial systems which can aid in the implementation of state policies and which can help to maintain the fiscal integrity of the state; and provide and promote opportunities for the continued professional development of staff members. (Budget Office)
- To provide timely and quality legal services at a reasonable cost to state/county agencies (Attorney General/County Attorney).

The development of good goal statements cannot be done in a vacuum or simply as a groupthink process. While it is important to cast a wide net in developing goal statements, especially to involve those who have leadership roles in meeting the goals, it is important that the processes be informed by objective data that answer the following kinds of questions: (1) Is the goal theoretically achievable at some future date? (2) Do we have the resources, or the potential resources, to achieve the goal over an extended period of time? (3) How big a role does our organizational unit have in the achievement of this goal? (4) Can we develop the political support necessary to achieve this goal? and (5) What qualities and characteristics do we want to express in achieving the goal? All of these questions require data gathering and data checking from a variety of sources. What follows are some strategies for acquiring this data and establishing work unit goals:

- Focus on outcome conditions that represent improvements in the community or to the client base (cf. Oregon Progress Board 2012).
- Review existing **budget requests**, especially the objective hierarchy section for the program.
- Interview governing body members, program administrators, managers, and supervisors.
- Review legislative and governing body actions that mandate or authorize the program.
- Review legislative and governing body budget hearings.
- Review grant applications and federal mandates that fund a program.
- Review what professional associations say the goals of a program should be.
- Review "goal setting" efforts by other comparable departments in other jurisdictions and organizations.
- Review summaries of the job responsibilities for the major leaders/supervisors who are responsible for the achievement of the goals.
- Review complaints and concerns of residents in the community.
- Review complaints and concerns of clients of the program.
- Review the operating and service characteristics (particularly the various activities) of the agency (what it is actually doing).
- Review the results of previous program evaluations.

Exhibit 12.2 provides a summary framework that will result in the creation of meaningful, doable, and affordable organizational goals. A goal should fully express and implement authorizing laws, but if a particular program or service is only tangentially authorized, it may signal the need to consider reprioritizing or discontinuing the activity. The questions in Exhibit 12.2 help to curb even well-intentioned mission creep and activities sustained by historic but outdated political agreements and policy interpretations.

The outcome focus of effective goals shifts attention away from a short-term focus on the next fiscal year and from protecting organizational turf and historical patterns of doing things simply out of inertia. Instead, attention is placed on the conditions needed to achieve substantial and practical results. This focus on the future may require a sustained commitment over many years or decades, or it may require the integration of a broad array of resources from many sources. Extended goals provide a long-term compass for short-term objectives and annual spending and investments. The outcome-driven focus of goals allows leadership to develop complex initiatives and programs that involve staff, capacity, and administration from several departments, divisions, or programs. Goals are boundary spanning, which contrasts with the fund structure and accounting-based rigidity of the line-item budget format. The boundary spanning ability of PPBS is especially helpful in larger organizations, where functional departments and their agencies are separated by different cabinetlike heads, legal authorizations, and reporting structures. For example, effective recovery of endangered Pacific Northwest anadromous salmon and steelhead fisheries may require program and budget contributions from agencies within the federal departments of the Interior, Commerce, Agriculture, Energy and Defense, as well as within state/local governments, tribes, and special districts. Formal coordination among these entities requires the vertical involvement of administrators from the field to the secretarial level and horizontally across many semi-sovereign

Exhibit 12.2

Suggestions for Minimizing Problems in Establishing Work Unit Goals

The application of several caveats will help administrators and speed the development of program and work unit goals.

- Include members of the staff in the process. Interview as many of your staff as possible, at least through the supervisory level, for their ideas on what the goals of the organization are or should be.
- Review all of the major programs of service that subordinate organizational units provide to the community or to other agencies.
- Review goal statements of subordinate units that collectively are responsible for the achievement of the goals.
- Be sure the goal statements are broad enough to cover all the functions legally authorized for the organization or program.
- Be sure the goals statements are limited to the functions authorized for the organization or program.
- Be aware of duplication of goals among programs/divisions. In some instances, eliminating duplication may be in order; in others, duplication may enhance quality, effectiveness, and be legally mandated.
- Recognize that goals may be timeless because their accomplishment is continuous. Goals may also define an end state or final condition that may take an extended period to accomplish.

governing jurisdictions. PPBS structured goals provide a means of keeping the program focus on salmon and steelhead recovery, which may take decades of program commitment and hundreds of billions of dollars from dozens of jurisdictions and organizations in the public, private, and nonprofit sectors.

In the same manner, PPBS outcome-driven goals can bring integration to local community problem solving. If local governments, state agencies, community foundations, consolidated intermediary nonprofits, and service delivery organizations can concede at least to some degree on a common set of goals, then short-term objectives, annual funding, and performance responsibilities can be allocated to the different actors according to their strengths. For example, community organizations—including local government, community foundations, consolidated intermediary nonprofits, religious organizations, and service providers—may develop a 10-year initiative to stamp out homelessness in their community. Goals in a PPBS structure provide the outcome-driven vision of the conditions that need to be in place in order to ensure success. PPBS keeps the initiative of the various partners focused on the long-term outcome over the course of 10 or more fiscal years. PPBS also provides an umbrella of goals under which different loosely coupled organizations may work together to achieve a larger shared vision.

PPBS Element 3: Formulating Objectives

Much of what we have described for the formulation of goals in the previous section also applies to the formulation of objectives. An **objective** is a desired result in which the achievement is measurable within a given time frame at a specified level or increment of cost. The primary difference between a goal and an objective is that objectives more concretely describe the specific sets of activities that will be undertaken within a specified period of time and what it will cost to perform those activities. Objectives answer the question: How are we going to achieve a specified goal? Good objective statements answer the following four questions (City of Portland 1979):

1. What specific activities will be undertaken to achieve the goal?
2. When will these activities be accomplished?
3. How much will it cost to achieve these objectives?
4. How are we measuring the completion and achievement of our objectives?

Objectives should be stated in terms of a needed result or outcome conditions, not as a set of processes, a set of **inputs**, or a set of activities. Exhibit 12.3 provides several examples of objective statements to illustrate this important point. In reviewing the examples, ask whether the objective statement answers each of the four questions we have set forth for a good objectives statement.

The examples in Exhibit 12.3 illustrate the importance of specifying the outcome and program detail for each objective. This includes a statement of what will be accomplished, how, and at what cost. Since governments characteristically provide service rather than produce products, outcomes are commonly expressed as levels of service provided by the government to its citizens and clients. A *level of service* defines the service delivery volume and service quality provided to citizens or clients. For example, a small city police department might define a level of police patrol services in one of its annual budget objectives. The department uses two measures to define the level of coverage: the amount of coverage as measured by the number of sworn officers per 1,000 population, and the quality of coverage as measured by service call response times. The department estimates that it can meet the objective and provide a specified level of service for a requested level of funds. The department may also recognize that the community has a stable population of relatively wealthy individuals. Gang activity and substance abuse crimes may be minimal, and the department may propose a service level of sworn officers per 1,000 at a rate below the national standard rate. The lower standard may be acceptable to the community and require less expense.

The level of service concept implies that changes in the criteria and specifications in a budget objective lead to a corresponding change in budget expenses or needed revenues. This opens up an opportunity for budget choice, as well as for the consideration of alternative service levels and alternative management configurations for providing those services. By working in terms of detailed objectives and activities with varying criteria, PPBS can help to effectively frame comparisons of service alternatives and expenses. The performance metrics and performance analysis techniques we discuss in the next chapter provide the tools for the analysis and comparison of service level alternatives. The capability of PPBS to compare the relative costs of different levels of service and alternative service delivery configurations was an important feature behind Secretary McNamara's application of the system at the Pentagon.

The review of objectives during annual budget preparation also provides an occasion for program managers to reassess the construction of each objective as a planning element, program descriptor, and outcome or output measure. At the same time, managers and analysts can assess organizational progress in the achievement of program objectives by asking the following questions:

• Was the prior year's objective achieved?
• Was the objective overstated? If so, should the objective be reduced to conform more accurately to the available resources, or should resources be increased to make it possible to achieve the overstated objective?
• Was the objective understated? If so, should the objective be increased to reflect increased productivity, or can resources be reduced?

Exhibit 12.3

Qualities of PPBS Objectives

Objectives should be results oriented	Objectives should not be process or input oriented
In the next year install x number of traffic signals at 80% of the locations designated in the traffic master plan.	Complete x number of traffic studies.
Reduce by x % the level of congestion at y % locations by resetting the traffic timing intervals at z number of intersections.	Undertake traffic studies at the 10 most congested locations.

Specifies cost parameters	Does not specify cost parameters
In the next year install x number traffic signals at 80% of the locations designated in the traffic master plan at a total cost of y.	Install x number of traffic signals.
Reduce by x % the level of congestion at y % locations by resetting the traffic timing intervals at a cost no greater than 110% of what was spent last year (total requested cost = z).	Complete x number of traffic studies.

Objectives should be realistic	Objectives should not be unrealistic
Resolve x % of citizen and public agency complaints regarding traffic congestion within two weeks of receipt at a cost no greater than what was spent on such activities last year (total requested cost = y).	Resolve x % of citizen and public agency complaints regarding traffic congestion within two weeks.
Ensure effective enforcement of code violations by reducing the number of violations from x % in FY1 to y % in FY2, at a cost no greater than 105% of what was spent for code enforcement last year.	To correct 80% of the violations by FY2.

Objectives should be specific	Objectives should not be general
Increase available on-street parking space by x % in walking districts, y % in scooter districts, and z % in outlying districts, through effective enforcement of parking regulations ordinance in FY2 compared to FY1.	Increase parking spaces.
Increase the use of the auditorium for visual arts displays by increasing the percentage of time available for temporary visual arts displays by x % in FY2.	Increase the use of the auditorium.

Objectives should be measureable in a defined time frame for accomplishment	Not measureable, lacks a defined time frame for accomplishment
For the one-year period of FY2, increase available on-street parking space by x % in walking districts, y % in scooter districts, and z % in outlying districts relative to FY1 levels, through effective enforcement of parking regulation ordinance.	Increase downtown parking spaces.
To eliminate x % of grass and weed violations at least once within the 120-day period between June 1 and October 31 in those neighborhoods identified as problem areas.	Improve the environment of the county.

- Should resources be shifted among programs or activities to achieve greater overall productivity?
- To what degree should annual objectives be adjusted upward or downward as a result of periodic reviews during the year?

These questions provide concrete illustrations of the importance of collecting extensive data prior to the creation of objectives, and of analyzing and discussing the significance of this data among those responsible for executing the activities associated with the objective statement. The same strategies we have outlined regarding data collection for the establishment of goals applies equally well to the setting of objectives.

There are at least three consequences of this data-driven process for setting objectives. First, it places a large amount of control of program budgeting in the hands of *the doers,* those who have access to the information related to operational success. Without using this knowledge to set objectives, there's little chance that the objectives will accurately reflect what is reasonably possible and doable. In addition, involvement provides the opportunity for incorporating and generating creative ideas and developing ownership of the process. This ownership becomes essential for the creation and accurate reporting of the performance data.

A second consequence of the data-driven process is that if the operational data does not exist, then it needs to be collected and tested, which increases the amount of time it may take to implement PPBS. For instance, in developing performance measures, it may become apparent that some of the objectives need reworking. In listing activities and functions performed by an organization, it may become clear that the goal statements have been too narrowly defined or that previously listed objectives are no longer feasible. Or, there may be changes in the organization that need to be taken into account. As these and other problems surface during the program planning process, time needs to be factored in to make the necessary adjustments. These adjustments may also have important implications for the development of performance measures. An overriding concept to remember is that there should be flexibility in any program planning and performance measurement system.

A third consequence of the data-gathering focus of PPBS is that it can be threatening to those responsible for the operational achievement of the objectives. Frequently, managers become preoccupied with lingering fears (1) that the information may be used to punish the organizational subunits and individuals in leadership positions if an objective is not met, or (2) that these units and individuals will not be rewarded when an objective is met or exceeded. This fear factor cannot be ignored, which usually means that PPBS needs to be piloted on a trial basis for at least one year after it is put in place. Adjustments may be needed, and the organizational leadership must demonstrate that the system will be used for positive—not punitive or negative—purposes.

When all of the consequences of a data-based approach to objective setting are added together, it means that PPBS requires three to four years to develop, implement, and test. First, it takes at least a year to develop objectives if the data is readily available. If the data is not available, it may take two years to develop realistic objectives. Once the objectives have been developed, it takes another year to connect those objectives to the budget process. Then, another year is needed to allow for adjustments in the objectives that will alleviate the fear factor and ensure a high level of correspondence between the objectives and program operations. In many jurisdictions and organizations, this lengthy process can lose steam as administrative and political priorities of both elected and appointed leaders change. To be successful, PPBS requires a sustained commitment from elected officials and senior administrative leaders over a period of several years.

In addition to using a data-driven approach to objective development, we offer a series of recommendations on the development of goals and objectives:

- Review and be familiar with organizational goals. Objectives should have a clear relationship to their respective goals.
- Interview governing board/legislative members, program administrators, managers, and supervisors.
- Review objectives established by other comparable agencies.
- Establish organizational goals before attempting to formulate objectives.
- Be sure objectives support the goal statement.
- Carefully select the language of the objective statement to clearly state exactly what service will be provided. The language should "screen out" those variables that may affect your organization's performance but over which you have no control.
- Be sure that the objective is results oriented and deals with effectiveness (quality and/or quantity), efficiency (quantity-cost), a level of service, or a combination of the three.
- Include reasonable targets of performance in the objective statement. Review department historical data so realistic targets are established.
- List all activities and functions to guarantee that objectives cover everything the organization's authorization and goals allow.
- Prepare objectives carefully, with an eye toward reducing the amount of time spent on developing performance measures.
- Periodically review objectives: Objectives are not static.

PPBS Element 4: Determining Program Activities to Achieve an Objective

Activities perform the actual work of an organization and provide the critical link that connects the PPBS budget to program operations. Objectives cannot be established without a very clear understanding of the concrete organizational activities that need to be undertaken and sequenced in order to achieve them. Direct service delivery to external clients is the most evident form of activity, but some activities provide critical internal support to service delivery. For fire, police, and public safety departments, training programs are an activity in themselves. Training not only ensures high performance in service delivery but also lowers the organization's performance liability. Support activities include procurement and purchasing, human resources, general counsel and legal services, finance, information technology, motor pool services, and radio/telecommunications. While support activities do not actually deliver a service to external clients, they enable other programs to do so. Analysts and administrators may need to define several service delivery and training activities, and then link to several support activities provided by other organization units to fully implement a single objective. For example, increasing the responsiveness and efficiency of a permit center may require linking several sets of program activities located in different departments, like planning, transportation, building services (inspectors), public utilities, and legal counsel. Support activities use the same detailed activity definitions and descriptions as do service delivery activities. A full definition of activities for an objective requires: (1) establishing work plans and workflow; (2) defining the direct service delivery activities; (3) recognizing and integrating training and support activities; (4) defining the role of contracts and partnerships; and (5) integrating capital equipment, information technology, and facilities. The integration and scheduling of all these different activities and resources into a coordinated program to meet an objective demonstrates the programming aspect of PPBS.

The detail for each activity should include the necessary staff positions, FTEs, and work team organization. The performance outcomes and criteria established in an activity should relate directly to the annual or biannual personal performance evaluation criteria of its work team members and administrators. A completed activity description includes a total expenditure estimate. This total estimate sums the expenditure estimates from all the component activities.

The PPBS focus on the activity as a unit of cost establishes a fundamental unit for analysis and budget construction. Rather than focus on aggregated categories of cost as in the line-item format, PPBS attempts to use the actual cost of providing an activity to develop cost projections for the parent objective. Complete cost development includes both directly attributable costs and an assigned share of the organization's administrative overhead costs. Activity level costs make a critical contribution to performance measurement systems and to performance budgeting, as we will see in the next chapter. By focusing at the activity level, analysts can often separate low- and high-cost clients and then move away from a reliance on average annual costs. **Activity based costing** and its related tools form the basis of many performance analysis and measurement systems (Stenzel and Stenzel 2003; Garrett and MacDonald 1996).

The extension and programming of objectives into activities is not particularly esoteric or uniquely demanding. It is what good managers and supervisors do. The difference in effective PPBS is that the management and supervision is guided by a clear and mutually shared understanding among *all* who have leadership responsibility of the objectives that *every* one of the individual activities is intended to accomplish. This is a group ownership model that may not fit easily with many conventional bureaucratic models designed on the basis of individual roles and responsibilities. How does one square this individual-centered model of responsibility with group ownership and group responsibility? Our answer is **coproduction**.

Coproduction is a group and team process of building agreement on the goals and their importance to the organizational unit. Once there is agreement on the goals, then there needs to be a deliberative process that explores all of the pathways to achieve the objectives, with agreement on which pathways should be given the highest priority for a given period of time. This deliberative process of constructing agreement on the ends and the means to get there enables those with official role responsibilities in the bureaucratic hierarchy to maximize the achievement of the agreed-upon goals and objectives, as illustrated in Exhibit 12.4.

ORGANIZING OBJECTIVES INTO A PROGRAM

Our discussion of PPBS so far suggests that the program budgeting model is a top-down linear and instrumentally rational process. By starting with a mission and then proceeding in a linear fashion from goals to objectives, one moves from the larger purposes to ever narrower instrumental and operational issues involving the best way to achieve these purposes. The ideal setting for undertaking PPBS is in the initial stages of defining a new initiative or starting a new program. This ideal, however, is exceedingly rare and not the normal circumstance that prevails in most public organizations. Typically, activities in a given organizational program are added incrementally, without any well-thought-out plan or rationale that connects all of the parts to a larger whole. How can PPBS be put into place in an environment where this is the norm? What happens when there is no incentive to do PPBS from the top? Conversely, what happens when there is such an initiative, but you have existing collections of activities that don't lend themselves very well to the PPBS format? We will address these two questions in the paragraphs that follow.

It is important to remember that the PPBS protocol can be applied to any set of cohering activities. For example, a Parks Department or the larger jurisdiction may have no interest in creating a formal system of PPB. But those in charge of a given park or a given set of activities (like after-school, summer, and other programs) can apply the PPBS technique to all or a portion of their portfolio of activities. If PPBS can assist you in making better decisions and involving your staff in a more productive way in the planning, implementation, and overall decision-making process, then use it.

Much like organizing multiple partners into community initiatives and programs, PPBS also can be used to help rationalize a hodgepodge of existing programs and collections of activities that have developed over time without a clear strategic plan. In fact, the American political process operates

Exhibit 12.4

Activities Related to an Objective: A Hypothetical Example

Objective: In the next two fiscal years, install traffic signals at 80% of the locations designated in the traffic master plan (12 intersections) at an expected cost not to exceed $3.5 million.

Direct Service Activity 1: Use three in-house crews to complete preparation of land-use plans, permits, and engineering design at the 12 intersections specified in the traffic master plan. Complete at least five plans by six months into the fiscal year. Each crew will have a lead design engineer (1 FTE), an engineering technician (1 FTE), and a traffic engineer (0.25 FTE), and consult the county engineering staff as necessary. As necessary, crews will: visit the site and conduct field analysis of soils; assess existing sidewalks, drainage, vegetation and other structures; identify electricity sources and access; identify electrical boxes, vaults, and hardware necessary; identify need for road structure modifications and under road surface installation; consider traffic flow patterns and flow levels at average levels, high and low peaks; and prepare engineering designs and plans for installation. Crews will prepare and file all necessary state, county, and city permits for signal installation and construction. Crews will have access to and use: engineering design software, spreadsheet and office software, light duty trucks and cars from the county motor pool, and engineering and land survey instruments by rental or from county ownership. Conduct quarterly reviews to assess progress on activity accomplishment.

Total Cost: $850,000

Total FTEs: 6.75

Direct Service Activity 2: Based on preliminary engineering plans and final plans available six months into the fiscal year, conduct a procurement process for construction professional services to install traffic signals at five designated locations. Complete procurement process no later than the end of the tenth month of the fiscal year. Procurement team will formulate and announce a request for qualifications for the project; update the existing county professional engineering services roster; formulate and announce a request for proposals for the project; hold a competition and make a selection from the professional services roster; negotiate final contract agreement with winning bidder; conclude contract terms and sign a contract; and help to arrange pre-work meeting. Procured installation activities shall include: road bed and traffic flow and pedestrian pattern modifications; drainage, sidewalk, utility box and vault, and other needed facility construction; signal pole, arm, and gantry installation; installation of signal lights; installation of electric wiring; testing and setting of traffic signals; and a two-year post-installation service guarantee. Establish a procurement team that includes: senior design engineer (0.5 FTE); procurement specialist II (0.2 FTE); coordination and support from the two design engineers; and support from county general counsel's office. County general counsel will support administration as necessary up to 0.1 FTE; over that level, office of counsel will charge engineering program for additional time (refer to indirect support activity below).

Total FTEs: 0.7 FTE, contingent additional 0.1 FTE

Total Cost: $80,000

Direct Service Activity 3: Implement and administer a construction contract to install traffic signals at five designated locations. Establish a contract administration and performance compliance team to represent the county for the contract. Contract compliance team shall include a designated contracting officer (procurement specialist II for 0.1 FTE) and contracting officer's field representative (senior design engineer for 0.5 FTE). Following selection of a winning bid and contract finalization, conduct a pre-work meeting; establish work completion mileposts, a production schedule, and partner roles; establish contract partnership; monitor work progress; provide routine progress accomplishment reports to the contracting officer and to the contractor; inspect completed work for quality and acceptance; assess any bonus incentives or penalties as needed per contract. Administration crew will enter all contract-related communication and reports into the county procurement records system. Administration crew will have access to and use light duty trucks and cars from the county motor pool.

Total FTEs: 0.6 FTE **Total Cost: $40,000**

Professional services construction contract estimated level:
Bidding process will establish the final total cost of the traffic signal installation contract. **Total Cost: $2,500,000**

Contract Management and Timeline
Finalize contract terms by end of tenth month of budgeted fiscal year. Begin contract execution in final two months of the budgeted fiscal year. Contract expected to continue for all of the 12 months of the next fiscal year (fiscal year +1), with contract completion expected by the end of the first month of fiscal year +2. Total contract elapsed time expected at 15 months. Contract provisions will likely include a cost escalation provision triggered by the U.S. Federal Reserve inflation multiplier at month 8. Acceptance of a contract opens the county to an array of performance and financial liabilities. Contract provisions will be included to minimize these risks.

Indirect Support Activity 1: Office of County Counsel will provide consultation services and legal advice in support of procurement and contract administration for the traffic signal installation project at five sites across the county. Counsel's office will provide service up to the budgeted amount. Service needs above the 0.1 FTE will require negotiation with the county executive, the county counsel, and the engineering department director.

Total FTEs: 0.05 FTE counsel rate, 0.05 FTE paralegal rate **Total Cost: $30,000**

Total Objective Costs:

Total FTEs 8.15 FTEs

Total county staff and operational costs $1,000,000

Professional services construction contract estimated cost $2,500,000

Total expected cost to meet budget objective $3,500,000 in large part in this way, especially at the state and national levels of government. Over the past several decades, most members of state legislatures have experienced budget and staff limitations, which means that there may not be much analysis or time invested in figuring out all of the details of a proposed piece of legislation. Elected officials seize on windows of opportunity to push legislation with the understanding that "we will figure out the details later." The "we" is often the career administrators who are responsible for managing programs that don't quite fit what they are already doing. Under such circumstances, PPBS can be used to reconstruct legislative intent or intentions, with the goal of getting greater clarity about how a program needs to be managed. The enacted statute and accompanying legislative committee reports may serve as the PPBS "plan" by providing the key elements for an agency and program mission statement, goal statements, and even objectives.

PPBS can also be used periodically to gain a better understanding of how the existing array of loosely coupled programs might be better reconfigured to work more efficiently and effectively. The goal- and objective-setting process is a useful exercise in data gathering. It helps illuminate where there might be potential synergies among existing sets of activities, and whether these activities could be put to higher and better use through some organizational realignment. Under this scenario, PPBS is used to jump-start a strategic planning process, rather than serving as the end product of a process. With this kind of occasional use of PPBS, there is no reason to assume that one needs to tie the process permanently into the larger organization's budget process.

PROGRAM BUDGET EXERCISE

By completing a program budgeting exercise, one can gain an appreciation for the utility, complexity, and potential disadvantages of PPBS. In the exercise presented in Exhibit 12.5, you are asked to develop a hypothetical PPB structure for a small program or small portion of your organization. The textbook website (www.pdx.edu/cps/budget-book) offers a more complete exercise in PPB hierarchy development. As you work, remember the importance of tightly linking the objectives to the goals and developing objective statements that specify which activities will be undertaken, at what cost, and within what specified time period.

Completing a PPBS exercise requires you to be very specific in establishing goals and in breaking down these goals into achievable and measureable objectives that are causally linked back to your goal statement. The PPBS exercise gives you a better appreciation for the power of program budgeting, but it also makes clear that a considerable amount of time and the heavy involvement of operational staff are needed for its successful completion. Time limitations are especially constraining when PPBS is conducted on an annual basis.

ADVANTAGES AND DISADVANTAGES OF PROGRAM BUDGETING

Program budgeting offers three sets of advantages to public administrators, particularly at the local level of government. First, it focuses the attention of managers on the effectiveness of administrative work. As we have already pointed out, PPBS was originally designed as a tool to help managers improve the effectiveness of their organizations, especially those having several operating units that provide dissimilar services. How does the department head of a public health unit determine whether money should be cut from public education and outreach in order to support more direct service to vulnerable populations? Program budgeting is intended to help answer this question by creating clearly defined goals and objectives. Goals and objectives, when tied directly to budgeted resources, represent an overall plan for operating units and their parent agency or department.

A second advantage of PPBS is that the exercise of preparing goals and objectives enables an organization to periodically revisit what it intends to achieve as a result of changes in the external environment. Without realistic goals and objectives, it is difficult for an organization to know and to communicate to others whether it is functioning efficiently and effectively or even if it is providing those services to the community approved by the board, council, or legislature. Goals and

Exhibit 12.5

Program or Small Organization PPBS Self-Assessment Exercise

Mission Statement:

Program Description:

Goal No. 1: _____
_____
_____

Goal Aggregated Total Cost Estimate: $_____
(Obj. 1 cost + Obj. 2 cost)

Objective No. 1: _____
_____
_____

Aggregated Objective 1 Total Cost Estimate: $_____
(Sum of No. 1 activity costs)

Object No. 1 Activities:

Activity 1.1 (Direct service delivery or task): _____
_____
_____

Activity 1.1 Total Cost Estimate: $_____

Activity 1.2 (Training, supporting, or overhead): _____
_____
_____

Activity 1.2 Total Cost Estimate: $_____

Objective No. 2: _____
_____
_____

Aggregated Objective 2 Total Cost Estimate: $_____

Object No. 2 Activities:

Activity 2.1 (Direct service delivery or task): _____
_____
_____

Activity 2.1 Total Cost Estimate: $_____

Activity 2.2 (Training, supporting, or overhead): _____
_____
_____

Activity 2.2 Total Cost Estimate: $_____

objectives provide a visual way for everyone in a community to see the correspondence between what is intended by a government, nonprofit, or foundation's policy board and the actual translation of those intentions into concrete program activities. This kind of objectification of intentions also provides a rationale for budget approval, and, if adopted, a contract for assessing accountability/ effectiveness. This accountability feature of program budgeting has made it very popular with grant funders and contractors. It enables them to define a clear scope of work and hold grantees and contractees accountable for performance. Many nonprofit organizations use some form of PPBS budgeting (in addition to line-item budgeting) because (1) they are frequently required to do so by funders, and (2) it provides a clear way of communicating to board members and the larger public the bundles of activities which are being undertaken for specific target populations.

In addition to providing clarity about the goals and objectives of an organization, a third advantage of PPBS is that it provides the structure for determining the costs of services and the relative importance of activities carried out by employees within the organization. The relationship between the hierarchy of goals and objectives developed by departments and programs on the one hand, and the dollars budgeted to achieve them on the other, reveals what is important and why. This information has become increasingly important—in fact, essential—for programs that are expected to be self-supporting from the fees that are charged for services. For example, it is increasingly common practice to charge fees for various types of building permits and inspections (i.e., construction, electrical, engineering, and plumbing). It has also become common to charge fees for recreation programs, for access to public lands, and for the purchase of services like water, electricity, sewer, fire, and similar kinds of public goods. In these cases, the provision of public services may be conducted on a cost of service basis. This simply means that individuals are charged for what it costs to collect, produce, and distribute the water they have consumed, or to perform the code compliance inspection they have received, or to maintain the public lands and facilities that recreation users are enjoying (i.e., maintenance of trails, campsites, toilets, and boat ramps). In such cases, it is essential for program managers to keep track of the cost information to deliver a specified set of services. This information serves as the basis for establishing fees that can be defended. State and federal utility commissions that license private-sector suppliers to provide electricity, water, wastewater management, and other public goods rely heavily upon program budgeting techniques and protocols for documenting requests for fee increases and adjustments.

Another example of the importance of program-level information to managers is illustrated in Exhibit 12.6. Once programmatic information is available, it becomes clear that most of the responses to calls by fire departments has less to do fires than with the demographics of America's aging population. Fire departments around the nation spend more time responding to 911 calls from health care facilities and aging residents than they do to fires. This information raises important questions about whether the service delivery system is best aligned to deliver the most efficient and effective services to the clients in question. Line-item budgeting systems would obscure this information.

A traditional line-item budget, aggregated to the department (organizational) level, is still useful for internal management. In keeping with our fire example, emergency response is provided by firefighter/paramedics who are cross-trained for *both* fire and medical emergencies, and who drive fire trucks to medical calls. But for budget policy decision making, it is helpful to aggregate line-item expenses to the *program* level. In some cases, this requires some analysis to break apart line-items by asking questions like, What *percentage* of the time are firefighter/paramedics responding to fire calls, and what percentage of the time is a fire truck being used to respond to medical calls?

In this example, the program budget reveals to the public and to policy makers (the fire district board or city council) that the fire department is really functioning as a public health department— information that is hidden in the traditional line-item/organizational budget.

Aside from the internal advantages that PPBS provides to the organization, the information generated by the PPB process provides important management information to the council, board, or legisla-

Exhibit 12.6

Program Budget for a Fire Department

| Programs | Organizational Units | | | | Total by Program |
	Administration	Emergency Response	Training	Vehicle Fleet	
Fire Suppression	$200	$2,000	$250	$100	$2,550
Emergency Medical Service	$1,650	$17,900	$250	$880	$20,680
Prevention	$150	$100		$20	$270
Total by Organization Unit	$2,000	$20,000	$500	$1,000	

ture. Information on the objectives of departments and the degree to which the objectives are achieved can reduce the element of risk taking in council, board, or legislative decisions. Understanding the potential for accomplishment is important in making policy and resource decisions. After two or three years of budgeting by objectives, the board, council, or legislature will have accumulated historical cost information on services provided by a department. This information can aid the governing body in budgetary decision making and show the direction in which a department is moving.

In addition to providing managers and the governing body with aids for decision making, another advantage of program budgeting, especially when coupled with performance data, is that it can provide citizens with information on the levels of services provided by agencies and, after council approval of the budget submissions, the costs of those services. Citizens are becoming increasingly interested in what their tax dollars are buying, including the productivity and the efficiency of the provision of government services. One of the purposes of both program and performance budgeting is to enable citizens to have easier access to usable information.

But there can be clear disadvantages in relying mainly on program-based budgeting information. First, the lack of detailed line-item historical information can obscure frequent subprogram changes and information on the efficiency of a program's operation. This is especially the case in larger units of government, where the definition of *program* may be so broad that it covers most of a unit's activities. Changes within these units may be significant over time but never show up in the budget process for much centralized review because the name of the program and the total dollar amount being spent from year to year hasn't appeared to change very much. For example, a police department may have a patrol or community policing program, but over the years the composition of the patrol function may have shifted away from responding to all calls to responding only to those where there is an immediate threat to life and property. Or the community policing function may have shifted away from an emphasis on developing neighborhood watch programs to the prevention of gang violence. The department or organization may not even fully recognize that the shift in purpose has occurred. Periodic review of the department mission and goals provides one remedy to organizational drift.

A second disadvantage of PPBS is related to the political consequences of organizing the expenditure of public funds around programmatic activities. The establishment of program goals and objectives identifies the political stakeholders much more clearly than is the case with line-item budgeting. Stakeholders seldom organize around the object codes of "personnel," "materials and supplies," "capital outlay," and "interfund expenditures." But they do organize around programs that serve specific target populations or that deliver defined sets of services. As a result, this makes it much harder to cut program budgets than it is to cut line-item budgets. There are two reasons for this: First, it is much easier to see who the losers are when there are program cuts than is the case with across-the-board monetary cuts in a line-item budget. It takes a while to see exactly what the consequences of a given set of line-item budget cuts will be. For example, if the organization must make permanent cuts in the number of full-time employees, the program consequences of these cuts may not be known until the final decision is made and until all of the employee rights of seniority have played out within the organization. The delayed implications emerge as the remaining individuals move from one position to another and from one program to another as a result of exercising their seniority bumping rights under the union contract and civil service rules. Second, budget cuts are more difficult to make with PPBS than under line-item budgets because PPBS recognizes and responds to the integration and interconnectivity of the whole organization. PPB requires this kind of preplanning and sustained integration over a period of years. Once goals and objectives have been carefully decided and linked through time-consuming analysis and discussion by program managers and their staff, it is very hard to disassemble one of the parts without affecting the whole. Aaron Wildavsky has likened PPB to buying a complete suit of clothing, including perfectly matching accessories. This kind of wardrobe makes it difficult to make adjustments if one of the parts is lost or becomes worn (Wildavsky 1978, 503). With PPBS, there is less flexibility in making adjustments, and the political transaction costs of making the adjustments may be high compared to line-item budgeting.

In Exhibit 12.7 below, we provide a summary overview of the advantages and disadvantages of PPB from the perspective of the various actors in the budgeting process. From this summary, one gains an appreciation of why PPB was unable to be successfully applied across all federal departments (DeWoolfson 1975; Harper, Kramer, and Rouse 1969; Schick 1973; Lyden and Lindenberg 1983, 92). The PPB experience has been more successful at the state and local levels (Howard 1973; O'Toole and Stipak 1988, 1992) and in a few federal departments, such as the Army Corps of Engineers (Lord 2005).[2]

Why? Primarily because PPBS requires a great deal of time, commitment, and political and administrative leadership to ensure development and implementation. PPBS works well for the Army Corps of Engineers because the Corps is legally required, for many of its activities, to budget by programs that show cost-share matches with local partners. Professional managers in local jurisdictions, with part-time elected officials, can make use of PPBS because they have longer time-horizons and a stable of known services. This is not the case for many senior managers working in a more mercurial political and policy environment at the state and federal levels of government. Merewitz and Sosnick argue that for these reasons, it is "unwise to impose program accounting, to tabulate future expenditures for established programs, to prepare statements of purpose, to defend budget requests without referring to the size of previous appropriations, or to undertake quantitative evaluation of alternatives whenever possible" (1971, 12). However, they do defend the value of pursuing the purposes of program budgeting on a selective basis and in other ways, as we have argued above.

A second reason that PPBS has not been a vast success is that it is misaligned with the interest group nature of the American public policy process (Wildavsky 1979b, 1984, 1992). This process places a premium on compromise, taking advantage of windows of opportunity and the mobilization of political support. The public policy process does not thrive on, or depend on, extensive systematic analysis and data collection. In fact, such analysis can inject additional complexity and controversy to the process (Wildavsky 1979b, v, 166–167). Local governments, especially those that operate on a nonpartisan basis, provide a much better enabling environment for PPBS as a long-term budget strategy. Moreover, for nonprofit organizations, PPBS is especially important for demonstrating accountability to grantors and contractors.

The application of PPBS marked a quality improvement in local government and nonprofit budgeting. Budget instructions and organizational leadership prescribe the exact application of PPBS in annual budget preparation, but even a partial application of the system helps to provide ground-

Exhibit 12.7

PPBS Summary

Purpose? Central question? Problem to be solved?	Chief characteristics	Central actors	Conditions for success	Strengths	Weaknesses
• Program accountability • Is the program achieving its goals and objectives? • Program effectiveness	• Focus is on program plans, goals, and objectives. • Requires budgeting to a plan.	• Program managers and program analysts.	• Requires the necessary time, staff, and resources to develop program plans, goals, and objectives.	• Provides clear linkage between program activities and budget allocation. • Links parts to whole. • Links immediate investments to downstream future financial commitments. • Works well in partnership and network setting.	• Requires considerable investment of resources. • High potential for conflict.

ing and context to the finance-centered line-item budgeting format. The PPBS format explains to the community what its money is purchasing and what activities government or a nonprofit will produce over the coming fiscal year. The planning and programming aspects of PPBS provide important value to public budgets, and when coupled with performance information, the approach provides a whole new level of benefits. We turn to the addition of performance data in the next chapter.

STUDY QUESTIONS

The textbook website (www.pdx.edu/cps/budget-book) provides budget data and organizational information that may be helpful in answering one or several of the following study questions.

1. What does the term *program budgeting* mean? When, why, and by whom was PPBS first used extensively in the public sphere? Examine the budgets (e.g., Budget Data and Plan) on the textbook website (www.pdx.edu/cps/budget-book). Which of these budgets provides a good example of "program budgeting"?
2. What is the role of the chief executive and the legislature in undertaking PPBS? How does PPBS affect the balance of power between the executive and deliberative branches of government?
3. What conditions are necessary for the implementation of PPBS?
4. Which budget and organizational actors tends to gain and to lose in adopting PPBS?
5. What efforts have been made by your agency in recent years to implement a PPBS system? What have been the results of that experience?
6. Why is PPBS effective in budgeting for multiyear, multidepartment programs and organizational initiatives?
7. Why has it been said that PPBS has failed? Based on your organizational experience and your experience with PPBS (including completion of budgeting exercises), do you believe the reasons for the failure of PPBS in public-sector organizations are justified? Why? Why not?
8. What organizational and leadership factors contribute to the relatively successful implementation of PPBS at the state or local level of government? Are these factors present or absent at the federal level of government?
9. What are some reasons you might use PPBS concepts and formats even if you would not adopt it as an annual part of your agency/department budgeting process?
10. Identify a PPBS budget from a government or nonprofit in your region or state. Compare the budget to your own organization's budget regarding its ability to explain and justify public expenditures and to build public confidence.
11. Practice program and PPBS budgeting with exercise 12.1 PPBS Program Budgeting from the textbook website (www.pdx.edu/cps/budget-book).

NOTES

1. Planning, Programming, Budgeting System (PPBS) is a particular version of program budgeting that was popularized by Secretary of Defense Robert McNamara in the 1960s. Like all program budgeting, it breaks budget expenditures out by types of activities. But unlike simple program budgeting, PPBS emphasizes linking these activities systematically to goals and budgets so that the three parts function together as an integrated system. When we use the term program budgeting throughout the chapter, we are using it the strong PPBS sense.

2. For a local government example of a PPBS/line-item hybrid budget, consult Tualatin Valley Fire and Rescue district budgets at www.tvfr.com (accessed October 22, 2012). For a historical summary of the U.S. Army experience with PPBS and extensive detailed guidance on how the army implements PPBS in the setting of an extremely large federal agency, consult Lord 2005 (www.globalsecurity.org/military/library/report/2005/htar2005ch9.pdf).

13   PERFORMANCE BUDGETING

Political rationality is the fundamental kind of reason, because it deals with the preservation and improvement of decision structures, and decision structures are the source of all decisions. . . . There can be no conflict between political rationality and . . . economic rationality, because the solution of political problems makes possible an attack on any other problem. . . . In a political decision . . . action is never based on the merits of a proposal, but always on who makes it and who opposes it. . . . Compromise is always a rational procedure, even when the compromise is between a good and a bad proposal.

(Paul Diesing 1982, 198, 203–204, 232)

Government performance needs to be viewed from the perspective of the organic wholeness of a political system in which the public, private, and nonprofit sectors work together to create the uniqueness of a given political community. This view emphasizes the synergistic influence of history, social institutions, and culture in creating a shared system of values, agreement on governance processes and structures and the respective roles that the private and nonprofit sectors play in the creation of the common good.

(Douglas F. Morgan and Craig Shinn, 2014, 6)

As the opening epigraphs for this chapter illustrate, what counts for performance is very much a contested issue. Like the Great Wall of China or a simple ax, it depends on whose perspective is being used to test its performance. The opening teaching case for Part III of this book illustrates the concrete ways in which differences in perspective take on organizational expression in the budgeting process. Budget and Finance director Spiro Augustine understands performance improvement as a process of organization and process reform. City department and program directors likely see the new performance effort as conflicting with their current, often successful, efforts to improve productivity. City budget analysts wonder what the new mayor's performance initiative means for the procedures and requirements of budget preparation, and social service advocates and rank-and-file city staff readily interpret the new initiative as an excuse to undertake more and deeper cutbacks. While a performance orientation to budgeting may be in the eye of the beholder, there is general agreement that performance budgeting provides an analytic perspective and approach to budgeting that draws on data and information derived from **performance measures** and comparisons. Our primary purpose in this chapter is to build a basic understanding of performance measurement and explain how it can integrate into the budgeting system and support the preparation of a **budget request** through performance budgeting.

Our secondary purpose is to demonstrate that a performance approach to budgeting is necessarily a political question: What kind of information should be collected and how should it be assessed to improve the public good? The etymological origins of the term *performance* reflect the broadening perspectives by which we have come to judge the performance of government and its various activities. Originally, the term *performance* was attached to carrying out a promise or duty, but over time it has broadened to include anything that is performed, especially entertainment. The democratization of the term *performance* has important implications for public budgeting, where the terms *budgeting* and *performance* have become increasingly linked. By connecting the two, *performance* becomes fundamentally a political question of deciding what people value and whether they are getting their money's worth.

The discussion of performance in this chapter is arranged in four parts. In the first part, we describe the performance budgeting technique and how it relates to our earlier discussions of PPBS and program budgeting. We give examples to illustrate what it looks like in practice. In the second part, we review the purpose, history, and contextual setting that creates an enabling environment for a performance orientation to budgeting. In the third part, we discuss some of the enabling conditions for making performance budgeting work in practice. In the fourth part, we assess the strengths and weaknesses of performance budgeting and discuss strategies for building a performance orientation into a range of other activities that government undertakes.

THE TECHNIQUE OF PERFORMANCE BUDGETING

Performance budgeting is a term that applies broadly to any number of budgeting strategies and formats that attempt to incorporate the measurement of results and costs as an important consideration in the allocation of budget resources. Unlike PPBS and program budgeting, where the goal is to assemble and budget to program objectives or goals, performance budgeting systematically incorporates performance and cost measurement information into the budgeting process and uses this information to allocate scarce public resources. You can have program budgeting without performance measurement and you can have performance measurement without program budgeting. For example, provision of services to juveniles can be organized into programmatic sets of distinct activities with clear and separable objectives and overall costs without a commitment to systematic measurement. By contrast, you can have systematic measurement of process costs and, say, apply that to the number of miles of road paved by a department of transportation without necessarily having these activities organized along programmatic lines. Or you can measure the number of HIV cases successfully treated with refined cost information without having a distinct and separate HIV program. In short, if outcomes and process cost data are measured but are not taken into consideration in the allocation of public resources, you may have some kind of performance system; however, you do not yet have performance budgeting. For example, many jurisdictions may have a strategic plan or a community visions document that sets forth the aspirations and the priorities of a community, but unless these documents play an important role in determining the level of resources to allocate to various programs and agencies, the jurisdiction does not have performance budgeting.

Examples of Performance-Based Budgeting

Exhibit 13.1 presents a simple performance budgeting example that builds on the community corrections example we used at the beginning of the previous chapter to illustrate how the planning, programming, budgeting system (PPBS) works. Extending the PPBS to include performance indicators makes performance budgeting the natural and final step in the preparation of goals and objectives. While performance measures can be used without systematically linking them to a causally linked hierarchy of goals and objectives, this is not the preferred approach when doing *performance-based* budgeting. In the community corrections example, notice the need for several performance measures for a given objective and the need for several objectives for each goal. All performance measurements should include cost information, since few activities undertaken to achieve objectives are cost free. Performance measures can also relate to published standards.

Using standard measures allows the comparison of program performance across jurisdictions and organizations with respect to efficiency, effectiveness, and other performance indicators. The number of recommend police offers per 1,000 residents or the recommended criteria for replacement of motor vehicles are examples of these standard-based forms of measurement. There may be valid explanations that justify lower performance standards, but inefficient process performance is often the root cause of high costs for reduced outputs.

Compare the example in Exhibit 13.1 to the program example in the previous chapter on program budgeting. The difference between the two examples illustrates the difference between program budgeting and performance budgeting. In program budgeting, we identified the total costs of meeting goals and objectives. The cost figure often represents the historical cost of providing the desired services. But in Exhibit 13.1, we add detailed performance measurements and criteria as the basis for allocating scarce public resources. When performance measures are added to a set of goals and objectives, there are several important considerations to keep in mind:

- One needs to develop measures of both input and output in order to have a comprehensive understanding of performance. For example, if your goal is to pave additional miles of road over the current fiscal year, it is not enough to know what the outcome performance measures are going to be (for example, 1,000 miles of road paved at x standard of asphalt). A more complete answer to a performance-based orientation is that you are able to assess what you are accomplishing in relationship to what it will cost to do the additional work.
- The cost of accomplishing an identifiable set of activities needs to be translated into the implications for next year's budget. For example, if you need two additional field employees to achieve your projected work objective of paving an additional 1,000 miles of road, you need

---

Exhibit 13.1

Community Corrections Budget for FY5

Goal: To rehabilitate clients on parole and probation so they can return as productive members of society.

1. Objective: To increase FY2 employment references of clients by 10 percent over FY2 with no budget increase over what was allocated for these activities in FY1.

   Performance Measures:

   a. Number of FY2 employment references are at least 10 percent more than FY1, and
   b. at a total cost that is equal to or less than what was allocated in FY1

2. Objective: To double total mental health consultations experienced by clients in FY2 compared to FY1 at a cost of 1.0 FTE Mental Health Nurse.

   Performance Measures:

   a. Total mental health consultations in FY2 is double the total mental health consultations in FY1 and
   b. costs no more than $65,000

3. Objective: To limit FY2 parole and probation violations to 15 percent of Corrections clientele by introducing a bracelet monitoring program at a cost that does not exceed the total budget allocation expended in FY1 for parole and probation monitoring.

   Performance Measures:

   a. FY2 parole and probation violations are 15 percent or less than the FY1 parole and probation violations and
   b. the total costs do not exceed what was allocated in FY1 for the bracelet program

to know the amount of costs associated with accomplishing your objective. This includes the salary and benefit costs of the new employees, but also additional supplies, equipment, and staff support.
• Once you have linked program performance with budget information, you have lots of discretionary choices concerning how to frame this linkage, as the following discussion of performance, productivity, and other types of performance information will illustrate.

Types of Performance and Cost Measures

As the previous discussion makes clear, if you want to do performance-based budgeting, you need to have increasingly sophisticated cost-related information. This information has grown in urgency as public bodies are attempting to offset shrinking resources and an inflation-related loss of purchasing power with improvements in productivity. The legal restrictions that have been put in place to limit new revenues, coupled with a faltering economy, have increased the incentive for local government jurisdictions to develop some clear measures of performance for the allocation of tax dollars. There are many ways to approach and define performance, as the following sections will illustrate.

Productivity and Performance

While the concepts of **productivity** and performance measurement are not synonymous, they are very closely linked. Without a system for measuring the changes in actual performance, it is very difficult to determine if any strides are being made toward increasing productivity. The concept of productivity implies a ratio of the quantity and/or quality of results (**output**) to the resources (**input**) invested to achieve them. Productivity has two dimensions: *effectiveness* and *efficiency*. Effectiveness focuses on the extent to which governments achieve their program objectives, and it can be assessed through a combination of *qualitative* and *quantitative* measures. Qualitative measures collect information on the satisfaction and quality of a given product or service, while quantitative measures collect information on the number and kind of services delivered to x number of clients.

Whether one is concerned with measuring the quality or the quantity of an objective, the objective itself can take several different forms. For example, an objective may focus on impacts, outcomes, outputs, or results. The combination of ways in which objectives can be defined and quantitatively and/or qualitatively measured produces many discretionary possibilities in taking a performance-based approach to budgeting. For example, the assessment of a local school reading program could be defined in terms of quantitative scores on a nationally standardized examination. Or it could be measured in terms of the qualitative impact the program has on a student's sense of well-being and improved performance in other areas of development. Or it could be measured in terms of successful performance in college or in one's career.

In contrast to **effectiveness measures**, which focus on outputs, outcomes, results, or impacts, efficiency focuses on the ratio of a unit of goods and/or services produced in relationship to the amount of resources required to produce it. For example, a reading program may prove to be highly effective in achieving a set of predefined objectives, but the cost per student could turn out to be significantly higher than other alternative programs. If this proved to be the case, we would describe the program as being effective, but not as efficient as other alternative programs that are operated at a lower cost per student. In short, a concern for productivity does not predetermine the pathway to success. For example, higher productivity can be achieved by:

1. keeping expenditures constant and improving effectiveness and/or efficiency;
2. keeping effectiveness and/or efficiency constant and reducing expenditures; or

3. increasing expenditures but improving effectiveness and/or efficiency at a higher proportional rate.

As this list of productivity improvement strategies suggests, productivity that focuses only on the relationship of inputs to outputs is a limited perspective at best. In addition to reaching and maintaining a given service-level target for the community, it is also important that the qualitative nature of that production does not diminish and that costs per unit of service do not skyrocket in the process. In summary, performance measurement involves monitoring the varying degrees of effectiveness and efficiency in performance that result from the production of public goods and services. When measurement of these dimensions of public service are systematically related to planned goals and objectives, performance measurement becomes an integral part of the man-agement planning cycle—that is, the development of goals and objectives (a plan for resource allocation), process implementation (the comparison of inputs to outputs in order to determine productivity), and performance measurement (efficiency and effectiveness determination). In fact, performance budgeting completes the planning cycle that is an integral part of PPBS.

Any indicator that seeks to measure the success of a government unit's achievement of its goals or objectives can be considered a performance measure. The three types of performance measurements are (1) effectiveness measures, (2) efficiency measures, and (3) workload measures. Definitions and examples of each are provided in the sections that follow.

Measures of Effectiveness

Effectiveness is a result-oriented concept. It focuses on how well a goal or objective is accom-plished independent of cost or other inputs. Examples may include:

• Percentage of improved neighborhood traffic realignment projects in which through traffic is no greater than 1,000 vehicles per day one year after installation of the improvement.
• The average number of highway deaths from drunken driving in FY2 compared to the aver-age rates in FY1.

Neither of the above examples provides very precise information on the activities to be under-taken to produce the named results. And they do not provide information on the cost or efficiency of producing the result. They only give us information about outcomes, outputs, results, or impacts. When the effectiveness of a specific goal is explicitly connected to an intentional set of activities, the conditions are in place to create one of the following four kinds of effectiveness measures.

Targeted Goal or "Percent of Perfect" Performance Measures. This is the most desirable measure if it can be developed for an activity. The actual result is expressed as a **target** rate—a percentage of the most desirable result. Example: the percentage of neighborhood locations with traffic bar-riers in which through traffic is greater than 1,000 vehicles per day one year after barriers have been installed.

Result Characteristic Measures. When a base standard cannot be established, then one can use various characteristics of an activity to determine meaningful measures of the effectiveness of the activity. Examples include:

• Service complaints per year per 1,000 clients.
• Response to complaints within *x* days.
• Successfully resolved complaints measured by *x* criteria.

Compliance with Standards Measure. With many routinely provided services, it is possible to develop performance standards that measure the success of that activity against the developed standards. No additional credit is given for exceeding the standard. Note that the measure is similar to the "percent of perfect measure." The important difference is that in using a "compliance with standards measure," 100 percent is theoretically achievable and may be expected. Examples of compliance measures with standards include the following:

- 100 percent compliance with EPA and EQC Clean Air regulatory standards within one year for a minimum of 95 percent of the individual emission standards established by the regulatory process.
- Number of citations issued by regulatory agencies for permit violations per million gallons of wastewater processed (used to measure 100 percent compliance with federal and state public health and regulatory agency requirements).

Subjective Measures. At times it is necessary to rely on the subjective views and attitudes of those persons involved in the activity. Although less reliable, these measures should not be ignored. In some areas, it is extremely difficult to develop other acceptable measures. When subjective measures are used, the following steps should be taken to improve consistency and reliability:

1. Identify the fact that a subjective effectiveness measure is being used.
2. Develop a checklist of points to be evaluated for each measure.
3. Try to have evaluators use simple scales to help organize their evaluation, for example: outstanding, very good, good, average, below average, and poor.
4. Use more than one evaluator and take samples at a number of points, then average the results.
5. Have the evaluation made by people other than those responsible for the activity. For example, in surveying the satisfaction level of the business community with parking enforcement, the evaluation should be undertaken by someone other than those responsible for enforcement activities.

Examples of subjective measures include the following:

- Percentage of business people surveyed who perceive the enforcement of parking regulations as helpful.
- Percentage of customers/clients reporting satisfactory service delivery by agency personnel.

Measures of Efficiency

Efficiency is a process-oriented concept. It focuses on how well resources are used without particular regard for the amount of service output produced in relationship to the amount of resources required. Process efficiency measures can be defined in an engineering context by the amount of ingredients, time, and effort needed to produce an output. But purchasing or valuing inputs redefines many efficiency measures into costs that define the relationship between the funds needed for process inputs and a corresponding output or outcome. Carefully constructed cost measures can evaluate process performance, compare performance to published standards, and provide a basis of comparison across budget needs. Examples of efficiency measures include:

- Cost per participant in a tuition reimbursement program.

- Cost per million gallons of wastewater processed.
- Cost per installation of traffic control devices.

Efficiency measures relate output to the applicable input, generally dollars, and tend to fall into two groups:

Cost per Unit of Output Measures. This measure is the most direct. It relates the cost to the actual output or result and is expressed in dollars per unit of output. Examples include the following:

- Cost per dry ton of sludge processed.
- Cost per person hour to maintain and operate one pumping station.

Cost per Other Base Measure. This measure is used where the cost cannot be directly related to output (as in prevention-oriented activities). Rather than measuring on a per individual basis, costs are scaled to appropriate orders of magnitude, such as the costs per one hundred, per thousand, per ten thousand, or per million basis. Using costs on a scaled basis results in a more easily understood measure rather than do costs with excessive leading zeros or of large size. Examples of costs per base measure include the following:

- Cost per 1,000 licensed drivers for traffic safety.
- Cost per million lane miles for traffic fatalities.
- Cost per million gallons of water treated.

Measures of Workload

Workload measures, as the name implies, track the amount of work that is done within a specified period. While common, they do not provide information on issues of efficiency, effectiveness, or how to reallocate resources to higher priority public goals. However, workload measures are essential for managers and unions who are interested in standardizing expectations with regard to what can be accomplished in a given amount of time. It is common, for example, to use workload measures to judge the amount of resources needed in managing permit centers, emergency rooms, and case managers in probation/parole/social service programs. Examples of workload measures include the following:

- Number of traffic lights installed.
- Number of public requests for parking enforcement resolved.
- Number of calls answered.

Workload measures are most commonly used by supervisors and serve various operational purposes, but they indicate little about the quality of the work performed. However, workload measures can be utilized to develop effectiveness measures by conversion to a rate or normalized basis, as the following example illustrates: Number of public requests resolved within the established response time compared to the number received. Workload measures can also be utilized to develop efficiency measures by conversion to a cost or input: Cost per traffic light installed.

Types of Costs as a Refinement of Performance Measurement

Costs are a specific type of efficiency performance measure that relates inputs of resources and funds to measured outputs and outcomes. Costs, however, reflect several different aspects of resources used in the production process. Understanding the different types of cost is critical for the development of budget estimates and for gaining productivity improvements. Efficiency and workload measures are often related by using one or more of the following cost measures (Lyden and Lindenberg 1983, 70–74):

- *Fixed Costs.* A fixed cost input covers the resources needed to operate the program or service at any level of service or complexity. A program must have basic office space, utilities, information technology and communications accessibility, supporting administrative services, and organization administrative relationships and oversight.
- *Variable Costs.* Costs that change proportionally as the size of the program or service increases or decreases are considered variable costs. Variable costs are often defined on a per individual basis. Typically, as more customers or individuals are served, the costs increase in a continuous curve. Variable costs increase with increasing numbers of students at a school, patients in a hospital, or inmates in a prison. For example, a state youth authority pays increasing food costs in direct positive proportion to the number of offenders and at-risk youth in a given population.
- *Incremental or Step-Increase Costs.* These costs are a variation of the variable cost examples described above. Instead of changing on a per individual basis, incremental costs change by a defined unit of capacity. For example, a state youth administration buys 40 passenger buses to transport offenders. Once the first bus is filled, the next increment is another 40 passenger bus with its added capital cost, driver, and maintenance.

The total of all fixed, variable, and incremental costs represents the total cost of providing a service to a specified level or number of individuals. The total cost at any specified level contains all fixed costs, the proportional variable costs, and the lowest level of incremental costs needed to meet service-level needs. Based on the per unit cost rates, analysts can estimate the costs for smaller or larger program levels. This forms the basis for allocating resources for next year's budget. The *level of service* represents the amount of workload accomplished to a specified standard within a given time span. The gross amount of product or service can be calculated using the following equation:

$$\text{Service Level} = \text{Workload} \times \text{Specified Standard} \times \text{Duration}.$$

Two examples of the application of this formula follow:

- Number of 911 calls responded to within 15 minutes during FYx.
- Percent of customer complaints successfully resolved within seven days during FYx.

The service-level calculation in the above examples refines the level of service costs used in program (PPBS) budgeting (see discussion in chapter 12). The total cost to meet a level of service reflects the number of units in the workload and the cost per unit to meet the specified standard over a specified duration. It is important to note that as the level of service rises, fixed costs can be shared over a larger number of individuals, resulting in a smaller share per individual. For example, the construction and start-up costs of a new school auditorium and theater complex can be shared or amortized over the student population in an inverse relationship. At the same time, variable and incremental costs will increase in proportion to the number of individuals served.

Defining a cost in terms of the total fixed, variable, and incremental costs per number of individuals served represents an average cost value for each individual. This may provide a useful model for many applications, including budget estimation. For example, hundreds of offenders in a youth corrections facility include both heavy teenage eaters and light eaters, but on balance, an average level of food consumption supports effective purchasing and budgeting. However, effective performance and cost analysis often must move beyond average values to identify classes of individuals that incur relatively high or low costs. Cost averages mask important variations that lead to effective cost reduction. For example, Oregon Health Science researchers (Dorr 2007) estimate that 3 to 5 percent of Oregon Medicare patients account for about 50 percent of state Medicare expenditures. These patients have an intense level of service need and are typically elderly, with multiple—and oftentimes related—chronic diseases, along with other social and financial issues. Establishing a medical "home" for these patients and instituting coordinated team-based care may be one pathway for controlling these concentrated high costs. Focusing performance improvement and cost reduction efforts on the most expensive 5 percent would bring the greatest return for the improvement effort. Determining costs by categories of clients is important for water, sewer, fire, public health, and police services.

Benchmarks and Comparison to Established Standards

Performance measures are often custom designed to the context, program structure, and client base of a government or nonprofit program. These measures may provide effective information for budgeting and for cost analysis and monitoring. But without some sort of comparison to other providers or some type of published benchmark, administrators have no idea if their organization is meeting the highest possible level of efficiency and effectiveness. Standardized performance measures, or **benchmarks**, set by national professional organizations, state regulatory standards, federal agencies or federal grantors, major foundations, or published research can be used as a means of making comparisons across peer organizations. At least one of the performance measures developed for a program should match or reflect a standard measure or benchmark. Expressing performance measures as a standard ratio and scaling the ratio to a standard form enhances comparisons.

In chapter 11 on line-item budgeting, we introduced the concept of a current service baseline as the level of funding needed to continue the quantity and quality of this year's services into the next fiscal year. In the line-item case, we assume that organization and program productivity will remain the same year to year. But with a greater understanding of productivity and performance measurement, we can question that assumption and compare an organization's performance to the performance of peer organizations. The *current service level* approach implies that a jurisdiction can benchmark its performance in various categories of public service against what it *should be performing* or what other comparable jurisdictions are providing. For a good example of this approach, see the annual *Current Services Level Reports* prepared by the City of Portland Auditor's Office (City of Portland, Auditor's Office 2010). Exhibit 13.2 provides an example of the performance of the Parks and Recreation Bureau in 2010 on a variety of workload, efficiency, and effectiveness measures, including its performance in comparison to other cities.

As Exhibit 13.2 illustrates, a variety of workload, efficiency, effectiveness, and comparative performance information can be collected and published that is of potential value to citizens, managers, and elected officials. Exhibit 13.2 also illustrates how a variety of different ways of measuring performance can be linked to budget information. But there is an ongoing debate as to how closely this information should be linked to the budget development and allocation process. The most extreme linkage would use the information in Exhibit 13.2 to determine how much more or how much less the Parks Bureau should get for next year's budget. In the sections that follow, we use the history of a performance orientation to governance to explore in greater detail the enabling conditions that need to be in place to make performance-based budgeting possible and some of the technical considerations that make it possible to link performance metrics to resource allocation decisions.

Exhibit 13.2

Example Performance Report

Portland Parks & Recreation

MISSION   Portland Parks & Recreation contributes to the City's vitality by:

- Establishing and safeguarding the parks, natural resources, and urban forest, thereby ensuring that green spaces are accessible to all.

- Developing and maintaining excellent facilities and places for public recreation, and building community by providing opportunities for play, relaxation, gathering, and solitude.

- Providing and coordinating recreation services and programs created for diverse ages and abilities that contribute to the health and well-being of community members.

INPUT MEASURES	05-06	06-07	07-08	08-09	09-10
Expenditures (millions, adjusted):[1]					
Operating	$62.0	$63.2	$65.9	$[1]	$73.3
Capital	$7.2	$13.5	$26.8	$[1]	$8.7
TOTAL	$69.2	$76.7	$92.7	$[1]	$82.1
Permanent staffing (FTEs)	412	408	414	437	445
Seasonal staffing (FTEs)	284	298	320	335	381
Volunteers (FTEs)	219	221	223	224	222
Total volunteer hours	457,307	461,274	462,877	465,353	460,746
Total paid staff hours (millions)	1.4	1.4	1.5	1.6	1.7

WORKLOAD MEASURES	05-06	06-07	07-08	08-09	09-10
Service population	556,370	562,690	568,380	575,930	582,130
Number of Parks & Facilities:					
Sports fields[2]	—	—	—	351	351
Community centers	12	12	12	12	12
Arts centers	6	6	6	6	6
Pools	13	13	13	13	13
Golf courses	5	5	5	5	5
Off-leash dog areas	31	31	32	32	32
Skate parks	1	2	3	5	5
Community gardens	31	31	32	32	35
Park acres:					
Developed parks	3,257	3,260	3,272	3,274	3,417
Natural areas	7,074	7,140	7,263	7,287	7,523
Undeveloped	282	285	228	234	207
TOTAL	10,613	10,685	10,763	10,795	11,147
Building square footage	1,081,712	1,081,712	1,091,944	1,117,922	1,120,035
Estimated recreation visits (millions):					
PP&R–sponsored recreation programs and facilities[2]	—	—	—	—	3.7
Sports programs using PP&R–managed fields	2.0	2.1	2.2	2.3	2.3

EFFICIENCY MEASURES	05-06	06-07	07-08	08-09	09-10
Operating spending per capita (adjusted)[1]	$111	$112	$116	—[1]	$126
Capital spending per capita (adjusted)[1]	$13	$24	$47	—[1]	$15
Cost recovery for fee-supported programs[1]	33%	34%	33%	—[1]	34%
Workers compensation claims/100 workers	7.3	8.3	8.4	8.3	7.6
Percent of maintenance done that is preventive (hours spent, goal: 52%)	55%	53%	49%	46%	58%
Volunteers hours as percent of paid staff	33%	32%	30%	29%	27%

EFFECTIVENESS MEASURES	05-06	06-07	07-08	08-09	09-10
Residents living within ½ mile of park (goal: 100%)	75%	75%	76%	76%	77%
Park acres per thousand residents (goal: 19 acres per thousand residents)	19.1	19.0	18.9	18.7	19.1
Facilities Condition Index (0.05–0.10 = good)	0.05	—	—	0.05	0.06

	2006	2007	2008	2009	2010
Customer ratings (Community centers & pools):					
Percent rating overall quality good or very good	—	—	—	96%	95%

COMPARISON TO OTHER CITIES	05-06	06-07	07-08	08-09	09-10
Parks operating budget per capita (adjusted):[3]					
City of Portland	$94	$91	$98	$102	$109
6-city average[4]	$103	$111	$113	$103	$96

[1] Data not reliable for FY 2008–2009, due to midyear accounting system change.
[2] The Bureau improved the methodology for counting sports fields (2009) and recreation visits (2010). Prior year data is not shown because the numbers are not comparable.
[3] For comparison purposes, enterprise activities such as Portland International Raceway are excluded from these numbers.
[4] Charlotte, Cincinnati, Denver, Kansas City, Sacramento, and Seattle are the cities we used for comparison.

For more information about Portland Parks & Recreation, click or go to:
www.portlandoregon.gov/parks/

HISTORICAL PERSPECTIVE ON PERFORMANCE-
BASED BUDGETING AND GOVERNANCE[1]

In the previous section, our discussion of performance-based budgeting focused on the conceptual categories, techniques, and methodologies required when taking a performance-based orientation to the budget allocation process. But, as we argued in our introduction to this chapter and as illustrated in the master case to Part III (Expenditure Formats for Decision and Control), performance is a matter of reconciling competing perspectives as to what truly counts for performance. We have argued that performance-centered budgeting is not simply a matter of mastering the technical expertise to understand the conceptual categories and methodological techniques of performance and measurement; rather, it is a matter of deciding what counts for the successful political performance of the governance system as a whole. And here, the perspective of citizens is important, as one would assume in a democratic system of government. But citizens have not been of equal mind on this issue, as a brief history of what counts for performance will illustrate.

Early Concerns of Public Administration for a Performance Orientation

The concern for performance is not something new. In fact, one can argue that the founding of the American political system was driven by a concern for performance. The English governance system in place in the 13 colonies was not performing to the satisfaction of colonists, so they took the initiative to alter the status quo. The American Revolution began to reveal the weaknesses of the Articles of Confederation, so there was another initiative to alter the system in ways that would bring it into better alignment with the performance needs and expectations of citizens.

In fact, from a historical perspective, the history of American government can be viewed as a nearly constant effort of performance realignment and change. The Jacksonian Era introduced *rotation in office* as a performance tool to check the disproportionate influence of commercial elites on the policy-making and implementation process. The Populist Era introduced civil service reform, the initiative, referendum, recall, nonpartisan local elections, citizen boards and commissions, and an expansion in the number of elected offices at the state and county levels of government out of a concern for better government performance. This tradition was continued with the Progressive movement at the turn of the nineteenth century, which introduced a wide variety of new performance initiatives (Morgan et al. 2013, chap. 5; Stever 1988). These included research bureaus that for the first time emphasized data-based policy recommendations and evaluation of results. Research bureaus laid the groundwork for performance measurement of managerial operations, which could then be fed into the budget allocation process. The Progressives championed the council-manager form of government as a governing structure that would bring increased attention to issues of business efficiency and effectiveness, especially as an alternative to the commission form of government that was currently in vogue (Morgan, Nishishiba, and Vizzini 2010, 280–283). The council-manager model embodies the Progressives' reliance on professionals to meet the needs of citizens, whether through social work, public health, public works, law enforcement, or the management of the general affairs of the community (Stever 1988; Stivers 2000).

The New Deal continued America's historical preoccupation with finding new ways of improving government performance. The vision that guided the New Deal was clearly articulated in a famous report by one of the intellectual leaders of the New Deal, Louis Brownlow. The Brownlow Committee Report (Roosevelt 1937) provides the underlying rationale for more than 100 executive-level reorganization plans submitted to Congress since 1939.[2] It places priority on the dual principles of centralized political accountability and administrative efficiency.

The Rise of New Public Management (NPM)

A concerted effort was made from 1980 through 2010 to reframe the model of public administration from a rule-centered system of accountability to one more focused on businesslike performance. This movement, called **new public management (NPM)**, strives to make the services provided by government more responsive and accountable to citizens by applying businesslike management techniques with a strong focus on competition, customer satisfaction, and measurement of performance. There is general agreement among scholars and practitioners alike that these efforts to measure what gets done have produced a variety of worthwhile results:

- Measures of efficiency and effectiveness have inspired managers, supervisors, and frontline employees to improve their capacity to diagnose and correct operational problems (Ammons and Rivenbark 2008).
- An emphasis on performance measurement has heightened interest in creating systems that improve the overall management and governance of political entities (Hatry 2002, 2010; Moynihan and Pandey 2005; Wholey and Hatry 1992).
- Performance measurement systems have expanded to embrace an increasingly larger array of values, including cost and efficiency measures; various effectiveness measures like outputs, outcomes, and impacts; and qualitative measures like satisfaction, responsiveness, and quality of life (O'Flynn 2007; Stoker 2006; Jørgensen and Bozeman 2007).

But there are two major weaknesses in using private-sector business principles to improve the performance of government, regardless of what gets measured. First, there is no common denominator—like profit, market share, or return on investment—that can serve as a common comparator across the very wide range of criteria that defines *government performance*. These criteria and the way they are handled can either build or erode people's sense of trust and legitimacy in their political institutions. Efficiency, effectiveness, and responsiveness to citizens (customers) do not exhaust the legitimating possibilities. Values like fairness, equity, protection of rights, and transparency play important roles in determining the legitimacy of political institutions, processes, and outcomes (Cooper 2003; Rosenbloom 2003; Moe 1994; Moe and Gilmour 1995; Lynn 1998; Kelly 1998; Moore 1994, 1995; Hefetz and Warner 2004). How do you put these more elusive values on the same plane as those that can be more easily measured? And how do you create a common denominator that allows for meaningful comparisons?

The second weakness inherent in using private-sector models for improving government performance is that the public sector consists of increasingly fragmented structures of authority that confound the possibility and even desirability of moving in a straight line from goals and objectives to instrumentally and rationally linked performance measures. The proliferation of local governments we described in Part I of this text, coupled with the entrepreneurial push to outsource public service to nonprofit- and private-sector organizations, shifts performance away from a single-minded focus on the efficient, effective, and customer-sensitive achievement of goals and objectives. Organization now must also focus on achieving and sustaining agreements between and across structures of authority. This has been described as "leading in a power-shared world" (see Bryson and Crosby 1992; Morgan et al. 2013, chap. 12) and is the focus of a body of literature called **new public governance (NPG)**, which began to emerge in the early 1990s (Osborne 2010).

To summarize, the NPM agenda is based on a truncated view of the purpose of government. Government is not simply the agent of accountability to citizens or the agent of efficiency and effectiveness; it is also responsible for collecting the values of the community and creating integrated responses to these values across increasingly fragmented government systems (Kelly 1998;

Lynn 1998). When the values of the community are in conflict, or when they are contrary to the interests of significant minorities, government officials have a fiduciary responsibility to make decisions that are in the larger public interest. This kind of accountability model has faded into the background with the emergence of NPM. In a previous day, whether it was the scientific management movement of the early twentieth century or the efficiency and effectiveness initiatives of the Brownlow and Hoover Commission reports in the 1930s, 1940s, and 1950s, the discussion of performance was framed within a larger discussion. This larger discussion focused on the respective roles of the executive and legislative branches in making the overall system of government work (see especially Cook 1996, 119–120; Stever 1988, 1990). Performance was not stripped down to the simple issue of business efficiency and effectiveness. It was treated as an important part of a larger set of governance issues—issues that were an integral part of building trust and legitimacy in governing institutions and their leaders. This larger, more holistic and organic perspective has been largely missing from the proponents of the NPM movement over the past three decades. These concerns have spawned the rise of the new public governance movement (NPG).

Performance and the Rise of New Public Governance (NPG)

Concerns with NPM spawned a countermovement by both practitioners and academics to place substantive political values more at the center of the governance debate than has been the case with NPM's narrow instrumental focus. This countermovement emphasizes three characteristics of public governance that are important for building trust and legitimacy but are undervalued by NPM. First, NPG is value-centered. It argues that the goal of government is to promote the larger common good. Mark Moore has called this new emphasis "the public value" approach (Moore 1994, 1995), while Stoker and others have called it "the collective preference" approach (Stoker 2006; Alford 2002). NPG is interested in advancing the value created by the whole of government activities, not just improved efficiency, effectiveness, or responsiveness in the implementation of a given program. This shift has broadened the objectives of performance measurement and management to include service outputs, satisfaction, outcomes, a wide array of substantive political values, and, ultimately, citizen trust and the very legitimacy of government itself.

A second characteristic of NPG is that it emphasizes the importance of creating government processes that facilitate the generation of implementable agreements among wide-ranging stakeholders who may disagree on what courses of action will produce the maximum public value (Yang and Holzer 2006; Sanger 2008). This is because NPG views politics as the politically mediated expression of collectively determined preferences that the citizenry determines to be valuable (Alford 2002; Moore 1995; O'Flynn 2007). This contrasts with NPM, which views politics as the aggregation of individual preferences. The consequence of this difference is well-illustrated by the major steps the United Kingdom (UK) has taken over the past decade to reform the delivery of its social, education, medical, and justice services to citizens at the local government level. In recent years, public officials in the UK have chosen to treat government performance not as a set of rationally planned objectives but as a process of political mediation among contending stakeholders. These stakeholders have very legitimate differences regarding the public values that need to be preserved to ensure the integrity of the larger public good. Such efforts have resulted in the creation of a wide variety of new policy instruments, negotiated agreements, and performance measures that would have been difficult, if not unthinkable, under NPM (Brookes and Grint 2010; Osborne 2010, especially chaps. 16, 19, and 22).

A final characteristic of the NPG movement is that it views the creation of the public good as a coproduction process involving the public, private, and nonprofit sectors (see chapter 1 discussion on intersectoral interdependence; see also Crosby and Bryson 2005; O'Toole 1997, 2006; Osborne 2008). Under this model, the role of government is not simply to regulate, distribute, or redistribute public benefits but to serve as a catalytic agent to invest private and nonprofit stakeholders in shared ownership of the public good. This can take the simple form of community policing programs or a much more complicated form of networked governance such as watershed management over a very large geographic area involving multiple stakeholders and structures of authority. It is important to distinguish NPG's approach to partnerships with the private and nonprofit sectors, compared to NPM's approach. The latter is primarily interested in using the private and nonprofit sectors to deliver a service cheaply, efficiently, and effectively (Osborne and Gaebler 1992), while NPG is interested in enhancing the capacity of local organizations as a means of building civic infrastructure and the overall capacity of a community to be self-authoring (Smith and Lipsky 1993; Smith and Smyth 2010).

The three characteristics of NPG discussed above emanate from a common belief that government performance needs to be viewed from the perspective of the organic wholeness of a political system. In such a system, the public, private, and nonprofit sectors work together to contribute to the distinctive way of life of a political community. This view emphasizes the synergistic influence of history, institutions, and culture in creating a shared system of values and shared agreement on governance processes and structures—both formal and informal. In chapter 2, we introduced the concept of polity budgeting to capture this more holistic and integrated approach to public budgeting. It draws from the resurgence of scholarship that uses *polity* or *regime* as the unit of analysis for understanding performance, political change, governance, and leadership development (Rohr 1989; Ozawa 2005; Johnson 2002; Stone 1989, 1993; Leo 1997, 1998; Lauria 1997). We believe this framework is especially useful in broadening the focus of performance away from program metrics to include building bridges across sectors and across organizations, thereby leveraging the maximum resources possible to promote the larger good of the community.

Current State of Performance-Based Budgeting: Performance as Ideology

Over the past four decades, a steady ideological shift has arisen that calls into question the paradigm represented by the New Deal. With this shift has come an increased interest in a performance orientation to the budgeting process and growing doubts about the effectiveness of the New Deal model of an activist government. As noted in our discussion of new public management and new public governance, there is general agreement between the two major political parties that the government has a central role in managing the economy, but this agreement does not extend to other roles, especially those that make government an active agent of managing social service, public health, environmental pollution, and consumer protection programs. Such initiatives can often compromise economic prosperity. For example, adding government regulations to control pollution, protect public health, and ensure consumer safety frequently increases the cost of doing business, even though long-term health costs for the nation as a whole may be considerably less.

Consider, for example, the information found in Exhibit 13.3. In his last year in office, President George H.W. Bush presented a federal budget for FY1992 that included the information in Exhibit 13.3. The information on first glance is shocking. Federal regulatory efforts are extraordinarily costly. Whether the information contained in Exhibit 13.3 is accurate or paints a fair picture of the overall federal regulatory environment is not the point for purposes of discussion here. Viewed in the larger context of an ideological debate over the size, role, and expense of government that was occurring during this period, the budget information in Exhibit 13.3 is part of a larger systematic campaign by presidents to alter the implementation of public policy in the United States.

The ideological shift to reduce the role, size, and cost of government has continued unabated since the 1980s and has played an important role in the budgeting processes of both democratic and republican administrations. For example, shortly after becoming president, Bill Clinton promulgated Executive Order 12866 (1993), the key provisions of which are summarized in Exhibit 13.4. This order sets out a new philosophy intended to guide the work of federal administrative agencies.

Exhibit 13.3

Cost Effectiveness of Selected Regulations

Regulation	Agency	Cost per premature death averted (in millions of $ in 1990)
Space Heater Ban	CPSC	0.1
Aircraft Cabin Fire Protection Standard	FAA	0.1
Auto Passive Restraint/Seat Belt Standards	NHTSA	0.1
Steering Column Protection Standard	NHTSA	0.1
Underground Construction Standards	OSHA	0.1
Trihalomethane Drinking Water Standards	EPA	0.2
Aircraft Seat Cushion Flammability Standard	FAA	0.4
Alcohol and Drug Control Standards	FRA	0.4
Auto Fuel-System Integrity Standard	NHTSA	0.4
Standards for Servicing Auto Wheel Rims	OSHA	0.4
Aircraft Floor Emergency Lighting Standard	FAA	0.6
Concrete and Masonry Construction Standards	OSHA	0.6
Passive Restraints for Trucks & Buses (Proposed)	OSHA	0.7
Crane Suspended Personnel Platform Standard	NHTSA	0.7
Children's Sleepwear Flammability Ban	CPSC	0.8
Auto Side Door Support Standards	NHTSA	0.8
Side-Impact Standards for Autos (Dynamic)	NHTSA	0.8
Low Altitude Wind Shear Equipment and Training Standards	FAA	1.3
Electrical Equipment Standards (Metal Mines)	MSHA	1.4
Traffic Alert and Collision Avoidance (TCAS) Systems	FAA	1.5
Trenching and Excavation Standards	OSHA	1.5
Hazard Communication Standard	OSHA	1.6
Side-Impact Standards for Trucks, Buses, and MPVs (Proposed)	NHTSA	2.2
Grain Dust Explosion Prevention Standards	OSHA	2.8
Rear Lap/Shoulder Belts for Autos	NHTSA	3.2
Benzene NESHAP (Original: Fugitive Emissions)	EPA	3.4
Radionuclides in Uranium Mines	EPA	3.4
Ethylene Dibromide Drinking Water Standard	EPA	5.7
Benzene NESHAP (Revised: Coke Byproducts)	EPA	6.1
Asbestos Occupational Exposure Limit	OSHA	8.3
Benzene Occupational Exposure Limit	OSHA	8.9
Electrical Equipment Standards (Coal Mines)	MSHA	9.2
Arsenic Emission Standards for Glass Plants	EPA	13.5
Ethylene Oxide Occupational Exposure Limit	OSHA	20.5
Arsenic/Copper NESHAP	EPA	23.0
Hazardous Waste Listing for Petroleum Refining Sludge	EPA	27.6
Cover/Move Uranium Mill Tailings (Inactive Sites)	EPA	31.7
Benzene NESHAP (Revised: Transfer Operations)	EPA	32.9
Cover/Move Uranium Mill Tailings (Active Sites)	EPA	45.0
Acrylonitrile Occupational Exposure Limit	OSHA	51.5
Coke Ovens Occupational Exposure Limit	OSHA	63.5
Lockout/Tagout	OSHA	70.9
Asbestos Occupational Exposure Limit	OSHA	74.0
Arsenic Occupational Exposure Limit	OSHA	106.9
Asbestos Ban	EPA	110.7
Diethylstilbestrol (DES) Cattle Feed Ban	FDA	124.8
Benzene NESHAP (Revised: Waste Operations)	EPA	168.2
1,2 Dichloropropane Drinking Water Standard	EPA	653.0
Hazardous Waste Land Disposal Ban (1st 3rd)	EPA	4,190.4
Municipal Solid Waste Landfill Standards (Proposed)	EPA	19,107.0
Formaldehyde Occupational Exposure Limit	OSHA	86,201.8
Atrazine/Alachlor Drinking Water Standard	EPA	92,069.7
Hazardous Waste Listing for Wood Preserving	EPA	5,700,000.0

Source: From the U.S. Budget for Fiscal Year 1992, Table C-2, Part II, p. 370.

Exhibit 13.4

Excerpt from Executive Order 12866

Regulatory Planning and Review

September 30, 1993

The American people deserve a regulatory system that works for them, not against them: a regulatory system that protects and improves their health, safety, environment, and well-being and improves the performance of the economy without imposing unacceptable or unreasonable costs on society; regulatory policies that recognize that the private sector and private markets are the best engine for economic growth; regulatory approaches that respect the role of State, local, and tribal governments; and regulations that are effective, consistent, sensible, and understandable. We do not have such a regulatory system today.

With this Executive order, the Federal Government begins a program to reform and make more efficient the regulatory process. The objectives of this Executive order are to enhance planning and coordination with respect to both new and existing regulations; to reaffirm the primacy of Federal agencies in the regulatory decision-making process; to restore the integrity and legitimacy of regulatory review and oversight; and to make the process more accessible and open to the public. In pursuing these objectives, the regulatory process shall be conducted so as to meet applicable statutory requirements and with due regard to the discretion that has been entrusted to the Federal agencies.

Section 1. Statement of Regulatory Philosophy and Principles

(a) The Regulatory Philosophy

Federal agencies should promulgate only such regulations as are required by law, are necessary to interpret the law, or are made necessary by compelling public need, such as material failures of private markets to protect or improve the health and safety of the public, the environment, or the well-being of the American people. In deciding whether and how to regulate, agencies should assess all costs and benefits of available regulatory alternatives, including the alternative of not regulating. Costs and benefits shall be understood to include both quantifiable measures (to the fullest extent that these can be usefully estimated) and qualitative measures of costs and benefits that are difficult to quantify, but nevertheless essential to consider. Further, in choosing among alternative regulatory approaches, agencies should select those approaches that maximize net benefits (including potential economic, environmental, public health and safety, and other advantages; distributive impacts; and equity), unless a statute requires another regulatory approach.

(b) The Principles of Regulation

To ensure that the agencies' regulatory programs are consistent with the philosophy set forth above, agencies should adhere to the following principles, to the extent permitted by law and where applicable:

(1) Each agency shall identify the problem that it intends to address (including, where applicable, the failures of private markets or public institutions that warrant new agency action) as well as assess the significance of that problem.

(2) Each agency shall examine whether existing regulations (or other law) have created, or contributed to, the problem that a new regulation is intended to correct and whether those regulations (or other law) should be modified to achieve the intended goal of regulation more effectively.

(3) Each agency shall identify and assess available alternatives to direct regulation, including providing economic incentives to encourage the desired behavior, such as user fees or marketable permits, or providing information upon which choices can be made by the public.

(4) In setting regulatory priorities, each agency shall consider, to the extent reasonable, the degree and nature of the risks posed by various substances or activities within its jurisdiction.

(5) When an agency determines that a regulation is the best available method of achieving the regulatory objective, it shall design its regulations in the most cost-effective manner to achieve the regulatory objective. In doing so, each agency shall consider incentives for innovation, consistency, predictability, the costs of enforcement and compliance (to the government, regulated entities, and the public), flexibility, distributive impacts, and equity.

(6) Each agency shall assess both the costs and the benefits of the intended regulation . . . [and] adopt a regulation only upon a reasoned determination that the benefits of the intended regulation justify its costs.

(7) Each agency shall base its decisions on the best reasonably obtainable scientific, technical, economic, and other information concerning the need for, and consequences of, the intended regulation.

(8) Each agency shall identify and assess alternative forms of regulation and shall, to the extent feasible, specify performance objectives, rather than specifying the behavior or manner of compliance that regulated entities must adopt.

(9) Wherever feasible, agencies shall seek views of appropriate State, local, and tribal officials before imposing regulatory requirements that might significantly or uniquely affect those governmental entities. [A]s appropriate, agencies shall seek to harmonize Federal regulatory actions with related State, local, and tribal regulatory and other governmental functions.

(10) Each agency shall avoid regulations that are inconsistent, incompatible, or duplicative with its other regulations or those of other Federal agencies.

(11) Each agency shall tailor its regulations to impose the least burden on society . . . taking into account, among other things, and to the extent practicable, the costs of cumulative regulations.

(12) Each agency shall draft its regulations to be simple and easy to understand, with the goal of minimizing the potential for uncertainty and litigation arising from such uncertainty.

The philosophy embodied in Executive Order 12866 puts all federal administrators on notice that they bear a much heavier burden in justifying all regulatory activity than had been the case in the past. It clearly expresses the countervailing values that should be given increased weight in the regulatory balance: protecting the private marketplace from unnecessary rules, reducing the costs of government regulations, placing higher priority on the role of states and Native American tribes, reducing paperwork, improving the readability of rules, and providing greater attention to the liberty and privacy interests of those being regulated. Another step in President Clinton's campaign to change the implementation philosophy of administrative agencies was the designation of Vice President Al Gore to implement Executive Order 12866 and carry out what came to be called the National Performance Review Initiative.[3] This initiative received widespread media coverage and formed an important cornerstone of Gore's subsequent campaign for the U.S. presidency. Taken together, the executive order, the National Performance Review Initiative, and the systematic media campaign succeeded in significantly altering the implementation of public policy at the national level.

The performance focus of the Clinton and the elder Bush's presidential initiatives has existed in all subsequent presidential administrations. President George W. Bush used the Office of Management and Budget to create a new Program Assessment Rating Tool (PART) that facilitated the establishment of program-level performance measures across federal programs (Mullen 2006; Kamensky 2011; although no longer an actively maintained website, see ExpectMore.gov for an explanation and illustration of PART). Each PART questionnaire includes 25 questions divided into four sections.

- The first section of questions asks whether a program's purpose is clear and whether it is well designed to achieve its objectives.
- The second section involves strategic planning and weighs whether the agency establishes valid annual and long-term goals for its programs.
- The third section rates the management of an agency's program, including financial oversight and program improvement efforts.
- The fourth section of questions focuses on results that programs can report with accuracy and consistency.

The answers to questions in each of the four sections result in a numerical score for each section from zero to 100 (100 being the best score). Because reporting a single weighted numerical rating could suggest false precision or draw attention away from the very areas most in need of improvement, numerical scores were translated into qualitative ratings. Exhibit 13.5 presents a summary of the bands and associated ratings used in the PART process.

Exhibit 13.5

PART Rating Range

Effective	85–100
Moderately effective	70–84
Adequate	50–69
Ineffective	0–49

President Obama and Congress have moved beyond the PART approach and replaced it with the Government Performance and Results Modernization Act of 2010 (GPRA Modernization Act 2010). GPRMA does not grade programs as being *successful* or *unsuccessful;* instead, it requires agency leaders to set priority goals, demonstrate quarterly progress in achieving goals, and explain performance trends. The GPRMA definition of *goal* reflects both cross-agency federal priority goals and initiatives, and agency-level priority strategic goals (Kamensky 2011). The GPRMA calls for each agency of the federal government to make a strategic plan available on its public website. The plan must contain a comprehensive mission statement covering the major operations of the agency; general goals and objectives, including outcome-oriented goals; a description of how the goals and objectives are to be achieved; and an identification of key factors external to the agency that could significantly affect the achievement of the goals and objectives. The act also calls for the establishment of a balanced set of performance indicators to be used in measuring or assessing progress toward each performance goal, including customer service, efficiency, output, and outcome indicators. The means used to verify and validate measures must be described, as well as how the agency will ensure the accuracy and reliability of the data. An additional effect of GPRMA is that it requires states receiving federal funds to measure their performance with those funds and to report on a regular basis to the responsible federal agency. GPRMA requirements for quarterly reporting and Internet-based communication of results are transforming the timescale of performance reporting into near real-time information. This short time frame contrasts with the static, annual performance reports used in most budget decision making. Reinforcing direct performance reporting, the American Recovery and Reinvestment Act of 2009 (Recovery Act) included an enhanced accountability system to track oversight and employment performance at the grant and contract level (Kamensky 2011).

The aforementioned examples from the last three decades illustrate the heightened importance of performance information to justify the continued existence of many public programs. But even when data does not support ideological predispositions, it can be used under certain conditions to force a rethinking of public policy that was originally driven by an ideological agenda. As the following section illustrates, this rethinking is occurring with the mandatory prison sentencing policies that swept across most states in the 1980s; such policies were part of a larger, ideologically driven bandwagon of reform supported by very little real data.

Performance Measurement as a Mediating Influence on Ideology: The Prison Problem

During the last quarter of the twentieth century, the states experienced a heightened interest in strategies that would reduce the growing crime rate. The most common response was to pass mandatory minimum sentences for different categories of crime, thus reducing the discretion of judges. One of the most famous mandatory sentencing initiatives was California's "three strikes law," which was the first mandatory sentencing law to gain widespread publicity. The law required imprisonment for a minimum term of 25 years after a defendant was convicted of a third felony. Similar laws were subsequently adopted in most states.

These laws were passed without much analysis of the long-term financial consequences, which have been tectonic. States are now spending $50 billion a year nationwide on incarceration. Corrections is the second-largest state expenditure behind Medicaid. One out of every 15 state dollars is spent on corrections. Not coincidentally, one in 31 American adults is incarcerated. It costs taxpayers, on average, $7.47 per day for parole and $78.95 for incarceration. The total annual cost per prisoner in California is $44,563, nearly the same price as a year at a major university with room and board (Skolnick 2011).

In South Carolina, the prison population tripled between 1983 and 2009, with a 500 percent increase in spending totaling $393 million (Skolnick 2011). California's prison system has been in crisis mode during this period as well. With the need to cut the budget, its prisons filled to over 160 percent capacity. Thirty-three of the state prisons were operating at double capacity in 2011. Temporary beds, half of which were filled by probation or parole violators, were triple stacked in gyms and classrooms and crowding out rehabilitation programs. Sometimes two and three inmates shared a cell designed for one person. These conditions resulted in a lawsuit in which the U.S. Supreme Court mandated that the California Department of Corrections and Rehabilitation (CDCR) reduce the prison population to 137.5 percent capacity by 2012 (*Brown v. Plata* 2011). As a result of the decision, nearly 23,000 prisoners in California were released, all of whom were nonviolent and deemed to be low risk re-offenders (Vara and White 2011).

The problems described above have triggered the production of an avalanche of prison budget performance data: medical and mental health costs; labor and benefit costs; recidivism rates; post-prison employment rates; capital development and operating costs; the comparative costs and benefits of alternative strategies, including parole, probation, community service, employment, education, and others; and contracting out services to private prisons.[4] The collection of this information is having some dramatic policy consequences as each state scrambles to control its runaway corrections costs (Zaitz 2010; Skolnick 2011; Vara and White 2011). The most dramatic reversal is occurring in South Carolina, which, with help from the Pew Foundation for the States, passed the Omnibus Crime Reduction and Sentencing Reform Act of 2010. The act redirects investments in prisons to investments in probation, parole, and alternative service programs. It is projected to save $175 million in construction and $66 million in operational costs over the next five years (Pew Center on the States 2010b).

The summary point we wish to make in this section is that performance information that is connected to the budget allocation process can add up to a difference that counts in how taxpayer money gets spent—and on what kinds of programs. This can occur even when there are serious ideological differences of opinion among citizens and organized interest groups. But elected officials have to be convinced that the performance information being collected is aligned with a political agenda that can acquire the support of those upon whom they depend for their political and financial electoral success. It is much easier for this to occur at the local level than at the state and federal levels of government.

REDEEMING PERFORMANCE FROM IDEOLOGY: WHAT LOCAL GOVERNMENTS CAN DO TO MAKE PERFORMANCE BUDGETING SUCCESSFUL

Performance budgeting has enjoyed much greater success in local jurisdictions than at the state and federal levels (O'Toole and Stipak 1995; O'Toole and Marshall 1990; O'Toole, Marshall, and Grewe 1996).The reasons include the smaller scale and complexity of many local governments, the absence of highly partisan political parties, and the existence of strong mayor and council-manager forms of government that allow for more centralized control and direction over administrative agencies by the executive branch. When administrative agencies operate with more than one master (as is the case at the federal level, where strong interest groups, divided government, and the separation of powers system vie for influence), it becomes difficult for agencies to sustain the will to implement performance budgeting over an extended period. This is especially the case where there is concern by strong unions that performance budgeting may threaten jobs and pay increases for employees. In the sections that follow, we will go beyond our discussion of the importance of performance information in budget decision making to focus specifically on what it takes to create and implement a performance-based budgeting system at the local budget level.

Practical Questions for Doing Performance Budgeting

Performance budgeting is partly art and partly science. It is therefore useful to learn from the experience of those who have developed performance metrics, especially with the goal of tying them to the budget allocation process. The following "baker's dozen" list of questions is based on our compilation of the experience of practitioners who have taken our public budgeting course over the past 20 years and who possess considerable experience with various forms of performance budgeting.

1. Is there a strong causal connection between the performance measure and the objective? For example, if reduction of crime is the objective, it would make little sense to use increased police response time as a performance measure if that did not have much influence on the reduction of crime. On the other hand, if the objective is to reduce the *fear of crime*, then a quicker response time may have a more causal influence on the achievement of the objective. In other words, when selecting a performance measure, you need to ask whether there is any real connection between the performance measure you have chosen and the objective you are seeking to accomplish.
2. Does the performance measure overstate or understate how much of the objective can be achieved by the chosen measure? For example, how much can AIDS be reduced by a public education campaign? By a needle disposal program at selected sites throughout a jurisdiction? By an aggressive safe sex program? These questions illustrate one of the reasons for the resistance by some career administrators and program managers to performance measures. They resist being held accountable for the achievement of results through limited specified performance measures.

3. Are your performance measures minimally necessary? Frequently, more than one measure needs to be developed for an objective, especially if you are seeking to incorporate quantitative, qualitative, and cost information. But ask yourself, How many measures are minimally necessary to determine how well my organization is achieving its stated objective? Data collection, management, and analysis are a cumulative cost to the organization. So collecting information that is not needed—or where less expensive data is sufficient—is an important consideration.

4. Is the measure valid? Does the indicator measure the effectiveness or efficiency of the objective?

5. Can the measure be quantified? The better quantified the measure, the easier it will be to use.

6. Is the data required to develop the measure available? The more available the measure, the easier it will be to implement and operate.

7. Is the measure as simple as you can make it? The simpler the measure, the easier it will be for all concerned to understand and use.

8. Is the measure acceptable to those who are likely to care about its use? Ask whether people will accept it as a valid measure.

9. Does the measure give you timely information? Will the measure reveal problems soon enough to permit corrective action before significant loss of service occurs?

10. Can the information be collected and sustained over a broad enough sample and period to provide you with a reliable measure? How dependable is the data collection system?

11. Can the information be collected at a reasonable cost?

12. Are you spending so much time on the development of performance measures that service delivery is suffering? It is possible to become so involved in improving efficiency that service objectives are nearly forgotten and effectiveness impaired.

13. Previous measures may no longer be adequate, and they should be changed and refined to a point of general managerial acceptance. Experience may show managers that the information being tracked is irrelevant. If any of these problems occur in the year or two after objectives have been established and performance measures have been developed, time needs to be built into the process to correct the situation prior to the following fiscal year's budget submission. This will enable the necessary changes to be reflected in the budgetary plan for the upcoming fiscal year. The important thing to remember is that there should be flexibility in any program planning and performance measurement system.

Some Examples of How to Link Performance Measures to Objectives

One of the more difficult challenges in doing performance budgeting is choosing measures that are *causally linked* to the objectives you are trying to achieve. For example, a public safety department may have an objective of "reducing homicide crimes by 10 percent over the previous year." But if the department chooses to measure the response time to calls, this may have little or no impact on the actual reduction of homicide crimes. Similarly, the timely response to citizen and victim complaints may have little influence on the factors that contribute to the complaints in the first place. It is important, then, to select performance measures that are causally linked to the actual achievement of the stated objective. Exhibit 13.6 provides some examples that illustrate this causal connection.

Exhibit 13.6

Example Causal Connections

1. Housing and Community Conservation

Objective: To reduce abandoned vehicle violations in FY2 by 10 percent or greater over FY1 in each neighborhood with a high number of violations, at a cost no greater than 5 percent above FY1.

Performance Measure: Ratio and cost of abandoned vehicle violations in high violation neighborhoods compared to the previous year in the same neighborhood.

2. Performing Arts

Objective: To increase potential usage of all related facilities by referring inquiries when Performing Arts Auditorium is unable to accommodate.

Performance Measure: Percentage of inquiries referred in FY1 compared to FY2.

3. Public Works

Objective: To operate treatment facilities at a cost no greater than the previous three years' average cost, with 100 percent compliance with federal and state public health requirements.

Performance Measure: Cost of operation in FY4 compared to average cost of FY1–FY3.

Performance Measure: Number of citations issued by public health agencies for permit violation per million gallons of wastewater processed.

4. Financial Management Services

Objective: To provide revenue estimates that are within a 5 percent range of accuracy at a cost no greater than the previous year.

Performance Measure: Accuracy of revenue projections within a variance of 5 percent.

Performance Measure: Total cost of operation in FY2 compared to total cost in FY1.

5. Police

Objective: To ensure that the average response time for all calls for service does not exceed x minutes.

Performance Measure: Response time = Average response time per call

Number of calls

6. Fire

Objective: To contain the dollar and life loss per fire at a level not to exceed x percent of the average for the past three years.

Performance Measure: The dollar loss per fire and the life loss per fire for next year as compared with the average dollar loss per fire and life loss per fire for the previous three years.

7. Executive

Objective: Ensure that progressive discipline training is provided to 50 percent of new supervisory personnel appointed in FY5 at a unit cost of $100 per person.

Performance Measure: The percentage of new supervisors appointed in FY5 who received progressive discipline training.

Performance Measure: The total cost of progressive discipline training for FY5 divided by the total number of new supervisors trained in FY5.

Performance Budgeting Exercise

One of the best ways to appreciate the intricacies and complexities of performance budgeting is to actually experience the task of doing it. Using the form provided in Exhibit 13.7, prepare some performance measures for goals and objectives you have developed. You can use an example from your own experience, build on the examples from chapters 11 and 12, or draw from the data provided on the accompanying website for this book. Remember to tightly link the performance measures to the objectives and to include a performance measure on costs. Costs may not be as relevant or as easy to quantify when dealing with mandated or constitutionally required activities, such as first and fourth amendment rights, due process, and regulatory requirements. But even in these cases, there are discretionary administrative choices that need to be made within the required parameters. From doing the exercise, one can quickly see why it takes three to four years to put such a system into place. This cannot be accomplished without incentives for elected officials to use the performance information to make budget allocations easier rather than more difficult.

Creating the Enabling Conditions for a Performance Budgeting Orientation

More often than not, practitioners are motivated to collect and use performance information when it helps solve practical public policy and budget problems rather than make the problems more difficult. This may sound obvious, but it is an essential starting point for understanding what it takes to create incentives for public officials (both elected and career) to place increased emphasis on the use of measurement in the budget allocation process. It is quite rational for public officials to resist spending their time and the public's money to undertake extensive performance analysis when there is strong political support to continue with business as usual. And it is even more rational for them to resist analytic information when it generates considerable political resistance, as Budget and Finance director Spiro Augustine came to realize in the teaching case for Part III. As Kettl (2000) points out, "Most discussions of public management reform begin with a flawed premise: that management reform is most fundamentally about management. . . . Elected officials do not pursue management reform for its own sake but because they believe it helps them achieve a broader political purpose" (67). This means that important incentives are needed in the political environment for performance information to be collected and used in the budget allocation process (Hatry 2010; Lynn 1998). There are several external factors currently at play that create positive incentives in favor of a performance approach to budgeting.

External Drivers Create Incentives to Undertake Performance Budgeting

We write this book on local public budgeting in the midst of widespread ideological dissensus over what American citizens want their government to do. But there is growing evidence that all parties in the debate are relying more and more on the collection and use of performance information to make their case. This dependence on performance information has been significantly aided and abetted by a growing bipartisan recognition that many state and local governments simply can't afford to continue doing what they have done in the past; without important changes in the way all levels of government run, Americans may feel they are being pushed to the edge of bankruptcy and tethering future generations to very high rates of taxation, fees, and charges for government programs and services. Together, these conditions create incentives for elected officials to make use of performance data and to tie the measurements to the budget allocation process. While the debate over what to cut and what not to cut will remain fierce at the national level, where party partisanship will continue to use major government programs (i.e., social security, health care, food stamps, business tax credit, etc.) as symbolic "weapons" of mass destruction against their

Exhibit 13.7

Practical Exercise: Performance Budgeting

Goal No. 1: _____

_____

_____

Objective No. 1: _____

_____

_____

    Performance Measure No. 1: _____

    _____

    _____

    Performance Measure No. 2: _____

    _____

    _____

Objective No. 2: _____

_____

_____

    Performance Measure No. 1: _____

    _____

    _____

    Performance Measure No. 2: _____

    _____

    _____

opponents, at the local levels of government these debates are significantly tempered by a focus on how to make basic services more efficient, affordable, and accessible. For these reasons, we are optimistic that the trend for local jurisdictions to rely on the collection and analysis of performance information in making budget allocations will continue to grow in the future. In fact, according to an April 2013 report by the Center for American Progress (Shah and Costa 2013),

New York City is now piloting the use of **social impact bonds**, a relatively new outcome-based strategy in which the government pays for a contracted service only after there has been an audit by a third party verifying the achievement of the agreed-upon contract outcomes or results. Under this performance-based model, a government agency or agencies define a specific, measurable social outcome they want achieved in a given population over a certain period of time, such as reducing the number of asthma-related emergencies in low-income children by 15 percent over five years in a small city. They then contract with an external organization that pledges to achieve that outcome within the specified time. The external organization—sometimes called an intermediary—raises money from private investors to fund the interventions and actions needed to achieve the outcome. If an independent assessor verifies through a rigorous evaluation that the outcome has been achieved, the government releases an agreed-upon sum of money for the outcome, and the external organization repays its investors with a slight return for shouldering the financial risk. If the external organization fails to achieve the outcome, the government doesn't pay, and the investors stand to lose their capital (Shah and Costa 2013). We anticipate that such performance-oriented innovations will become increasingly more common at the local government level.

The Importance of Getting Agreement on Goals: The Example
of Using Government to Manage the Economy

As we argued earlier, unless elected officials can reach agreement on goals and priorities, it will be very difficult to make performance budgeting a way of life. Our example in the previous section of getting agreement to reduce asthma-related emergencies in certain target populations is relatively easy to achieve compared to getting policy agreement on how to manage and provide services to the local homeless population. But once this agreement is achieved, a performance orientation can quickly become the norm for doing government business. A dramatic example that illustrates this point is the political agreement among both Democrats and Republicans following World War II on using government to manage the economy. For the first half of the twentieth century, there was profound partisan disagreement over the role of the government in managing the economy, as evidenced by the New Deal debate over whether the government programs created during this period represented the advancing guard of socialism. But this partisan divide ended in 1946, with the passage of the Full Employment Act. In this bipartisan postwar act, both Democrats and Republicans agreed to lay the responsibility for economic stability (as measured by inflation and unemployment) onto the federal government (Stein 1969). The act did not specify how this was to be done, thus leaving open the question of whether it should be done through Keynesian policies of increased government spending during troubled times or fiscal policies that focused on control of the money supply through interest rates and taxation.

The Full Employment Act created the Council of Economic Advisers (attached to the White House), which provides analysis and recommendations, as well as the Joint Economic Committee of Congress, consisting of members of both houses and both major political parties. This bicameral and bipartisan structure has played a powerful role in norming expectations about the role of government in the economy and the role of analysis in measuring government economic performance. This is in evidence on a daily basis in our media coverage. For example, when a report is issued on the current unemployment rate, the inflation rate, or the rate of growth in a given sector of the economy, there is seldom ideological debate over the accuracy of the numbers. Instead, there is debate over who is at fault for the inadequate progress or which strategies will work best to increase economic performance.

The larger point to be made from this example is that the chances for linking performance metrics to budget allocation increase significantly where there is agreement on the goal. Without agreement between Democrats and Republicans that government has the central role in managing the economy, there would be far more debate over the meaning and value of the data that is collected, its use in measuring and managing the state of the economy, and paying for the salaries and programs to make this management effective. The lesson for local government officials is that political agreement on goals is critical to the success of performance budgeting. If goals are not understood, or if there is disagreement over their value or priority, no amount of data is likely to make much difference. Our discussion of planning and goal setting in chapter 10 and priority-based budgeting in chapter 14 have important implications for the success of performance-based budgeting. These chapters set forth various strategies and techniques for getting political and community agreement on budget priorities, which is the necessary precondition for the long-term political survival of performance-based approaches to budgeting.

ADVANTAGES AND DISADVANTAGES OF PERFORMANCE BUDGETING

The completion of the budget exercise in the previous section provides the basis for summarizing the key advantages and disadvantages of doing performance budgeting.

Why a Focus on Performance Is Important

There are many reasons for focusing on performance in the public sector. The conventional view is that public-sector organizations are much more concerned about creating and running programs that meet the pleasure of elected officials and vested interest groups than about being efficient and effective. Therefore, one of the primary purposes of performance budgeting is to temper the influence of political pressures on the resource allocation process with a strong dose of rational assessment of what is being purchased with tax dollars. This concern is real, especially at the federal and state levels of government.

Frequently, elected officials and their constituents press for passage of programs that do not necessarily represent an effective or efficient expenditure of tax dollars. As we discussed earlier, mandatory sentencing is an example of where this has occurred, resulting in extensive expansions of correctional facilities that are now too expensive to maintain. Had there been clear and long-term analysis of the budget consequences of these decisions before they were made, maybe the outcomes would have been different . . . but maybe not, since such laws frequently are passed when the heat of public passions are high and where there is little time or patience for preparing and debating various kinds of performance data. As we pointed out in chapters 1 and 7, the taxpayer revolts starting in the 1970s did not provide the opportunity for passions to be tempered by the hard facts of the longer-term reality that would result from property tax limitations. However, one of the secondary consequences of both of these populist initiatives is that they have heightened interest in performance measures as a way of demonstrating to citizens what their taxes are purchasing in the way of both outcomes and efficiencies. One way of viewing the politics of performance budgeting is to see it as a struggle between a *constituent service/clientele* and a *taxpayer perspective*, with the latter more interested in performance measures than the former.

In addition to these political reasons for undertaking performance measurement, there are important management purposes served by performance budgeting. For example, performance information provides an opportunity for managers to determine whether an organization is achieving its general and specific goals. Because of resource limitations, a manager must be able, at least periodically, to assess the current situation against some agreed-upon criteria. As achievement is measured, this information provides the basis upon which to make program adjustments. Measuring the achievement of an objective can also provide an improved basis for developing succeeding managerial strategies, alternative budget proposals, and service level objectives. In short, a performance system has several managerial benefits:

- Performance measurements can be used to evaluate specific program or project proposals by comparing planned to actual achievements. Programs can be evaluated in terms of improved performance while at the same time considering whether changes are cost effective.
- Performance measurements can be used to forecast resource requirements.
- Performance information provides an important rationale to justify budgetary resource requests. Performance-based rationales supplement, and sometimes counter, the arguments made by political interest groups in favor of and in opposition to public programs and services. This is especially important during a period of declining resources with pressures to reduce personnel costs. Without productivity information, it becomes difficult for both labor and management to defend the number of staff on the payroll without some kind of productivity measurement system.

The Barriers and Disadvantages of Performance Budgeting

Despite the seemingly obvious advantages of using performance measures, little widespread interest has surfaced in systematically using such information in the budget allocation process. There are several reasons for this. First, performance measurement takes considerable time and energy to execute over time, especially if reliability is an important concern. The rule of thumb is that it takes three years to develop, implement, and test a performance-based budgeting system. This is about the length of an election cycle, which means that sustained political support over time is needed to create and maintain a performance budgeting system.

There are many factors that contribute to the need to take time in the development of performance budgeting. Not only is the technical aspect of the task difficult and time-consuming, as we have already illustrated in previous sections of this chapter, but the development of performance measures may be threatening to program managers and their staff, especially if there is the perception that the performance measures will be used to justify program and staff cuts. But managers also might resist performance budgeting for the same reason they resist program budgeting: It limits their flexibility to shift dollars from one set of activities to another. As we noted in our discussion of program budgeting in the previous chapter, over time strong constituency support can develop around defined sets of activities and programs, thus constraining managerial flexibility.

Another barrier is that many units of government may find it difficult to measure outcomes, especially in the short run. For example, there are a variety of social service programs for children, addicts, battered women, and the mentally ill that encounter difficulty crafting adequate, valid, and reliable longitudinal measurements. Even when such measurements can be constructed, the time and expertise required to do so can end up reducing the resources available for direct service. Finally, some public programs are not nearly as popular as others. When this is the case, program supporters and advocates frequently argue that high measures of performance will not fundamentally change the support they are likely to receive from the general citizenry. For instance, there is abundant evidence that building more prisons and expanding mandatory punishment for various categories of criminal activity will not reduce the crime rate or do much good for the incarcerated. Despite this performance information, the general public has generally supported incarceration over treatment or rehabilitation.

Finally, and perhaps most important, performance budgeting has been resisted in some cases by elected officials and their constituents. Elected officials and their staff frequently judge a program negatively if they receive a large number of complaints about it from their constituents. Conversely, a program is judged positively if it has considerable constituency support. The development and use of performance measures may significantly upset this political calculus. For example, programs that may have strong support from a powerful few may not stack up well on the basis of performance measures. Likewise, politically weak constituents may have a strong case to be made in their favor on the basis of performance measures.

Performance Budgeting in a Community Network Context

A results-oriented, outcome-driven focus on performance quickly moves beyond the boundaries of a single local governmental organization and into its service-delivery network of intergovernmental, nonprofit, and for-profit partners.[5] New public management and new public governance encourage these extensive external partnerships to focus attention on creating greater governmental efficiency and effectiveness. However, partnered service delivery brings an array of challenges in measuring, reporting, and assessing partner and network performance. Network governance decisions to revise service delivery programs and arrangements, to change previous allocations of grant or contract funding, or to eliminate inefficiencies in performance often bring political and even legal challenges.

As in the organizational context, effective performance budgeting by a community network requires planning and agreement on joint missions, goals, and work objectives. The PPBS/program budgeting format provides an umbrella structure under which many community actors can contribute policy recommendations, funding, service, and administrative capacity. Effective planning identifies the mission and goals for the community network as an entity. Additionally, plans must allocate resource and performance expectations to each member organization and to its subnetwork constellation of contractors, grantees, subgrantees, and collaborative partners. For performance budgeting to work, all members of the network must consistently collect detailed cost, accomplishment, and productivity information, and communicate that information to budget analysts with the network lead organizations.

The criteria for measuring efficient and effective network performance and accountability vary with an observer's perspective and role responsibility. Network member organizations and the network leadership must respond to and communicate performance accomplishments and quality with at least the following three perspectives in mind (Provan and Milward 2001; Bardach and Lesser 1996):

- an external view of the network as a community responder and system;
- an internal view of the network as a single integrated entity of members, resources, administrative systems, and service delivery systems; and
- an internal view of the network that takes account of the individual organization/participant as a member of the network.

The criteria for measuring successful accountability and performance will vary according to the needs of the three perspectives just listed. Lead administrative organizations in a network, including lead local governments and community intermediaries and foundations, will need accomplishment, cost, and productivity information to support their annual budgeting processes and budget decision making. The budget decisions made by these lead organizations must respond primarily to the external community and to the function of the network as an integrated system. The network and its leadership may need to make compromises and trade-offs to demonstrate successful performance among the three levels. Slippage on the part of one member's performance measures may be necessary to ensure the performance of the larger network (Bardach and Lesser 1996, 204). Performance measurement under the NPM framework would place the greatest emphasis on the community-level outsider's viewpoint. NPM would ask how efficiently and effectively the partner or network arrangement responded to the community's issues and needs. While the NPG framework recognizes the importance of the external community viewpoint, it also takes into account the health of the network as a civic entity and the well-being of the member organizations as long-term contributors to the civil society. Bardach and Lesser (1996, 201) argue that networks are accountable not only for results but also for the governance issues of choosing priorities wisely, targeting their resources and professional discretion, and overseeing system modification and redesign.

The capacity to measure the performance of individual network members and of an entire network rests on the authorities and requirements embedded in the relationships between and among network members. Network relationships fall into four broad categories: intergovernmental agreements (IGAs), short- to medium-term contractual relationships, long-term public-private partnerships, and collaborative partnerships. Cost data in the form of budget line-item funding and contract/grant costs are typically available from governmental or nonprofit organization procurement and finance systems. IGAs for services between local governments do not necessarily require performance measurement or reporting features, although local government councils, commissions, or governance boards could add agreement provisions to develop program goals and objectives and to collect and report accomplishment, cost, and productivity information. With this information, government analysts, executives, and elected officials can then apply various performance budgeting techniques.

Accomplishment and performance measures may be readily available in many short- and medium-term contractual relationships. Contract and grant performance requirements and assessments may provide work accomplishment and quality measures that closely reflect efficiency and effectiveness measures (see chapter 17; Farris 2009). Contract reporting requirements ensure a steady flow of information to the contracting organization. However, to determine whether external contracting is more or less efficient and effective than in-house program delivery, the contracting government or organization needs to collect internal costs, industry benchmark costs and performance data, as well as contractor costs and performance results (see U.S. Government Accountability Office [GAO] 2007).

Long-term public-private partnerships are often results oriented and outcome focused, and partner performance may be measured by required criteria. No matter the exact structure of these formal partnerships, the contracting or granting government or the lead network nonprofit must collect, organize, and report on the partnership performance and costs for its subsequent use in performance budgeting. Collaborative partnerships present the most challenging relationships on which to measure performance. The very mention of performance measurement and verification can transmit a lack of trust and confidence in the partner or relationship. Many smaller collaborating nonprofits may rely extensively on volunteer labor, which does not lend itself to performance enforcement. Negotiated agreements of accountability between partners can help to provide a limited means of performance responsibility between the partners. Reliance on the partner's organizational procedures and reporting may provide an information source on which to construct network performance (Morgan et al. 2013, Figure 14.8, 448).

The performance-based budgeting decisions by the lead government agencies, community foundations, or federated intermediaries may have implications throughout the community network. Public perception of poor performance by one network member tends to implicate all the other network members (Bardach and Lesser 1996, 208). Making governance decisions to revise the structure of the joint network or to replace a network partner to increase efficiency or effectiveness requires both procedural transparency and extensive communication between network members and the public. For a participant-governed network (Provan and Kenis 2007) of relatively equal organizations, a decision to modify the network likely requires dialogue and broad agreement. For networks organized around a lead organization or external network administrator, the policies and procedures of the lead organization would provide network governance procedures. Federal or state contract or grant requirements may provide additional procedures for managing subcontracts or subagreements with service providers.

The results of performance measurement and analysis may imply the need for revised funding levels and revised policies. Network governance decisions that change network structures to increase performance or to eliminate a poorly performing member require careful attention to timing and the potential reaction of participants across the network. Contract or grant completion and consideration for renewal provide a natural opportunity for participants in network and intergovernmental agreements to rethink and restructure partnerships, cost structures, and performance requirements. This may be the time to undertake an objective analysis and use the information to replace a poorly performing partner or to reconfigure the network to increase efficiency and effectiveness. But frequently, the contracting and grant processes operate within a relatively short time frame—one that is not well suited to a performance-based analysis and discussion. Unless the performance criteria have been established at the outset of the contract, grant, or intergovernmental agreement, it will be difficult to use the end of the process to acquire the kind of information that is needed for a thorough performance-based dialogue and a consideration of alternatives strategies. And pushing changes without the data to support it may open the contracting or granting organization to legal liability. It is also frequently the case that replacing major governmental or major nonprofit network funders or participants is extremely difficult, even in the presence of rival large organizations (Bardach and Lesser 1996, 205). Large community foundations and intermediary organizations have a major presence in the community polity.

In the face of the difficulties of linking performance to contract and grant renewal, community leaders and elected officials may provide an alternative remedy for poor performance by major organizations. Contracts and memoranda of agreement sometimes serve as a means to clarify responsibilities and roles and to ensure performance and accountability among major network members. Negotiations and political pressure may be the only means of encouraging more efficient and effective performance by collaborative members of a network with interpersonal and informal ties to the larger group.

CONCLUSION

We conclude this chapter with the observation that performance budgeting will become increasingly important in the future, despite all of the barriers that stand in the way of its successful application in the public sector. There are two reasons for this conclusion. The first has to do with the state of the economy for the foreseeable future. When the economy is growing, the justification for adding new public programs is commonly a matter of generating the political support needed to authorize it and get it funded; however, when the economy is declining, public budgets and programs have to be cut. Political support, however important, is not enough to save the day. This is especially the case when program cuts operate against the popular will or prevailing ideology of the day, as has been the case with prison reform. In these cases, performance information becomes an increasingly urgent and even normal part of the budgeting process.

There is a second reason that performance budgeting will become more important in the future. Despite the barriers to implementing performance budgeting on a systemwide basis and getting agreement by elected officials on community-wide goals and priorities, individual program managers will still be motivated to use performance budgeting to achieve a variety of administrative objectives within their scope of authority. Their ability to do so will vary, of course, with the type of work they are managing. For example, it would probably be much easier for the manager of a road crew to develop performance measures than it would be for the manager of a group of neighborhood associations. But the general pressure on managers "to do more with less" and to justify their existing base budgets creates the kind of incentives that make performance budgeting here to stay—if not for elected officials, at least for professional career managers.

STUDY QUESTIONS

Completion of the performance budgeting exercise in Exhibit 13.1 and making use of appropriate data on the textbook website (www.pdx.edu/cps/budget-book) may be helpful in answering one or several of the following study questions.

1. What is meant by the term *performance budgeting*"? When, why, and by whom was performance budgeting first used extensively in the public sphere?

2. What are the differences (the strengths and weakness) between performance budgeting and PPBS?

3. What are the various ways of measuring the performance of an organization so that it can be tied to budget allocation?

4. How does the role of the chief executive (CEO) and the legislature differ in performance budgeting and PPBS?

5. What conditions are necessary for the successful implementation of performance budgeting?

6. Who tends to gain and who tends to lose in adopting performance budgeting?

7. What efforts have been made by your agency in recent years to implement a performance budgeting system? What have been the results of that experience, or what might the results be if your agency were to attempt to implement performance budgeting?

8. What factors account for the success of productivity-oriented budgeting approaches at the local government level?

9. What explains the differences in performance-oriented budgeting efforts at the federal government level from those attempted at the state and local levels?

10. To what extent do you believe performance measurement can be successfully incorporated into your own organization's budget development and implementation process?

11. To what extent can/should performance improvement be included as a major purpose of the public budgeting process?

NOTES

1. For this section, we have drawn from previous work published in the *Foundations of Public Service* (Morgan et al. 2013, chap. 5).

2. See Franklin Roosevelt's "Summary of the Report of the Committee on Administrative Management," January 12, 1937; Richard Nixon's "Special Message to the Congress on Executive Branch Reorganization," March 25, 1971; Mansfield (1969); Nathan (1976); Rohr (1986, chap. 9); National Academy of Public Administration (1983); and Gore (1993).

3. For a history of the National Performance Review Initiative, relevant documents, and its accomplishments, see Kamensky 2001. Significant groundwork for the National Performance Review Initiative had been laid in the previous administration of President George H.W. Bush, who established a Council on Competitiveness in 1989. Bush charged Vice President Quayle with responsibility for reducing the regulatory burden on the economy. On June 15, 1990, the president expressly directed the council to exercise the same authority over regulatory issues as the former Task Force on Regulatory Relief. Executive Orders 12291 and 12498, issued on February 17, 1981, and January 4, 1985, respectively, set forth the specific procedures for the regulatory review process and served as the legal authority for council activities. Initially, the council considered issues in four different areas: preserving free enterprise, access to capital, bringing science to market, and development of human resources. In President Bush's 1992 State of the Union address, he announced a 90-day regulatory moratorium followed by a 120-day moratorium extension on agency rulemaking. During this period, federal agencies submitted lists of then-current rulemaking and cost estimates to the council for review and consideration.

4. There are a variety of analytic and performance-based studies and reports that have been undertaken by foundations (see Pew Foundation Public Safety Performance Project at www.pewstates.org/projects/public-safety-performance-project-328068), private-sector consulting companies, the U.S. Department of Justice, the National Institute for Justice and state-level studies undertaken by the department of corrections. These sources provide good examples to illustrate a performance-based approach intended to make significant policy changes and to shift public budgeting priorities.

5. We draw on Morgan et al. 2013 (chap. 14, 438–449) to support this discussion.

14 PUBLIC-SECTOR INNOVATION AND ZERO-BASE BUDGETING

No longer can we take for granted the existing budget base and simply be responsible for reviewing proposed increases to continue programs and add new ones. . . . I will insist that the entire range of State services be re-examined and will cut back or eliminate established programs if they are judged to be ineffective or low priority.

(Georgia governor Jimmy Carter, January 15, 1971, quoted in Schick 1987)

State programs are not, in practice, amenable to such a radical annual re-examination [required by ZBB]. Statutes, obligations to local governments, requirements of the federal government, and other past decisions have many times created state funding commitments that are almost impossible to change very much in the short run. Education funding levels are determined in many states partly by state and federal judicial decisions and state constitutional provisions, as well as by statutes. Federal mandates require that state Medicaid funding meet a specific minimum level if Medicaid is to exist at all in a state. Federal law affects environmental program spending, and both state and federal courts help determine state spending on prisons. Much state spending, therefore, cannot usefully be subjected to the kind of fundamental re-examination that ZBB in its original form envisions.

(National Conference of State Legislatures [NCSL] 2010a)

Zero-base budgeting (ZBB) is a budgeting approach that requires government programs and services to undergo rejustification on a regular basis. In this chapter, we use ZBB as the occasion for focusing on the larger issue of incentivizing **innovation** in the public sector. As discussed in the previous chapters, over the past three decades there has been a heightened focus on improving government performance on a variety of fronts: increased effectiveness of management systems, especially in the implementation of public programs; enhanced customer satisfaction; more efficiency; greater responsiveness to citizens and stakeholders; and the inculcation of a heightened concern for innovation. All of these goals require the constant reexamination of current practices to see if better ways can be found to do the public's business. Constantly rethinking *what we do* and *how we do it* are essential preconditions for innovation.

Think of how much innovation has occurred in the field of technology over the past 30 years. Who would have imagined in the 1970s that cell phone and computer technology would change so dramatically in such a short period of time? We have rapidly moved from telephone lines, to fiber optics, to cyberspace transmission with ever smaller and more powerful computer capacity. Advances in microscopy have made possible the emergence of nanotechnology, which enables us to focus on the manipulation of atomic particles instead of the silicon wafers to store, transfer, and manipulate information. All of this has the potential for faster, smaller, and cheaper systems that improve the human condition. If such remarkable things can happen in the private sector, why can't they happen in the public sector? In this chapter, we will answer this question. We begin this chapter with a focus on the use of zero-base budgeting to drive reexamination of the status quo—a spark to incentivize new and innovative approaches to public service. At the end of the chapter, we broaden the discussion to a more general consideration of how well the budgeting process can be used to incentivize innovation in the public sector compared to other strategies.

ZERO-BASE BUDGETING: A FORMAT TO INCENTIVIZE INNOVATION

Since the very beginning of the American democratic republic, the encouragement of innovation has been viewed as an important purpose of government. In fact, the founders in Article I, Section 8 of the U.S. Constitution authorized Congress to grant patents "by securing for limited Times to Authors and Inventors the exclusive Right to their respective Writings and Discoveries."[1] Innovation was part of the general Enlightenment belief that the progress of science and the free exchange of ideas needed to be encouraged for the continued improvement of the human condition (Kors 2003; Headrick 2000). The general belief in the value of innovation was not limited to government's role in encouraging it in the private sector, but included drawing on innovative ideas to improve the performance of government itself. In fact, Alexander Hamilton made this argument to persuade his colleagues to take on the difficult task of creating an entirely new form of government. He argued in Federalist No. 9 that the new "science of politics," like most other sciences of the day, had improved sufficiently to make this difficult task possible (Hamilton, Madison, and Jay 1787/1961).

Over the course of American history, state, federal, and local levels of government have engaged in various kinds of innovation to improve performance and build democratic trust and legitimacy. We have argued throughout this book that local governments are entering a prolonged period of resource constraints that will create pressures on government and nonprofit administrators to find, develop, and adopt new ways of administering programs and delivering services (Damanpour and Schneider 2008).

Innovation can take a variety of forms. Hartley (2005) classifies several broad categories but recognizes that any particular innovation often reflects several categories:

- Product innovation: new durable and consumable goods;
- Service innovation: new ways of providing services to citizens, clients, and consumers, innovation may change the relationship between providers and clients;
- Process innovation: new front- and back-office process changes;
- Position innovation: new use of positions;
- Strategic innovation: new goals or purposes of the organization or community;
- Governance innovation: new ways of involving citizens and strengthening democratic institutions; and
- Rhetorical innovation: new language or concepts to describe a longstanding service or program.

Effective innovation is more than having a good idea. Gaining the maximum benefit of innovation requires an organizational process of (1) identifying new ways of doing business, (2) experimenting with scaled-down versions, (3) developing the ideas into appropriate reforms, (4) initiating the innovation into the organization, (5) adopting the innovation as a permanent practice, and (6) measuring the innovation outcome to assure increased public benefit. This latter point is especially critical. Undertaking an innovative change does not guarantee improved efficiency, increased public value, or improved quality of services or governance (Hartley 2005, 30). That is why measurement of results is so important.

Opening an organization to innovation can be especially challenging. Organizational structure, procedures, resource allocation, information flows, culture, and institutional values may all respond sufficiently well to demands and forces of the external environment, and small incremental changes may be sufficient to keep an organization responsive to its environment. The organization may respond to the environment and perform at a sufficient level, but the organizational and institutional forces of stasis can prevent the achievement of a highly responsive, high-performing organization. Without major internal or external threats to its survival, an organization remains in relative stasis with its environment and remains resistant to change (Hartley 2005, 31; cf. Gersick 1991, punctuated equilibrium model).

ZBB provides a controlled exercise to break down and challenge organizational and institutional structures and traditions. It allows the development of innovative scenarios (1) for eliminating parts of an organization and shedding service responsibility to other providers, (2) for reconfiguring the organization for better service delivery, or (3) for utilizing external service providers, including contractors, grantees, or partner governments. ZBB has been especially focused on developing service innovation, process innovation, position innovation, and strategic innovation.

Our discussion of ZBB follows the organizational design we have used in the three previous chapters on budget formats. We first discuss the origins and purposes of ZBB, provide some examples, summarize the strengths and weaknesses of this format, and end with a practical exercise.

THE ORIGINS AND PURPOSE OF ZERO-BASE BUDGETING

Peter Phyrr, a private-sector entrepreneur at Texas Instruments Corporation, invented zero-base budgeting (ZBB) in the late 1960s. Texas Instruments was an early leader in the application of computer chip technology in the manufacture of computers, watches, and other timing devices. Phyrr's goal was to create a decision-making mechanism that would force Texas Instruments to remain competitive in a rapidly changing set of market conditions. He believed this could best be done by putting managers in the position of constantly asking: Why are we doing what we are doing? Should we be using our resources to do something else? These questions were asked from a shared set of assumptions and a common purpose: to produce better products at a cheaper price than the competition. One of the best ways of forcing managers to rethink what they have been doing is to begin each budget year without assuming that they will have the resources they received last year. What if you had to start over from scratch each year and justify everything you were doing from the ground up? In short, why not create a level playing field for everyone and assume that you could stop what you have been doing and use the resources to do something else instead? Wouldn't this generate more innovation and new product lines, thus ensuring a company's competitive edge in the market place? Peter Phyrr thought so and created ZBB to achieve this goal. His book remains the most definitive and comprehensive treatment of ZBB to date (Phyrr 1973).

The philosophy of always questioning why we should continue doing what we have been doing in the past is the heart and soul of ZBB. Like all other budgeting formats, ZBB should be viewed as a way of structuring the universe of budget discourse. By altering the kinds of questions that get asked and the rules of evidence for answering these questions, ZBB assumed that budgeting could be used as a driving force for generating more creativity by administrators in the budget development and policy implementation process. When Jimmy Carter assumed the office of governor of Georgia in 1971, he became the first chief executive to adopt ZBB on a government-wide basis in the public sector.

In practice, ZBB commonly exists only in modified form in the public sector, usually as **decision packages** or **add packages** that require managers to submit discrete activities or programs for funding above a predetermined reduced level of the previous year's budget. For example, modified

ZBB may ask managers to reduce their budget to a 70–85 percent level from the previous year and then add back requests that they want approved for funding. While the modified approach encourages managers to put some existing programs into competition with new programs, it saves them from the severe strain of justifying *all* programs from the ground up. The modified approach has become common simply because it is too hard—as well as legally impossible—to change what agencies have been funding from one budget year to the next for all of the reasons outlined in the chapter's opening quotation from the National Conference of State Legislatures.

The size and extent of a *modified* application of ZBB varies. At the modest end of the innovation spectrum, budget preparation instructions may direct budget analysts to consult with their department heads and program directors and to conduct a quick paper exercise based on existing position counts and funding levels. This type of mini-exercise fits within the purview and time frame of the annual budget cycle. While this type of exercise generates reflection and learning, it produces a top-down product with little or no organizational support. On the more innovative end of the spectrum, ZBB can be applied as an organizational development and internal planning process that requires extensive involvement of representatives from across the organization, as well as from the community polity. Program clients, constituent group advocates, and community leaders may have unique perspectives on how government can best be shaped to deliver its services. Conducting a more extensive and involved ZBB process requires sufficient time to accomplish the process steps, along with time for reflections and reactions from participants. This information is then used to formulate proposals for new ideas by those responsible for assembling the budget. This may require a full year of process time. Ultimately, the results must be reduced to **budget packages** and decisions that are integrated into the annual budget cycle. Budget process leaders must carefully plan the ZBB exercise and ensure the integration of its results into the larger budget process.

The ZBB format typically builds from the line-item budget format and includes several key concepts: decision units, a base budget, an adjusted level budget, a reduced level budget, and decision packages that are ranked for comparison. A **decision unit** is an element of the organization with responsibility for the delivery of a specified program or activity of the organizational mission. The **base budget** is defined as the most recent legislatively adopted budget for the previous or current fiscal year. The **reduced level budget (RLB)** is a budget with all line-items adjusted downward by a specified percentage from the base budget levels. The budget instructions prepared by the central budget office and the chief executive officer (CEO) (see discussion in chapter 10) will provide guidance on how far each program or department will be reduced as part of the ZBB exercise. The reduced level budget includes services considered critical or essential, but may include new or existing programs. Some jurisdictions make use of what is called an **adjusted level budget (ALB)**. When you see such a term being used, it normally reflects adjustments to the reduced level budget (RLB) necessary to maintain ongoing service levels at next year's prices using the same productivity. The ALB adjusts the RLB by the rate of inflation and by other programmed cost increases in labor contract and service contracts. **Decision packages** are discrete additions to the reduced level budget ranked in priority order to maintain existing programs, serve increased workloads, or add new programs.

ZERO-BASE BUDGET EXAMPLE

Exhibits 14.1–14.5 display the essential elements and characteristics of a zero-base budget exercise for a hypothetical county community corrections department. The tables include a base budget, an RLB, and three decision packages. Exhibit 14.6 provides a summary that rank orders the decision packages with the accumulated totals that would support a **budget request**. In our example, the community corrections department would have a decision unit manager, likely a senior administrator who has a degree of objectivity from any proposed changes. The decision unit manager will convene the ZBB process, coordinate the process with the department budget analysts and other budget actors, and keep communications flowing with labor union representatives, clients, and advocacy groups to prevent unnecessary rumors. As process convener and manager, the decision unit manager has some control over the process outcome in how cutbacks are made, how decision packages are developed, and how they are ranked and compared.

Exhibit 14.1 summarizes the base budget for the corrections department. The department operates a residential corrections center for all levels of offenders, a Restitution Center residential facility for low-level offenders, an extensive field services program to reenter probationers and parolees back into the community, a support services program to contract with professional providers, and an administrative function. The base level budget supports 51 FTEs with expenditures of about $3.59 million.

Exhibit 14.2 summarizes the reduced level budget, a 20 percent reduction from the base budget level in Exhibit 14.1. Most of this reduction represents cuts in the Restitution Center program. The RLB could be set for any percentage desired by the central budget office and the CEO of the organization. RLB reductions usually range from about 5 percent to more than 25 percent. Whatever amount is set, the percentage reduction is established with the goal of stimulating some creative thinking, innovation, and discussion. The reduction's impacts must be sufficient to confront ZBB participants with a reality that differs from the one they are accustomed to dealing with, thus triggering the need for new, innovative responses. The percentage reduction may also reflect the sideboards of falling revenue forecasts. In our example in Exhibit 14.2, department expenses have fallen by 20 percent to about $2.87 million, and FTEs have fallen in rough proportion to 41.5. The table also displays a variety of impacts on the department, its clients, and the community.

The RLB is followed by three decision packages (Exhibits 14.3–14.5), which are each summarized as stand-alone activities. This is in keeping with the goal of ZBB, which is to fund identifiable packages of activity that have clearly stated objectives. Exhibit 14.3, Decision Package 1, provides an example of a package that "purchases back" an eliminated program without substantial programmatic or administrative changes. The Restitution Center program funded by the package is highly effective in reducing offender recidivism and downstream costs, but was the least critical of the department's core programs under the RLB scenario. The package details indicate that the restoration of the program funding will come from county general fund dollars, departmental revenues, and from beginning fund resources.

Exhibit 14.4, Decision Package 2 ("The Job Development Coordinator"), provides an example of a package that is centered on program, process, and position innovation. The package indicates that this new FTE coordinator position is funded by a combination of reductions in the parole and probation staff and reductions in the professional services contracting line-item. The department's accounting will recognize $83,000 in internal transfers to fund the new position, but overall, department spending and FTE totals remain unchanged. This package represents a position redefinition that will more effectively respond to client needs and reduce future recidivism costs more effectively than would an FTE focused on parole and probation services.

Exhibit 14.5, Decision Package 3, seeks to add a new program that is expected to increase process efficiencies. The new technology of remote bracelet monitoring will drive process innovation and a reduction in probation violations. Reducing the base budget to the RLB level resulted in the loss of 2.0 FTEs in the field services department that includes probation and parole officers (Exhibit 14.2, Program Staffing Adjustments). This decision package will replace 1.0 FTE of that loss with a new mental health coordinator and a technology package. The ZBB process participants expect that savings will include reduced personnel costs (a net loss of 1.0 FTE) and stronger monitoring of parolees with fewer violations.

The table in Exhibit 14.6 provides a summary overview of the reduced level budget and each of the decision packages that are rank ordered with dollar amounts attached to each package. As in

Exhibit 14.1

ZBB Package Impact Assessment Form: Example Base Budget

Department: Community Corrections
Organization Unit/Code: 242
Budget Fund Code: 130

Budget or Package Description:

Base Budget Community Corrections Dept.

Purpose: To operate the Community Correction Department at the adopted budget funding level (FY4).
Goal for Community Corrections Center: Provide a structured residential environment for residents and integrate them back into the community with appropriate support strategies.
Goal for Field Services: Provide community supervision of adult probation and parole offenders who reside in the county.

Base Budget Program Staffing Levels:
- Operate the Community Corrections Centers (residential, 10 FTEs) and the Restitution Center (5 FTEs) total: 15FTE.
- Operate Field Services parole and probation at 30 FTE.
- Operate Program Services at 2.0 FTE.
- Administrative Support Division at 4.0 FTE.
Total Department Staffing = 51.0 FTE

Programs: Community Corrections Center (residential) and the Restitution Center (residential) are staffed and operated by county personnel.
Field Services (parole and probation services) are staffed and operated by county personnel.
Program Services is staffed and operated by county personnel, but maintains extensive contracts with mental health, employment training, and pre-release professionals.
Administrative Services is staffed and operated by county personnel.

Impacts:
- The Community Corrections Center remains the primary residential facility for the Department: an estimated 1700 cases in FY4.
- The Restitution Center is a residential facility for low-risk offenders; receive services and may earn restitution compensation to victims: 400 cases this fiscal year, with an expected increase to 750 cases in FY5.
- Field Services currently operates at 2300 cases with 30 FTEs.

Measures:
- Inmate cases
- Avg length of offender stay in residential facility
- Cases per staff FTE
- Cases per 1,000 residents
- Recidivism rate

Budget: **Total Dept. FTE:**   **51.0**
Personal Services $2,949,041
Materials & Supplies $637,350
Revenue Sources
General Fund (20.8 %) $747,111
Departmental (including intergovernmental) $2,439,266
Beginning Fund Balance $400,014
Total Request $3,586,391

Exhibit 14.2

ZBB Package Impact Assessment Form: Example Reduced Level Budget (RLB)

Department: __Community Corrections__
Organization Unit/Code: __242__
Budget Fund Code: __130__

Budget or Package Description:

Reduced level budget (RLB) @ 80 percent of base

Purpose:
To operate Community Correction Department at a funding level of 80% of the base budget.
Goal: Transition offenders back into the community with full assurances of community safety.

Program Staffing Adjustments:
- Discontinue Restitution Center (–5.0 FTEs) = 0.0 FTE
- Reduce Community Corrections Center (residntl) (–2 FTEs) = 8.0 FTE
- Reduce Field Services parole and probation (–2 FTEs) = 28.0 FTE
- Reduce Administrative Staff (0.5FTE) = 3.5 FTE
Total Staff Reduction: (–9.5 FTEs) Remaining FTEs = 41.5 FTE

Program Adjustments:
Restitution Center
1. Discontinue and shift all offenders to parole and probation program.
Community Corrections Center
1. Reconfigure residential center staffing to retain existing capacity. Eliminate a package of transition services.
2. New professional services contract to partially offset staff reduction.
Field Services
1. Retain field services to greatest degree, but reduce capacity and increase remaining parole and probation officer caseloads.

Impacts:
- Discontinuing Restitution Center will shift 750 cases mostly to parole and probation program increasing the workload on a smaller staff.
- Parole and probation officer caseload will grow by about 25 cases per year.
- Release of low-risk offenders directly into the community may result in a decrease in community safety.
- Low-risk offenders will not have the structured support of an outpatient transition program.
- Community Corrections Center offender wait time to participate in group treatment activities will now be 7 days. Early release offenders will not be able to access this limited treatment.

Measures:
- Community Corrections center will maintain the same level of in-facility and community safety as under full funding.
- Reductions will be focused on life skill and transition programs.
- Community Corrections Center staff to offender ratio.
- Parole and probation officer staff to offender ratio.
- Offender wait time for treatment.
- Parole and probation offender incident rate per 1,000 offenders.

Budget:　　　　　**Total Dept. FTE:**　　**41.5**
Personal Services　　　　$2,359,233
Materials & Supplies　　　$509,880
Revenue Sources
General Fund (15%):　　　$430,726
Departmental (including intergovernmental)　$2,073,376
Beginning Fund Balance　$365,011
Total Request　　　　　$2,869,113

Exhibit 14.3

ZBB Package Impact Assessment Form: Example Decision Package 1

Department: Community Corrections Organization Unit/Code: 242 Program Unit Code: 2420 Budget Fund Code: 130	Budget or Package Description: **Decision Package 1: Restore Restitution Center** **Restoration from: RLB (80%)**
Purpose: • To maintain capacity to house nondangerous offenders while providing assistance in obtaining education, training, and employment. • To improve post-transition offender behavior and community safety.	**Recommended Programs:** • To maintain operation of the Restitution Center, a minimum security housing and training center for low-risk offenders. • Operate as a county provided service at FY4 staffing and funding levels. • Restore 5.0 FTE for restitution center staffing. • Increase administrative support staffing by 0.5 FTE.
Program Alternatives: 1. Buy back some residential and program services for a reduced program of about 50 percent of the base levels (FY4). 2. Contract out restitution center operations to private sector. 3. Contract with other relevant public agencies in nearby jurisdictions to provide part, or all, of the program level. 4. Partner with state public safety department to assume some responsibilities for parole and probation. Institute a cost share agreement.	**Impacts:** • Retaining the Restitution Center allows operations of program to continue at previous year level. • Lessen caseload on Community Corrections center staff (by about 2 cases). • Lessen caseload on Field Services parole and probation staff (by about 25 cases). • Eliminating program creates need to find other methods to provide services to further the rehabilitation of offenders.
Measures: • Track number of inmates housed in Restitution Center and compare recidivism rate to comparable record of inmates who do not have access to Restitution Center.	**Budget: Package FTE: 5.5 Total Dept. FTE: 46.5** **Expenditures** Personal Services (5.5 FTE) $451,721 Materials & Supplies $76,877 **Revenue Sources** General Fund (57%) $300,000 Departmental (including Intergovernmental) $198,598 Beginning Fund Balance: $30,000 **Total Package Request** $528,598

Exhibit 14.4

ZBB Package Impact Assessment Form: Example Decision Package 2

Department: <u>Community Corrections</u>
Organization Unit/Code: <u>242</u>
Program Unit Code: <u>2421</u>
Budget Fund Code: <u>130</u>

Budget or Package Description:

Decision Package 2: Job Development Coordinator

Restoration from: RLB (80%)

Purpose:
- To expand the capacity of the Community Corrections Department to rehabilitate offenders and make them self-sustaining, productive citizens.
- To enhance service capacity, and to improve employee and resident security, of the Community Corrections Center.
- To decrease the overall demand for parole and probation services and to increase community safety.

Methods:
- Add position: 1.0 FTE Job Development Coordinator (+1.0 FTE)
- Fund position through two sources:
- Reduction of department budget for contracted professional services (line item 2219).
- Reduction of Field Services parole and probation (−1.0 FTE of Parole/Probation Officer Aide position).

Package FTE: 1.0 new hire   Package Net FTEs = 0.0

Alternatives:
- Fund position completely (100%) from line item 2219 (contracted professional services).

Impacts:
- Addition will lower parole/probation violations by an estimated 10–15%.
- Without this position, only 0.5 FTE Mental Health Worker is available in the Corrections Center and no staff expert on duty for work placement.

Measures:
- Track percent of violations of successfully placed compared to those who are not placed.

Budget: Package Net FTE: 0.0   Total Dept. FTE: 41.5

Expenditures	
Personal Services (1.0 FTE)	$60,000
Materials & Supplies (2219)	$23,000
Other Expenditures	$0
Revenue Sources	
General Fund (54%)	$45,000
Departmental (including Intergovernmental)	$38,000
Beginning Fund Balance:	$0
Total Package Request	$83,000

Exhibit 14.5

ZBB Package Impact Assessment Form: Example Decision Package 3

Department: __Community Corrections__
Organization Unit/Code: __242__
Program Unit Code: __2422__
Budget Fund Code: __130__

Budget or Package Description:
Decision Package 3: Bracelet Monitoring Program
Restoration From: RLB (80%)

Purpose:
To decrease parole probation violations by 15% through remote bracelet-monitoring program.

Methods:
- Add 1 FTE Mental Health Coordinator I to supervise remote bracelet-monitoring program.
- Purchase 50 units of bracelet hardware and monitoring system software upgrades.

Package FTE: 1.0 new hire   Package Net FTEs = +1.0

Alternatives:
1. Contract out for all services and hardware.
2. Divert FTEs devoted to bracelet program.

Impacts:
- Reduce parole probation violations to 15% of clientele served.
- Self-supervision results in a savings of 1.0 FTE probation supervisor time.

Measures:
- Number of parole and probation violations in FY4 compared to FY5.
- Number of parole and probation violations per staff member and per staff hours.

Budget: Package Net FTE: +1.0   Total Dept. FTE: 42.5

Expenditures	
Personal Services (1.0 FTE)	$85,074
Materials and Supplies	$40,000
Revenue Sources	
General Fund (25%)	$31,269
Departmental (including Intergovernmental)	$93,805
Beginning Fund Balance:	$0
Total Package Request	$125,074

Exhibit 14.6

Summary of RLB and Prioritized Decision Packages with Base Budget Comparison

Budget or Decision Package	By Decision Package					Cumulative Totals				
	Gen. Eval. Fund	Departmental	Beg. Fund Balance.	Package Total	FTEs	Gen. Eval. Fund	Departmental	Beg. Fund Balance	Cumulative Total	Cumulative FTE
RLB	$430,726	$2,073,376	$365,011	$2,869,113	41.5	$430,726	$2,073,376	$365,011	$2,869,113	41.5
Package #1 Restore Restitution Center	$300,000	$198,598	$30,000	$528,598	5.5	$730,726	$2,271,974	$395,011	$3,397,711	47.0
Package #2 Job Development Coordinator	$45,000	$38,000	$—	$83,000	1.0	$730,726	$2,271,974	$395,011	$3,397,711	47.0
Package #3 Bracelet Monitoring Program	$31,269	$93,805	$—	$125,074	1.0	$761,995	$2,365,779	$395,011	$3,522,785	48.0
Base Budget	$747,111	$2,439,266	$400,014	$3,586,391	51.0	$747,111	$2,439,266	$400,014	$3,586,391	51.0

our exhibit, the aggregate costs of the packages (1, 2, and 3) added to the RLB often will not sum to the original base budget level. Here, purchasing package 3 will push the general fund dollars over the base budget level while leaving extra dollars seemingly available in the departmental and beginning fund balance columns. The departmental and beginning fund dollars may be restricted to specific purposes and thus not available for a general purchase that general fund dollars can make. To purchase both package 1 and package 3, the corrections department will need to either free up some restricted departmental funds or request a small increment of additional funds from the county commissioners. These examples are presented in a format that is typical of the ones used in practice by ZBB process participants, executives, and elected officials to decide on a set of packages to fund for the coming fiscal year. In fact, at the close of this section on the mechanics of ZBB, we will use this format for purposes of practicing ZBB with your own data set or one provided as part of this text.

After the decision packages have been developed, they are ranked in priority order by a process determined by the decision unit manager and forwarded to the next higher level of review. Decision package priorities from multiple decision units are integrated, so ultimately there is one department-wide list of prioritized decision packages.

If the process is done effectively, top management of an organization will have gained both a planning tool and a budget management tool. Decision unit managers will have had an opportunity to express their priorities, and middle and upper management will have integrated the unit manager lists to meet overall organization objectives. Top management will have some assurance that, if the lowest priority decision packages are not financed, the least important contributions to achieving the organization's objectives have been deleted. The format requires decision unit managers to provide a clear statement of what will be accomplished if a decision package is adopted, as well as summary of the consequences if the agency/program is not funded.

KEY ELEMENTS OF ZERO-BASE BUDGETING

There are four key elements or steps needing completion in sequence in order for ZBB to be successful. First, those in charge of the budgeting process at the top of the organization have to decide on the decision units and the decision unit managers who will have responsibility for creating decision packages. Normally, these decision units and their managers correspond to the existing organizational units that compose the bureaucratic hierarchy, but this need not be the case. Second, the CEO has to specify the rules or formula that will be used to create an adjusted level budget and a reduced level budget. Third, managers must develop a series of innovative packages to improve organization and program effectiveness. Fourth, decision unit managers need to be provided with guidelines (if there are any) for rank ordering decision packages. We discuss each of these steps in the sections that follow.

Selection of Decision Units and Decision Unit Managers

As a first step in the budgeting process, the CEO asks each department to identify and submit for approval the program structure proposed for use in presenting the budget request. This process formalizes the selection of decision units, which is another way of determining the level of discretionary budget authority in the organization. The common presumption on the part of the organizational staff, management, external partners, and constituent group advocates is that the decision units will coincide with the existing organization structure. While this presumption may be reasonable, it is important to remember that the purpose of ZBB is to "shake things up" by questioning existing assumptions. Managers can use the selection of decision units as an opportunity to accomplish this goal. For example, a sergeant within the gang division of the public safety department may have engaged in conversations with the manager of the domestic violence unit and community nonprofit and school partners about effectively leveraging public resources to deal with gang issues in certain neighborhoods and public schools. The creation of a new decision unit may provide the opportunity to do some further exploratory work that legitimizes the expansion of conversations to those outside the immediate organization structure. Of course, such a move would not be made without the full knowledge and approval of the manager's organizational superiors. That is why departments are required to submit their proposed list of decision units to the central budget office for review and approval.

Small departments, which have previously presented their budgets as a single program, may wish to identify only a single decision unit. Larger departments may wish to use the existing organizational structure or may alter the number or size of decision units in order to stimulate creative thinking about how to get better results out of existing resources. For example, a police gang unit in public safety may decide to join with the domestic violence unit, the community policing unit, and a drug unit to create a new structure and set of skills that redefine the current approach that has been taken to deal with gang crime issues. ZBB is intended to encourage this type of new thinking by building into the front end of the budgeting-making structure an opportunity to alter the status quo.

The selection of a large number of units for purposes of preparing decision packages greatly increases the amount of paperwork and detailed supporting data required of a department. A large number of packages can also increase competition and the difficulty of prioritizing packages from different parts of the organization. Selecting too few decision units, on the other hand, may compromise the purpose of the unit by combining such dissimilar responsibilities that agreement on a clear set of policy objectives becomes impossible. These difficulties have generated some "best practices" for selecting decision units:

- A decision unit should be able to undertake actions during the budget year that are capable of producing measurable accomplishments.
- A decision unit needs to have one or more individuals who are accountable for the accomplishments of the unit. In short, the organizational structure of authority needs to align with the personnel structure of authority.
- A decision unit needs to have available specific fiscal and accomplishments information, both historical and projected.
- A decision unit needs to be large enough to represent a set of policy priorities that are important to the organization but not so large that significant priorities lose their visibility.

One of the most important questions surrounding the selection of decision units is how far down the organizational hierarchy one should go in encouraging the submission of decision packages. Under traditional line-item budgeting, this question is answered by who has the authority within the organization to approve the expenditure of money by object code. Decision unit packages would normally be prepared for each of these levels of authority. But such an approach can result in an excessive number of decision packages and create the problem of deciding who and where authority is lodged for prioritizing and deciding which packages are allowed to go forward and which ones are not. Let us illustrate this problem by using a simplified organizational structure of authority in Exhibit 14.7.

In Exhibit 14.7, the executive leadership of the organization might conveniently settle on level 2 departments as the appropriate decision units. In this case, the department heads would take responsibility for determining how to generate decision packages and for prioritizing them. This

390

Exhibit 14.7

Simplified Organizational Structure of Authority Chart

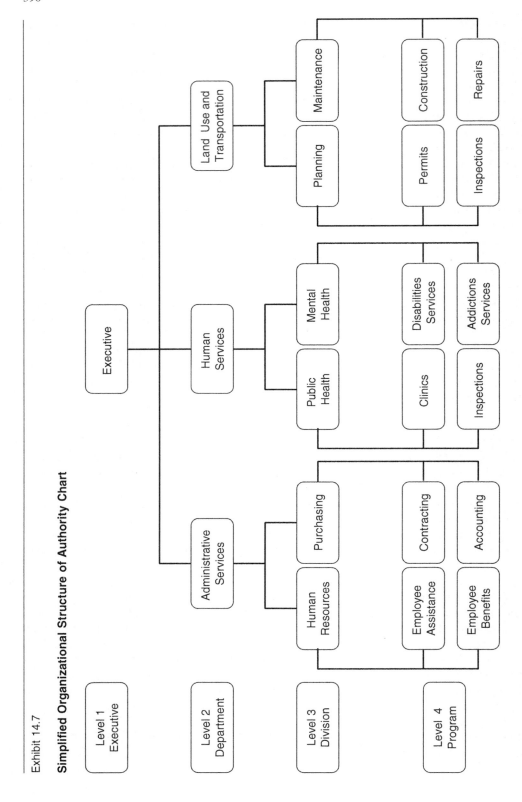

could result in considerable variation among departments, as each department head decided how to generate an RLB and a list of decision packages. For example, a department head might choose to go to level 3 to allow for more specific budget presentations and priority development. The level 3 division managers might decide to involve level 4 program managers, and some may not.

The point of our discussion here is that the selection of decision units and method of setting decision package priorities are far from standard and could result in considerable variability across an organization. For this reason, and because of the tendency to default to past practices, responsibility for the preparation of decision packages usually falls into the hands of those who have traditionally been responsible for preparing and submitting budget requests. This customarily begins with level 4 program managers and proceeds hierarchically up the chain of organizational command. At each level of the hierarchy, the senior manager has the responsibility of winnowing and sorting the decision packages that float up from the bottom of the unit into an RLB and prioritized list of decision packages for that level of the organization. But even this traditional process can produce unexpected friction. For example, differences in the way managers involve others in priority setting, coupled with wide variation by managers in the involvement of lower-level staff in the budget-making process, can quickly produce political rumblings throughout the organization that have little to do with budgeting and a lot to do with issues surrounding the use of power and authority.

The selection of decision units goes hand in hand with the selection of decision unit managers. Just as decision units can diverge from the organizational structure of authority, so can decision managers diverge from the formal structure of authority. For example, a sergeant within the gang division of the police department may be working with other community partners to explore more effective ways of combating youth gangs. It may be reasonable for the director of the gang division to appoint the sergeant to be the decision unit manager for a new community-based initiative. This is a key decision to be made early in the budgeting process.

While it is desirable to have one individual responsible for each decision unit, it is also quite appropriate to appoint a working team to emphasize the importance of a more participatory management approach to problem solving. In such cases, a team leader needs to be designated in order to ensure accountability and responsibility in the budget development and implementation process. It is also appropriate for a decision unit manager to be responsible for more than one decision unit. In the example above, the sergeant in the gang division might serve as the decision unit manager for a new community initiative, while also being the decision unit manager of the dog patrol or community outreach program. Whether an individual or a team, the decision unit managers should be able to complete the following ZBB tasks successfully:

- Assess the decision unit's area of responsibility and determine which of the activities are most essential to meeting assigned objectives.
- Develop a summary of measurable accomplishments that can be achieved at reduced or alternative budget levels.
- In coordination with participating units and budget staff, prepare the fiscal data for different budget levels.
- Prepare incremental decision packages beyond the reduced level budget.
- Rank these decision packages in priority order.

The Reduced Level Budget (RLB) and the Adjusted Level Budget (ALB)

The reduced level budget (RLB) provides the monetary baseline for constructing a zero-base budget. The RLB is calculated by reducing the previous year's adopted budget by a stipulated percentage. Normally, the previous year's budget is defined as the most recent legislatively adopted budget, which includes any amendments to the original adopted budget. The most recent adopted budget serves as the ZBB base budget. For example, if managers are instructed to develop a budget from an 80 percent base, then the RLB is simply 20 percent of the previous year's adopted budget. It is important to distinguish between the previous year's legally adopted budget and what was actually spent (called the actual budget, see chapter 10). The base budget does not take into account any inflationary cost increases over the past year. If a budget is reduced by 20 percent and there has been a 4 percent average increase in costs, the real reduction is 24 percent. To account for inflation, the RLB is sometimes adjusted upward to take into account inflationary and other cost increases. This adjustment produces what is called the adjusted level budget (ALB). The budget instructions manual (see chapter 10) will provide guidance to managers on inflationary factors they need to use for various categories of expenses.

The ALB represents the financing needed to maintain existing adopted programs through the next budget year at the reduced level. The ALB reflects the same series of inflation, contractual, and equity obligations described in chapter 11 for development of the current service baseline (CSB) budget. All of these adjustments are attenuated to match the reduced base of the RLB. If there were no percentage reduction in the RLB, the ALB with its adjustments would equal the current service baseline budget. The ALB takes into account the following additional costs above the previous year's legally adopted budget:

- full financing of salary levels at next year's salary rates;
- full financing of all benefit increases (such as health care, sick leave, and vacation pay);
- documented inflationary and other cost increases for materials and supplies (M&S) and capital outlay;
- inflation cost adjustments per contractual requirements of all ongoing purchases, contracts, grants, and partnerships;
- legislatively mandated programs and activities; and
- the costs of excluded categories, such as debt service, capital construction and capital improvement projects, and restrictive grants.

The ALB sets a department-wide control figure, not a budget plan or a limit for each and every program unit within the organization. In the organizational chart in Exhibit 14.7, the ALB is applied to level 2 of the organization, with the discretion by each department head to determine the number and kind of packages that are produced by levels 3 and 4 of the organization. The goal of the ALB is to create some flexibility for senior managers to try new things or to do existing things a bit differently. The preparation of the RLB and ALB allows managers to grandfather in programs with little or no justification during the budget process. This is intended to free up managers to focus more of their attention on innovative changes rather than invest their time in creating and justifying several decision packages that add marginal increases to the established ALB base.

Development of the RLB forces managers to identify the core or most important objectives for which they are responsible. Most public agencies spend close to 90 percent of their budget on personnel. Cutting your budget back by 20 percent of what you had last year requires careful consideration of which functions are core. A 20 percent reduction in department size requires a similar level reduction in personnel numbers, along with a reconfiguration of staff positions and duties. However, departments with substantial expenditures in professional service contracts and grants may be able to reduce these expenditures with external partners in lieu of cutting staff FTEs and employees. Such a consolidation will still reduce program size and most likely result in a combination of service reductions and productivity efficiencies. Understanding the exact implications of the RLB requires cost and performance data and careful analysis.

An RLB budget, however, must also recognize that most public-sector organizations are required by law to carry out a set of designated functions. Sometimes there is considerable discretion as to how best to meet a particular set of legal obligations, but in other cases the discretion can be quite limited. For example, judges operating under statutorily mandated sentencing requirements create budget obligations for corrections, parole, and probation that cannot be easily changed without fundamental changes in the law. This is also true of debt service, most entitlement programs, and personnel costs that are governed by union and civil service requirements. For these reasons, public agencies cannot markedly change directions from one year to the next. That is why zero-base budgeting is known as *modified ZBB* when applied in the public sector.

Multifunded departments may be tempted to reduce departmental funded or federally funded programs while protecting general fund programs. This is not likely to pass the scrutiny of the analysts in the central budget office. As stated earlier, the reduced level budget figure is a control figure only. Within that figure, departments may:

- include new programs or program enrichments at the expense of existing programs;
- increase expenses for one category (personal services, services and materials, etc.) at the expense of another; or
- shift expenditures from one decision unit to another.

Development of Decision Packages

Following the creation of an RLB, unit managers develop decision packages that do not exceed the amount specified in the budget instructions. For example, the central budget office may ask departments to submit decision packages that do not exceed 110 percent of the base budget. Given these instructions, departments would submit decision packages in increments that do not exceed the specified 110 percent limit. Illustrations are provided above in Exhibits 14.1–14.5 of decision packages. You can use these examples to test the extent to which they meet the criteria for "good decision packages" discussed in the paragraphs to follow.

Several commonly accepted criteria or principles guide the preparation of decision packages. First, each decision package should represent a single, clear policy decision. It should include the specific accomplishments to be achieved and all costs to be incurred during the year. This is in keeping with ZBB's goal of getting participants in the budgeting process to focus on the whole, including what a set of activities is supposed to accomplish and how these accomplishments will contribute to the mission of the organization. A package would normally not be prepared for a single position, one piece of equipment, or one item of expenditure for services and supplies. Instead, all related costs necessary to accomplish a program objective should be identified.

A second principle in the preparation of decision packages is the need to include estimates of the fiscal and program impact of the proposal beyond next year. This is particularly true if the proposal represents a new program or if a planned change in the financing base will take place in the future. If the package is expected to produce substantial matching revenue from other jurisdictions or would generate other revenue, analysts would explain the conditions of this new revenue in detail. This is particularly true if failure to approve the package would eliminate revenue that has been received by the department during the previous year, or would jeopardize continuing a project with a partner agency, organization, or jurisdiction. The analysis should explain whether generated revenues are restricted in use to the particular program arrangement, or are unrestricted and available to offset costs in other programs.

Several common practices undercut the primary ZBB goal of preparing decision packages that initiate some kind of innovation. Decision packages are often designed to simply restore program cuts through the RLB reductions. However, a restored package should clearly demonstrate an effective program with substantial current or future benefits above costs (for an example, see the Restitution Center in Exhibit 14.3). A sufficient number of restorative packages can result in pushing the RLB up to the base budget level with little or no creative thinking or innovation. It is also common for packages to focus on program expansion based on anticipated workload demands or program enrichment to improve the quality of service. ZBB process managers and decision unit managers must consistently work to limit these types of packages, which skirt the innovative goal of ZBB.

Decision Package Ranking Process

Since one of the goals of ZBB is to facilitate the establishment of priorities, decision packages are rank ordered as they are sent forward in the organizational chain of command. This priority **ranking** provides managers and political decision makers at higher levels of the organization with important information in deciding how to allocate scarce resources.

In order for the ranking process to be effective, department managers must develop a specific method of analysis before making recommendations. Agency and program objectives must be identified. Decision unit managers must develop packages that relate accomplishments to objectives. Finally, management must be able to judge the relative importance of decision packages of both similar and dissimilar functions. The creation of a ranking process helps to address this challenge.

The ranking process starts with the decision unit manager. This allows the individual who developed the decision packages (and is accountable for the proposed accomplishments) to do the initial ranking of the relative importance of the proposals. The ranking process above the decision unit level will depend on department program and/or organization structure. In most cases, program decisions will coincide with the organizational structure of authority. In multiprogram settings and complex organizations, program decisions may cross organizational lines.

We have already discussed the problem of deciding how far down the organizational chain managers are requested to prepare decision packages, as was illustrated in Exhibit 14.6. Depending on the breadth of organizational units and the levels within the hierarchy, the problem of ranking decision packages can become an onerous technical and political challenge. We illustrate the difficulty in Exhibit 14.8 below for a medium-sized department with five decision units and two major programs.

At decision unit level C, 5 managers must rank from 3 to 9 packages within each of their respective decision units. At level B, program managers must rank 10 and 18 packages, respectively. Finally, the administrator (A) must rank 28 packages involving 2 programs and 5 decision units (7 if B1 and B2 are treated as independent decision units from those at level C).

Although the unit administrator may be able to evaluate the number of packages in this example, in large organizations the volume may be too great. Therefore, some form of consolidation may be

---

Exhibit 14.8

Sample Decision Packages Aggregated by Organizational Level

A
28 Packages

B1
10 Packages

B2
18 Packages

C1	C2	C3	C4	C5
4 Packages	6 Packages	3 Packages	9 Packages	6 Packages

necessary to focus management's attention on the most critical decisions. This is where ranking approaches become useful, if not necessary.

RANKING APPROACHES

Ranking ZBB packages must be performed with a clear understanding as to who is responsible for decisions and what criteria are to be used to judge among packages. Ranking may be done by individual managers or by some form of management committee. A committee allows for the use of more than one perspective in the ranking of decision packages. If a committee is used, it should include individuals who have substantive operational knowledge of the units whose packages they are responsible for ranking, and, if possible, include the decision unit manager who developed the initial package. Whether the ranking is undertaken by a committee or done by an individual manager, four ranking approaches are most commonly used.

Single Standard

The single standard approach is the simplest and best for dealing with a single program or several programs. Under this method, all decision packages are evaluated against a single criterion such as dollar savings, cost-benefit ratio, increased effectiveness, or known public demand for the services. The key element is that all packages must be considered in terms of their common characteristic. For example, a road maintenance department may decide on repaving priorities based on the single standard of pavement age.

Weighting

Because many programs are complex and a single standard may not provide enough information for effective ranking, a more sophisticated method called *weighting* may prove more useful. Under this approach, several criteria are used, with each receiving a different value. Thus, a self-supporting activity might be worth four points, while a program enrichment activity might be worth one point. The point counts of the packages are then reviewed, differences are resolved, and a consensus rank is passed up to the next level of management.

Multiple Standards

A multiple standards approach, another variation of the weighting system, is more complex in that it focuses on management considerations as well as economic merits. Under this approach, the decision to implement a package may depend on answers to the following kinds of questions:

- Is there a demonstrated demand for the service by the public?
- Do we have the necessary technical skills?
- Will line management accept and execute the program?
- Can we afford not to act?
- What are the political consequences of acting? Of not acting?

Major Categories

A variation on the multiple standards approach is to create categories into which decision packages may be grouped. This places packages from throughout the organization into categories for ranking. Major categories might include:

- packages that generate a positive net revenue;
- packages that pay for themselves in the first years;
- efforts of substantial long-term economic benefit;
- mandatory packages that are required by federal or state law or by contractual obligation;
- packages that have an identified revenue source;
- packages that must compete for revenue from general sources;
- packages that have been previously scheduled but not accomplished; and
- all other remaining packages.

Decisions on what kind of ranking system should be used will, of course, depend on the needs of the department and should be kept as flexible as possible. Statutory authority to perform certain activities is not, in itself, a desirable criterion for ranking priorities. One of the goals of ZBB is for administrators to assist the executive and legislative bodies in identifying the activities that are most critical in achieving the department's overall responsibilities. Just because a department has statutory authority to undertake its current set of activities does not mean that these activities are the best way to spend public funds to fulfill the department's larger set of responsibilities.

Much time and energy can be expended by various layers of the organization on the ranking process. Doing so runs the danger of making the process more important than the outcome. For this reason, departments should not devote an inordinate amount of time determining whether package number 4 is more important than package number 5, but should be more concerned that packages ranked 4 and 5 are more important than package 9, and that package 9 is more important than package 14.

ZBB EXERCISE GUIDELINES

Prepare a zero-base budget for your work unit or for one of the programs in the data set that is provided on the textbook website (www.pdx.edu/cps/budget-book). Keep it simple and prepare no more than three decision packages for a program or a subset of program activities. Use Exhibits 14.1–14.5 as the format for preparing your decision packages and for summarizing the results of your work. Be certain to capture this information by properly labeling the summary information at the top of each form. Use the example provided at the beginning of this chapter to guide your work. Once you have completed the five forms, transfer the FTE, budget, and revenue sources data (bottom right corner of the form in Exhibits 14.1–14.5) to the comparison chart in Exhibit 14.6. Calculate the cumulative costs in the columns provided. Finally, be prepared to discuss and explain your program's reduced level budget and decision packages in the meeting with other department heads to balance next year's budget.

SUMMARY: STRENGTHS AND WEAKNESSES
OF ZERO-BASE BUDGETING

Completion of the ZBB exercise in the previous section provides you with a better appreciation for the strengths and weaknesses of this format. Like PPBS/program and performance budgeting, ZBB is intended to introduce a more systematic planning and analytic perspective into the decision-making process for the allocation of scarce resources. Instead of focusing on performance measures (as does performance budgeting) or the achievement of objectives (as does PPBS), ZBB structures the process so that participants are forced to consider whether current resources might be better spent on other activities. But like all other budgeting formats, there are strengths and weaknesses that benefit some stakeholders and put others at a disadvantage. No format, as we have argued throughout this book, is politically neutral.

Strengths of ZBB

How successful has the ZBB reform initiative been? One way of measuring the success of ZBB is to see how much of it has survived since it was first introduced into the public sector in 1971. ZBB has been especially well suited to meet the needs of nonprofit organizations that provide discrete programs to target populations. Many of these programs have earmarked sources of funding that require some form of ZBB to establish ranked priorities in order to operate within budget guidelines and meet the performance expectations of external funders (Dropkin, Halpin, and La Touche 2007; Finkler 2010). In public-sector organizations, two commonly used budgeting practices have their roots in ZBB, even though users may be unaware of their origins: (1) reduced level/decision package budgeting and (2) **priority budgeting**. We elaborate on each of these more fully in the sections that follow.

Reduced Level and Decision Package Budgeting

There are some important advantages of the ZBB format and its procedures in preparing public and nonprofit managers for certain real-world surprises that they may not have anticipated. Take, for example, the public safety services levy presented in the teaching case at the beginning of Part II of this text. That case is built upon the real-world experience of a county government that had long depended on a supplemental property tax levy for about 17 percent of its law enforcement and corrections budget (Danks 2004). Faced with a crowded ballot, voters rejected a five-year renewal levy with major consequences to the county sheriff, corrections department, youth services department, and prosecuting district attorney. While unthinkable among county leaders before it occurred, scenario planning with an RLB that was based on a 15 to 20 percent reduction would have provided some preparation to meet this major loss in tax revenues.

Several additional examples reinforce episodes of severe revenue reductions as part of organizational life. The severe drop in sales and income tax revenues faced by many local governments following the economic downturn of 2007–2009 resulted in the need to make major reductions in staff, services, and programs. We presented an exhibit in chapter 10 of a large school district undergoing massive personnel cuts because of limited property taxes and a continuing loss of state support. In a very similar context, nonprofit organizations often face the loss of a major grant or contract that provided a substantial portion of organization revenues. The ZBB exercise of developing an RLB gives administrators insight into the challenges of quickly and deeply cutting back and reducing their organizations.

ZBB provides a framework for thoughtful cutback management. When faced with the need to reduce the budget, it is important to understand the external and internal political and technical factors that have an impact on the organization. Are the reductions necessitated by episodic factors with the potential for rebound, or are they a result of permanent changes in the environment that require the development of a new strategic plan, business model, and program configurations? Where the reduction appears episodic and short- to medium-term in nature, the ZBB process can be used to retain and protect organizational and institutional capacity. This includes planning and working to (1) retain key staff technical expertise and institutional memory and (2) protect the core administrative and process functions and systems that can subsequently be used to restore program capacity.

If budget reductions are the result of permanent changes in the external environment, then the ZBB process, in combination with other approaches (like priority budgeting discussed in the next section), can be used to identify and protect the core activities essential to the mission. Whether undertaking temporary reductions or resetting priorities because of permanent changes, the ZBB process provides an opportunity for transparent budgeting. But transparency occurs only when those engaged in the preparation of decision packages communicate with affected internal and external partners, especially with contractors, grantees, and community partners. This communication is even more critical when the goal is to maintain high performance at reduced budget and program levels. This cannot be done without maintaining and building trust among affected partners (Pandey 2010).

Many jurisdictions have incorporated the ZBB principles of reduced level budget and decision packages as common operating procedures within their budget preparation process. As a regular part of the budget process, some jurisdictions assume that revenues are likely to fall short of needed and requested expenses. In anticipation of this outcome, those managing the budget development process rely on the notion of a reduced level budget and the preparation of add packages as an instrument of self-control. This approach pushes the decision-making responsibility downward in the organization when it comes to deciding exactly which cuts to make and how deep to make them. In short, the concepts of reduced level budget and decision packages have generally been used to control budget growth rather than used as originally intended by Peter Phyrr to focus on higher priority uses of existing resources. But, the growing fiscal inability of local jurisdictions to fund all of their current programs and activities has spawned a variation on ZBB, called priority budgeting.

Priority Budgeting

In addition to initiating the practice of preparing decision packages, ZBB has helped to institutionalize the practice of frequently thinking through program and organizational priorities and doing so with a careful eye toward both the costs and the benefits involved. In fact, ZBB has prepared the way for what has come to be called priority budgeting (Government Finance Officers Association [GFOA] 2011c). **Priority budgeting** asks executives, department heads, and program managers to decide what services and activities matter most and to identify the sources of revenue they can draw from to support these priorities. Effective prioritization requires a frank and difficult examination of what activities and service levels are of the most critical need to most members of the community. Alternatively, prioritization encourages leaders to identify programs that deserve funding because they generate large impacts in the community for a relatively small investment. Establishing priorities provides guidance to executives, the central budget office analysts, elected officials, and board members as to how best to disassemble the organization under reduced funding. Strategic disassembly of programs and service elements helps to maintain professional expertise, information systems and procedures, and core service capacity in the face of reduced funding and reorganization. Similarly, prioritization of services gives guidance on how to reconfigure services and capacity; ZBB packages summarize the extent to which such a reconfiguration represents innovation or is simply an add-back package that has been previously funded. Recent budgets from the City of Chandler, Arizona, have applied priority budgeting as part of a program and performance formatted budget (see City of Chandler, AZ 2013–2014). There is a growing interest in using priority budgeting to enable state budgets to remain balanced (Tabor 2012). The approach is especially popular with advocacy groups who want to rebalance the relationship between individual liberty and government control (for good examples, see Fiscal Policy Center 2014 and American Legislative Exchange Council 2014).

To summarize, the advocates of ZBB and its newfound variations of priority budgeting and reduced level budgeting argue that these formats help political and administrative leaders "better articulate why the services we offer exist, what price we pay for them, and, consequently, what value they offer citizens" (GFOA 2011c, 2). This is because these approaches place an emphasis on the following budget activities:

- *Prioritization*. Political and senior administrative leaders are required to reach a consensus on why programs and activities are being funded in lieu of other possibilities.

- *Community transparency and accountability.* Clear establishment of priorities provides citizens with a better understanding of the reach and limits of government services, the results of those services, and how they are connected to achieving larger community goals.
- *Doing the important things well.* With gradual but extensive declines in revenue, it is no longer possible for governing jurisdictions to do everything equally well. Attempts to continue funding activities and programs through traditional line-item budgeting can lead to the gradual withering of all services with incremental cuts from one year to the next. Priority and reduced level budgeting encourage political and administrative leaders to identify services that "offer the highest value and continue to provide funding for them, while reducing service levels, divesting, or potentially eliminating lower value services" (GFOA 2011c, 2).
- *Knowing the costs and managing them within the constraints of government's core business.* Priority and reduced level budgeting can result in more members of the organization having greater knowledge of (1) the overall budgeting process, (2) the costs of doing business, and especially (3) the interplay between managing programs and people within a fixed set of resources. But this requires a deliberate strategy to obtain widespread participation both inside and outside organizational and jurisdictional walls in the budget development process.
- *Constant questioning of past practices.* The involvement of first-line supervisors and street-level service providers builds organization-wide ownership of constantly questioning past practices. This ownership decreases the likelihood that the momentum of the past will secure the future of programs when they have lost their purpose for existing.

Weaknesses of ZBB

The chief weakness of applying ZBB in the public sector, as we have pointed out, is that most governmental programs are legally fixed and cannot be changed extensively in a short period of time without changes in the law. Under these conditions, it makes little sense to undertake the considerable work required by ZBB only to discover that programs ranking low in terms of benefits and high in terms of costs have strong political support with key decision makers in the budget process. That is why it is important to invest political leaders in ownership of ZBB. Laws may need to be changed and elected officials and other political leaders will need to carry the political consequences that come from making such changes. ZBB or any other budgeting format cannot solve what is fundamentally a political problem.

This key issue can be illustrated with a simple summary of the normal budget approval process. When budgets are submitted to the legislative body for review and approval, they are usually taken up one department at a time. This provides no opportunity for legislative members to examine and compare decision packages across multiple departments. And even if this could be done, it would likely result in too many decision packages to be digested during the limited time available for the budget approval process. The implication of these political realities is that administrators have to be convinced that ZBB is worth doing despite the additional burdens it attaches to the traditional line-item budgeting process we described in chapter 11.

Since more people need to be involved at lower levels of the organization in preparing and executing the budget, the ZBB process is more complex, time-consuming, and costly than traditional object code budgeting. By focusing attention on the ends, purposes, and new directions for the future, the ZBB process increases the possibilities for conflict and the need for additional time to resolve these conflicts. Many programs, like a suit of clothes, are interactive with other programs and activities. The creation of independent and self-standing decision packages burdens those responsible for these synergistic and interdependent kinds of activities. The systematic weighting and ranking of decision packages provides an opportunity for ZBB to appear far more rational than it may actually be in practice. The need to choose criteria and then to decide on what the weighting should be opens up opportunities for considerable subjective judgment. Furthermore, elected officials, the executive, and other leaders must be willing to abide by the results of a rational ranking, even when those results are politically difficult to accept. To illustrate this point, examine the criteria ranking framework for capital budgeting discussed in chapter 16. In the example, it is not clear how the nine stated criteria for ranking capital projects was determined. Most priority ranking systems usually are the result of some kind of planning process or a discussion among the senior leadership team, not the result of systematic gathering and analysis of empirical data from a multiplicity of stakeholder groups.

STUDY QUESTIONS

The datasets on the textbook website (www.pdx.edu/cps/budget-book) provide budget data, staffing levels and positions, and other information that can be used to prepare practice ZBB decision packages. The information may also be helpful in answering one or several of the following study questions.

1. What is the rationale behind the adoption of a ZBB system?
2. To what extent does this rationale make sense in light of the conditions that prevail in your agency?
3. What conditions are necessary for the implementation of ZBB? To what extent are these conditions present in your organization/agency/program? What major changes in revenue sources or flow might trigger the need to introduce ZBB into your organization's budget processes?
4. How could you apply ZBB in your organization to stimulate innovation and enhance performance?
5. Who tends to gain and who tends to lose when a local government adopts ZBB?
6. What has been the experience of those agencies, departments, etc., that have adopted ZBB?
7. What are the most difficult practical problems in constructing a zero-base budget?
8. Place yourself as a department or program leader with budget instructions to provide a reduced level budget (RLB) at a 90 percent level, and budget alternatives at the 93 and 95 percent levels. What steps and procedures would you use to adjust department outcomes and outputs, and to identify the personnel reductions necessary to meet these reduced budget levels? If you have limited experience or need data to develop an answer, access the ZBB exercises on the textbook website (www.pdx.edu/cps/budget-book). The county budget dataset on the website provides sample department budgets with detailed positions lists.

NOTE

1. For the history, purpose and reach of copyright law in the United States, see the U.S. Copyright website (www.copyright.gov/). This site provides information on the development of copyright policies since the founding of the American constitution, how these policies have changed, and what is required to file a copyright claim.

PART III SUMMARY

THE COMPARATIVE STRENGTHS OF BUDGETING FORMATS AND THEIR CONTRIBUTIONS TO DEMOCRATIC GOVERNANCE

Democratic discourse implies relevant and valid information. The classical political problems with information are (a) that knowledge is never neutral, so ignorance may be seen as serving the interests of some political actors, and (b) that experts may not be neutral and may manipulate political actors by misrepresenting knowledge.

(James G. March and Johan P. Olsen 1995, 81)

Since the creation of line-item budgeting at the turn of the twentieth century, there have been repeated attempts to supplement it with other budgeting formats. As we have seen in the previous chapters in this section, line-item budgeting fails to provide the information needed to answer the following questions:

1. What are we achieving with the expenditure of tax dollars (PPBS/program budgeting)?
2. How efficient and cost effective are we in the expenditure of these resources (performance-based budgeting)?
3. Should we be doing this at all? Or should we spend tax dollars on *x* rather than *y* (ZBB)?

Each of the four budgeting formats we have examined in Part III—line-item (object code); planning, programming, budgeting system; performance budgeting; and zero-base budgeting—attempts to bring these questions to the center of the budget deliberations by restructuring what gets asked and the decision rules and evidence needed to give the answers. Exhibit P3.1 summarizes the comparative characteristics of the four budgeting formats we have examined in Part III of this book.

As Exhibit P3.1 illustrates, line-item budgeting has high value for those in the political arena who must reach decisions relatively quickly on complex conflict-ridden issues. It is not very useful in providing analytic information on various kinds of performance accountability or in incentivizing innovation. By focusing on dollars, coupled with the infinite ability to divide dollars into ever more finite increments, issues of conflict, interdependence, and analytic sophistication get obfuscated with line-item budgeting. The other formats put considerable pressure on analysis, focus attention on important programmatic consequences of budget increases or decreases, and require extensive attention to program complexities and interdependencies. PPBS, performance, and ZBB

Exhibit P3.1

Budget Format Comparisons

	Purpose? Central question? Problem to be solved?	Chief characteristics	Central actors	Conditions for success	Strengths	Weaknesses
Line-item/ object code/ incrementalism	• Financial accountability. Is the money being spent according to intention? • Preventing misappropriation of funds.	• Focus is on past, with last year as the "base." • Use of formulas like "fair share" to balance the budget.	• Accountants and central office budget managers interested in balancing the budget. • Constituency advocates in the legislature.	• Minimum amount of staff time and expertise is needed to create and track the budget.	• Works well when time is short, there is considerable complexity, multiple stakeholders, and high potential for conflict.	• Not good for dealing with questions of efficiency, effectiveness, future and/ or neglected concerns.
Planning, programming, budgeting system (PPBS)	• Program accountability. Is the program achieving its goals and objectives? • Program effectiveness.	• Focus is on program plans, goals, and objectives. • Requires budgeting to a plan.	• Program managers and program analysts.	• Requires the resources necessary to develop program plans, goals, and objectives.	• Provides clear linkage between program activities and budget allocation. • Links parts to whole and present to future.	• Requires considerable investment of resources. • High potential for conflict.

Performance budgeting	• Program efficiency/ effectiveness. • Is the program cost-effective? Is the program effective? • Measures of what is being accomplished.	• Measurements are created for workload activities, efficiency of resource allocation, and effectiveness.	• First-line supervisors and street-level bureaucrats.	• Requires considerable resources to develop reliable measures. • Requires time to develop confidence of those needed to create performance measures.	• Provides objective ways of documenting accomplishments.	• Time-consuming and expensive. • High potential for resistance because of fear of measures being used to penalize.
Zero-base (ZBB) and priority budgeting	• Priority and appropriateness of what is and should be done. • What should we be doing? Are we giving appropriate priority to current programs and activities? • Deciding whether to continue doing what has been done in the past.	• Systematic reexamination of some portion of current program activities from the ground up.	• Depending on the primary locus of authority, ZBB can be done at any and all levels of the organization.	• Requires considerable time and resources to reexamine activities from the ground up. • Requires self-confident staff and managers.	• Provides opportunity for existing assumptions and activities to be re-examined. • Provides opportunity to reallocate resources.	• Places a high burden on organizational resources. • Is threatening, usually creating resistance. • Difficult to achieve comparability across org. units.

add a higher level of analytic oversight, which is useful in tempering the influence of those who are inclined to allocate the budget on the basis of the strength of organized political preferences. But these methods also add to the complexity of the budgeting process, and they give considerable influence to career professionals who are in charge of creating the categories of analysis and the data that, taken together, give meaning to those participating in the budgeting process. These consequences frequently encourage participants to fall back onto line-item budgeting in order to make the process more manageable and to give more influence to organized stakeholders. There are several summary conclusions that one can draw from Exhibit P3.1 and the multiple purposes served by the four formats discussed in Part III.

CONCLUSION 1

The choice of formats and the combination of those formats is a function of the purposes and complexity of a given organizational setting. In fact, one of the goals of Part III of this text is to sensitize readers to the importance of choosing a combination of formats that work both politically and organizationally. In Exhibit P3.2, we provide a summary of some of the key characteristics of an organizational setting. Exhibit P3.2 enables you to assess the conditions that exist within your program/agency and the likelihood of success for each of the respective budgeting formats.

CONCLUSION 2

In addition to contextualizing the importance of budgeting formats, Exhibits P3.2 and P3.3 call attention to the importance of one of the most important foundational questions of the American system of democratic rule: Who should rule? How much influence should be lodged on the one hand with budget analysts and program managers and on the other with elected officials and citizens? Answers to these questions ultimately turn on one's theory of democratic governance. Program, performance, and priority-based budgeting can give disproportionate influence to career administrators, experts, and senior political leaders at the expense of grassroots voices in the system.

CONCLUSION 3

The history of efforts to implement budgeting reform ultimately turns on the fundamental questions of American democratic governance: Which problems of preserving a regime of ordered liberty are most important to address at a given point in time? Do you think responsiveness to the organized voices in the community is the most important? If so, line-item budgeting will be your preference. But what about the unorganized voices and their unaddressed needs? If this is a major concern, then line-item budgeting will not be your choice. You will favor an approach that gives more influence to professional career administrators and analysts who can identify the larger needs of the community and the strategies necessary to address them. Any format that emphasizes community-based strategic planning and needs assessment will accomplish this goal. These issues take us back to our discussion in chapter 2 and the theory of democratic governance that informs our participation in the budgeting process. Do we think our local democratic system needs more responsiveness to the voices of citizens? Or does it need more expertise to ensure efficient and effective management? Or does it need more external scrutiny to allay suspicions that agencies and program managers develop budgets with an eye toward their own growth and expansion? Answers to such questions ultimately turn on what dangers individuals believe are most important to guard against in the budget development and implementation process. Viewing budgeting from this larger perspective means that budgeting formats are an integral part of the history of democratic reform over the course of American history.

Exhibit P3.2

Characteristics of the Budgeting Environment: Which Format Works Best?

	Low 1	2	3	4	5	6	7	8	9	High 10
Degree of organizational complexity	Performance			ZBB			Program			Line-item
Potential for conflict	Performance				ZBB		Program			Line-item
Informational/analytic capacity of organization	Line-item					Program			Performance	ZBB
Degree of expertise available in organization	Line-item				Program				Performance	ZBB

CONCLUSION 4

Exhibit P3.1 illustrates the increasing importance of the executive branch of government and career public administrators in the budgeting process. Line-item budgeting, which requires some auditing and accounting expertise, was put in place to control corruption. But as questions of efficiency and effectiveness grew in importance, other kinds of expertise became increasingly important, and reform systems were put in place to address those concerns as well. And as new reforms were occurring, other steps were being taken on other fronts to improve government performance. The use of sunset laws, the establishment of citizen/professional oversight committees, rotating performance audits, strategic planning, contracting out, and performance-based personnel systems have been used alongside the budgeting process to improve government performance. All of these approaches rely on analytic techniques that are designed to introduce more systematic analysis and evaluation into public decision making at all levels. Most advanced of the formats, ZBB heavily relies on performance information and a high level of analytic skills to describe program levels of service and performance (Exhibit P3.2). ZBB also requires a very high level of administrative skills in organization development and process innovation. These approaches share a common desire to correct the defects of the incremental consequences of the political process, which tends to rely on *satisficing* rather than *optimizing* as the standard for deciding what to do.

In Exhibit P3.3, we illustrate the role that budgeting formats play within a much larger debate over the course of American history. This debate continues to center around the dangers considered most critical to a regime of ordered liberty, and which combination of solutions are best suited to ameliorate these dangers (for an extended discussion of this issue see Morgan, et al. 2013, chap. 5). The list in Exhibit P3.3 is only partial and intended to be suggestive of the broad array of policy and strategy tools that are available to achieve a given set of objectives (Salamon 2002). Exhibit P3.3 is also a reminder that budgeting formats are one of many tools available to accomplish a set of government purposes, whether it is cost savings, incentivizing innovation, or getting community agreement on priorities.

Personnel systems, management structures and processes, community engagement strategies, and any number of other approaches can be used separately or in tandem with the budget development and implementation process. Thinking strategically about what is most needed in the long term, what is possible within the context of a given community, and what personnel, planning, auditing, citizen engagement, and other tools can be mobilized will prevent the budgeting process from collapsing under the weight of more burdens than it can bear. A failure to consider other strategies that can be used in tandem with the budgeting process is why most budget reformers have been disappointed with the results of their efforts.

STUDY QUESTIONS

1. What are the essential differences between the assumptions of performance budgeting, PPBS, and ZBB systems?
2. How does the role of the chief executive officer and the legislature differ under a ZBB format in comparison either to line-item or PPBS formats?
3. What are the overall strengths and weaknesses of ZBB in comparison to other budgeting alternatives?
4. What combination of budgeting formats makes the most sense for your organization? Your jurisdiction? Why?
5. Choose a budget objective you would like to see achieved for your organization. What nonbudget strategies and administrative functions would you consider using in tandem with the budgeting process to help achieve your specific budget objective?

Exhibit P3.3

Summary Characteristics of Budget Formats and Other Reform Initiatives to Preserve a Regime of Ordered Liberty

Purposes of Reforms: Types of Accountability

	Responsiveness/prevent government abuses	Efficiency/effectiveness	Innovation/entrepreneurialism	Community-centered governance
Types of Reforms and Tools	• Initiative/referendum/recall • Line-item format • Civil Service reform • Financial disclosure • Open gov't laws • Freedom of information • Anti-nepotism rules • Audits • Post-employment prohibitions • Conflict of interest • Rights of privacy • Rulemaking	• Program format • Performance format • City Manager movement • New management theories (for example, Y and Z) • Performance audits • Cost-benefit analysis • Operations research • Critical path analysis	• ZBB and priority format • Reinvention of government movement • Sunset laws • Contracting out • Cost-of-service budgeting • Block grants	• ZBB and priority format • Community-based strategic planning • Network governance models • Polity leadership model

PART IV

EXECUTIVE PRIORITIES, BUDGET ADOPTION, AND IMPLEMENTATION

NEGOTIATIONS WITH CITY UNIONS THREATEN TO DISRUPT THE BUDGET PROCESS

CASE NARRATIVE

Budget deliberations can be contentious, but they can be made even more so if union contract negotiations are taking place simultaneously. That's precisely what occurred in the hypothetical City of Upper Cascadia.

At first, it seemed like it would be a normal budget year for the city, but events ended up colliding into budgetary confusion and political recriminations. The city's three largest unions—police, firefighters, and trades—were all in the final year of a three-year contract. The city had anticipated and prepared for these labor negotiations, but unexpectedly the nation had just been thrust into a major economic downturn. The City of Upper Cascadia had not escaped the downturn's far-reaching economic and financial effects.

In the immediate path of this collision was City Manager Mark Duncan. Duncan had been hired four years earlier to help spearhead economic development in Upper Cascadia. Known as the consummate professional, yet sometimes strident protector of management discretion, Manager Duncan had locked horns not only with the unions on more than one occasion but with the city council as well. In fact, less than two years earlier, the police union had helped engineer his firing by an outgoing city council prior to the election of new council members. In the weeks following the election of new council members, however, the new majority on the council rehired Duncan after a bitterly fought election. Buoyed by his rehiring, Duncan had set out to delineate the boundaries between council policy setting and city manager administrative responsibilities, including negotiations with employee groups.

Upper Cascadia's three major unions had received 3 to 3.5 percent cost of living increases over the past five years during rapid growth periods for the city. Sizeable increases in retail and automobile sales, as well as growth in residential and commercial property values, had fueled a strong rise in tax revenues. The cost of living increases were in addition to the normal salary step increases given each year to employees who had not topped out of their pay range. Between the two, represented employees could receive up to an 8.5 percent annual wage increase. Union leaders expected to win support for at least the step increases going into negotiations for the next bargaining agreement.

Department directors who had received only minor budget reduction targets during the prior year expressed alarm with the 4 percent cuts that the city manager had telegraphed at the start of the budget process. Reflecting the economic downturn, the budget office had just forecast as much as a 15 percent drop in local sales tax revenues for the coming fiscal year—not a small decline in a city where sales taxes comprised more than 40 percent of the general fund budget. The prospect that the economy would turn around within the next few years did not look promising. Rather than make across-the-board cuts, department directors looked at some alternative budget reduction approaches to propose to the city manager. Manager Duncan indicated to the group that he was open to an alternative approach, although privately he was skeptical that they would be able to make the tough decisions.

Although union leaders knew full well that the city's budget situation was not unique, they believed they had an ace up their sleeve. The city's general fund opening balance totaled about $100 million, with general fund operating expenditures of about $220 million. A 50 percent reserve was on the high end of reserve levels for any local government. Surely, the city could allocate a few million dollars from those reserves to fund pay increases for city employees. As time would tell, however, several city council members came to believe that reserves should *not* be tapped to make pay raises when a growing share of the city's citizens faced layoffs as well as pay cuts. Nonetheless, with elections less than a year away, council members had to be wary of disgruntled union members who, in the past, had provided both campaign donations and volunteer help. At least five members of the Upper Cascadia City Council had been elected or defeated over the years depending upon how they were viewed by union leaders and the rank and file.

In response to the executive management team's request and the union's demands to use reserves for wage increases, City Manager Duncan tasked Budget Manager Sue Wilson with developing an alternative budget approach to cutbacks and a defense for preserving current reserve levels. Wilson and her team faced a nearly insurmountable task. One approach that had seen some success in a few other jurisdictions relied on service priority-setting as a way to parse out reduction or savings targets. With this approach, departments would first inventory and cost out all their services. Based on the inventory and costs, the departments would then prioritize their services based on several criteria, including (1) how well the service met community goals (e.g., safe and healthy community); (2) whether the service was required by law or available from another source such as the private sector; and (3) whether demand for the service had increased or decreased in recent years. This process would produce service *scores* that would help identify the relative importance of every program the city operated. The downside to this approach was that it was fairly time intensive and would require at least four or five months to complete. However, the budget office didn't have much more time than that to submit budget proposals to the city manager. Nonetheless, Wilson figured she had nothing to lose by suggesting it to the executive management team.

With regard to the general fund reserves, Budget Manager Wilson felt more confident about the viability of the city's approach. For half of the reserves ($25 million), Upper Cascadia had a long-standing policy of maintaining 12 percent of its general fund revenues as a contingency in the event of a financial emergency or natural disaster. The city had never tapped into those reserves, nor did it intend to unless dire circumstances dictated. The other half of the reserves was not designated for a specific purpose, and the credit rating agencies liked it that way. Some of these unassigned reserves had been tentatively set aside for future economic development or for capital projects. In the past, Upper Cascadia had great success entering into agreements for major economic development projects, where the city either offered to fund the public infrastructure improvements needed for the project or offered cash incentives if the firm relocating to the city met certain job creation targets. The flexible, unallocated reserves provided important resources for economic development at the moment of a falling economy. Upper Cascadia's large reserves contributed to the city's AAA bond ratings earned from two of the three major credit rating agencies. These sterling bond ratings helped to lower long-term borrowing costs for numerous capital improvement projects. Wilson was certain that these uses of the reserves would hold sway during budget deliberations.

The unions were equally confident that the reserves were the answer to their wage demands. They largely dismissed the city's retort that use of reserves, even if advisable, would violate the city's financial policy of using one-time funds only for one-time needs. Union leadership countered that a few million dollars in wage increases could be sustained with one-time funds for a few years until the economy rebounded and ongoing revenues returned to levels sufficient to pay for those increases and more. Armed with information that the city's reserves bested any other city in the state and most cities in the nation, the unions bided their time in negotiations until the deadline for a settlement grew closer, which conveniently coincided with the council's review of the city manager's proposed budget.

Following a briefing with the city manager, Budget Manager Wilson met with the executive management team to discuss her office's idea for budget reductions. To prevent the team from lowballing their budget cuts, the city manager had instructed Wilson not to set a specific reduction goal, but rather charge the team with identifying all reasonable reductions in priority order. However, the budget office did issue some guidelines on how to identify services and set priorities that were much more streamlined than reduction strategies that had been used by other government jurisdictions.

City Manager Duncan knew he faced some big hurdles with the defense of reserves and sizeable cuts in services. Not known for possessing stellar bargaining skills, Duncan relied on Mayor King to test the waters with other members of the council. In his second term as mayor and term-limited to leave in less than four years, King was well respected in the community, but he too was not particularly known for consensus building, nor did he have an ability to line up votes on the council if he needed to. Nonetheless, King could recognize when adoption of a budget, as the manager had outlined, was in trouble. He dutifully reported back that key members of the council were not convinced that budget reductions of the magnitude to which the city manager hinted were necessary.

During normal budget times, the city manager might schedule a few community meetings to solicit input from residents before putting the finishing touches on his proposed budget. Other than some informal one-on-one discussions with council members, the council as a whole would not be briefed on budgetary issues before the proposed budget was formally submitted by the city manager. Duncan knew that this budget year would be different from any other year: He would have to brief the council on key budget issues before finalizing his budget. This would serve several purposes. First, it would provide council with a preview of the budget office's forecast for revenues and expenditures over the next three to five years. This would help to demonstrate the seriousness of the revenue troubles. Second, it would give the manager a barometer of whether the council was inclined to challenge his budget assumptions. Third, if he could demonstrate effectively that the budget troubles were not short-lived, perhaps he could neutralize the union's influence with council concerning their wage demands. Having council member support would avoid a showdown during the council's budget deliberations. The city manager scheduled three briefings with the council before he was scheduled to complete and submit his proposed budget.

In the interim, the budget office continued its work with the executive management team on budget reductions. A first round of meetings focused on describing current services and service levels. Department directors took turns explaining their programs and associated costs to other members of the team. In the next round, directors identified potential cuts that they could make in their programs. After the "easy" cuts had been identified, the team decided they needed a specific dollar reduction target from the city manager. Without it, they knew that directors would play a game of "hide and seek" to prevent cuts to their own programs. Manager Duncan recognized the directors' dilemma, even though he wasn't particularly sympathetic. He set a goal of $4 million in budget reductions. In the budget office's five-year forecast, a budget deficit was projected for the first three years because of drastically falling tax revenues and continuing levels of labor and program costs. Managers Wilson and Duncan knew that budget reductions would be necessary over that same period. The budget gaps totaled some $17 million over those three years or almost 10 percent of the operating budget. After nearly a decade of nonstop growth that filled the city's coffers, Wilson and Duncan concluded that city staff and elected officials, as well as the community at large, might find it difficult to cut back so much in such a short period of time. Duncan tasked Wilson to come up with a plan to soften the blow.

The briefings to council highlighted the shortcomings of looking only at the near term when making budgetary decisions. The briefings showcased a single issue at each of the three sessions: (1) the five-year budget forecast with successive years of budget deficits, (2) the gap between funding sources and proposed capital project spending over the same period, and (3) the expected drawdown of fund balance over the next several years without any further spending commitments (e.g., wage increases). The five-year budget forecast matched falling tax revenues with a continuation of the existing level of personnel and program costs into the future. The reaction to the presentations was not unexpected: The unions questioned the veracity of the forecasts and once again argued that short-term use of reserves for wage increases would not bankrupt the city, much less balloon future budget deficits. Although there was some turnout by members of the community at large, comments from that group raised concerns about the prospect of increased taxes to close the budget gap. Tax increases were never a real possibility. With layoffs and unemployment on the rise, elected officials couldn't fathom raising taxes—either sales or property—even if it was targeted at budget shortfalls. At the briefings, council members didn't doubt the budget office's forecast but understood the further out the forecast went (years 3 through 5), the less reliable it would be. They also fully understood that a brake had to be put on capital projects. They could easily explain to constituents that delaying the projects would forestall tax increases, but there was a division among council members over the use of fund balances. In fact, at the session on that subject, three of the six council members cornered the budget director during the break and pointedly asked, "If our contingency reserve is the equivalent of a rainy day fund, how much worse does it need to get before it could be used?"

The executive management team finished its work and presented its recommendations to the city manager. Four million dollars in cuts made a significant dent in the first year's budget deficit, but the manager was still $2 million short in closing the gap. Duncan turned to his budget manager for some answers. Wilson had been working a plan for a few weeks; she believed she had something that would work but didn't know if he would embrace it. Her plan was simple and straightforward yet seemed to run counter to Upper Cascadia's established financial policies. The heart of the plan used up to $9 million to create a budget stabilization reserve that could be tapped over the next three years to make up the difference between budget cuts and the remaining budget gap projected in each of the three years. One-time funds, in combination with cuts, could be used to close the budget gap for those years. If, by the end of the third year, revenues did not grow sufficiently to cover the remaining budget gap, the difference had to be made up in cuts. Wilson had consulted with the city's financial advisor, who assured her that the credit rating agencies would be okay with this budget balancing approach because use of the reserves had a precise time frame and because it specified the amount of money that could be used. Wilson reasoned that the same rationale would support the use of one-time resources ostensibly for ongoing costs without violating the city's long-standing financial policy. Duncan accepted the plan but wondered if the unions would turn it against him during budget deliberations and labor negotiations.

With a budget finally balanced, City Manager Duncan submitted his proposed budget to the council for consideration and adoption. A full day of briefings had been scheduled so staff could explain to the council members what comprised the operating and capital budgets. The city manager and budget manager took the lead to explain the budget challenge and the proposed deficit reduction plan. Department directors followed with a comprehensive review of their budget reductions and the team effort that went into prioritizing reductions. Council members had a chance to ask questions throughout the day and directed most of their questions to specific reductions, such as the reduction in library hours and increases in fees. Overall, they seemed pleased that the city manager had come up with creative way of closing the budget gap. It was not clear, however, whether they would accept the budget proposals or amend them to provide additional resources for wage increases.

The opportunity for public input came a week later at a formal budget hearing. Nearly 50 residents showed up to express their concerns with a reduction in library hours and deferred park development. The largest turnout, however, was generated by union members and their families—more than 100 in total—including a number who testified. The arguments sounded familiar—police officers put their lives on the line every day and at the very least should receive their 5 percent step increases. Moreover, they argued that the city could easily afford the increases with the tens of millions of dollars sitting in a "slush" fund. The rhetoric was shrill, and at times police union members questioned the council members' concern for the public's safety. The trades union made similar arguments but pitched the argument that its members were the lowest paid of the city's workforce. Interesting enough, the firefighters union, which was the most influential in the city, made an appeal for higher wages so as not to lose financial ground, but added that they would understand if the council did not see it the same way given the state of the economy.

One week divided the public hearing meeting and the budget adoption meeting. Mayor King already communicated to City Manager Duncan that the substance of his proposed budget would remain intact, but a growing majority appeared ready to support the restoration of a few services, such as library hours, with the use of additional reserves. At the closed executive session prior to the budget adoption, City Manager Duncan would learn whether the unions had convinced council to tap reserves to provide step increases to their members. They had not; the police and trades unions had overplayed their hands. The council believed the wrath of voters would be much greater than the loss in union support if they had supported wage increases. Besides, the city manager had already included non-base step increases in his budget that affected a small percentage of the workforce and didn't commit the city to permanent wage increases. The city manager's proposed budget passed that night with a few amendments to restore library hours and some public safety positions. The strategy outlined by Wilson and Duncan managed to balance the budget over multiple years without wage increases.

DISCUSSION QUESTIONS

Consider and answer the following questions as you prepare to discuss this case:

- What were the biggest factors that undermined the unions' demands for higher wages?
- How did the city manager avoid violation of the city's financial policy to use one-time funds only for one-time needs? Did he hold true to the policy?
- What were the potential ramifications if the city had failed to balance its budget? Was that a choice it could make?
- How did the personal styles of the city manager and the mayor play into their strategies for winning adoption of the proposed budget?
- Did inclusion of amendments by the council for service restorations, funded by additional reserves, pose any particular risks for the city?
- How was the budget process unusual, if at all, from the processes with which you are familiar? How important do you think it is for the budget process be adaptable to changing circumstances?
- How did the city manager and the budget manager define the "base budget" to include one-time wage increases? What are the dangers of defining a base budget in this way?

TEACHING CASE

COUNTY BOARD CONSIDERATION OF A CAPITAL PROJECT THAT COULD JEOPARDIZE THE COUNTY CREDIT RATING

CASE NARRATIVE

Finance Director and Budget Officer Elizabeth Brown of Upper Cascadia County learned on Monday that a major manufacturing firm, Smith & Co., had committed to locating an 800-employee plant in an unincorporated area of the county. In return, Smith & Co. asked the county to commit to installing sewer and road infrastructure serving the plant and providing workforce-training funds to support skill-based training for the firm's employees.

Workforce training funds were not a major obstacle. The state was still reallocating leftover ARRA grant dollars from the federal government, and this project appeared to meet all of the grant criteria.[1] Infrastructure funding, however, was a different story and one that posed policy, political, and economic benefit challenges for Finance Director Brown as well as for the county board.

Within the past month, the county board had adopted a five-year capital improvement plan (CIP) setting forth the new capital projects the county planned to initiate in the coming fiscal year, along with its best estimate regarding projects to undertake in the remaining four fiscal years. Suffice it to say, the road and sewer infrastructure project for Smith & Co. was not part of that plan. Even worse, more than $75 million worth of projects previously included in the plan had been deferred for lack of sufficient funding and were no longer scheduled for implementation over the next five years.

At the initiative and encouragement of Finance Director Brown, two years earlier the county board had adopted a comprehensive set of financial policies. Among those policies was one that required the county to maintain minimum reserves in its general fund at 15 percent of current budgeted revenues. In addition to this emergency reserve or *rainy day fund*, the county maintained a capital project reserve of $10 million, which could grow or shrink by vote of the board.

The economic boost offered by Smith & Co.'s proposal to open a major manufacturing facility would be constrained by the county's limited financial resources and the demands of constituent groups for long-awaited community facilities. The fundamental question vexing county officials is: Should Upper Cascadia County gamble on the hopes of long-term economic gain by investing in facilities that primarily benefit a private entity—even in the face of community backlash?

Director Brown had worked long and hard to secure approval from the county board of financial policies governing capital improvements. Her efforts to get these policies in place was prompted by the continued experience of having a new county administrator or a cast of new board members make capital project budgeting decisions based on the program or project initiative that garnered favor at the time. One program or project alone would not place county finances at risk, but a compilation of them over time without the numbers to back them up could erode budget stability. Financial policies, particularly those governing budget reserves, could provide a backstop to protect against the commitment of county financial resources that had not yet materialized or that the county could not reasonably sustain over time.

While these reserves were high enough to provide adequate protection in the event of a financial emergency, erosion of these reserves over time could adversely impact the county's credit rating with agencies who evaluated the county's creditworthiness. A lower evaluation increased the county's costs of borrowing money. Finance Director Brown had to remind management and the board regularly that those emergency reserves were just that—to be used only in extreme situations, if at all. But preserving the integrity of the county's financial policies understandably was a low priority for Economic Development Director Susan George. She had met a few weeks earlier with representatives of Smith & Co. to discuss their request for county financial support for public infrastructure to serve their new manufacturing plant. The proposed plant needed dedicated lines to provide water and sewer, as well as an extension to the sewer trunk line to serve the new plant. The trunk and line extensions were estimated to cost just over $15 million. Extension of roads to serve the facility would require another $5 million.

Funding for this infrastructure would be expected to come from the issuance of county bonds, which would require annual debt service of $2 million over the next 20 years. The county's credit rating of AA+ meant a possible savings of $150,000 annually over the next highest rated bonds, AA.

The prospect of creating 800 jobs, which the company projected would contribute $4 million annually in new sales and property tax revenues, proved very attractive to three of the seven county commissioners. One commissioner was undecided, while the three remaining—including the county board's chair, Thurston Huston—supported two neighborhood groups that saw the funding of infrastructure for the plant as a threat to the construction of a county regional park, Upper Cascadia Lake, which had been on the drawing board for nearly a decade.

The two neighborhood groups, Red Oaks and Strawberry Way associations, had pushed hard for development of the Upper Cascadia Lake regional park for years. For members of the associations and surrounding small communities, the proposed park represented one of the few recreational opportunities within a 20-mile radius. For those closest to the park site, it would be the next best thing to a neighborhood park—a place for children and families to enjoy the outdoors or hold family gatherings. The proposed development—including roads, water, and sewer; a boat landing and dock; picnic areas; three ball fields; and five miles of bike and running trails—had an estimated cost of $18 million.

The two associations succeeded in getting a bond measure on the ballot, which voters approved three years ago. A recession intervened, however, and property values dropped to the point that a tax rate increase would have been necessary to undertake the design and construction of Upper Cascadia Lake. A tax rate increase during the height of the worst recession since World War II was not in the political cards. What few dollars were available to cash fund public projects went for road maintenance. With property values beginning to inch their way up once again, association members saw an opening to resurrect Upper Cascadia Lake. What stood in their way was the prospect that public infrastructure for a major manufacturing plant would divert all of the pay-as-you-go funding away from the more essential regional parks improvement projects such that upcoming bond issues could not be used for the new park's construction.

Looking for alternative funding for the manufacturing plant projects, the Red Oak and Strawberry Way associations set their eyes on the county's $40 million in general fund reserves. They reasoned that if the plant would add $4 million to the county's property and sales tax revenues, it would take only 5 years to replenish the county's reserves. Moreover, if the overall economy improved at the same rate that accompanied the rebounds from other recessions, increased property tax revenues would be sufficient to issue bonds for the regional park in three years, which could in turn reimburse the general fund for the cash advanced from general fund reserves. Association leaders had already spoken to Chair Huston and Economic Development Director George about their funding proposal and received a favorable first reaction. The first public hearing on the Smith & Co. infrastructure project was scheduled two weeks out, and the clock was ticking to win support from other board members.

Director Brown learned of the associations' proposal from Director George and worried that if it were adopted, it would not only undermine the county's financial policies but also jeopardize the county's favorable credit rating; once lost, an AA+ rating is very difficult to regain. Finance Director Brown knew that she had very little time to advance a cogent argument against drawing on the county's reserves and weighed whether the cost-benefit of the competing projects would make a better case than the potential loss of the county's credit standing and the need to preserve reserves to address unforeseen fiscal problems. She pondered her next move as she prepared for a meeting with Chair Huston and two other commissioners. How would you advise Director Brown?

DISCUSSION QUESTIONS

Review and answer the following questions as you consider and discuss this case.

- Should the board choose between the two competing projects or find a way to do both, even if means drawing down county reserves?
- What is Director Brown's strongest argument for protecting the county's reserves and credit rating?
- What factors should a cost-benefit analysis of the two projects take into account?
- How do the estimated operating costs of each project factor into the decision, if at all?
- What precedent might be set if the board chose to authorize a project that hadn't previously been evaluated and vetted through the capital improvement planning process?
- How could the county be assured it would receive a return on its investment if the Smith & Co. plant closed down after a few years?

NOTE

1. American Recovery and Reinvestment Act of 2009 (ARRA; also known as The Recovery Act), Pub. L. No. 111–5, 123 Stat. 115.

15 EXECUTIVE BUDGET PREPARATION AND LEGISLATIVE BODY APPROVAL

The responsible administrator is one who is responsive to these two dominant factors: technical knowledge and popular sentiment.

(Carl J. Friedrich 1940, 12)

The function of the public and of its elected institutions is not merely the exhibition of its mastership by informing governments and officials of what it wants, but the authority and power to exercise an effect upon the course which the latter are to pursue, the power to exact obedience to orders.

(Herman Finer 1941, 337)

We have considered both the factual and legal aspects of the challenges that the petitions present. . . . We conclude that the provisions of Oregon Laws . . . that eliminate the annual assumed earnings rate credit to PERS Tier One members' regular accounts impair a contractual obligation of the PERS contract in violation of the . . . Oregon Constitution.

(*Strunk v. Public Employees Retirement Board*, Oregon Supreme Court, March 8, 2005)

The role of the chief executive officer (CEO) in the preparation and approval of the budget is both technically complex and politically complicated, as the opening epigraphs suggest. In this chapter, we will explore in detail the nature of the executive's role. We open with an overview of the tensions inherent in the executive's role. We then discuss the various factors that contribute to the technical and political complexities of preparing the budget and obtaining approval by the **legislative body**. The most important of these factors consists of the behavioral and strategic roles of the executive and legislative actors in the local government budgeting process. We follow this discussion with an examination of the mechanisms available to the executive to control and influence the compilation and integration of a proposed budget.

We then examine the technical mechanics of developing a **proposed budget**, also known as a **requested budget**. CEOs most likely will not perform these budget mechanics personally, but they must have a full understanding of the procedures and decisions that fold into the preparatory activities. These decisions include management of the **general fund (GF)**, oversight of **internal charges for services**, oversight of **interfund transfers**, and ensuring short- and longer-term balanced budgets. Employee health care costs and retirement benefits are two categories of growing and uncertain cost that make budget preparation difficult. The CEO needs to understand recent changes in these uncontrolled external costs, and their implications on general fund resources and on efforts to balance the proposed budget. Executive framing of budget decisions and the executive responses to the political needs and expectations of the legislative body round out our discussion of proposed budget development. The chapter then turns to legislative body review and the consideration and adoption of the proposed budget. We close the chapter with a discussion of how **budget adoption** decisions by local governments and major nonprofits can affect community resources and partner decisions within the community network of resource and service providers.

SUMMARY OVERVIEW: BALANCING COMPETING TENSIONS

More than any other person in the budgeting process, the chief executive officer is faced with balancing multiple and frequently competing tensions during budget preparation and approval. The CEO serves the full organization, and the proposed budget is a financial, policy, and managerial statement expressing the CEO's agenda and vision for the entire organization. For elected CEOs, strong mayors, and county executives, the agenda and vision embedded in a proposed budget reflect direct political responsiveness to the voters, but even for appointed CEOs, city managers, and general managers, the budget presents an opportunity to exert leadership over the entire organization. This leadership role necessarily requires balancing competing tensions between meeting the internal managerial, technical, and professional needs of the organization, and being responsive to external community needs and wants. The consolidated executive budget gives concrete expression to how this balance is achieved. The CEO, his or her finance director (CFO), budget officer, and the central budget office staff must attend to numerous professional best practice requirements as they compile a proposed budget.[1] These include recommendations from the Government Finance Officers Association (GFOA), applicable state government laws or regulations, and professional guidelines (the Governmental Accounting Standards Board [GASB] and other professional groups). The organization's financial and budget policies round out these professional standards (chapter 10).

The technical aspects of the executive's proposed budget include and catalog all budgeted funds established by the organization. The budget for each fund documents the **reserves**, estimated inflow of revenues, expected outflow of program expenses, and desired closing fund balance. However, to present a consolidated analysis, the CEO's proposed budget must extend beyond the individual department and program budgets to detail an integrated picture of general fund spending, **interdepartmental transfers**, and **internal service charges**. The management and allocation of general fund resources becomes a critical aspect of the consolidation exercise. As we discussed in considerable detail in chapter 9, general government departments and programs are nearly completely dependent on general fund support; without it, these programs would cease to exist. Numerous other programs are partially dependent on general fund support for a portion of their resources. Some partially dependent programs may be able to generate additional charge and fee revenues, but general fund support is typically a critical resource that enables such programs to maintain full program operation. The CEO plays a decisive role in determining the degree of general fund support that will be provided to departments and programs. The exception is when the elected body has made a policy decision regarding the guidelines to be used by the CEO in the allocation of general fund revenues.

The executive's proposed budget must also balance, especially for the upcoming budget year. For the general fund and all other governmental funds, the beginning fund balances plus expected revenues must equal program expenditures plus a desired ending fund balance and fund reserve. All of this work requires considerable technical information, assumptions, and long-term **forecasts** and informed guesswork about economic conditions and business cycles that are beyond government control.

Another set of factors that the executive must take into account in preparing the budget are employee salaries and benefits, as the first teaching case in Part IV demonstrates. The continuing increase in health care benefits for employees, along with their partners and dependents, remains a major cost driver in local government spending. Externally imposed costs add major challenges to the development of an executive's proposed balanced budget. Many of these costs follow trends tied to demographics, employee longevity, and state-mandated payments. Obligations to state-sponsored **public employee retirement system (PERS)** funds or to local public employee retirement system trust funds continue to grow as these funds struggle to maintain solvency (Pew Center on the States 2010a). Retiree health care benefits add another category of unchecked costs to the budget balancing calculus. In some states, the retirement and retiree health care trust fund contributions passed on to local governments have grown so significantly that they are displacing program and service delivery spending. Debt service on borrowed funds provides another category of required payments. To assure a continued favorable credit rating, local governments must meet the agreed-upon payment schedules for interest and principal repayment. In developing a proposed budget, the executive and central budget office must take into account these spending mandates, which often can come at the expense of funding programs and service delivery.

Other expenditure requirements are more nuanced. Responding to community requests and to the political needs of the city council, county commission, or other legislative board members presents a more ambiguous and fluid set of requirements. In the end, the development of the executive's proposed budget represents a financial balance of limited resources and expenditures, and a political balance of responses to many competing demands (Forsythe 2004).

The multiple tensions described above put the CEO in the catbird's seat of local democratic governance and return us to an age-old issue of how much initiative and **administrative discretion** the executive office should exercise in the budget development process. The Carl Friedrich epigraph above (1940) argues for a strong, independent executive role that responds primarily to technical competence and community responsiveness. This model is the most common. In most cases, the CEO controls the department and program budget preparation through the budget instructions and through the review of department and program requests that are conducted by the central budget office. The executive also exerts control by consolidating department and program requests into an integrated document. In the process, the executive plays a decisive role in determining how much general fund support departments and programs will receive. In short, development of the consolidated budget document allows the executive and staff wide latitude to ensure the fiscal integrity of the budget, and to enfold and express the executive's policy agenda.

As the Finer (1941) epigraph reminds us, an excessively dominant role of the executive in the public budgeting process can easily compromise the role of the legislative body in providing policy and political guidance in budget preparation. Finer favored a system that ensured legislative dominance of administrators and the administrative function—a degree of control that might make sense in the British parliamentary system most familiar to Finer, but one that the local public budgeting process in the United States does not provide. Elected city councils, county commissions, and boards of directors are typically not provided with the technical and analytic capacity to exercise this supervening role. Elected officials can set policy priorities; they can request analyses and information from the staff; and they can influence the process and pace of budget preparation. However, in most local government arrangements, they have little control over the vast majority of resource allocation, policy compliance, and financial decisions in the CEO's proposed budget. In many jurisdictions, the executive and legislative body work collegially to make decisions and to develop a budget in a transparent manner. Yet, even in these situations of joint relationships and mutual trust, the role of the legislative body serves as a check on executive action. Finer reminds us that the legislative body—city council, county commission, special district board, or even nonprofit board—plays a critical role in gathering and expressing public concerns in a final **adopted budget**. In the end, only the legislative body can make law and adopt a local government budget.

SOCIAL ROLE BEHAVIOR OF BUDGET DECISION MAKERS AND PARTICIPANTS

A CEO's proposed budget is only as good as its likelihood for acceptance by the legislative body. How each legislative body reviews, vets, and comes to accept and adopt a budget is a unique process. However, all local government jurisdictions must develop and adopt a new budget in time for their new fiscal year. While each jurisdiction's budget process demonstrates a unique expression of the standard steps, the actors in the process tend to enact recognizable role behaviors and strategies. Understanding such role behaviors and strategies is a skill that can speed budget review and acceptance. As a foundation for executive budget development and legislative adoption, we extend our earlier work in chapter 4 to include an additional typology of budget actor roles in this chapter.

Budget Actor Behavioral Roles

The authors have observed a predictable pattern of behavioral roles performed by the different budget actors in budget preparation, review, and adoption. In chapter 4 ("Budget Actors: Conflicting Perspectives"), we categorized budget actors according to their primary orientation: professional/ technical or political. This breakdown provides a basic understanding of budget actor motivations, but a more refined categorization of behavioral and strategic roles provides additional insight into the dynamics of proposed budget preparation and its subsequent consideration and adoption. Exhibit 15.1 identifies the key participants in decision making and their role(s).

Decision Makers

Decision makers are those who actually make budget decisions. The CEO and the legislative body have primary responsibility for developing a proposed budget and its adoption. The CEO plays the heavy lead in overseeing and influencing the budgeting process. The CEO's chief of staff, the chief finance officer (CFO), or the budget director may act as a representative and surrogate for the executive in many budget review and preparation activities, but at critical points in the process and in decision making, the CEO must step in personally to make key decisions. The legislative body also plays a principal role in the budget process. As we noted in chapter 5, the town or city council, county commission or board, or special district board must follow public process steps and make the final decision on budget adoption. However, the CEO and the legislative body are more than simple participants in the budget process. These two actors must also bring process

---

Exhibit 15.1

Decision-Making Participants and Roles

Participant	Role(s)
Chief executive or administrative officer (CEO)	Solicitor, gatekeeper, negotiator, decision maker
Legislative body and citizen advisory committees	Solicitor, negotiator, decision maker
Staff (program managers, analysts)	Gatekeeper, influencer
Community leaders, advocacy group leaders, service delivery network members	Influencer

management and political management skills to the undertaking. The CEO and the legislative body are both the conveners and the primary decision makers of the budget process.

Gatekeepers

Gatekeepers are participants, who by their position of authority or assigned tasks in the budget process, can control what is included in the budget or what information is made available to assess budget proposals. The CEO is the primary gatekeeper in the budgeting process, but program managers, department directors, the finance director/chief financial officer, as well as central budget staff can also exert controlling influence on how issues are framed for debate and decisions. Gatekeepers typically determine which data is selected and presented to support arguments, how issue arguments are constructed, and how information is presented in the budget document and public presentations. Ultimately, these staff administrators will have important influence on what is considered for funding in the budget.

Influencers

Influencers are process participants who are not responsible for making budget decisions, but who can influence the outcome, directly or indirectly. Because they have direct access to decision makers and have insights into the organization and the programs and services it delivers, department managers and central budget office analysts can influence decisions even if they do not have a particular bias for or against a particular program. Those who do have a special interest in a particular program or service—most often community leaders, interest groups, and service delivery network members—do have a particular bias and are intent on influencing budget decision making.

Negotiators

Negotiators are often the decision makers themselves, who mediate differences of opinion or positions on budget proposals. They can alter the makeup or outcome of budget decisions through their efforts to find common ground or form alliances among decision makers. There are times when a non–decision maker known for his or her expertise or familiarity with a particular issue will be asked to serve in the negotiator role.

Solicitors

Solicitors are those participants who actively request input from other participants in the process or from members of the community at large. Again, these are usually the decision makers themselves, who have the legal authority and responsibility to seek input into the budget process through formal public hearings. Alternatively, solicitors may seek input from individuals, groups, or network members who can support or form alliances on a particular budget issue or proposal.

The different behavioral roles appear and often reappear throughout the budget process. During the executive budget formation phase, gatekeepers and influencers make a substantial contribution through their management of information content and flow. Gatekeeper and influencer contributions often reflect and reinforce the preferences and priorities of the CEO. However, gatekeepers and influencers may advocate and work for a contrasting position based on technical, financial, or even political reasons, which stimulates debate and conflict within the organizational hierarchy. These are largely healthy conflicts that serve to strengthen analysis and issue positions. However, such conflicts must be resolved before the CEO's proposed budget is released to the public and the legislative body.

Release of the CEO's proposed budget to the public and the legislative body places the document under public scrutiny. To the analysts who toiled to build an accurate and technically correct budget, public review can feel threatening, even adversarial. If the CEO and the organizational leadership can reframe public scrutiny into a testing and review that makes for a persuasive, more responsive budget, the threatening feelings can be minimized. Budget actors who serve as solicitors play a critical role at this point. The very acts of reviewing the proposed budget and of delivering information to the CEO and staff are part of the process of meeting the responsiveness test needed to build trust and legitimacy in both the process and content of the budget. Solicitors make a critical contribution during the public hearings that precede budget adoption. Adoption of the budget requires behind-the-scenes negotiations between the CEO, members of the legislative body, and issue advocates. The adoption process places a premium on solicitation, negotiation, and decision-making behaviors.

Personal Styles of Participants

Like most other organizational activities, the personal styles of the participants influence how budget decisions are reached. Participants, the roles they perform, and how they go about their duties can have a bearing on the outcomes. If budget decision making is dependent upon interactions among individuals and groups, the personal styles of the individuals involved will influence how successful those interactions are or whether any single individual or group dominates the process.

Studies of personality types suggest that personal styles influences how one approaches decisions and how well one works with others to reach consensus, both of which are key ingredients in the policy formation and budget-making processes. Some decision makers look inward for answers rather than engaging others in negotiations or collaboration. Other decision makers, with personal styles that thrive on engaging others, are more inclined to depend upon negotiation or active collaboration to arrive at major decisions. These different approaches may not result in different decisions, but they may require a flexible budget process—or modifications to it—in order to accommodate the preferences or styles of participants. Elements of personality and various methods of interaction may well explain why a defined set of decision-making models does not exist in the world of public budgeting, or if it appears to, its precepts are frequently altered, adapted, or ignored.

EXECUTIVE CONTROL OF BUDGET COMPILATION

In each step of the process, the CEO is assisted by a finance director and a budget officer or analyst. This technical support can range from the clerk in very small towns or special districts, to a designated business manager or analyst from the finance department, to a central budget office staff in large cities and counties. The staff members from those offices serve as the gatekeepers that drive the process by determining what information needs to be gathered, how that information will be evaluated, and what will be presented to the CEO for review and discussion. The CEO may review progress at key points, and if necessary, take leadership to produce a package responsive to current needs and to the CEO's agenda. Under this arrangement, a small group of analysts and administrators takes control of the budget and assumes responsibility for delivering a budget package to the CEO. Few of the program staff employees throughout various levels of the organization are aware of the ongoing budget development activities. Fewer still pay attention to the process procedures or understand the mechanics. The CEO is typically responsible for submitting a proposed budget to the legislative body. In his or her capacity as the organization executive, the CEO shapes the development of the budget through the following steps in the executive-level process:

- issuance of budget guidelines;
- compilation and review of budget requests;
- input from the departments;
- final decisions on what to include in the proposed budget; and
- formal submittal of the proposed budget.

Issuance of Budget Guidelines

In chapter 10, we detailed the purpose and content of executive budget guidelines and preparation instructions. These instructions provide a foundation for the preparation of the program- and department-level requests. Budget guidelines or instructions direct the department analysts and managers on what information, and in what format, they need to present their budget proposals or requests for consideration by the CEO. These guidelines can be highly technical, containing instructions that range from how to enter information into the budget database and computational system, to the accepted methods for performing analyses and making cost increase assumptions, to a full schedule of due dates. Budget guidelines and instructions are also often policy oriented, with instructions on the size of funding reallocations/reductions and policy changes that need to be reflected in departmental budget submittals. Changing levels of service demand, revenue availability, policy requirements, and the executive agenda all contribute to the allocation and size of reductions or increases in the department requests. As we pointed out in chapter 5, all departments and programs within an organization expect to receive their *fair share* of any resource increases or reductions. A refinement of this equal treatment is to ask departments and programs to take a **proportionate share** of reductions or increases. Simply stated, a proportionate reduction requires departments to reduce their budgets in a share roughly equal to the proportion their budget represents of the total general fund budget. So, a department that receives 15 percent of the general fund budget would be responsible for absorbing 15 percent of a total general fund reduction. To keep internal strife to a minimum, CEOs rely on some form of proportional and fair share concepts in their budget preparation guidelines.

Review and Compilation of Budget Requests

Once the departments submit their requests, the finance director/CFO, budget officer, central budget office staff, or clerk will act as a finance surrogate for the CEO and embark on the task of both validating requests and compiling information for the CEO's review and consideration. This review ensures that departments have (1) accurately forecast their revenues and expenditures, (2) complied with the budget instructions, and (3) followed the CEO's fiscal and policy guidelines. The requested information is then compiled into a standard format that allows for ease of review and comparison. The standard format also supports presentations by the budget officer or the central budget office analysts to the CEO, as well as subsequent discussion and recommendations over how best to allocate limited resources to competing needs.

Program- and unit-level line-item requests serve as the foundation and building blocks of the organizational budget. The program-level line-item requests are grouped and *rolled up* or aggregated by line-item and expense category to the next higher level of the organizational hierarchy, which could include the bureau, division, or program office level. After review of this second level of requests, the line-item schedules are rolled up again to the department or **functional area** level. The final **roll-up** consolidates the departmental or functional area requests into an organization-level budget. Automation has transformed the roll-up process that once required hours of hand computations. Whether by a simple electronic spreadsheet or by a sophisticated and integrated budgetary software system, these building blocks of individual cost estimates are aggregated electronically, simultaneously, and virtually instantaneously.

We demonstrated in chapter 9 on budget funds that each local government department is linked to one or several budget funds for resource support and for managerial controls. Exhibit 9.2 demonstrated the varying degree to which departments are dependent on support by the jurisdiction's general fund. Also in chapter 9, we explained the numbering system and coding commonly used to designate budget funds. These explanations come into our discussion here. Exhibit 15.2 presents a crosswalk between programs and departments for the hypothetical medium-sized City of Upper Cascadia and the sources of funds upon which they rely. Each program or service (top vertical titles) is tied to one or several of 20 budget funds with resources (left column).

Exhibit 15.2 demonstrates a typical arrangement, in which the general fund (001) provides the primary share of revenues for all the programs in the policy and administration and community services departments. The general fund also contributes funds to the parks and grounds and to the planning programs. Dedicated revenue funds (100s) support the building inspection program and the parks capital improvement program. The enterprise funds (400s) support the water service, storm sewer, and sanitary wastewater sewer programs. The city facilities fund (200) supports the maintenance of city-owned property. The two local improvement funds (220s) support the engineering and the streetlights programs for community enhancement. Two funds support debt service for bonds (300s). Finally, the central services funds (500) provide a means for one city program to purchase services from another. This includes the direct interdepartmental purchase of services, and the coverage of indirect, shared administrative costs. All programs and departments must pay a share of these allocated general administrative costs. We provide additional discussion on internal charges for services later in this chapter.

The shift in perspective embedded in Exhibit 15.2 is very important. Program and departmental requests reflect the internal concerns of programs, their unique funding streams, and the legal requirements associated with each of those streams. These are all critical concerns for effective service delivery to clients, but the perspective is limited. Shifting the perspective from the level of individual programs and departments to the integrated level of the general fund and the central services fund puts programs into context with the full organization and its strategic mission.

Input from Departments

While budget software may be able to quickly and efficiently roll up the program and department requests into an organization-level budget, the human relationships of executive decision making move at a slower pace. Once the information from departmental budget requests is compiled, the finance director, budget officer, and central budget office staff typically meet with the CEO to brief him or her on departmental proposals for funding, policy, and program changes. The meetings between the CEO and budget staff provide a neutral setting in which central budget office participants can candidly express concerns about particular proposals without fear of alienating departmental directors, managers, and operating-level staff. Once those initial reviews are completed and any needed clarification is sought from departments about their proposals, the CEO will often meet with department heads to discuss specific remaining concerns. This is an opportunity for the officer to either convey tentative decisions or directly solicit additional input from departments before making final decisions.

Final Decisions on What to Include in the Proposed Budget

The CEO must take into consideration a host of factors before making decisions about what goes into the proposed budget. The list of factors can be exhaustive or short, depending upon the CEO's view of what is important, but the list usually will include the following:

- community preferences and tradition;
- interests of influential individuals or groups;
- compatibility with strategic goals and policies;
- impact on the organization;
- impact on service delivery partners; and
- views and positions of legislative body members.

These factors do not necessarily become a checklist for everything included in the proposed budget, but rather a sieve to identify those issues that are likely to receive the most attention or to create controversy during final deliberations on the budget. Most funding issues escape scrutiny even during times of significant cutbacks. Except for extreme financial crises such as the threat of default or bankruptcy, major shifts in priorities or funding levels are rare. As we have stressed in chapters 5 and 11, incremental changes are still the foundation for, and bane of, organizational budgeting, in both the governmental and nonprofit sectors.

To assess whether any of the above bulleted factors will or should play a part in shaping the content of the proposed budget, the CEO will want to survey the political landscape. Where the interests and concerns of particular individuals or groups are in play, the CEO or his or her surrogates (department heads or key staff) may need to talk one-on-one with the interested external parties. If these discussions uncover opposition to important proposals from influential budget participants or key members of the legislative body, the CEO may attempt to alter that proposal to secure sufficient support for its passage.

Part of the predecisional outreach includes contacts with service delivery and community partners. The budget decisions in the proposed budget may have major implications for the contractors, grantees, and intergovernmental partners who have formal agreements with the local government. The CEO's budget decisions can also stretch to affect informal partnership relations with community groups and citizens. The pathways of communication to the service delivery and policy partners may be affected by the structure of the community network (Robinson and Morgan 2014). In informal networks and in participant-governed networks, the network members may need to work through a dialogue to generate a recommendation on the CEO's budget proposal. One or several partners in the network may act as information solicitors from the other partners. The solicitation role allows for a flow of interpersonal communication from throughout the network back to the government CEO. In more structured networks, the lead organization or administrative organization might exercise a policy process to develop a response and comments to budget proposals. Regardless of the structure of the local network, everyone realizes the importance of getting information on the CEO's proposed budget prior to formal submission to council. Once the proposed budget is finalized for submission to the legislative body, it becomes much harder to influence the outcome of budget review and deliberations.

One group that requires at least symbolic outreach and for which established lines of communication on the budget do not typically exist is the community at large. The CEO or his representatives may choose to hold special community meetings or informal hearings before final decisions are reached on the proposed budget. Other avenues for these outreach efforts are community television programs, electronic forums, and online survey tools. Even if this outreach does not attract many participants, the efforts are a way for the CEO and the government organization to demonstrate a commitment to engaging residents and taxpayers in the budget process.

In the end, the overriding consideration for budget decisions is the need to balance total resources (i.e., revenues, transfers in, and on-hand resources) with total requirements (i.e., expenditures, transfers out, and ending balances). This balancing requirement spans the budget process from start to finish. If the budget is out of balance, reductions and funding adjustments may be neces-

Exhibit 15.2

City of Upper Cascadia: Budget Fund Support and Obligations by Program Function

Fund Code	Fund Name	Policy & Administration											Community Services			
		Mayor & Council	City Mgr. & Exec. Staff	Human Resources	Inform. Tech.	Risk Management	Finance Admin.	Financial Operations	Admin. Services	City Attorney	Technology		Police	Library	Social/ Community Events	
001	General Fund	P	P	P	P	P	P	P	P	P	P		P	P	P	
400	Sanitary Sewer Fund															
410	Storm Sewer Fund															
430	Water Fund															
450	Water CIP Fund															
100	State Motor Fuels/Gasoline Tax Fund															
110	Traffic Impact Fee Fund															
120	Electrical and Plumbing Inspection Fund															
125	Parks CIP Fund															
135	Criminal Forfeiture Fund												C			
140	Insurance Receipt and Self-Insurance Fund							P								
145	Building Permit Revenue Fund															
165	Street Maintenance Fee Fund															
200	City Facilities Fund															
220	Green St LID/CIP Fund															
225	Wall Street LID Fund															
350	General Obligation Debt Service Fund							O								
300	Bancroft Debt Service Fund/ Local Imp. Dist.															
500	Central Services Fund	I	I	I	I	I	I	I	I	I	I		I	I	I	
550	Fleet/Property Management Fund	I	I	I	I	I	I	I	I	I	I		I	I	I	

Source: Adapted from City of Tigard, OR 2004, 280–352.

Notes: P = Primary Resource Support
  I = Internal Service Charge or Transfer; C = Contributing Resource Support;
  O = Obligated Payment

Exhibit 15.2 *(continued)*

Fund Code	Fund Name	Public Works									Development Services					
		Public Works Admin.	Parks & Grounds	Sanitary Sewer	Storm Sewer	Water Services	Street Maintenance	City Fleet Maintenance	City Property Maintenance		Community Dev. Admin.	Building Inspection	Current Planning	Long Range Planning	Engineering	Street Lights & Signals
001	General Fund	P	C						C		P		C	C		
400	Sanitary Sewer Fund			P												
410	Storm Sewer Fund				P											
430	Water Fund					P										
450	Water CIP Fund					P										
100	State Motor Fuels/Gasoline Tax Fund						C									
110	Traffic Impact Fee Fund						C									
120	Electrical and Plumbing Inspection Fund											P				
125	Parks CIP Fund	O	P													
135	Criminal Forfeiture Fund															
140	Insurance Receipt and Self-Insurance Fund															
145	Building Permit Revenue Fund												C	C		
165	Street Maintenance Fee Fund						C									
200	City Facilities Fund								P							
220	Green St LID/CIP Fund														C	C
225	Wall Street LID Fund														C	C
350	General Obligation Debt Service Fund										O					
300	Bancroft Debt Service Fund/Local Imp. Dist.										O					
500	Central Services Fund	I	I	I	I	I	I	I	I		I	I	I	I	I	I
550	Fleet/Property Management Fund	I	I	I	I	I	I	I	I		I	I	I	I	I	I

sary to reach balance. In those cases, the officer might need to confer again with key participants to ensure they concur with those adjustments.

Formal Submittal of Proposed Budget

The last remaining act in the first half of the budget process is the production of the proposed budget document. Although many of the decisions may already have been made about what ends up in the final adopted budget, it is in the **proposed budget** that the details and rationale behind the numbers are revealed. The proposed budget is the vehicle for presenting the financial and organizational information upon which budget decisions are based. It also serves as the device through which the CEO conveys his or her spending priorities and initiatives for upcoming fiscal years.

Makeup of Proposed Budget Document

Unlike annual financial reports (see chapter 18) that have a standard format, the budget documents from any two jurisdictions are never exactly alike. These differences reflect minimal requirements in state regulations and guidance, the issues of controversy, the CEO's priorities, and the finance and budget officer's professional preferences. A quick visit to local government websites for views of current and past budget documents will highlight these differences. However, the Government Finance Officers' Association (GFOA) Distinguished Budget Presentation Awards program provides a list of criteria that serve as a uniform standard for local government budgets.[2] While state law or local ordinance may require the inclusion of specific content or analyses, budget documents for a proposed budget typically contain the following information:

- *Budget Message:* chief executive or administrative officer explains the major initiatives or changes, and the factors and assumptions underlying the budget proposals contained in the document.
- *Spending and Revenue Summaries:* Condensed summaries of revenue, expenditures, and personnel details, perhaps by department, fund, and major object of expenditure (i.e., personal services, materials and services, and capital outlay).
- *Revenue and Debt Analysis:* Description of underlying assumptions, trends, and capacity of the jurisdiction's revenues, reserves, and borrowing.
- *Operating Detail:* Typically presented department by department, the operating detail or budget notes usually include a mission statement; description of major services; programmatic objectives for the upcoming fiscal year; spending by major object for the prior year, current fiscal year, and upcoming fiscal year; perhaps some key performance measurement data; and explanations of any changes in program size, delivery, content, or funding.
- *Capital Project Summaries:* Usually a summary of more detailed information presented in the jurisdiction's multiyear capital improvement plan (CIP).

A key element of the proposed budget package is the CEO's **budget message**. The CEO prepares a budget message and transmittal letter to the legislative body and to the public at large. It outlines his or her view of the most pressing budgetary issues and concerns, along with recommendations for addressing them in the budget. In some cases, the message may be little more than an articulation of program or service priorities and funding levels that the CEO is proposing those priorities should receive. For example, the message may contain a specific recommendation to add police patrol officers in response to an increase in crime. However, the most effective messages will look beyond the upcoming budget year to several years out to set forth a strategic approach for dealing with long-term trends, developing challenges, and potential opportunities that the community may want to pursue and in which local decision makers may want to invest through the budget. The CEO might decide, for instance, that additional patrol officers are not necessary because long-term trends do not show an increase in crime. The CEO may conclude that funding might be better allocated to technological approaches to crime prevention rather than the more traditional "putting boots on the street." The budget message presents an effective vehicle for explaining this situation and the CEO's decision. Whatever its scope and nature, the budget message often represents the most important policy presentation in the budget. The budget message content, presentation, and issue framing can set the tone and context for the deliberations and negotiations that follow during the remainder of the budget process.

EXECUTIVE OVERSIGHT OF ORGANIZATIONAL-LEVEL ISSUES

The proposed budget represents an organizational-level perspective on the local government that corresponds with the CEO's responsibility for the entire organization. The finance director or CFO, budget officer, and central budget office staff share this broader perspective, which allows these actors the ability to see the entirety of decisions, linkages, implications, and context, which are often obscured from the department and program analysts. The organizational-level perspective allows the CEO and his or her staff to place budget decisions into an extended financial context and into a strategic context of community service needs and programs. The organizational level raises issues for the CEO in a short-term budget-year frame, and in a mid-term to long-term frame of sustained financial balance. In the short run, the allocations, linkages, and performance requirements in the proposed budget are the levers that refine the budget to support the CEO's agenda. The CEO also holds the ultimate responsibility for the technical quality of the budget and for ensuring a **financially sustainable** organization over the middle and long terms. Achieving these goals often requires implementing previously adopted financial policies (chapter 10) on budget reserves, contingency and rainy day funds, interfund transfers, "one-time" revenues, and unidentified and unexpected costs and obligations. The proposed budget provides the CEO and the finance director or CFO with the opportunity to proactively respond to and manage long-term financial issues. It also frames these issues for consideration by the legislative body, which may place higher priority on other more pressing needs and politically driven obligations. Organizational-level budget issues that require CEO oversight and decisions typically include:

1. *General Fund Resource Allocations:* The allocation of general fund resources to general fund programs, and the use of general fund resources to supplement nongeneral fund programs.

2. *General Fund Balance and Reserves:* The management of the general fund balance, including the establishment of, or replenishment of, contingencies and reserves; the identification of end-of-year carryforward needs and closing balances; and the identification of resources and controls to meet those balances.

3. *Internal Charges for Services (Interdepartmental Charges):* The identification of service purchases by one department or program from another, and the allocation of overhead and administrative support costs to all departments and programs.

Exhibit 15.3

City of Upper Cascadia: 100 General Fund (GF) Budget

	Current Year Adjusted FY4	Requested Preliminary FY5
RESOURCES		
Beginning Fund Balance	$7,065,185	$7,751,279
Revenues		
Property Taxes	$9,115,977	$9,443,080
Intergovernmental	$2,250,690	$2,484,669
Fees & Charges	$693,000	$806,769
Fines	$434,127	$592,840
Franchise Fees	$2,508,866	$2,693,727
Interest & Rentals	$156,304	$172,500
Other Revenues	$36,032	$68,200
Total Revenues	$15,194,996	$16,261,785
Transfers In from Other Funds		
Building Permit Rev Fund	$64,754	$64,503
Criminal Forfeiture Fund	$62,200	$50,000
Elect & Plumbing Inspt Fund	$16,891	$16,826
City Facilities Fund	$0	$0
State Mtr Fuel/Gas Tax Fund	$1,155,255	$1,083,085
Sanitary Sewer Fund	$113,414	$149,055
Storm Sewer Fund	$257,988	$122,593
Street Maintenance Fee Fund	$0	$20,800
Traffic Impact Fee Fund	$74,163	$82,206
Water Fund	$325,189	$366,963
Total Transfers in Other Funds	$2,069,854	$1,956,031
TOTAL RESOURCES	**$24,330,035**	**$25,969,095**
REQUIREMENTS		
Program Expenditures		
Policy and Administration	$310,775	$336,635
Community Services	$9,629,511	$10,168,132
Public Works	$2,473,000	$2,407,459
Development Services	$2,398,228	$2,499,824
Total Program Expenditures	$14,811,514	$15,412,050
Debt Service	$0	$0
Capital Improvements	$0	$0
Transfers Out to Other Funds		
Building Fund	$39,052	$28,280
Central Services Fund	$2,517,189	$2,391,733
Central Services Reserve	$375,000	$350,000
City Facilities Fund	$450,000	$250,000
Fleet/Property Mgmt. Fund	$563,479	$777,022
State Mtr Fuel/Gas Tax Fund	$0	$0
Total Transfers out to Other Funds	$3,944,720	$3,797,035
Contingency		
General Contingency	$829,414	$1,000,000
Designated Contingency	$0	$0
Total Contingency	$829,414	$1,000,000
Total Budget	**$19,585,648**	**$20,209,085**
Ending Fund Balance		
Undesignated Fund Balance	$4,744,387	$5,760,010
Total Ending Fund Balance	$4,744,387	$5,760,010
TOTAL REQUIREMENTS	**$24,330,035**	**$25,969,095**

Source: Adapted from City of Tigard, OR 2004, 282–286.

4. *Interfund Transfers:* CEO oversight of major transfers between budget funds.

5. *Multidepartment Initiatives:* The review of special program initiatives that require resource contributions, coordination, and program elements from multiple departments and budget funds. The identification of implications and costs unapparent to program- and department-level analysts.

6. *Unidentified Costs:* To ensure a financially sustainable organization, the identification and forecasting of unidentified and unexpected costs not fully recognized in previous operating budgets.

7. *Appropriate Use of Nonrecurring "One-Time" Resources:* The careful use of nonrecurring "one-time" revenues to prevent unexpected downstream future payment obligations.

8. *Financially Sustainable Organization:* The development and maintenance of a structurally balanced budget and a financially sustainable organization over the long term.

General Fund Resource Allocations

In full-service local governments, the general fund may be relatively small compared to internal/central services funds and enterprise funds (water service, wastewater, or transit systems), but it is the principal source of financing for the most visible community services, including police, fire, parks and recreation, and libraries. Except for county governments, which often are responsible for administering state government social services and health programs, public safety programs (police, fire, and emergency medical services) often are the largest recipients of general fund dollars. In some cities, public safety comprises as much as 70 percent or more of total general fund spending. Dollars from the general fund are highly sought after and spur stiff competition among many of a jurisdiction's services and programs. The general fund budget often becomes the focus of the CEO's attention and decision making during the budget development and legislative review process.

Because general fund resources frequently are dwarfed by competing needs and requests, the CEO must find ways to prioritize or otherwise winnow down those requests. Oftentimes a CEO's budget instructions and guidelines serve this purpose—establishing criteria for funding programs and services, or limiting how much funding a particular program or service can receive. However, and more often than not, the CEO will leave ambiguity and vagueness in the guidelines in order to maintain his or her discretion or flexibility on funding issues. In these cases, the review phase of the proposed budget development process is used to ascertain what those general fund allocation priorities should be. Such decisions are likely to be subjective, reflecting what the CEO believes are in the best interests of community or are most likely to gain the greatest political support. In the end, the CEO must be concerned that the members of the legislative body will provide sufficient votes to win adoption of the budget.

Exhibit 15.3 summarizes the general fund schedule for the hypothetical City of Upper Cascadia. Notice that this schedule is at the aggregate, not the line-item level: Revenues are listed by type, the program expenditures are listed by department, and the transfers to and from the general fund are clearly detailed. The schedule also includes two contingency reserves, which we will describe shortly.

General Fund Balance and Reserves

Another source of resources for general fund programs and services are the fund balances or designated reserves within the fund balance of the general fund. The size of reserves, and their withdrawal and use, may be specifically limited by the jurisdiction's financial policies, or by state law and regulations. You will recall that we mentioned in chapter 10 that reserves are an important part of a jurisdiction's financial policies. General fund reserves may be established to accumulate and maintain sufficient resources to fund two months of the fund's annual operating expenses, or at a specified percentage (e.g., 5 percent) of general fund unrestricted resources. The reserve may be held as part of the general fund balance, or it may be transferred to a formally designated **rainy day fund, contingency reserve fund, emergency fund,** or **revenue stabilization reserve fund**. The use of formally designated reserves is typically restricted by the jurisdiction's financial policies for use in specific circumstances of emergency, financial, or economic conditions. Meeting the policy criteria would trigger the use of these funds. Under all other conditions, the reserves normally remain unavailable to general spending. Typically, once conditions are triggered for use of the reserves, the legislative body must endorse tapping the reserve and execute an **appropriation** of reserve funds.

In addition to specifically designated reserves, jurisdictions accumulate positive balances in the various subaccounts within the general fund because of the underspending of program funds or the appearance of unexpected revenues from prior years. If these funds are not restricted by a specific purpose (**carryforward**) or by a contract-related encumbrance, these surpluses are available to spend for lawful public purposes in future budgets. Because a surplus is by its very nature a one-time resource—that is, there is no guarantee it will reoccur—it should be spent only for **one-time expenditures** such as the acquisition of equipment or the construction or repair of a capital improvement. Financial policies should address the use of one-time, nonrecurring resources only for one-time spending.

The CEO and the finance director play critical roles in establishing and protecting reserves. During the development of the proposed budget, the CEO and his or her directors and staff can, without political pressures, prioritize the general fund allocations to include building reserves as well as funding programs. After release of the proposed budget, pressure for the use of reserves can increase, as the first teaching case in Part IV on labor union negotiations demonstrates. Notwithstanding previously adopted finance policies and best intentions, reserves are often readily tapped by CEOs and legislative bodies willing to make difficult choices that could reduce programs. A more likely scenario, though, is that the undesignated fund balance will be so small that its use will have little impact on the maintenance of service levels. The jurisdiction's finance director and central budget office staff are the primary monitors of general fund reserves.

Enterprise funds and other budget funds often have reserves, but management of these reserves typically falls under the purview of the responsible department. Reserves in entrepreneurial funds may grow to substantial size, and CEOs and legislative bodies may take a careful interest in the management of such resources. The development of the proposed budget provides a venue for CEO oversight, while budget adoption provides a chance for the legislative body to conduct oversight on entrepreneurial departments. With enterprise funds, continued levels of reserves in excess of operating and capital needs may indicate that the organization is charging excessively high rates for services relative to the expected costs, or that excessive reserves are being maintained at the expense of service delivery. Conversely, continued drawdown of reserves in enterprise funds can mean that rates are being held artificially low to assuage ratepayers even though, over the long term, the drawdown can create financial troubles for the enterprise.

Internal Charges for Services: (Interdepartmental Charges)

External revenues—such as general-purpose taxes and charges and fees for services—are not the only source of general fund revenues. Jurisdictions typically establish charges for services purchased and provided internally between departments. These charges are known as **internal charges for services, internal service charges**, or **interdepartmental charges** and are usually used for services that are provided by a single department, to other departments or to the full organization to avoid duplication of effort and gain economies of scale. These central services include information technology, geographic information systems (GIS) and mapping support, facilities and building maintenance, fleet maintenance and fuel, printing services, and mail services. The transactions for these services may be organized into specific internal service funds (e.g., Exhibit 15.2, 500 Central Services Fund, and 550 Fleet/Property Management Fund) to help ensure that charges are adequate and are restricted in their use for the services that they were intended to finance. In theory, revenues and spending within these internal service funds should balance over the long run, although in any one year or series of years, the revenues collected from purchasing departments may well exceed short-term spending needs. Such imbalances are common where reserves are established within internal service funds to cover the replacement of equipment or facilities that support those specific services.

In many instances, the internal service charges are identifiable to the needs of the purchasing program or department. These charges can be fully assessed to the purchasing program or department. Different from direct interdepartmental purchases, indirect charges are established for those functions that are generally considered governance-related or administrative in nature. These functions do not necessarily have a cost-of-service basis; and they are generally performed regardless of demand or need for them by any one department or program. Examples of such functions include executive functions, such as the CEO's office; legislative department expenses—the city council, commission, or board; legal services; human resources; audit; general finance functions; and purchasing and procurement services. In some cases, indirect charges may include services such as systems support for information technology, where it is difficult to assess charges for services rendered or the benefit of service accrues to the organization as a whole.

Objective criteria are generally established to allocate those indirect costs to departments in a manner that in some fashion resembles the benefit received or workload created for these indirect functions. Two examples demonstrate such allocations. First, the costs of a finance department may be allocated to other departments based on the combination of several criteria, such as the number of staff in a department, the size of its budget, or the number of transactions that are processed for it (GFOA 2013a). The second example presents a larger system of cost allocation for a medium-sized city government, which uses the following criteria as the basis for determining the burden of internal service charges carried by each of its departments (City of Gresham, OR 2013):

- Size of operating budget
- Size of payroll
- FTE count
- Square footage of facilities
- Number of computers
- Number of telephones
- Information technology programming hours (three-year average)
- Number and type of vehicles
- Historic fuel usage
- Attorney hours (three-year average)
- Property insurance
- Workers compensation claim history (three-year average)

Exhibit 15.4 demonstrates the relative burden of internal service charges by department for the City of Gresham, Oregon, for 2013–2014. The general fund departments and programs pay the greatest load (45 percent). Other budget funds contribute a smaller allocation of the total charges. The general fund departments include the city's police and fire services with extensive facilities, capital equipment purchasing, information technology, and human resource needs—thus, they carry the heaviest burden of shared costs.

The CEO typically does not get involved in determining the budgets for direct or indirect internal services because those costs and charges are based on established guidelines approved by the CFO. The responsibility for assessing charges will generally fall either to the department providing the service or, in the case of indirect cost allocations, to the central finance department, which has detailed allocation information readily available. The CEO may get involved where it is apparent that overcharging or undercharging for an indirect or direct service is occurring and the situation has the potential for adversely affecting the viability of funding sources or assets of the jurisdiction.

Interfund Transfers

A CEO or legislative body is more likely to become involved in budgeting of interfund transfers. **Transfers**, unlike internal service charges, frequently do not have a sound financial basis for their size and composition. Their intended purpose is often to shift resources from a fund with significant resources, often an enterprise fund, to a fund with inadequate resources, more often than not the general fund. Unless there is an expressed prohibition on their use, transfers can become a significant source of revenue for the general fund. However, in states with prohibitions, enterprise funds are defined as being self-supporting operations that are limited to charging the costs of services. These prohibitions prevent using excess enterprise fund revenues and net operating resources to supplement the jurisdiction's general fund.

Political expediency may push legislative bodies to violate policies on interfund transfers. In many cases, it may be easier for a legislative body to increase rates for enterprise services (such as water and wastewater treatment) than it would be to increase rates for general-purpose taxes (such as property taxes). Increasing charges on water, wastewater, and other utilities may provide a viable means of raising new revenues when property tax limitations have reduced tax revenues to untenable levels. Using increased fees and interfund transfers, however, shifts the burden of providing tax-supported public services like public safety and libraries away from general taxpayers to utility ratepayers. In most cases, but not always, these two constituencies are one and the same. But if those utility services are disproportionately paid for by a segment of the customer base that is not representative of the general taxpayers within the community, then it may be easier for decision makers to shift that burden. The imposition of an enhanced utility fee may represent sound governance, if the proposal is well vetted by the community, supported by transparent analysis, and adopted by the legislative body after public hearings and public listening sessions. The CEO plays a significant role in the consideration and adoption of enhanced fees and subsequent interfund transfers.

Interfund transfers need not be limited to enterprise operations and funds, but generally those are the only funds that hold assets significant enough to withstand transfers without being irreparably harmed over the long term. It is the responsibility of the finance director, the budget officer, and the CEO to monitor and assess the viability of interfund transfers to ensure (1) that harm is not done, (2) that the general fund does not become too reliant on those transfers as a growing source of its funds, and (3) that transfers are made in conformance with established financial policies.

Exhibit 15.4

Allocation of Internal Service Fund Collections by Budget Fund

Internal Service Fund

Revenues:

Interest income	$	x,xxx
Misc. income		x,xxx
Internal service charges		x,xxx
Beg. Balance		x,xxx
	$	x,xxx

Requirements:

Dept. operating	$	x,xxx
Contingency		x,xxx
	$	x,xxx

ISC Collection by Fund

General Fund	45.0%
Transportation Fund	7.1%
Streetlight Fund	0.5%
Rental Inspection Fund	0.9%
Infrastructure Development Fund	2.2%
Urban Design & Planning Fund	3.0%
Dedication Revenue Fund	1.1%
Building Fund	2.8%
Urban Renewal Support Fund	2.6%
Water Fund	9.2%
Stormwater Fund	6.9%
Wastewater Fund	14.2%
Facilities & Fleet Management Fund	0.4%
Information Technology Fund	0.5%
Legal Services Fund	0.2%
Utility Financial Services Fund	2.3%
Administrative Services Fund	1.1%
Total ISC Collected	100%

The distribution of charges is based on a set of defined drivers which allocate the cost based on usage

Source: City of Gresham, OR 2013.

Multidepartment Special Initiatives

The individual departmental and program budget requests submitted to the CEO reflect the program capacity, needs, and issues of the particular department. However, new issues or problems, or campaign promises made by the CEO or other elected officials, may require blending the services and capacities of two or more programs or departments into a special initiative or task group. A state-level example demonstrates such a situation. The closure of timber harvest programs on a state forest may leave large numbers of unemployed forest and wood products industry workers. Retraining and reemploying these workers will require the services of the state forestry department, the state employment agency, regional community colleges, and even the state universities. A comprehensive forest-worker reemployment and retraining program must integrate program goals and resources across these different state agencies. The governor's budget would provide a mechanism for exerting leadership on this issue by organizing a multidepartmental response.

In towns, small- to medium-sized cities, and many special district governments, these types of multidepartmental integrated service delivery initiatives may take place quietly and seamlessly. Department heads and midlevel staffs meet to coordinate goals and program objectives, and internal service charges or budget transfers for staff time and services provide the needed joint resources. However, in larger city and county governments, as well as in state and federal governments, a more formal set of coordination procedures may be required to generate a comprehensive response to an issue or problem. This may necessitate the establishment of a special initiative or task group to ensure sufficient organization attention, resources, contracting authority, administrative system support, and public visibility to the issue. PPBS/program budgeting (see chapter 12) provides an effective tool for this type of response through the establishment of overarching goals. Once the initiative goals are established and clarified, the task group can define program objectives and work activities that tap into and integrate units and program capacity from different departments across the organization.

Developing a special initiative requires coordination across departments and programs. Department and program budget analysts, however, are limited in the perspectives and abilities to link across departments; thus, the organization budget officer and the central budget office analysts become critical actors in organizing and programming multidepartmental initiatives. CEO support for a special initiative also helps to give it prominence in the proposed budget and in the CEO's budget message.

Unidentified Costs

One of the bigger challenges of municipal budgeting and, to a degree, of nonprofit budgeting, is hidden costs. These costs are not purposely hidden; rather, they simply are not immediately obvious to decision makers. Unidentified costs can be classified into three categories: (1) undercharges and the understatement of true costs; (2) the appearance of unbudgeted expenditures; and (3) unfunded liabilities that can be attributed to past decisions or current services but that remain unfunded.

Undercharges and Understatement of True Costs

Undercharges and understatements of costs often occur when the central services cost allocation system fails to capture and transfer the full cost load to the benefiting department or program. For example, the costs of maintaining a fleet of police vehicles should be fully allocated to the police department as the benefiting department, and the police department should fully reimburse the fleet maintenance group for its vehicle maintenance activities and purchases of parts, tools, and consumables. The criteria in the central cost allocation system may provide a good—but not an exact—cost allocation to the police department, with the result that the fleet maintenance group is left short of reimbursement revenues to cover its costs. If the full charges and costs are not reflected as an expense in the receiving department (e.g., the fleet maintenance group), the cost of the program or service benefiting from the internal service (police department) is understated by the difference in costs. When this situation occurs, the CEO and legislative body may not know the true costs of those services when making budget decisions. If not disclosed, it could mean those costs may not be accounted for when the operating department receives a budget increase or is subjected to a budget reduction; hence, the real cost of the budgetary action may not be known at the time the increase or reduction is made.

Appearance of Unbudgeted Expenditures

Another class of unexpected charges includes expenses generated by one program or capital investment but left for another program or department to pay. Again, this situation arrises because program and department budget preparation occurs within a limited perspective of a single organizational unit. For example, costs that seem sensible to the public works or community development department may have ramifications for parks department operations. The central budget office plays a critical role in identifying, linking, and managing these interdepartmental implications. These types of costs often occur with capital improvement projects. For example, the construction of a new municipal facility likely will result in the addition of operating costs such as increased utilities, maintenance, and program staffing. It is not unusual for proposed capital improvements to fail to estimate the full operating budget impact of a given improvement; as a result, decision makers may not know the cost of operating that facility when they approve the project. The city council or board may just assume that the city has sufficient funds to operate the facility when it comes on line. Again, one budgetary decision may lead to other cost increases that were either unknown or not considered significant at the time.

More and more jurisdictions have begun to address the issue of hidden costs by including an estimate of the operating budget impact of projects in their capital improvement plan and, in some cases, automatically including a request for an operating budget increase to cover those costs in their proposed budget. Estimates for these types of costs can reflect several years of **phase-in** or **start-up costs**. Similarly, unbudgeted expenses may appear when facilities are closed or decommissioned. Multiyear **phase-out** or **close-out costs** may occur at this end of the project or facility life cycle.

Unfunded Liabilities from the Past or from Current Programs

Unfunded liabilities often appear unexpectedly. For example, poor financial decisions and undocumented interfund transfers may leave liabilities from the past with the jurisdiction's current CEO, CFO, and legislative body. Judicial decisions or arbitrator rulings may leave the jurisdiction with unexpected costs and payments. Unexpected increases in retirement fund and personnel benefits costs, as we will discuss later, can also appear as unfunded liabilities. Because these costs usually are not integrated into the budget development process, it would otherwise fall to the central budget office to call them out in budget discussions with the CEO and possibly in presentations to the legislative body. It then rests with the CEO or the legislative body to decide whether to take those costs into account when making budgetary decisions. Maintenance of a sufficient general fund reserve can buffer the effects of smaller unfunded liabilities, but explicit expenditures from the general fund may be needed to cover larger unfunded liabilities. The CEO, finance director, budget officer, and the central budget office staff will play an important role in handling these issues, which can affect the entire organization.

Appropriate Use of Nonrecurring "One-Time" Resources

From time to time, the jurisdiction may receive time-limited, **"one-time" nonrecurring revenues** from a variety of sources. These temporary windfalls include federal and state grants, unanticipated tax revenues, or an excessive accumulation of reserves and unrestricted opening fund balances. In times of financial strength, one-time monies used as **nonrecurring appropriations** or **one-time expenditures** can allow a jurisdiction to accomplish numerous tasks not tied to the recurrent level of expenditures and program capacity. For example, one-time monies can remove case backlogs, cover independent urban renewal projects, perform maintenance in advance, or pay down debt in advance. But, one-time monies must be used with care to ensure that they do not inflate the recurring level of expenditures above **recurring revenues**, or that they do not trigger future expenditure obligations. For example, federal grants to local governments to hire new police officers and firefighters often include contract clauses that require the local jurisdiction to fund those positions permanently after the first two or three years of federal cost share. In times of financial stress, CEOs and legislative bodies may be tempted to use one-time revenues to balance the budget and to maintain program levels. This abuse comes at the expense of making decisions to resize programs to meet recurring revenues. CEOs and CFOs can use the proposed budget to manage the use of one-time revenues. There may be a case to use one-time revenues to fill revenue shortfalls for a single transition year, but if tax, fee, or intergovernmental revenues have fallen on a consistent trend, the CEO and CFO need to exert leadership to begin discussions to reduce program capacity. The first teaching case in Part I of this book gives an example of program realignment and reduction triggered by a long-term pattern of revenue declines and expense growth.

Ensure the Financial Stability of the Organization

This chapter has stressed that keeping individual funds and the larger budget in balance is the overriding imperative for the CEO, finance director/CFO, and central budget office staff. The obsession with balance leads to a balanced proposed budget, which serves as the framework for adoption of a balanced budget by the legislative body. However, a budget balanced for the short run may not be financially sustainable over the long run. Changing economic conditions may hold general tax and fee revenues flat or in decline, and at the same time, expected and unexpected future spending commitments folded in the currently balanced budget may appear and demand increasing levels of resources. In addition to ensuring the short-term balance of the budget, CEOs, finance directors, budget officers, and the legislative body must commit to a **structurally balanced budget** (GFOA 2013b; Forsythe 2004). With a structurally balanced budget, an organization takes a major step toward becoming **financially sustainable**. Failure to adopt a structurally balanced budget leaves the organization in **structural deficit** and financially unsustainable over the long run.

A jurisdiction's financial policies (chapter 10) typically detail how it will attain and maintain financial sustainability, but it falls to the CEO, the finance director, budget officer, and the legislative body to take action to become sustainable. The careful management of recurring revenues and spending, the filling and maintenance of general fund reserves, the establishment and filling of rainy day and contingency fund reserves, the careful use of one-time monies, and an awareness of unfunded liabilities and unanticipated costs are all critical elements of ensuring financial sustainability.

In a structurally balanced budget, **recurring resources** are equal to **recurring expenditures** for multiple years into the future. Recurring resources are those that appear annually with a high degree of certainty by law or are the result of economic conditions that are consistently better than expected. As examples, property tax revenues from the permanent tax base will fluctuate with property values, but local governments can rely on these revenues as stable into the future; or retail sales tax revenues may fluctuate with the strength of the local economy, but trends of historic sales data should indicate a floor of sales activity and of corresponding tax revenue. Supplemental tax levies can provide revenues with certainty over the defined period of the levy measure, but as we saw in the second teaching case in Part III, the public may reject what appears to be the most basic of tax levies. To reach a structurally balanced budget, recurring expenditures must be sized to recurring resources. This means sizing program capacity to match a dependable recurring level of resources. Recurring expenditures are those that are made each year, including personnel services and materials and supplies expenditures. Labor contract agreements and service contract agreements define the periods of recurring expenditures, as do special programs or projects receiving **continuous appropriations** that span multiple fiscal years. Long-term **financial forecasts** of three or more years (chapters 7 and 10) provide the tools for identifying and forecasting recurring revenues, recurring expenditures, and expected future service caseloads.

Debt service requirements and major capital investments in facilities and large equipment present another set of recurring costs with a long-term horizon of up to 20 or 30 years. We address the larger issue of a jurisdiction's borrowing capacity and its management in chapter 16. The management of the general fund reserve and contingency reserve funds provide the CEO, CFO, and the staff with tools to buffer spikes and changes in the recurring revenue and expenditure levels. The careful and restrained use of one-time resources by the CEO and the legislative body also helps to support a structurally balanced budget.

EXTERNAL FINANCIAL PRESSURES: EMPLOYEE BENEFIT COSTS

While financial forecasts can capture many recurring costs, employee benefit costs lurk as uncontrolled and uncertain costs in both the short- and long-term outlook. These uncontrolled costs include employee health insurance for current active employees and their partners and dependents, retirement fund contributions for both current active and retired employees, and health care benefits for retirees. The unfunded liability for future retiree benefits is one of the largest uncontrolled costs faced by local governments. These cost categories have grown explosively over the past two decades because of an aging public-sector workforce, insufficient employer contributions, unrealistic investment assumptions, and deferred recognition of the cost of benefits (McLoughlin and Stephens 2012). While individual governments may be able to marginally control these costs through labor negotiations and adroit benefit package selection, their growth is largely beyond their control. Insurance companies, state public employee retirement systems (PERS), and locally established retirement systems typically present next year's costs as near-mandatory payments. Local government budget analysts can only do their best in forecasting the growth and volatility in these cost trends. Budget analysts and human resource staff members can present their forecasts and actively work with the CEO to present to the legislative body a full description of the expected future commitments and their implications. Additional presentations should keep local labor union leadership, state legislators, and the community informed of these growing commitments.

Active Employee Health Care Costs

Employee health care benefits for current active employees and their partners and dependents remain a major uncontrolled cost for local governments. State and local governments financed 17 percent of all U.S. health care costs in 2011 (CMS 2013). U.S. health care costs nearly quadrupled between 1990 and 2011; they doubled between 2000 and 2011 (Young 2013). For both public and private employers, health care insurance premiums grew 138 percent between 1999 and 2010 (GFOA 2011d). The increase in premiums was reflected in sustained 6, 10, and even greater annual percentage increases in local government expenditures for employee health care benefits. Possibly reflecting the impacts of the economic downturn of 2007–2009, this rising cost trend has moderated. In each of the past three years (2009–2011), the increase in health care costs rose only 3.9 percent annually (CMS 2013). The future growth rates of health care costs, insurance premiums, and health benefit expenditures are of course uncertain, but CEOs, CFOs, budget analysts, elected officials, and labor union leaders must remain aware that health care costs will have a major impact on all future local government budgets. GFOA (2011d) describes a number of strategies and techniques for managing health care costs by changing benefit levels, managing the choice of providers, sharing costs with employees, reducing employees' use of health care resources, and rightsizing health care benefits.

At the beginning of 2014, it was too early to tell what impact the Patient Protection and Affordable Care Act (PPACA, "Affordable Care Act") would have on the costs of retiree and current public employee health care benefits. This adds another level of uncertainty to forecasts of employee benefit costs and budget expenditures. Provisions within the PPACA, combined with the laggard recovery of local government finances from the economic downturn of 2007–2009, could place pressure on employee bargaining units to forego future wage and benefit increases (Taylor 2013). One PPACA provision, the so-called Cadillac tax, imposes a tax or a fee on employers who would provide plans to employees and retirees with premiums costing annually in excess of certain threshold (e.g., $10,200 for individual coverage for current employees). Benefits in excess of the thresholds will be taxed or assessed at 40 percent of their costs in excess of their limit. Because public employees and retirees traditionally have received richer benefits than have their private-sector counterparts, the impact on public employers and employees could be greater. The full effect of the PPACA on public employee benefits probably will not be fully understood or felt for several years.

Pension Fund Contribution Costs

Public employee retirement system (PERS) obligations present local governments with especially troublesome financial uncertainties. PERS cost liability for annual contributions and supplemental payments appears in the current year, but cost liability often balloons into even larger required payment obligations in the future. State PERS plans are typically managed by state commissions, state agencies, and state legislatures, which set the plan structure, investment objectives, forecasts of investment returns, payout commitments, and annual contribution schedules. In most cases, PERS retirement funds are structured as investment trust funds, which use a major portion of the annual contributions from participating local governments as investment capital. Ideally, retirees receive payouts from the annual investment returns generated by the fund principal. However, many state PERS are underfunded and face substantial unfunded liabilities.

Estimates place the unfunded liabilities of state and local government retirement plans between $703 million and $4.4 trillion, and unfunded liabilities of state and local retiree health care is estimated at more than $500 million (DePaul 2012; Pew Center on the States 2010a; Collins and Rettenmaier 2010). An **unfunded liability** indicates that the current and future contributions and revenues generated from retirement fund investments would not cover current or future retiree demands on the system's resources. The PERS retirement and retiree health care fund liability by state varies greatly, as does the demand for increased payments from local governments. In some states, efforts to ensure PERS fund viability have required the payment by local governments of supplemental premiums above the historic level of annual payments. In some cases, local governments must make increased payments immediately in order to provide the principal for added investment growth into the future; in other cases, they must pay to ensure sufficient cash to meet current payment obligations, especially if financial market returns sag below forecasts. These supplemental payments often come from the local jurisdiction's general funds, which creates funding competition with service delivery programs and capital investments. Facing substantial obligations, some local governments borrow funds to make annual payments and stretch the repayment schedule over an extended period of several decades. This may make the immediate obligations for general funds more tolerable, but it affects the jurisdiction's credit rating and debt capacity (chapter 16).

Locally established public employee retirement systems serve a specific group of public employees tied to one or several local governments, or even particular departments within a government. Police and firefighters may have local retirement funds. The relatively small size and large number of these plans makes it difficult to understand the full picture of current and future total liability. But as with state-level plans, the local governments with these plans must make continuing contributions on behalf of the current and future retirees at a sufficient rate to cover payouts and to maintain fund solvency into the future.

The type of retirement plan used by many local governments aggravates the uncertainty of PERS and local retirement system obligations. Unlike the private and nonprofit sectors, the majority of state and local governments offer employees **defined benefit (DB) pensions** that guarantee employees a permanent monthly income upon retirement. The amount of the benefit is usually based on the number of years of service and the average of the highest salary received by the employee while employed. In contrast, **defined contribution (DC) pensions** are plans used largely by private employers; they provide a benefit entirely dependent on the amount of assets accumulated by the employee over time, including plan contributions by the employee and employer and the investment earnings on those contributions over time (e.g., 401(k) and 403(b) accounts). DC plans transfer investment risk and contribution responsibility to the employee and away from the retirement fund and the local government organization. Over the past 15 years, 16 states have shifted their state retirement fund plans to full or partial defined contribution arrangements (Thom 2013). These shifts were taken in part to reduce financial obligations and liability to state retirement funds and their member governments. However, as the third epigraph at the beginning of this chapter reminds us, retirement and pension benefits are often interpreted by state courts as contractual obligations. Modification of benefits for current retirees may take the passage of statutes by state legislatures, but even then, such modifications are often interpreted by retirees and public employee unions as a breach of contract by the state government. State supreme courts have reinforced the terms of original retirement system provisions and obligations—no matter how costly. The strength of contractual terms makes retirement system and pension reform especially difficult.

Retiree Health Care Costs

Unlike most retirement plans that set aside assets for future payments, albeit often at inadequate levels, faster growing retiree health benefits are often funded on a **pay-as-you-go** basis. This implies paying funds only for the current year's expenses and leaving all future year's expenses for subsequent fiscal years. This approach leaves proportionally higher unfunded liabilities for future generations to bear. Again, the level and form of debt liability for public employee retiree health care varies by state, and annual costs to local governments reflect this variation in liability. One obvious solution for retiree health benefits that mirrors the solution for retirement benefits is **prefunding**. Prefunding presumes that the cost of benefits should be recognized as they are earned, and it sets aside assets toward paying future costs and supplements them with investment earnings (Tatum 2012). The additional options for funding these and other retirement benefits is to work with current employees to restrict eligibility for maximum benefits, reducing benefits, increasing cost sharing with employees, and transitioning from a defined benefit to a defined contribution plan with a capped contribution from the local government.

Each of the uncontrolled costs described above can be addressed in the local proposed budget without major reforms. Analysts can respond to uncertainty by identifying their financial implications and estimating their cost, and by requiring one-time funding to close the gap in future funding needs. Whether these costs are addressed in the budget will depend largely upon the interest, attention, and leadership they receive from the budget office, the CFO, and the CEO.

EXECUTIVE FRAMING OF BUDGET DECISIONS FOR LEGISLATIVE ADOPTION

Conformance to professional standards and extensive analysis will not guarantee a smooth public review and adoption of the CEO's proposed budget. An effective budget must respond not only to the CEO's agenda but also to the political needs of members of the legislative body and to the community's issues and needs. The successful CEO uses his or her **administrative discretion** to actively frame the proposed budget to respond to these political dimensions of the budget process. This active framing involves defining problems and issues, ensuring that issues of concern are fully analyzed, and clearly presenting this information for legislative and public decision making. The Friedrich and Finer epigraphs at the beginning of this chapter remind CEOs and budget staff to exercise caution in how they frame budget issues and debates. Friedrich calls on administrators to be directly and actively responsive to the public. This responsiveness comes easily to elected chief executives but not necessarily for appointed city managers and district executives. Finer reminds administrators to follow the guidance and limits set by the legislative body. The exact degree of deference often reflects the traditions and expectations of the jurisdiction, the clarity of the legislative guidance, and the personalities and expectations of the legislative body members. CEOs have control over how collegial or adversarial their relations are with the city council, commission, or board. In any case, the CEO, the finance director, and the budget office staff must assess the political and issue environments, prepare budget documents, and prepare budget presentations to meet multiple and sometimes conflicting political expectations. All of these activities serve to facilitate successful budget adoption.

The budget preparation and adoption process necessarily requires CEOs to play an important political role, even if they hold to Finer's view of simply implementing the orders of their elected superiors. City council members, township selectmen, county commissioners, and special district board members all must stand for election and build support from the electorate. The budget review and adoption process provides an opportunity for elected officials to demonstrate responsiveness to voter preferences. The process may also provide a venue for the critical review of specific budget issues that are of significant concern to select but vocal groups of community stakeholders. On occasion, the budget-making and approval process may reflect deeper ideological and philosophical differences regarding the role of government and how to address an issue. The process can also provide an opportunity for elected officials and community stakeholders to stand up to and control the CEO and the bureaucracy. Effectively handled, all of these motivating and sometimes cross-cutting political influences can be used by the CEO to build public confidence in the budget. However, the CEO and staff may decide to push back on political pressures. A clear response helps to ensure that the short- and long-term political ramifications of changes to the budget are fully displayed and understood before final budget adoptions by the general public and by all elected officials. Two aspects of preparation help to prepare the political environment and legislative body for budget adoption: (1) identifying issues that could stall or inflame budget review and adoption; and (2) recognizing the size and extent of the organization and its programs in the community.

Nature and Severity of Budgetary Issues

The CEO and staff should actively identify and respond to factors that can influence the decision-making process. Many of these issues will emerge or evolve during the budget process, but the most pervasive are:

- economic conditions;
- financial requirements and compliance;
- labor relations;
- public infrastructure needs and financing; and
- service levels.

If not carefully managed, any one of these issues can dominate or commandeer budget decision making or otherwise become the singular focus of budget deliberations. Issues do not necessarily appear in isolation; in fact, they are many times interrelated and interdependent. For example, a local jurisdiction facing budget cutbacks may not be able to sustain service levels that the community has come to expect and demand. These financial or budget woes may be spurred by an economic downturn, which was the case for many governments during the 2007–2009 recession. In such a case, very few if any programs manage to escape budget reductions, and budget adoption decisions revolve around the method for allocating cuts and perhaps setting criteria for exempting some programs from the chopping block. In the face of drastic revenue shortfalls, program additions and service enhancements rarely receive consideration. The focus is limited to reducing the impact on the budget status quo. These examples demonstrate the importance of evolving economic conditions and changing revenue forecasts. The most recent budget-cycle revenue forecast may confirm previous long-term forecasts or may indicate fast-changing conditions that require adjustments to the CEO's proposed budget. The importance of updated revenue forecasts is especially important at the state level, where a state legislature may take three to six months to consider the governor's proposed budget and to adopt a final budget for the fiscal year or biennium.

The variability of the economy and its impact on government revenues has placed a greater emphasis on long-range financial forecasts and financial plans at the local government level (chapter 10). The more prevalent long-range forecasts usually project operating revenues and expenditures as well as fund balances 3 to 10 years out into the future (chapter 7). The value of these forecasts is magnified when they clearly illustrate the impact of proposed budget decisions on future spending and fund balances. The CEO will often rely on long-range forecasts prepared by the central budget office to predict future surpluses or deficits within the general fund. These forecasts provide a base for advocacy for or against particular budget proposals. For example, if the CEO can illustrate that the addition of a program or service level for a current program will contribute to the possibility of a future deficit, then a case might effectively be made to the legislative body that the addition of funding for that program is not in the best interests of the entity. Conversely, if the CEO can show that revenues can be expected to grow at a reliable rate adequate to accommodate additional program funding, a case could be made for enhanced services.

The long-term utility of these financial forecasts will be measured largely by their reliability and credibility. If the forecasts consistently fail to provide reasonably accurate predictions, then their usefulness as a decision-making aid will eventually be questioned and their value diminished. The CEO must be careful not to use the forecasts simply to achieve easy political wins.

Since personnel costs can comprise as much as 60 to 70 percent of a jurisdiction's general fund budget, labor relations can weigh heavily on the budget process. As the first teaching case in Part IV demonstrates, negotiations over wages and benefits can frequently affect the budget preparation and adoption phases unless multiyear labor contracts are in force. Even then, as we discussed in chapter 11 on the incremental aspects of line-item budgeting, the financial commitments embodied in those agreements will drive the level of funding needed to accommodate negotiated wage and benefit increases. Meeting new contractual requirements can dominate the budget decision-making landscape.

Service-level changes and public infrastructure issues also can become important matters for consideration in budget deliberations. For example, whether police officers should be added to deal with actual or perceived increases in crime activity or whether a vacant public property should be converted to a park are the kinds of issues that pervade many budget discussions.

Organizational Size and Complexity

The degree and type of involvement of budget participants will depend upon the size and complexity of the organization, the nature and severity of budgetary issues, and the personal styles of the budgetary participants. Generally, the larger the government, the greater the number of participants likely to be involved in the process. In larger governments, particularly in urban jurisdictions, many programs and services—each with its own administrators and advocates—will compete for limited budget resources. Since the organization is larger and more complex, the budget process becomes more complex, and budget process participants will be assigned fewer tasks. This tends to narrow the participants' frames of reference. Integrating requests and information from numerous departments and programs, gaining clearances from several lead executives and administrators, and integrating resources and programs across multiple departments, all on tight schedules, requires effective coordination and interpersonal cooperation to meet process deadlines. For example, budget staff may be assigned singular tasks such as revenue forecasting because of the sheer number and diversity of revenue sources. But exclusive attention to revenue forecasts prevents an analyst from fully understanding of the details of expenditure development and computation. This separation reinforces the necessity of internal staff communications and coordination during budget production.

Organizational complexity, however, does not necessarily dictate the complexity of the decision-making process. Even in small jurisdictions, decision making can be complex, particularly if tasks are not sufficiently defined or institutional knowledge is lost when key participants leave the organization or are no longer active in the process. Conversely, decision making can be relatively straightforward and uncomplicated in large jurisdictions if the policy preferences and alliances of key participants are well known and represent the majority interests of the legislative body. Sometimes, it may be something as simple as electoral representation that dictates how budgetary decisions are made. Legislative body members elected by district, rather than at large, naturally are focused on the parochial interests and concerns of their constituents. When the interests and concerns of the jurisdiction at large are sacrificed routinely to the interests of districts, decision making becomes more predictable and regimented. In a variation of proportional and fair share allocations, program services and benefits are divided up in a "budget allocation by district," where some level of spending is determined through simple math (i.e., divide a budget appropriation by the number of electoral districts). With highly competitive tension between voter districts or wards, proportional allocation by district can be a large determinant of where the focus of decision making lies and how much support the rest of the budget will garner from the legislative body. Reciprocal support by members of the legislative body for each other's funding levels is somewhat the equivalent of pork-barrel spending at the federal level.

LEGISLATIVE BODY CONSIDERATION AND ADOPTION

By the time the proposed budget reaches the legislative body, decision making is typically anticlimactic. Many of the major decisions (unless the chief executive officer has made those decisions in isolation) have already been fleshed out. The exception may be where a major unsuspected financial or service-related crisis engulfs budget development and requires a sudden and major shift in funding, spending levels, or priorities. Otherwise, most decisions left to the legislative body are on the margin.

The role of the legislative body is twofold: (1) to ensure that issues and concerns of budget participants and the community at large have been properly aired and considered, and (2) to serve as a "check and balance" for the decisions or recommendations made by the chief executive or administrative officer. Without their involvement, the budget process and decisions that flow from it lack legitimacy and official sanction, for it is the legislative body that ultimately decides what is funded. The legislative body uses the following mechanisms to ensure that its approval and oversight role is carried out: budget notes, hearings, amendments, adoption, vetoes, and production of the final **approved budget** document.

Budget Detail and Budget Notes

As the earlier sections on construction of the CEO's proposed budget demonstrate, rolling up the individual department requests into an integrated organizational-level document generates vast amounts of detailed information. This information, known as the **budget detail,** is critical and useful to the department and central budget office analysts, and to analysts who work for advocacy groups; however, members of the legislative body have neither the time nor the financial expertise to wade through the minutia underlying the proposed budget. The **operating detail**, or **budget notes,** with summary tables provides a means to reduce the proposed budget into a manageable, concise package that is helpful to elected officials for oversight and decision making. Budget notes may provide information and detail at the department level or at the major program level. Either way, the notes summarize each operational department or program into a few pages that follow a standard format. The notes for a department or program typically include:

- Summary line-item table of revenues and expenditures by major line-item category for the previous and current years, and of the proposed levels for the budget year.
- General fund supplement proposed, and status of dedicated revenue funds.
- FTE by major positions and in total.
- Performance accomplishments against goals and objectives from the past year.
- Performance and productivity accomplishments as compared to standardized benchmarks.
- Program goals and objectives for the coming year.
- Summary of the major program components and issues facing each component.
- Rationale and explanations justifying requests for policy changes, program revisions, personnel changes, funding-level changes, and any continuous appropriations.
- CEO recommendation to fund the department at the proposed level.

The CEO's budget message provides an organizational-level justification for the proposed budget and its spending levels. The budget notes provide explanation and justification of the CEO's budget at the department and program levels. Presenting this more refined level of information helps to organize and structure oversight by the legislative body. In working through the budget notes, members of the legislative body have sufficient information to review the organization and its programs systematically, without getting lost in line-item details. This information allows board members to ask questions of the CEO and department managers at an insightful level and to probe deeper into issues of performance if warranted. The budget notes present each program in a standard format with common information, guaranteeing a consistent level of data for oversight and comparison of funding levels, performance, and productivity.

Summary tables that aggregate information from the program and department levels provide a bridge to the organization level. This type of aggregation and consolidation is also important because funding allocations, expenditure decisions, and policy guidance are typically reduced to a few lines per department or program in the budget adoption ordinance.

Budget Hearings

The legislative body uses public hearings, both formal and informal, to carry out its budget review and adoption responsibilities. By law, all local jurisdictions are required to hold public hearing(s) on the proposed budget. The budget notes often structure the flow of public hearings as the legislative body and citizen advisory budget committees work systematically through the organization's budget. Responsibility for conducting these hearings resides with the legislative body. Minimum requirements, including the number, notification, timing, and purpose of budget hearings, are set forth in state law and local ordinance. At these legally required hearings, everyone is afforded the opportunity to testify on the proposed budget and sometimes on amendments. These legal gatherings may be supplemented by formal hearings held by one or more standing committees of the legislative body to focus on particular topics or aspects of the budget. For example, a public works subcommittee might convene to hold hearings on capital projects proposed for inclusion in the budget. In some states, a budget committee of citizens and elected officials reviews the CEO's proposed budget as a precursor to full legislative body adoption. These meetings provide additional opportunities for public input as well as a public forum for legislative body members to stake out their position on particular elements of the budget. Budget hearings are not the only avenue for participants. Individual members of the legislative body may decide to hold community meetings in their districts to make presentations on the proposed budget and to solicit public comment.

Amendments

The legislative body's opportunity to modify the proposed budget, other than through informal discussions and negotiations with the CEO or his/her staff before the proposed budget is introduced, is through the budget amendment process. Amendments are formally introduced by standing committees of the legislative group or by individual members, usually after the legally required public hearings. The amendments may be introduced in regularly scheduled meetings a week or more before the meeting dedicated to adoption or even at the budget adoption meeting.

These amendments may alter the budget in any way provided the budget remains in balance. Typically, the amendments will focus on individual programs, services, or projects. They may not involve large funding changes, since the authors know they will need to identify the sources for additional funding, which will likely involve cuts in other programs or projects. This reallocation ritual, even though marginal, serves an important purpose: to demonstrate the member or coalition's commitment to mitigate the impact of a budget reduction or add resources to provide a higher level of service or finance a special project. The committee or member introducing the amendment must garner enough support from other members to achieve a majority to secure passage. Amendment authors may enlist the support of the CEO, CFO, or other influencers in the decision-making process to persuade other members to vote for the amendment. The earmarking of resources or spending for a specific program or purpose is another tool used by legislators to build support for budget passage. An **earmark** lists out in the budget ordinance or appropriations bill a defined level of resources or spending dedicated to a specific program or service task. Earmarking is more commonly used in state and federal legislatures where members may trade dedicated funding in an earmark for political support.

Adoption

Once amendments are considered and approved, the legislative body is ready to vote on the budget as a whole. Separate votes may be taken on the operating budget and on the capital budget. In some states, local governing bodies are also required to take a separate vote on the property tax rate and/or tax levy. Before the vote is taken on the operating budget, the budget staff may be asked to confirm that the budget has remained in balance. Again, the final votes, after the ritual comments by members to urge support or defeat, are often anticlimactic because the outcome is already known. A simple majority vote is typically all that is required to approve the budget.

Vetoes

The legislative body's work is not complete once the budget is adopted. In many jurisdictions, the elected chief executive officer (e.g., strong mayor, elected county executive, village president, or the like) has veto authority. The elected CEO may have a week or more to issue his or her budget vetoes. In many cases, the vetoes are directed at amendments approved by the full body. It is rarer for them to target proposals submitted in the proposed budget that reflect their own initiatives and decisions. Once those vetoes are issued, the legislative body must act at its next regularly scheduled meeting to either affirm or overturn the vetoes. In many cases, the body needs a two-thirds majority to overturn a veto. Of course, the veto process is not applicable in council-manager systems of local government because the city administrator or manager works for the council.

Production of Final Document

The final act in the budget-making process is to publish and post online the adopted budget document. The final budget document is usually nothing more than a slightly altered version of the CEO's proposed budget reflecting the changes approved by the legislative body, an appropriation ordinance or legislative resolution listing appropriations at a fund or department level, and perhaps a transmittal letter with a final budget communication by the CEO or administrative officer. The last remaining task in the budget process is the uneventful yet laborious task of uploading budget appropriations, at the line-item level of detail, into the jurisdiction's financial system (chapter 17). This task is left to the finance and budget office staff, who are the only participants involved in the budget process from start to finish.

NONPROFIT AND COMMUNITY BUDGET ADOPTION

State statutes and regulations, along with professional best practice standards, provide extensive guidance to local government CEOs, elected officials, and staff on how to conduct the public budgeting process, including developing the CEO's proposed budget, budget review, and budget adoption. Nonprofit organizations follow a similar set of budget development, review, and adoption activities. In the following section, we review the similarities and differences between local governments and nonprofit organizations. The decisions that arise from budget adoption by governments and nonprofits have effects outside of the organization. Effective public budgeting requires CEOs, elected officials, and nonprofit board members to look broadly at community needs and at the contributions of other organizations before adopting a new annual budget.

Nonprofit Organizations Follow Similar Procedures

Local government accounting and financial management practices place emphasis on using designated budget funds and commonly accepted accounting methods as a means of control and communication. As we have discussed above, even a small city typically uses 10 to 20 different funds to segregate and track general funds, special revenues, one or more enterprise operations (e.g., water and wastewater), debt service, and internal service charges. Budget construction is partly a matter of integrating numerous funds into a single budget document. As noted earlier, the CEO plays a decisive role in this process by deciding the level of general fund resources or internal service charges to allocate to a particular department or program.

In contrast to the fund-based budget of local governments, nonprofit organizations rely on relatively fewer funds, but with greater attention to the likely future availability of resources. For example, pledges may be made by donors, but until those pledges are collected, they are not usable revenues. Other donations may have restrictions that limit their availability to future years and in limited increments. For small nonprofits, budget construction by the executive director, treasurer, or small budget committee may rely on balancing a single current service fund that includes capital purchases of equipment. Budget review and ratification may follow straightforward discussion and a vote by the board members.

Larger nonprofit organizations typically follow a budget development and adoption process (Dropkin, Halpin, and La Touche 2007) that closely parallels the local government process. Rather than the CEO providing budget process oversight, the CFO may take the lead in budget preparation and financial policies. In preparing the budget, the CFO will review department requests, allocate shared administrative costs, and adjust program size and staffing to meet expected revenues. The complete integrated budget document is accompanied by a letter of transmittal. The budget presentation typically includes an organization-wide budget summary, department and program summaries, an organization-wide line-time expense schedule, and line-item expense schedules for each operating unit of the organization (Dropkin, Halpin, and La Touche 2007, chaps. 15–17, 20).

Rather than focus on public review of the budget, the nonprofit CEO prepares a proposed budget for review by the board of directors. The proposed budget is delivered in advance to the board members. The CEO and the board chair and/or the chair of the board's budget and finance committee manage the presentation of the budget and other important financial information to the full board. These tasks include framing and managing issues and controversy, and managing the timeline for board members to receive, read, and digest the budget document. As in local government, the CFO, staff, and the CEO stand ready to answer questions and to perform additional analyses if necessary. Unlike the public focus of local government budget adoption, the politics of budget consideration and adoption are internal to the nonprofit. Organization members, clients, issue advocates, and community members must all advocate and communicate with the board members to have their concerns addressed in the final approved budget (Dropkin, Halpin, and La Touche 2007, chap. 21).

Community Implications of Government and Nonprofit Budget Adoption

Release of a proposed budget and budget adoption by local governments and nonprofit organizations do not occur in a vacuum. Contractual partners monitor budget deliberations closely to assess continuing support for joint projects. For local governments, these include partners in intergovernmental agreements, contractors with multiyear agreements, and partners in extended programmatic relationships—all of whom are seeking reassurance that promised funding and policy support will continue in the coming fiscal years. For large intermediary nonprofits and foundations, contractual partners and informal noncontractual partners are also seeking assurances of continued support.

Local governments and nonprofits in complex network settings must take care in monitoring their partners' budgeting decisions. As the first teaching case in this book demonstrated, decisions by one network partner quickly affect the rest of the network. Budget decisions by one major fund provider in a network will reduce a degree of freedom and limit the flexibility of other members to provide the funding needed to accomplish network objectives. Preparation of the CEO's proposed budget and budget adoption by the legislative body provide important opportunities for local governments and nonprofits to listen to partner concerns and to respond to potential gaps in support for community services. These responses become especially important if gaps in service have been exacerbated by large reductions in contributions by larger network members. In such cases, it is common practice among network members to caution their peers that they will not be the funder of last resort after everyone else has reduced their contributions. Deciding how much resource is needed and how best to deliver reduced services among providers puts network governance to a severe test. Budgeting as a member of a community network requires CEOs, elected officials, and board members to take a broader perspective that considers the funding levels and support contributed by other network members. In informal and participant-governed networks, members will tend to rely on personal relationships and personal communication to share information on budget decisions. In networks with a lead organization or a network administrative organization (NAO), the leadership and staff of the lead organization will take on the tasks of dispersing information on combined network revenues, on the contribution decisions made by larger network members, and on network program and capacity decisions.

SUMMARY

The release of the CEO's proposed budget marks an important turning point in the budget process. For the first time, the public and the legislative decision makers see an integrated budget that represents all funds and functions of the organization. While seemingly a technical exercise, the integrated budget is much more than this. For the career professionals who have prepared the budget, it represents a test of their acumen in successfully integrating complex technical and political information. For the organization, it provides an important opportunity for the various departments and programs to discuss the value of their work on behalf of the community. And for the community, it provides an important opportunity to test and renew trust in the organization.

The process of reviewing and adopting the budget is both technical and political. It marks the culmination of nearly a year of information gathering, analysis, assembly, and negotiation. For the budget office staff responsible for preparing the budget, most programs and services are the products of political decisions made years ago. This eases the burden of deciding the allocation of resources, which are largely incremental unless a major crisis or series of events has arisen before or during the budget process. The political incrementalism of the process means that those who have led responsibility for preparing the budget can focus their attention on the two technical dimensions of budget preparation that are essential: meeting the organization's performance requirements, and meeting the legally required budgeting and accounting procedures.

Whether that of a local government or a nonprofit organization, the CEO's proposed budget presents the community with a picture of how the organization understands the community's needs, and how the organization believes it can best respond to those needs. This picture establishes the foundation for building citizen confidence in the organization. For local governments, review and discussion of the proposed budget forces department and program directors and the organization's staff to face elected representatives and to describe the value they bring to the community. For nonprofit organizations, review of the CEO or CFO's budget offers a similar process of scrutiny and exposure. The review process provides a primary opportunity for all members of the organization to build public confidence in the budget and in the organizational mission.

In their most encompassing role for both nonprofit and government organizations, the budget review and adoption procedures are trust-building exercises with the community. Adoption of a final budget by the legislative body represents a commitment by the organization to the community. For a local government, this commitment takes the form of a budget ordinance, an enforceable legal statute. Budget adoption by a nonprofit organization is less binding, but for major intermediary nonprofits and foundations the budget represents a public commitment to its partners and to the community. This community-building role of budget preparation and adoption is the most valuable function of executive-level budgeting.

STUDY QUESTIONS

The textbook website at www.pdx.edu/cps/budget-book may provide data and exercises that may assist you in answering these study questions.

1. Give an example of how personal styles of budget decision makers exert an impact on budget decisions.
2. What mechanisms can the CEO or administrative officer use to shape the budget proposals submitted by departments?
3. What are key sections or categories of information that a proposed budget document should contain?
4. What is the role of the CEO's budget message or transmittal letter to the legislative body? How can this role be used to facilitate budget adoption?
5. What is the purpose of direct interdepartmental transfers in the proposed budget? What is the purpose of indirect internal service charges for administrative expenses in the proposed budget? How are these costs captured in a consolidated all funds budget?
6. What role, if any, does the press play in the budget preparation and approval process?
7. What purpose(s) are served by the public hearings and other community meetings on the budget?
8. How do labor agreements, debt payments, external cost drivers (i.e., health care and retirement) and contract payment requirements from past years condition funding allocations in a proposed budget? How do these constraints influence budget actor behaviors?
9. How should local governments and intermediary nonprofits integrate the concerns and advocacy of their network partners during budget review and adoption? Should partners who have a contractual or formal intergovernmental relationship with a local government or intermediary receive a preferential voice? How might unaffiliated citizens or organizations feel about any special preference?

NOTES

1. As we discussed in chapter 5, we use the term proposed budget as a generic name for the organization-level, all funds, balanced budget prepared under the executive's guidance for release to the public and for consideration by the legislative body. State statutes, regulations, or manual guidance may use other terms for the proposed budget such as approved budget, executive recommended budget, executive requested budget, and requested budget.

2. See the GFOA website (www.gfoa.org/) for further explanation of the Distinguished Budget Presentation Awards program.

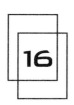

CAPITAL BUDGETING AND FINANCING

This $54 million tunnel is worth celebrating because now drivers and pedestrians alike can count on a safe and quick commute. The project created Washington jobs for the past two years. The completed tunnel embodies the renewed spirit of progress and hope that can be witnessed all across our great state.

(Governor Chris Gregoire [D-WA] at the
Bremerton, Washington, tunnel opening, July 6, 2009)

The number of water, sanitary and storm drain replacement and rehabilitation projects has been growing in comparison to the number of capacity-increasing projects. As the City's infrastructure gets older, many underground facilities reach the end of their service life and require replacement.

(City of Beaverton, Oregon, Capital Improvements Plan, 2011)

Capital improvements and infrastructure are the physical embodiment of a community and its governance decisions. Roads and streets, city halls, libraries and other public buildings, parks and recreation facilities, justice centers, and drinking water and wastewater systems all demonstrate community decisions to invest in long-term commitments that improve the general welfare. These systems touch us repeatedly throughout our day, and we place high personal and societal confidence in their continued function. Building a capital project brings an immediate burst of construction employment that stimulates the local and regional economies; furthermore, successful capital projects leave a political and physical legacy to community leadership and vision. But the decision to build a capital project carries long-term ramifications and out-year financial commitments that extend over generations of citizens. Appropriately, the debt financing of capital projects spreads the financial burden over the useful life of the facility.

Capital infrastructure financed, built, and maintained by local governments includes a wide range of facilities. Cities, towns, and townships are typically responsible for local roads, residential neighborhood streets, and traffic control signals. County governments often have responsibility for rural roads and arterial roads and highways. From a driver's perspective, local and county government roads must seamlessly connect and integrate with the state road system and the federal interstate highway system. However, mixed ownerships, along with varying ages and road conditions, often leave a patchwork system of local city streets, county roads, and arterials and state highways with fragmented and confused responsibilities for transportation planning, road design, maintenance, and reconstruction.

Additionally, local governments and special districts are often responsible for drinking water collection, purification, storage, and distribution systems. These systems include watersheds, storage dams, wells, transfer pipelines, purification plants, above- and below-ground storage tanks, and distribution pipe networks to homes and businesses. Similarly, local governments build and operate wastewater systems, including residential and commercial collector pipes, sewer trunk lines and transfer networks, stormwater drains and surface runoff collectors, and wastewater treatment facilities. In some states, municipalities and special districts provide electric power to homes and businesses. These jurisdictions build and maintain electrical transmission lines, transformer switching facilities, and neighborhood distribution systems.

Local governments and special districts build and maintain a full range of public buildings and transit facilities. Public buildings include schools, community college campuses, fire stations, city halls and courthouses, justice centers and jails, libraries, public hospitals, community centers, and emergency communication centers. Many of these facilities must be specially designed and reinforced at extra cost to withstand major natural disasters. Parks, swimming pools, athletic fields, recreation facilities, bike paths, sidewalks, and streetlights represent another group of capital facilities. Large specialized equipment purchases including fire pumper and ladder trucks, hazardous material (hazmat) trucks, ambulances, police cars, and even school buses may be considered capital purchases and financed over extended periods of use. Still another category of local infrastructure includes transit system facilities and bus and rail vehicles. This category can include: city buses; bus stop and transit station buildings and equipment; and rail tracks, signals, and rolling stock. Regional port special districts are often responsible for airport facilities and for marine terminal facilities.

As the second extract above points out, capital facilities have a useful lifespan. The excitement of building and commissioning new facilities quickly faces the unglamorous reality that all capital investments depreciate and wear out. Many capital projects provide the heavy maintenance, reconstruction, and replacement that keep basic public service systems operating. Where governments fail to perform scheduled maintenance or replacement, capital infrastructure degrades at accelerated rates, which only shortens its useful lifespan and increases reconstruction costs.

Capital budgeting is an adjunct to the annual or biennial operating budget process. Capital budgeting is used to plan and finance the physical infrastructure and other physical assets of a local government. Unlike operating budgets, the **capital budget** is—by its nature and necessity—a long-range view that extends beyond one fiscal year. The **capital budget request** covers only one fiscal year period, and it is frequently drawn from a long-range **capital improvement plan (CIP)** that usually spans from three to five years in length.

The reasons for planning and budgeting separately from operating spending are manifold, but include the following:

- Capital assets or projects constitute one-time, large expenditures.
- Capital spending, due to its financial largess, needs to be spread across fiscal years.
- Projects usually do not compete with operating needs for the same sources of funding.
- Physical infrastructure projects typically have long, useful lives that require advanced and protracted planning.
- Bond financing is a unique source of financing for capital projects not used for operating purposes.

Capital budgeting does share many of the same characteristics of operating budgeting in at least three ways. First, competition for resources is intense for both capital and operating needs, especially during economic downturns. Because raising revenue is subject to political inhibition and legal constraints such as tax limitations, it's likely that spending needs will greatly outstrip available resources, whether for operating or capital purposes. Second, special interests, typically singularly focused, can greatly influence budget decisions. On the capital side, those groups will frequently favor a particular project and then press the governing body to allocate funding for that purpose. For example, neighborhood organizations usually spearhead efforts to secure funding for street improvements and parks in their respective neighborhoods. Third, due to limited resources and the influence of special groups, efforts are made on both the operating and capital budget sides to rationalize spending decisions. Some sort of priority-setting or ranking process is commonly used to sort out those decisions initially.

Because capital budgets are the culmination of multiyear planning, the process followed by many jurisdictions can be more extensive and methodical than the process used for the operating budget. Although not practiced by every jurisdiction, the following steps typically comprise the capital improvement planning and budgeting process:

- setting capital budget and finance policies;
- inventorying existing capital assets;
- identifying capital project needs;
- determining capital financing options and potential; and
- making a capital plan and budget decisions.

Nonprofit organizations also engage in capital projects, as discussed in Exhibit 16.1, but not nearly to the extent that public entities, responsible for critical infrastructure, do. That does not mean, however, that capital projects for nonprofits do not require a significant investment of financial resources.

CAPITAL BUDGET POLICIES

A jurisdiction's financial management policies typically include capital budgeting policies. Sometimes these policies spell out the process for approving projects; more often than not, they will define what qualifies as a capital project (GFOA 2011b).

Although it can vary from one jurisdiction to the next, most localities will set a minimum dollar value and minimum useful life for an asset to be considered a capital project. As noted earlier, a capital project is usually defined as a physical asset (land, facilities), other infrastructure (streets, sidewalks, parks, buildings, water, and wastewater facilities), and any improvement or major rehabilitation to those assets. The minimum dollar value and useful life is established so that minor equipment or routine maintenance that should be funded as part of the operating budget does not become part of the capital budget. This separation reserves the capital budget for major assets that have longer useful lives and that can be funded with bonded indebtedness, if necessary and desired.

Minimum qualifications for capital projects can vary widely, often reflecting differences in state law. Local jurisdictions typically define a capital asset as a capital project with minimum total project cost of $50,000 to $100,000, and a useful life of five to seven or more years.

Other capital budget policies will establish parameters for other facets of the capital improvement planning and budgeting process, including:

- length of the capital improvement plan (CIP) (e.g., three or five years);
- legal requirements for design and construction or procurement of major equipment;
- criteria for prioritizing projects;
- sources for capital financing;
- public involvement in the process;
- governing body approval process;
- integration of capital budget into the operating budget; and
- amendment of capital budget during the fiscal year.

These policies, like other financial management policies, may or may not be formally adopted; if followed religiously by the finance department, however, they can replicate the force of law.

Exhibit 16.1

Nonprofit Hospitals Contribute to Community Infrastructure

Local governments are not the only developers of community public buildings and infrastructure. Nonprofit organizations make a major contribution to the buildings and campuses used for health, education, religious, and social services. Nonprofit organizations follow many of the same needs assessment, facilities planning, financing, and decision-making steps used by local government in developing capital projects. However, unlike governments, which can use tax revenues, nonprofits normally use charitable and philanthropic giving to raise funds to pay for capital projects. Service delivery nonprofit organizations such as hospitals and universities typically establish an independent nonprofit foundation to raise funds for major capital projects and for other investments. Funds raised through a capital campaign may be used to pay for a capital project on a pay-as-you-go basis, or to make a down payment on an extended loan or bonds. In many states, health, educational, and cultural nonprofits have access to state-sanctioned municipal bonds, which can greatly lower the cost of borrowing funds for capital projects. A composite case of actual fundraising experiences demonstrates how nonprofit hospitals in small to medium cities use fundraising campaigns to upgrade diagnostic and treatment equipment and to build new facilities.[1]

The Upper Cascade Community Hospital was established as a nonprofit community hospital in the 1950s. The mission of the hospital is to provide high-quality health care to patients of all income levels and faiths. The hospital serves a medium-sized city of 85,000, an adjacent town, and the surrounding rural areas. Many of the hospital's clients earn limited incomes, and the hospital prides itself on providing substantial amounts of free and subsidized care.

To help build its facilities and programs, the hospital leadership used the form of a **corporate foundation** and established the Upper Cascade Hospital Foundation. The hospital itself also developed a strategic master plan and vision document. At its inception, this plan envisioned a multiyear strategy to develop a health care campus with expanded facilities and ties to university medical schools. The plan mapped out future investments in real estate, facilities, and major equipment. However, the rapid advancement in medical technology had led to a constant effort by the foundation staff to raise funds to upgrade and replace medical equipment.

To enhance women's health services, the hospital foundation (at the request of the hospital leadership) undertook a two-year fundraising campaign to raise $2 million for a cancer treatment facility. A second campaign to raise $1.25 million for new breast cancer detection/diagnostic equipment took place eight years later. In planning the campaigns, the foundation board, staff, and consultants performed a careful assessment of service demand and local community support for such facilities. This assessment included identifying all other recently completed, ongoing, or pending capital fundraising campaigns in the community that might compete with a new campaign. The assessment also evaluated the potential for grants and donations from major local-, regional-, and state-level donors, estimated the potential for smaller donations from individuals and businesses, and evaluated the regional economy and business cycle. The campaigns began with an initial nonpublic phase in which the foundation staff and foundation board secured the support of several major donors whose donations would act as catalysts for other major donations and citizen contributions. In public events, these major donations were announced, and the hospital foundation board members themselves provided personal contributions to the efforts. The foundation staff held annual fundraising dinners and events and established partnerships with local businesses that would hold a fundraising event and contribute a share of their daily income to the campaign. A number of grants from the local community foundation and one from a regional foundation combined with donated funds to reach the campaign goals. Once the facilities were built, equipped, and completed, the hospital and foundation held well-publicized open houses to celebrate the community's accomplishment.

[1]This minicase integrates similar capital campaign experiences from three small-to-medium hospitals. See the Harrison Medical Center in Bremerton, Washington (Harrison Foundation 2013); the Clark Fork Valley Hospital Foundation website (Clark Fork Valley Hospital Foundation 2013); and the Tuality Healthcare Foundation in Hillsboro, Oregon (Tuality Healthcare 2013).

State procurement laws and regulations may also reinforce the local government definition of a capital purchase. For example, in Washington State, any public works project for new construction, facility replacement, or reconstruction costing over a specified amount ($35–$50,000) must go out for competitive bid (Washington State Municipal Research and Service Center 2010). This regulation reinforces the distinction between construction and routine maintenance, the latter being covered as an operating budget expense.

INVENTORYING EXISTING CAPITAL ASSETS

Local governments manage and finance much of the nation's public infrastructure. In 2013, the American Society of Civil Engineers (ASCE) issued a report on the condition of the nation's public infrastructure and gave it an overall grade of D+. The report estimated it would require $3.6 trillion in investments between 2013 and 2020 to restore America's roads, bridges, airports, water treatment facilities, and other infrastructure to a safe, dependable condition.

The gap between infrastructure funding needs and actual spending is not a recent phenomenon, but it is one that has been growing in recent years as the nation's infrastructure has aged, as demands on government spending have grown, and as resources have shrunk under economic downturns. For these reasons, as well as simply the need to know when a jurisdiction's physical assets require improvement, replacement, or major maintenance, some method for inventorying a community's facilities and other infrastructure and their condition is essential. Many jurisdictions conduct and periodically update an inventory and use it in part to develop and update their capital improvement plans. When a centralized inventory is maintained, it typically includes the following information:

- Asset name, type, and location
- Size or other measurement of the asset
- Year acquired, constructed, or last improved
- Original cost
- Estimated replacement cost
- Physical condition of the asset
- Remaining useful life or year expected for major improvement or replacement

Except for the smallest jurisdictions, these inventories are usually computerized as part of an integrated financial and human resources management system or asset management system. These systems not only provide the information needed for capital budgeting but also maintain information for day-to-day repairs as well as the asset valuation required for annual financial reporting. If the recordkeeping is not centralized, it is commonplace for larger departments—particularly those involving capital-intensive operations such as water utilities or public works departments—to maintain their own records for capital budgeting purposes. Exhibit 16.2 provides an example of such a record.

The exhibit illustrates an inventory included in a multiyear CIP. Much of the information in the inventory is a best guess, with the exception of the "Year Built/Acquired" and "Original Purchase/Construction Cost." The purpose of the inventory is to provide some idea of the timing and relative cost of the next addition, replacement, or improvement of the asset. A better estimate of those factors is determined as the associated capital project moves up on the priority list of projects to be budgeted. For the same reason, the condition assessment of the assets is more qualitative than quantitative.

Exhibit 16.2

Example Inventory of Major Capital Assets

Department:		Prepared by:		Date:		Page No.
Regional Parks and Greenspaces Department				Aug. 6, 1997		1 of 4
Asset	Year built/ acquired	Original purchase/ construction cost	Latest major investment/repair	Condition	Target replacement year	Estimated replacement cost*
Blue Lake Park						
• 185 acres and house	1960	$613,000	N/A	A	2040 House	$2,780,300
• Bathhouse (old swim center building)	1962	$141,258	N/A	D	2005	$196,100
• Pool and concrete dock	1962	$85,293	1992 Dock & Perimeter Renovation	A	2017	$238,600
• Refreshment stand/bldg. (food concession)	1965	$68,263	1989 Exterior Renovation	B	2025	$93,000
• Curry Building (office and warehouse)	1965	$60,731	N/A	A	2025	$81,900
• Sanitary sewer system	1969	$57,709	N/A	A	2019	$75,800
• Picnic shelters (3)	1987	$177,800	N/A	A	2017	$197,200
• New swim beach and building	1989	$465,400	N/A	A	2049	$506,500
• Road system realignment	1989	$225,000	N/A	A	2014	$244,700
• Lake house and food conc. exterior renovation	1989	$80,000	N/A	B	2019	$87,000
• Wetland, pathway, and rail	1989	$165,000	N/A	A	2014	$178,000
• Picnic shelters (2)	1990	$154,900	N/A	A	2020	$166,800

Source: Metro Regional Government, Portland, OR. 1997. Metro Adopted Capital Improvement Plan for 1997–98 through FY 2001–02 (April).
*Estimated replacement cost in 1997 dollars based on a 1.1% per year increase over purchase/construction cost per Risk & Contract Management Division of the Administrative Services Department.

The condition assessment in this exhibit is based on a letter scale of A to D, defined as:

A   Excellent   No discernible deficiencies; no major repairs are anticipated within the next 5 years.

B   Good   Deficiencies that are not potentially urgent, but which, if deferred longer than 3 to 5 years, will affect the use of the asset or cause significant damage to it.

C   Fair   Potentially urgent deficiencies which, if not corrected within 2 years, will become urgent needs.

D   Poor   Urgent needs to be completed within one year, such as correcting a safety problem, eliminating damaging deteriorations, or complying with environmental regulations or other mandates.

Normally, the asset listed in the inventory is the entire asset, such as a building, unless a component part (e.g., heating, ventilation, and air conditioning [HVAC] system) meets the minimum dollar and useful life threshold for a stand-alone capital project.

IDENTIFYING CAPITAL NEEDS

The inventory provides the most important source of capital improvement needs identified in the capital planning and budgeting process. As mentioned earlier, deferred asset maintenance is a big contributor to capital funding requirements because it is a major drain on infrastructure longevity. Improperly maintained or neglected infrastructure can shorten the useful life of capital assets. For example, streets and roads that go years without regular maintenance and rehabilitation, such as through sealcoating, will deteriorate more quickly and require full replacement within a shorter time frame than properly maintained streets and roads. The cost of maintenance on consistently well-maintained roads is much less per mile than the maintenance costs per mile on partially deteriorated streets and roads (Griffin-Valade, Kahn, and Woodward 2013). Failure to spend funds to perform routine maintenance digs a jurisdiction into an ever more costly maintenance and reconstruction backlog. Consistent spending on road and infrastructure maintenance allows a community to obtain the maximum service length from its capital investments at minimal cost.

Ultimately, all pieces of capital infrastructure must be rebuilt or replaced, and capital reconstruction and replacement is a major if not the dominant part of many local government capital plans and budgets. Capital plans should clearly schedule and forecast the estimated costs of the reconstruction and replacement of a jurisdiction's capital inventory over the medium and long term.

Improvements to existing infrastructure or new improvements make up the remaining portion of local government capital asset needs. Identifying these particular needs can be done in any number of ways. Other planning processes done for a jurisdiction such as general land-use plans or plans prepared for particular purposes (such as master plans for parks, economic redevelopment plans, or facility plans for fire and police stations) are a typical source for assessing capital asset needs. Normally, the department responsible for preparing a plan will be responsible for bringing those facilities or improvements requests forward to the capital improvement planning process.

The master or facility plans usually provide a fair amount of detail regarding a proposed new facility or improvement, including the purpose, scope, basic design, and projected costs. The plans also detail how the improvement fits within the network of related or similar facilities, and the strategic purpose it serves for a particular government function. This information is often adequate for capital planning purposes and may only need to be updated if the underlying plan is somewhat dated.

These plans provide an added advantage. A public participation process frequently is included in the plan development. At one or more stage of the preparation, the general public and specific stakeholders may be asked to comment and make suggestions for facilities and improvements that are being considered for inclusion in the plan. This serves two purposes: (1) it gives community members an opportunity to identify what they believe are critical or high-priority facility needs, and (2) it helps unveil any opposition or support to a particular facility or improvement. Early public input can change the order of priority or makeup of a project long before it becomes a part of a formal plan that is reviewed and acted upon by the governing body.

The capital improvement planning process begins in advance of the operating budget planning process to allow time to develop requests, evaluate funding options, prioritize projects, and assess the impact of projects on the operating budget (GFOA 2006). This process needs to allow sufficient time for the consideration of projects tentatively scheduled for the ensuing fiscal year. Any associated operating budget increases would need to be reviewed and considered in tandem with the capital budget requests by the chief executive, the council, or the board. Exhibit 16.3 is an example of a form or schedule used to compile information by departments for projects for consideration and ultimate inclusion in the CIP. The "Project Detail," as shown in this exhibit, provides detailed information within several categories, including:

- *Department Priority:* displays the department's ranking for the project among all of its projects submitted;
- *Project Estimates:* estimated capital costs and recommended funding sources for the project as a whole and during the plan years;
- *Project Description/Justification:* includes use or purpose of the project and any unique features;
- *Annual Operating Budget Impact:* shows the estimated increase or decrease in operating costs or revenue generated from the operation and maintenance of the capital project, including the first full year of operation.

The Project Detail Sheet provides a uniform and consistent way of presenting key information to establish a basis for comparison among projects and ultimately prioritizing projects and making decisions.

EVALUATING AND PRIORITIZING PROJECTS

Prioritizing capital projects for scheduling and adoption by the city council or other legislative body requires blending an evolving mix of needs and resources. Local government departments will often use their own criteria for ranking or prioritizing their own projects. Ranking projects may be as simple as reaching consensus among department managers or as complex as running and interpreting sophisticated computer models. More often than not, ranking may entail relying on the policies and priorities set in the local government's master facility plans described earlier. Prioritizing or ranking projects across department lines, however, is a different story. Dissimilar purposes or missions, such as fire suppression and recreation, make it difficult to judge priorities among projects that serve wholly different purposes. If the funding source is restricted to specific purposes or projects, prioritization may be left to the department responsible for those projects. For example, wastewater projects funded through bonds financed through wastewater rates will be left largely to the wastewater utility or department responsible for projects. Even in that case, coordination with other departments may be necessary to ensure proper timing with other projects impacted by those wastewater projects, such as streets that may need to be reconstructed when a new sewer line is installed.

A capital projects advisory committee, composed of representatives from different departments, may be established to evaluate and rank projects that are competing for the same source of funds. Alternatively, the chief executive or administrative officer (CEO), who submits the proposed budget and capital improvement plan to the governing body, will need to work through those assessments; ultimately, the executive who submits the proposed budget decides what is included in the plan. However, the executive's job is made much easier by assistance from others who can provide technical advice and recommendations.

463

Exhibit 16.3 **Example Capital Project Detail Sheet**

PROJECT DETAIL

Project Title: METRO CENTRAL EXPANSION OF HAZARDOUS WASTE FACILITY

TYPE OF PROJECT: ☐ New ☑ Expansion ☐ Replacement	DEPARTMENT/DIVISION: Regional Environmental Management Engineering & Analysis				TYPE OF REQUEST: ☑ Initial ☐ Continuation ☐ Revision	DATE:
SOURCE OF ESTIMATE: ☐ Preliminary ☐ Based on Design ☐ Actual Bid Documents	PROJECT START DATE: Winter 1998	PROJECT COMPLETION DATE: Fall 1999			DEPARTMENT PRIORITY: 12	PREPARED BY:

PROJECT ESTIMATES	PRIOR YEARS	1998-98	1999-2000	2000-01	2001-02	2002-03	BEYOND 2003	TOTAL
CAPITAL COST:								
PLANS & STUDIES		$30,000						$30,000
LAND & RIGHT-OF-WAY		50,000						200,000
DESIGN & ENGINEERING			$150,000					
CONSTRUCTION								
EQUIPMENT/FURNISHINGS								
PROJECT CONTINGENCY								
1% FOR ART								
OTHER								
TOTAL		$80,000	$150,000					$230,000
FUNDING SOURCE:								
FUND BALANCE-CAP./OP. REV.		$80,000	$150,000					$230,000
GRANTS								
G.O. BONDS								
REVENUE BONDS								
OTHER								
TOTAL		$80,000	$150,000					$230,000

PROJECT DESCRIPTION/JUSTIFICATION:
The expansion would be approximately 800 square feet and would occupy the existing loading dock, which is not used. The expansion is necessary to supplement existing flammable storage that is inadequate and to accommodate the Reuse Program. No significant increase in operating costs is expected as a result of this expansion.

These costs reflect construction that meets the standards for a hazardous waste facility which may not apply to this addition's principal use as storage.

ANNUAL OPERATING BUDGET IMPACT:	
PERSONAL SERVICES COSTS	
MATERIALS & SVC. COSTS	$1,200
CAPITAL OUTLAY COSTS	
OTHER COSTS	
(REVENUES)	
NET ANNUAL OPERATING COSTS	$1,200
RENEWAL & REPLACEMENT CONTRIBUTION	N/A
FIRST FULL FISCAL YEAR OF OPERATION:	2000-01
FUND(s): Solid Waste Revenue Fund, General Acct.	

Source: Metro Regional Government, Portland, OR. 1997. Metro Adopted Capital Improvement Plan for 1997–98 through FY 2001–02 (April).

An evaluation tool such as the one shown in Exhibit 16.4 can provide a uniform method for scoring similar or dissimilar projects and, in the process, aid in determining which ones should be recommended for inclusion in the capital plan and budget, and possibly in what order and in what year they should be implemented. This evaluation sheet helps to score projects individually, based on a number of criteria on a scale of one to five. Presumably, those projects with the highest total points move forward in the process. Even with the advisory committee, these qualitative tools are not the be-all and end-all. Other considerations—like the number of projects any one department has garnered support for—can be determining factors in which projects are advanced in the process.

Qualitative tools are not the only evaluation methods available to choose among projects. Quantitative financial analysis such as a **net present value (NPV)** analysis, which evaluates the project costs and income along with the interest cost of money over the extended time frame of the project, can assess which project alternatives have the greatest rate of benefit or return. Although not all projects lend themselves to this sort of analysis, projects that represent alternatives to the same purpose or outcome, and whose costs and benefits can be clearly calculated, can benefit by this analysis approach.

DETERMINING CAPITAL FINANCING OPTIONS AND POTENTIAL

Whether a project ranks high or one project option supersedes another, the availability of funding will be the ultimate barometer of whether a project moves off the drawing board. In most situations, there are only two methods of financing a **capital project**: (1) **pay-as-you-go**, and (2) **debt financing**.

Pay-As-You-Go Financing

This method of financing capital projects relies on funding from current revenues. Because available dedicated funds and general funds are typically limited, unless the jurisdiction receives formula-based grant dollars such as gas tax revenues for road projects, the number and scope of projects that can be funded through this method is also limited. Paying as you go requires a flow of funds over the course of a project's implementation. The revenue sources of funding for pay-as-you-go projects can be as varied as a jurisdiction's sources of operating funds, including taxes, user fees and charges, and special assessments. Unless the projects are small, however, sufficient resources will not be available to fund many projects unless a jurisdiction has built up cash in a reserve fund or expects to receive a capital grant or large donation. Pay-as-you-go financing does force governments to pay for projects with already available funds rather than incur the additional cost of borrowing. In addition to the funding limits of this option, another downside is the exclusive reliance on current taxpayers and ratepayers to pay for the cost of facilities that have useful lives of many years and possibly decades. This places an inequitable financial burden on a community's current residents for a facility that will clearly benefit future residents who will not share in the original cost of that facility. Pay-as-you-go financing is effective for smaller, expected, routine projects such as carpet replacement in public buildings, basic facility upgrades, and information system upgrades.

Debt Financing

One way to correct the intergenerational inequity created by pay-as-you-go financing is to borrow monies for the **major construction/acquisition** of facilities and improvements. Borrowing and repayment spreads the cost of financing over many years and hopefully over the entire useful life of the facility, thereby requiring, in theory, both current and future users of the facility to pay for the capital cost. More important, borrowing allows jurisdictions to pay back the cost of funding over many years instead of financing upfront. This avoids having to reserve cash for many years, perhaps well beyond when need for a facility first arises. Borrowing also avoids the necessity of imposing significant tax or user charge rate hikes to provide a large infusion of cash to pay for

Exhibit 16.4

Example Capital Project Evaluation Tool

$$\boxed{\text{ATTACHMENT "A"}}$$

CITY OF TRACY
CIP PROJECT SCORING
(For Staff Use)

CIP #:_____   PROJECT #:_____

PROJECT NAME: _____   RATER DEPARTMENT:_____

INSTRUCTIONS: Provide a score from 1 to 5 to assist in determining how well the project supports the stated criteria.
1 = Does not support stated criteria.   3 = Neutral or moderate impact regarding stated criteria.
5 = Supports or enhances stated criteria.
Note: Highest and lowest scores from the group will be discarded and the remaining scores will be averaged to produce an AVERAGE ADJUSTED SCORE for a project.

	CRITERIA	1	2	3	4	5	TL
Public Safety	Does the project eliminate or prevent an existing health, environment, or safety hazard? *Example: Improvements to playgrounds that would protect children from traffic or hazardous equipment.*						
Neighborhood / Community Impact	Does the project enhance property or increase quality of life within the City of Tracy? *Example: New ball fields or expansion*						
Legal Requirements	Is the project in accordance with state, local and federal laws or regulations? *Example: ADA compliance*						
General Plan	Does the Project advance the goals of the *City of Tracy's General Plan*? *Example: Increase or expansion of Passive Recreation, Expansion of bikeways.*						
Population Served By Project	Who in the community/region will the project serve? *Example: All customers in City vs. a small segment of the population.*						
Fiscal Impact	Will the project have a net positive, neutral or negative impact on the City's finances? Does this project represent good financial value for the cost? Does the project have high ongoing operational and maintenance costs? What's the Phase-ability of the project? *Example: Upgrade in lighting might have a savings in energy costs. The ongoing O & M is significantly high and unbudgeted;*						
Life Expectancy	How long is the improvement expected to last? *Example: A new roof may extend the life of a building 20 years.*						
Economic Development	Does the project promote Economic Development Goals? infrastructure opportunity sites opportunity *Example: Enhances the City's Infrastructure (i.e. in undeveloped opportunity sites) Sports Park (Promotes Regional community draw & increases revenue (sales & TOT taxes)*						
Sustainability	Does the project promote sustainability efforts? *Example: Fuel efficient Vehicles, Sustains existing assets, results in energy-saving measures*						
					TOTAL SCORE		

Source: City of Tracy, CA. n.d. redistributed by the California State Municipal Finance Officers Association December 12, 2012.

very expensive projects. These rate spikes, if they are associated with property taxes, may not be practical for governments subjected to tax limitation laws (chapter 7). Nor would they necessarily endear governing body members to taxpayers or ratepayers who elected them.

Three types of borrowing are available to most local governments: general-obligation (GO) bonds, revenue bonds, and leasing. All three types require a dedicated source of revenue from taxes or charges. Only leasing, which is often reserved for financing large equipment purchases, is reversible with nonappropriation clauses (i.e., releasing future governing bodies from the obligation to continue the lease) and relinquishment of the leased asset.

General obligation (GO) bonds are backed by the full faith and credit of the jurisdiction issuing them, which legally and morally obligate the government to repay the debt. This is accomplished typically through a dedicated tax or a pledge of other revenues. With these added assurances, a jurisdiction can obtain a lower interest rate than through other forms of borrowing. Issuance of local government debt is tightly controlled by state governments because of the potential negative impact that a default or excessive borrowing can have on the credit rating of all governments within a state. Consequently, state law commonly controls how much debt a local government can issue, what it can be issued for, whether voter approval is required, and how it will be financed.

The most frequently used sources of revenue for GO debt include property tax, sales tax, and special assessment revenues. Taxes are used because the tax rate can be increased to the exact amount necessary to specifically pay for the **debt service** (i.e., principal and interest on the bonds). In fact, in some states, local government must adopt a special tax levy for debt service. GO bonds are often used to cover general government projects such as the construction of public buildings like a new city hall. GO special assessments are also levied for sidewalks, street lighting, and other infrastructure that abuts private properties. The property owners who benefit from the improvement repay the assessments.

Revenue bonds are borrowed funds repaid with user charge and fee revenue specifically related to the use of enterprise facilities (municipal water or wastewater facilities, for example). Because they are not backed by the full faith and credit of the issuer, those bonds typically carry a higher interest rate. The charge and fee revenues, however, are often generated by highly dependent clients and customers of public utilities, transportation systems, and public services.

Known as *municipal bonds* by investors, most local government bonds benefit from their tax-exempt status. This means that the interest income received by bondholders is exempt from federal income taxes and income taxes in the state in which the bonds are issued. The benefits of tax exemption on the interest income offset the lower interest payments an investor receives relative to typical for-profit corporate bonds. Nonprofit organizations often have access to the tax-exempt bond market through state financing agencies (e.g., Washington State Higher Education Facilities Authority; Arizona Health Facilities Authority; and the Colorado Educational and Cultural Facilities Authority). Nonprofit colleges and universities; nonprofit museums, arts, and cultural organizations; and nonprofit hospitals and medical services organizations frequently rely on state government backing to enable the construction of major facilities and campus buildings. Typically, the state provides financial backing on the bond issue, and the nonprofit organization pledges a stream of revenue from charges on clients and customers. For example, students at a private nonprofit university might pay a semester building use charge or an increased tuition payment to generate bond repayment revenues.

The biggest challenge facing jurisdictions and organizations issuing bonds is assessing their tax and other revenue capacity to support debt service requirements. Most local governments and nonprofit organizations will procure the services of a financial advisor to help with that assessment. Financial advisors not only know the intricacies of debt burden and bond costs but also the vagaries of the bond market. Both come in handy when structuring a debt issue (i.e., determining the size, maturities, and type of bonds), and assessing **debt capacity** (i.e., availability of revenues to repay the debt and restrictions on how much debt can be issued). The number and type of bonds carried by the government or organization under previous issues, along with a history of successful repayment, contribute to the interest rate charged on new debt issues. Assessing debt capacity entails projecting the revenue streams available to repay the bonds as well as determining how much debt can be issued within legal restrictions. For local governments, the latter, with some exceptions, is not a particular problem because the debt ceiling is so high that the jurisdiction would not likely reach it. The former is more of challenge because it requires making assumptions about the rate and speed at which the revenue repaying the bonds will grow and how much support exists among governing body members for necessary tax rate hikes.

Small-scale bond issues usually are not directly rated by an independent credit rating agency. They are often issued through a state finance authority, financed by a promissory note, or borrowed directly from a bank, and they do not exceed the federal limits of $20 million. Larger bond issues proposed by a local government or nonprofit organization receive review and scrutiny by independent credit rating agencies. The credit rating agency examines the organization's debt capacity and the certainty of its revenue streams and then issues a letter rating or **bond grade** of the bonds to be issued. The higher the quality of the **bond rating**, the lower the organization's debt service and interest costs to borrow funds. Maintaining and protecting the organization's credit rating becomes a critical effort for its executive, finance officer, and council or board members.

Exhibit 16.5 offers a graphical example of the debt capacity analysis for a local government. The government has established a debt service budget fund from which to pay its bond obligations of interest and principal repayment. The graph plots property tax revenue dedicated to debt service ("secondary property taxes" in this example), debt service costs, and debt service fund balance. The graphs shows that with two consecutive years of double-digit declines in property assessed values (−10 percent in FY12/13 and then −7 percent in FY13/14) available revenues fall below the annual payment requirements. These declines are followed by three percent growth in values in each consecutive year thereafter. But even with the stabilization and increase in property values and revenues, the generated revenues fall short of the annual payment requirements. The debt service fund balance line indicates the accumulated yearly shortfalls over the decade. There is insufficient property tax revenue available to support existing debt service, much less new debt service, for more than five years. The underlying spreadsheet allows staff to ascertain what tax rate increases would be needed to issue new debt. Alternatively, it can be used to determine how many capital projects would have to be deferred to cover existing debt service payments.

Leasing is an alternative method for acquisition or rental of major equipment and facilities. **Capital lease** agreements can vary in length, but they usually do not exceed 10 years. Municipal leases, which are available only to state and local governments, are tax exempt, which means they carry a lower interest rate than a commercial lease. Their greatest advantage is their nonappropriation clause, which allows the jurisdiction to cancel the installment contract following the close of any given budget year. Their disadvantage is the jurisdiction may not own the asset at the end of the lease agreement if it does not opt to execute the purchase. A **certificate of participation** (COP) is a form of leasing agreement in which the issuer sells shares of the lease to investors. The investors receive interest income that is often exempt from federal and state income tax.

Integrating Diverse Funding Sources

The funding of a proposed project reflects its revenue authorizations and characteristics. We have described how local governments use pay-as-you-go and debt financing of eligible projects. But a project may be eligible to receive revenues from several sources. For example, a local city government primarily funds street and road resurfacing and reconstruction from its street maintenance and reconstruction budget fund; however, if a road project requires the construction of a new storm drain, money from the stormwater budget fund could contribute a secondary source of resources. Similarly, sewer collector replacement to repair a broken sewer main as part of a larger street pavement maintenance project would allow the use of sewer funds in the project. Resources from

Exhibit 16.5

Example Debt Capacity Analysis (in millions)

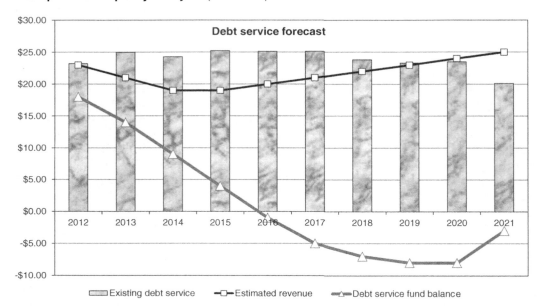

Source: City of Chandler, AZ. 2012 (January). Prepared by Gregory Westrum, City of Chandler budget manager for an internal financial plan.

Note: This estimated forecast assumes the following conditions:
- –10% Secondary Assessed Value Decrease in FY12/13;
- –7% Secondary Assessed Value Decrease in FY13/14;
- no new debt for 5 years;
- no tax rate increase.

a drinking water capital budget fund for a water main replacement, or a parks capital budget fund for a new adjacent bike path could also complement street fund resources. Resources from the government's general fund can also be integrated to support projects on a pay-as-you-go basis.

Integrating available and future funding across multiple capital budget funds is an important step in the project planning and scheduling process. This type of integration can also extend across agencies. A county government may share funding with a local sewer and stormwater management special district to develop an integrated sewer and stormwater capital project. The ability to garner funding from several sources may move a project up the priority list over projects with a single limited source of funding. Local governments gain efficiencies by performing several related **capital construction** tasks within a single project. The careful planning and integration of funding sources and project tasks serves to stretch public resources to their maximum benefit.

MAKING CAPITAL PLAN AND BUDGET DECISIONS

Debt capacity as explained in the preceding discussion may be the most important factor in deciding how many and which capital projects are included in the multiyear capital improvement plan and, even more important, within the capital budget request for the ensuing fiscal year. The CEO, however, will have to weigh a myriad of other factors before submitting a proposed CIP and capital budget request to the council, the commission, or the governing board.

In order to move a CIP and a capital budget request through the budget adoption process, the

CEO must communicate with and build support from several key budget actors. These actors include elected officials, key administrators within the organization, leaders and decision makers in other partner agencies, and key advocacy group and constituent group leaders. Some local governments recruit citizens to serve on a capital plan advisory committee, which serves as a link between the community on the one hand, and elected officials and administrators on the other. The advisory committee reviews the proposed list of projects and funding arrangements in the CIP and the capital budget request and forwards its recommendations to the CEO and the board, usually after consultation with public works and finance directors. Other governments use an internal project review and selection committee of department directors and key managers. Typically, the CEO independently consults with the department directors and key allies on the governing body before making decisions. Depending on whether a project was already part of the CIP preparation, efforts also may be made to solicit public input on proposed projects, although those efforts can be handled concurrently with public involvement efforts for the operating budget. Ideally, decisions on the CIP will be timed to coincide with decisions on the operating budget if the jurisdiction makes it a practice of including increases or decreases in operating costs associated with capital projects in the operating budget. Beyond the first year of the CIP, which is only part of the plan that is funded (e.g., the capital budget request), the chief executive or administrative officer will be interested in which projects are included in the out-years of the CIP. The symbolism of including a project in a multiyear CIP, even if it changes in subsequent years, may be enough to satisfy proponents of the project and dissuade them from seeking a reordering of projects once the CIP makes it way to the governing body for review and adoption.

The proposed CIP submitted to the governing body will include a number of schedules and accompanying narrative. The following are some of the more commonly found features.

- a message or transmittal letter from the chief executive or administrative officer;
- a summary of capital spending by function and department;
- sources of funding for capital projects;
- debt capacity analysis;
- project detail sheets for each project included in the first year, at a minimum;
- capital asset inventory;
- status of existing capital projects; and
- a list of unfunded projects by department.

The city council, county commission, or governing board may choose to assign the plan to a finance or public works subcommittee for review and recommendations, or simply take it up as a body of the whole when it considers the proposed operating budget. Similarly, it may choose to hold public hearings on the CIP in conjunction with hearings on the operating budget. In any event, the pressure to modify the capital plan may not be as great as the pressure to allocate more dollars to specific services or programs. Only a project with significant and widespread community or neighborhood support could prevent such a transfer of general funds from program operating expenditures. Administrators and elected officials must take a strong leadership role to ensure full community support and resources for less glamorous replacement, reconstruction, and heavy maintenance capital projects.

The adoption of spending for the capital budget request by the governing board covers only the first year of the CIP. Unlike appropriations in the operating budget that control spending at the program, department, or fund level, appropriations for capital projects are typically made at the project level. The governing council or board may amend the capital budget and adjust funding levels at the time of award or amendment of the design and construction contracts associated with projects. These contract awards and amendments take place as the project contracts come forward to the governing body for approval during the fiscal year. The monitoring and administration of capital projects during the year usually falls to the project managers in an engineering division or to staff in the sponsoring department. Reporting on projects to the governing body aside from consideration of contracts is not normally done during the fiscal year and may not occur until the next year's CIP is released.

It is important to note that once an organization appropriates first-year funds for a multiyear project, it commits itself to continuing funding in the project's second and later years. These obligations are reinforced through any procurement and contract language with contractors and suppliers. Adopting and executing a multiyear capital project requires finance officers and project administrators to reserve, or encumber, sufficient funds to meet future obligations. These obligations add constraints that limit decision flexibility in future years' budgets. PPBS/program budgeting (chapter 12) that focuses on holistic goals and objectives provides a framework that can explain multiyear projects. A jurisdiction may choose to pull the plug on a multiyear project, but this typically results in claims of legal liability from contractors, the admission of "sunk costs" or wasted funds spent on the project to date, and increased public and media scrutiny of a bad decision and poor project management. Terminating a capital project prior to its completion is an admission that the most cost-effective option is immediately to tie off any work and to pay off any downstream costs and liabilities.

SUMMARY

Capital improvements are an expression of a community's sense of self, and they constitute a significant portion of a local government's budget. Because they can have such a huge impact on the size of annual budgets and require considerable lead time to implement, multiyear plans are prepared and debt financing is employed to allow a longer planning horizon and to spread the cost of pricey improvements over many years. Dedicated streams of revenue from special property tax levies, sales tax increments, or charges for services assure dedicated funding to make debt payments over the life of a bond. Despite this long-term approach, it is only the first year of the CIP that constitutes the capital budget request. Consideration of requests by the governing board subjects projects to many of the same political pressures and bargaining that departments and programs face in the operating budget. Capital improvement plans are usually updated annually, and the process to develop them begins a bit before the operating budget process so that the two dovetail when the timetable dictates that budget decisions have to be made.

STUDY QUESTIONS

1. How and why should the capital improvement planning process complement the operating budget process?
2. Why is it important to identify the operating budget impact of capital projects as decisions are made about which projects are to be considered for funding?
3. What factors will dictate whether debt should be used to finance a capital project?
4. How is decision making on which capital projects should be funded similar and dissimilar to the decision making on which programs and services should be funded?
5. How might projects be evaluated for their importance and priority as part of the capital planning and budgeting process?
6. Consider the capital plan for your local jurisdiction. What proportion of projects are new construction, and what share are replacement and reconstruction?
7. How does your jurisdiction integrate resources from different capital construction funds to support a large, complex project? How might a project integrate funding from several government agencies?
8. Does your local jurisdiction adequately fund the maintenance of its capital infrastructure? By what standards would you judge *adequacy*?
9. Attempt the capital budgeting exercise on the textbook website at www.pdx.edu/cps/budget-book.

17 | BUDGET EXECUTION

The administration of government . . . falls peculiarly within the province of the executive department. The actual conduct of foreign negotiations, the preparatory plans of finance, the application and disbursement of the public moneys in conformity to the general appropriations of the legislature. . . .

(Alexander Hamilton, Federalist No. 72, 1788,
quoted in Rossiter 1961)

In the months between the time the budget preparations begin and final approval . . . , the environment has probably changed. But the assumptions behind the budget remain. A static document in an active world, it reduces the organization's flexibility to respond to change.

(Ram Charan and Larry Bossidy 2002, 230–231)

The management of financial resources is a year-round effort, much like the management of services and programs. The local government budget need not remain in **balance** at any given time during fiscal year, but resources must equal requirements at the beginning and the end of the fiscal year or biennium. Unlike in the private sector and in some government enterprises, most local jurisdictions do not have very much flexibility to adjust total resources and spending to adapt to changing circumstances once the budget is adopted. In many ways, this limits local entities' ability to adapt to emerging issues and events. That does not mean, however, that local entities cannot make budgetary changes following adoption so long as they abide by state and local legal constraints. In many jurisdictions, managers and legislative bodies are allowed to adjust budgets following adoption within departmental- and fund-level appropriations, respectively.

The budget process does not end with the adoption of the budget. Numerous changes in conditions inevitably occur after the legislative body has approved taxation and appropriation limits for a given jurisdiction, necessitating administrative adjustments throughout the legally established budgetary cycle. For example, a jurisdiction may receive a grant midyear that they did not anticipate at budget adoption and may need additional appropriation authority to spend those grant revenues. Natural disasters will drive the need for disaster relief, including local spending that is not fully reimbursed with federal funds. For whatever reason, funds may be withheld, appropriations may be supplemented, positions may be frozen, and transfers may be authorized. By the end of the fiscal year, the budget may look very different from the one adopted at the beginning of the year. For these reasons, most jurisdictions pay considerable attention to budget implementation. This attention focuses mainly on controlling the timing of spending and on the actual amount departments are permitted to spend, despite what may have been authorized and appropriated by the legislative body.

Because the budget is only a plan, a best estimate of revenues and expenditures, all jurisdictions have a set of mechanisms in place to monitor, control, and report on actual budgetary results throughout the year. If the budget includes performance goals and action plans, an additional process exists to track and report on those results. The central budget office and the departments usually split responsibility between them for monitoring, control, and reporting. Discretion may also be granted to the chief executive officer (CEO) and to department heads to make budget adjustments. Ultimately, the responsibility for amending the adopted budget lies with the legislative body. Departments also should conduct a formal review of financial and program performance at year's end to determine how well they have met their targets.

Budget adjustments may be a necessity because economic conditions change and because revenue and spending forecasting is not a perfect science. However, budget adjustments may also be used to advance political and policy agendas in off budget cycle months of the fiscal year when they do not have to compete with higher spending priorities. For example, legislative body members may propose budget amendments to restore cuts made to their favorite programs if revenues come in higher than expected during the fiscal year. This may amount to only a one-time increase, but it can establish a precedent for continuance of the restoration during the following budget. The extent to which these and other adjustments can be made is rooted in the local charter, ordinances, or financial management policies.

Nonprofit organizations typically adopt flexible budgets that allow the board, or in some cases the executive director, to increase the total budget as resources become available during the fiscal year. Dropkin, Halpin and La Touche (2007, 129) strongly encourage nonprofit executives and boards to carefully monitor their budget performance and respond to changes in budgeted revenues and expenses. This may include modifying the adopted budget. The reporting and budget adjustment methods described in this chapter for local governments apply in much the same way to nonprofit organizations, but without the public notice and disclosure requirements. However, major nonprofit intermediaries and foundations may wish to make public disclosures of budget changes to notify their partner organizations and contractors of possible changes to funding streams.

Whether for a local government or a nonprofit organization, budget execution begins by communicating budget funding levels and decisions to the organization leadership and staff and to the organization control systems. This chapter identifies the major elements of this communication and transfer process, beginning with a summary of financial policies that define and set procedures for financial transactions, administrative transfers of funds, and budget amendments. The chapter then describes techniques for monitoring and controlling spending, and goes on to identify several of the most common monitoring reports. These reports not only analyze and document the organization's budget performance through the flow of expenditures and the inflow of revenues but also serve as early warning signs of changing conditions—indications of a need to make revisions and amendments to the adopted budget. The back half of the chapter explains the procedures for modifying a budget to meet changing conditions and follows up with a description of the end-of-year reporting that completes the implementation cycle and provides timely information for budget development for the next fiscal year. The chapter closes with a short discussion of network-level budget execution and reporting.

FINANCIAL MANAGEMENT POLICIES

Minimum standards and requirements for financial operations, including budget execution, are typically established through a comprehensive set of financial management policies that the legislative body may or may not formally adopt (chapter 10). Budget policies related to budget execution cover a wide range of practices with a particular focus on appropriation control, budget adjustments and amendments, and periodic budget status reports. Policies will also likely speak to the level of authority (up to a dollar limit) the chief executive officer (CEO), or their designated staff, must possess to transfer spending authority between appropriations. The policies may also prescribe whether that authority allows transfers between line-item objects or expenditures, organizational subunits, or programs. If these policies are codified through ordinance or resolution, they have the force of law, and an independent auditor will likely review compliance as part of the jurisdiction's financial audit. Otherwise, the policies may simply be included in the published budget document with the jurisdiction's finance director responsible for ensuring compliance.

MONITORING AND CONTROLLING SPENDING

The budget authorizes the raising and spending of government resources for specific purposes. The four most frequently used controls to ensure that the budget is implemented as authorized are allotments, position controls, appropriation controls, and encumbrance controls, as described next. However, before these controls are put into operation, final budget decisions in the legislatively adopted budget are transmitted to departments and budget amounts recorded in the accounting system. This ensures that the jurisdiction has provided accurate notice of the final budgets and that its record of revenue raising, spending, and staffing is known and understood by the central budget office, the finance office, and the departments and their programs.

Allotments

Once the legislative body adopts the budget, departments may not be automatically authorized to spend against their appropriations. At the federal and state levels and in some larger local jurisdictions, the budget office prepares an allocation plan (i.e., **allotment**) that spreads spending authority for each agency or department over the fiscal year or biennium. Funds may be allotted on a quarterly, semiannual, or annual basis. Federal agencies and large state agencies also allocate funds to their major divisions and programs. Federal and state agencies more commonly use allotments and allocations than do local jurisdictions. This periodic release of funds serves several purposes:

- avoiding the premature exhaustion of funds;
- maintaining a balanced budget;
- preventing deficits; and
- diminishing the need for supplemental budgets or amendments.

Allotments can be of equal amounts over the course of the fiscal year or can be sized to follow historical or seasonal spending trends. Two examples demonstrate the effective use of allotments. Oftentimes, discounts can be realized by paying an insurance premium at the beginning of a fiscal year rather than in monthly installments. A lump-sum allotment at the beginning of the fiscal year would make such a discount available to a local government. Budget allotments can be used to provide funds to match variable levels of program activity. Forestry and natural resource management agencies must respond to wildfires during the hot, dry months of the year. Careful budget allotments provide funds for early season preparations, but then increase to high levels of funds to pay for wildfire suppression crews, heavy equipment operators, support logistics, and command teams. Allotment levels fall off during the wetter off-season months. As an additional control, funds can be allotted as a lump sum or allocated to a department or program based on one or more expenditure categories of related line-items. The fewer the categories within which funds are allotted, the more discretion departments have to adjust spending throughout the year.

Position Controls (FTEs)

The adopted budget normally identifies the number and types of positions authorized for each department or program. The budget office may review requests to fill new positions or to reclassify existing positions to ensure that adequate position and expenditure authority is available. These reviews, called **position controls**, are done not only to ensure authorization but also to guarantee that adequate funds are available for wages and benefits. This is particularly important during times of fiscal troubles, when hiring freezes may have to be imposed to protect against budget problems.

Appropriation Controls

Appropriation control is a form of line-item authority (chapter 11). State budget law normally spells out the level of appropriation at which a department head needs to seek permission from the legislative body in order to exceed a spending limit. Appropriation controls can be set at any level of spending category. For example, appropriation levels could exist at a department or fund level, or, alternatively, at a program or division level within the department. The higher the level of appropriation, the greater flexibility the department head has to manage the department's funds. For example, a department head could transfer $50,000 between two divisions if the appropriation control was at the departmental level because the division level is lower than that of the department.

The task of the budget office and departmental finance staff is to monitor departmental spending **outlays** to ensure that all resources are expended as planned and that appropriation levels are not exceeded without a budget amendment.

Encumbrance Controls

An **encumbrance** is a commitment of appropriated funds to purchase an item or service. Similar to **restricted funds**, when funds are **encumbered**, they are set aside or committed for a specified future expenditure. Encumbrances are established in the accounting system. For example, if a department executes a contract to purchase electrical repair services during the fiscal year, an encumbrance is established in the accounting system to show that the funds needed to cover the cost of the repair services have been designated for that future purchase. A department that encumbers funds avoids erroneously obligating the same funds for another purpose.

The encumbrance control prevents the overspending of accounts. When the department or program obligates or assigns funds for a purchase, the department business manager and central budget office recognizes a reduction in available resources. Accounting staff can then recompute the department's actual accumulated expenditures to date, its encumbered future commitments, and its remaining available resources.

BUDGET AND PERFORMANCE STATUS REPORTS

The three control measures described above help ensure that the departments stay within their budgets. To determine how well the controls and action plans are working, it is common practice for the central budget office or department finance staff to issue regular budget and performance status reports. These reports help managers and elected officials throughout the year to assess budgeted versus actual results, thus ensuring budgets remain within appropriation, and to monitor progress toward performance goals. Status reports can be prepared as frequently as needed but normally are prepared quarterly. The advent of online data entry for financial transactions allows instantaneous access to the report information, which lessens the delay and rigidity of a quarterly reporting, review, and oversight cycle

Three types of performance reports are normally prepared and periodically reviewed: (1) an expenditure budget status report, (2) a revenue budget status report, and (3) a performance status report. These reports are not substitutes for detailed accounting reports, but they provide information related to budget control and monitoring on a real-time basis.

Status reports demonstrate how the government is fulfilling its budget obligations and how revenues are flowing. Status reports also provide useful information to polity network members, including contractors, grantees, intergovernmental partners, and informal community nonprofit and foundation partners. Reports of substantial changes in governmental revenues, expenditure rates, or program performance allow network partners to compensate if necessary with other funding sources and staffing.

Expenditure Budget Status Report

The **expenditure budget status report** provides a periodic budget summary to managers. This summary serves two important purposes. It tells whether expenditure **outlays** for a particular budget category (such as a "fund" or a "department") are within the budgeted amounts, and it identifies how much money is still available for expenditure. The most common types of expenditure reports are the fund budget and the department budget status reports. They follow the same format and give the same information, the first at the fund level and the second at the department level. The following information may be provided for each expenditure category or line-item object code (e.g., travel) enumerated within the report.

- *Adopted budget:* This identifies the amount appropriated for each budget category for the specified fund. Within the appropriated amount, the adopted budget may bring forward any applicable encumbrances from previous fiscal years.
- *Amended budget:* If the legislative body or other authorized individual has amended the budget, this identifies the amended budget amount for this category of expenditure. In the federal budget system, a **supplemental appropriation** increases the funding to an agency, department, or program, while a **rescission** withdraws funding.
- *Expended through this period:* This identifies the actual expenditures through the reporting period (e.g., month or quarter). Exhibit 17.1 lists expenditures through the seventh month of the fiscal year (January 2012). This expenditure summary normally includes all encumbrances recorded in the jurisdiction's financial information system.
- *Percentage expended:* This category shows the percentage of actual expenditures for this period of the amended or adopted budget.
- *Budget remaining:* This category provides a summary of the amended or adopted budget amounts minus actual expenditures, including encumbrances for this period.
- *Percentage expended for this period in the last and previous fiscal years:* There are separate columns for each of these percentages. These last two columns provide valuable comparisons with prior fiscal years. If the percentage expended during the current year deviates significantly (e.g., 10 percent or more) from the two prior fiscal years, further review will need to be done to determine the cause. Significant deviations may be early warning signs that expenditures are running ahead of budget projections because of increased demand for services. In such a case, preventive measures need to be taken to avoid budget overruns.

Exhibit 17.1 provides a seven-month (fiscal year began previous July 1) expenditure status report for the departments and major programs within the general fund for the city of Chandler, Arizona. This type of report is prepared and submitted to the city council at the close of every month. The report displays the adopted budget for each department or program. The Expenses and Encumbrances column combines accumulated expenditures and remaining encumbrances to show what has been committed and/or spent to date.

This format provides a quick snapshot of potential underspending or budget overruns for the pending five months of the fiscal year. Exhibit 17.1 compares the current year period expenditures and encumbrances with those of the same period in the prior year. This is highlighted by showing actual expenditures as a percentage of total budgeted expenditures for the same period in both years—a method that provides a quick comparison to help decision makers determine whether spending is running ahead or behind the prior year. Only the current year shows the actual budget

Exhibit 17.1

Example General Fund Expenditure Summary

CITY OF CHANDLER GENERAL FUND EXPENDITURE SUMMARY
THROUGH JANUARY 2012

Department	Adopted Budget	Adjusted Budget	Expenses & Encumbrances Thru Jan 2012	Percentage of Adjusted Budget Expended & Encumbered Thru Jan 2012	Percentage of Adjusted Budget Expended & Encumbered Thru Jan 2011	Over/Under Last Year's Percentage
City Clerk	$ 560,098	$ 582,960	$ 303,008	52.0%	62.0%	-10.0%
City Manager and Organization Support*	15,041,173	16,463,634	8,946,833	54.3%	54.0%	0.4%
Communications & Public Affairs	2,217,658	2,509,840	1,197,930	47.7%	49.7%	-1.9%
Community Services	28,707,174	30,104,245	17,675,842	58.7%	59.3%	-0.5%
Fire	27,529,396	27,363,432	15,702,140	57.4%	53.7%	3.7%
Law	3,149,461	3,198,576	1,697,054	53.1%	55.3%	-2.3%
Magistrate	3,851,242	3,901,343	1,928,154	49.4%	52.8%	-3.4%
Management Services	5,856,855	6,092,883	3,219,342	52.8%	53.0%	-0.2%
Mayor and Council	784,017	800,630	422,334	52.8%	52.7%	0.0%
Police	56,907,724	58,324,289	33,753,311	57.9%	56.4%	1.4%
Transportation & Development	16,842,086	18,787,562	10,008,428	53.3%	58.7%	-5.5%
Non-Departmental (Personnel Services and O&M)	4,758,380	7,300,522	3,508,584	48.1%	34.9%	13.1%
Subtotal Prior to Contingencies/Reserves	**$ 166,205,264**	**$ 175,429,916**	**$ 98,362,960**	**56.1%**	**55.1%**	**0.9%**
Non-Departmental Reserves (Carryforward, Utility, Fuel & DT)	12,802,989	4,115,500	-	0.0%	0.0%	0.0%
Non-Departmental Contingencies (12% & Council)	19,832,074	19,268,888	-	0.0%	0.0%	0.0%
TOTAL	**$ 198,840,327**	**$ 198,814,304**	**$ 98,362,960**	**49.5%**	**48.4%**	**1.0%**

* Organization Support includes Information Technology, Human Resources, Economic Development and Neighborhood Resources

Adopted Budget: Includes estimated reserves for encumbrance carryforward from the previous fiscal year and full Council approved reserve/contingency established in the budget.

Adjusted Budget: Includes movement of estimated reserves for encumbrance appropriation to Departments based on actual end-of-year encumbrances and Council approved contingency transfers. Reserves/Contingency appropriation cannot be spent from Reserve/Contingency line items; it must be moved to spendable lines within Departments.

NOTE: The total Adopted budget compared to the total Adjusted budget always equals when viewing **all** funds. When looking at the General Fund only, it is not uncommon for the amounts to differ. This is due to estimated carryforward appropriation, personnel adjustment appropriation or Council approved contingency transfers being moved to other funds, as directed by Council authorized by the Budget Resolution.

and actual expenditures and encumbrances. The exhibit shows that the city clerk's expenditures have fallen by 10 percent as compared to the previous year. The clerk's office either has a smaller program or has increased efficiency to generate this reduction. In contrast, the nondepartmental category has increased by over 13 percent, while most other departments and programs are nearly the same as last year. Large increases or decreases in department or program expenditures can reflect many factors. A department may begin payments on a new service contract that will increase spending rates over the previous year. Completion and closure of a contract without a replacement will help to decrease spending. Improvements in productivity will help to lower spending rates. However, where program spending remains constant, changes in spending rates can indicate changing program demand or difficulties and delays in program performance.

Revenue Budget Status Report

Revenue budget status reports serve two important purposes. They tell how much revenue is actually being collected or accrued to the fund compared with the estimates developed for the budget, and they identify potential revenue shortfalls in time to make spending adjustments. The reports can present budgeted versus actual data similar to that presented in the expenditure budget reports. A comprehensive revenue status report might provide revenue data and comparisons for:

- amended budget;
- amount received through this period;
- percentage received;
- budget remaining;
- percentage received this period last fiscal year; and/or
- percentage received this period in previous fiscal years.

The sample revenue report in Exhibit 17.2 presents a more a comprehensive variation analysis by including historical and prior year comparisons. The historical comparison displays percent of budget spent in the same period over the prior three years. This allows the users to compare how well revenues are doing on a historical basis rather than just on an actual basis. Such a comparison is a better measure of whether revenues are running ahead of or behind in recent years and hence a better early indicator of whether the jurisdiction may fall short or exceed budgeted revenue targets by year's end.

The finance department normally provides this information for each current revenue source or other financing source (e.g., interfund transfer) that finances the fund. Fund balances typically are not included in this report because they have been set in the adopted budget, and they do not increase or decrease during the fiscal year. Fund balances are changed only at the beginning or end of the fiscal year.

As in the expenditure budget status reports, a graph or series of graphs can accompany the financial data in the revenue budget status report to help the reader focus on potential problems or opportunities. Retail sales and use tax revenues are a critical revenue source for most local governments and demand detailed reporting. Exhibit 17.3 reports local sales tax monthly revenue collections in tabular form. The chart compares the actual monthly collections from the previous fiscal year with the monthly collections to date in the current year. The year-to-date total collections (seven months) are aggregated on the bottom line. Year-to-year percentage differences are also displayed. Exhibit 17.4 presents a matched bar graph of the same information. The graph quickly communicates the year-to-year changes in monthly revenue collections.

Exhibit 17.2

Example General Fund Revenue Summary

CITY OF CHANDLER REVENUE SUMMARY

FY 2011-12 Year-To-Date Actuals Through January 2012

GENERAL FUND REVENUES	BUDGET		ACTUALS			COMPARISON TO PRIOR YEAR ACTUALS		
	FY 2011-12 Adopted Budget	FY 2011-12 Budget Prorated Based on Historical Trend	FY 2011-12 Actual Revenue YTD	+ or - of Actual to Budget Based on Historical Trend	% Change of Actual to Budget Based on Hist. Trend	FY 2010-11 Actual Revenues for Same Period	Difference + or (-) from FY 2010-11 to FY 2011-12	% Change of Actuals to Same Period FY 2010-11
Local Sales Tax Collections	$ 84,500,000	$ 50,563,138	$ 55,500,854	$ 4,937,716	9.8%	$ 49,417,222	$ 6,083,632	12.3%
Local Sales Tax Fees, Audit Assessments, Penalties, Interest	2,525,000	1,573,740	1,598,723	24,983	1.6%	1,842,730	(244,007)	-13.2%
Total Local Sales Tax Revenue	87,025,000	52,136,878	57,099,578	4,962,699	9.5%	51,259,952	5,839,626	11.4%
Franchise Fees	2,766,000	1,449,239	1,159,583	(289,657)	-20.0%	1,328,995	(169,412)	-12.7%
Primary Property Taxes	8,243,200	4,417,174	4,377,097	(40,077)	-0.9%	5,188,439	(811,342)	-15.6%
State Shared Sales Taxes	17,387,400	8,529,901	8,805,704	275,802	3.2%	8,292,346	513,358	6.2%
Auto Lieu Tax	7,962,700	4,005,290	3,957,831	(47,458)	-1.2%	3,745,336	212,495	5.7%
Urban State Revenue Sharing	19,929,800	11,625,920	11,624,881	(1,040)	0.0%	13,106,792	(1,481,911)	-11.3%
Licenses & Permits	3,302,000	1,754,208	3,716,168	1,961,959	111.8%	1,612,197	2,103,971	130.5%
Charges for Services	9,888,150	4,929,022	6,393,794	1,464,773	29.7%	5,316,680	1,077,114	20.3%
Fines & Forfeitures	3,615,000	2,012,708	1,785,141	(227,567)	-11.3%	1,855,154	(70,014)	-3.8%
Interest & Investments	1,700,000	956,070	366,138	(589,931)	-61.7%	864,978	(498,840)	-57.7%
Other Revenues	1,114,700	650,242	398,429	(251,813)	-38.7%	615,951	(217,523)	-35.3%
Indirect Cost	7,966,900	4,647,358	4,647,358	(0)	0.0%	4,705,692	(58,333)	-1.2%
TOTAL GENERAL FUND REVENUES	$170,900,850	$ 97,114,011	$104,331,701	$ 7,217,690	7.4%	$ 97,892,512	$ 6,439,188	6.6%
Prior Month	$170,900,850	$ 81,634,883	$ 88,376,430	$ 6,741,547	8.3%	$ 81,753,321	$ 6,623,110	8.1%
Change from Prior Month	$ -	$ 15,479,128	$ 15,955,271	$ 476,143	-0.9%	$ 16,139,191	$ (183,922)	-1.5%

479

Exhibit 17.3

Example Sales Tax Revenue Summary

City of Chandler Local Sales Tax Revenue
Monthly Actuals Compared to Prior Year

Local Sales Tax Collections	Monthly Collections FY10/11	Monthly Collections FY11/12	$ Difference +/(−) FY11/12 over FY10/11	% Difference +/(−) FY11/12 over FY10/11
July	$7,331,796	$8,322,663	$990,867	13.5%
August	$6,957,679	$7,862,658	$904,979	13.0%
September	$6,660,351	$7,544,324	$883,973	13.3%
October	$6,925,112	$8,265,131	$1,340,019	19.4%
November	$6,614,552	$7,180,223	$565,671	8.6%
December	$6,529,493	$7,272,209	$742,716	11.4%
January	$8,398,239	$9,053,647	$655,408	7.8%
February	$6,176,403			
March	$6,413,130			
April	$7,468,956			
May	$6,748,194			
June	$7,748,036			
YTD Totals	$49,417,222	$55,500,854	$6,083,632	12.3%

Exhibit 17.4

Example Sales Tax Revenue Graph (in millions $)

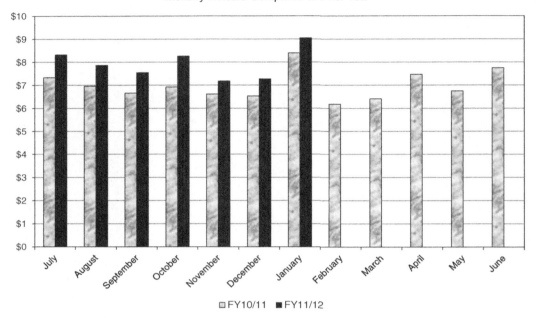

City of Chandler Local Sales Tax Revenue
Monthly Actuals Compared to Prior Year

□ FY10/11   ■ FY11/12

Cash Flow Status Report

Exhibit 17.5 shows a variation on the expenditure and revenue status reports previously presented. This report is a **cash flow status report**. The flow of property tax revenues, intergovernmental and grant payments, and other revenues often appears at different times in the fiscal year than the flow of spending. To make timely payments, the organization's finance office must accumulate sufficient resources for periods when expenses are paid. For example, property tax revenues might be received in May and November on a six-month interval, but public safety program expenses occur fairly evenly over the year. *Cash* is the resource from revenues and carryforward savings available to make payments. The adopted budget sets the planned levels of revenues and expenses for a fund or department at the beginning and close of the fiscal year or biennium, but the actual cash availability and flow may vary widely within that period. The cash flow status report shows the status of revenues and expenditures as well as other financing sources and the resulting available cash balance. These cash flow reports are particularly important in determining (1) when spending is running ahead of, behind, or on pace with available resources; (2) how much is available for investing and for how long; and (3) whether interfund or external borrowing is needed to bridge uneven cash flows during the fiscal year. Such information is the basis for effectively managing cash flow.

Monitoring cash flow is especially important toward the end of the fiscal year or biennium. Once resources have been spent earlier in the fiscal year, available cash becomes unavailable to meet unexpected last-minute expenses. In other instances, a failing economy may result in drastically reduced sales and income tax revenues late in the fiscal year, after expenses have been incurred.

If available cash and reserves are spent, and bridge loans are not available, the only alternative is to temporarily reduce program services, which can have a drastic effect on clients. Cash management and its timing becomes challenging because the adopted budget requires that all resources be expended by the close of the fiscal year or biennium.

The cash flow analysis in Exhibit 17.5 is a simplified example that shows the monthly cash balance forecast for a small but representative selection of the city of Chandler's budget funds. The city's general fund, several enterprise operating funds, debt service funds, and the medical self-insurance fund are listed. The report shows each fund individually and collectively. The analysis forecasts a snapshot of the fund balance on the first of each month. The difference between the monthly balances indicates the net change in cash balance from one month to the next (table bottom line). The monthly balances are projected based on the pattern of major receipts, encumbrances, and disbursements experienced in prior years. This information typically is downloaded from the jurisdiction's financial system at the close of each month. Major receipts include property, sales, and other tax revenues, fee and charge revenues, routine state intergovernmental payments, and other expected revenues. Disbursements include expected program expenditures, expected personnel wage and benefit costs, health care costs, retirement fund payments, expected contract and procurement expenditures, scheduled payments for encumbrances, debt payments, and leasing payments. Not included in this analysis are invested funds, which are tracked separately and can be drawn from—depending on their liquidity—to fill gaps in consecutive months of negative balances. Conversely, these cash flow projections can assist finance staff in determining when large sums of cash are available to invest and for how long.

Exhibit 17.5 forecasts that the city's general fund will begin the year at almost $166 million, but will fall to $132 million by the close of the fiscal year. The forecast implies falling revenues against stable or rising expenditures. The Water Operating Fund shows variation but forecasts a slightly higher closing balance at the end of the fiscal year. Higher revenues and increased efficiencies might explain this forecasted improvement. The Airport Operating Fund shows an expected drop from a zero-dollar opening balance to a $287,500 deficit. While this is a relatively small deficit relative to other funds, resources from other accounts such as the general fund may be needed to cover the shortfall. Finally, the Medical Self-Insurance Fund covers the cost of health care for employees and their dependents. The increasing balance in this fund points to limited revenues and sharply increasing costs. This is a cash flow report, not a budget status report, so variations at the beginning or ending periods are not necessarily an indicator of ending revenues and expenditures that have been accrued.

Like local governments, nonprofit organizations face a similar need to closely monitor their monthly cash flows (see Finkler 2010, chap. 7). A sufficient reserve of cash helps to cover basic expenses between major revenues, but an excessive reserve withholds needed resources from program clients and patients. Nonprofits build their budgets on the best available forecasts of revenues, cash reserves, and program levels, but donor pledged revenues may not materialize, new grants may appear unexpectedly, program operations may cost more than expected, or personnel may not be hired as planned. In some instances, donor payment policies exacerbate cash flow issues, including after-the-fact funding arrangements that make payment only after services are provided and billed; delayed fund delivery from donors; and delays from funders to continue previous programs (Dropkin, Halpin, and La Touche 2007). Nonprofit organizations should establish policies for managing working capital, modify their budgets when necessary to reflect new realities, and routinely forecast cash flows. Most important, nonprofit executives must identify cash flow issues early and then respond promptly and aggressively to solve potential problems. Delayed action often makes cash flow issues worse. The cost control activities described above for governments are often applicable to nonprofits, but nonprofits can adjust fee revenues and conduct additional fundraising efforts.

Exhibit 17.5

Example Cash Flow Status Report

City of Chandler Estimated Cash Flows for Selected Funds
Monthly Estimates for FY 2010–11 with Year-End Final Estimate

Fund	Actual Cash Net Balance 7/1/2010	Actual Cash Balance 8/1/2010	Actual Cash Balance 9/1/2010	Actual Cash Balance 10/1/2010	Actual Cash Balance 11/1/2010	Actual Cash Balance 12/1/2010
101-General Fund	$165,942,562	$168,864,360	$167,586,136	$134,763,393	$140,051,620	$141,041,337
605-Water Operating	25,038,430	26,196,497	28,861,517	30,730,176	30,851,364	33,350,830
615-Wastewater Operating	19,608,799	22,242,064	24,259,318	23,039,304	24,656,271	25,492,590
424-Parks Impact Fees	6,592,907	6,772,427	6,927,127	7,089,747	7,223,313	7,427,453
635-Airport Operating Fund	0	843	(6,927)	(32,842)	(43,728)	(60,413)
460-Police Bonds	1,847,342	1,847,342	1,453,063	1,454,222	1,049,522	915,495
310-GO Debt Service Fund	19,083,092	19,083,092	19,160,411	19,232,474	20,515,382	35,584,647
741-Medical Self-Insurance	5,361,952	6,193,638	6,763,034	6,556,766	6,192,576	7,743,891
Total Cash Balance	243,475,083	251,200,262	255,003,678	222,833,239	230,496,321	251,495,830
Net Change from Prior Month		7,725,179	3,803,416	(32,170,440)	7,663,082	20,999,509

City of Chandler Estimated Cash Flows for Selected Funds
Monthly Estimates for FY 2010–11 with Year-End Final Estimate

Fund	Actual Cash Net Balance 1/1/2011	Actual Cash Balance 2/1/2011	Actual Cash Balance 3/1/2011	Actual Cash Balance 4/1/2011	Actual Cash Balance 5/1/2011	Actual Cash Balance 6/1/2011	Year-End Final Estimate
101-General Fund	142,070,920	131,591,870	133,151,846	133,973,401	130,568,310	136,487,442	132,190,010
605-Water Operating	35,791,519	34,426,159	36,740,339	39,029,381	41,339,629	43,615,782	31,112,864
615-Wastewater Operating	25,144,186	22,217,994	21,356,499	20,184,902	18,946,869	17,410,822	3,915,914
424-Parks Impact Fees	7,631,311	7,683,307	7,736,637	7,789,698	7,842,494	7,895,556	7,948,529
635-Airport Operating Fund	(96,200)	(111,610)	(128,581)	(145,630)	(162,864)	(180,687)	(287,541)
460-Police Bonds	801,456	675,114	549,174	422,698	294,102	164,394	33,387
310-GO Debt Service Fund	39,833,872	33,607,905	34,088,285	34,734,316	35,878,811	39,984,965	15,378,529
741-Medical Self-Insurance	9,139,282	10,560,649	12,016,674	13,440,935	14,874,819	16,312,876	17,744,943
Total Cash Balance	260,316,347	240,651,388	245,510,873	249,429,702	249,582,171	261,691,150	208,036,636
Net Change from Prior Month	8,820,517	(19,664,959)	4,859,485	3,918,829	152,469	12,108,979	(53,654,514)

Performance Status Reports

Performance plans are a jurisdiction's plan for implementing strategic goals and objectives during the fiscal year (chapters 12 and 13). Unless these goals and objectives are presented within the budget document, **performance status reports** usually are internal reports. In these reports, the budget office will typically update the jurisdiction's progress toward meeting those goals and objectives by reporting on measures or indicators of success for key goals and objectives. Exhibit 17.6 provides an example of a performance status report.

Unlike budget status reports, performance status reports are usually done on a quarterly basis and may include the following kinds of information:

- *Goals and Strategies for the FY:* Enumerates a department's priority goals or strategies adopted for the fiscal year.
- *Target vs. Actual Completion:* Enumerates the actual performance level or indicator attained during the prior quarter in comparison to the targeted performance measure or level budgeted.
- *Notes:* Provides a brief explanation of any events or circumstances that resulted in the failure to achieve, or in the overachieving of, a particular performance level.

Exhibit 17.6 presents one page out of a much larger quarterly performance report for a large city government. In the full report, all city functions are measured and reported. This page details the Finance, Fire, Fleet Management, and Grants Monitoring & Administration functions. This format includes the annual performance target, the quarterly performance target, and the quarterly actual result. The few reported performance measures serve as indicators of broader program performance, including a measurement of program accomplishment toward the annual goal. Used in combination with a corresponding department or program quarterly expenditure status report, the performance measures report can indicate productivity rates. Reduced levels of performance with high levels of expenditure may indicate performance difficulties or inefficient processes.

BUDGET AND PLAN ADJUSTMENTS

Through regular monitoring of and reporting on the status of the adopted budget, cash flow and cash reserves, and action plans, the central budget office or department finance staff can obtain early warning of potential problems or opportunities during the fiscal year. The following situations, when discovered, trigger the need for adjustment:

- Budget authorization in danger of being exceeded (e.g., 90 percent of budget is spent by the third quarter of fiscal year).
- Revenue shortfall or overspending (e.g., license fees fall short of budgeted estimate).
- Significant delay or change in action plans or capital projects (e.g., a building project that may be delayed beyond the fiscal year).

The first two bulleted situations listed above have legal implications for a jurisdiction. The third may not pose legal problems, but it can have a significant bearing on the jurisdiction's credibility or capacity to carry out its mission. To avoid these situations (and otherwise act decisively before they create problems) requires different types of adjustments. A transfer of spending authority or a budget amendment may be called for, or the jurisdiction may need to impose spending cutbacks or modify an original budget or action plan in order to keep it on track with the department's goals and objectives. We describe four types of adjustments below.

Exhibit 17.6

Example Performance Measures

City of San Antonio Performance Measures		1st Quarter FY 2010	

Finance	Annual Target	1st Qtr Target	1st Qtr Result
Achieve composite score of 85 in the ability to plan, direct, monitor and control the financial resources of the City of San Antonio	85	85	85
Achieve composite score of 85 in accuracy, efficiency and timeliness of processing and recording financial transactions in support of the City's financial operations	87	87	77

Fire	Annual Target	1st Qtr Target	1st Qtr Result
Average response time to emergency incidents from dispatch to arrival (in minutes)	5.92	5.92	5.81
Percent of Customer Satisfaction rating for public education presentations and training sessions	98%	98%	96%
Percentage of all medical calls responded to by fire trucks/units	51%	51%	50%
Average number of Fire Prevention inspections performed per day per Fire Prevention Inspector	6	6	6
Percentage of time Advanced Life Support unit arrives on scene in 8 minutes or less	81.4%	81.4%	79.7%
Percentage of time first unit/ladder arrives on scene within 5 minutes	68%	68%	68%

Fleet	Annual Target	1st Qtr Target	1st Qtr Result
Perform at 95% technician efficiency for all Preventive Maintenance - Schedule A work orders for Police Cruisers	95%	95%	97.5%
Achieve a 100% notification compliance rate for all Preventive Maintenance	100%	100%	100%
Achieve and maintain 90% customer satisfaction rating	90%	90%	94%

Grants Monitoring & Administration	Annual Target	1st Qtr Target	1st Qtr Result
Provide advanced professional training for 50% of GMA Staff	100%	50%	50%
Conduct two monitoring reviews for each agency scheduled for compliance review	100%	25%	25%
Conduct quarterly performance reviews with each agency funded through the entitlement program	100%	25%	25%

Source: This example is drawn from the City of San Antonio, Texas, for the first quarter 2010. For 2012, San Antonio has enhanced its quarterly performance reporting with graphical displays. Performance reports for 2012 and earlier years may be found at City of San Antonio, TX 2013 (www.sanantonio.gov/Budget/Budget-Archives.aspx#311956-fy-2012).

Delegated Transfer of Spending Authority

A **transfer** of spending authority gives a chief executive or department head the legal authority to modify the budget and to transfer resources between accounts without formal approval from the chief executive or legislative body (e.g., council, commission, or board of directors). This type of transfer typically occurs between one or more departments, divisions, or programs, or between major expenditure categories (e.g., personnel/personal services) *within* a department's appropriation. It is used when the likelihood exists that the department's budget authorization will be exceeded. For example, if a department head has the authority to transfer funds between appropriations within the department, budget overruns can be avoided. Federal agency administrators often receive the same type of authority to **reprogram** resources under a specified amount and rule limitations from Congress.

Managers might initiate a transfer by a simple request to the budget office or through the financial information system if it has that capability. If the appropriation control level is at the departmental or fund level, a transfer may not be necessary so long as the control level is not exceeded at the end of the budget year. If local ordinance or policy does not give managers the authority to make such transfers, they will need approval and passage of a formal budget amendment by the legislative body.

Budget Amendments

The transfer of funds *between* budget appropriations or the approval of supplemental budgets requires a **budget amendment (amendment)**. Typically, local budget ordinances and appropriation language dictate when budget amendments are required and permitted. Legal provisions often govern the following:

- Dollar limits above which transfers will require legislative board approval
- Maximum dollar amounts that can be transferred
- The source for supplemental appropriations
- Vote of legislative body required to approve amendments (e.g., simple majority of those present)
- Requirement for public hearings, if any
- Cut-off dates for requesting budget amendments

State law may establish restrictions on budget amendments for local jurisdictions. However, more often than not, the appropriation ordinance adopted along with the local budget stipulates such restrictions.

Spending Cutbacks

When revenue shortfalls or overspending becomes severe, spending cuts may be necessary to avoid budget overruns and to preserve reserves. Imposing hiring freezes and spending freezes are two of the more common ways to prevent overspending during the budget year. **Hiring freezes** prohibit departments from filling vacant positions unless they can document (1) that the vacancy creates a threat to public health or safety; or (2) that external grant revenue or enterprise revenue funds the position. **Spending freezes** restrict departments from spending budgeted funds for certain categories of expenditures such as travel or equipment. Either of these freezes can be effective tools to prevent budget overruns, but they are normally used sparingly to avoid service or program disruptions. These tools remain available if a severe fiscal crisis develops.

Plan Modifications

Changes to operational and business/action plans may be needed as new or unforeseen events occur. Authority is often granted to the staff responsible for programs or projects to make plan modifications without requiring formal approval. Where the overall budget, scope of a project, or strategy is affected, managers need to have a method in place for notifying decision makers and stakeholders of any impending changes and for seeking formal approvals for changes. The responsible administrators should keep the legislative body (council or board) advised of evolving conditions and potential major program changes in a timely manner. For example, if the budget or scope of a capital project has to be modified because of an anticipated problem or event (say the site chosen for a new facility must be abandoned due to environmental problems that were uncovered subsequent to budget adoption), the method in place should include a mechanism for amending the capital plan and the related budget. This mechanism allows the budget oversight committee or the legislative body itself to approve changes to the scope of the project as long as they do not exceed the total appropriated for capital projects.

The ability to make changes in performance plans is normally much greater than is the case with changes to the operational budget or capital plan (CIP). As long as major goals or strategies (e.g., reduce juvenile delinquency through intervention programs) are not altered, the department responsible for program administration usually needs only to notify the legislative body of strategic plan changes. What is required in the way of notice is always governed by the conventions and political agreements of the moment. For example, a department that has recently gone through a highly controversial set of changes that have been fully vetted by the board will be treated differently than a department that has had no major changes in the past several years.

FINANCIAL AND PERFORMANCE EVALUATION

The last step in the budget execution cycle is to evaluate financial and program performance. The evaluation should be done after the final budget and performance data are available and before work begins on the next year's budget. The purpose of this evaluation is threefold:

- To determine whether the department's resources are adequate to sustain current service and program levels over the long term.
- To assess whether the department is achieving its strategic goals.
- To measure the outputs and results of programs and services.

The most effective way to conduct this evaluation is through an update and analysis to the long-range financial forecast and/or strategic plan and performance measures. We provide additional discussion of financial and performance evaluation as part of end-of-year external reporting in chapter 18.

Financial Forecast Updates

The central budget office normally provides updated financial forecast information to departments when the year-end data is available. Departmental-level staff use this information to identify potential budget gaps or surpluses in the second half of the fiscal year. If the forecast predicts budget shortfalls, staff must review a variety of measures that can be taken to avoid fiscal problems, including program or service reductions, increased efficiencies, and revenue enhancements.

Program or Service Reductions

These include cuts in service levels on a short- or a long-term basis. These service reductions may include:

- Deferred spending
- Across-the-board reductions
- Elimination of nonessential programs
- Reductions in programs and service levels (e.g., hours of operation)

Increased Efficiencies

These measures seek to save costs through one or more of the following combination of activities:

- Contracting out or privatizing a specific service or program
- Evaluating opportunities for applied technology
- Adopting energy conservation techniques

Revenue Enhancements

These activities focus on ways of increasing revenues, including:

- improving cash management and investment;
- identifying new revenue sources;
- reviewing and updating existing user charges and fees (making sure that they are competitive with those of neighboring jurisdictions and capture actual charges for service rather than what the market will bear or what other jurisdictions are charging); and
- assessing temporary tax or fee surcharges.

Strategic Plan Reviews and Updates

Long-term goals and strategies need an annual review to determine whether they are still relevant or require revision or elimination. Even successful strategies or goals need to be maintained or succeeded by other strategies or goals. The annual review is usually undertaken first by the division or program manager, followed by a review session with the department head. For each strategy or goal, weaknesses and strengths are identified and recommendations made regarding the strategy or goal's continuation, modification, or elimination in the next fiscal year.

Performance Measures Report

This is the final step in the budget and plan cycle. The budget or finance officer should do a year-end review and prepare a report of budgeted versus actual results for all output, efficiency, and outcome indicators if a performance budget or plan is prepared. The report should include an explanation of (1) major deviations from the adopted budget and (2) recommended changes to programs and services that attain improvements in the next fiscal year.

The completion of this last step in the budget and planning cycle sets the stage for the first phase of the cycle for the next fiscal year or biennium. The work invested in developing the financial and planning tools presented in this chapter will produce huge returns in future years as they are perfected and fine-tuned.

NETWORK AND COMMUNITY BUDGET EXECUTION AND PERFORMANCE

This chapter has described the budget monitoring and reporting techniques used at the organizational level by local government and nonprofits, but we have argued that public service program delivery often relies on a diverse array of contractual agreements, partnerships, and networked relationships. As with government and nonprofit organizations, issues of transparency and public confidence in government also apply to multimember service delivery arrangements. Partner organizations each contribute funds, staff time, and other resources to the multimember arrangement, and one or several members of the arrangement remains responsible for demonstrating two things: (1) effective service delivery accomplishment, and (2) the rationale for and advantages of the collective arrangement. Budget execution provides a tool by which collective arrangements can demonstrate their trustworthiness and value in delivering services to the community.

In the multimember collective context, budget execution returns to several basic themes: aggressive compliance with financial controls and transparency in spending; demonstrated performance and delivery on outcomes; and timely reporting with useful reports and performance indicators. Fulfilling these analysis and communication tasks becomes especially difficult in the partnership or network context because the internal control systems used within member organizations have limited reach beyond the organization's boundary. Effectively demonstrating financial compliance and task accomplishment performance requires data collection, analysis, and reporting at both the organizational and the collective levels. Reflective of the problems with using secondary data in research, aggregating organizational data to the partnership or network level is often difficult because of inconsistencies in member indicator variable definitions, data collection protocols, and report contents and formats. A joint commitment of staff time and resources, along with mutual agreement on definitions and report content, are necessary when developing quality financial controls, data collection, and reporting standards at the collective level.

Budget execution in the context of intergovernmental relationships is perhaps the most straightforward of the multimember arrangements. Each partner government follows its own budget process and contributes a defined share of resources to the joint project. The intergovernmental agreement should define these contributions. Each organization's financial and performance systems assure administrative accountability, and elected officials assure political oversight. For example, a small suburban city might purchase law enforcement service from the county sheriff. Oversight by the city council and the county board of supervisors would assure accountability through an intergovernmental agreement. Public complaints would also be handled by city administrators. Budgeting and financial reporting would follow the protocols established by each organization.

Contracted relationships between a local government and a nonprofit or for-profit provider are governed by procurement contracts and other formal agreements. These are a second group of multimember arrangements. Contracts and agreements provide the tools for program spending and performance reporting. Here, the service provider may engage a subcontractor, but responsibility often rests with the contracted primary provider for performance. Extended public-private partnerships are grounded in formal contracts but require extensive, positive relationships and informal controls for program success. In this context, local governments must follow transparent public procedures and reporting for budget execution. These provide a measure of accountability for the relationship, but the nonprofit or private party in the relationship remains a competitive actor with limited requirements for full disclosure of performance and productivity information (Cooper 2003). The contract or partnership agreement may specify the release of specific performance and productivity data by the private partner, but this may still leave some data undisclosed. High levels of trust and goodwill in the relationship may lead to informal controls and result in the release of additional information.

Organizations join a multimember network arrangement because membership generates benefits beyond the capacity of the individual organization (Bardach and Lesser 1996, 203). Network accountability should measure outcomes generated by both the full network and by individual members, with the recognition that optimal production by the full network may require suboptimal production by individual network members. Network members must be accountable to each other in order to generate excellent performance (Bardach and Lesser 1996, 204). Broadly, network members enforce accountability between themselves through formal and informal mechanisms (Bardach and Lesser, 205; Romzek, LeRoux, and Blackmar 2012), but the structure of member relationships within a network conditions the form and expression of accountability mechanisms (Robinson and Morgan 2014).

Provan and Milward (2001) recognize three aspects of network performance effectiveness. These include (1) external relationships to the community, (2) member relationships to the network as an entity, and (3) internal relationships between each member organization to the larger network. Issues of budget execution focus most heavily on two of these three aspects: The first is network external relationships with the community, which answers the question, Is the network delivering for the community, clients, and advocates? The second is network internal relationships as a measure of the value of the organization's participation in the network, which answers the question, Is membership worth the cost?

Informal-spontaneous networks (Isett et al. 2011; Imperial 2005) tend to have decentralized structures with members who have relatively equal power. Trust-based relationships form the basis of network production and administration. When such spontaneous networks generate enough momentum to become ongoing agents of change, the collection, sharing, and use of resources creates the need for a system of accountability. Such systems are normally governed by member resource contributions and member reporting requirements. Any network-level decisions and reporting are likely driven by group agreement, consensus, and informal enforcement mechanisms.

Participant-governed networks (Provan and Kenis 2007) also have decentralized structures and an equitable distribution of power across member organizations, but these networks have greater stability and permanence in the community. Member organization procedures, controls, and reporting requirements provide the first level of network budget execution. However, the network members must negotiate agreement on administrative procedures and commit resources to network-level data collection, financial and performance analysis, and monthly, quarterly, or annual reporting.

In the **lead-organization network** form (Provan and Kenis 2007), the lead organization typically dictates administrative procedures and reporting requirements for its contractors and partner members in the network. In networks with several lead organizations, this can cause conflicting expectations and multiple sets of reporting requirements for network members. To increase administrative efficiency, the lead organizations may negotiate out a common set of administrative and reporting requirements. For example, a state social service agency and a local intermediary organization may each provide substantial resources to provider organizations. The two leads might be able to agree on a common format for performance and financial analysis and reporting.

Networks led by a **network administrative organization (NAO)** rely on guidance from the NAO on financial controls and reporting (Provan and Kenis 2007). As an independent organization, the NAO has independent finances, which require annual budgeting, board oversight, budget execution, financial controls, and regular reporting. Regional councils of government organizations and most trade associations provide these types of administrative services. The NAO budget often represents both the administrative organization's operating expenses and members' contributions toward the network's larger mission and goals.

SUMMARY

Governmental and nonprofit budgeting remains a dynamic process throughout the fiscal year, and the different phases of the budget cycle are virtually always in play. Hence, managers and elected officials need ways to monitor, control, and adjust authorized revenue raising and spending to keep budgets in balance during budget implementation. The common devices for controlling spending are position controls, appropriation controls, and encumbrances. Periodic reports are prepared throughout the biennium or fiscal year to ensure that revenue raising and spending stay on target. If adjustments are needed, budget transfers or amendments typically are employed. If economic and financial conditions change dramatically, spending cuts or tax increases may be used to maintain a balanced budget. Before the end of each fiscal year, program and financial performance reports at the organization, partnership, and network levels are commonly used to assess the changes needed for the next budget.

STUDY QUESTIONS

1. What factors ensure that the budget remains a dynamic process following its adoption?
2. What mechanisms are used to control and monitor the budget during the fiscal year? Who is responsible for exercising these controls?
3. What are some of the major reasons for amending a budget?
4. What purposes do expenditure and revenue status reports serve? What type of information is typically presented in those reports?
5. What devices are employed to adjust budgets? Which of those devices require formal involvement of the governing body?
6. What steps might a department take to stay within its budget if spending looks like it will exceed its authorized level?
7. Consider an intergovernmental network or a public-private service delivery network in your community. Research and reflect on network-level budget execution and reporting.

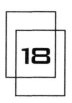

AUDIT AND PERFORMANCE EVALUATION

MARTHA SCOTT*

Performance by another that entails consistency, competence, and reliability is likely to enhance greatly the likelihood of the development of a relationship of trust.

(Valerie Braithwaite 1998, 52)

Seattle Lax in Tracking Federal Grants, State Auditor Concludes.

(Lynn Thompson, *Seattle Times,* 2012)

Massachusetts Auditor . . . Cites Wrongdoing by Former Official at Springfield Technical Community College.

(Dan Ring, *The Republican,* 2012)

State Auditor Implicates Ex-PUD Employee.

(Paul Gottlieb, *Peninsula Daily News,* 2012)

Some level of citizen skepticism and distrust in government has existed since the founding of the American Republic (chapter 3). Over the past two decades, trust in government organizations has declined considerably, owing in part to the kind of performance issues reflected in the opening extracts. While many factors have contributed to this decline in citizen trust and confidence in government, an important primary trust criterion is dependable technical performance (Braithwaite 1998, 47). Demonstrated compliance with financial reporting standards, clean audits, compliance with contract and grant requirements, and meeting performance expectations all stand as demonstrations of dependable institutional and administrative performance.

Administrators from program directors to department heads to the chief executive officer (CEO) make key contributions to ensuring financial performance, program performance, and reliable communication with elected officials and the public. In addition, the information generated through the end-of-year financial and audit processes provides the data necessary to support the budget development process and its related decision making. Financial and performance audits verify the information provided by an organization and validate the efficacy of its internal systems, which reinforces opportunities to build citizen trust.

With demands for increased accountability from citizens and elected officials over the past decade, local governments have improved budgeting procedures, implemented more detailed budget requirements, and increased monitoring of budgets throughout the fiscal year. In addition, many governments have expanded year-end reporting to include both financial and performance reporting. Currently, most state statutes require annual independent audits of all local governments,

---

*Martha Scott, CPA, MPA, is the retired Controller of the City of Portland, Oregon.

and expanded audit procedures have been mandated by federal statutes for those organizations that receive federal funding. These required reviews by third parties help build confidence in government and provide assurances that government is acting in the best interest of its citizens.

In this chapter, we will discuss common year-end accounting and reporting processes in local governments and the audits that follow the year-end process. First, we begin with a discussion of the year-end accounting process, including an overview of common year-end tasks. Second, we discuss year-end financial reports, including the comprehensive annual financial report (CAFR) and year-end performance reports. Third, we provide an overview of the various types of audits, including financial audits, single audits required by federal grantor agencies, and performance audits. We also provide a summary of the year-end and audit process for nonprofit agencies.

THE YEAR-END CLOSE OUT AND FINANCIAL REPORTING PROCESS

While state and local governments monitor revenues and expenditures periodically throughout the year (chapter 17), the final phase of the budget cycle takes place at the end of the fiscal year, when the government closes the accounting records. Year-end budget adjustments that increase or reduce budgeted amounts or transfer resources between funds generally must be approved by the legislative body prior to the end of the fiscal year. Though most unused budget allocations expire at fiscal year end, some governments have the option to carry over certain budgetary items prior to year end, or to reestablish budgeted amounts for the next fiscal year.

In addition, local governments are required to submit an annual financial statement to meet the statutory requirements within a prescribed amount of time after the end of the fiscal year. For a small organization, this annual report may be limited to cash basis (see chapter 9 for further information on cash basis accounting) reporting of revenues and expenditures by fund and a separate expenditure report for any grants received. For larger governments and nonprofits, statutes often require more complex reporting and most large governments choose to prepare a CAFR. Though many of the technical tasks involved in closing the fiscal year and preparing the CAFR are completed by the finance or accounting office, there are a number of tasks that are the responsibility of department or program staff.

Year-End Tasks and Adjustments

Ideally, departmental and program staff should review monthly departmental financial reports (chapter 17), identify any errors that have taken place during the month, and make the required adjustment to the records prior to receiving the following month's reports. This periodic monitoring ensures that revenues and expenses have been charged to their proper categories and are properly reported. In reality, this review may be delayed until year's end, allowing errors to accumulate and go uncorrected for several months. This makes the year-end review of departmental reports a much larger task.

Performance of year-end tasks and adjustments helps ensure that year-end records are accurate and that year-end financial statements meet accounting standards. Year-end adjustments can vary between governments; however, a number of adjustments are common across all organizations. To facilitate the year-end process, the finance or accounting department typically sends a memo to the departments and programs with end-of-the-year closeout instructions. This memo includes a list of required tasks and a schedule of due dates. Common tasks on this schedule include the adjustments detailed below.

Adjustments for Payroll Cutoffs

Payroll and payroll-related expenses for governments often constitute two-thirds of total expenses. Thus, governments and programs must accurately report these expenses on year-end reports.

Year-end payroll account balances often need to be adjusted to accurately reflect these expenses. Generally, employee timesheets must be submitted several days prior to payday to allow time to process the payroll. For organizations that pay employees monthly or semi-monthly with payroll cutoffs at the end of each month, no year-end payroll adjustments are usually required. However, for employers that pay employees weekly, biweekly, or using a delayed cutoff, a year-end adjustment is usually necessary to split the paycheck paid in the new fiscal year into the portion worked before and the portion worked after the end of the fiscal year. This adjustment allows accurate reporting of payroll costs in the correct year. Assistance from department payroll staff may be required to provide the information needed to make these adjustments.

Purchasing Cutoffs

One area where actual activities may differ from budgeted activities is in the area of purchases made close to the end of the fiscal year. Regardless of when purchases are budgeted, accounting standards require that goods or services be received by the government prior to the end of the fiscal year in order to be charged to the current year's budget. Goods and services received after the end of the fiscal year must be charged to the new fiscal year's budget. To facilitate this process, most government purchasing departments publish a schedule of purchasing cutoff dates to ensure that purchases made close to the end of the fiscal year will be charged as intended. Departmental and program business staff often need to communicate with program managers and other employees to encourage them to comply with purchasing cut off dates established by central purchasing departments.

Accounts Receivable/Billing Cutoffs

Accounts receivable refers to those amounts owed to the local government by outside individuals or organizations for the purchase of goods and services. Similar to the purchasing cutoff requirements, accounting standards require that billings for goods or services provided by the government be billed in the year in which the goods or services were provided. Billings for goods or services provided after the end of the fiscal year must be recorded in the new fiscal year. Department staff may be required to review departmental records to identify unbilled amounts.

Grant Expenditures and Billings

Organizations that receive federal grants or other grant funding must be especially careful at year's end to ensure that grant expenses are recorded in the year that the grant activity takes place and within the period allowed by the grant agreement. Additional information on year-end grant requirements is covered in the "Single Audit" section later in this chapter.

Petty Cash, Purchasing and Credit Card Reconciliations, and Travel Reimbursements

For those organizations that use petty cash accounts, purchasing or credit cards, or employee travel reimbursements, the finance office normally establishes a cutoff date designed to ensure that these types of expenses are processed in the year in which they were incurred. Departmental staff often need to communicate with their program managers and other employees to encourage them to submit these types of transactions for processing in a timely manner.

After the Fiscal Year Ends

Deadlines for year-end budget adjustments and reporting vary depending on state statutory requirements for local governments; however, the year-end adjustments and preparation of the year-end financial reports usually continue for weeks or months beyond the end of the fiscal year. While the year-end process continues, the newly adopted fiscal year's budget has been recorded in the government's financial records and ongoing programs continue to operate in the new year (see chapter 5). As the finance department completes the year-end processes, the normal budgetary and accounting procedures for activities in the new fiscal year must also be processed. In Exhibit 18.1, we provide an example of the importance of year-end budget adjustments and reporting and the potential adverse consequences when established procedures are not followed.

Exhibit 18.1

The Importance of Accounting Cut-Offs

The transportation staff in the hypothetical city of Upper Cascadia were delighted that they were finally going to be able to construct a major new interchange in town. The construction would add additional lanes, redesign the interchange to improve safety, and reduce congestion as the town continued to grow. The project was funded in large part by federal transportation grants with additional funds provided by local transportation fees. Design work for the $23.9 million construction project was completed and actual construction began in the fall of 2011. The contractor billed the town quarterly based on progress reports submitted to the town engineer. For some unknown reason, the progress reports at year-end were delayed and the quarterly billing of $1.9 million was not processed until several months after the end of the year. Though the town accounting staff sent several emails to all departments reminding them to get their year-end invoices to accounting within 60 days after year-end, the quarterly billing for the interchange construction was not processed until after the accounting records were closed and the financial statements finalized.

During the annual audit, the audit staff performed a common audit procedure to identify unrecorded liabilities and found that the $1.9 million payment to the contractor should have been recorded in the prior year. This error resulted in an audit finding for inadequate internal controls, which was included in the audit report and was reported to the federal granting agency. The federal government will consider this negative finding in any of the town's future grant applications and may categorize the town as a "high risk" applicant, which would subject it to increased audit requirements and extra costs. While clean audit reports are seldom reported by the local press, negative audit findings are almost always covered by the media. Public awareness of unfavorable audit findings contributes to the loss of citizen trust in local governments.

ANNUAL FINANCIAL AND PERFORMANCE REPORTING

Though statutes vary from state to state, virtually all local governments are required to prepare a year-end financial report and various other required year-end schedules. A **schedule** is a supporting set of calculations, data, information, or analysis that shows or amplifies how figures in financial statements are derived (e.g., your personal federal income tax return is a set of schedules). The standards for the preparation of these reports are **generally accepted accounting principles (GAAP)**, which are established by the **Governmental Accounting Standards Board (GASB)**. Some smaller jurisdictions have the option, based on population or revenue thresholds, to prepare less complex reports, generally on a cash basis. While cash basis reporting can reduce audit costs and simplify report complexity, reporting in accordance with GAAP promotes fiscal accountability, transparency, and consistency of practices across multiple organizational and jurisdictional boundaries. The more comprehensive GAAP standards allow citizens to better evaluate a government's financial status or position, and GAAP-level reporting is often required to meet federal grant requirements.

The Comprehensive Annual Financial Report

We have previously identified the budget and accounting funds as the primary unit of government budgeting and financial management (chapter 9). This focus on individual funds highlights program and departmental spending but does not allow users to easily view the financial status of the organization as a whole. The **comprehensive annual financial report (CAFR)** solves this problem and integrates a fund-focused view with a consolidated reporting view of the entire government and all of its funds. The report includes a reconciliation between these two views. The fund accounting view mirrors the budget funds structure introduced in chapter 9, and it demonstrates that fund resources have been spent in accordance with statutory and budgetary restrictions on the use of public funds. The fund level view places a focus on the current budgetary cycle, one fiscal year, or a biennium if applicable. The fund reports are prepared using the **full accrual basis** of accounting for proprietary-type funds, and the **modified accrual basis** of accounting for governmental-type funds, consistent with the types of transactions and events reported in those fund types (see chapter 9).

In contrast to the fund view, the consolidated or government-wide view provides a broad overview of a government's finances separated into governmental activities and business-type activities. This view has a long-term focus. Governmental activities are those activities that are financed through taxes, intergovernmental revenues, and other nonexchange revenues. These activities are reported in the general fund, special revenue funds, debt service funds, capital project funds, and permanent funds. Business-type activities are those activities financed in whole or in part by fees charged to external parties for goods and services. Business-type activities cover revenues for utility services, including water, sewer, and electric services, which are normally reported in enterprise funds. The government-wide reports convert all data to the full accrual basis of accounting, which provides a broad overview of government finances. The "notes" to the financial statements give additional disclosures necessary to provide a complete picture of the information presented in the statements. Exhibits 18.2 and 18.3 display sample government-wide reports for the hypothetical city of Upper Cascadia.

The statement of net assets in Exhibit 18.2 provides a snapshot of the financial position of the hypothetical city of Upper Cascadia as of the last day of the fiscal year. The statement is classified into major groupings of **assets, liabilities**, and **net assets**. Assets represent the value of resources and investments held by the city. Current assets include financial resources of cash, investments, and expected revenues from taxes, fees, intergovernmental sources, grants, and internal payments. These assets are typically readily available as unrestricted current assets. Saleable inventories of goods and equipment are a less available form of asset, but these could be sold relatively quickly for cash. The total current assets line in Exhibit 18.2 indicates that Upper Cascadia has a total of $19.6 million in current assets. It is important to note that a portion, but not all, of the current assets are available to spend on liabilities as they come due. For example, receivables cannot be spent until they have been received. Inventories and capital assets cannot be spent unless sold. A group of current restricted assets is available in cash and other liquid forms, but these may be used only for specified purposes.

Governments, especially cities and counties, frequently have large investments in capital assets such as land, buildings, vehicles, and electric, water, or sewer infrastructure, which will probably never be sold and converted to cash. These are denoted as noncurrent assets. According to Exhibit 18.2, Upper Cascadia has $132.2 million in capital assets. Upper Cascadia's assets of all kinds total $151.8 million.

Exhibit 18.2

Example Statement of Net Assets

CITY OF UPPER CASCADIA
STATEMENT OF NET ASSETS
12/31/20XX

	Governmental Activities	Business-Type Activities	Total
ASSETS			
Current Assets (unrestricted):			
Cash	$9,669,239	$148,405	$9,817,644
Investments	3,032,697		3,032,697
Receivables			
Taxes	522,440		522,440
Intergovernmental	3,520,603		3,520,603
Accounts	1,893,785	177,715	2,071,500
Internal balances	3,522	(3,522)	0
Inventories	34,182		34,182
Deferred charges	175,844		175,844
Current Assets (restricted):			
Cash and investments	313,063		313,063
Receivables			
Accounts	42,152		42,152
Grants	75,483		75,483
Total Current Assets	19,283,010	322,598	19,605,608
Noncurrent Assets:			
Capital assets, not being depreciated	13,229,076	98,004	13,327,080
Capital assets, net of accumulated depreciation	109,688,748	9,196,190	118,884,938
Net Capital Assets	122,917,824	9,294,194	132,212,018
Total Assets	142,200,834	9,616,792	151,817,626
LIABILITIES			
Current Liabilities (payable from unrestricted assets):			
Accounts payable	2,200,000	67,644	2,267,644
Accrued liabilities	1,009,911		1,009,911
Accrued interest payable	402,785		402,785
Unearned revenue	314,547		314,547
Bonds payable	1,350,000		1,350,000
Current Liabilities (payable from restricted assets):			
Accounts payable	1,594,000		1,594,000
Total Current Liabilities	6,871,243	67,644	6,938,887
Noncurrent Liabilities:			
Notes payable	241,902		241,902
Bonds payable	38,000,000		38,000,000
Total Noncurrent Liabilities	38,241,902	0	38,241,902
Total Liabilities	45,113,145	67,644	45,180,789
NET ASSETS			
Invested in capital assets, net of related debt	81,360,747	9,294,194	90,654,941
Restricted for:	0		
Parks endowment fund-nonexpendable	313,063		313,063
Unrestricted	15,413,879	254,954	15,668,833
Total Net Assets	$97,087,689	$9,549,148	$106,636,837

The statement of net assets in Exhibit 18.2 also lists the jurisdiction's liabilities. Liabilities are the debt or claims the city must pay to vendors, partners, investors, and others. Liabilities match the three categories of assets: current liabilities payable from unrestricted assets; current liabilities from restricted assets; and noncurrent liabilities. This last category includes capital debt for major infrastructure purchases. So while Upper Cascadia has just over $132.2 million in capital assets, it has liabilities for future principal repayment on bonds of $38.2 million. At year's end, Upper Cascadia has more assets than liabilities in both their governmental- and business-type activities, which results in a positive figure in both restricted and unrestricted net assets. The fact that both restricted and unrestricted net assets are positive is one indication of a healthy financial position.

The statement of activities in Exhibit 18.3 provides a summary of the activities of the hypothetical city of Upper Cascadia for the 12-month period ending December 31 of the fiscal year (or for 24 months for a biennium). The presentation focuses on the programs and departments operated by the city, and it provides a summary view of program revenues and expenses for each. This type of report is related to departmental revenue and general fund revenue breakout described in Exhibit 9.1. For each program, Exhibit 18.3 details the expenses incurred. The report then details program-generated revenues, including charges for services, grants revenue, and other contributions. The three columns on the right detail the net of program expenses less program revenues. For example, the parks and recreation department spent $1.63 million and had departmental revenues of $1.02 million, which left a negative net **balance** of $613,091. This negative net amount required support from the city's general fund (general revenues). In contrast, we can see that the water department is self-supporting with fees and grant revenues exceeding expenses by about $51,914. Aside from the water department, the other programs require some support from general revenues in addition to revenues generated by the program.

At the organizational level, this statement also shows that total revenues exceeded expenses for the business-type activities (a positive $11,521), but that total expenses for the year exceeded revenues for governmental activities (a negative $385,671). The bottom line is that total expenses for the city were more than total revenues, which resulted in a decrease in net assets from the end of the prior year (column on the far right, a negative $374,150). During the budget development for the next year, city elected officials and managers will want to consider this negative trend and create a budget that will either slightly cut spending or increase revenues to increase the total net assets for the following year. In addition to the organizational level statements presented above, the CAFR includes detailed information on each individual budgetary fund.

Most governments post several years of CAFRs on their website to enable citizens and other users to have easy access to financial information about the government. As with the Distinguished Budget Presentation Awards program mentioned in chapter 9, the Government Finance Officers Association has established a Certificate of Achievement for Excellence in Financial Reporting program (GFOA 2013c). This program identifies and rewards local governments that go beyond the minimum requirements of generally accepted accounting principles to prepare CAFRs that evidence the spirit of transparency and full disclosure.

Generally, the end-of-year final budget to actual spending comparisons (chapter 17) for individual funds is included in the CAFR. However, the location and presentation of these reports varies depending on (1) whether the fund had a legally adopted annual budget, (2) the size of the individual funds, and (3) the legal level of budgetary control. Smaller governments that use a cash budgetary basis, which is different from GAAP, may need to convert their accounting to the GAAP standards for reporting. Some of the year-end adjustments to report transactions in accordance with GAAP may result in unexpected overspending. For this reason, department staff should carefully monitor monthly budgetary reports late in the fiscal year to develop an awareness and understanding of how the year-end adjustments may impact budget to actual reporting.

Exhibit 18.3

Example Statement of Activities

CITY OF UPPER CASCADIA
STATEMENT OF ACTIVITIES
FOR THE YEAR ENDED DECEMBER 31, 20XX

Functions/Programs	Expenses	Program Revenues			Net Revenues (Expenses) and Changes in Net Assets		
		Charges for Services	Operating Grants and Contributions	Capital Grants and Contributions	Governmental Activities	Business-Type Activities	Total
Governmental Activities:							
Parks and recreation	1,635,514	272,661		749,762	(613,091)		(613,091)
Community development	2,241,062	489,934	574,468		(1,176,660)		(1,176,660)
Public safety	8,804,243	189,173			(8,615,070)		(8,615,070)
Legislative and support services	1,163,683	97,487			(1,066,196)		(1,066,196)
Transportation	42,227,879	1,299,973	15,676,752	364,361	(24,886,793)		(24,886,793)
Interest on long term debt	1,601,756			67,925	(1,533,831)		(1,533,831)
Total governmental activities	57,674,137	2,349,228	16,251,220	1,182,048	(37,891,641)	0	(37,891,641)
Business-Type Activities:							
Sewer	351,151	199,308				(151,843)	(151,843)
Water	334,562	227,429		159,047		51,914	51,914
Total business-type activities	685,713	426,737	0	159,047	0	(99,929)	(99,929)
Total Primary Government	$58,359,850	$2,775,965	$16,251,220	$1,341,095	(37,891,641)	(99,929)	(37,991,570)
General revenues:							
Property taxes					36,569,603		36,569,603
Investment earnings					398,723	3,064	401,787
Miscellaneous revenues					641,127	4,903	646,030
Transfers					(103,483)	103,483	0
Total general revenues and transfers					37,505,970	111,450	37,617,420
Change in net assets					(385,671)	11,521	(374,150)
Net Assets, beginning					97,473,360	9,537,627	107,010,987
Net Assets, ending					$97,087,689	$9,549,148	$106,636,837

Most governments have a central accounting or finance department that is responsible for the preparation of the CAFR. In a centralized organization, this department may perform all of the tasks necessary to complete the CAFR. In a more decentralized organization, departmental staff may assemble much of the data and prepare some of the supporting information required for the CAFR, with the central accounting staff performing a quality control function for the information provided by departmental staff. As an example, in decentralized organizations, departmental staff often prepare schedules of accounts payable and accounts receivable accruals to identify items billed but not yet paid or revenues earned but not yet billed at year's end. Departmental staff also may reconcile interfund billings between departments; perform fixed asset inventories to validate accounting records for buildings, equipment, and infrastructure and prepare related fixed assets schedules; and prepare unrecorded liability schedules to identify payments owed to vendors but not yet billed. Regardless of the level of centralization, departmental staff should review all fund reports for their department funds for accuracy and reasonability prior to completion of the CAFR.

Annual Performance Reports

In addition to preparing year-end financial statements, some governments that use the program and performance budgeting techniques previously discussed in chapters 12 and 13 prepare **Service Efforts and Accomplishments (SEA)** or other year-end performance reports. We also discussed a monthly version of SEA reports in chapter 17. These reports communicate the actual performance results and compare them to the expected goals and objectives identified during the budget development process. Used in conjunction with the financial information provided in the financial statements, this report provides a more comprehensive view of the efficiency and effectiveness of government operations. The Governmental Accounting Standards Board (GASB 2010), Government Finance Officers Association (GFOA 2011a), International City/County Management Association (Ammons 2008), and others have issued guidelines for reporting performance information, but currently there is no recognized standard for this type of reporting. In addition, the federal government has been implementing performance management for several years in response to requirements established by the Government Performance and Results Modernization Act of 2010 (GPRA Modernization Act 2010). This act requires federal agencies to prepare and display strategic plans on public websites, establish performance indicators to measure progress toward performance goals, and report performance regularly to responsible federal agencies (see chapter 13 for an additional discussion of these issues).

The GASB has identified four essential components for effective SEA reporting:

- A statement of the purpose and scope to convey what portion of a government the report covers and why the performance information is being reported.
- Identification of the major goals and objectives related to the programs and services included in the report.
- Key measures of SEA performance identified by the government that reflect the government's efforts toward achieving the identified major goals and objectives.
- A discussion and analysis of the factors that affected the level of achievement of the results and the government's plan for the future.

To complete the program and performance budgeting cycle, governments should incorporate the data reported in the year-end performance report into the development of budget priorities for the following year (chapter 17).

Current Issues and Challenges in Financial Reporting

Timeliness of Reporting

To be of greatest use in the development of the next year's budget and to better assist decision makers, bondholders, and investors, year-end reports must be available as soon after year's end as possible. There has been a growing movement to encourage governments to provide annual financial information more quickly after the end of the fiscal year. A recent survey by the Association of Government Accountants (2012) found that state and local government comprehensive annual financial reports are typically issued six months after the close of the fiscal year. In contrast, federal agencies issue their year-end financial reports 45 days after the end of the federal fiscal year, but the federal reports include less information than the CAFR. Since the CAFR includes the formal audit opinion, to issue the local CAFR more quickly, governments would also have to be able to complete the audit process sooner. Reducing the time required to produce the CAFR would increase work pressures and audit costs for thousands of state and local governments.

The U.S. Securities and Exchange Commission (SEC) has also expressed a need for more timely financial reporting from local governments that issue municipal bonds (chapter 16). An SEC analysis (U.S. Securities and Exchange Commission 2012) of the municipal securities market indicates that by the time municipal financial statements are available to investors and the public, the reported information is too stale to provide an accurate picture of the particular government's current financial status. Since investors depend on this information to make informed investment decisions, having access to current information is critical for building investor confidence. Fortunately, municipal securities have significantly lower default rates than corporate or foreign government bonds, but municipal securities occasionally do default, with resulting negative impacts on investor confidence in the larger local municipal bond market.

A faster year-end financial reporting process would likely increase preparation and audit costs and would necessitate significant changes to current government processes. The changes would be especially difficult for decentralized governments that depend heavily on department and program staff to assemble year-end data and prepare year-end schedules.

Proliferation of Accounting Standards

Since its inception in 1984, the Governmental Accounting Standards Board has worked to improve accounting and financial reporting for governments. To that end, the GASB has issued new accounting requirements each year. These new requirements routinely entail an analysis of current organizational accounting practices by state and local government staff. While the new requirements are designed to provide greater fiscal transparency and improve consistency of treatment in financial statements, some governments question the benefit of these new standards. Smaller local governments that use cash basis accounting often do not have an adequate staff to prepare reports in accordance with generally accepted accounting principles (GAAP). These smaller governments will be less able to comply with accounting requirements as they become more complex. In contrast, driven by the recent revenue challenges surrounding the public sector, some governments have developed creative enterprise business solutions that drive a need for new current accounting treatments. These complex governments would benefit from a more timely response to these immediate needs.

AUDITS OF LOCAL GOVERNMENTS

An **audit** is an examination of an organization's financial, grant, or performance records or reports to determine the validity or reliability of the information reported. Given the need for accountability and legal compliance in local government, the audit takes on special importance. Through the audit process, governments are able to meet the demand for oversight and control by elected officials and public-sector managers. Audits also confirm the reliability of financial reports, show compliance with legal requirements, and demonstrate quality performance. Audits are generally classified as either financial or performance based. Financial audits are performed by independent, external auditors employed by either private firms or state audit offices and focus on the reliability of financial reports. Performance audits are often performed by internal auditors who are employees of the government and focus on the efficiency and effectiveness of government operations. In Washington State, state agency auditors routinely conduct both financial and performance audits of local governments.

Most audits, regardless of type, follow a standard protocol that includes an entrance conference; a phase of gathering and analyzing data; an assessment of the soundness of **internal controls** and business systems; testing of internal controls to ensure proper operation; periodic discussions with management regarding preliminary observations; preparation of draft and final reports, with opportunities for management to respond to the draft report; and follow-up during future audits to determine if issues have been resolved. The quality and efficacy of an organization's internal controls is a critical aspect of a financial audit. Internal controls are an integrated set of policies and procedures established by the organization to ensure reliable financial reporting, effective and efficient operations, and compliance with applicable laws. The length of time required for the audit will vary depending on the size and complexity of the government and the number of auditors assigned to the engagement.

Financial Audits

The focus of the **financial audit** is to provide users of financial reports with assurance that financial statements are accurate and can be relied on by citizens, managers, and credit rating agencies. This reality conflicts with a commonly held belief among the general public that the purpose of an audit is to find fraud. While new audit standards designed to increase fraud detection were established following the Enron and WorldCom scandals, the fact is that no matter how strong an organization's internal controls, fraudulent department managers and elected officials can always override them.

Audits of state and local governments are controlled by two sets of standards: Generally Accepted Auditing Standards (GAAS) issued by the American Institute of Certified Public Accountants (AICPA 2012) and Governmental Auditing Standards (commonly referred to as the *Yellow Book*) issued by the federal Comptroller General of the United States (2011). While GAAS applies to audits of both private and public organizations, *Yellow Book* standards apply only to governmental audits. These standards establish the general framework of the audit and provide guidance for audit planning and communications, risk assessment, fieldwork, and audit reporting.

State statutes vary as to whether the annual financial audit must be performed by audit staff from a state audit office or can be performed by appropriately trained auditors employed by local audit firms. As of 2009, 34 states had state audit organizations that audit local governments, including school districts (22 states), counties (24 states), cities (17 states), towns and villages (18 states), and nonprofit/for-profit organizations receiving federal/state funds (11 states) (National Association of State Auditors, Comptrollers, and Treasurers 2009). The remaining states rely on local private-sector audit firms. During the audit, the audit team members review the organization, evaluate internal controls over financial transactions, analyze transactions and account balances, and issue a report that expresses the auditor's opinion on the accuracy of the financial statements. A clean audit opinion will state that the financial statements of the organization are free from material misstatements and are prepared in accordance with generally accepted accounting principles

(GAAP). If there are **audit findings** included in the report, the report will identify areas where the organization's financial statements deviated from GAAP or where the organization needs to improve its internal controls. Audit findings need to be corrected prior to the next audit.

Many governments have an audit committee of citizens and elected officials whose members are independent of the management of the organization. This committee is responsible for hiring, evaluating, and retaining the independent auditor and overseeing the audit process. While the audit committee oversees the audit, the government's finance or accounting office has the primary responsibility for coordinating the audit and working with the independent auditor during the audit. The accounting office provides audit staff with access to electronic files and documents required for the audit and coordinates auditor requests for information located in other government departments.

The audit process includes the application of a number of analytical procedures that independent auditors tailor to meet the needs of the government being audited. Audit standards require that the audit staff review internal controls over budget planning, preparation, adoption, execution, and reporting. In addition, the audit generally requires that the auditor evaluate compliance with state statutes governing the budgetary process and determine whether budgets have been prepared and adopted in compliance with those requirements. Depending on state statutes and the way the budget to actual reports are presented in the CAFR, the audit may include a detailed analysis of the budget to actual comparisons presented, including an explanation of any significant variances identified. If the organization has a process in place for regular monitoring and amending budgets, this analysis is usually straightforward. If not, it can be complex and can require significant work by both finance and departmental staff.

In response to the WorldCom and Enron financial scandals, Congress passed the American Competitiveness and Corporate Accountability Act of 2002 (Sarbanes-Oxley Act; SOX). This act requires publicly traded corporations to (1) increase internal financial and accounting controls with personal certification by the chief executive and chief financial officers, (2) increase external controls through enhanced audit committee responsibilities and auditor independence, and (3) support evidence protection and whistleblower protection. Though Sarbanes-Oxley applies only to the publicly traded firms, the impact of the act has been much broader. Several states apply Sarbanes-Oxley–type requirements to nonprofits. California became the first state to adopt state-level accountability controls with the California Nonprofit Integrity Act of 2004. New Hampshire recently passed a law in 2004 requiring nonprofits with revenues in excess of $500,000 to submit audited financial statements with their IRS Form 990s, the annual IRS report required for organizations exempt from income tax. Maine, in 2004, and Connecticut and Kansas in 2005, passed similar laws. No new legislation has been introduced that would impact local governments directly, but some audit firms have been warning government entities that special interest groups and oversight agencies can be expected to take a closer look at their practices in the current environment (Gentry 2008).

Federal Single Audits

Local governments and nonprofit organizations often receive substantial financial assistance in the form of grants from the federal government. As recipients of federal financial assistance, these organizations are subject to additional audit requirements of the federal Single Audit Act of 1996. In general, those organizations that expend $500,000 or more per fiscal year in federal funds must have an audit performed in accordance with the requirements of the Single Audit Act. Proposed federal regulations would raise this limit to $750,000 (U.S. Office of Management and Budget 2013). The act adds an additional layer of testing and reporting requirements to the GAAS and *Yellow Book* standards discussed earlier. Recipients of federal awards are required to:

- maintain internal controls over federal programs to ensure compliance with grant requirements;
- comply with federal laws and regulations applicable to its awards;
- prepare year-end financial statements;
- prepare the year-end Schedule of Expenditures of Federal Awards (SEFA);
- monitor subrecipient activity; and
- follow up and take corrective action on audit findings.

Grant compliance requirements vary depending on the type of grant and the granting agency. The different requirements are identified in the federal Office of Management and Budget (OMB) Circular No. A-133, *Audits of States, Local Governments, and Non-Profit Organizations* (2007), which is often supported by an annual compliance supplement (U.S. Office of Management and Budget 2012). However, OMB published final guidance rules in December 2013 describing extensive changes to the administrative requirements, cost principles, and audit requirements for federal grants. Federal agencies are responding to this guidance by promulgating new conforming regulations that are scheduled to take effect in December 2014 (U.S. Office of Management and Budget 2013). Since many governments receive grants from multiple federal grantor agencies, it is important that departmental staff who work in grant-related programs are familiar with compliance requirements for each of their grants and that they monitor compliance during the grant period. During the audit, audit staff will identify and evaluate compliance with each set of compliance requirements based on information and documentation provided by program staff. In addition, the audit staff will evaluate the effectiveness of internal controls over federal programs and review the SEFA for accuracy.

One area of confusion concerning grants relates to subrecipient grantees. Grant subrecipients are local governments or nonprofits that receive federal funds through another agency to carry out the activities of a federal program. The pass-through agency may be a state government agency, a county government, or it may be another local government. The subrecipient organization uses the pass-through funds for actual program service delivery. It is the responsibility of the pass-through entity to inform the subrecipient organization of the grant requirements and to monitor the subrecipient organization to ensure compliance with laws, regulations, and the provisions of contracts or grant agreements. Depending on the size and number of the grants received, the subrecipient may also be required to have an audit done by a qualified auditor. Alternatively, the firm that audits the pass-through agency may be permitted to perform additional audit procedures on the subrecipient organizations.

Since most federal grants are provided on a reimbursable basis, any delay in processing requests for reimbursement can cause cash flow problems for the government (chapter 17). Many governments have a central grants department within their finance office that coordinates grant applications, federal reports, and reimbursement requests. If such a department exists, staff from that department can provide valuable assistance and support to program staff assigned to grants. Other governments rely on departmental staff to complete grant applications, federal reports, and reimbursement requests. It is important that program staff understand the processes in place in their organization and ensure that these important tasks are completed promptly and in accordance with federal requirements. Exhibit 18.4 provides an example of the audit process for pass-through grants and the implications of errors in tracking financial transactions that are grant funded.

Performance Audits

Performance audits measure program performance and make recommendations for ways to improve the program. The focus of the audit can be an entire organization, a single department, or an activity or function within or across departments. Generally, the audit evaluates the depart-

Exhibit 18.4

The Impact of Disallowed Grant Expenditures

The hypothetical city of Upper Cascadia received federal Community Development Block Grant (CDBG) funds to assist low-income homeowners with the installation of weatherization and other energy saving projects. The city contracted with a local nonprofit agency, Energy Savers SE, to perform energy assessments, identify qualified homeowners, arrange low-cost financing, and select local contractors to install the upgrades. Homeowners applied to the city and, once approved, received the energy assessment free of charge. Energy Savers SE staff processed the applications and performed the energy assessment. Based on the energy assessment, Energy Savers SE staff prepared an estimate of potential weatherization costs and expected savings and worked with homeowners to select a contractor and obtain financing. The grant contract specified that the nonprofit bill the city monthly to reimburse the actual costs of the program. The city began receiving applications from homeowners for processing by Energy Savers SE in the spring of 2011. In March 2011, Energy Savers SE began billing the city for $200,000 monthly to reimburse for costs incurred by the program. Energy Savers SE continued to bill the city $200,000 each month through the end of the project. During the annual audit of the city of Upper Cascadia, auditors noticed that the city was being billed the same amount each month to reimburse Energy Savers SE for costs related to the Energy Efficient Block Grant and requested documentation to support the monthly billings. Energy Savers SE staff was unable to produce such documentation and told audit staff that they based the billings on a prorated share of the total grant and that they were unaware that they needed to provide documentation of actual costs. Audit staff worked with Energy Savers employees to determine the actual cost for each month of the program from the Energy Savers SE financial records and determined that Energy Savers SE had been paid a total of $43,765 more than the actual costs incurred by the program. In addition to generating an audit finding, the city was required to repay the unsupported amount to the federal granting agency.

ment or activity in terms of the economy and efficiency of operations, effectiveness in achieving desired results, and compliance with relevant policies. Examples of performance audits include: an identification of services that can be reduced or eliminated; an analysis of a new or ongoing program to determine if it meets program objectives; an analysis of services to identify gaps or overlaps in programs or services; a review of the cost effectiveness of alternative methods of service delivery; or an analysis of departmental performance data, performance measures, and self-assessment systems.

Standards for performance audits come from two sources, the federal *Yellow Book* (Comptroller General of the United States 2011) and the Institute of Internal Auditors (IIA) (2013). While the *Yellow Book* includes standards for both financial and performance audits, the IIA *International Standards for the Professional Practice of Internal Auditing* establishes standards for internal audits, including local government performance audits. Similar to the standards for financial audits, these standards establish requirements for staff qualifications, auditor independence, field work, and reporting for performance audits.

Performance audits can be performed by an in-house internal audit organization, by an external state audit organization or contract auditor, or by a combination of internal and external auditors. Twenty-five states mandate performance audits of state agencies or local governments by a state audit organization (National Association of State Auditors, Comptrollers, and Treasurers 2009). In medium- to large-sized governments, internal auditors are usually employees of the government they audit. They report either to an elected or appointed official and are independent from the activities they audit. An internal audit department becomes part of the internal controls of the organization and provides information to management to help improve government operations. In some states, state auditors have the statutory responsibility and authority to carry out performance audits of state agencies and local governments. Depending on the state, these audits may respond to the concerns of citizens, management, or elected officials. Those organizations without an internal audit function and no access to a state audit function may choose to contract with outside auditors or specialized consulting firms to provide required performance auditing expertise. In contrast to financial auditors, performance auditors usually focus on a specific department or activity. Performance auditors typically work directly with departmental staff to obtain information. The required information varies, depending on the goals of the audit, but often auditors will want to review organizational charts, department policies and procedures, process flowcharts, program performance data, and financial reports.

The organizational structure of the audit department and the process for identifying the focus of a performance audit may be established by statute or based on other criteria. In local governments, the internal audit departments may report directly to the mayor, to the elected council, to an audit committee, or to an elected auditor. The organizational structure has a major impact on the way the audits are selected and whether performance audits are politically or professionally motivated. If the audit department reports to the elected officials, audits tend to be more politically focused on those areas that respond to constituent concerns and further the political agendas of the elected officials. If the audit department reports to an elected auditor or to an audit committee, audits tend to focus on those areas that will increase the efficiency and effectiveness of individual programs and of the organization as a whole.

Year-End Reports and Audits of Nonprofit Organizations

The year-end and audit processes for nonprofit organizations are similar to those described above for state and local governments in many ways, but there are some important differences. Each state defines nonprofit organizations differently, and the reporting requirements in each state reflect these differences. Nonprofits are required to file an annual federal IRS form 990 (for organizations exempt from income tax), and most states require nonprofits to also file an annual financial report with the state agency that oversees nonprofit organizations. Some states allow nonprofits to complete the basic part of the required state form and attach the form 990, but each state has its own requirements. Nonprofits must establish year-end cutoffs and procedures identical to those described earlier for state and local governments.

Nonprofits do not publish CAFRs; rather, they publish consolidated financial statements. These statements are similar to government financial statements but focus on the restrictions placed on donor contributions and on the use of these contributions. Expenses are divided between program and support services and are shown for each program. The nonprofit financial statements may consist of the basic reports required by state statutes for a small organization. A large nonprofit may prepare a comprehensive consolidated financial statement including the audit report, explanatory information about the organization, detailed financial statements, and detailed notes to the financial statements.

In certain circumstances, federal, state, or grantor agencies may require nonprofits to provide audited financial statements annually or as part of grant application processes. As audit requirements have increased and driven up the cost of audits, smaller nonprofits may want to consider not having an audit or having a different kind of audit that provides a lower level of assurance. However, organizations that receive $500,000 or more in a single year in direct or pass-through federal funds are required by law to have an audit, as discussed in the Single Audit section above (pending $750,000 limit; U.S. Office of Management and Budget 2013). Depending on the size of the organization, smaller nonprofits might be able to use a financial review or other agreed-upon audit procedures in lieu of a full audit. Another alternative might be to provide the form 990 to financial statement users as a substitute for an audited financial statement.

In contrast, larger nonprofits such as hospitals, colleges, and major foundations may choose to have a complete audit, even if not required to do so, to provide greater transparency and accountability to contributors, governing boards, and the media. Many of these same organizations have voluntarily, or in response to the new state requirements, adopted practices required of public companies by the Sarbanes-Oxley Act.

In many communities, the availability of federal grant funds is a major driver in the development of a complex network of funding that involves federal, state, and local governments; nonprofit service providers; and local vendors. The federal government works in partnership with state agencies and local governments to establish criteria and standards for awarding funds to local governments and nonprofit service providers. Local governments and nonprofits may in turn contract with other nonprofits or vendors to provide services to recipients. In these instances, the federal government and the pass-through government act as network lead organizations that define the internal controls and audit standards for a large segment of a community's service delivery network. Based on the flow of federal funding, federal grant audit standards have become widely known among nonprofit financial and administrative professionals (Farris 2009). Any negative audit reports by a subrecipient may have adverse consequences on the pass-through organization and its audit record.

SUMMARY

In this chapter, we have discussed the year-end and financial statement preparation process and annual audit as the final steps in the budget process. Together, these procedures work to communicate a positive message to citizens that government employees and elected officials are competent and can be trusted to protect public assets and use public money as intended. This message, together with the financial information generated at year-end meets the accountability and transparency needs of citizens and elected officials in the twenty-first century.

STUDY QUESTIONS

1. Consider the government or nonprofit programs in your experience. What year-end procedures do they have in place?
2. Consider the government or nonprofit programs in your experience. What type of year-end financial statements and annual performance reports do these organizations issue?
3. Consider the government or nonprofit programs in your experience. Do these organizations have an annual audit? What does the audit report include?
4. Consider the government or nonprofit programs in your experience that receive federal grant funds. Select a grant. What federal regulations apply to one of the federal grants received by the organization?
5. How might the year-end financial statements for a small nonprofit like a local hiking club differ from the financial statements for a major social or youth services provider?
6. How does year-end information in a local government contribute to the annual budget development process?
7. Consider the government or nonprofit programs in your experience. How do these organizations develop, use, and report performance information?
8. Consider the government or nonprofit programs in your experience. How might the Sarbanes-Oxley requirements apply to these organizations now or in the future?

19   LOCAL BUDGETING FOR THE COMMON GOOD

The purest form of political expression in a representative system of governance is the adoption of a budget.

(Mike Gleason 2013, retired city manager)*

We will work in a collaborative, powerfully aligned way with our partners—in business, in the foundation community, in local and state government, and in the community at large—to solve systemic and increasingly complex human services issues in the face of growing local and state government resource constraints.

(United Way of King County [UWKC] Strategic Plan 2010)

MAJOR THEMES REVISITED

In this final chapter, we revisit the major themes of this book with an eye toward their implications for the key budgeting issues that will face local governments and communities in the foreseeable future. Rather than attempt a grand synthetic summary, we draw from the various topics, themes, and substantive budgeting information we have covered in the separate chapters of this text to shed light on these issues.

Throughout the book we have emphasized the following eight themes.

1. Local Government Uniqueness and Wide Variation

There is considerable variability in local governing structures of authority, and they have an important influence on both the process and outcomes of local public budgeting.

2. Governance Context for Budgeting, Revenues, and Finances

Local budgeting is seriously constrained by financial conditions and the legal framework that structures the types of revenue that are available for budget allocation.

3. Administrative Behavior and Discretion

Given the part-time role of most elected officials in local government, career administrators are positioned to play a central role in the budget development, approval, and implementation process. This unique position, however, heightens their moral responsibility for understanding the competing core values that are essential for making our systems of constitutional democracy work and the role that all of the participants play in America's mixed economy. Administrators balance numerous ethical and political pressures in the role of a Democratic Balancewheel.

---

*This chapter was coauthored by Mike Gleason, local government city and county administrator for 30 years (now retired) and local government consultant for the past 20 years.

4. America's Mixed Economy and the Implications for Coproducing the Public Good

America's complicated mixture and interdependence of organizations in the government, for-profit, and nonprofit/civic sectors requires those responsible for local public budgeting to have an understanding of why, how, and to what end budgets are viewed and used by the respective coproducers of the public good.

5. Citizen Confidence in Budgeting and Taxation

Citizens play a critical role in shaping the legitimacy and success of local public budgeting because of America's system of decentralized control over revenue generation and budget allocation.

6. Polity Budgeting for Networks and the Community

America's legal tradition of local control and sectoral differentiation among the government, for-profit, and civic/nonprofit sectors creates an opportunity for career public administrators to play a synergistic role in integrating and coordinating the allocation of resources among the sectors to maximize the achievement of the common good.

7. Multiple Budgeting Systems and Purposes of Control

Over the decades, multiple and sometimes conflicting budgeting systems have been created with systems of control that depend increasingly on the expertise of various career professionals (auditors, program managers, executive-level administrators). These multiple systems have heightened tensions not only among the sometimes competing systems and their purposes but also between experts and career professionals on the one hand, and the elected officials and citizens they serve on the other.

8. Mastering the Language of Budgeting

Throughout this text, we have emphasized the importance of knowing how to read budgets and understand what they mean. This is not because we expect our readers to become professional budgeters (although our text provides rich opportunities to master such skills for those who have these aspirations), but because there are essential rules of syntax and grammar associated with the world of public budgeting and finance that are as important to understand as the syntax of languages is important for acquiring linguistic competence.

In this final chapter, we will extend the core themes of the previous chapters to explore two key challenges that will confront those responsible for local public budgeting in the decades ahead. First, local elected officials and executives will be pushed to use the budget process to achieve goals that are beyond its capacities. Continued scarce resources in the face of public concerns for performance and accountability will press officials to use the annual budgeting process to undertake a combination of the following initiatives: resolving major policy issues, establishing performance analysis systems, initiating organization reform processes, and framing organizational- and community-centered strategic planning efforts. The budget process can contribute useful information and organization to these other processes and functions, but it cannot substitute for them.

Second, citizen concerns over taxation, excessive government, and "getting their money's worth" require a polity-centered approach to local budgeting. Budgets structured solely on local government jurisdictional authority once provided sufficient financial and performance accountability. But with the increased reliance on extensive service contracting and partnerships, what has been called new public governance (NPG), this control has vanished. Continued reliance on the traditional organization-centric perspective obscures the reality of public service delivery. For these reasons, we have argued for a polity-centered approach to public budgeting that takes into account the complex interactions of civil society, intergovernmental arrangements, and service delivery networks of nonprofit and for-profit providers. We have argued throughout the book for an extended perspective of public budgeting applied at the network level. However, insightful budgeting at the network level opens up numerous issues that need to be addressed, including joint capacity, coordination, responsiveness to tensions between local and regional needs, and accountability of the regional governance and provider systems. These are governance issues that require separate policy and planning initiatives and governance systems to resolve. But, in performing their annual budgeting processes, government and nonprofit officials will continually bump up against the challenges of ensuring control, accountability, and performance from complex and extended service delivery arrangements. Public budgeters will face these challenges for decades to come.

In addressing these two challenges, it is important to remember an underlying budget reality that is common to both challenges and, in fact, frames the problematic of local public budgeting throughout this book: how to manage and coordinate multiple budgeting systems. Local budgeting over its many decades of evolution has grown increasingly complex as its goals have been expanded and diverse professional competencies have been added to support the achievement of these goals. As we observed in Part III, the budgeting process initially was formalized in order to maximize fiscal accountability. This system requires the competence of auditors and accountants.

But other kinds of accountability grew in importance, requiring the addition of different knowledge and skill sets to the budgeting process. For example, effectiveness requires the expertise of program specialists and analysts who have the substantive knowledge to understand how to articulate meaningful operational program goals and to link these to tactical management plans to achieve them (see chapter 12).

Other budgeting systems focus on efficiency, which starts with the knowledge of program specialists who can articulate operational goals, but ends with cost accountants who can track expenditures and compare the outcomes of various program initiatives with what it costs to obtain them (see chapter 13). Still other systems seek to incentivize innovation and the search for better ways of addressing public problems and achieving established goals (see chapter 14). The system established to achieve this kind of accountability requires different processes and competencies than is the case for financial control-oriented, efficiency-oriented, and effectiveness-oriented budgeting systems.

Layer after layer of systems have been added to the budgeting process: planning systems (chapter 10), capital budgeting systems (chapter 16), expenditure control and performance systems (chapters 17 and 18). These multiple systems require considerable expertise by professional career administrators to manage and coordinate. But these management- and expertise-centered systems ultimately must be carried out in the service of the political goals of the community as these find expression through the local political process. This local political system is the first among equals of the various systems that professional career administrators must coordinate and manage in partnership with the elected officials and citizens they serve. In small jurisdictions and those with part-time elected officials, career public servants play a critical facilitative and educational role in enabling elected officials to successfully carry out their supervening fiduciary and oversight responsibilities of the budget development, approval, and oversight processes. But behind this outer political layer that most citizens equate with local public budgeting stands a complex and interdependent infrastructure of sub-budgeting systems.

In the sections that follow, we discuss two major tensions that arise out of the need to balance the sometimes competing goals of various budgeting systems and subsystems. We believe these tensions will grow in importance in the decades ahead. The first section focuses on the tendency to try and use the political system that produces an adopted budget to address issues that really require resolution by other processes. The second section focuses on the consequences of the misalignment between the structures of political authority around which budgets are currently organized and the complex networks of public intergovernmental, private, nonprofit, and for-profit service providers that coproduce the public good. This lack of alignment in a scarce resource environment will require a polity-centered approach to budgeting, not a jurisdictional-centered approach. In each of the next two sections, we will first identify the major characteristics and parameters of the challenges and then offer some strategies that can be used to mitigate them. Together, our discussion of future local budgeting challenges and mitigating strategies constitutes our crystal ball vision of what the future world of local public budgeting might look like.

ALIGNING THE PURPOSES OF A LOCAL PUBLIC BUDGET WITH ITS POLITICAL FUNCTION

In this section, we return to our opening epigraph and argument that a local government budget document, and the political process that produces and adopts it, creates the most significant and binding declaration of collective action that a community can make. This declaration is more a political act than a technical one. And it is the legal demarcation that differentiates public government service from nonprofit and private-sector enterprise. This is because a government budget is a binding social contract between those who govern and those they serve. Once adopted, the budget becomes a codified legal document that compels action. It is enforceable in a court of law, and it is an authoritative political force. Once it is grafted into its parent organization as a tangible act of political will, budget managers have a fiduciary obligation to honor both its intent and expressed declaration. The process by which a budget comes to fruition represents both the gas pedal and the steering wheel of democracy. As a steering wheel, it establishes the discretionary boundaries within which administrators can pursue the policy goals agreed upon as being most appropriate by the community through their elected representatives. As a gas pedal, it provides the energizing authority to pursue those goals as robustly, effectively, and efficiently as possible.

The budget document adopted by local governing bodies can be used to serve a multitude of purposes, some of which are more compatible with the fundamental political nature of the budget-making process than others. One of the reasons that the budget reforms we discussed in Part III of this text have largely failed at the state and federal levels of government is that the budget-making process at those levels has been used to address challenges that are either poorly suited to the political purposes of a budget or are more managerial than allocative in nature. For example, problems of program effectiveness, management efficiency, and interjurisdictional collaboration/coordination are better left to nonbudgetary discussion forums. These issues and problems include:

- Improvements in management structures and processes;
- the examination of human resource recruitment, training, and deployment;
- a consideration of how data information, collection, use, and evaluation can be used to improve the delivery of public services;
- ongoing dialogue among intergovernmental service providers as to how they can coordinate the delivery of public services to reduce costs, increase effectiveness, and build citizen trust and satisfaction; and
- conversations with the network of civic and nonprofit organizations as to how coordination might improve the amount and quality of services provided in the local community.

   Pressures to use the budget to achieve management goals will not go away; in fact, they are likely to increase. Elected officials will find "improved performance" an attractive agenda to ameliorate citizen concerns about big, expensive, and inefficient local government. What can career administrators do about this? The fortunate answer is that they are in a legal and functional position to resist the inappropriate expectations placed on the budgeting process. First, with part-time elected officials who have no staff, career administrators have a unique opportunity to play a critical educational role among both elected officials and the larger political community. But to perform this role, career administrators must fully understand and defer to the political primacy of the budget development, approval, adoption, and oversight processes. This means that they are public servants who must subordinate their own agendas to the political wishes and desires of their elected superiors. Second, career administrators must take the initiative in using their management expertise to address issues of performance (i.e., productivity, efficiency, and effectiveness). And, finally, they must take the lead in norming the mutual role expectations of the administrative staff, elected officials, and the larger community through the preparation of critical guidance documents. We will elaborate more fully on each of these strategies in the sections that follow.

THE BUDGET IS A POLICY DOCUMENT
THAT DEFINES THE PUBLIC GOOD

Borne out of local politics, a budget is primarily a policy document. Once adopted, it provides political guidance to the governing agency's managers and legally authorizes the organization to begin administering service operations. By definition, the adopted budget represents the most current and complete statement of public purposes for which that particular governmental agency is responsible. The budget gives concrete meaning to the public interest. In fact, one can argue that local public budgeting is the only political context in which the public interest is not an abstraction but a fact of day-to-day governing.

   In Exhibit 19.1 we provide a comprehensive list of 85 public goods and services that we have identified in our research and which are provided by the various 89,400 governments within the United States.[1] These products and services are nested within 13 macro or overarching public systems. This product and service list was compiled after examining the chart of accounts representing a complete range of government organizations (states, counties, special districts, municipalities, school districts, metro-area governments, and the federal government). There are only 6 categories of services that are exclusively provided by the federal government, with the remaining 79 governmental products and services provided by state and local jurisdictions. Although the federal government has just 6 exclusive service roles, it is a major player in the majority of the other 79 products and services through policy guidance, financial support, and procurement and contracting regulations and provisions.

   What emerges is a complex tapestry of service producers woven around and through the daily lives of 320 million citizens. The common thread for all of these 89,400 governmental agencies is the budget process, which codifies and authorizes the delivery system. While the exact number and methods for categorizing these services can vary depending on the goals and purposes of the task at hand, for our purposes we developed an outline that represents the common elements of the public process found within the budgets of these government agencies. These 85 products and services will be found in the accounting tables and the chart of accounts that make up the architecture of the budget reporting documents. The 13 macrosystems under which the 85 products and services are nested represent the major categories of work and organization that governments use to classify job duties.

   Exhibit 19.1 does not represent an organizational chart or even an operational map. It implies nothing about who should provide these services, nor does it represent a comprehensive list of

Exhibit 19.1

Summary of Public Goods and Services

Courts
- Adjudication
- Prosecution
- Public defense
- Records and warrants
- Appellate review

Education
- Facility operation
- Research and development
- Publications
- Educational instruction maintenance

Emergency operations
- Planning and training
- Assessment
- Response teams and operation centers
- Rehab and repair

Fire operations
- First responder
- Prevention
- Special teams
- Training and certification
- Water supply management
- Communications

Governance
- Organizational management and administration
- Voting operations and regulations
- Long-range planning and forecasting
- Tax collections and regulations
- Financial and budgetary operations
- Policy and research analysis
- Intergovernmental relations
- Governing board administrative support
- Public records and citizen input

Incarceration
- Facilities operation
- Diversion
- Parole and probation

Park cultural services recreation and open space
- Land and facilities operations
- Museums, cemeteries, and historical sites
- Libraries and document repositories
- Arts and cultural amenities
- Public assembly facilities and spaces
- Recreation programming
- Open-space management

Police operations
- Administration
- Patrol and prevention
- Investigations
- Training and certification
- Records and evidence control
- Special teams
- Dispatch and emergency communications and coordination

Planning and economic development
- Business regulations
- Market development
- Industrial regulation and market support
- Land-use planning and regulations
- Housing supply and regulations
- Infrastructure planning and private integration
- Public health
- Facility operations
- Safety inspections
- Product regulation and testing
- Immunization
- Epidemiology
- Research and development

Social services
- Grants and provision of various forms of social insurance
- Emergency shelters
- Food and income support
- Emergency medical aid
- Social behavioral interventions
- Mental health

Transportation
- Public transit
- Roadbed construction and repair
- Heavy rail and freight regulation
- Air system
- Water transport
- Private conveyances regulation
- Pipeline conveyances

Utilities
- Electrical supply and distribution
- Water supply and distribution
- Wastewater treatment and collection
- Stormwater treatment and collection
- Natural gas regulation and distribution
- Right-of-way regulation and control
- Solid waste collection and treatment
- Energy research development and regulation

Unique federal authorities
- Interstate commerce services and regulations
- Regulation of the commons (airway, bandwidth, etc.)
- National defense and security
- International relations treaties and agreements
- Money coinage, supply, treasuries, and commercial regulations
- Judicial enforcement of federal laws and U.S. Constitution

services that are being provided to the community as a whole by various nongovernmental entities. It represents only the most common rhetorical dialogue among the public, political, and organizational players that finds expression in the local public budget process. This public service political map explains the service types, but it does not explain the organization that produces the products and services. The determination of which providers in the governmental, for-profit, or nonprofit sectors produce which product, or parts of a product, is idiosyncratic to the geographical location and sometimes to the citizen who is using the product or service. What is common is that the end user will receive and recognize the vast majority of these services at the local level. And, it is the locally elected official to whom they will generally take their demands and grievances, even when the service is provided by a contracted third party. That is why some scholars argue that local elected officials "cannot escape from their fellow citizens," and why these officials make the most important decisions about the "matters of direct and compelling interest to the mass of citizens" (Elkin 2004, 55). The former Speaker of the U.S House, Tip O'Neill, drove this point home when he quipped that "all politics is local." In making these local decisions, elected officials cannot dismiss the interconnections between the claims of various interests and the larger interests of the local community. For all these reasons, local elected officials must, as Elkin suggests, think constitutionally.

At the heart of thinking constitutionally is the tension between what is considered a matter of individual freedom and what is considered a legitimate need of the collective (see chapter 2). For academics, this tension is a theoretical one; for politicians and their constituencies, it is largely rhetorical; for elected officials, it requires action. Elected officials must resolve the tension through political debates that are given concrete expression through the adoption of the budget. Adoption of the budget temporarily casts in stone the answer to what is private and what is public. Local elected officials cannot escape this fiduciary responsibility. In order for a governing body to spend public money, it must make a determination that a particular product or service is in the public's interest. It must make this decision in the open and in a public meeting and at the political peril of its elected members.

Once the political body officially adopts the budget document, it becomes an empirical action statement and ceases to be theoretical or rhetorical. The debate is settled for that year, and it is memorialized as a live, social contract between the elected officials of the jurisdiction and the citizens they serve. It also creates the platform for debate for subsequent years' budgets, based on the tangible actions of the agency during the adopted budget period.

Taking Management Initiative to Improve Performance

We argued in chapter 10, on budget planning, that while the budgeting process and its supporting systems rely heavily on strategic planning results, strategic planning is a separate administrative system. Strategic planning issues reach across the community with implications beyond the budget and finance systems, and an independent system is required to develop an effective plan. Developing a strategic plan requires extensive public involvement that exceeds the capacity of an annual budget process. However, both the planning system, and the revenue and budgeting systems contribute information to operational plans and programming (see chapter 12). The annual budget process provides the opportunity to draw on the information in operational plans to develop an annual program of resources, expenditures, and performance expectations. The adoption phase of the budget process provides an opportunity to review the intentions of the strategic plan and to reassess its conformity with long-term financial projections and policies.

While the public budget contributes to the planning functions, it is largely useless as a method for creating organizational productivity, effectiveness, and efficiency. Think of what it takes to increase public service outputs (productivity), ensuring that you are accomplishing your goals (effectiveness), and/or that you are getting the most "bang for the buck" (efficiency). As we have argued throughout Part III of this book, these objectives are a by-product of analyzing the systems and subsystems of work activity used to create a public service. For example, if you want to increase the productivity of the miles of streets swept, you need to acquire extensive and detailed operational and cost data from those who actually do the work; then, you have to compare this information with alternative approaches to street sweeping. Similar kinds of data and information are needed for improving effectiveness. If the current sweeping regimen is not effective in achieving the goal of clean streets, is there another way of achieving the goal that might be more effective? This requires cost-benefit analysis of the public goal that includes work mapping to forecast costs of different types of related products (for example, flushing the street with water from the fire hydrant instead of sweeping). Understanding effectiveness also requires an analysis of how clean is clean. Similar questions arise if we are interested in achieving "more bang for the buck." We need extensive cost data and information on each of the major stages in the work process, as well as alternative management strategies for organizing the workflow.

The kinds of information and expertise needed to improve program and organizational performance is the responsibility of the professional administrative staff. They need to take the initiative in persuading elected officials to commit to the development of a performance enhancement system for their jurisdiction, especially since in local governments the failure to address performance issues can quickly result in a decline in citizen trust and confidence. The performance system that is developed stands as an independent organizational system that links to the budgeting and other financial systems. In large and medium organizations, this often means dedicating a staff leadership position to performance improvement, establishing a cost and performance analysis system, and reforming the culture of the organization to embrace systems change and performance improvements. Failure to establish and maintain an independent performance function contributes to the budgetary process being hijacked by an attempt to use it as a tool for achieving greater productivity, effectiveness, or efficiency. Ironically, such efforts can create the opposite effect by decreasing the organization's capacity to perform. This happens when the demarcation between organizational performance issues is confused with the local politics that are a natural and necessary part of the budget process. If allowed to operate without the proper constraints, the organization itself will become a part of the political process. This can be observed when the organization starts to place its own needs before those of the bill-paying public.

Funding a dedicated position to oversee performance enhancement is beyond the capacity of many microsized and small local governments and nonprofits. Here, the task falls to the CEO and the clerk, finance officer, or administrative officer to assure attention to performance enhancement, but in a manner that will not confound performance enhancements with budgetary decision making. The budgeting system receives and reports information from the performance system, but is not a substitute for it.

Taking Administrative Initiative to Norm Governing Role Expectations

We have argued throughout this book, especially in chapter 2, that local government administrators have a lead role responsibility in maintaining a balanced system of democratic government. We define *balance* in terms of maintaining the commensurate equality among the following competing values that are at the core of the American rule-of-law system: responsive government, efficient and effective government, protection of minority rights, and sensitivity to the unique values of the local community. In local governments with part-time officials and no administrative support staff, professional career administrators take on major responsibility for this balancing role. In doing so, they help to norm the role expectations of the elected officials, the administrative staff, and the larger community.

Over the course of many decades of studying the relationship between elected bodies and city managers, James Svara has concluded that a successful working relationship between the council and professional managers results from agreement on two fundamental questions (Svara 1990, 2004, 2008). The first is agreement by members of the elected council on what kind of role they would like the city manager or CEO to play in relation to council members and the council as a whole. Do they want the manager to be proactive in highlighting problems and issues that need attention? Do they want a manager who anticipates stakeholder concerns and takes a hands-on approach to addressing these concerns before they become issues for the elected officials? Or do they want a city manager who is not a politically active problem-solver for members of council? (See the summary of the classic Friedrich-Finer debate in chapter 15.)

The second issue that members of a council and the city manager must agree on is the kind of managerial role that the community as a whole would like the city manager to play in relation to other members of the council. For example, a city with a visibly strong mayor who performs mainly a ceremonial role will likely expect the city manager to play a supporting role to the mayor. By contrast, it is common for the board chair of school systems and other special districts to develop an informal understanding that results in the superintendent or the chief executive officer playing a key representational role. But in each case, it is best that these informal understandings be made explicit and not simply be taken for granted. They should be memorialized in a policy document, adopted in a public meeting (preferably with a public hearing), and reviewed each year as governing board members change. This document becomes a foundational element in the annual performance review of managers by the governing body and plays a key role in shaping the budget process and its political dynamics.

There are several concrete actions that the legislative body and the administrative leadership team can and should take to facilitate norming the role expectations of board members and their relationship with those who have lead responsibility for managing the organization. In Exhibit 19.2, we summarize the major policy, financial, and organizational instruments that are used to create a mutual understanding of roles and responsibilities of the elected officials and the career public personnel.

Following are the collective goals that are achieved by producing the documents listed in Exhibit 19.2:

1. Establishment of a community-supported service system, designed to improve and enhance the health, welfare, and safety of the citizenry.
2. Creation of a capital improvement program that adequately maintains and enhances the publicly owned assets over their useful lives.
3. A performance-based provision of services that is measured and tested to assure maximum reasonable efficiency and effectiveness.
4. Prudent and professional managerial and financial practices to assure a well-managed and financially accountable government.
5. Explicit role differentiation with respect to governance, policy, and operational practices.
6. Organization capacity to perform in perpetuity with a focus on serving constituencies as the first priority.
7. An annual approved budget that supports adopted council goals and policies.

As we have argued in chapter 10 on budget planning and in chapter 15 on the executive budget, chief executives, chief finance officers, budget officers, and other senior and midlevel administrators play critical roles in convening and shaping the budget process and its decision making. Through their vision of the process and behaviors, administrators structure the roles of budget

518

Exhibit 19.2

Policy, Financial, and Procedural Documents to Norm Governance Role Expectations

Documents	Purpose	Advantages
Annual council goals with debate and citizen input	To establish service priorities in advance of the annual budget development process.	Enables elected officials to take charge of the budget preparation process and provides the CEO with budget development guidelines.
Annual budget assumptions	To officially memorialize the following assumptions in preparing the annual budget: • Inflationary cost increases by category • Increases/decreases in services • Changes in revenue from all sources • Salary adjustments • Amount to be budgeted for reserves	Enables elected officials to have control over major cost drivers of the budget process prior to budget preparation and official submission to the elected board.
Separate operating and capital budgets with a requirement that they be sustainable	To ensure that both the operating and capital budgets can fund services and capital maintenance on a sustainable basis. To prevent the operating budgets from being used to fund capital replacement by optimizing utilization and minimizing long-term life cycle costs.	Provides for separate capital and operating budgets with sufficient funds allocated on an annual basis (1) to cover needed expenditures to maintain capital, and (2) for capital budgets that fund capital replacement.
Long-term operating and capital expense projections	To provide governing body and administrators with at least a six-year projection of operating and capital expenses.	Provides administrators and elected officials with the lead time necessary to make program adjustments as a result of changes in revenue and demand for services. Reduces surprises and allows time to make needed policy changes.
Internal cost allocation plan	To determine the cost of providing central business management services and/or indirect costs to the various operating funds.	Ensures that the necessary central business functions will survive during budget adjustments and limits propensity to obtain cost savings through reductions in maintenance and use of reserves.
Policy on management of budget funds	To ensure that funds are managed independently according to generally accepted accounting principles and practices. Policies should include the amount and use of reserves.	Ensures that budget funds are not comingled and that they are being balanced with the dedicated revenues legally linked to the fund.
Financial control and reporting	To maintain financial control by providing monthly reporting to elected council of revenue and expenditures at the line-item detail and reconciliation of all accounts.	Provides spending control by giving managers the information they need to identify positive and/or negative trends. Future evaluation of these trends also allows for more precise future budget estimates.
Financial accountability	To ensure comprehensive annual financial reporting at the end of the budgeting year, with the elected board having the advice of independent certified public accountant staff to report on the condition and accuracy of the financial and reporting systems.	Ensures that adequate reporting systems are in place and are being properly used.
Long-range fiscal impact statements for new programs	To provide the legal and policy justification for new programs, sources of revenue to be used with assessment of alternative approaches.	Provides governing body with the information needed to make long-term commitments.

process actors, define and structure budget process activities, contribute to structuring decisions, and build internal and external relationships with other budget actors. As process conveners, administrators have the unique perspective to see the whole of the budget process and to keep track of the details that integrate into the entirety of the budget as a governance system.

POLITY BUDGETING: A JURISDICTIONAL VERSUS A COMMUNITY-CENTERED APPROACH TO BUDGETING

As we mentioned at the beginning of this chapter, future local budgeting will face two major challenges. We have already discussed various strategies that local administrators can use to protect the budgeting process from being overburdened with other purposes that must be addressed outside the formal budgeting process. The second major challenge is the need to address the ever-present concern by citizens that they are receiving inadequate value from government programs in relation to the taxes and fees they pay. While many citizens are unaware of its full extent, most governments have shifted a substantial portion of their service production to external intergovernmental agreements, service contracts, extended public-private partnerships, and networked coproduction. Government has largely followed the tenets of **new public management** (NPM) and "hollowed out" its productive capacity (Milward and Provan 2000). Broadly, governments have let their production capacity atrophy to minimal levels. In many instances, this major shift exceeds the capacity of governmental control and performance systems to significantly ameliorate the challenge of providing responsive and high-performing programs.

Throughout this text, we have emphasized the tension between a jurisdictional approach to local public budgeting, and a service-centered or function-based approach that takes into account all of the assets that are being used by various public, private, and civic associations to promote the common good of the community (see chapter 1, especially Exhibits 1.8 and 1.9). Overall, we have tended to place more emphasis on the jurisdictional aspects of the public budget process because local governing bodies have a legal obligation to adopt a balanced budget and to implement that budget in ways that meet the political and legal accountability requirements that are in place for the jurisdiction. While this jurisdictional perspective will continue to dominate the local budgeting process, we believe a *community-centered approach*, or what we have labeled a **polity** approach, will grow in importance as local governments seek ways of responding to citizen concerns about the quality and cost of the provision of local services.

Our use of the term *polity* calls attention to two important dimensions of the local public budgeting context that are not adequately captured by a jurisdictional approach. The first is the network of local and regional government services providers who will be challenged to coordinate and maybe even consolidate services in an effort to lower costs and increase performance. How to fund and size the intergovernmental service network will become a strategic issue with implications for annual budgeting decisions. One option is to use the budgeting process to incentivize the larger intergovernmental network. Another option is to create additional network leadership organizations—possibly in the form of loosely coupled leagues or organizations—that are given significant regionwide policy and budgeting authority. We believe that citizens have come to expect the delivery of a minimal level of services. For the most part, they are not especially interested in the fine points of which jurisdiction provides these services, as long as they have access to influencing budget and policy decisions when they become disenchanted.

The second dimension of local budgeting that tends to get short shrift with a jurisdictional approach is the network of civic, nonprofit, and for-profit organizations that work together to coordinate and improve the delivery of community services. Local governments provide only a portion of the services that contribute to the well-being of our local communities. Nonprofit and for-profit organizations fill in the gaps of government capacity desired by the community. These networks may be informal and loosely coupled (e.g., informal-spontaneous or participant-governed networks), or they may take the form of "holding" companies with considerable authority to collect and distribute community resources (e.g., lead-organization and NAO-led networks). Local governments in the future will need to pay much more attention to the role of these networks in the budgeting process. In the next two sections, we will explore two dimensions of these network service delivery issues in greater detail.

The Rise of Interjurisdictional Coordination

The American system of federalism gives local governments extensive authority to collect taxes and to provide the services about which citizens are most concerned. In many major metropolitan areas, once rural towns and villages that reflect historic independent identities are now small- to medium-sized cities or towns of the metropolitan region. Each of these jurisdictions provides a relatively similar set of basic services to its citizens, possibly refined to reflect the unique preferences and tastes of its taxpayer customers. In other instances, county governments have attempted to remove themselves from the business of providing local services with the intent of concentrating on regional issues. This abdication has resulted in the establishment, and voter acceptance, of a wide array of special district governments and special taxing districts for police, fire, and emergency medical services; parks and recreation; water provision; and wastewater collection and treatment. In other instances, local governments have realized that an integrated approach is more effective and consequently have established regional-level service districts for wastewater collection/treatment and for drinking water provision. These types of governmental arrangements have resulted in enormous overlapping and conflicting service delivery systems in every metropolitan area in the nation. It has also resulted in a gross underinvestment in the public infrastructure (see chapter 16). In many cases, the individual governing bodies have very little understanding of the degree and the kind of overlap under which the local and regional systems suffer. Local government elected officials, administrators and technical staff may have some understanding of how their jurisdiction's service systems contribute to the larger regional system. But, the authority of local officials is limited to their individual jurisdictions, and they have no real authority over how sister governments will coordinate and contribute to combined regional services. Local government budgets prepared at the organizational level reflect this narrow focus. We argue in this closing chapter that local government administrators in the decades ahead will focus more of their budgeting attention on revisiting these intergovernmental arrangements. The incentive for doing so is illustrated by the following short example.

In a major metropolitan area, the county sheriff organization provides services for patrol, investigations, and special skills teams to unincorporated areas of the county.[2] The sheriff also provides these services to 14 incorporated cities and towns within the county on a contract basis. The contracts take the form of extended intergovernmental agreements with a defined service level and an annual schedule of payments. The defined payment schedule has two advantages in that it assures an annual base level of resources to the sheriff's department, and it sets a defined annual charge for service to each of the member cities and towns. The sheriff's department, however, also relies on county general fund monies to support its services. When the economy declines and property tax and sales tax revenues fall, the department is left with extensive service commitments despite a shortage of resources. The sheriff is reduced to pleading with the county commission for increased general fund revenues. As a fairness issue, should each of the 14 purchasing cities and towns step up and increase their contribution to the department? Or should each jurisdiction decide to accept a lower level of service based on the funds at hand? These are questions that an annual budget process should address. However, a broader functional approach to intergovernmental budgeting encourages the elected officials in each jurisdiction to respond to the situation and needs of the full law enforcement network. Intergovernmental coordination reaches beyond staff-level relationships; it includes functional budgeting that considers the funding decisions by neighboring jurisdictions and community-level needs. Piecemeal annual budgeting by the individual client jurisdictions cannot solve the larger issue—that is, sizing the sheriff's office to meet the service needs of all of the partners in the intergovernmental network. The county sheriff as the lead organization in this network must gather all the client jurisdictions and the unincorporated voices together for discussions on how to size and plan for law enforcement services across the full county.

In addition to the episodic incentives of the kind described above, there are other important historical factors that will contribute to a more coordinated approach to budgeting across multiple jurisdictions in the decades ahead. First, there is a surprising uniformity of citizen expectations for a consistent package of basic service in urban and suburban areas. Second, there is a uniformity of accepted standards that norm budgeting expectations and processes across jurisdictional boundaries, thus making it easier to have service coordination discussions and agreements. We will elaborate more fully on each of these incentives in the sections that follow.

National Uniformity and Variability in Public Services:
Implications for Interjurisdictional Coordination

Comprehensive local governments from towns to major cities provide a standard menu of services, including police, fire, and emergency medical; land-use planning, roads, and transportation; drinking water; wastewater management; library; and cultural and economic development. County governments may perform many of these same services in unincorporated areas. Depending on state law, larger cities may handle airports, hospitals, and even the local public schools. The exception to the model of comprehensive service delivery appears in rural areas and urban areas that have taken advantage of the legal option to form special service districts. As we have indicated, special districts engage in specialized delivery of one primary service, often over an extended area of multiple local jurisdictions. Special district service specialties match most of those provided by comprehensive governments. For example, these services include water, sewer, police, fire, parks, library, and similar general government responsibilities. Comprehensive governments may have central coordination, but special district arrangements may actually increase the incentive for geographic-wide coordination, especially in rural areas.

Earlier in this chapter, we identified 85 different public products and services typically produced by government agencies (see Exhibit 19.1). The 89,400 local governing jurisdictions in the United States deliver 79 products and services, with only 6 provided by the national government. Given the large geographic expanse of the United States and the variability of local government structures and processes (see chapter 2), one might expect a correspondingly wide variety of public services. But this is not the case. While there is great diversity in local governing systems, there is great uniformity across the United States both in local budgeting systems and in the services they provide. Some economists argue that the variety of local government jurisdictions allows citizens to self-select the services they want based on their ability to pay (Tiebout 1956). This argument explains in part the large growth in special districts that has occurred over the past several decades (Burns 1994). We also believe this desire for local political control over the quality, amount, and cost of public services will facilitate future intergovernmental discussions regarding the most efficient and responsive systems of service delivery.

In rural areas, the incentive for geographic coordination arises from a different combination of incentives than those at play in an urban setting. In a study conducted by Heflin and Miller (2011), the authors found that in rural service delivery (1) there are fewer options, (2) the demand is higher than the supply, (3) the costs are higher, and (4) the service needs of the population are greater than their urban counterparts. The authors concluded that the need for integrated human service delivery may be even more critical in nonmetropolitan areas than metropolitan areas (Heflin and Miller 2011, 19; also see Gutierrez et al. 2010).

Another set of factors that has contributed to a uniformity of service provision across widely diverse geographic expanses is the role of the national associations in establishing technical and performance standards. For example, national standards define the expected levels of coverage, staffing, equipment, and training for local fire departments. Local government fire and police departments participate in certification programs to demonstrate high levels of performance quality to their citizens. Attainment of certified status implies compliance with nationwide professional standards. Professional training and attendance at professional meetings by local government staff provide another unifying force on performance standards (e.g., DiMaggio and Powell 1983). No matter the jurisdictional configuration of general purpose governments and special districts, professional training and standards serve to standardize the form and level of governmental services.

To summarize, while there may be variability in the amount and quality of services listed in Exhibit 19.1, at least in urban areas these services are the political result of 200 years of responding to human needs. As a consequence, they have acquired the status of political entitlements. Such expectations create considerable incentives for public leaders to undertake intergovernmental initiatives for the coordination, consolidation, and delivery of services.

National Budgeting Standards and Expectations Support Coordination

A second set of factors easing the way for greater interjurisdictional coordination in the future is the emergence over the past 75 years of a national set of budgeting standards and expectations. This is partly the result of requirements by the federal government and partly the result of work by professionals in charge of public finance, accounting, and budgeting systems.

The federal government has played a major role in establishing national accountability standards through (1) grants that support various kinds of infrastructure development and the delivery of social services, and (2) regulatory requirements dealing with clean water, air, public health, and the like. In all cases, these federal programs have assumed that state and local governments would administer federally funded programs. One of the most beneficial but unintended outcomes of this approach has been the creation of a uniform national accounting and reporting system (e.g., chapter 18's discussion of federal Single Audit requirements; Farris 2009). This system is now nearly universal and has improved government accountability by a remarkable degree.

The creation of a uniform national accounting system has also been aided and abetted by a constituency of practitioners and politicians who rely on the system to demonstrate public accountability. As we mentioned in chapter 9 (on budget funds and accounting), Robert Anthony (1985) lamented the lack of effective controls in governmental accounting. Without effective means to track the delivery and utilization of money granted to local governments, universities, hospitals, and nonprofit service providers, it was impossible for congressional and presidential activists to motivate political action groups and for Congress to authorize appropriations. But in the past 30 years, common reporting and accounting requirements have been put into place that are now used by the private sector as the basis for (1) determining government accountability, (2) assessing financial risk, and (3) determining eligibility for selling bonds and borrowing money from banks. At the same time, the Governmental Accounting Standards Board (GASB), the Government Finance Officers Association (GFOA), and the accounting and budgeting professions have pushed to develop common coding, accounting, and tracking procedures (as we discussed in some detail in chapters 9, 17 and 18). As a result, the budget of any particular government can be compared to any other with a reasonable expectation that it will represent a common, universal standard of measurement. A person who is involved in the budgetary process for the school district in Biloxi, Mississippi, would theoretically (and almost certainly) recognize the elements of discussion, the procedures for measurement, and the political processes necessary to gain agreement if they suddenly moved to San Jose, California, and were involved in a discussion with the city council about their expenditures for personnel in the fire department.

To summarize, the mosaic of local governments in most regions reflects historical factors, citizen preferences, decisions by previous elected officials and voters, geography, and installed infrastructure. Providing sufficient resources to the intergovernmental network presents a public budgeting challenge that will grow in significance in the decades ahead. This provides an opportunity for those responsible for public budgeting to revisit age-old democratic governance issues—namely, how to balance the need for responsiveness and political control against the need for effective and efficient service delivery. The ultimate question upon which future interjurisdictional coordination and cooperation rests is what combination of arrangements will produce the greatest trust and confidence in government by the citizens and taxpayers who fund its existence. This "measure of success" reinforces the major theme we set forth at the beginning of the book: Budgeting is not about numbers but about what kind of democratic system of governance we want.

Polity Networks and Nongovernmental Service Providers: Some Implications for Local Public Budgeting

In addition to the questions of interjurisdictional coordination raised in the section above, a second major polity issue that local budgeting government officials will face in the future concerns nongovernmental service providers, specifically, how best to take into account those nongovernmental providers and civic organizations that make substantial contributions to the larger common good. This has been a central theme throughout the book. We introduced the concept of polity budgeting in chapter 1 (see especially Exhibits 1.8 and 1.9), and carried this theme through our various chapters. Our approach to the issue of the role of nongovernmental service providers in the local budgeting process began with an introduction to the concept of networks. We identified the following four types of networks (see chapter 4): the informal-spontaneous network; the participant-governed network; lead-organization network; and NAO-led network. In addition to tracking all four forms throughout the various phases of the budget process, we demonstrated that the approaches and techniques for budgeting and financial administration are different for each network type. The operational and tactical techniques of network budgeting and financial management raise two important issues for those in charge of local public budgeting in the decades ahead: (1) What role should the government play in sizing network capacity to meet local needs? (2) How does government ensure network transparency and accountability? We will explore each of these issues more fully in the sections that follow.

The Role of Government in Sizing Service Networks

In chapter 8, which deals with nonprofit sector revenues, we developed a vision of integrated community-level resources that includes the business, government, nonprofit, and civil society sectors. We argued that extensive contracting for services by local governments, extended public-private partnerships, and the rise of quasi-governmental foundations have blurred the bright-line distinction among the sectors. A polity network that once discretely separated actors is now integrated contractually, financially, by policy, and by opportunistic arrangements. This blurring has forced a recasting of the public revenue framework away from just government resources to include revenue sources from the charitable, philanthropic, civic, and for-profit sectors. We pointed out that this shift in focus raises several important policy issues.

One of the most important issues is government's role as a member of the local polity network. For example, if severe economic conditions force a major drop in philanthropic giving and a reduction in intermediary and foundation grants, should governments step up to fill part of the gap with tax revenues? Another policy issue asks how government should behave as a major community donor. Should government have the authority to take the lead in providing the initial "seed" grant donation against which private donors can leverage their funds? Understanding how state agencies and local government revenues and resources fit in context with other nongovernmental resources in the community is an important step in community or polity budgeting.

The economic downturn of 2007–2009 demonstrated the poignancy of these types of financial questions. The loss of revenues from foundation and philanthropic sources and from declining government contracts placed severe pressure on nonprofit service providers in many communities (see the teaching case in Part I). Longstanding nonprofit organizations were forced to close facilities, stop service delivery, lay off staff, reorganize, or consolidate their remaining capacity to a smaller, more sustainable level. Nonprofit organizations serving as partners and subcontractors to larger nonprofit organizations were affected in turn. The closure or retrenchment of nonprofits across a community raised issues of how the community as a polity would deliver needed services. Forecasts of local government revenues and program support can raise the issue of whether the community needs to raise new revenues or to adjust program capacity. Major nonprofit intermediaries, community foundations, and nonprofit service providers can contribute important information to this discussion, but each may have to make independent decisions on costs and service levels to prevent collusion and to ensure compliance with federal antitrust laws.

The challenges of sizing the service network to match revenue fluctuations and changes in service demand ultimately fall back to financial policies and the annual budgeting decisions made by each member organization. These organizations, along with local governments, contribute resources and their name to the network and its function. Each member organization reviews its commitment as a member of the larger network, and assesses the effectiveness of the network in meeting its goals of service delivery to the community. The annual budget process provides a limited forum for network oversight. However, to assure network performance, the board members, the elected officials, and the executives of each member organization must enlarge their perspective from a narrow jurisdictional and organizational view to a broader functional view of the service delivery system, including both the desired outcomes and the processes for achieving them.

Limited resources and public expectations of detailed accountability may drive elected officials and nonprofit boards to mandate changes to a network that will better match resources to capacity and responsiveness to needs. Independent network-level governance processes and structures provide an important complement to member-level decision making and oversight. However, as we have argued throughout this text, the "how" of network governance is critical to its acceptance and application. Careful planning may enhance the success of network establishment and development (Goldsmith and Eggers 2004). Human and Provan (2000) remind us that network establishment requires building internal legitimacy among network members and the network entity, along with external legitimacy among clients, the community, and governmental and nonprofit leaders. Network reform and redesign may take substantial administrative and political effort and require an independent planning, dialogue, and decision process.

Again, the type of network involved is critical to the success or failure of a design. Informal-spontaneous networks rely on a decentralized authority structure, the free flow of dialogue, and high-trust relationships to make decisions and enforce performance. The imposition of formal directives from a local government or a major network member to adjust the network size and capacity would likely stifle the sense of trust and fairness among members, the spontaneity of civil society, and any sense of member initiative. In a similar manner, participant-government networks—again with decentralized authority and high-trust relationships—rely heavily on dialogue and relationships for network governance. Such dialogues would be essential following the individual annual budgeting decisions by the network members. To summarize, in working with informal-spontaneous and participant-governed networks, local governments need to exercise great care in their presence and communication with other network members (Goldsmith and Eggers 2004).

By contrast, in lead-organization networks, decisions by the local governments, intermediary nonprofits, and other lead members can more responsively increase or decrease the capacity and procedural functions of the whole network. Here, lead organization board members can make decisions with an expectation of a resulting effect. Similarly, in NAO-led networks, policy and budgeting decisions by the NAO board of directors and executive set the direction and service capacity for the entire network membership.

Community capacity mapping (McKnight and Kretzmann 1996) and creative applications of geographic information systems (GIS) enhance the ability of community leaders and network designers to see the community and its resources as an integrated entity.[3] The difficulties of network design and the spontaneous aspects of network establishment and growth reinforce the need for a separate planning and design effort. The design effort, however, will likely draw on information and decisions developed through the annual budgeting process of organizations from different sectors in a community.

Government Leadership in Network Transparency and Accountability

Sizing the capacity of the polity network is only part of what is needed to build citizen confidence in local governments and nonprofit organizations. The network must also function in a way that demonstrates transparency and accountability. A network that demonstrates effective accomplishments to the community will engender support for public and donor resources. If citizens perceive the network and its members as engaged in conflict, or in confused and inefficient service delivery, support for public involvement and financial contributions will decline for all parties. Similarly, major intermediary nonprofits will face probing questions from their board members over continued network membership, or of the contribution of resources to the network in the face of limited donor resources. Beyond budgeting and financial reporting, the network must demonstrate effectiveness in its service delivery and political responsiveness.

The first line of defense in ensuring accountability and transparency consists of the financial reporting standards and requirements of the network members. We summarized the role of the CAFR for governmental organizations and of annual financial reporting for nonprofits. The enhanced reporting requirements for the Sarbanes-Oxley Act have added another reporting protocol to ensure nonprofit organizational performance. However, a functional view of standard financial reports must take an integrated approach across network member organizations. Network members must have access to each other's budget and financial reports in order to generate mutual confidence.

The mutual sharing of budget and financial data may present a challenge for members of an informal-spontaneous network. In many instances, this type of network reflects spontaneous civil society. Many members of this type of network might be very small nonprofits, individuals, and ad hoc community groups. These members may not have fully functioning financial systems, and funding and budgeting may be spontaneous. Rather than request financial information, local government and chartered nonprofits can lead by example by proactively sharing their financial documents for all to review in a nonthreatening manner. With information on the table, government and nonprofit group representatives can then engage the network members in a governance dialogue using conciliatory practices.

For the more fully developed and stable network forms, local governments and chartered nonprofit members can take the lead in supporting network governance by committing analyst time and talent, as well as financial information. Interpreting network-level performance requires dedication and a willingness to dig for detailed understanding by board members and organization executives. We extended these themes in chapter 17 (on budget execution) with a full discussion of how networks jointly execute programs and ensure performance. To gain the resources and support for network administrative activities, organization executives and administrators must build support among board members and elected officials. Executives must explain the importance of transparency in network finances as a precursor to public support for networked service delivery.

CONCLUDING MESSAGE

Successful budgeting requires the capacity to manage multiple budget systems with competing purposes. It requires balancing tensions between what people want and what they need; between being efficient and effective and being responsive; between doing what is merely legal and what is morally, politically, or organizationally right; between a jurisdictional-level approach to budgeting and a polity-level approach; between an expert-centered and a political-centered perspective; and between a community-oriented versus a government-oriented focus. These tensions are not simply the artifact of the accidents of history. They result in large part from the deliberate design of our political economy to balance the competing needs of a democratic society: enough government, but not so much that it endangers liberty and undermines local control.

We began this book with an argument that, because of the large number of local governments in the United States and our decentralized system of legal authority, the success of democratic government depends on how the tensions inherent in American democratic government get managed by local governing officials through the budget process. There is some irony that we conclude this book with a call for local elected officials to broaden their focus and become more proactive in identifying and using the assets of the entire community in a more strategic fashion. But, it is only ironic if you equate *small government* with *passive government*.

Much of the heavy lifting in gathering, analyzing, and using information to enable government to carry out its polity-focused responsibilities will fall on the shoulders of local career administrators. This leadership role goes to the heart of American democratic governance. The health of the larger body politic depends on how well our local government administrative leaders engage citizens, elected officials, and the larger network of service providers in conversations about the ongoing nature of the common good.

STUDY QUESTIONS

1. What evidence of budgetary stress exists within your community or public service organization?
2. To what extent is the response to budgetary stress characterized by managerial responses (i.e., increased emphasis on efficiency, effectiveness, and various forms of "doing more with less") rather than political responses (i.e., engaging citizens and community partners in discussions about leveraging community resources and deciding what service elements and amounts are essential to the common good)?
3. This chapter has emphasized the importance of placing expectations on the budgeting process that it can successfully bear. Evaluate the extent to which your organization or jurisdiction has created appropriate and sufficient complementary planning, policy, performance, and other systems that complement the budgetary process and expectations.
4. To what extent is your organization or community jurisdictional centered rather than polity centered in its approach to public budgeting? To what extent do you see evidence of change? What are the forces driving this change? How do these forces compare to those discussed in this chapter?

5. If there is a predisposition by the community or your public service organization to take a polity-centered approach, to what extent is this predisposition informed and guided by the different forms and types of networks discussed in this chapter?

NOTES

1. This summary of services has been calculated by Mike Gleason from the chart of accounts from more than 100 local jurisdictions (including counties, cities, and special districts) as well as the U.S. federal government.
2. Sources for this example include King County Sheriff 2013; City of Sammamish, Washington 2012a; and Ervin 2010.
3. There are a variety of tools that will become increasingly important to facilitate polity-centered budgeting. These tools fall into two broad categories: analytic and conciliatory practice.

Analytic Tools

One of the challenges of undertaking a polity-level approach to local-level budgeting is the general inclination of citizens to be satisfied with the status quo. But there are analytic mapping tools that can be used to assist citizens and stakeholder groups in seeing new patterns of social service needs and resources that remain invisible to the naked eye.

Spatial Mapping

The most common form of social mapping is *geographic information systems (GIS)*. These systems are being used in a variety of creative ways—for example, to map capital infrastructure systems, civic infrastructure systems, and health systems. In all of these cases, we can create maps that describe the spatial position of humans with a point placed where they live, or with a point located where they work, or by using a line to describe their weekly trips; we can overlay this map with a map of the services consumed, the supplier of these services, and the comparative costs. We can add complexity by changing the unit of analysis from individuals to groups, types of organizations, businesses, etc. Each of our service-mapping choices has dramatic effects on the techniques that can be used for the analysis and on the conclusions that can be obtained.

Asset Mapping

Another form of mapping that has proven very successful in generating different kinds of conversations about the common good is called *asset mapping*. It was first popularized by Kretzmann and McKnight (1993), who argued that traditional planning based on a needs or deficits approach undervalues the assets that are already present in the community but have never been identified, mobilized, and targeted to achieve a shared common good. The model's simplicity is part of its power in transforming local communities.

Conciliatory Practice Tools

Polity budgeting requires not only the acquisition of information regarding politywide resources (through tools like spatial and asset mapping) but also the mobilization of political agreement to do something with these resources that can be supported by the majority of stakeholder groups in the community, even under conditions of considerable conflict. Over the past several decades, scholars and practitioners have developed a growing body of knowledge and practices called *conciliatory practices,* the goal of which is to facilitate community agreement, even in the face of seemingly intractable conflicting views. These practices provide administrators and elected officials with the knowledge and tools to answer the following questions (Morgan et al. 2013, 374–377; Shinn, Hallmark, and Singer 2010):

- How do you choose whom to involve?
- How do you manage conflicting values?
- How do you keep everyone committed to the process?
- How do you manage decision making in conciliatory processes?

We believe that conciliatory practices, in combination with spatially displayed data on community resources and assets, can be used to develop a polity-oriented focus to local public budgeting. Spatially displayed data can provide a visual picture of a community that is different from the community experienced by citizens in their daily lives. This data can be used by experts in conciliatory practice to facilitate community conversations about the values, beliefs, and community cultural norms that may or may not match up with the prevailing balkanized service map characteristic of many local communities. Surely, some of these discussions will be hotly contested as participants are reminded of the unique and sometimes idiosyncratic rationales that resulted in the creation of service systems—rationales that may no longer have any basis in current reality. Communities need to have these discussions, especially given the growing irreconcilable conflict between what citizens want and what they are willing to pay for. Such discussions will motivate elected officials to temper their jurisdictional-centered predispositions.

GLOSSARY

Glossary terms are emboldened on first use, on primary definition, or on major discussion in the text. The numbers in parentheses (#) following each glossary entry indicate, in priority order, the chapter of definition, explanation, or application of the term in the text. Glossary entries are alphabetical and include references to similar or contrasting terms.

Accounting fund (9): A fund established to accumulate related transactions performed for a specific purpose over the course of a fiscal year or biennium. An accounting fund records revenue inputs, resource balances, and spending transactions. An accounting fund directly corresponds to its counterpart budget fund. *See also* fund; budget fund.

Activity (12): A primary structure of program/PPBS budgeting. A process or operation undertaken by an organization specifically designed to meet an objective. The process or operation is very clearly defined with a specified time frame, resource needs, staffing, and a measurable outcome. One or several activities contribute to meeting an objective. *See* planning, programming budgeting system; goal; objective.

Activity based costing (12): An accounting and performance measurement perspective that focuses on production costs as the critical measure of organization performance in the production of outputs and outcomes. For examples see Michel (2004) and Stenzel and Stenzel (2003). An activity based costing system is one element in an organization's performance improvement system. This system should be independent of, but contribute information to, the budgeting system. Activity based costing information can help support performance and PPBS budget decision making.

Add package (14): A budget package (budget decision package) used in a zero-base budgeting (ZBB) context. A discrete bundle of resources and program capacity designed specifically to meet an objective or to produce an activity or outcome. Add packages are developed to innovate new approaches, maintain existing programs, serve increased workloads, or add new programs. Typically, several competing add packages are ranked in priority order, with a preferred combination of packages selected to restore funding from the reduced level budget (RLB) toward the level of the adjusted level budget (ALB). *Relate to* budget package, decision package.

Adjusted level budget (ALB) (14): In zero-base budgeting (ZBB), the adjusted level budget reflects the necessary adjustments to the reduced level budget (RLB) to maintain ongoing service levels at next year's prices using the same productivity. The ALB typically adjusts the RLB by the rate of inflation and by other programmed cost increases in labor and service contracts.

Administrative discretion (2, 15): The behavioral and policy flexibility, initiative, and degree of choice inherent in an administrative position and its performance. The degree of discretion granted to an administrator derives from many factors, including the design of the position, the specific delegation of legal authority to the position, the role expectations of the position inside the organization, the community expectations of the position, and the personal attributes and skill of the incumbent. See chapter 15 for a summary of the Friedrich/Finer debate on administrative leadership and discretion.

Adopted budget (15): For government jurisdictions, an adopted budget is the budget that has been adopted by statutory ordinance by its legislative body (council, commission, or board, etc.). The adopted budget sets legally binding spending limits for different budget funds and/or departments for the designated fiscal year or biennium. The adopted budget is built from the executive's proposed budget (also known as the executive approved or executive recommended budget). The legislative body may make amendments to the executive's proposed budget before its adoption. For nonprofit organizations, the board of directors adopts, with any modifications, the executive's proposed budget by motion and vote. The adopted budget may also be amended by the board or legislative body throughout the budget year, in which case the most recent amendments represent the adopted budget. *See also* appropriation, budget adoption, amendment.

Allotment (17): A portion of the funds appropriated to a department or program under an adopted budget. Allotment controls are used to meter out resources on a quarterly or monthly basis to meet expected levels of expenditures. Allotment controls may be adjusted to meet periods or seasons of increased or decreased program spending, but they are always managed to maintain a sufficient reserve in the fund to prevent overspending at the close of the fiscal year. Allotments are more commonly employed by state governments than local governments.

Amendment; also, **budget amendment (17):** In local government budgeting, an amendment is a budget resolution or ordinance to revise the previously adopted fiscal year budget. An amendment can provide additional funds, can rescind or take back unneeded or unused funds, or can reprogram or transfer money between budget funds. Once adopted as an ordinance, a budget amendment has the force of law and revises the original adopted budget. *See also* supplemental appropriation; rescission; reprogram; current service baseline; adopted budget.

Anti-Federalists (2): A group of American founders who favored the creation of a weak and decentralized government with reliance on small homogeneous communities to protect liberty from abuse by over-reaching public officials. *See also* civic republic tradition, coproduction. *Contrast with* Federalists.

Appeal (7): *Related to* appraisals. *See* board of property tax appeals; board of equalization.

Appointed board; also, **appointed commission (4):** A small group of citizens nominated by the chief executive officer of a governmental jurisdiction, and often confirmed by the legislative body (council, commission or board), to support governmental activities. A board or commission may have an advisory role to the chief executive and legislative group, or may have delegated executive powers, legislative and policy decision authority, or adjudicative authority within a defined area of administrative or technical law. Decisions by boards and commissions may often be appealed to the legislative body. For example, a local planning commission interprets the development code and adjudicates permit applications. Appeals of planning commission rulings are typically presented to the city council or commission.

Appointed commission (4): *See* appointed board.

Appraisal (7): The determination of the value of a piece of property susceptible to property taxation. Typically, staff assessors under the direction of a county assessor appraise or value each piece of designated property in the jurisdiction on a prescribed time cycle. The appraisal becomes the basis for computing the property tax on a property.

Appropriation (4, 15): An official action taken by the governing body of a jurisdiction to authorize the expenditure of a specified amount of money from a specified budget fund for a specific program or department in a specified fiscal year; spending authority. Most local government appropriations are made through the budget ordinance at adoption of an annual budget; however, some local governments are able to appropriate during the fiscal year, typically from unanticipated revenues or form available fund balances. *See also* adopted budget.

Appropriation committee also, **budget committee (5):** Standing committee of a legislative body, especially at the state and federal levels of government, that is given the authority to review budget requests and to approve budget spending authority for programs, departments, and agencies.

Appropriation control (17): The level in the budget above which administrators and managers must seek permission from the legislative body, often through adoption of a budget amendment, to transfer funds between budget funds or program units. *See also* amendment (budget amendment); transfer.

Approved budget (5, 15): A proposed budget to which the chief executive (CEO) has given his or her approval as the final proposal ready for legislative consideration. This version of a jurisdiction or nonprofit's budget reflects the compilation of all department and program requests into an integrated budget that shows the amount of money the CEO (governor, city manager, mayor, etc.) proposes to spend on various programs for the jurisdiction/organization. Also known as executive recommended budget, executive requested budget, and proposed budget.

Asset (18): Cash, receivables, securities and investments, tangible items and real property (e.g., land, infrastructure or facilities, equipment or inventory), marketable intangible intellectual property (e.g., software or brand) owned by a government, nonprofit, or for-profit organization.

Audit (18): A formal and legally official examination of an organization's financial, grant, or performance records and reports based on the use of established criteria or standards.

Audit findings (18): Areas of potential control weakness, policy violation, or other issues identified during an official audit.

Authorization (4): An official legal action taken by the governing body of a governmental jurisdiction, often by a committee's legislative members, to: (1) define a program and its related strategy; (2) approve the expenditure of funds, FTEs, and other resources for a specified set of program activities; and (3) set budget levels for a program. Authorization is typically performed as a separate legislative action in state legislatures and in the U.S. Congress. Once a program is "authorized," the legislative body still needs to determine how much money will be "appropriated" for expenditure during each fiscal year or biennium. Many programs have received authorization but have failed to receive the appropriations necessary to execute the fully authorized program.

Balance (9, 17, 18): For a fund to balance at the close of the fiscal year, the opening resources in the fund at the start of the year (opening fund balance) plus all new revenues collected over the year, plus transfers in of funds from other departments or funds, must equal all expenditures made over the year, transfers out to other departments or funds, and the closing fund balance remaining in the fund.

Base budget (5, 11, 14): Multiple uses: (1) a budget actor behavior which assumes that last year's budget will serve as the starting point for the political and financial development of the next year's budget request. (2) In line-item budgeting, the most recent version of the legislatively adopted budget adjusted to remove one-time, nonrecurring revenues and expenditures. The base budget forms the starting point for any percentage adjustment to individual line-items as part of the development of a budget request for the next fiscal year. *Contrast with* current service baseline. (3) In zero-base budgeting (ZBB), the most recent legally adopted budget for the previous or current fiscal year. It forms the starting point for preparing a reduced level budget (RLB) and an adjusted level budget (ALB), which takes into account inflationary and other cost increases.

Baseline forecast (7, 10). *See* baseline run.

Baseline forecast; also, **baseline run (7, 10):** A forecast (often for revenues, expenditures or caseloads), a "run" of a statistical or mathematical model, or a planning scenario that serves as a comparison point against which other forecasts or runs are compared. The baseline run or scenario often has the highest quality statistical and contextual fit to real world conditions, or has been seen as the most likely scenario, or has been identified as a preferred scenario. Sensitivity analysis procedures then incrementally vary the assumptions and data used in the baseline run or scenario to produce forecasts, runs, or scenarios that contrast with the baseline. A sufficient number of varying contrasting runs provides indications of the baseline's behavior under widely changing conditions. *See also* sensitivity analysis.

Basis (9): An accounting analysis and reporting perspective that reflects professional standards and practices. *See* cash basis; full accrual basis; modified accrual basis.

Beliefs and values statement (12): A statement that defines the values that guide the work of an organization, suborganization unit, or program. One of three components of a detailed, well-developed mission statement. *See also* planning, programming budgeting system; mission statement; vision statement.

Benchmark (13): One or several performance measures that portray governmental accomplishment, productivity, and status of community conditions. Benchmark measures often track changes in condition over an extended time frame and are closely linked to government-wide or professional standards. Governments and nonprofits frequently compare their actual performance against benchmark standards to measure their effectiveness or to determine progress against community goals and needs.

Biennium (5): A defined two-year period that segregates all revenues and expenditures transactions from earlier and later periods. For governments that practice a two-year budget cycle, this is the amount of time that a budget is legally in force. For example, for the State of Oregon, the biennium begins on July 1 of odd-numbered years and ends on June 30 of the next odd-numbered year (e.g., 2013–2015). *Compare to* fiscal year.

Board of equalization (7). *See* board of property tax appeals.

Board of property tax appeals; also, **board of equalization (6, 7):** A county- or local government–level citizen board that hears citizen appeals of assessor valuations of property. Typically, citizens may further appeal a board's opinion through the courts or a state-level property tax appeal board. Names for this board and appeal procedures vary by state.

Bond grade (16). *See* bond rating.

Bond rating; also, **bond grade (16):** A letter-based quality rating that is given by a private bond-rating organization to the bonds being issued for sale by a jurisdiction or organization, typically for a capital purchase. The bond rating reflects the risk to the bondholder for the timely repayment of the borrowed funds and interest. A jurisdiction or organization's tax base value, economic health, identified revenues, past repayment history, and financial management history all contribute to the rating assigned to a bond issue. A bond rating is analogous to a personal credit score.

Borough (1): A local unit of government that varies in its size and responsibilities for local service provision. In Alaska, boroughs are similar to county governments, while in the eastern states, boroughs are subunits of cities or independent units smaller than a city.

Budget (3): A plan identifying and organizing the revenues, expenditures, position types and FTEs, capital resources, indirect and administrative cost allocations, and performance expectations to support a department, program, or project over a fiscal year or biennium.

Budget adoption (5, 15): For local government organizations, budget adoption consists of the passage by the legislative body (e.g., town or city council, commission, special district board) of an ordinance or resolution that contains spending authorizations, allocations of resources for all budget funds and/ or departments, and spending-related policy guidance for the prescribed fiscal year. For nonprofit organizations, budget adoption consists of the passage by the board of a resolution containing spending authorizations and resource allocations for all budget funds for the prescribed fiscal year. *See also* adopted budget.

Budget amendment (17): *See* amendment.

Budget cycle (5): A specified set of administrative and public activities that supports the planning, preparation, adoption, execution, and evaluation of a budget for a specific fiscal year or biennium.

Budget-cycle revenue forecast (7, 10): A revenue forecast prepared specifically to support the preparation and adoption of the executive's proposed budget, as well as the execution of an adopted budget over the fiscal year or biennium. The forecast takes into account the most recent economic and demographic conditions that could affect governmental revenues. *Contrast with* long-term revenue forecast.

Budget detail (15): Data and reports from the most detailed level of budget line-item accounts and raw data. The detailed data and information is used to build the department and program budget requests.

Budget-driven state (7): A tax system characteristic that defines how local governments perceive the relationship between revenue generation and budget development. In a budget-driven state, local governments prepare a preliminary or proposed budget and then request a tax increase to cover any gap between existing tax revenues and the budgeted level. *Contrast with* rate-driven state.

Budget fund (9): A fund established for use in the budgeting process for segregating and tracking related expected revenues, available resources, and expected spending. Budget funds are financial concepts and professional practices used to separate unrelated resources and spending. A budget fund directly corresponds to its counterpart accounting fund. *See also* fund; accounting fund.

Budget guidelines (10): *See* budget instructions.

Budget instructions; also, **budget guidelines (10):** Detailed guidance prepared under the direction of the chief executive officer (CEO) to guide the preparation of the departmental and program budget requests. Budget instructions provide analysis directions, instructions for data entry and software, basic assumptions, policy guidance, and an extensive and detailed schedule of due dates. Budget instructions provide one means for the executive to assert a policy agenda into the proposed budget.

Budget message (15): The transmittal cover letter that accompanies the executive's (CEO) proposed budget document. The budget message explains any major initiatives and changes, as well as the factors and assumptions underlying the budget.

Budget notes (15): *See* operating detail.

Budget officer (4): A position designated by the chief executive officer (CEO) and/or the chief finance officer/director (CFO) of a governmental organization with primary responsibility for the execution of the annual budget process in full compliance with state law. The organizational-level budget officer often has departmental- and program-level counterparts responsible for the budget process at their level of the organization. *Compare to* chief financial officer (CFO).

Budget package; also, **decision package, package (12, 14):** A package is an integrated plan of activities and specified resources designed to meet an objective or defined outcome. The resources integrated in a package typically include funding, FTEs, contracting authority, organizational support services, and external partner support. The terms may be loosely applied, where a "package" may cover funding for an entire department, a program, or just a portion of a program. In PPBS and performance budgeting, several budget packages may be designed as competing funding or program alternatives. The CEO and the legislative body (council, commission or board members) decide which combination of packages constitutes the most effective and low-cost response to community needs. *See also,* add package. *Related to* policy request package.

Budget request (5, 11, 12, 13, 14): The unit- or program-level request made to the chief executive (CEO) or finance officer by an agency, department, or program. These requests are submitted in response to and in conformance with budget instructions prepared by the central budget office, finance officer, or office of the executive. The budgeting formats discussed in chapters 11, 12, 13, and 14 separately or in a blend, provide the framework for an organization's, department's, or program's budget request.

CAFR (5, 18, 9): *See* comprehensive annual financial report.

Capital budget (16, 4, 11): The capital budget documents the revenues and expenditures associated with the acquisition of capital purchases during the fiscal year or biennium. This budget includes costs associated with the purchase of land, the construction and reconstruction of buildings and facilities, infrastructure development/replacement, and major equipment. Funds for these projects are usually appropriated from surplus funds, earmarked revenues, savings, or bond sales. The capital budget may be part of, but is often separate from, the jurisdiction's operating budget. *Contrast with* operating budget.

Capital budget request (16): A budget request for the pending fiscal year or biennium that is separate from the operating budget request and contains a list of proposed infrastructure construction and major equipment purchases and their financing. The list of projects is typically selected and prioritized from the jurisdiction or organization's capital improvement plan (CIP). *Contrast with* major construction/acquisition.

Capital construction (16): *See* major construction/acquisition; capital improvement.

Capital improvement (16): A classification of smaller capital purchases or projects. Each jurisdiction establishes a specific dollar threshold and useful life that defines a capital improvement. For example, a capital improvement may be any project that costs $50,000 or more in land costs, construction, purchasing, or renovation costs and whose underlying asset will have a useful life of at least 5 years. It can also include the purchase of major equipment with a long useful life.

Capital improvement plan (CIP) (16, 10): A multiyear strategic and operational plan that organizes a jurisdiction or organization's capital infrastructure, new construction, reconstruction, and major equipment needs into a schedule of projects and their likely funding sources. CIPs are typically based on an inventory of capital assets, including buildings and their component systems, roads, bridges, utility distribution systems and facilities, parks and recreation facilities, other facilities, and major equipment (including specialized vehicles). The first year of the CIP typically constitutes the capital budget for the fiscal year or biennium.

Capital lease (16): The leasing of a capital asset such as a building or major piece of equipment over an extended payment period. The lease agreement may, or may not, have an early cancellation clause. A capital lease may be an alternative to the purchase of a capital asset. *See also* certificate of participation (COP).

Capital outlay; also **capital outlay category (11):** Capital outlay consists of expenditures for minor or small capital purchases (typically $10,000 or less) of durable goods (depreciated) tied to the operations of a program or department. Line-items in this category of expenditures typically cover furniture and furnishings; power tools and specialized computer hardware; maintenance, minor reconstruction, and remodeling to facilities; and (if not covered through a central fund) automobiles and vehicles, and computer hardware and software.

Capital project (16): A transaction purchasing a major construction project, reconstruction project, or a major piece of equipment that is used more than one time and that lasts more than two years or over a depreciation schedule; a large purchase of a fixed asset such as land, buildings, water and sewer infrastructure, etc. State law or jurisdiction policies establish a specific dollar threshold that defines a capital project. A capital project may be financed by one or a combination of methods including pay-as-you-go, debt financing, or leasing methods.

Carryforward (15): The portion of an appropriation that is carried forward to the following fiscal year or biennium to permit the completion of particular project(s) or contracts. Although carryforwards are typically disclosed in the budget, they do not necessarily need to be expressly authorized because they were already appropriated by the legislative body. The jurisdiction's financial policies or budget ordinance will spell out generally when and how carryforwards may be executed.

Cash basis (9): An accounting practice and perspective that focuses strictly on the flow and accumulation of cash assets in an accounting fund. *Contrast with* full accrual basis; modified accrual basis.

Cash flow status report (17): A routine monitoring report, typically prepared monthly, that combines elements of the expenditure and revenue status report to detail the accumulation of revenues and carryforward savings (cash) to make payments. The adopted budget may set the planned level of revenues and expenditures, but the actual flow of revenues may vary widely within the fiscal year or biennium. The cash flow status report gives an indication of whether spending is running ahead, behind, or on pace with available resources. *See also* expenditure budget status report; revenue budget status report; carryforward.

CBO (5): *See* Congressional Budget Office.

CEO (3, 4): *See* chief executive officer.

Certificate of participation (COP) (16, 8): A certificate of participation (COP) is a tax-exempt government security used to raise funds for capital leases to improve and construct buildings or to purchase equipment. COPs are used to finance capital costs related to construction or acquisition, and may not be used to finance ongoing operating costs. COPs are sold to investors. In return, the investors receive COP payments, which include interest income that is often exempt from federal and state income tax.

CFO (3, 4): *See* chief financial officer.

Charge for service (6): *See* fee for service.

Charitable giving (8): Typically personal and relatively small size giving to an intermediary nonprofit or public service organization, often with income tax benefits. Frequently distinguished from philanthropic giving, which often is on a larger scale and made under a strategic plan. *Contrast with* philanthropic giving (Frumkin 2010).

Chart of accounts (9): A master list of all the budget funds and object codes (line-items) used to construct the budget for an organization. The chart of accounts defines the fund numbers and coding system used by the organization to link departments and programs (organization units) to revenues and resources and to expenditures or expenses as detailed by refined object code (line-item) categories. The chart of accounts also forms the basis of the organization's accounting systems and transaction ledgers.

Chief executive officer (CEO) (3, 4): An individual who holds the most senior authority to carry out and enforce the jurisdiction's laws and to act on behalf of the organization. The executive may be an elected official (e.g., a strong mayor, or county executive) or an appointed officer (e.g., a city or town "manager" or nonprofit "executive") depending on the structure and charter of the jurisdiction or organization. In some organizations, the CEO may have the title of "chief administrative officer," or "administrative officer." *See also* manager.

Chief financial officer (CFO) (3, 4): The senior-most position in an organization with responsibility for financial and budgeting issues (may have the title "finance director" in governmental organizations). The CFO typically reports directly to the CEO as a member of the executive management team. CFO responsibilities may also include procurement and contract services, investments, risk management, and other business activities. The CFO may serve as the governmental jurisdiction's budget officer with primary responsibility for the execution of the budget process, or may delegate these responsibilities to an independent budget officer position. *Compare to* budget officer.

CIP (16, 10): *See* capital improvement plan.

City (1): A local unit of government established under statutory authority from the state government. Incorporated cities operate under a charter approved by their voters and with the authority to levy taxes and collect fee revenues. Cities typically provide public safety, transportation, planning and land use, parks and recreation, water provision, wastewater management, cultural and library, and other municipal services. *See also* town.

Civic republican tradition (2): A democratic theory of governance often associated with Thomas Jefferson and the Anti-Federalists, who emphasized the importance of small geographic units composed of like-minded citizens who take an active and vigilant role in preserving the values of a democratic government. *Contrast with* procedural republican tradition; *see also* Anti-Federalists, coproduction.

Civil society (4): Citizen-generated governance activities and capacity often spontaneously initiated in response to a community issue or need. Civil society actors may organize through an informal-spontaneous network (Isett et al. 2011; Imperial 2005). *See also* informal-spontaneous network.

Close-out costs (15): *See* phase-out costs.

Commission form of city government (1, 2): An organizational arrangement for city and town governance with an elected city council and an elected mayor; the elected mayor acts as the primary and integrative executive, but each council member serves as the executive officer for a portfolio of departments and programs.

Community foundation (8): A legal structure and nonprofit organization that raises and accumulates funds for making grants that provide services and benefits to the community. Community leaders and major donors often sit on the boards of community foundations.

Comprehensive annual financial report (CAFR) (5, 18, 9): A final accounting of a jurisdiction or organization's finances for a fiscal year or biennium. A CAFR includes integrated financial statements covering the entire organization, summaries for individual accounting funds, and the independent auditor's report. CAFR reports comply with generally accepted accounting principles (GAAP) and state financial reporting standards. Completion of a CAFR is recommended by the Government Finance Officers Association (GFOA), and it serves as an important source of information in the review of the organization's financial condition by credit rating agencies.

Congressional Budget Office (CBO) (5): The congressional counterpart to the President's Office of Management and Budget (OMB) that was created by Congress in 1974 to provide independent estimates on the president's budget request and on any proposed budget and spending legislation.

Contingency reserve fund (10, 15): A budget and accounting fund set apart to provide for unforeseen expenditures or for anticipated purposes of uncertain amounts. *Related to* emergency fund; rainy day fund; revenue stabilization reserve fund. *Contrast with* reserves.

Continuous appropriations (15): Agency authority that has been granted by the legislative body to spend money on an ongoing basis without the need for new appropriation approval at the end of each fiscal year or biennium.

Contract for service (1, 4, 8, 11): An agreement for service performance for compensation with specific obligations of time duration, task description, performance, and administration. In the government sector, service contracts typically are secured through a competitive procurement process. Contractors and their subordinate subcontractors may appear as members of a service delivery network. *See also* grant; partnership contract; lead-organization network; network.

Coproduction (2, 12): A group or team leadership and management process that (1) builds agreement on the goals and their relative importance to the organizational unit, and (2) effects a deliberative process with partners, clients, and citizens that explores all of the pathways to achieve the goal and objectives for a given time period. Service delivery pathways to achieve the goals and objectives often include citizen and civic association participation in service delivery.

COP (16, 8): *See* certificate of participation.

Corporate foundation (8, Exhibit 16.1): A legal structure established by an organization to raise funds and to make grants that benefit the community. A corporate foundation established by a for-profit organization may use corporate revenues or endowment proceeds to fund grants (Frumkin 2010). A corporate foundation established by a nonprofit raises funds through philanthropy and charitable giving to support the programs and capital purchases of the parent nonprofit. *See also* foundation.

Council-manager form of city government (1, 2): An organizational arrangement for city and town governance with an elected council and a weak mayor either elected or appointed from the council members. The council hires a professional administrator to act as the chief executive officer who runs the government organization, including preparing and proposing a budget. Special purpose districts and some nonprofits use a similar arrangement of an elected or appointed board that hires an executive director to lead and administer the organization.

County (1): In almost all states, counties are local units of government that serve as an agent of the state, but with wide variation of state-delegated authority and service responsibility. In the New England states, counties are limited to judicial and sheriff's services, but in the other parts of the country, county governments provide a wide array of local- and regional-level services. Mega-counties often serve millions of residents and have all funds/budgets comparable to those of small state governments.

CSB (11): *See* current service baseline.

Current expense fund (9): *See* general fund.

Current service baseline (CSB) (11): A budget that continues the current fiscal year's programs at the same program content, quantity, quality, and efficiency levels through the upcoming fiscal year or biennium. Development of a current service baseline budget begins with the most recent legislatively adopted budget. The adopted budget is then adjusted to reflect forecasts of inflation/deflation, cost of living adjustments, and personnel wage step increases; mandatory caseload and workload increases; any phased-in or phased-out programs; any government-wide benefit program changes; adjustments for annexations and demographic changes to ensure uniform services across all citizens or clients; and a number of other factors defined in a jurisdiction's financial policies. Once computed, the current service baseline serves as a comparison point for alternative line-item budgets. *Contrast with* base budget.

Current unrestricted fund (9): A nonprofit organization budget or accounting fund with resources that the organization can use for any authorized use in the current fiscal period. Comparable to a government organization's general fund.

DB pension (15): *See* defined benefit pension.

DC pension (15): *See* defined contribution pension.

Debt capacity (16): A dollar limit of the amount of debt that a jurisdiction or organization may take on. Debt capacity may be based on several factors, including tax and revenue base wealth (e.g., percentage of total assessed value of all property within the jurisdiction); revenue availability, stability, and consistency; credit rating and debt repayment history; and the financial soundness of the jurisdiction or organization. State law may set indebtedness limits for local governments based on debt load as a percentage of the jurisdiction's total assessed property valuation.

Debt financing (16): Using some form of borrowed funds, typically bonds, to finance a capital infrastructure or major equipment lease or purchase. *See also* certificate of participation (COP); general obligation (GO) bonds; revenue bonds.

Debt service (16): Repaying the principal and interest on a jurisdiction's debt. The jurisdiction's debt is typically the bonds and certificates of participation (COPs) it has issued to raise money. Debt service is typically tied to capital expenditures.

Decision package (12, 14): *See* budget package.

Decision unit (14): In zero-base budgeting, an element of the organization with responsibility for the delivery of a specified program or activity of the organizational mission.

Dedicated revenue fund (9): A budget and accounting fund that segregates revenues from a specific source or set of sources to ensure their expenditure on solely authorized expenses. *Contrast with* general fund; *see also* restricted funds.

Defined benefit (DB) pension (15): A retirement benefits plan that pays a defined monthly benefit beginning at employee retirement until the death of the employee. In some programs, a partial benefit may be paid to the surviving spouse after the employee's death. The benefit is fully funded by the local jurisdiction. The benefit level is often determined as a percentage of the employee's years of highest wage levels. *Contrast with* defined contribution pension.

Defined contribution (DC) pension (15): A retirement benefits plan in which the employee contributes resources to an employer-sponsored savings plan. The employer—a local government, nonprofit, or for-profit organization—may contribute a defined annual amount to an employee's plan either as a specific amount or as a match of the employee's annual contribution. The retirement benefits received by the employee are determined by the amount of contributions and the investment earnings on those contributions. *Contrast with* defined benefit pension.

Democratic Balancewheel (2): A democratic theory of governance that emphasizes the importance of balancing the tensions among the often competing values of efficiency/effectiveness, civic engagement, responsiveness, and protection against tyranny by the majority or by governing officials.

Departmental revenues (9): Revenues generated by departmental or program activities used to fund departmental activities. Departmental revenues may flow through the general fund or through a dedicated fund.

Dillon's Rule (1): A legal doctrine derived from the "states reserved powers" clause of the Tenth Amendment of the U.S. Constitution, which holds that the states provide for the establishment of local governments and delegate authority to local governing bodies that otherwise hold no independent authority. Judge Dillon first articulated this doctrine in *Clinton v. Cedar Rapids and Missouri River Railroad* (1868). *Contrast with* Fordham Rule.

Directed giving (8): Charitable or philanthropic giving specified by the donor to a particular program or service outcome. Directed giving contrasts with funds donated to an intermediary nonprofit organization for its discretionary allocation to multiple service providers and community needs. *Contrast with* unspecified giving.

Discretionary funds (9): General funds and current unrestricted funds that may be used by the organization for any authorized purpose.

Donor-advised fund; also, **gift fund (8):** A fund, typically managed by commercial financial services entities, that makes charitable and philanthropic donations using the resources of—and on the direction of—its member investors. The investor donors typically conduct their own research into the charities and community needs; the funds verify the tax-exempt status of the recipient, make payments, and keep records of the donations. Donor-advised funds are similar to intermediary nonprofits in that they act to collect and distribute funds to designated organizations, but they do not provide the professional strategic advice, program evaluation, and oversight of a federated intermediary. *Contrast with* federated intermediary nonprofit; intermediary nonprofit; community foundation.

Earmark(15): The designation by one or several members of a legislative body of an expenditure, or of certain sources of revenue to support specific programs or agencies by statutory provision. Often used at the state and federal levels during adoption of appropriations bills.

Economic downturn (1): A general term used to describe a lower level of performance of the market economy based on commonly accepted measures. More specifically and recently, the term refers to the contraction of the national business cycle beginning in December 2007 and reaching bottom in June of 2009. The lagging effects of the downturn continued in 2011, with depressed real estate values in most markets (S&P Indices 2011) and double-digit unemployment in rural areas of the country.

Effectiveness measure (13): The systematic collection of data to determine whether a program or set of activities is achieving some combination of desired outputs, outcomes, results, or impacts. *See* productivity; planning, programming, budgeting system; performance measure; performance status report; Service Efforts and Accomplishments (SEA) Report.

Emergency fund (15): In addition to or as an alternative to a contingency reserve fund, an organization may establish a separate fund (called an emergency fund) to store resources to meet unforeseen events and budget needs. *Related to* contingency reserve fund; rainy day fund; revenue stabilization reserve fund.

Encumbered (9, 17): *See* encumbrance.

Encumbrance; also, **encumbered (9, 17):** The commitment of appropriated funds to purchase an item or service. An obligation or reservation of appropriated funds that is typically spent within the fiscal year. If an encumbrance is made near the end of the fiscal year, the expenditure will need to be made within 30 to 60 days of the end of the fiscal year. If the appropriated fund is an all-years fund for capital or grant expenditures, the encumbrance can extend into the new fiscal year, but the related expenditure must be made within a payment time frame specified by policy. *See also* ending fund balance; carryforward.

Ending fund balance (9): The level of resources remaining in a fund at the close of the fiscal year or biennium after all revenues have been received and all expenditures have been completed. As part of the ending fund balance, state regulations may specify a reserve balance that equals a specified portion of general fund total spending; another portion of the ending fund balance may be encumbered for contractual commitments; other funds may be carried forward for authorized purposes; still other funds may be restricted for other specific future purposes. The remaining portion may be unrestricted and available to use without restrictions for spending in the next fiscal year. *See also* opening fund balance; carryforward; encumbrance (encumbered).

Endowment (8): An accumulation of funds invested for growth, but also to generate annual interest and other income. The principal of the endowment is maintained and grown, while the annual income is used to make grants or to cover defined expenses. *Related to* foundation; trust.

Enterprise fund (9): A budget or accounting fund containing revenues and expenses of self-supporting business operations. Local governments typically operate utility enterprises for water, wastewater, and in some states electricity. Transit special districts that operate bus and rail transit systems are typical operated as enterprise funds. *See also* proprietary funds.

Enterprise zone (8): A political district, often with taxing authority, established to stimulate economic growth within its boundaries. Enterprise zones are typically authorized under state laws. Businesses agreeing to locate in the zone may receive tax relief in exchange for guaranteeing defined levels of employment, infrastructure investment, compensatory payments to local governments for services, and operations for a defined period of time. *Related to* tax increment financing (TIF).

Escrow account (6): *See* escrow fund.

Escrow fund; also, escrow account (6): Established to hold funds separately in trust for another party, often as part of a transaction. Escrow funds allow purchasers and sellers, or contributors and beneficiaries, to see the amount and availability of funds set aside for their mutually defined purpose.

Estimate (7): A numerical prediction of future values or quantity, typically based on historical and recent data, and made using quantitative techniques tempered by professional judgment.

Excise tax (6): A sales tax collected on the sale of a specified type of good or service, often on a per unit basis, with revenues typically dedicated to a particular governmental program or service. For example, a motor fuels per gallon sales tax dedicated to road maintenance or construction; a tax on lodging, food and beverage, and car rentals dedicated to tourism and convention facilities.

Executive recommended budget (5, 15, 4): *See* proposed budget.

Executive requested budget (15): *See* proposed budget.

Expenditure (9): *See* expense.

Expenditure budget status report (17): A monitoring report, typically reported monthly, that identifies the amount of money spent to date, and remaining to be spent, in the fiscal year or biennium. Often the expenditure status report is prepared at the control level of the budget fund or the department; the report indicates whether spending is within budgeted amounts, and how much money is still available for expenditure. *See also* revenue budget status report; cash flow status report.

Expenditure code budgeting (11): *See* line-item budgeting; object code budgeting.

Expense; also, expenditure (9): Transaction that spends money from a fund to obtain goods or to provide services. An expense applies under full accrual accounting; an expenditure applies under modified accrual accounting (cf. Granof and Khumawala 2011, chap. 4, 5).

Fair share (5, 11): A budget actor behavior which assumes that, in the face of any major changes from the previous year's budget levels, all increases or cuts will be shared fairly or uniformly by all departments and programs.

Family foundation (8): A legal structure and nonprofit organization that receives funds from a family estate or family income, accumulates and manages the funds, and then makes grants to further a defined philanthropic agenda. Family members typically control the board of a family foundation. *See also* trust; private foundation.

Federalists (2): A group of American founders who favored the creation of a strong national government with adequate powers and a system of checks and balances that would attract highly qualified and experienced officials; those officials would use their expertise to craft wise policies that could be implemented efficiently, effectively, and energetically. *See also* procedural republican tradition. *Contrast with* Anti-Federalists.

Federated intermediary nonprofit (8): A nonprofit organization that raises funds on behalf of numerous member or partner organizations. The organization may or may not have an endowment. *See also* intermediary nonprofit.

Fee for service; also, charge for service (6): 1. Revenue collected in return for a service. In some contexts, the fee is charged on a per unit of service rendered basis; in other contexts, the fee is a general charge or assessment that broadly covers the cost of a service. Applicable to both governmental and nonprofit organizations. 2. The concept of charging a fee only to those citizens or clients who actually use or benefit from the service, e.g., the students paying college tuition are the beneficiaries of that service.

Financial audit (18): Examination of an organization's accounting records by a certified public accountant to express an opinion on whether the financial statements are presented in accordance with generally accepted accounting standards.

Financial forecast (10, 15, 7): A strategic forecast of a government jurisdiction's long-term (three- to 10-year) financial environment, including long-term revenue forecasts; forecasts of fund balances and reserves; long-term expenditure forecasts based on forecasts of caseloads, service demand, and client need; expected commitments for personnel salary and benefit costs; expected and unexpected costs for public employee retirement system obligations (PERS); expected expenditures and commitments for service contracts and partnerships; anticipated maintenance and capital outlay expenses; future credit obligations; regional demographic trends; federal economic and financial policies; and the state and federal political environment surrounding intergovernmental revenues. Financial forecasts are typically developed for all major budget funds (general funds, major enterprise funds, and major special revenue funds). A key element of an organization's financial strategic plan. *See also* long-term revenue forecast; strategic plan.

Financial policies (10): Definitions and statements adopted by the jurisdiction or organization to define procedures and practices and to guide decision making related to finance and budgeting. Local government financial policies must also reflect applicable state law and regulations.

Financially sustainable (15): A financially sustainable organization has the resources to meet all extended term debt, midterm debt, and near-term operational obligations. It is able to endure extreme financial conditions because it maintains a structurally balanced budget with sufficient recurring revenues and resources meeting or exceeding recurring expenditures in all future time periods. A financially sustainable organization maintains sufficient reserves and contingency reserve funds to respond resiliently to the financial stress of severe reductions in revenues or sharp increases in expenditures. *Related to* structurally balanced budget; recurring expenditures; recurring revenues; recurring resources; contingency reserve fund.

Fines and forfeitures (6): A class of governmental revenues generated from citizen or client failure to comply with program requirements or regulations, failure to pay taxes due, or violation of criminal codes.

Fiscal year (FY) (5): A defined one-year period that segregates all revenue and expenditure transactions from earlier and later periods. The dates of local governmental fiscal years are typically defined by state statute. Nonprofits may set their fiscal year according to need and policy. The fiscal year may or may not coincide with the calendar year—often it does not. For governments that practice a one-year budget cycle, this is the amount of time that a budget is legally binding. The years following the abbreviation FY are the years in which the fiscal year begins and ends, e.g., FY12–13. Common local government fiscal years are July 1 to June 30, or January 1 to December 31. *See also* biennium.

Fixed cost (7): A cost incurred to operate a program that occurs at any level of program size. Typically, fixed costs include program capital costs, program facilities use costs, basic utilities, and basic communications and information technology. Jurisdictional or organizational financial policies may define administrative costs as fixed, or as incremental or variable costs. *Compare to* incremental cost (step cost); variable cost.

Fordham Rule (1): The Fordham Rule says that home-rule governments should be allowed maximum authority, except in areas of civil relations and felony criminal law. The rule was used by Jefferson Fordham in 1953 as the basis for the American Municipal Association's model home-rule charter. The rule contrasts with the opposite principle in Dillon's Rule, in which local governments only have the authority specifically enumerated to them by the parent state government. *Contrast with* Dillon's Rule.

Forecast (7, 10, 15): A set of estimates of future conditions. Analysts typically forecast future revenues, expenditure trends, and service caseload demand. When data is available, forecasts apply mathematical and statistical techniques to quantify past trends, cycles, and predictable variation as evidence of future behavior. A clear understanding of the assumptions underlying the data and techniques is critical to a valid forecast. Recent and current information may also color a forecast. *See also* estimate; budget-cycle revenue forecast; long-term revenue forecast; financial forecast.

Foundation (8, 3): A legal structure and organization that raises and accumulates funds for making grants to further a defined agenda. The foundation organization has a board that sets policy and the philanthropic agenda. Family members typically control the board of a family foundation, and community leaders sit on the boards of community foundations. Foundations often accumulate and grow funds in an endowment with annual giving sized to match annual income.

Founding Beatitudes (2): A set of teachings by the American founders regarding the four values essential for the preservation of democratic liberty: majority rule, competent government (i.e., efficiency and effectiveness), civic engagement, and protection against majority tyranny. *See also* Democratic Balancewheel.

Full accrual basis (9, 18): An accounting practice and perspective that focuses on the timing of an economic benefit of a purchase or revenue. Under the full accrual method, costs are accrued and matched with appropriate revenues over the life of an investment. *Contrast with* cash basis; modified accrual basis (cf. Granof and Khumawala 2011, chap. 4, 5).

Full-time equivalent (FTE) (11): A formula for calculating the duration, intensity, and cost of staff positions. One (1) FTE equates to a specified number of service hours worked over the full 12-month fiscal year as designated in a personnel services or negotiated union labor contract. A partial FTE is the prorated cost based on the proportion of annual hours worked. For example, for a half-time employee (0.5 FTE), the employee may work 6-months at full-time, or 12 months on a half-time basis. In the end, however, the employee will work one-half the hours specified in the contract for one FTE.

Functional area (15): A broad grouping of related and complementary services provided typically by several agencies, government departments, or major programs. A budget aggregation level above the department level and below the full organization. The name of the functional area is typically descriptive of the area's general purpose and services, e.g. General Government, Public Safety and Justice, Transportation and Planning, Health and Human Services, National Defense, Natural Resources and Environment.

Fund (9): A set of related accounts and transactions that must balance at the close of the fiscal year or biennium. In application, a fund is used in budgeting as a budget fund, and as a related accounting fund to record transactions. Governmental budgeting uses multiple funds to segregate revenue sources according to their legal authorization. Governments also use multiple funds to enhance transparency. *See also* balance.

FY (5): *See* fiscal year.

GAAP (9, 18): *See* generally accepted accounting principles.

GASB (9, 18): *See* Governmental Accounting Standards Board.

General fund (GF); also, current expense fund (9, 15): Receives revenues not designated to any other fund maintained by the jurisdiction. A general fund receives revenues from taxes, fees, interest earnings, and other unrestricted sources. For local governments, most of this money comes from property taxes, retail sales and use taxes, and fees and charges for services. General funds may be used to pay any authorized purpose but most often are used to support program operations and maintenance. *Compare to* current unrestricted fund.

General fund department (9): A local government departmental unit or program defined as wholly or partially dependent on resources from the jurisdiction's general fund for operations and maintenance. *Contrast with* self-supported department.

General obligation (GO) bond (16): A finance instrument in which the jurisdiction or organization borrows funds for an extended period and repays the debt with interest over that period. General obligation bonds are backed by the full faith and credit of the jurisdiction issuing them, which legally and morally obligates the government to repay the debt from any received revenues, including general fund revenues.

Generally accepted accounting principles (GAAP) (9, 18): Professionally accepted accounting and financial procedures and reporting formats. In the case of local governments, the standards promulgated by the Governmental Accounting Standards Board (GASB) are accepted as GAAP rules. In the case of nonprofits, the Financial Accounting Standards Board (FASB) establishes the GAAP rules. GAAP standards help to ensure fiscal accountability, transparency, and consistency of practice across governmental jurisdictions or nonprofit organizations.

GF (9, 15): *See* general fund.

Gift funds (8): *See* donor-advised funds.

GO bonds (16): *See* general obligation bonds.

Goal (12): A primary structure of program budgeting and PPBS designed to achieve part of the organization's mission. A goal defines the purpose of an organization, organization unit, or program in terms of a community impact or societal outcome. A goal statement expresses values and often is without a time frame in that the service or activity outcome is continually needed into the future. A goal defines the outcome condition (or "what") of organizational or program action. *See also* planning, programming, budgeting system; mission statement; objective.

Governmental Accounting Standards Board (GASB) (9, 18): The national professional organization responsible for promulgating the professional standards for finance and accounting (GAAP) that govern the financial procedures and reporting required of local governments. *See also* generally accepted accounting principles.

Governmental foundation (8, 6): A nonprofit foundation established to support and to augment the mission of a governmental agency (e.g., local school district to a federal agency or installation). The foundation is a quasi-public entity in that is typically chartered as a private nonprofit organization that raises private revenues but has some degree of authorization, resource support, governance (board membership), and oversight from a public governmental organization or legislative body. Typically blends the attributes of a corporate foundation and a community foundation in support of a governmental agency and its mission.

Governmental funds (9): Monies used for functions and services inherent to government, which typically do not generate sufficient revenues to fund their operation, e.g., elections, property assessment, and taxation. *Contrast with* proprietary funds; enterprise funds; trust and agency funds.

Grant (4, 8): A service agreement that often includes the performance of professional skills and professional judgment in return for payment. The procurement process may not require competitive bidding. *Compare with* contract for service.

Hamiltonian leadership model (2): A public service leadership model that emphasizes the importance of innovation and an entrepreneurial spirit in building democratic trust and legitimacy.

Hiring freeze (17): A strong form of a position control. A prohibition by the CEO, central budget office, or legislative body that prohibits departments from refilling vacant positions or from filling new positions, usually as means to save money under very difficult financial circumstances. Typical exceptions to hiring freezes involve positions related to public health and safety, or positions that are funded from external sources such as enterprise fund revenues or grants. *See also* position controls; spending freeze.

Horizontal equity (6): The equal treatment of an individual taxpayer relative to all other taxpayers with the same familial, demographic, revenue, and economic factors. A measure of the fairness of a tax system. *Compare with* vertical equity.

IGA (1, 4): *See* intergovernmental agreement.

Income tax (6): A tax levied on personal, business, or corporate income, including employment salary wages and benefits, investment revenues, retirement and benefits payments, and business income. Income taxes are typically levied by states and by the federal government, but are levied by local governments as allowed by state law. *Contrast with* wage tax.

Incremental budgeting; also, incrementalism (5, 11): A term that describes the common practice of most public agencies. This practice requires that only additions or deletions to current budgeted expenditures be explained and justified. Funding decisions are made on the margin, based on the justification for the increased costs of operating agencies or programs. This process can be used in conjunction with either line-item budgeting or program (PPBS) budgeting.

Incremental cost; also, step cost (7): A cost structured to increase or decrease by a series of steps or increments over the full range of output production. Each increment reflects a defined range of production output, with the cost remaining uniform across the defined range. Capital equipment and vehicle costs, along with facilities-use costs driven by client numbers, can be structured as incremental costs. Jurisdictional or organizational financial policies may define administrative costs as fixed, incremental, or variable. *Compare to* fixed cost; variable cost.

Incrementalism (5, 11): *See* incremental budgeting.

Independent foundation (8): *See* private foundation.

Informal spontaneous network (4, 17): (Isett et al. 2011). A network arrangement characterized by trust-based relationships and a decentralized structure with relatively equal distribution of authority and power; such networks are transitory in duration, and contingent or spontaneous in establishment. The informal-spontaneous networks often channel and express the concerns and energy of civil society in response to issue developments. *See also* network; *contrast with* participant-governed network.

Innovation (14): The development of new ideas or behaviors, and the adoption of their use into organizations and service delivery (see Damanpour and Schneider 2008; Hartley 2005).

Input (12, 13): The resource put into a program. Examples are dollars, number of employees, and equipment.

Interdepartmental category (11): *See* interfund category.

Interdepartmental charges (15): *See* internal charge for service.

Interest group liberalism (2): A democratic theory of governance that emphasizes the dominating role of interest groups led by professional experts; influence is exercised at the subgovernmental level of operations (i.e., congressional subcommittees and executive-level agencies and bureaus).

Interfund category; also, **interdepartmental category (11):** In a line-item budget schedule, a category of expenditures that covers internal purchases of services by a department or program from another, or by a department or program from a central services or other fund. The category typically includes line-items for the direct purchase of services needed for department or program operation, and in some jurisdictions the purchase of allocated administrative costs in the form of internal charges for services. *Related to* internal charge for service (interdepartmental expenditure).

Interfund transfer (15, 9): *See* transfer.

Intergovernmental agreement (IGA) (1, 4): A formally defined relationship between two or more governmental organizations stating a common understanding on policy or service provision. *See also* interlocal agreement.

Intergovernmental revenues (6): Revenues authorized by a state or federal program delivered to local governments for specified programs or grants or for general fund use. In many instances, the state government acts as a tax collection agent that returns the proportional share of the collected revenues to each local government; in others, intergovernmental revenues are distributed by formula or under grant or contract provisions.

Interlocal agreement (1, 4): An intergovernmental agreement between two or more local-level governments. Local governments would include county, township, city, town, and special purpose district or authority. *See also* intergovernmental agreement (IGA).

Intermediary nonprofit (3, 8): A nonprofit organization that raises funds for redistribution to other service providers, typically by grant or service contract. May be organized as a federated intermediary, foundation, or service provider. Examples: local United Way chapters, Salvation Army chapters, and Catholic Relief Services.

Internal charge for service; also, **internal service charge, interdepartmental expenditure (9, 11, 15):** 1. The purchase of services within an organization by one department or program from another. Internal service charges occur in two forms: the direct purchase of goods and services to support program activities, and the payment for a share of central services and commonly shared administrative costs allocated to each operating department in the organization. Central services and shared costs include: human resources, information technology (IT), communications, building and facility maintenance, and vehicle maintenance and vehicle fuel. Internal service charges are often entered and cleared through a central services fund. 2. A category of expenditures in the line-item budget schedule for such internal charges. *See also* interfund category (interdepartmental category).

Internal controls (18): The integrated set of policies and procedures established by an organization to ensure reliable financial reporting, effective and efficient operations, and compliance with applicable laws and regulations.

Internal service charge (15): *See* internal charge for service. *Related to* interfund category (interdepartmental category).

Jeffersonian leadership model (2): A public service leadership model that emphasizes the importance of civic engagement and local control in building democratic trust and legitimacy.

Jurisdiction: A local government.

Lead-organization network (4, 17): (Provan and Kenis 2007) A multiparty network with authority, administration, resource control, and performance compliance centered in one or several dominant "lead" organizations. *See also* network.

Leasing (16): Using pay-as-you-go or debt financing to cover regular payments for major equipment use or purchase over the useful life of the equipment. A jurisdiction or organization may be able to break a lease and return the equipment partway through the lease period. *See also* certificate of participation.

Legislative body (4, 10, 15): The group of elected or appointed officials of a government (e.g., town or city council, county commission or court, or special district board) that represents the citizens and creates the jurisdiction's laws and policies. The body also decides how government will be financed and holds responsibility for budget adoption. For a nonprofit organization, the board of directors serves as the legislative body that sets policy and adopts a budget for the organization.

Leverage (8): To combine a philanthropic donation with other funds to gain sufficient resources to accomplish a defined goal. Contribution of the donation may be conditioned on the previous or simultaneous donations of other donors. *See also* seed donation.

Levy (6, 7): *See* tax levy.

Liability (18): Amount owed to creditors of the government or other organization.

Line-item budgeting (11, 9): A budget analysis strategy and format that categorizes all expenditures by refined numerical object codes or lines of expenditure. Line-item expenditures typically fall into several major classes: personal services, materials and supplies, capital outlay, interdepartmental, and contractual services. Line-items are the focus of development, analysis, authorization, and control of the budget. *See also* object code budgeting.

Long-term revenue forecast (7, 10): A revenue forecast of extended time frame (3- to 10-years) to support financial strategic planning and extended financial forecasting, and to provide context to annual budget construction. Long-term revenue forecasts are typically prepared for each recurring revenue used by a jurisdiction or organization. A recurring revenue consistently produces a level of revenues within its generating capacity under varying economic conditions. The goal of the forecast is to predict revenue generation under the most likely economic scenarios. *See also* recurring revenues; financial forecast; *contrast with* budget-cycle revenue forecast.

Lottery revenues (6): Money that a local jurisdiction receives from the state government as intergovernmental revenues generated by people who play state-sanctioned lottery games.

Madisonian leadership model (2): A public service leadership model that emphasizes the importance of negotiation and compromise among competing interests in building democratic trust and legitimacy.

Maintenance of effort (6, 9): Consistent and sufficient expenditures by a government to demonstrate continued commitment and involvement in a jointly funded program. Failure to make sufficient and timely maintenance of effort payments may result in the discontinuance of grant funds from a state or the federal government.

Major construction/acquisition (16): A type of capital expenditure defined by law and/or by jurisdiction that exceeds a dollar threshold, such as a major construction or purchase to build, buy, or change a facility, or to purchase land. *Contrast with* capital improvement.

Manager (4): A professional executive at the county, city, village, or town level who is appointed by the legislative body to oversee and direct the day-to-day responsibilities of the jurisdiction as the chief executive or administrative officer (CEO). Along with many other duties, the manager is responsible for preparing and proposing a budget. *See also* chief executive officer (CEO); council-manager form of city government.

Materials and supplies category (M&S); also, **materials and services category (11):** In a line-item budget, a category of line-items or object codes that include nonpersonnel consumable goods and services to operate a program and to deliver services. It usually includes expenditures to support contracted, professional, and jointly partnered services. In some jurisdictions, the category may include the internal charges for services to cover the facilities, central services, and administrative costs allocated to the program. *See also* personnel category (personal services category); capital outlay category; interfund category (interdepartmental category); internal charge for services. In recent years in many jurisdictions, the purchase of contracted and professional services has increased to far exceed spending on consumable materials and supplies. This has led to a renaming of the category as "materials and services."

Millage rate (7): A property tax rate applied to $1,000 of assessed property value.

Mission statement (12): A statement of the purposes an organization or program intends to achieve, typically applied in a broad, long-term strategic context. Well-developed mission statements may include the separate or combined subelements of a mission/purpose statement, a beliefs and values statement, and a vision statement. *See also* planning, programming budgeting system; beliefs and values statement; vision statement.

Modified accrual basis (9, 18): An accounting approach and perspective often used by local governments to highlight activity in the short-term fiscal period. The approach identifies revenues and costs as recorded when the benefit is identified or occurs, and when resources are available for receipt or payment. *Contrast with* other accounting approaches, such as cash basis and full accrual basis (cf. Granof and Khumawala 2011, chap. 4, 5).

NAO (1, 4, 17): *See* network administrative organization.

Net assets (18): The difference between the assets and liabilities of a government. Total assets less total liabilities equal net assets.

Net present value (NPV) (16): A quantitative analysis of an investment's costs and benefits that considers the cost of the money and interest used to make the investment or perform the project over its lifetime. This method is often used to value and to compare alternative capital investments.

Network (1): A relationship of at least three autonomous organizations that work together to address an issue of common concern and to achieve their own organizational goals (Provan and Kenis 2007, 231). Networks may be informal or formal (Isett et al. 2011), and be self-initiated or established by contract or mandate (Provan and Kenis 231). *See also* informal spontaneous network; participant-governed network; lead-organization network; network administrative organization.

Network administrative organization (NAO) (4, 17): (Provan and Kenis 2007). An independent organization that provides administrative and leadership services to a multiorganization network (NAO-led network). Network members may elect a governing board that authorizes the NAO to act on behalf of the network. A large portion of the authority in the network is concentrated in the NAO and its policies. *See also* network.

New public governance (NPG) (13): (Osborne 2006, 384) An academic and practitioner movement in public administration that emerged in response to new public management (NPM). NPG emphasizes the joint and often networked production of public services by government, nonprofits, and for-profit organizations, and, in so doing, recognizes trust, relational capital, and relational contracts as the foundation of much of modern-day governance and the joint production of the common good.

New public management (NPM) (2, 13, 19): (Osborne 2006, 379) An academic and political movement that began in the 1980s and applied for-profit–sector performance management techniques to government program implementation. The movement organizationally separated policy development from policy implementation, encouraged market alternatives to the government delivery of services, and widely embraced competitive contracting and public-private–sector partnerships as a means to increase the efficiency and effectiveness of public service delivery.

Nonmarket goods and services (6): Economic goods or program services that cannot easily be valued, or are purposefully not valued, through market exchange transactions. For example, governmental protection of the civil rights of citizens, arrestees, convicts, and governmental employees are nonmarket services.

Nonrecurring appropriation; nonrecurring expenditure also, **one-time expenditure (15, 10):** Purchase or appropriation made for one-time items or projects. Examples include capital equipment purchases, special studies, pilot projects, and nonrecurring information technology upgrades. *Contrast with* recurring expenditure.

Nonrecurring revenue; also, **one-time revenue (15):** A revenue not tied to the jurisdiction's normal flow of tax, fee, intergovernmental, or other routine source. For example, a federal grant for a single purchase or project. *Contrast with* recurring revenues.

NPG (13): *See* new public governance.

NPM (2, 13): *See* new public management.

NPV (16): *See* net present value.

Object code budgeting (11, 9, Exhibit 9.1): The practice of relying on predetermined categories of expenditure in the budget process for analysis and budget control. Commonly used "object classification" categories include personal services, materials and supplies/services (M&S) and equipment, capital outlay, and interdepartmental/internal service charges. Some states impose a standard system of object classification codes on all local government budgets. See example in Exhibit 9.1. *See also* line-item budgeting.

Objective (12): A primary structure of program/PPBS budgeting that defines, typically in detail, how an organization or program will attain a goal in total or in part. An objective is a desired result in which the achievement is measureable within a given time frame at a specified level or increment of cost. An objective must have a specified time frame and specified outcome condition to define its completion. *See also* planning, programming, budgeting system; goal; activity.

Office of Management and Budget (OMB) (5): An executive-level office of the U.S. government that ensures the technical integrity of federal agency budget requests, compliance with the president's political and policy agenda, and the preparation of an integrated proposed budget that the president presents to Congress for debate and approval in January of every fiscal year. *Contrast with* CBO.

OMB (5): *See* Office of Management and Budget.

One-time expenditure (15): *See* nonrecurring appropriation.

One-time revenue (15, 10): *See* nonrecurring revenue.

Opening fund balance (9, 6): The level of resources in a budget fund at the beginning of the fiscal year or biennium. The opening fund balance is equal to the ending fund balance from the previous fiscal year. Portions of the opening fund balance may be encumbered or reserved for specific purposes; other portions may be unrestricted and available for spending in the coming fiscal year. *See also* ending fund balance.

Operating budget (3, 4, 5, 11): The budget established for the operation of a jurisdiction's departments, agencies, and programs, and often includes funding for routine maintenance (e.g., Operations & Maintenance, O&M). Typically, the operating budget is approved by the jurisdiction's legislative body (commission, council, board), or in the case of grants, contracts, etc. by the contracting/granting authority. *Contrast with* capital budget.

Operating detail; also, budget notes (15): A moderately detailed report with summary information supporting the CEO's proposed budget, typically presented on a fund-by-fund or a department-by-department basis. The operating detail usually includes a mission statement, description of major services, programmatic objectives for the upcoming fiscal year, spending levels by summary line-item code for the prior year, adopted spending levels for the current fiscal year, proposed spending for the upcoming fiscal year, expected revenues, and perhaps key performance measurement data. May also include comparable revenues. *Contrast with* budget detail.

Outcome; also, outcome measure (13): An outcome is an indicator or measure to assess the actual impact of an agency's/program's actions. Outcome measures often reflect more than a strict quantitative measure of production (output). Outcome measures also attempt to recognize attributes such as quality, fit to the situation, value, unmeasureable qualities, and effect on community status. An outcome measure is a means for qualified comparisons between the actual result and the intended result. An example is reducing the rate of infant mortality by a certain percentage.

Outlays (17): The use or spending of appropriated funds by an agency or program through expenditure transactions. Outlays may be lower than what has been appropriated (adopted for expenditure during a given budget year), or what has been authorized (approved for potential expenditure).

Output; also, output measure (13): The quantitative number or indicator of a good or service produced by an agency. An example is the number of personnel trained by a vocational education organization, but without qualitative or cost inferences.

Package (12): *See* budget package.

Participant-governed network (4, 17): A durable network characterized by relative equality of authority and power decentralized over all members, trust-based interpersonal relationships, mutual decision making, and mutual enforcement of norms and performance (Provan and Kenis 2007). *See also* network; *contrast with* informal spontaneous network.

Partnership agreement (1): A loose understanding or a formal agreement between multiple organizations or citizen groups to respond jointly to an issue or community situation through resource contributions, policy intention, organizational action, and shared expertise. A partnership agreement often serves to identify network membership, member roles, rules, performance expectations, and procedures.

Partnership contract (4): A service delivery contractual relationship of broad program scope and extended duration that is often structured to bring private-sector professional expertise to the partnership. The broad scope and extended duration of partnership contracts limit the effectiveness of direct contract enforcement and administration provisions and techniques. Strong, trust-based, interpersonal relationships may become the key to a successful partnership contract. *Contrast with* contract for service.

Pay-as-you-go financing (16, 15): A method of financing capital projects that relies on funding from current year's revenues or from funds saved in advance in a reserve fund. *Contrast with* prefunding.

Payroll tax (6): *See* wage tax.

Performance audit (18): An assessment of a program's performance against objective criteria.

Performance budgeting (13): A method of allocating resources based on various measures of results, which can include efficiency, effectiveness, customer satisfaction, and other similar performance criteria. Performance budgeting requires the clear specification of goals and objectives and the systematic collection of data to measure the achievement of these goals and objectives.

Performance measure (13): A standard or indicator used by agencies/departments/programs to measure operational performance and progress toward the achievement of the objectives and goals adopted by an organization on behalf of the community. *See also* benchmark; outcome; output; performance status report.

Performance status report (17): A routine reporting of performance measures and indicators as a means to measure attainment of the program goals and objectives. If the goals and objectives are included in the adopted or amended budget, the performance status would be reported internally and externally. If the goals and objectives are not included in the budget, they are often just reported internally. The performance report may be prepared on a monthly or quarterly basis. *See also* performance measure; effectiveness measure; Service Efforts and Accomplishments (SEA) Report.

Permit and license revenues (6): A fee charged by a governmental organization that allows the citizen or client to undertake, at his or her discretion, an activity regulated by that government.

PERS (15, 10, 11): *See* Public Employee Retirement System.

Personal services category (11): *See* personnel category.

Personnel category; also, **personal services category (11):** In line-item budgeting, the cost category that covers employee costs. This category typically includes line-items for regular, overtime, temporary, and vacation salaries; medical and dental benefits; pension fund and retirement contributions; unemployment compensation; and other benefit costs. *See also* materials and supplies category; capital outlay category; interfund category (interdepartmental category).

Phase-in costs; also, **start-up costs (15):** The amount of operational and maintenance expenditures needed to establish and build up a new program to its full operational level. For the fiscal year or biennium following the phase in/start up, the program will need expenditures at the full level to continue operation.

Phase-out costs; also, **close-out costs (15):** The opposite of "phase-in costs," it is the amount of operational and maintenance funds for part of a fiscal year or a biennium to wind down and close out a program.

Philanthropic giving (8): A typically larger scale donation often made under a structured or strategic plan for coordinated donations, recipient performance requirements, and tax and financial benefits. Philanthropic giving is distinguished from less strategic, smaller-scale charitable giving (Frumkin 2010). *Contrast with* charitable giving.

Planning, programming, budgeting system (PPBS) (12): A particular version of program budgeting that was popularized by Secretary of Defense Robert McNamara in the 1960s. Like all program budgeting, it breaks budget expenditures out by types of activities. But unlike simple program budgeting, PPBS emphasizes systematically linking activities, goals, and budgets together into an integrated system. *See also* program budgeting.

Policy request package (10, Exhibit 10.3): A departmental or program request for changes in statute, regulations, policy, or guidance necessary to implement a proposed budget package. A policy change request will often complement its companion program budget package. *Related to* budget package, decision package, add package.

Polity (1, 8, 19): A Greek term for the form or constitution of an organized unit of governance. The term emphasizes the organic and interrelated social, economic, cultural, and political components of a community that combine to give a community its distinct identity and character. We use the term throughout the book to focus attention on the community as a whole, not just the formal structures and processes of government.

Position controls (17): Central budget office or executive review of all department and program requests to fill new positions or to reclassify existing positions; position controls are set in an effort to assure sufficient position and expenditure authority to cover the cost of additional wages and benefits. A technique to help limit expenditures and to protect against budget problems.

PPBS (12): *See* planning, programming, budgeting system.

Prefunding (15): A term used relative to retiree health care. It recognizes the cost of a retiree future benefit as it is "earned" or first established by the beneficiary, and pays ahead for a future retiree benefit rather than waiting to pay for a benefit when it is actually used years or decades in the future. Prefunding, like an investment trust fund, accumulates assets toward paying future costs and supplements those assets with investment returns. *Contrast with* pay-as-you-go financing.

Preliminary budget (5): An early stage of the budget developmental process, which consists of the budgets compiled from all department and program requests awaiting approval by the executive officer. On executive approval, the preliminary budget becomes the proposed, approved, or requested executive budget. In some states, the preliminary budget also formally proposes the tax and other revenue levels needed in a final adopted budget. The proposed revenue levels must be publicly advertised and adopted by the legislative body in advance before the executive can formally propose a complete budget. *See also* proposed budget; executive requested budget.

Priority budgeting (14): A budgeting procedure that asks executives, department heads, and program managers to rank the relative importance of services and activities, and then to identify sources of revenue to support the ranked priorities (see GFOA 2011c). Frequently, this process is part of a larger community-wide or council-centered strategic planning activity that creates broad guidelines for the priority setting undertaken by departments heads and program managers.

Private foundation; also, **family foundation, independent foundation (8):** Typically, a nonprofit organization established and directed by an individual, family, or private group for philanthropic gifting. The foundation may directly gift revenues from its owner or often may establish an endowment fund to generate investment earnings, which are then used to support gifting. *Contrast with* trust.

Procedural republican tradition (2): A democratic theory of governance often associated with James Madison and Alexander Hamilton, who emphasized the importance of a procedural system of checks and balances and separation of powers to produce policies based on knowledge and experience and to secure liberty against the usurpation of authority by overreaching government officials and tyrannical majorities. *See also* Federalists; *contrast with* civic republican tradition.

Productivity (13): A ratio of the quantity and/or quality of results (output) to the resources (input) invested to achieve them. Productivity has two dimensions: effectiveness and efficiency. Effectiveness focuses on the extent to which an organizational unit achieves its program objectives and can be assessed through a combination of qualitative and quantitative measures. Efficiency focuses on the ratio of a unit of goods and/or services produced in relationship to the amount of resources required to produce it.

Program budgeting (11): A budgeting approach that appropriates money based on careful consideration of program goals and expected results. A program is a separately identifiable and managerially discrete function within an organization designed to meet a statutory requirement or a defined set of public goals. Program budgeting focuses on the identification of all of the resources necessary to accomplish goals, objectives, and program activities, often over multiple fiscal years. PPBS is one version of program budgeting. *See also* planning, programming, budgeting system.

Progressive tax (6): *See* progressive tax structure.

Progressive tax structure; also, **progressive tax (6):** A quality of vertical tax equity or fairness with an increasing or heavier relative tax rate or tax burden applied to increasing levels of taxpayer income, wealth, or consumption. *See also* vertical equity; *compare to* proportional tax structure (proportional tax rate); regressive tax structure (regressive tax).

Property tax (6, 1): An ad valorem or value-based tax on real property. Personal property taxes are imposed on land and real estate (homes and lots), and in some states on vehicles, boats, and trailers. Property taxes levied on businesses typically include real estate, equipment, inventory, and furnishings.

Proportional tax (1, 6): *See* proportional tax structure.

Proportional tax structure; also, **proportional tax rate (6):** A quality of vertical tax equity or fairness that uses a tax rate of constant proportional value applied uniformly across the range of taxpayer income, wealth, or consumption. Also known as a "flat tax" because the tax rate remains constant across all classes of taxpayers. *See also* vertical equity; *compare to* progressive tax structure (progressive tax rates), regressive tax structure (regressive tax).

Proportionate share (15): A proportionate reduction or increase requires departments to reduce or increase their budgets roughly equal to the proportion their budget is to the total general fund budget.

Proposed budget (5, 15, 4): A balanced, consolidated, all-funds budget prepared under direction of the chief executive officer (CEO), chief finance officer (CFO), or central budget office. The executive approves the proposed budget before it is released to the public and to the legislative body for review, consideration, amendment, and final adoption. Alternate and similar terms: approved budget; executive recommended budget; executive requested budget; recommended budget, requested budget.

Proprietary funds (9): Budget and accounting funds with revenues and spending related to government business operations, including enterprise funds, internal (interdepartmental) service funds, payment service funds, and debt service funds. *Contrast with* governmental funds; trust and agency funds.

Public employee retirement system (PERS) (15, 10, 11): A retirement savings, investment, and benefit disbursement system for state and local government public employees, typically established at the state level for efficient administration and to pool resources for investment purposes. State agencies and local governments make contributions to PERS on behalf of their employees. PERS are often administered by state government citizen-appointed boards or commissions that follow policy mandates or guidance from the state legislature. Local governments may establish local public employee retirement systems to serve similar functions as a predecessor to, or alternative to, a state-level system. *See also* defined benefit pension; defined contribution pension.

Public foundation; also, quasi-governmental foundation (6): A foundation established by a governmental agency to collect nongovernmental revenues and to make grants and contracts to extend the mission of the agency. Such a foundation is often not under the full control of the government agency because the foundation has a separate board of directors, takes in and manages private donations, and may report as a private nonprofit corporation. *See also* foundation.

Public goods (1, 6): The benefit of a good or service available to any citizen without reducing the value of the good or service to other consumers. It is a good or service to which an exclusive property right cannot be assigned. The ownership of the rights are jointly held by all members of the community.

Public involvement (5, 10): Opportunities in the public budgeting process for citizens to review budget recommendations and offer comments and suggestions to elected officials and administrators.

Quasi-governmental foundation (8): *See* public foundation.

Rainy day fund (15): A separate accounting or budget fund established to hold reserves as a hedge against risk, and as a cushion for emergencies, economic downturns, or unexpected expected expenses. *See also* contingency reserve fund, emergency fund, revenue stabilization reserve fund; *contrast with* reserves.

Ranking (14): In zero-base budgeting and priority budgeting, a listing and numerical rank order is used for comparison of alternative budget packages or funding levels based on one or several criteria.

Rate-driven state (7): A tax system characteristic that defines how local governments perceive the relationship between revenue generation and budget development. In a rate-driven state, property, sales, and other tax rates deliver a predetermined level of revenues. Local governments then prepare a proposed budget based on the available revenues. *Contrast with* budget-driven state.

Recommended budget (5, 4): *See* proposed budget.

Recurring expenditure (15): Expenditure that occurs with annual regularity at consistent levels or at levels with defined growth (e.g., labor contracts, multiyear service contracts with defined payment provisions). *See also* structurally balanced budget; *compare with* nonrecurring appropriation (one-time expenditure).

Recurring resources (15): Accumulated fund balances based on a consistent level of recurring revenues, generating a consistent level of fund reserves, and a consistent generation of unrestricted fund balances over an extended financial planning period of multiple fiscal years. *See also* structurally balanced budget; recurring revenues.

Recurring revenues (6, 15): Revenues collected at consistent levels over many years within the capacity of the tax or fee base. *See also* structurally balanced budget; *compare with* nonrecurring revenue (one-time revenue).

Reduced level budget (RLB) (14): In zero-base budgeting, a budget with all account or activity items adjusted downward by a specified percentage from the base budget levels.

Referendum (6, Pt II—Teaching Case): A measure or ordinance adopted by a local government council, commission, or board to be referred to or placed before the voters for ratification. Proposals to increase property tax rates or levies are placed before voters as referenda. The process allows citizens to make laws—similar to a citizen initiative.

Regressive tax (6): *See* regressive tax structure.

Regressive tax structure; also, regressive tax (6): A quality of vertical tax equity or fairness with a decreasing or lighter relative tax rate or tax burden applied to increasing levels of taxpayer income, wealth, or consumption. *See also* vertical equity; *compare to* proportional tax structure (proportional tax rate); progressive tax structure (progressive tax).

Reprogram; also, reprogram authority (17): Authority given by standing policy or a budget amendment to a government department or program to use money that has been approved for one purpose to reprogram the use for another purpose. For example, the Department of Transportation may be given authority to "reprogram" up to a fixed dollar amount of its Road Repair Funds to the Emergency Repair and Service Fund. *See* transfer; amendment.

Reprogram authority (17): *See* reprogram.

Requested budget (5, 15): *See* proposed budget.

Rescission (17): Legislative action by council, committee, board, or legislature taking back previously appropriated funds for the current fiscal year. *See* amendment; *contrast with* supplemental appropriation.

Reserves (15): The portion of a fund balance set aside as a hedge against risk (GFOA 2013b). The GFOA recommends a minimum general fund reserve level that is no less than two months of regular general fund operating revenues. *Contrast with* rainy day fund, contingency reserve fund, and revenue stabilization reserve fund, which transfers and stores the reserve monies in a separate fund rather than as part of the fund balance.

Resources (9): The money accumulated in a budget or accounting fund. Resources include revenues added to the fund, transfers from other funds, and the money already in the fund from previous years. Some resources may be restricted or encumbered for specific purposes, while other unrestricted resources may be available for spending on any authorized purpose during the fiscal year.

Restricted funds (9, 17): Resources carried forward, encumbered, or reserved for a specific future use and specified conditions. Funds may be "current restricted," which allows use in the current period for specified expenses; "long-term restricted," which delays access into the future and on specified conditions; or "permanently restricted," which limits access to the interest generated annually. *See also* encumbrance (encumbered); carryforward; current unrestricted fund.

Retail sales tax (6): A tax levied at the point of final sale to the consumer based on the value of the sale. Retail sales taxes are assessed as a percentage of the sale value. Often authorized and collected by the state government for itself and on behalf of local governments. *See* tax; *contrast with* value-added tax.

Revenue (9): Money entering a budget or accounting fund (e.g., tax levied and collected by a jurisdiction for its own purposes and attributed to a specific fiscal year or biennium).

Revenue bonds (16): A finance instrument in which the jurisdiction or organization borrows funds for an extended period and repays the debt with interest over that period. Revenue bonds are repaid with user charge and fee revenue specifically related to the use of enterprise facilities, such as municipal water or wastewater facilities. Because they are not backed by the full faith and credit of the issuer, those bonds typically carry a higher interest rate than general obligation bonds. *See also* general obligation (GO) bonds; certificate of participation (COP).

Revenue budget status report (17): A monitoring report for budget execution that details and compares the actual revenue collected or accrued with the estimates developed for the budget. As a basis of comparison, the report often presents the revenue collections at the same period in previous fiscal years. The report is typically prepared on a monthly basis at the fund or at the department level. *Compare to* expenditure budget status report; cash flow status report.

Revenue committee (5): A standing committee of a legislative body that is given the authority to review and approve all proposed revenue measures. For example, the Ways and Means Committee of the U.S. House of Representatives.

Revenue forecasting (7): The estimation of revenue using a combination of the following information: historical data; analytical techniques (mathematical, financial, or statistical); contextual demographic, social, and economic assumptions; and professional judgment. A revenue forecast may be designed to focus on the upcoming budget cycle (budget cycle forecast), or on an extended period (long-term forecast) for financial and strategic planning purposes. *See* budget-cycle revenue forecast; long-term revenue forecast.

Revenue manual (7): A catalog of all revenue types and sources used by a governmental jurisdiction or organization that details, in a consistent format for each revenue type, the authorization and source of the revenue, the forecast estimates, the method used to forecast, the key assumptions behind the analysis and forecast, and a discussion of the limitations and key factors that could affect the forecast estimates.

Revenue stabilization reserve fund (15, 10): *See* contingency reserve fund.

Ripper clauses (1): Ripper clauses specifically forbid state legislatures from delegating powers of interference in municipal functions to special commissions, private corporations or associations, or any other entities that would work on behalf of private interests over local public interests.

RLB (14): *See* reduced level budget.

Roll-up (15): A computer systems and data processing term to gather and aggregate the data from multiple lower-level sources (e.g., program level) into larger groupings with computed group totals (e.g., division or bureau level). Roll-up enables the gathering and aggregation process to be successively repeated at higher levels (department, agency), ultimately including the full organization.

Sales tax (6, 7): *See* retail sales tax.

Schedule (18): A supporting set of calculations, data, information, or analysis that shows or amplifies how figures in financial statements are derived. For example, your personal federal income tax return is a set of schedules.

SEA Report (18): *See* Service Efforts and Accomplishments Report.

Seed donation (8): An initial contribution or donation that encourages giving by other individuals and entities, typically with the intent of aggregating multiple donations into a sufficient amount to accomplish a defined purpose. *See also* leverage.

Self-supported (9): A government department or program that through the course of its operations generates a major portion of the revenues needed to fund its own operations, and thus is not dependent on substantial support from the organization's general fund. *Contrast with* general fund department.

Sensitivity analysis (7, 10): A technique for assessing the variability of forecasts or other outputs generated by complex mathematical and statistical models. With a preferred forecast as a baseline, a sensitivity analysis makes a series of runs of the forecast model that incrementally varies one or a few data inputs or assumptions from those of the preferred forecast. The results of the series of runs are compared to the preferred revenue forecast as context for variability and quality. *See also* baseline forecast/baseline run.

Service Efforts and Accomplishments (SEA) Report (18): A performance report that tracks and compares actual program and service accomplishments to planned and funded targets. Often prepare at the end of the fiscal year or quarterly. *Similar to* performance status report.

Severance tax (6): A tax levied on the extraction or harvest of a natural resource, often on a per unit basis. For example, a timber harvest severance tax would be levied on the volume of timber cut on a cubic meter, cubic foot, or board foot measure.

Social entrepreneurism (8): Nonprofit organization operation of commercial activities to generate revenues. The commercial activities (e.g., snack bars, gift stores, athletic club memberships) may or may not align closely with the organization's religious, charitable, or educational mission.

Social impact bonds (13): These are new financial strategies first pioneered in Great Britain; public, nonprofit, and philanthropic resources are leveraged to undertake an innovative social service initiative in which government agencies pay only for improved social outcomes *after* those outcomes have been achieved and verified.

Special district; also, special purpose district (1): A public corporation established to provide a specific set of services to all citizens and residents within defined geographic boundaries, often with the authority to levy and collect tax and fee revenues. The statutory requirements for establishing special districts vary by state. Typical special district purposes include mass transit, port, hospital, K–12 schools, wastewater management, library, drainage and flood control, cemetery maintenance, and emergency medical services.

Special payments: These payments are made directly to persons, contractors, or others. The payments also go to local governments such as counties or school districts.

Special purpose district (1): *See* special district.

Spending freeze (17): A severe form of appropriation control. Prohibitions or restrictions from the CEO, central budget office, or legislative body preventing spending for specific line-items or categories of line-items, e.g., prohibitions on travel or equipment purchases. Typically applied in times of severe fiscal stress. *See also* hiring freeze; appropriation control; position controls.

Start-up costs (15): *See* phase-in costs.

Statistical fit (7): For forecasts made with statistical techniques, using statistical quality measures (e.g., correlation coefficients, r-square values, and confidence bands) as a measure of the fit of the computed estimates to the data set.

Step cost (7): *See* incremental cost.

Strategic financial plan (10): A major element of a jurisdiction or nonprofit organization's strategic plan that assesses the current and future external financial environment and the organization's response to those external conditions. A strategic financial plan includes long-term financial forecasts of revenues, expenditures, and balances for each budget fund in the operating budget. The plan also assesses the organization's financial policies and systems. A third important element of a strategic financial plan is forecasts of current and future debt obligations and debt capacity based on the organization's capital improvement plan. *See also* financial forecast; capital improvement plan (CIP); financial policies.

Strategic plan (10, 12): A plan prepared by an organizational entity that uses an extended time horizon to take into account the impact of future political, social, economic, community, and other environmental influences on shaping the goals and success of the organization. A general strategic plan may have complementary subplans covering specific topical areas, including financial, revenues, office space, and infrastructure. *See also* mission; vision; beliefs and values statement; strategic financial plan.

Strong mayor form of city government (1, 2): An organizational arrangement for city and town governance with an elected city or town council and an independently elected mayor who acts as the chief executive and administrative officer of the government. County governments can follow this structure with elected commissioners and an elected county executive.

Structural deficit (15): Deficits that occur when the forecast growth in revenues from taxes and other revenues sources are less than the forecast growth in spending needed to maintain current services and to meet future financial obligations. A downward trend in future revenues or an unexpected increase in future costs over multiple fiscal years leads to a structural deficit. Typically in some combination, a lack of new construction assessed value, depressed real estate valuations, a loss of intergovernmental revenues, and rapidly increasing pension fund costs are pushing local governments toward structural deficit.

Structurally balanced budget (15): A budget in which recurring revenues equal recurring expenditures (GFOA 2013b). Recurring revenues are revenues that are collected at consistent levels over many years within the capacity of the tax or fee base. Recurring expenditures are expenditures that occur with annual regularity at consistent levels or levels with defined growth (e.g., labor contracts, multiyear service contracts with defined payment provisions). A structurally balanced budget is one indicator of a financially stable organization. *See also* recurring revenues; recurring expenditure; *contrast with* nonrecurring revenue (one-time revenue); nonrecurring appropriation (one-time expenditure).

Supplemental appropriation (17): Supplemental appropriation is an additional appropriation made by the legislative body to a department or program during the current operating fiscal year to cover unforeseen events, to cover projected overexpenditures, to take advantage of new revenues, or to replace revenue shortfalls; additional funds over the adopted level. Term most often used at the state and federal levels. *See also* amendment (budget amendment).

Target (13): The desired value of an output or outcome at a particular point in time. For example, the year 2015 target for the rate of child abuse and neglect was 6 out of 1,000 persons under the age of 18. *See also* outcome; output.

Tax (6, 7): A charge broadly imposed by a government on an economic base or activity to cover the cost of services. Tax bases include wealth (property); income; and economic activity (sales). Taxes are intended to recover revenue from all citizens who benefit from public goods, nonmarket goods, and often market-valued services provided by government. *Related to* excise tax; income tax; property tax; retail sales tax; value-added tax (VAT).

Tax and expenditure limitation (TEL) (7): One or several of a set of approaches to limit the collection of tax revenue or to limit total government spending. Chapter 7 includes a summary of the different TEL approaches on tax rates, property valuation, total levy, and total spending. TELs are typically applied at the state level to property tax mechanisms with implications for local governments. California's Proposition 13 and Colorado's Taxpayer Bill of Rights (TABOR) are widely known TELs.

Tax code area (7, Exhibits 7.1, 7.2): An area of a local governmental jurisdiction with the same combination of overlapping tax districts. A property owner in a tax code area will face tax assessments from each of the several districts. The owner's total tax rate will equal the combined rate of all the applicable district assessments. A government jurisdiction will typically contain several tax code areas. See Exhibits 7.1 and 7.2 for an example and further explanation. *Related to* tax district.

Tax district (7): The tax base established by a local government under state law. A property tax district defines the geographic areas on which the tax will be assessed. A sales tax district would define the boundaries where such a tax would be applied. Local governments and special district governments often overlap, but each has a geographically defined tax district. The unique overlap of districts defines a tax code area: *See* tax code area.

Tax expenditure (8): A policy decision by a government to forego and not collect potential tax revenue. In not collecting the potential revenue from a particular source or group, the government in effects makes an expenditure of money to the group receiving the expenditure, commonly called a "tax break." All other taxpayers must increase their contributions to meet total revenue needs. Chapter 8 describes the use of tax expenditures to support nonprofits, government, and economic development.

Tax increment financing (TIF) (8): A land-use and financing procedure used by local governments to remove blight and to encourage economic development in a prescribed tax district. Within the designated district, property taxes are frozen as of a given date. If the property values within the district increase, any tax revenue generated on the added value is diverted to renewal activities or to bonds for capital projects. After any debt is repaid on a designated date, the property reverts to the general tax base.

Tax levy (6, 7): The total potential burden or cost of a tax; the total potential tax revenue generated by a tax; the tax rate applied to the tax base over a prescribed time period.

TEL (7): *See* tax and expenditure limitation.

TIF (8): *See* tax increment financing.

Town (1): A small local government with a charter of incorporation adopted by its voters. Popularly understood as smaller in population and size than a city, but may be statutorily equivalent to a city under state law. Towns have the authority to levy taxes and collect fee revenues. *See also* city.

Township (1): A local government that provides municipal services similar to those provided by an incorporated city or town, but to unincorporated areas. Townships typically are granted the authority, expressly limited by state law, to raise revenues through taxes and fees and to spend money. A local unit of government in the mid-Atlantic, New England, and midwestern states.

Transfer; also, interfund transfer (9, 15, 17): A general term used to describe a shift of funds from one budget fund to another, or to shift funds from one program to another. Administrators may transfer or reprogram (federal) funds within a fund or department, or between programs up to a level specified in previously adopted financial policies without legislative approval. Above the specified level, the legislative body must adopt a budget amendment to authorize a transfer of monies between funds. A budget may transfer monies from one fund to another to fund a program (e.g., the legislative body may use general fund dollars to support an emergency purchase in an enterprise fund). Most commonly, funds are transferred to pay for a specific interdepartmental purchase or internal charges for services. *See also* reprogram.

Trust (8): A legal structure used to direct the transfer of personal or family wealth. *See also* family foundation.

Trust and agency funds (9): Governmental budgeting and accounting fund designations for monies held by government for other individuals or groups. These funds include retirement pension and employee medical benefit funds and trust funds. *Contrast with* governmental funds; proprietary funds.

Unfunded liability (15): Refers to the excess of payment obligations compared to the available funds, future contributions, and investment returns for a given fund or combination of funds. Often identified as the insolvency condition of many state and local pension funds.

Unfunded mandate (6): Performance and expenditure burdens and limitations on revenue collection placed on one level of government by another. Typically expressed as the federal and state government placing requirements and limitations on local governments, or the federal government on state governments. Examples include occupational safety and health requirements, environmental regulations, land-use planning requirements, and wage and working conditions, just to name some of the most common categories of unfunded mandates.

Unspecified giving (8): Charitable and philanthropic donations made without donor restrictions on their use. Unspecified giving allows the recipient organization the opportunity to allocate funds to program and administrative expenses as deemed necessary. *Contrast with* directed giving.

Use tax (6): A tax imposed on the use of a good or service rather than on the sale of the item or service. Use taxes are imposed when sales taxes inadequately cover a particular good or service. For example, a state may charge automobile owners a use tax at the time of registration rather than a sales tax at the time of purchase.

Value-added tax (VAT) (6): A tax on the increase in value of a good or product at each step of the production or economic process. Retail sales and excise taxes collect revenue at the last step of the economic process. A VAT collects tax revenue at each phase of a manufacturing process that added value, including the raw material purchase, component purchases, wholesale purchases, and retail sale. VATs are not used in the United States, but are common in European countries and nations in the current and former British Commonwealth.

Variable cost (7): A type of cost that varies in proportion to the number of units produced. Jurisdictional or organizational financial policies may define and allocate administrative costs as fixed, incremental, or variable costs. *Compare to* incremental cost (step cost); fixed cost.

VAT (6): *See* value-added tax.

Vertical equity (6): The relative tax burden over the range of all taxpayer wealth, income, or consumption. A quality of the equity or fairness of a tax over all taxpayers. *See also* progressive tax structure/rate; proportional tax structure/rate; regressive tax structure/rates. *Compare with* horizontal equity.

Vision statement (12): A subelement of a broader mission statement that provides clarity on how the organization or program defines success. *See also* planning, programming, budgeting system; mission statement; beliefs and values statement.

Wage tax; also, **payroll tax (6):** A tax levied on employee wages, salaries, and compensation by local governments. *Contrast with* income tax.

Warrant (6): Short-term governmental borrowing in the form of a bank loan or short-term note in which future tax revenues serve as the collateral for the loan.

Washingtonian leadership model (2): A public service leadership model that emphasizes the importance of systematic planning and the values of efficiency and effectiveness in building democratic trust and legitimacy.

Ways and means committee (5): A standing committee of the U.S. House of Representatives or in a branch of a state legislature that is given the authority to review and approve all proposed revenue measures.

Weak mayor form of city government (1): An organizational arrangement for city and town governance with an elected council and an elected mayor with limited authority or with largely ceremonial duties. The executive authority is lodged in the council or in an appointed (hired) city administrator. The council-manager form is one version of the weak major form of city government. *See also* council-manager form of city government; strong mayor form of city government.

ZBB (14): *See* zero-base budgeting.

Zero-base budgeting (ZBB) (14): A budgeting procedure that subjects all programs, activities, and expenditures to justification, in contrast to incremental budgeting. Funding requests, recommendations, and allocations for existing and new programs are usually ranked in priority order on the basis of alternative service levels, which are lower, equal to, and higher than current levels. This process can be used in conjunction with either line-item budgeting and/or program (PPBS) budgeting.

BIBLIOGRAPHY

Adair, Douglass. 1974. *Fame and the Founding Fathers*, ed. Trevor Colbourn. New York: Norton.

Alford, J. 2002. Defining the client in the public sector: A social-exchange perspective. *Public Administration Review* 62, no. 3: 337–346.

Allen, Greg. 2009. Property tax revenue drop adds to counties' woes (radio news report). Morning Edition, National Public Radio, June 11. www.npr.org/templates/transcript/transcript.php?storyId=105225149.

American Institute of Certified Public Accountants (AICPA). 2012. Generally accepted auditing standards. www.aicpa.org/Research/Standards/AuditAttest/DownloadableDocuments/AU-00150.pdf.

American Legislative Exchange Council. 2014. "The state budget reform tool-kit." www.alec.org/wp-content/uploads/Budget_toolkit.pdf (accessed May 6, 2014).

American Recovery and Reinvestment Act of 2009 (ARRA) ("Recovery Act"), Pub. L. No. 111–5, 123 Stat. 115.

American Society of Civil Engineers (ASCE). 2013. *2013 Report Card for America's Infrastructure.* www.infrastructurereportcard.org/a/#p/grade-sheet/americas-infrastructure-investment-needs (accessed July 3, 2013).

American Society of Public Administration (ASPA). 2013. About ASPA: Our mission. www.aspanet.org/public/.

Ammons, David N., ed. 2008. *Leading Performance Management in Local Government.* Washington, DC: International City/County Management Association (ICMA) Press.

Ammons, David N., and Newell Charldean. 1989. *City Executives: Leadership Roles, Work Characteristics, and Time Management.* Albany: State University of New York Press.

Ammons, David N., and William C. Rivenbark. 2008. Factors influencing the use of performance data to improve municipal services: Evidence from the North Carolina benchmarking project. *Public Administration Review* 68, no. 2: 304–318.

Anderson, James E. 2003. *Public Policy Making: An Introduction.* 5th ed. New York: Houghton Mifflin.

Anderson, Nathan B., and Jane K. Dokko. 2009. Mortgage delinquency and property taxes. *State Tax Notes* 52 (April 6): 49.

Andreoni, James, Brian Erard, and Jonathan Feinstein. 1998. Tax compliance. *Journal of Economic Literature* 36, no. 2 (June): 818–860.

Anthony, Robert N. 1985. The games that government accountants play. *Harvard Business Review* 63, no. 5 (September–October): 161–170.

Arizona Department of Public Safety. 2013. Mission/vision. www.azdps.gov/about/Mission_Vision/.

Arizona State Land Department. State Land Department Historical Overview. www.azland.gov/history.htm (accessed January 23, 2014).

Arrillaga-Andreessen, Laura. 2012. *Giving 2.0: Transform Your Giving and Our World.* San Francisco, CA: Jossey-Bass.

Association of Governing Boards of Universities and Colleges. 2013. Term limits. http://agb.org/knowledge-center/briefs/term-limits (accessed January 10, 2013).

Association of Government Accountants. 2012. *Charting a Course Through Stormy Seas: State Financial Executives in 2012.* NASACT-AGA 2012 Survey of State Financial Executives. Alexandria, VA: August. www.nasact.org/nasact/publications/papers/GT_AGA_StateSurvey2012_04.pdf (accessed September 14, 2013).

Association of Washington Cities. 2010. Statement of the Director and Financial Conditions, 2010 Survey Results. September 9. Olympia, WA.

Augstums, Ieva M. 2008. Losses jolt financial sector. *The Oregonian,* July 23, B1.

Axelrod, Donald. 1995. *Budgeting for Modern Government.* 2d ed. St. Martin's Press: New York.

Babwin, Don. 2010. Job cuts kill company tax breaks: Cities, counties enforce "clawbacks." *Seattle Times,* January 3, A6.

Baden, Ben. 2011. Public sector job cuts threaten recovery. *US News and World Report,* July 8. http://money.usnews.com/money/careers/articles/2011/07/08/public-sector-job-cuts-threaten-recovery (accessed December 11, 2012).

Banovetz, James M. 1994. City managers: Will they reject policy leadership? *Public Productivity & Management Review* 17, no. 4 (Summer): 313–324.

Bardach, Eugene, and Cara Lesser. 1996. Accountability in human services collaboratives: For what? And to whom? *Journal of Public Administration Research and Theory* 6, no. 2, (April): 197–224.

Barone, M. 1996. The road back to Tocqueville; at last, 19th century values stage a revival. *Washington Post*, January 15, 21–23.

Barron, David J. 1999. The promise of Cooley's city: Traces of local constitutionalism. *University of Pennsylvania Law Review* 147, no. 3, 487–611.

Bartle, John R. 2003. Trends in local government taxation in the 21st century. *Spectrum: The Journal of State Government* 76, no. 1 (Winter): 26–29.

Beal, Jason, and Bipin Prabhakar. 2011. Chapter 20: Public-sector ERP. In *Readings on Enterprise Resource Planning*. Montreal: HEC Montreal. Preliminary version. http://bealbudgeting.com/web/wp-content/uploads/2011/09/Readings_on_ERP_Public-Sector-ERP_chapter20.pdf (accessed August 28, 2012).

Beaverton School District. 2012a. Budget teaching session of staff & community members. Handout with simulation. Beaverton, OR: March. https://docs.google.com/a/beaverton.k12.or.us/presentation/pub?id=11StXTQ4gbv2I7omF8ZSHVgZWWKw9Di2NWAqMCUxnJso&start=false&loop=false&delayms=60000#slide=id.p14 (accessed October 1, 2012).

———. 2012b. Superintendent budget listening session. Handout, January 17. www.beaverton.k12.or.us/depts/business/budget/Documents/2012-13%20Budget%20Year/1-17-12%20Listening%20Session/Listening%20Session%20011712%20Handouts.pdf (accessed February 27, 2014).

Behn, Robert D. 1995. Creating an innovative organization: Ten hints for involving frontline workers. *State and Local Government Review* 27, no. 3 (Fall).

Behrs, Jan. 2011. Tax the lot, not the house. *The Oregonian,* May 1, H1. http://blog.oregonlive.com/homes-rentals/2011/04/post_1.html (accessed May 19, 2011).

Bellah, Robert N., Richard Madsen, William M. Sullivan, Ann Swidler, and Steven M. Tipton. 1985. *Habits of the Heart: Individualism and Commitment in American Life*. New York: Harper & Row.

Berlin, Isaiah. 1969. *Four Essays on Liberty*. London: Oxford University Press.

Berman, David R., ed. 1993. *County Governments in an Era of Change*. Westport, CT: Greenwood Press.

Berman, Evan M. 2007. *Essential Statistics for Public Managers and Policy Analysts*. 2d ed. Washington, DC: CQ Press.

Berry, Jeffrey M., and David F. Arons. 2003. *A Voice for Nonprofits*. Washington, DC: Brookings Institution Press.

Biddle, Bruce J., and David C. Berliner. 2002. Unequal school funding in the United States. *Educational Leadership* 59, no. 8 (May): 48–59.

Blank, Rebecca M. 2002. Evaluating welfare reform in the United States. *Journal of Economic Literature* 40 (4): 1105–1166.

Blinder, Alan, and Mark Zandi. 2010. *How the Great Recession Was Brought to an End*. July 27. www.economy.com/mark-zandi/documents/End-of-Great-Recession.pdf (accessed April 2011).

Boris, Elizabeth T. 2001. Foundations. In *Understanding Nonprofit Organizations: Governance, Leadership and Management*, ed. J. Steven Ott, 231–238. Boulder, CO: Westview.

Box, Richard C. 1998. *Citizen Governance: Leading American Communities into the 21st Century*. Thousand Oaks, CA: Sage.

Braithwaite, Valerie. 1998. Communal and exchange trust norms: Their value base and relevance to institutional trust. In *Trust and Governance*, eds. Valerie Braithwaite and Margaret Levi, 46–74. New York: Russell Sage Foundation.

Braybrooks, Melissa, Julio Ruiz, and Elizabeth Accetta. 2011. *State Government Tax Collections Summary Report: 2010*. Government Division Brief G10-STC. Washington, DC: U.S. Census Bureau, March. www2.census.gov/govs/statetax/2010stcreport.pdf (accessed November 4, 2011).

Brinkley, A., N.W. Polsby, K.M. Sullivan, and A. Lewis. 1997. *New Federalist Papers: Essays in Defense of the Constitution*. New York: Twentieth Century Fund.

Brookes, S. 2008. Responding to the new public leadership challenge. Paper presented at the Herbert Simon 2nd Annual Conference, Manchester, England.

Brookes, S., and K. Grint, eds. 2010. *The New Public Leadership Challenge*. New York: Palgrave Macmillan.

Brown, Kate. 2012. *Oregon's Counties: 2012 Financial Condition Review*. Oregon Secretary of State Audit Report no. 2012–17. Salem, OR: Secretary of State Audits Division, May. www.sos.state.or.us/audits/pages/state_audits/full/2012/2012-17.pdf (accessed November 29, 2012).

Brown v. Plata, 563 U.S. _____. 2011. Supreme Court Slip Opinion. www.supremecourt.gov/opinions/10pdf/09-1233.pdf.

Browning, Edgar K., and Jacquelene M. Browning. 1992. *Microeconomic Theory and Applications*. 4th ed. New York: HarperCollins.

Bruce, Donald, and William F. Fox. 2004. *State and Local Sales Tax Revenue Losses from E-Commerce: Estimates as of July 2004.* Knoxville, TN: Center for Business and Economic Research, University of Tennessee. www.ncsl.org/print/press/Ecommerceupdates.pdf.

Bruce, Donald, William F. Fox, and LeAnn Luna. 2009. *State and Local Government Sales Tax Revenue Losses from Electronic Commerce.* Knoxville, TN: University of Tennessee, April 13. http://cber.utk.edu/ecomm/ecom0409.pdf (accessed April 22, 2011).

Bryson, John. M. 1995. *Strategic Planning for Public and Nonprofit Organizations: A Guide to Strengthening and Sustaining Organizational Achievement.* Rev. ed. San Francisco, CA: Jossey-Bass.

————. 2001. Strategic planning. In *Understanding Nonprofit Organizations: Governance, Leadership and Management,* ed. J. Steven Ott, Chapter 10. Boulder, CO: Westview.

————. 2005. The strategy change cycle: An effective strategic planning approach for nonprofit organizations." In *The Jossey-Bass Handbook of Nonprofit Leadership and Management* (2d ed.), ed. Robert D. Herman and Associates. San Francisco, CA: Jossey-Bass.

Bryson, John M., and Barbara C. Crosby. 1992. *Leadership for the Common Good: Tackling Public Problems in a Shared-Power World.* San Francisco, CA: Jossey-Bass.

Burns, Nancy. 1994. *The Formation of American Local Government: Private Values in Public Institutions.* New York: Oxford University Press.

Byrtek, Megan C. 2011. Leverage Points for Sustainability: A Case Study in Organizational Performance. Portland, OR: Executive MPA Capstone Project, Division of Public Administration, Hatfield School of Government, Portland State University, June.

Carrington, Paul D. 1997. Law as "the common thoughts of men": The law-teaching and judging of Thomas McIntyre Cooley. *Stanford Law Review* 49: 495–546.

Carroll, Deborah A. 2009. Diversifying municipal government revenue structures: Fiscal illusion or instability? *Public Budgeting and Finance* 29, no. 1 (Spring): 27–48.

Carroll, Deborah A., Robert J. Eger III, and Justin Marlowe. 2003. Managing local intergovernmental revenues: The imperative of diversification. *International Journal of Public Administration* 26, no. 13: 1495–1518.

Carroll, Deborah A., and Terri Johnson. 2010. Examining small town revenues: To what extent are they diversified? *Public Administration Review* 70, no. 2 (March/April): 223–235.

Carter, Jimmy. 1971/1987. Budget message to the Georgia general assembly (January 15, 1971). In *Perspectives on Budgeting,* ed. Allen Schick, 115. Washington, DC: American Society for Public Administration.

Catalogue of Federal Domestic Assistance (CFDA). 2011. *CFDA.Gov Public User Guide 2.0.* Washington, DC: CDFA, February 11. www.cfda.gov/downloads/CFDA.GOV_Agency_User_Guide_v2.0.pdf (accessed November 11, 2011).

Center for Budget and Policy Priorities (CBPP). 2013. Policy basics: Taxpayer bill of rights (TABOR). Washington, DC: Center for Budget and Policy Priorities, February 15. www.cbpp.org/cms/index.cfm?fa=view&id=2521 (accessed August 3, 2013).

Center for Economic Development. 2012. Subsidies and incentives. In *A Guide to Economic Development Practice* (online). Cleveland, OH: Maxine Goodman Levin College of Urban Affairs, Cleveland State University. http://urban.csuohio.edu/economicdevelopment/knight/tools/operatingcosts/subsidies.htm (accessed January 29, 2012).

Center for Medicare and Medicaid Services (CMS). 2013. National health expenditure 2011 highlights. www.cms.gov/Research-Statistics-Data-and-Systems/Statistics-Trends-and-Reports/NationalHealthExpend-Data/downloads/highlights.pdf (accessed August 7, 2013).

Cerra, Michael F. 2007. Forms of Government. *New Jersey Municipalities* (March). www.njslom.org/magart0307_p14.html (accessed March 1, 2011).

Chandler, John. 2006. Don't build schools on bad public policy: Systems development charges. *The Oregonian,* December 22, D9.

Charan, Ram, and Larry Bossidy. 2002. *Execution: The Discipline of Getting Things Done.* New York: Crown Business.

Chen, Greg G., Dall W. Forsythe, Lynne A. Weikart, and Daniel W. Williams. 2009. *Budget Tools: Financial Methods in the Public Sector.* Washington, DC: CQ Press.

Chery, Sharonda D. 2009. "The Personality of Nature." *Poetry in Nature.* www.poetryinnature.com/nature/poetry.asp?poem=1841 (accessed May 3, 2014).

Childs, Richard S. 1963. The enduring qualities of a successful manager. *Public Management* 45: 2–4.

Christensen, Peter, Jeff McElravy, and Rowan Miranda. 2003. What's wrong with budgeting: A framework for evaluating and fixing public sector financial planning processes. *Government Finance Review* 19, no. 5 (October): 11–20. www.gfoa.org/downloads/GFROct03.pdf (accessed August 24, 2012).

Christie, Jim. 2010. Bankruptcy talk spreads among California muni officials. Reuters News, May 27. www.

reuters.com/article/2010/05/27/us-economy-california-munibankruptcy-idUSTRE64Q6CQ20100527 (accessed March 2011).

City of Beaverton, Oregon. 2011. *Capital Improvements Plan for Fiscal Years 2011/12–2012/13,* Draft 2. Beaverton, Oregon.

City of Bellevue, Washington. 2005. *2004 Comprehensive Annual Financial Report.* June 29.

City of Camas, Washington. 2009. *City of Camas, Washington, Budget 2010.* www.ci.camas.wa.us/images/DOCS/FINANCE/REPORTS/2010budget.pdf (accessed April 2, 2011).

City of Chandler, Arizona. 2012. Strategic goals, financial policies and budget recommendations. In *Budget Highlights, 2012–2013 Proposed Budget.* Chandler, AZ: City Council. www.chandleraz.gov/content/20 13ProposedBudgetBookSection1BudgetHighlights.pdf (accessed August 10, 2012).

———. 2013–2014. Budget Highlights. Chandler, AZ: City Council, 22. www.chandleraz.gov/content/Budget%20Highlights%20Book%2013-14_CD.pdf (accessed September 16, 2013).

City of Gresham, Oregon. 2013. *Internal Service Charge Manual for Fiscal 2013/2014.* www.greshamoregon.gov/city/city-departments/finance-and-management/budget-division/ (accessed July 25, 2013).

City of Philadelphia, Pennsylvania. 2014. Earnings tax. www.phila.gov/Revenue/individuals/taxes/Pages/EarningsTax.aspx (accessed May 9, 2014).

City of Portland, Oregon. 1979. Goals, objectives, and performance measures. Portland, OR: The City of Portland Bureau of Management and Budget. January 26.

———. 2012. Current Service Level Annual Report, 2012. Portland, OR: The City of Portland Auditor's Office. www.portlandonline.com/auditor/index.cfm?c=53775&a=376731 (accessed May 5, 2012).

———. 2014. Portland Housing Bureau, Limited Tax Exemption Programs (LTE). www.portlandoregon.gov/phb/61182 (accessed May 9, 2014).

City of Sammamish, Washington. 2012a. *2013–2014 Biennial Budget: Investing in Our Community.* Sammamish, WA: The City of Sammamish Finance Department. www.ci.sammamish.wa.us/files/document/10803.pdf (accessed June 22, 2013).

———. 2012b. Interlocal agreements. Sammamish, WA. www.ci.sammamish.wa.us/about/InterLocal.aspx (accessed July 7, 2013).

City of San Antonio, Texas. 2013. Office of Management and Budget: Previous Budgets (Archives). www.sanantonio.gov/Budget/Budget-Archives.aspx#311956-fy-2012 (accessed May 23, 2013).

City of Seattle, Washington. 2006. Budget process diagram—2006 budget. *2006 Adopted Budget.* www.seattle.gov/financedepartment/06adoptedbudget/2006_Adopted_Budget_Process.pdf (accessed May 3, 2014).

City of Tigard, Oregon. 2004. *FY2004–2005 Adopted Budget.* Fund Summaries section, 280–352. http://publicrecords.tigard-or.gov/Public/DocView.aspx?id=298695&page=15&dbid=0.

City-data.com. 2010a. Louisiana—Local government. www.city-data.com/states/Louisiana-Local-government.html.

———. 2010b. New Jersey—Local government. www.city-data.com/states/New-Jersey-Local-government.html.

Civic Practices Network. 2013. http://cpn.org/tools/dictionary/civilsociety.html.

Clark County, Washington. 1999. *Clark County Revenues Manual.* Vancouver, WA: Clark County Auditor's Office. www.co.clark.wa.us/auditor/documents/financial/99revman.pdf (accessed February 11, 2013).

———. 2004. County fiscal policy. In *2005–2006 Clark County Budget.* Vancouver, WA.

———. 2010. *2011–2012 Biennium Financial Plan.* Vancouver, WA. http:www.clark.wa.gov/budget/2011-2012/5%20-%20Financial/11-12%20Financial.pdf#page=3 (accessed May 7, 2012).

Clark Fork Valley Hospital Foundation. 2013. About Clark Fork: Foundation. Plains, MT. www.cfvh.org/About/Foundation/default.aspx (accessed May 7, 2013).

Clinton v. Cedar Rapids and the Missouri River Railroad, 24 Iowa 455. 1868.

Cohen, Jean L., and Andrew Arato. 1992. *Civil Society and Political Theory.* Cambridge, MA: MIT Press.

Collender, Stanley E. 1996. *The Guide to the Federal Budget Fiscal 1997.* Lanham, MD: Rowman & Littlefield.

Collins, Courtney, and Andrew J. Rettenmaier. 2010. *Unfunded Liabilities of State and Local Government Employee Retirement Benefit Plans.* Policy Report No. 329: 2. Dallas, TX: National Center for Policy Analysis, July 29. www.ncpa.org/pub/st329.

Community Action Partnership. 2012. About CAAs. www.communityactionpartnership.com/index.php?option=com_content&task=view&id=21&Itemid=50 (accessed February 28, 2012).

Comptroller General of the United States. 2011. Governmental auditing standards. In *The Yellow Book.* Washington, DC: Government Accountability Office (GAO).

Congressional Budget Office (CBO). 1998. *The Economic Effects of Federal Spending on Infrastructure and Other Investments.* Washington, DC: CBO, June 1. www.cbo.gov/ftpdocs/6xx/doc601/fedspend.pdf (accessed April 26, 2011).

———. 2002. *The Future Investment in Drinking Water and Wastewater Infrastructure.* Washington, DC: CBO, November 1. www.cbo.gov/doc.cfm?index=3983.

Congressional Research Service. 2013. Water Infrastructure Financing: History of EPA Appropriations. www. fas.org/sgp/crs/misc/96-647.pdf.

Cook, Brian J. 1996. *Bureaucracy and Self-Government: Reconsidering the Role of Public Administration in American Politics.* Baltimore, MD: Johns Hopkins University Press.

Cooley, Thomas M. 1868. *A Treatise on the Constitutional Limitations Which Rest upon the Legislative Power of the States of the American Union.* 4th ed. Boston: Little Brown.

Cooper, Phillip J. 2003. *Governing by Contract: Challenges and Opportunities for Public Managers.* Washington, DC: CQ Press.

———. 2009. *The War Against Regulation: From Jimmy Carter to George W. Bush.* Lawrence: The University Press of Kansas.

Copley, Paul A. 2008. *Accounting for Governmental and Not-for-Profit Organizations.* 9th ed. Boston: McGraw-Hill Irwin.

Coppa, Frank J. 2000. *County Government: A Guide to Efficient and Accountable Government.* Westport, CT: Praeger.

Cordes, Scott, and Bob Winthrop. 2008. Making an argument for police enforcement costs: The St. Paul fee study experience. *Government Finance Review* 24, no. 5 (October): 31–34.

Cornia, Gary C., and Lawrence C. Walters. 2005. Full disclosure: Unanticipated improvements in property tax uniformity. *Public Budgeting and Finance* 25, no. 3 (Summer): 106–123.

Creighton, James L. 1992. *Involving Citizens in Community Decision Making: A Guidebook.* Washington, DC: Program for Community Problem Solving.

Crewson, Philip E. 1997. Public-service motivation: Building empirical evidence of incidence and effect. *Journal of Public Administration Research and Theory* 7, no. 4: 499–518.

Crewson, Philip E., and Bonnie S. Fisher. 1997. Growing older and wiser: The changing skill requirements of city administrators. *Public Administration Review* 57, no. 5 (September–October): 380–386.

Crosby, B.C., and J.M. Bryson. 2005. *Leadership for the Common Good: Tackling Public Problems in a Shared-Power World.* 2d ed. San Francisco, CA: Jossey-Bass.

Dahl, Robert A. 1989. *Democracy and Its Critics.* New Haven, CT: Yale University Press.

Damanpour, Fariborz, and Marguerite Schneider. 2008. Characteristics of innovation and innovation adoption in public organizations: Assessing the role of managers. *Journal of Public Administration Research and Theory* 19, no. 3 (July): 495–522.

Danks, Holly. 2004. Levy failure constricts county. *The Oregonian,* November 23, C1, C2.

Dartmouth College v. Woodward, 17 U.S. 518. 1819.

DePaul, Jennifer. 2012. Report: 100 largest public pension plans underfunded by $895B-$1.193T. *The Bond Buyer,* October 18. www.bondbuyer.com/issues/121_202/100-largest-pension-plans-report-assets-2-trillion-underfunded-1045074-1.html (accessed May 31, 2013).

DeWoolfson, B.H. 1975. Federal PPB: A ten-year perspective. *Federal Accountant* (September): 51–61.

Diamond, Martin. 1979. Ethics and politics: The American way. In *The Moral Foundations of the American Republic,* ed. Robert Horwitz, 75–108. Charlottesville: University Press of Virginia.

Diesing, Paul. 1982. *Reason in Society.* Urbana: University of Illinois Press.

DiMaggio, Paul J., and Walter W. Powell. 1983. The iron cage revisited: Institutional isomorphism and collective rationality in organizational fields. *American Sociological Review* 48 (April):147–160.

Dolan, Julia, and David H. Rosenbloom, eds. 2003. *Representative Bureaucracy: Classic Readings and Continuing Controversies.* Armonk, NY: M.E. Sharpe.

Dorr, David A. 2007. Medical homes in primary care: Policy implications from care management plus. Presentation to the Office for Oregon Health Policy & Research, Oregon Health Fund Board, December 12. www.oregon.gov/oha/OHPR/docs/healthreformresourcesdocs/medicalhomesinprimarycared.dorrohsu.pdf (accessed January 25, 2013).

Downs, Anthony. 1960. Why the government budget is too small in a democracy. *World Politics* 12, no. 4 (July): 541–563.

Dropkin, Murray, Jim Halpin, and Bill La Touche. 2007. *The Budget-Building Book for Nonprofits.* 2d ed. San Francisco, CA: Jossey-Bass.

Dugan, Ianthe Jeanne. 2010. Strapped cities hit nonprofits with fees. *Wall Street Journal,* December 27, A1.

Dye, Richard F., and David Merriman. 2006. Tax increment financing: A tool for local economic development. *Land Lines* 18, no. 1 (January). www.lincolninst.edu/pubs/1078_Tax-Increment-Financing (accessed May 20, 2011).

Ebdon, Carol, and Aimee L. Franklin. 2006. Citizen participation in budgeting theory. *Public Administration Review* 66, no. 3 (May/June): 437–447.

Eberly, Don E., ed. 1994. *Building a Community of Citizens: Civil Society in the 21st Century.* Lanham, MD: University Press of America and the Commonwealth Foundation for Public Policy Alternatives.

Economic Opportunity Act of 1964, Pub. L. No. 88–452. 78 Stat. 508. 1964.

Edwards, Mary. 2006. *State and Local Revenues Beyond the Property Tax.* Lincoln Institute of Land Policy Working Paper WP06ME1. Cambridge, MA: Lincoln Institute of Land Policy. www.lincolninst.edu/subcenters/teaching-fiscal-dimensions-of-planning/materials/edwards-revenue.pdf (accessed April 11, 2011).

Elazar, Daniel J. 1987. *Exploring Federalism.* Tuscaloosa: University of Alabama Press.

Elkin, Stephen L. 2004. Thinking constitutionally: The problem of deliberative democracy. *Social Philosophy and Policy* 21, no. 1: 39–75.

Elkin, Stephen L., and Karol Edward Soltan. 1993. *A New Constitutionalism: Designing Political Institutions for a Good Society.* Chicago, IL: University of Chicago Press.

Ervin, Keith. 2010. County council dems replace one tax-increase plan with another. *Seattle Times*, May 24. http://seattletimes.com/html/localnews/2011942030_salestax25m.html (accessed June 22, 2013).

Evans, Sara, and Harry Boyte. 1992. *Free Spaces: The Sources of Democratic Change in America.* Chicago: University of Chicago Press.

Executive Women International (EWI), Minneapolis. 2007. EWI Minneapolis Chapter Philanthropy Projects, Minneapolis, MN. www.ewimsp.org/forms_public/Philanthropy_Projects.pdf.

ExpectMore.gov. The program assessment rating tool (PART). http://georgewbush-whitehouse.archives.gov/omb/expectmore/part.html (accessed May 5, 2012).

Farris, Sharon. 2009. *Nonprofit Bookkeeping & Accounting for Dummies.* Hoboken, NJ: Wiley.

Federal Funds Information for States (FFIS). 2011. Major discretionary and mandatory program funding. Table, February 22. www.ncsl.org/documents/statefed/JimMartinTable.pdf (accessed November 13, 2011).

Finer, Herman. 1941. Administrative responsibility in democratic government. *Public Administration Review* 1 (Summer): 335–350.

Finkler, Steven A. 2010. *Financial Management for Public, Health, and Not-for-Profit Organizations.* 3rd ed. Upper Saddle River, NJ: Prentice Hall/Pearson.

Fiscal Policy Center. 2014. "Priority-Based Budgeting." http://tax.i2i.org/files/2010/11/CB_PriorityBudgeting.pdf (accessed May 6, 2014).

Fischel, William A. 2000. Municipal corporations, homeowners, and the benefit view of the property tax. Paper presented at the conference on Property, Taxation, and Local Government Finance, Paradise Valley, AZ, January 16–18. Cambridge, MA: Lincoln Institute of Land Policy. http://localgov.fsu.edu/papers/archive/Fischel_001.pdf (accessed May 9, 2011).

Fisher, Glenn W. 1997. Some lessons from the history of the property tax. *Assessment Journal* 4, no. 3 (May/June): 40–47.

Fletcher v. Peck, 10 U.S. 87. 1810.

Fong, Dominique. 2012. Rules clarify sports field use. *The Oregonian,* October 6, E1, E2.

Forrer, John, James Edwin Kee, Kathryn E. Newcomer, and Eric Boyer. 2010. Public-private partnerships and the public accountability question. *Public Administration Review* 70, no. 3 (May/June): 475–484.

Forsythe, Dall W. 2004. *Memos to the Governor: An Introduction to State Budgeting.* 2d ed. Washington, DC: Georgetown University Press.

Franklin, Linda. 2010. Property tax explanation. Office of the Clark County Washington Assessor. www.clark.wa.gov/assessor/documents/PROPERTYTAXEXPLANATIO1.pdf (accessed February 17, 2012).

Friedrich, Carl J. 1940. Public policy and the nature of administrative responsibility. In *Public Policy,* ed. C.J. Friedrich and E.S. Mason, 3–24. Cambridge, MA: Harvard University Press.

Froelich, Karen A. 2001. Diversification of revenue strategies: Evolving resource dependence in nonprofit organizations. In *Understanding Nonprofit Organizations: Governance, Leadership, and Management,* ed. J. Steven Ott, 182–194. Boulder, CO: Westview.

Frumkin, Peter. 2010. *The Essence of Strategic Giving: A Practical Guide for Donors and Fundraisers.* Chicago, IL: University of Chicago Press.

Gaid, Dawn Marie. 2009. *Changing Federal County Payments and Rural Oregon Counties: Analysis of Policy Impacts and Responses from Loss of Secure Rural Schools Funding in Selected Oregon Counties.* Working Paper 09–04. Corvallis, OR: Rural Studies Program, Oregon State University, October. http://ruralstudies.oregonstate.edu/sites/default/files/pub/pdf/RSP09-04.pdf (accessed January 28, 2013).

Gainer, Brenda, and Mel S. Moyer. 2005. Marketing for nonprofit managers. In *The Jossey-Bass Handbook of Nonprofit Leadership and Management*, ed. Robert D. Herman and Associates, 277–309. San Francisco, CA: Jossey-Bass.

Garrett, Michael R., and Todd MacDonald. 1996. Program/activity-based management at the Regional Municipality of Peel: An organization in transition. *Government Finance Review* 12, no. 4 (August): 7–15.

Garson, David G. 2006. *Public Information Technology and E-Governance: Managing the Virtual State.* Raleigh, NC: Jones and Bartlett.

Gelles, Erna. 2001. Fund-raising. In *Understanding Nonprofit Organizations: Governance, Leadership, and Management,* ed. J. Steven Ott, 175–181. Boulder, CO: Westview.

Genn, Adina. 2009. *The Everything Guide to Fundraising.* Avon, MA: Adams Media.

Gentry, James K. 2008. Sarbanes-Oxley impact extends far beyond public companies. BusinessJournalism. org. http://businessjournalism.org/pages/biz/2006/06/sarbanesoxley_impact_extends_f/index.html (accessed January 19, 2013).

Gersick, Connie J.G. 1991. Revolutionary change theories: A multilevel exploration of the punctuated equilibrium paradigm. *The Academy of Management Review* 16, no. 1 (January): 10–36.

Giving USA Foundation. 2011. *Giving USA 2011: The Annual Report on Philanthropy for the Year 2010 Executive Summary.* www.issuelab.org/resource/giving_usa_2011_the_annual_report_on_philanthropy_for_the_year_2010_executive_summary (accessed January 19, 2012).

Global Movement for Budget Transparency, Accountability and Participation, 2014. *Make Budgets Public Now.* http://globalbtap.org/2013/ (accessed May 2, 2014).

Goggin, M., A. Bowman, J. Lester, and L. O'Toole. 1990. *Implementation Theory and Practice: Toward a Third Generation.* Glenville, IL: Scott Foresman and Co.

Goldsmith, Stephen, and William D. Eggers. 2004. *Governing by Network: The New Shape of the Public Sector.* Washington, DC: Brookings Institution Press.

Goodnow, Frank Johnson. 1895/2008. *Municipal Home Rule: A Study in Administration.* New York: Macmillan and Co. Repr., Charleston, SC: BiblioBazaar.

Gore, Albert A. 1993. *Creating a Government That Works Better and Costs Less: The Report of the National Performance Review.* Phase I Report. Washington, DC: September 7.

Gottlieb, Paul. 2012. State auditor implicates ex-PUD employee. *Peninsula Daily News,* October 31.

Governmental Accounting Standards Board (GASB). 2010. *Voluntary Reporting of Service Efforts and Accomplishments (SEA) Performance Information.* Norwalk, CT.

Government Finance Officers Association (GFOA) of the United States and Canada. 1996. Best practice: Establishing government charges and fees. www.gfoa.org/index.php?option=com_content&task=view&id=1553 (accessed August 1, 2013).

———. 1999. Best practice: Financial forecasting in the budget preparation process. www.gfoa.org/index.php?option=com_content&task=view&id=1555 (accessed August 24, 2012).

———. 2000. Budget practices menu. In *Best Practices in Public Budgeting.* Chicago, IL: GFOA. www.gfoa.org/services/nacslb/budgetmenu.htm (accessed November 22, 2010).

———. 2005. Recommended budget practice on the establishment of strategic plans. www.gfoa.org/index.php?option=com_content&task=view&id=1554 (accessed August 24, 2012).

———. 2006. Best practice: Preparing and adopting multi-year capital planning (CEDCP). www.gfoa.org/index.php?option=com_content&task=view&id=1598 (accessed March 5, 2013).

———. 2008. Best practice: Long-term financial planning. www.gfoa.org/downloads/LongtermFinancial-PlanningFINAL.pdf (accessed August 24, 2012).

———. 2011a. Best practice: The overview of performance management: From measurement and reporting to management and improving. www.gfoa.org/index.php?option=com_content&task=view&id=2457 (accessed January 15, 2013).

———. 2011b. Best practice: Development of capital planning policies (CEDCP). www.gfoa.org/index.php?option=com_content&task=view&id=2455 (accessed March 5, 2013).

———. 2011c. *Anatomy of a Priority-Driven Budgeting Process.* Chicago, IL: GFOA. www.gfoa.org/downloads/GFOA_AnatomyPriorityDrivenBudgetProcess.pdf (accessed November 14, 2012).

———. 2011d. *Containing Health Care Costs: Proven Strategies for Success in the Public Sector.* Chicago, IL: GFOA. http://gfoa.org/downloads/GFOAContainingHealthCareCosts.pdf (accessed August 7, 2013).

———. 2013a. Best practice: Pricing internal service. www.gfoa.org/index.php?option=com_content&task=view&id=2600 (accessed March 5, 2013).

———. 2013b. Best practice: Structurally balanced budget policy. www.gfoa.org/index.php?option=com_content&task= view&id=2597 (accessed March 5, 2013).

———. 2013c. Certificate of achievement for excellence in financial reporting program (CAFR Program). www.gfoa.org/index.php?option=com_content&task= view&id=35&Itemid=58 (accessed January 23, 2013).

———. 2013d. Distinguished budget presentation awards program. www.gfoa.org/index.php?option=com_content&task=view&id=33&Itemid=57 (accessed May 31, 2013).

GPRA Modernization Act. 2010. Pub. L. No. 111–352, 124 Stat. 3866. 2011.

Granof, Michael H., and Saleha B. Khumawala. 2011. *Government and Not-for-Profit Accounting: Concepts and Practices*. 5th ed. Hoboken, NJ: Wiley.

Green, Richard T. 1993. Prudent constitutionalism: Hamiltonian lessons for a responsible public administration. *International Journal of Public Administration* 16, no. 2: 165–186.

———. 2012. Plutocracy, bureaucracy, and the end of public trust. *Administration & Society* 44, no. 1: 109–143.

Green, Richard T., and Douglas Morgan. 2014. Making the Constitution relevant to local governments, special districts and authorities. Panel paper presented at the American Society of Public Administration national conference, March 13–17, Washington, DC.

Green, Roy E. 1989. *The Profession of Local Government Management: Management Expertise and the American Community*. New York: Praeger.

Greenfield, James M. 2002. *Fundraising Fundamentals: A Guide to Annual Giving for Professionals and Volunteers*. 2d ed. Hoboken, NJ: Wiley.

Gregoire, Chris. 2009. Gov. Gregoire celebrates Bremerton tunnel opening. Press release, July 6. Olympia, WA: Office of the Governor, State of Washington. www.digitalarchives.wa.gov/GovernorGregoire/news/news-view.asp?pressRelease=1281&newsType=1 (accessed February 25, 2013).

Griffin-Valade, LaVonne, Drummond Kahn, and Beth Woodward. 2013. *Street Pavement: Condition Shows Need for Better Stewardship*. Portland, OR: Office of the City Auditor, City of Portland, February. www.portlandonline.com/auditor/index.cfm?c=60923&a=435217 (accessed March 7, 2013).

Grodzins, Morton. 1960. The federal system. In *Goals for Americans: Programs for action in the sixties, comprising the report of the President's Commission on National Goals and chapters submitted for the consideration of the Commission*, ed. The American Assembly. Englewood Cliffs, NJ: Prentice Hall.

Gross, Malvern J., John H. McCarthy, and Nancy E. Shelmon. 2005. *Financial and Accounting Guide for Not-for-Profit Organizations*. 7th ed. Hoboken, NJ: Wiley.

Gutierrez, M., K. Belanger, V. Clark, J. Friedman, J. Redfern, B. Weber, C. Fluharty and J. Richgels. 2010. *Rethinking Rural Human Service Delivery in Challenging Times: the Case for Service Integration*. Washington, DC: U.S. Department of Health and Human Services (DHHS), Office of Rural Health Policy.

Hale, M.L. 1989. The nature of city managers' work. In *Ideal and Practice in Council-Manager Government*, ed. H. George Frederickson. Washington, DC: ICMA.

Hamilton, Alexander. 1791/1966. "Report on Manufactures." In *The Papers of Alexander Hamilton*, ed. Harold C. Syrett and Jacob E. Cooke. Vol. 10, *December 1791–January 1792*. New York: Columbia University Press.

Hamilton, Alexander, James Madison, and John Jay, under pseudonym Publius. 1787–1789/1961. *The Federalist Papers*, ed. Clinton Rossiter. New York: New American Library.

Hannah-Jones, Nikole. 2011. County proposes less-severe budget. *The Oregonian*, May 5, B6. www.oregonlive.com/portland/index.ssf/2011/05/multnomah_county_chairman_jeff_2.html (accessed December 20, 2012).

Harper, Edwin L., Fred Kramer, and Andrew Rouse. 1969. Implementation and use of PPB in sixteen federal agencies. *Public Administration Review* 29, no. 6 (November/December): 623–632. Also in Allen Schick, *Perspectives on Budgeting* (Washington, DC: American Society for Public Administration, 1987), 91–102.

Harrison Foundation. 2013. Women's Health Screening Fund. In *Ongoing Funds & Priority Projects*. Bermerton, WA: Harrison Medical Center. www.harrisonmedical.org/giving/ongoing-funds-priority (accessed May 7, 2013).

Hartley, Jean. 2005. Innovation in governance and public services: Past and present. *Public Money & Management* 25, no. 1: 27–34.

Hartman, William. 2003. *School District Budgeting*. Lanham, MD: Scarecrow/Education.

Hatry, H.P. 2002. Performance measurement: Fashions and fallacies. *Public Performance & Management Review* 25, no. 4: 352–358.

———. 2010. Looking into the crystal ball: Performance management over the next decade. *Public Administration Review* 70, no. S1: s208–s211.

Headrick, Daniel R. 2000. *When Information Came of Age: Technologies of Knowledge in the Age of Reason and Revolution, 1700–1850*. Oxford, UK: Oxford University Press.

Hefetz, A., and M. Warner. 2004. Privatization and its reverse: Explaining the dynamics of the government contracting process. *Journal of Public Administration Research and Theory* 14, no. 2: 171–190.

Heflin, Colene, and Kathleen Miller. 2011. *The Geography of Need: Identifying Human Service Needs in Rural America*. Columbia, MO: Rural Policy Research Institute, June. www.rupri.org/Forms/Heflin-Miller_GeogNeed_June2011.pdf.

Heifetz, Ronald A. 1994. *Leadership Without Easy Answers.* Cambridge, MA: Belknap Press of Harvard University Press.

Held, Virginia. 1984. *Rights and Goods.* New York: Free Press.

Henkels, Mark. 2005. Fiscal policy. In *Oregon Politics and Government: Progressives Versus Conservative Populists,* ed. Richard A. Clucas, Mark Henkels, and Brent S. Steel. Lincoln: University of Nebraska Press.

Hinton, David W., and John E. Kerrigan. 1995. Tracing the changing knowledge and skill needs and service activities of public managers. In *Ideal & Practice in Council-Manager Government,* ed. H. George Frederickson, 120–129. Washington, DC: ICMA.

Hough, James A. (personal recollection of professional practice, Oct. 14, 2012).

Howard, S. Kenneth. 1973. Planning and budgeting: Who's on first? In *Changing State Budgeting,* ed. Kenneth S. Howard, 196–213. Chapel Hill, NC: The Council of State Governments. Also in *Government Budgeting: Theory, Process, and Politics*, ed. Albert Hyde (Pacific Grove, CA: Brooks Cole, 1992), 349–357.

Human, Sherrie E., and Keith G. Provan. 2000. Legitimacy building in the evolution of small-firm multilateral networks: A comparative study of success and demise. *Administrative Science Quarterly* 45, no. 2 (June): 327–365.

Hunsberger, Brent. 2011. Oregon municipal bonds get good marks, but look carefully. *The Oregonian,* March 12, 2011. http://blog.oregonlive.com/finance/2011/03/oregon_municipal_bonds_get_goo.html (accessed March 2011).

Imperial, Mark. 2005. Using collaboration as a governance strategy. *Administration & Society* 37, no. 3 (July): 281–320.

Institute of Internal Auditors (IIA). 2013. *International Standards for the Professional Practice of Internal Auditing.* Altamonte Springs, FL: IIA.

International Association of Assessing Officers (IAAO). 2011. Welcome to IAAO. www.iaao.org/index.cfm (accessed May 11, 2011).

International City/County Management Association (ICMA). 2006. Municipal form of government survey. In *The Municipal Year Book 2007.* Washington, DC: ICMA.

———. 2008a. Trends in Structure, Responsibility, and Composition. ICMA State of the Profession Survey. http://kcmayor.org/cms/wp-content/uploads/2013/06/Municipal-Form-of-Government-Trends-in-Structure.pdf (accessed May 9, 2014).

———. 2008b. Practices for effective local government management. http://icma.org/main/bc.asp?bcid=1 20&hsid=1&ssid1=308&ssid2=311 (accessed March 22, 2008).

———. 2009. Statistics and data. http://icma.org/en/icma/career_network/education/data (accessed May 2009).

Irvin, Renee A., and Patrick Carr. 2005. The role of philanthropy in local government finance. *Public Budgeting and Finance* 25, no. 3 (Fall): 33–47.

Isett, Kimberley R., Ines A. Mergel, Kelly LeRoux, Pamela A. Mischen, and R. Karl Rethemeyer. 2011. Networks in public administration scholarship: Understanding where we are and where we need to go. *Journal of Public Administration Research and Theory* 21, supplement no. 1 (January): i157–i173.

Itasca County, Minnesota. 2011. Section G. Real estate management. www.co.itasca.mn.us/Home/Departments/Land/Documents/LMPDocs/II.%20G.%20Real%20Estate%20Management.pdf (accessed April 8, 2011).

Jackson, Peggy M. 2007. *Nonprofit Strategic Planning: Leveraging Sarbanes-Oxley Best Practices.* Hoboken, NJ: Wiley.

Jacobson, Don. 2002. We are the key to reform. *Foreign Service Journal,* April. http://govleaders.org/reform.htm (accessed May 16, 2012).

Jeavons, Thomas H. 2001. Ethics in nonprofit management: Creating a culture of integrity. In *Understanding Nonprofit Organizations: Governance, Leadership, and Management,* ed. J. Steven Ott, 108–119. Boulder, CO: Westview.

Jeffery, Blake R., Tanis J. Salant, and Alan L. Boroshok. 1989. *County Government Structure: A State by State Report.* Washington, DC: National Association of Counties.

John, R.R. 1995. *Spreading the News: The American Postal System from Franklin to Morse.* Cambridge, MA: Harvard University Press.

Johnson, Donald Bruce, and Kirk H. Porter. 1973. *National Party Platforms, 1840–1972.* Urbana: University of Illinois Press.

Johnson, Fredrick J. 2011. Delinquent taxes on real estate stay with property. *Topeka Capital-Journal,* July 4. http://cjonline.com/news/2011-07-04/delinquent-taxes-real-estate-stay-property (accessed February 5, 2013).

Johnson, Laurence E., and David R. Bean. 1999. GASB statement no. 34: The dawn of a new governmental financial reporting model. *The CPA Journal* 69, no. 12 (December): 14–23. www.nysscpa.org/cpajournal/1999/1299/f141299a.html (accessed April 2, 2011).

Johnson, Nicholas, Phil Oliff, and Erica Williams. 2011. An update on state budget cuts: At least 46 states have imposed cuts that hurt vulnerable residents and the economy. Center on Budget and Policy Priorities, February 9. www.cbpp.org/cms/index.cfm?fa=view&id=1214 (accessed April 26, 2011).

Johnson, Steven. 2002. The Transformation of Civic Institutions and Practices in Portland, Oregon, 1960–1990. PhD diss., Portland State University, Portland, OR.

Jones, Alan R. 1987. *The Constitutional Conservatism of Thomas McIntyre Cooley: A Study in the History of Idea*s, New York: Taylor & Francis.

Jørgensen, T. Beck, and Barry Bozeman. 2007. "Public Values: An Inventory." *Administration & Society* 39, no. 3: 354–381.

Joyce, Philip G. 2005. Federal budgeting after September 11th: A whole new ballgame, or is it déjà vu all over again? *Public Budgeting and Finance* 25, no. 1: 15–31.

Kahn, Paul W. 1992. *Legitimacy in History: Self-Government in American Constitutional Theory.* New Haven, CT: Yale University Press.

Kamensky, John. 2001. *A Brief History of Vice President Al Gore's National Partnership for Reinventing Government During the Administration of President Bill Clinton, 1993–2001.* Denton: University of North Texas Libraries, January 12. http://govinfo.library.unt.edu/npr/whoweare/historyofnpr.html.

———. 2011. The Obama performance approach. *Public Performance & Management Review* 35, no. 1 (September): 133–148.

Karl, Barry. 1987. The American bureaucrat: A history of sheep in wolves' clothing. *Public Administration Review* 47, no. 1: 26–34.

Kass, Henry D. 2001. Is trust enough? The issue of reliance and reliability in public administration. Paper presented at Public Administration Theory Network (PATNET) Conference, Leiden, Netherlands, June 2001.

Kavanagh, Shayne C., and John Ruggini. 2006. Budgeting technology: A private-sector solution for an enduring public-sector problem? *Government Finance Review* 22, no. 6 (December): 11–16.

Kavanagh, Shayne, John Ruggini, Monica Na, Anne Kinney, Steve Kreklow, Joanna Greiner, and Amy Stewart. 2006. *Budgeting Technology Solutions.* Chicago, IL: Government Finance Officers Association. www.gfoa.org/services/documents/Budget_Technology_Report.pdf (accessed August 28, 2012).

Kelly, Janet M., and William C. Rivenbark. 2003. *Performance Budgeting for State and Local Government.* Armonk, NY: M.E. Sharpe.

Kelly, R.M. 1998. An inclusive democratic polity, representative bureaucracies, and the new public management. *Public Administration Review* 58, no. 3: 201–208.

Kemmis, Daniel. 1990. *Community and the Politics of Place.* Norman: University of Oklahoma Press.

———. 1995. *The Good City and the Good Life: Renewing the Sense of Community.* Boston, MA: Houghton Mifflin.

Kenyon, Daphne. 2007. *The Property Tax–School Funding Dilemma.* Policy Focus Report PF015. Cambridge, MA: The Lincoln Institute of Land Policy, December. www.lincolninst.edu/pubs/1308_The-Property-Tax-School-Funding-Dilemma (accessed April 26, 2011).

Kerth, Rob, and Phineas Baxandall. 2011. *Tax-Increment Financing: The Need for Increased Transparency and Accountability in Local Economic Development Subsidies.* Washington, DC: U.S. PIRG Education Fund, Fall. www.uspirg.org/sites/pirg/files/reports/Tax-Increment-Financing.pdf (accessed February 7, 2012).

Kettl, Donald F. 2000. *The Global Public Management Revolution: A Report on the Transformation of Governance.* Washington, DC: Brookings Institution Press.

King County, Washington. 2009. *2010 Executive Proposed Budget Book.* Seattle, WA: September. www.kingcounty.gov/operations/Budget/2010ExecutiveProposed.aspx (accessed April 8, 2011).

King County Sheriff, Seattle, Washington. 2013. Communities: Sammamish. www.kingcounty.gov/safety/sheriff/Communities/Sammamish.aspx (accessed June 22, 2013).

Kingdon, John W. 1995. *Agendas, Alternatives, and Public Policy.* 2d ed. New York: HarperCollins.

Klinger, Donald E., John Nalbandian, and Barbara S. Romzek. 2002. Politics, administration, and markets: Conflicting expectations and accountability. *American Review of Public Administration* 32, no. 2 (June): 117–144.

Kors, Alan Charles, ed. 2003. *Encyclopedia of the Enlightenment.* Oxford, UK: Oxford University Press.

Krane, Dale, Carol Ebdon, and John Bartle. 2004. Devolution, fiscal federalism, and changing patterns of municipal revenues: The mismatch between theory and reality. *Journal of Public Administration Research and Theory* 14, no. 4: 513–533.

Kratz, Robert. 1996. *A Primer on School Budgeting*. Lanham, MD: Scarecrow Press.

Kretzmann, John P. and John L. McKnight. 1993. Building communities from the inside out: A path toward finding and mobilizing a community's assets. Institute for Policy Research, Northwestern University, Evanston, IL. http://rally-foundation.org/projects/neighborood-info-initiatives/resources/Community%20 indicator%20Measurements/BuildingCommunitiesInsideOut.pdf (accessed May 6, 2014).

Lampel, Joseph, and Henry Mintzberg. 1999. Reflecting on the strategy process. *MIT Sloan Management Review* 40, no. 3 (Spring): 21.

Lauria, Mickey, ed. 1997. *Reconstructing Urban Regime Theory: Regulating Local Government in a Global Economy*. Thousand Oaks, CA: Sage.

Lawther, Wendell C. 2003. Contracting for the 21st century: A partnership model. In *The Procurement Revolution,* ed. Mark A. Abramson and Roland S. Harris III, 167–216. Lanham, MD: Rowman & Littlefield.

Lazenby, Scott. 2009. City Management Theory and Practice: A Foundation for Educating the Next Generation of Local Government Administrators. PhD diss., Portland State University, Portland, OR. July.

Leo, Christopher. 1997. City politics in an era of globalization. In *Reconstructing Urban Regime Theory: Regulating Local Government in a Global Economy,* ed. Mickey Lauria, 77–98. Thousand Oaks, CA: Sage.

———. 1998. Regional growth management regime: The case of Portland, Oregon. *Journal of Urban Affairs* 20, no. 4: 363–394.

LeRoux, Kelly, ed. 2007. *Service Contracting: A Local Government Guide*. 2d ed. Washington, DC: ICMA Press.

LeRoux, Kelly, Paul W. Brandenburger, and Sanjay K. Pandey. 2010. Interlocal service cooperation in U.S. cities: A social network explanation. *Public Administration Review* 70, no. 2 (March–April): 268–278.

LeRoux, Kelly, and Jered B. Carr. 2007. *Explaining Local Government Cooperation on Public Works: Evidence from Michigan*. Working Group on Interlocal Services Cooperation. Paper 26. http://digitalcommons.wayne.edu/interlocal_coop/26 (accessed January 2, 2013).

Levine, Charles H. 1978. Organizational decline and cutback management. *Public Administration Review* 38, no. 4 (July/August): 316–325.

Levine, Charles, and Glenn Fisher. 1984. Citizenship and service delivery: The promise of coproduction. *Public Administration Review* 44 (March): 178–187.

Lewis, Gregory. 1990. In search of the Machiavellian Milquetoasts: Comparing attitudes of bureaucrats and ordinary people. *Public Administration Review* 50, no. 2 (March–April): 220–227.

———. 1992. Men and women toward the top: Backgrounds, careers, and potential of federal middle managers. *Public Personnel Management* 21 (Winter): 473–492.

Light, Paul. C. 2004. *Sustaining Nonprofit Performance: The Case for Capacity Building and the Evidence to Support It*. Washington, DC: Brookings Institution Press.

Locke, John. 1980. *Second Treatise of Government,* ed. C.B. Macpherson. Indianapolis, IN: Hackett.

Lord, Harold. 2005. Chapter 9: Army planning, programming, budgeting, and execution process. In *How the Army Runs: A Senior Leader Reference Handbook, 2005–2006,* ed. U.S. Army War College. Carlisle, PA: Department of the Army. www.globalsecurity.org/military/library/report/2005/htar2005ch9.pdf (accessed November 8, 2013).

Lower Milford Township, Pennsylvania. 2011. *2012 Budget All Funds*. http://lowermilford.net/budget.pdf (accessed January 3, 2012).

Lowi, Theodore J. 1979. *The End of Liberalism*. 2d ed. New York: Norton.

Lowi, Theodore J., and Benjamin Ginsberg. 2000. *American Government: Freedom and Power.* 6th ed. New York: Norton.

Lyden, Fremont J., and Marc Lindenberg. 1983. *Public Budgeting in Theory and Practice*. New York: Longman.

Lynn, L., Jr. 1998. The new public management: How to transform a theme into a legacy. *Public Administration Review* 58, no. 3: 231–237.

Madison, James. 1787/1987. *Notes of Debates in the Federal Convention of 1787 Reported by James Madison,* ed. Adrienne Koch. New York: Norton.

Maher, Craig S., and Mark Skidmore. 2009. Voter responses to referenda seeking to exceed revenue limits. *Public Budgeting and Finance* 29, no. 2 (Summer): 71–93.

Mansfield, Harvey. 1969. Federal executive reorganization: Thirty years of experience. *Public Administration Review* 29(4), 332–345.

March, James G., and Johan P. Olsen. 1995. *Democratic Governance*. New York: The Free Press.

Marois, Deb, Terry Amsler, Greg Keidan, and JoAnne Speers. 2010. *A Local Official's Guide to Public Engagement in Budgeting*. Sacramento, CA: Institute for Local Government. www.ca-ilg.org/sites/main/

files/file-attachments/2010_-_Guide_to_Public_Engagement_in_Budgeting-w.pdf (accessed September 28, 2012).

Martell, Christine R., and Paul Teske. 2007. Fiscal management implications of the TABOR bind. *Public Administration Review* 67, no. 4 (July/August): 673–687.

Martens, Susan. 2011. Oregon property taxes. MovingtoPortland.net. www.movingtoportland.net/property_taxes.htm (accessed May 16, 2011).

Martinez, Amy. 2010. ACLU, Amazon face North Carolina tax collectors in Seattle court. *Seattle Times,* October 13. http://seattletimes.com/html/businesstechnology/2013154218_amazonlawsuit14.html (accessed April 22, 2011).

———. 2011. More states taking action to force Amazon to collect sales tax. *Seattle Times*, March 11. http://seattletimes.com/html/businesstechnology/2014471944_amazon12.html (accessed April 22, 2011).

Massarsky, Cynthia W. 2005. Enterprise strategies for generating revenue. In *The Jossey-Bass Handbook of Nonprofit Leadership and Management*, ed. Robert D. Herman and Associates, 436–465. San Francisco, CA: Jossey-Bass.

Mathews, Joe, and Mark Paul. 2010. *California Crack Up: How Reform Broke the Golden State and How We Can Fix It.* Berkeley: California.

McCaffery, Jerry, and John H. Bowman. 1978. Participatory democracy and budgeting: The effects of Proposition 13. *Public Administration Review* 38, no. 6 (November–December): 530–538.

McCaffrey, Scott. 2011. Tax-delinquency rate falls to another record low. *The Sun Gazette* (Arlington, VA), August 22. www.sungazette.net/arlington/news/tax-delinquency-rate-falls-to-another-record-low/article_69592d21-fcea-55b8-87d9-f20652f66272.html (accessed February 5, 2013).

McCullough, Thomas E. 1991. *The Moral Imagination and Public Life*. Chatham, NJ: Chatham House.

McGee, Patrick. 2011. Chapter 9 past may not be prologue: Priority uncertain for bondholders. *The Bond Buyer,* March 2. www.bondbuyer.com/issues/120_41/muni_bankruptcy-1023872-1.html (accessed April 27, 2011).

McKnight, John L., and John P. Kretzmann. 1996. *Mapping Community Capacity*. Evanston, IL: Institute for Policy Research, Northwestern University. www.racialequitytools.org/resourcefiles/mcknight.pdf (accessed January 28, 2013).

McLoughlin, Thomas, and Kristin Stephens. 2012. Municipal bonds: Pensions on our mind. *Wealth Management Research*. UBS Financial Services (September 18): 4–7. www.treasurer.ca.gov/cdiac/seminars/2012/20121017/supplement.pdf (accessed January 25, 2013).

Meier, Kenneth J. 2006. *Bureaucracy in a Democratic State: A Governance Perspective*. Baltimore, MD: Johns Hopkins University Press.

Merewitz, Leonard, and Stephen H. Sosnick. 1971. *The Budget's New Clothes: A Critique of Planning-Programming-Budgeting and Benefit-Cost Analysis*. Chicago, IL: Markham.

Metz, Rachel. 2011. States push harder for online sales tax collection. *Seattle Times*, March 20. http://seattletimes.com/html/localnews/2014552397_apustecamazononlinesalestax.html (accessed April 22, 2011).

Meyers, Roy T., and Philip G. Joyce. 2005. Congressional budgeting at age 30: Is it worth saving? *Public Budgeting and Finance* 25, no. 4s (December): 68–82.

Michel, R. Gregory. 2004. *Cost Analysis and Activity-Based Costing for Government*. Chicago, IL: Government Finance Officers' Association (GFOA).

Mikesell, John L. 2005. Changing revenue policy in the United States: Overview of the record and perennial puzzles. *Public Budgeting and Finance* 25, no. 4 (December): 99–126.

Milward, H. Brinton, and Keith G. Provan. 2000. Governing the hollow state. *Journal of Public Administration Research and Theory* 10, no. 2 (April): 359–379.

Missouri v. Lewis, 101 U.S. 22. 1879.

Moe, R.C. 1994. The "reinventing government" exercise: Misinterpreting the problem, misjudging the consequences. *Public Administration Review* 54, no. 2: 111–122.

Moe, R.C., and R.S. Gilmour. 1995. Rediscovering principles of public administration: The neglected foundation of public law. *Public Administration Review* 55, no. 2: 135–146.

Montjoy, Robert S., and Douglas J. Watson. 1995. A case for reinterpreted dichotomy of politics and administration as a professional standard in council-manager government. *Public Administration Review* 55, no. 3 (May–June): 231–239.

Moore, Mark H. 1994. Public value as the focus of strategy. *Australian Journal of Public Administration* 53, no. 3: 296–303.

———. 1995. *Creating Public Value: Strategic Management in Government*. Cambridge, MA: Harvard University Press.

———. 2000. Managing for value: Organizational strategy in for-profit, nonprofit, and governmental organizations. *Nonprofit and Voluntary Sector Quarterly* 29, no. 1 (March 1): 183–208.

Morgan, Douglas F. 2001. Ethics and the public interest. In *Handbook on Administrative Ethics,* ed. Terry L. Cooper, 2d ed., 151–175. New York: Marcel Dekker.

———. 2005. Oregon administrative structure. In *Oregon Politics and Government: Progressives versus Conservative Populists,* ed. Richard A. Clucas, Mark Henkels, and Brent S. Steel. Lincoln, NE: University of Nebraska Press.

Morgan, Douglas F., and Brian Cook, 2014. *Foundations of New Public Governance: A Regime Centered Approach,* eds. Douglas F. Morgan and Brian J. Cook. Chap. 1. Armonk, NY: M.E. Sharpe.

Morgan, Douglas F. and Craig Shinn. 2014. Foundations of new public governance. In *Foundations of New Public Governance: A Regime-Centered Perspetive.* eds. Douglas F. Morgan and Brian J. Cook. Chap. 1. Armonk, NY: M.E. Sharpe.

Morgan, Douglas F., Richard Green, Craig W. Shinn, and Kent S. Robinson. 2008. *Foundations of Public Service.* Armonk, NY: M.E. Sharpe.

———. 2013. *Foundations of Public Service.* 2d ed. Armonk, NY: M.E. Sharpe.

Morgan, Douglas F., and Henry D. Kass. 1993. The American odyssey of the career public service: The ethical crises of role reversal. In *Ethics and Public Administration,* ed. H. George Frederickson. Armonk, NY: M.E. Sharpe.

Morgan, Douglas F., Masami Nishishiba, and Daniel Vizzini. 2010. Keep Portland weird: Retaining the commission form of government. In *More Than Mayor or Manager,* ed. James Svara and Douglas Watson. Washington, DC: Georgetown University Press.

Morningstar, Inc. 2007. Municipal Bond Sectors. http://morningstardirect.morningstar.com/clientcomm/municipal_bond_sectors.pdf (accessed February 28, 2012).

Moynihan, Daniel P., and S.K. Pandey. 2005. Testing how management matters in an era of government by performance management. *Journal of Public Administration Research and Theory* 15, no. 3: 421–439.

Mullen, Patrick R. 2006. Performance-based budgeting: The contribution of the program assessment rating tool. *Public Budgeting and Finance* 26, no. 4 (Winter): 79–88.

Mullins, Daniel R., and Philip G. Joyce. 1996. Tax and expenditure limitations and state and local fiscal structure: An empirical assessment. *Public Budgeting and Finance* 16, no. 1 (Spring): 75–101.

Multnomah County, OR. 2014. "ITAX: Multnomah County Temporary Income Tax 2003–2005." http://web.multco.us/finance/itax-multnomah-county-temporary-income-tax-2003-2005 (accessed May 3, 2014).

Mulvihill, Geoff. 2011. Anger brews over government workers' benefits. Associated Press, March 8. www.washingtontimes.com/news/2011/mar/13/anger-brews-over-government-workers-benefits/?page=all (accessed March 8, 2011).

Municipal Research and Services Center (MRSC). 2009. *A Revenue Guide for Washington Cities and Towns.* Report No. 46 Revised. Seattle, WA.

———. 2013. Budget calendar for preparation of 2014 budgets in first (under 300,000) and second, and fourth class cities, code cities, and towns. March. www.mrsc.org/subjects/finance/budgets/budgcal.aspx (accessed June 7, 2013).

Nalbandian, John. 1991. *Professionalism in Local Government: Transformations in the Roles, Responsibilities, and Values of City Managers.* San Francisco, CA: Jossey-Bass.

———. 1994. Reflections of a "pracademic" on the logic of politics and administration. *Public Administration Review* 54, no. 6 (November/December): 531–536.

———. 2000. The city manager as political leader: A challenge to professionalism? *Public Management* 82, no. 3 (March): 7–13.

Natchez, Peter B., and Irvin C. Bupp. 1973. Policy and priority in the budgetary process. *The American Political Science Review* 67, no. 3 (September): 951–963.

Nathan, Richard. 1976. The administrative presidency. *The Public Interest* 44 (Summer), 40–54.

National Academy of Public Administration (NAPA). 1983. *Revitalizing Federal Management: Managers and Their Overburdened Systems.* Washington, DC: National Academy of Public Administration.

National Association of Counties (NACo). www.naco.org (accessed April 6, 2011).

———. 2011a. Payment in lieu of taxes (PILT) funding. Legislative Affairs Fact Sheet. Washington, DC: NACo.

———. 2011b. Key legislative priorities: Fiscal responsibility while creating jobs. Washington, DC: NACo.

National Association of Health and Educational Facilities Finance Authorities. 2008. Members [member listing by state]. www.naheffa.com/members.html (accessed February 28, 2012).

National Association of State Auditors, Comptrollers, and Treasurers. 2009. *Auditing the States: A Summary, 2009.* Lexington, KY: NASACT.

———. 2012. *Charting a Course Through Stormy Seas: State Financial Executives in 2012.* NASACT-AGA

2012 Survey of State Financial Executives. www.nasact.org/nasact/publications/papers/GT_AGA_State-Survey2012_04.pdf (accessed January 15, 2013).

National Bureau of Economic Research (NBER). 2010. U.S. Business Cycle Expansions and Contractions. Table, September 20. www.nber.org/cycles/cyclesmain.html (accessed April 14, 2011).

National Center for Charitable Statistics. 2009. Unified Chart of Accounts. http://nccs.urban.org/projects/ucoa.cfm (accessed July 30, 2012).

National Center for Educational Research. 2009. *Financial Accounting for Local and State School Systems, 2009 Edition.* Washington, DC: U.S. Department of Education. http://nces.ed.gov/pubs2009/fin_acct/index.asp (accessed January 20, 2012).

National Center for Education Statistics. 2009. "Revenues and Expenditures for Public Elementary and Secondary Education. http://nces.ed.gov/pubs2010/expenditures/tables.asp.

National Civic League. 1996. *National Civic League Survey.* Denver, CO: National Civic League.

National Commission on Fiscal Responsibility and Reform (NCFR&R). 2010. *The Moment of Truth: Report of the National Commission on Fiscal Responsibility and Reform.* Washington, DC: Executive Office of the President, December. www.fiscalcommission.gov/sites/fiscalcommission.gov/files/documents/TheMomentofTruth12_1_2010.pdf (accessed February 16, 2011).

National Conference of State Legislatures (NCSL). 1995. Fundamentals of Sound State Budgeting Practices. June. www.ncsl.org/issues-research/budget/fundamentals-of-sound-state-budgeting-practices.aspx (accessed May 19, 2012).

———. 2002. *A Guide to Property Taxes: Property Tax Relief.* Denver, CO: NCSL. www.leg.state.nv.us/73rd/otherDocuments/PTax/NCSL-gptrelief.pdf (accessed January 29, 2012).

———. 2007a. *Nexus in the New Economy: Ensuring a Level Playing Field for All Commerce.* www.ncsl.org/documents/standcomm/sccomfc/nexusneweconomyam2011.pdf (accessed November 27, 2007).

———. 2007b. Principles of a High-Quality State Revenue System. 4th ed. (2007 update). http://ltgovernor.ky.gov/taxreform/Documents/20120710_Kelly.pdf (accessed November 13, 2011).

———. 2008. Table 2–1: Budget cycle. In *Legislative Budget Procedures: Budget Framework,* December. www.ncsl.org/default.aspx?tabid=12645 (accessed July 24, 2011).

———. 2010a. *Fundamentals of Sound State Budgeting.* June 1. www.statebudgetsolutions.org/publications/detail/fundamentals-of-sound-state-budgeting-practices (accessed September 16, 2013).

———. 2011a. Legislative term limits: An overview. www.ncsl.org/LegislaturesElections/LegislatorsLegislativeStaffData/LegislativeTermLimitsOverview/tabid/14849/Default.aspx (accessed July 14, 2011).

———. 2013. Policies for the jurisdiction of the budgets and revenue committee. August 15. www.ncsl.org/ncsl-in-dc/task-forces/policies-for-the-jurisdiction-of-budgets-and-revenue-committee.aspx#Federal%20Mandate%20Relief (accessed May 4, 2014).

———. 2014. Standing Committee on budgets and revenue: Mandate monitor overview. www.ncsl.org/ncsl-in-dc/standing-committees/budgets-and-revenue/mandate-monitor-overview.aspx (accessed July 14, 2014).

National Philanthropic Trust. 2012. Charitable giving statistics. www.nptrust.org/philanthropic-resources/statistics/(accessed January 19, 2012).

Nishishiba, Masami, Margaret Banyan, and Douglas F. Morgan. 2012. Looking back on the founding: Civic engagement traditions in the United States. In *The State of Citizen Participation in America*, ed. Hindy Lauer Schachter and Kaifeng Yang, 27–36. Charlotte, NC: Information Age.

Nixon, Richard. 1971. Special message to the Congress on Executive Branch Reorganization. March 25. In *The American Presidency Project,* ed. Gerhard Peters and John T. Woolley. www.presidency.ucsb.edu/ws/?pid=2951.

Novick, David. 1992. What program budgeting is and is not. In *Government Budgeting: Theory, Process, and Politics,* ed. Albert Hyde, 342–348. Pacific Grove, CA: Brooks Cole.

Novick, David, and Daniel J. Alesch. 1970. *Program Budgeting.* Santa Monica, CA: Rand Corporation, 1–19.

Obama, Barack. 2011. Framework for deficit reduction. Speech transcript, April 13. www.whitehouse.gov/winning-the-future/fiscal-framework (accessed April 20, 2011).

O'Flynn, J. 2007. From new public management to public value: Paradigm change and managerial implications. *The Australian Journal of Public Administration* 66, no. 3: 353–356.

Okun, Arthur. 1975. *Equality and Efficiency: The Big Tradeoff.* Washington, DC: Brookings Institution.

Oregon Legislative Revenue Office. 1999. *1999 School Finance Legislation: Funding and Distribution.* Research Report #4–99. Salem, OR: State of Oregon Legislative Revenue Office, October.

Oregon Progress Board. 2012. Web page. http://benchmarks.oregon.gov/(accessed Oct. 19, 2012).

The Oregonian Editorial Board. 2010a. Oregon: Intel inside. *The Oregonian,* October 20. www.oregonlive.com/opinion/index.ssf/2010/10/oregon_intel_inside.html (accessed February 6, 2012).

———. 2010b. Sewer money for bikeways: Does it pass the smell test? *The Oregonian,* March 14. http://blog.oregonlive.com/opinion_impact/print.html?entry=/2010/03/sewer_money_for_bikeways_does.html (accessed July 19, 2012).

Organization for Economic and Community Development (OECD). 2014. *Best Practices for Budget Transparency.* Paris: OECD. www.oecd.org/gov/budgeting/best-practices-budget-transparency.htm (accessed May 5, 2014).

Osborne, David, and Ted Gaebler. 1992. *Reinventing Government: How the Entrepreneurial Spirit Is Transforming the Public Sector.* New York: Plume Penguin.

Osborne, David, and Peter Hutchinson. 2004. *The Price of Government.* Boulder, CO: Basic Books.

Osborne, Stephen P. 2006. Editorial: The new public governance? *Public Management Review* 8, no. 3: 377–387.

———. 2008. *The Third Sector in Europe: Prospects and Challenges.* London: Routledge.

———. 2010. *The New Public Governance? Emerging Perspectives on the Theory and Practice of Public Governance.* London: Routledge.

Osbourn, Sandra S. 1995. *Unfunded Mandate Reform Act: A Brief Summary.* CRS Report for Congress 95–246 GOV. Washington, DC: Congressional Research Service. http://digital.library.unt.edu/ark:/67531/metacrs259/m1/1/high_res_d/95-246_1995Mar17.html (accessed August 8, 2011).

Ostrower, Francie. 2007. *Nonprofit Governance in the United States: Findings on Performance and Accountability in the First Representative Study.* Washington, DC: The Urban Institute Press.

O'Toole, Daniel, and James Marshall. 1990. Budgeting trends: Implications for the future. In *School Business Management in the Twenty-first Century,* ed. Kenneth R. Stevenson and John H. Lane, 45–57. Reston, VA: Association of School Business Officials International.

O'Toole, Daniel, James Marshall, and Timothy Grewe. 1996. Current local government budgeting practices. *Government Finance Review* 12, no. 6 (December): 25–29.

O'Toole, Daniel, and Brian Stipak. 1988. Budgeting and productivity revisited: The local government picture. *Public Productivity Review* 12, no. 1 (Fall): 1–12.

———. 1992. Patterns and trends in budget format innovation among local governments. *Public Budgeting & Financial Management* 4, no. 2: 287–309.

———. 1995. Budgeting and productivity revisited: The local government picture. In *Competent Government: Theory and Practice,* ed. Arie Halachmi and Marc Holzer, 175–186. Burke, VA: Chatelaine Press.

———. 1999. Strategic planning and budgeting in local government. *Public Budgeting & Financial Management* 3, no. 2: 317–331.

O'Toole, Laurence J. 1997. The implications for democracy in a networked bureaucratic world. *Journal of Public Administration Research and Theory* 7, no. 3: 443–459.

———. 2006. *Bureaucracy in a Democratic State: A Governance Perspective.* Baltimore, MD: Johns Hopkins University Press.

———. 2010. The ties that bind? Networks, public administration, and political science. *Political Science and Politics* 43, no. 1: 7–14.

O'Toole, Randal. 2011. *Crony Capitalism and Social Engineering: The Case Against Tax-Increment Financing.* Policy Analysis No. 676. Washington, DC: Cato Institute, May 18. www.cato.org/pubs/pas/PA676.pdf (accessed February 7, 2012).

Ott, J. Steven, ed. 2001. *Understanding Nonprofit Organizations: Governance, Leadership, and Management.* Boulder, CO: Westview.

Owen, Wendy. 2012. Parents urged to attend budget-teaching lessons. *The Oregonian,* March 17, E4.

Ozawa, Connie, ed. 2005. *The Portland Edge: Challenges and Successes in Growing Communities.* Washington, DC: Island Press.

Paludan, Phillip S. 1975. *A Covenant with Death: The Constitution, Law, and Equality in the Civil War Era.* Urbana-Champaign: University of Illinois Press.

Pandey, Sanjay K. 2010. Cutback management and the paradox of publicness. *Public Administration Review* 70, no. 4 (July/August): 564–571.

Partnership for Public Service and Hay Group. 2011. Leading Innovation in Government. https://ourpublicservice.org/OPS/publications/viewcontentdetails.php?id=158 (accessed May16, 2012).

Patient Protection and Affordable Care Act of 2010, "Affordable Care Act" (PPACA), P.L. 11–148, 124 Stat. 119 through 124 Stat. 1025.

Payments in Lieu of Taxes Act (PILT). Pub. L. No. 103–397, 108 Stat. 4156. 1994.

Peisner, Lynn. 2006. Sandy Springs: The big experiment. *American City & County,* November. www.sandyspringsga.org/getmedia/c6725a70-6c1f-4a52-bd29-00623da4c561/AmCity.aspx.

People ex rel. Le Roy v. Hurlbut, 24 Mich. 44, 107–108. 1871.

Perrow, Charles. 1986. *Complex Organizations: A Critical Essay.* 3rd ed. New York: McGraw-Hill.

Pew Center on the States. 2013. "Long-Term Obligations Vary Across States," November 27, 2013, www.pewstates.org/research/analysis/long-term-obligations-vary-across-states-85899513708 (accessed April 23, 2014).

———. 2010a. *The Trillion Dollar Gap: Underfunded State Retirement Systems and the Roads to Reform.* Washington, DC: The Pew Charitable Trusts, February 18. www.pewtrusts.org/our_work_report_detail.aspx?id=57353 (accessed April 20, 2011).

———. 2010b. *South Carolina's Public Safety Reform: Legislation Enacts Research-Based Strategies to Cut Prison Growth and Costs.* Philadelphia: The Pew Charitable Trusts, June. www.pewtrusts.org/uploadedFiles/wwwpewtrustsorg/Reports/sentencing_and_corrections/PSPP_South_Carolina_brief.pdf (accessed May 6, 2012).

———. 2012a. *The Local Squeeze: Falling Revenues and Growing Demand for Services Challenge Cities, Counties, and School Districts.* Washington, DC: The Pew Charitable Trusts, June. www.pewstates.org/research/reports/the-local-squeeze-85899388655 (accessed June 18, 2012).

———. 2012b. Public safety. www.pewstates.org/issues/public-safety-328137 (accessed May 6, 2012).

Phillips, Matt. 2011. Fannie and Freddie: The saga in the charts. *Wall Street Journal,* February 11. http://blogs.wsj.com/marketbeat/2011/02/11/fannie-and-freddie-the-saga-in-charts/?KEYWORDS=Phillips+Fannie+and+Freddie (accessed April 26, 2011).

Phyrr, Peter. 1973. *Zero-Base Budgeting.* New York: John Wiley & Sons.

Plumb, Sally. 2010. "Underfoot." *Decanto Poetry Magazine.* (Littlehampton England). www.poetryinnature.com/nature/poetry.asp?poem=5435 (accessed May 5, 2014).

Pope, Alexander. 1732–1733/1994. *Essay on Man.* Repr., Mineola, NY: Dover Thrift Editions.

Port of Longview, Washington. 2010. *Annual Report 2009.* Longview, WA. www.portoflongview.com/Portals/0/Documents/Document-Library/Financial/2009%20Annual%20Report.pdf (accessed April 1, 2011).

Poston, William. 2010. *School Budgeting for Hard Times: Confronting Cutbacks and Critics.* Thousand Oaks, CA: Corwin Press.

Powell, Walter W., and Paul J. DiMaggio. 1991. *The New Institutionalism in Organizational Analysis.* Chicago: University of Chicago Press.

Provan, Keith G., and Kun Huang. 2012. Resource tangibility and the evolution of a publicly funded health and human services network. *Public Administration Review* 72, no. 3 (May/June): 366–375.

Provan, Keith G., and Patrick Kenis. 2007. Modes of network governance: Structure, management, and effectiveness. *Journal of Public Administration Research and Theory* 18, no. 2: 229–252.

Provan, Keith G., and Robin H. Lemaire. 2012. Core concepts and key ideas for understanding public-sector organizational networks: Using research to inform scholarship and practice. *Public Administration Review* 72, no. 5 (September/October): 638–648.

Provan, Keith G., and H. Brinton Milward. 2001. Do networks really work? A framework for evaluating public-sector organizational networks. *Public Administration Review* 61, no. 4: 414–423.

Purdy, Taryn. 2012. "Priority-Based Budgeting: Washington State's Priorities of Government." A Report Prepared for the Committee on Efficiency in State Government. Legislative Fiscal Division. Olympia, WA.

Putnam, Robert D. 1993. *Making Democracy Work: Civic Traditions in Modern Italy.* Princeton, NJ: Princeton University Press.

———. 2000. *Bowling Alone: The Collapse and Revival of American Community.* New York: Simon & Schuster.

Rawls, John. 1971/1999. *A Theory of Justice,* rev. ed. Cambridge, MA: Belknap Press of Harvard University Press.

———. 2001. *Justice as Fairness: A Restatement,* ed. Erin Kelly. Cambridge, MA: Belknap Press of Harvard University Press.

Reason, Tim. 2005. Budgeting in the real world: More companies are writing budgets that reflect strategy and reduce frustration. *CFO Magazine,* July 12. www.cfo.com/article.cfm/4124788 (accessed August 24, 2012).

Rebuilding Civil Society. 1995. A Symposium from *The New Democrat,* vol. 7, no. 2 (March–April).

Rice, Bradley R. 2010. "Commission Form of City Government." In *Handbook of Texas Online.* Denton: Texas State Historical Association. www.tshaonline.org/handbook/online/articles/moc01. (accessed July 19, 2014).

Rice, Robert. 1977. *Progressive Cities: The Commission Government Movement in America, 1901–1920.* Austin: University of Texas Press.

Richardson, James D., ed. 1899. *A Compilation of the Messages and Papers of the Presidents.* Vol. 10. Washington, DC: U.S. Government Printing Office.

Riley, Susan L., and Peter W. Colby. 1991. *Practical Government Budgeting: A Workbook for Public Managers.* Albany: State University Press of New York.

Ring, Dan. 2012. Massachusetts auditor Suzanne Bump cites wrongdoing by former official at Springfield Technical Community College. *The Republican,* October 11, 2012. www.masslive.com/politics/index. ssf/2012/10/massachusetts_auditor_suzanne_1.html (accessed September 9, 2013).

Ripley, Randall B., and Grace A. Franklin. 1991. *Congress, the Bureaucracy, and Public Policy.* 6th ed. Pacific Grove, CA: Brooks Cole.

Rivenbark, William C. 2003. Strategic planning and the budget process. *Government Finance Review* 19, no. 5 (October): 22–27.

Robinson, Kent S. 2004. "The Contribution of Social Trust and Reliance to Administrative Process." PhD diss., Portland State University, Portland, OR. DAI/UMI #: AAT 3150620.

Robinson, Kent S., and Douglas F. Morgan. 2014. Local government as polity leadership: Implications for new public governance. In *New Public Governance: A Regime Perspective,* ed. Brian Cook and Douglas F. Morgan. Armonk, NY: M.E. Sharpe.

Rohr, John A. 1989. *Ethics for Bureaucrats: An Essay on Law and Values.* 2d ed. New York: Marcel-Dekker.

———. 1986. *To Run a Constitution: The Legitimacy of the Administrative State.* Lawrence: University Press of Kansas.

———. 1981. "Financial disclosures: Power in search of policy." *Public Personnel Management* 10, 29–40.

Romzek, Barbara S., Kelly LeRoux, and Jeannette M. Blackmar. 2012. A preliminary theory of informal accountability among network organizational actors. *Public Administration Review* 72, no. 3 (May/June): 442–453.

Roosevelt, Franklin D. 1937. Summary of the Report of the Committee on Administrative Management (also known as the Brownlow Committee Report). January 12. In *The American Presidency Project,* ed. Gerhard Peters and John T. Woolley. www.presidency.ucsb.edu/ws/?pid=15342.

Rosenbloom, D.H. 2003. *Administrative Law for Public Managers.* Boulder, CO: Westview.

Rossiter, Clinton, ed. 1961. *The Federalist Papers.* New York: New American Library.

Rourke, Francis. 1984. *Bureaucracy, Politics, and Public Policy.* New York: Harper Collins.

Rove, B.J.D. 1999. Theory v. reality with the council-manager plan. In *Forms of Local Government: A Handbook on City, County, and Regional Options,* ed. Roger L. Kemp, 82–88. Jefferson, NC: McFarland & Company.

Rozwenc, Edwin C., ed. 1963. *The Meaning of Jacksonian Democracy.* Lexington, MA: D.C. Heath.

Rubin, Irene. 2006. Budgeting for contracting in local government. *Public Budgeting and Finance* 26, no. 1 (Spring): 1–13.

Ryan, Paul. 2011. *The Path to Prosperity: Restoring America's Promise.* Fiscal Year 2012 Budget Resolution. Washington, DC: U.S. House of Representatives, Committee on the Budget, April 5. http://budget.house. gov/UploadedFiles/PathToProsperityFY2012.pdf (accessed April 19, 2011).

Sabatier, Paul, and H. Jenkins-Smith, ed. 1993. *Policy Change and Learning.* Boulder, CO: Westview.

Salamon, Lester M. 1992. *America's Nonprofit Sector: A Primer.* 1st ed. New York: The Foundation Center.

———. 1999. *America's Nonprofit Sector: A Primer.* 2d ed. New York: The Foundation Center.

———, ed. 2002. *Tools of Government: A Guide to the New Governance.* New York: Oxford University Press.

———. 2012. *America's Nonprofit Sector: A Primer.* 3rd ed. New York: The Foundation Center.

Salamon, Lester M., S. Wojciech Sokolowski, and Stephanie L. Geller. 2012. *Holding the Fort: Nonprofit Employment During a Decade of Turmoil.* Nonprofit Employment Bulletin No. 39. Baltimore, MD: Center for Civil Society Studies, Johns Hopkins University, January. http://ccss.jhu.edu/wp-content/uploads/downloads/2012/01/NED_National_2012.pdf (accessed January 21, 2013).

Sanger, M.B. 2008. From measurement to management: Breaking through the barriers to state and local performance. *Public Administration Review* 68, no. 1: s70–s85.

Sarbanes-Oxley Act of 2002. Public L. No. 107–204, 116 Stat. 745. July 30, 2002.

Schaar, John H. 1964. Some ways of thinking about equality. *Journal of Politics* 26, no. 4 (November): 867–895.

Schambra, William. 1994. "By the people: The old values of the new citizenship," *Policy Review* (Summer 1994), 32–38.

Scheberle, Denise. 2004. *Federalism and Environmental Policy: Trust and the Politics of Implementation.* 2d ed. Washington, DC: Georgetown University Press.

Schick, Allen. 1966. The road to PPB: The stages of budget reform. *Public Administration Review* 26 (December): 243–258. Also in Albert Hyde, *Government Budgeting: Theory, Process, and Politics* (Pacific

Grove, CA: Brooks Cole, 1992), 46–60. Also in *Perspectives on Budgeting,*1980/1987 ed. Allen Schick, 46–67. Washington, DC: American Society of Public Administration.

———. 1973. Death in the bureaucracy: The demise of federal PPB. *Public Administration Review* 33, no. 2 (March/April): 146–156.

———. 1978. The road from ZBB. *Public Administration Review* 38, no. 2 (March/April): 177–180.

———. 1983. Incremental budgeting in a decremental age. *Policy Sciences* 16, no. 1: 1–25.

———. 1987. *Perspectives on Budgeting.* Washington, DC: American Society for Public Administration.

———. 2007. *The Federal Budgeting Process: Politics, Policy, Process.* 3rd ed. Washington, DC: Brookings Institution Press.

Scholz, John T. 1998. Trust, taxes, and compliance. In *Trust & Governance,* ed. Valerie Braithwaite and Margaret Levi, 135–166. New York: Russell Sage Foundation.

Schon, Donald A. 1983. *The Reflective Practitioner: How Professionals Think in Action.* New York: Basic Books.

Selznick, Philip. 1992. *The Moral Commonwealth: Social Theory and the Promise of Community.* Berkeley: University of California Press.

Serrano v. Priest, 5 Cal.3d 584 (1971) (also known as *Serrano I*); *Serrano v. Priest,* 18 Cal.3d 728 (1976) (also known as *Serrano II*); and *Serrano v. Priest,* 20 Cal.3d 25 (1977) (also known as *Serrano III*). http://scocal.stanford.edu/opinion/serrano-v-priest-27628 (accessed June 29, 2013).

Shah, Sonal, and Kristina Costa. 2013. "Social Impact Bonds: Pay-for-Success Programs Could Help OMB with Grant Guidance." Center for American Progress, April 26. www.americanprogress.org/issues/economy/news/2013/04/26/61415/pay-for-success-programs-could-help-omb-with-grant-guidance/ (accessed September 5, 2013).

Sherraden, Samuel. 2011. *Failing to Fill the Holes in State Budgets: Why the Recovery Act Spending on Infrastructure Fell Short.* Washington, DC: The New America Foundation, February 17. www.newamerica.net/publications/policy/failing_to_fill_the_holes_in_state_budgets_why_the_recovery_act_spending_on_infr (accessed April 15, 2011).

Shinn, Craig W., Elaine Hallmark, and Laurel Singer. 2010. *Introduction to Collaborative Governance.* Portland, OR: Executive Leadership Institute/National Policy Consensus Center, Portland State University.

Sickinger, Ted, and Brent Hunsberger. 2010. Are state workers overpaid? *The Oregonian,* October 24, A1, A12.

Siegel, Stephen A. 1984. Understanding the Lochner era: Lessons from the controversy over railroad and utility rate regulation. *Virginia Law Review* 70, no. 2: 187–263.

Simonsen, William, and Mark D. Robbins. 2000. *Citizen Participation in Resource Allocation.* Boulder, CO: Westview.

Single Audit Act Amendments of 1996, Pub. L. No. 104–156, 110 Stat. 1396. July 5, 1996.

Sirianni, Carmen. 2009. *Investing in Democracy: Engaging Citizens in Collaborative Governance.* Washington, DC: Brookings Institution Press.

Skocpol, Theda. 1997. The Tocqueville problem: Civic engagement in American democracy. *Social Science History* 21, no. 4: 455–479.

Skocpol, Theda, and Morris P. Fiorina. 1999. Making sense of the civic engagement debate. *Civic Engagement in American Democracy.* Theda Skocpol and Morris P. Fiorina. Washington, DC, Brookings Institution Press.

Skolnick, Adam. 2011. Runaway prison costs trash state budgets. *The Fiscal Times,* February 9. www.thefiscaltimes.com/Articles/2011/02/09/Runaway-Prison-Costs-Trash-State-Budgets (accessed May 5, 2012).

Smith, Steven R., and Michael Lipsky. 1993. *Nonprofits for Hire: The Welfare State in the Age of Contracting.* Cambridge, MA: Harvard University Press.

Smith, Steven R., and Judith Smyth. 2010. "The Governance of Contracting Relationships: 'Killing the Golden Goose'–A Third-Sector Perspective." In *The New Public Governance? Emerging Perspectives on the Theory and Practice of Public Governance,* ed. Stephen P. Osborne, 270–300. London: Routledge.

Sorenson, Richard D., and Lloyd Milton Goldsmith. 2006. *The Principal's Guide to School Budgeting.* Thousand Oaks, CA: Corwin Press.

Souder, Jon A., and Sally K. Fairfax. 1996. *State Trust Lands: History, Management, and Sustainable Use.* Lawrence, KS: University of Kansas Press.

Spar, Karen. 2013. *Community Services Block Grants (CSBG): Background and Funding.* CRS Report 7-5700, RL32872. Washington, DC: Congressional Research Service, May 24. www.crs.gov and at https://www.fas.org/sgp/crs/misc/RL32872.pdf (accessed May 4, 2014).

Spring, Joel. 2008. *The American School: From the Puritans to No Child Left Behind.* 7th ed. New York: McGraw-Hill.

S&P Indices. 2011. Home prices off to a dismal start in 2011 according to the S&P/Case-Shiller home price indices. New release, March 29. www.bloomberg.com/apps/news?pid=newsarchive&sid=agQSBAG7 mmf4 (accessed April 14, 2011).

State of Colorado, Department of Local Affairs. 2009. Active Colorado local governments (3,460 local governments). https://dola.colorado.gov/lgis/lgActiveAlpha.jsf.

State of Colorado, Taxpayer Bill of Rights [TABOR]. 1992. Article X, Section 20, Colorado Constitution. www.colorado.gov/cs/Satellite/CGA-LegislativeCouncil/CLC/1200536135614 (accessed April 19, 2014).

State of Oregon. 2010. *Tax Expenditure Report 2011–2013*. Salem, OR: Department of Revenue Research Section, Budget and Management Division, Department of Administrative Services, 280. www.oregon.gov/dor/STATS/docs/ExpR11-13/tax-expenditure-report-2011-2013.pdf (accessed January 21, 2013).

———. 2012. *2013–15 Tax Expenditure Report*. Salem, OR: Oregon Department of Revenue: Research and Statistical Reports, Property Tax Expenditures. www.oregon.gov/dor/STATS/Pages/tax-expenditure-report-2013-2015.aspx (accessed May 9, 2014).

State of Pennsylvania, Department of Community & Economic Development. 2013. "Tax Increment Financing (TIG) Guarantee Program." June 13. www.newpa.com/find-and-apply-for-funding/funding-and-program-finder/tax-increment-financing-tif-guarantee-program (accessed April 19, 2014).

State of Washington. 2008. *Proposed 2009–2011 Budget & Policy Highlights: Governor Chris Gregoire*. December. Olympia, WA: Office of the Governor.

———. 2009. Balanced but unjust: 2010 supplemental budget. Press conference remarks by Governor Chris Gregoire, December 9. www.ofm.wa.gov/news/release/2009/091209.asp (accessed December 20, 2012).

———. 2014. Revised Code of Washington (RCW), 35 RCW 35.32A, 35.33, 35.34.

Stein, Herbert. 1969. *The Fiscal Revolution in America*. Chicago, IL: University of Chicago Press.

Stenzel, Catherine, and Joe Stenzel. 2003. *Essentials of Cost Management*. Hoboken, NJ: Wiley.

Stever, J.A. 1988. *The End of Public Administration: Problems of the Profession in the Post-Progressive Era*. Dobbs Ferry, NY: Transnational Publishers.

———. 1990. The dual image of the administrator in progressive administrative theory. *Administration & Society* 22, no. 1: 39–57.

Stillman, Richard J., II. 1974. *The Rise of the City Manager*. Albuquerque: University of New Mexico Press.

———. 1977. The city manager: Professional helping hand, or political hired hand? *Public Administration Review* 37, no. 6 (November–December): 659–670.

Stivers, Camilla. 2000. *Bureau Men, Settlement Women: Constructing Public Administration in the Progressive Era*. Lawrence: University Press of Kansas.

Stoker, G. 2006. Public value management: A new narrative for networked governance? *American Review of Public Administration* 36, no. 1: 41–57.

Stone, Clarence N. 1989. *Regime Politics: Governing Atlanta*. Lawrence: University Press of Kansas.

———. 1993. "Urban regimes and the capacity to govern: A political economy approach." *Journal of Urban Affairs* 15, no. 1, 1–28.

Stone, Harold A., Don K. Price, and Kathryn H. Stone. 1940. *City Manager Government in the United States: A Review After Twenty-Five Years*. Chicago, IL: Public Administration Service.

Storing, Herbert J. 1981a. *The Complete Anti-Federalist*. 7 vols. Chicago, IL: University of Chicago Press.

———. 1981b. *What the Anti-Federalists Were For: The Political Thought of the Opponents of the Constitution*. Chicago, IL: University of Chicago Press.

Streamlined Sales Tax Project. 2005. Executive summary. www.streamlinedsalestax.org.

———. 2011. Frequently asked questions. www.streamlinedsalestax.org/index.php?page=faqs (accessed April 22, 2011).

Strunk v. Public Employees Retirement Board, S50593. Oregon Supreme Court. March 8, 2005. www.publications.ojd.state.or.us/docs/S50593.htm (accessed May 3, 2013).

Svara, James H. 1985. Dichotomy and duality: Reconceptualizing the relationship between policy and administration in council-manager cities. *Public Administration Review* 45, no. 1: 221–232.

———. 1990. *Official Leadership in the City: Patterns of Conflict and Cooperation*. New York: Oxford University Press.

———. 1991. City manager role: Conflict, divergence, or congruence? *Administration & Society* 23, no. 2: 227–246.

———. 1998. The politics-administration dichotomy model as aberration. *Public Administration Review* 58, no. 1: 51–58.

———. 1999. The shifting boundary between elected officials and city managers in large council-manager cities. *Public Administration Review* 59, no. 1: 44–53.

———. 2004. Achieving effective community leadership. In *The Effective Local Government Manager*, ed. Charldean Newell, 21–56. Washington, DC: ICMA.

———. 2006. Complexity in political-administrative relations and the limits of the dichotomy concept. *Administrative Theory & Praxis* 28, no. 1: 121–139.

———. 2008. *The Facilitative Leader in City Hall: Reexamining the Scope and Contributions*. Boca Raton, FL: CRC Press.

Swanson, Christopher J. 2008. Long-term financial forecasting for local government. *Government Finance Review* 24, no. 5 (October): 60.

Tatum, Adam. 2012. Our cities need preventive care too: How pre-funding and policy changes can help California's 20 largest cities manage their growing retiree benefit costs. *California Common Sense*, August 2, 2. www.cacs.org/images/dynamic/articleAttachments/16.pdf (accessed May 31, 2013).

Tax Policy Center. 2008. State and local tax policy: What are the sources of revenue for local governments? In *The Tax Policy Briefing Book*. www.taxpolicycenter.org/briefing-book/state-local/revenues/local_revenue.cfm (accessed April 26, 2011).

Taylor, Kate. 2013. Health care law raises pressures on public unions. *New York Times,* August 4. www.nytimes.com/2013/08/05/nyregion/health-care-law-raises-pressure-on-public-employees-unions.html?pagewanted=all&_r=0 (accessed August 10, 2013).

Tempel, Eugene R., ed. 2010. *Hank Rosso's Achieving Excellence in Fund Raising*. 2d ed. San Francisco: Jossey-Bass.

Teske, Paul, and Mark Schneider. 1994. The bureaucratic entrepreneur: The case of city managers. *Public Administration Review* 54, no. 4 (July–August): 331–340.

Thach, Charles C., Jr. 1969. *The Creation of the Presidency, 1775–1789*. Baltimore, MD: Johns Hopkins University Press.

TheCapitol.Net. 2009. *The Federal Budget Process: A Description of the Federal and Congressional Budget Processes*. Washington, DC: TheCapitol.Net Inc.

Thibaut, J., and L. Walker. 1975. *Procedural Justice: A Psychological Analysis*. Hillsdale, NJ: Lawrence Erlbaum.

Thom, Michael. 2013. Politics, fiscal necessity, or both? Factors driving the enactment of defined contribution accounts for public employees. *Public Administration Review* 73, no. 2 (May/June): 480–489.

Thompson, Lynn. 2012. Seattle lax in tracking federal grants, state auditor concludes. *Seattle Times*, October 31. http://seattletimes.com/html/localnews/2019573113_seattleaudit01m.html (accessed September 14, 2013).

Tiebout, Charles, M. 1956. A pure theory of local expenditures. *Journal of Political Economy* 64, no. 5 (October): 416–424.

Tims, Dana. 2011. Outlook grim for key services: Less federal and state money next year would bode ill for county programs. *The Oregonian*, April 16, E1, E2.

Tocqueville, Alexis de. 1835–1840/2000. *Democracy in America*, trans. and ed. Harvey Mansfield and Delba Winthrop. Chicago, IL: University of Chicago Press.

Transportation for America. 2011. The fix we're in for: The state of our nation's bridges. Washington, DC. http://t4america.org/resources/bridges/ (accessed April 26, 2011).

Tualatin Hills Park and Recreation District (THPRD). 2013. Final comprehensive plan update 2013 and financial sustainability analysis reports. Board of Directors meeting minutes, September 9. http://thprd.org/pdfs/document2310.pdf (accessed September 14, 2013).

Tuality Healthcare. 2013. Tuality Healthcare Foundation. Hillsboro, OR. www.tuality.org/home/index.php/about_us/foundation/ (accessed April 16, 2013).

Ullmann, John E. 1976. *Schaum's Outline of Theory and Problems of Quantitative Methods in Management*. New York: McGraw-Hill.

Umatilla County, Oregon. 2010. *FY 2010–2011 Adopted Budget*. Pendleton, OR.

Unfunded Mandates Reform Act of 1995 (UMRA), Pub. L. No. 104–4, 109 Stat. 48.

United Way of the Columbia-Willamette (UWCW). 2008. *Funding Trends Analysis 2008: Invest Now or Pay Later.* Portland, OR. www.unitedway-pdx.org/docs/whatwedo/united_way_funding_trends_analysis_2008.pdf (accessed February 8, 2011).

United Way of King County (UWKC). 2010. *Strategic Plan 2010–2015*. Seattle, WA: United Way of King County, June 1. www.uwkc.org/about/strategic-plan.html (accessed May 23, 2013).

———. 2011. United Way of King County funding principles. Seattle, WA: United Way of King County. www.uwkc.org/assets/files/non-profit-resources/grantee-materials/grantee-funding-principles.pdf (accessed September 18, 2012).

U.S. Advisory Commission on Intergovernmental Relations (ACIR). 1987. *The Organization of Local Public Economies*. Washington, DC.

———. 1993. *Local Government Autonomy: Needs for State Constitutional, Statutory, and Judicial Clarification*. Report A-127. Washington, DC: ACIR, October.

———. 1995. *Tax and Expenditure Limits on Local Governments*. Report M-194. Washington, DC: ACIR, March. http://digital.library.unt.edu/ark:/67531/metadc1198/m1/1/?q=Tax and ExpenditureLimits on LocalGovernments (accessed May 12, 2011).

U.S. Bureau of Land Management. 1974. *Manual of Survey Instructions*. Washington, DC: U.S. Government Printing Office.

U.S. Census Bureau. 2002. *Census of Governments*, Vol. 1, No. 1, *Government Organization*, Series GC02(1)-1. Washington, DC: U.S. Government Printing Office. www.census.gov/govs/cog/historical_data_2002. html.

———. 2003. Table 1: State and Local Government Finances by Level of Government and by State: 1999–2000. In *Government Finances 1999–2000*. Washington, DC: Governments Division, Census Management Staff, January. www2.census.gov/govs/local/00allpub.pdf (accessed September 16, 2013).

———. 2007a. *Census of Governments*. Washington, DC: U.S. Government Printing Office.

———. 2007b. Structure of governments, individual state descriptions. www.census.gov/govs/go/index. html (accessed November 15, 2011).

———. 2009. *Annual Surveys of State and Local Government Finances*. Washington, DC: U.S. Census Bureau. www.census.gov//govs/local/historical_data_2009.html (accessed November 11, 2011).

———. 2012a. Table 1: Intercensal Estimates of the Resident Population for the United States, Regions, States, and Puerto Rico: April 1, 2000 to July 1, 2010 (ST-EST00INT-01). State Intercensal Estimates (2000–2010). www.census.gov/popest/data/intercensal/state/state2010.html (accessed November 15, 2011).

———. 2012b. Table 1: State and Local Government Finances by Level of Government and by State: 2007–2008. From Historical Data: 2008, September 20. www.census.gov/govs/local/historical_data_2008. html (accessed September 16, 2013).

———. 2013. *Public Education Finances: 2011*. http://www.census.gov/govs/school/.

U.S. Department of Defense. 1984/2003. Directive 7045.14. May 22, 1984, certified current, Nov. 21, 2003. www.dtic.mil/whs/directives/corres/pdf/704514p.pdf (accessed January 25, 2012).

U.S. Department of the Interior, Bureau of Indian Affairs. 2011. *Tribal Leaders Directory, Spring 2011*. Washington, DC: BIA, March 31. www.bia.gov/cs/groups/xopa/documents/text/idc013398.pdf.

U.S. Department of Justice, Civil Rights Division, Disability Section. 2008. The ADA and city governments: Common problems. www.ada.gov/comprob.htm (accessed July 7, 2011).

U.S. Department of Justice, National Institute of Justice. 2012. Topical collection: Corrections. http://nij. ncjrs.gov/App/publications/Pub_search.aspx?searchtype=basic&category=99&location=top&PSID=18 (accessed May 6, 2012).

U.S. Environmental Protection Agency. 2013. "Drinking Water Infrastructure Needs Survey and Assessment: 2011." Fifth Report to Congress. Washington, DC: Government Printing Office.

U.S. Forest Service. 2014. "Agriculture Secretary Announces Rural Schools Payment." News release, April 4. www.fs.fed.us/news/2014/releases/04/rural-schools-payments.shtml (accessed May 10, 2014).

U.S. Government Accountability Office (GAO). 2007. *Cost of Prisons: Bureau of Prisons Needs Better Data to Assess Alternatives for Acquiring Low and Minimum Security Facilities*. Report GAO–08–6. Washington, DC: GAO, October 5. www.gao.gov/products/GAO-08-6 (accessed January 27, 2013).

———. 2012. *State and Local Pension Plans: Economic Downturn Spurs Efforts to Address Costs and Sustainability*. Washington, DC: Government Printing Office. www.gao.gov/assets/590/589043.pdf (accessed July 19, 2014).

Usgovernmentspending.com. 2014. "US Federal State Local Debt As Percent Of GDP." www.usgovernmentspending.com/federal_state_local_debt_chart.htm (accessed April 26, 2014).

U.S. Office of Management and Budget (OMB). 1992. "Budget of the United States." Table C-2, Part 2. Washington, DC.

U.S. Office of Management and Budget (OMB). 2007. Circular No. A-133: *Audits of States, Local Governments, and Non-Profit Organizations*. www.whitehouse.gov/sites/default/files/omb/assets/a133/a133_revised_2007.pdf (accessed January 19, 2013).

———. 2012. OMB Circular A-133: *Compliance Supplement 2012*. www.whitehouse.gov/omb/circulars/ a133_compliance_supplement_2012 (accessed January 23, 2013).

———. 2013. "Uniform Administrative Requirements, Cost Principles, and Audit Requirements for Federal Awards," 78 *Federal Register* 78590 (December 26, 2013). https://federalregister.gov/a/2013-30465 (accessed May 10, 2014).

U.S. Securities and Exchange Commission. 2012. *Report on the Municipal Securities Market*. Washington, DC: July 31. www.sec.gov/news/studies/2012/munireport073112.pdf (accessed January 15, 2013).

VanderHart, Dirk. 2010a. YWCA announces massive cutbacks. *The Oregonian*, December 16, C1, C2. http://blog.oregonlive.com/portland_impact/print.html?entry=/2010/12/portland_ywca_plans_significan.html (accessed December 14, 2012).

VanderHart, Dirk. 2010b. Portland YWCA plans significant staff, program cuts amid financial woes. *The Oregonian,* December 15. http://blog.oregonlive.com/portland_impact/print.html?entry=2010/12/portland_ywca_plans_significan.html (accessed December 14, 2012).

Vara, Vahini, and Bobby White. 2011. Prison ruling rattles California budget. *Wall Street Journal,* May 25. http://online.wsj.com/article/SB10001424052702303654804576343730209424422.html (accessed May 5, 2012).

Vision Action Network. 2010. *Annual Report 2010–2011.* Beaverton, OR: Vision Action Network of Washington County, OR.

Waldhart, Paul, and Andrew Reschovsky. 2012. *Property Tax Delinquency and the Number of Payment Installments.* La Follette School Working Paper No. 2012–013, October. www.lafollette.wisc.edu/publications/workingpapers/reschovsky2012-013.pdf (accessed February 5, 2013).

Walzer, Michael. 1992. "The Civil Society Argument," in *Dimensions of Radical Democracy: Pluralism, Citizenship, Community,* ed. Chantal. Mouffe, 89–107. London: Verso.

Wanat, John A. 1978. *Introduction to Budgeting.* North Scituate, MA: Duxbury Press.

Washington County, Oregon. 2000. *The County 2000 Financial Plan.* Hillsboro, OR: Washington County, Oregon County Government.

———. 2011. Property tax appeals and board of property tax appeals (BoPTA). www.co.washington.or.us/AssessmentTaxation/AppraisalsAppeals/PropertyTaxAppeals/index.cfm (accessed May 11, 2011).

Washington State BARS Manual. 2013. "Chart of Accounts, Account Structure." *Budgeting, Accounting and Reporting System (BARS): Cities, Counties and Special Purpose Districts (GAAP).* Olympia, WA: Office of the State Auditor. www.sao.wa.gov/local/BarsManual/Documents/GAAP_p1_Structure.pdf (accessed May 8, 2014).

Washington State Community Action Partnership. 2013. The community action network. www.wapartnership.org/we-are/what-community-action/ (accessed February 4, 2013).

Washington State Department of Revenue. 2010. Appealing your property assessment to the County Board of Equalization. http://dor.wa.gov/docs/Pubs/Prop_Tax/AppealProp.pdf (accessed May 11, 2011).

Washington State Municipal Research and Service Center (MRSC). 2010. *The Bidding Book for Washington Cities and Towns.* Report Number 52 Revised. Seattle, WA: MRSC. www.mrsc.org/publications/mrscpubs.aspx (accessed March 5, 2013).

Weintraub, Adam. 2011. California lawmakers approve Amazon tax compromise. Associated Press, September 10. http://finance.yahoo.com/news/Calif-lawmakers-approve-apf-4007609200.html (accessed September 10, 2011).

Weisbrod, Burton A. 1977. Toward a theory of the voluntary nonprofit sector in a three-sector economy. In *The Voluntary Nonprofit Sector: An Economic Analysis,* ed. Burton A. Weisbrod. Lexington, MA: Lexington Books.

———. 2001. Commercialism and the road ahead. In *Understanding Nonprofit Organizations: Governance, Leadership, and Management,* ed. J. Steven Ott, 231–238. Boulder, CO: Westview Perseus.

Whatcom County, Washington. 2010. Tax foreclosure sales process for real property. www.co.whatcom.wa.us/treasurer/auctions/foreclosures.jsp (accessed April 8, 2011).

Wheeland, Craig M. 2000. City management in the 1990s: Responsibilities, roles, and practices. *Administration & Society* 32, no. 3 (July): 255–281.

White, Leonard D. 1927. *The City Manager.* Chicago, IL: University of Chicago Press.

———. 1948. *The Federalists: A Study in Administrative History, 1789–1801.* New York: Macmillan.

Whitley, Glen B. 2010. State taxation—The impact of congressional legislation on state and local government revenues. Testimony before the U.S. House of Representatives Subcommittee on Commercial and Administrative Law. 111th Cong., 2nd sess., April 15. www.naco.org/legislation/policies/documents/finance%20and%20intergovernment%20affairs/whitley%20testimony%20_2_.pdf (accessed April 6, 2011).

Wholey, J.S. 1999. Performance-based management: Responding to the challenges. *Public Productivity and Management Review* 22, no. 3: 288–307.

Wholey, J.S., and H.P. Hatry. 1992. The case for performance monitoring. *Public Administration Review* 52, no. 6: 604–610.

Wildavsky, Aaron. 1961. Political implications of budgetary reform. *Public Administration Review* 21 (Autumn): 183–190.

———. 1964. *The Politics of the Budgetary Process.* Boston: Little, Brown.

———. 1966. The political economy of efficiency: Cost-benefit analysis, systems analysis, and program budgeting. *Public Administration Review* 26, no. 4 (December): 292–310.

———. 1978. A budget for all seasons. *Public Administration Review* 38, no. 6 (November/December): 501–509.

———. 1979a. *Speaking Truth to Power: The Art and Craft of Policy Analysis.* Boston: Little, Brown.

———. 1979b. *The Politics of the Budgetary Process.* 3rd ed. Boston: Little Brown.

———. 1984. *The Politics of the Budgetary Process.* 4th ed. Boston: Little, Brown.

———. 1988. *The New Politics of the Budgetary Process.* 1st ed. Glenview, IL: Scott Foresman.

———. 1992. *The New Politics of the Budgetary Process.* 2d ed. New York: HarperCollins.

———. 1993. *Speaking Truth to Power: The Art and Craft of Policy Analysis.* 2d ed. New Brunswick, NJ: Transaction.

Williams, Joan C. 1986. The constitutional vulnerability of American local government: The politics of city status in American law. *Wisconsin Law Review* 83: 105–111.

Wilson, James Q. 1989. *Bureaucracy: What Government Agencies Do and Why They Do It.* New York: Basic Books.

Winters, John V. 2008. *Property Tax Limitations.* FRC Report 179. Atlanta, GA: Fiscal Research Center, Andrew Young School of Policy Studies, Georgia State University.

Winthrop, Bob, and Rebecca Herr. 2009. Determining the cost of vacancies in Baltimore. *Government Finance Review* 25, no. 3 (June): 38–42.

Yang, K., and M. Holzer. 2006. The performance-trust link: Implications for performance measurement. *Public Administration Review* 66, no. 1: 114–126.

Young, Dennis. 2001. Nonprofit entrepreneurship. In *Understanding Nonprofit Organizations: Governance, Leadership, and Management,* ed. J. Steven Ott, 218–222. Boulder, CO: Westview.

Young, Jeffrey. 2013. Health care spending growth is slow for third straight year: Report. www.huffingtonpost.com/2013/01/07health-care-spending-growth-report_n_2426407.html (accessed August 7, 2013).

Zaitz, Les. 2010. Hard choices: Big part of Oregon prison budget is all locked up. *The Oregonian,* September 27. www.oregonlive.com/politics/index.ssf/2010/09/big_part_of_oregon_prison_budg.html (accessed May 5, 2012).

INDEX

Lakewood Plan (California), 37
Land Ordinance (1785), 22
Lead organization, 102
Lead-organization network, 490
Leasing method, 467
Legislative body
  budget actor role, 98, 109–10
  budget planning, 268
  executive budget development, 421, 448–51
Legislative committee, 110–12
Level of service, 331
Level of service costs, 352–53
Leverage donation, 234
Levy, 210–11
Liabilities, 497
Libertarians, 59–62, 73–74
Linear regression analysis, 206–7
Line-item budgeting. *See also* object code budgeting
  accounting funds, 246
  advantages of, 319
  behavior and techniques, 311–18
    average change calculation, 315
    cost estimations, 311–12, 313–14 (exhibit), 315
    current service baseline (CSB), 315–18
    historical data, 315, 316 (exhibit)
    percentage change calculation, 315
  capital budget, 307
  capital outlay category, 305 (exhibit), 307, 314 (exhibit)
  characteristics of, 309–11
    base budget principle, 309–10
    fair share principle, 309, 310–11
    incrementalism, 309, 310
  comparative summary, 401, 402–3 (exhibit), 404–6
  county increments/request computation example, 313–14 (exhibit)
  county worksheet example, 303, 304–305 (exhibit), 306–8, 311
  disadvantages of, 319–20
  expenditure code budgeting, 303, 304 (exhibit), 306
  full-time equivalents (FTEs), 306 (exhibit)
  interfund/interdepartmental category, 305 (exhibit), 307, 314 (exhibit)
  internal service charges, 305 (exhibit), 307
  material and supplies category, 304–305 (exhibit), 306, 313–14 (exhibit)
  object code, 303, 304 (exhibit), 306
  operating budget, 307
  origins and purpose, 87, 308–9
  personal services category, 304 (exhibit), 306, 313 (exhibit)
  program budget, 309
  study questions, 320–21
  value of, 303
Long-term restricted fund, 254
Long-term revenue forecast, 197, 281–82
Lottery revenue, 179

Louisiana
  parish governance, 20
  sales tax, 170

Madison, James, 39, 60
Madisonian interest group model, 78, 82 (exhibit)
Maine
  charter framework, 23
  intergovernmental revenue, 179
Maintenance of effort requirements, 179, 255
Major construction/acquisition, 464, 466
Majority Tyranny problem, 71 (exhibit), 73–74
Manager, 98
Managerial accountability, 90–91
Marshall, John, 16
Maryland
  income tax, 171, 172
  revenue burdens, 188
  school districts, 23
Massachusetts
  charter framework, 23
  intergovernmental revenue, 179
  revenue burdens, 188
Material and supplies category, 304–305 (exhibit), 306, 313–14 (exhibit)
McNamara, Robert, 87–88, 324
Michigan
  Detroit bankruptcy, 30–31
  income tax, 171, 172
  intergovernmental revenue, 179
Millage rate, 210–11
Mission statement, 326–27
Mississippi, 170
Missouri, 18–19
Missouri Constitutional Convention (1875), 18–19
Missouri v. Lewis (1879), 19
Mixed economy, 44, 45 (exhibit), 68, 69 (exhibit)
Modified accrual basis, 253
Modified ZBB, 379–80, 393
Montana, 169–70, 188
Municipal bonds, 466

National Association of Counties (NACo), 138, 181
National Bellas Hess, Inc. v. Department of Revenue (1976), 170
National Conference of State Legislatures (NCSL), 138, 180–81
National League of Cities (NLC), 138
National Performance Review Initiative, 362
Nebraska, 18
Net assets, 497
Net assets statement, 498 (exhibit)
Net balance, 499
Net present value (NPV), 464
Network administrative organization (NAO), 102, 490
Networked governance, 41
Nevada, 32
New Deal, 25, 356, 370

ABOUT THE AUTHORS

Douglas F. Morgan is professor emeritus of public administration and director of the MPA Program in the Hatfield School of Government at Portland State University. He has held a variety of public positions, both elected and appointed. His research interests focus on the role career public administrators play in ensuring effective and responsive systems of local democratic governance. He is coauthor of *Foundations of Public Service*, 2d ed. (M.E. Sharpe, 2013) and coeditor with Brian Cook of *New Public Governance: A Regime-Centered Perspective* (M.E. Sharpe, 2014). His work has appeared in the *Handbook of Administrative Ethics, Oregon Politics and Government, The International Encyclopedia of Public Policy and Administration, Public Administration Review, Administration & Society,* and *Administrative Theory & Practice*.

Kent S. Robinson is a senior fellow at the Hatfield School of Government at Portland State University. He was an assistant professor in the Institute of Public Service at Seattle University and an adjunct professor of public administration at Portland State. His main research focus is on the contribution of social trust to community governance and administrative practice. Prior to his academic career, he served as a budget and policy analyst on federal forestry and natural resource issues. He is a coauthor of *Foundations of Public Service*, 2d ed. (M.E. Sharpe 2013).

Dennis Strachota is a former local government finance director and budget manager. Most recently, he served as budget manager for the City of Long Beach, California. In his 35 years in state and local government finance, he served as Director of Educational Services for the Government Finance Officers Association (GFOA), responsible for its budget and cash management technical assistance programs, including the Distinguished Budget Presentation Awards program. Additionally, he served as coeditor of GFOA's publication, *Local Government Finance: Concepts and Practices* (1991) and is the author of *The Best of Governmental Budgeting: A Guide to Preparing Budget Documents* (1994).

James A. Hough has held numerous positions in city management, including that of city manager, interim city manager, assistant to the city manager, public works director, community development director, and chief financial officer. His professional practice focused on the needs of small- to medium-sized cities. He has served as coordinator of the ICMA city manager credentialing program for the Oregon City/County Management Association, and he authored *The Municipal Financial Indicators Evaluation Kit: The IndiKit,* published by ICMA. As a public administration consultant, Jim has provided a number of program evaluations and performance reviews for city governments. He has served as an adjunct professor with the Hatfield School of Government at Portland State University, where he taught public budgeting, public finance, and public works administration. Jim is city manager emeritus for the city of Banks, Oregon, having been the first and founding manager of that city.

Printed in Great Britain
by Amazon

44237547R00337